ENGLISH 102

Perspectives on Contemporary Issues

Cincinnati State Technical and Community College

Katherine Anne Ackley

Australia • Brazil • Japan • Korea • Mexico • Singapore • Spain • United Kingdom • United States

ENGLISH 102: Perspectives on Contemporary Issues, Cincinnati State Technical and Community College

Executive Editors:
Maureen Staudt
Michael Stranz

Senior Project Development Manager:
Linda deStefano

Marketing Specialist:
Courtney Sheldon

Senior Production/ Manufacturing Manager:
Donna M. Brown

Production Editorial Manager:
Kim Fry

Sr. Rights Acquisition Account Manager:
Todd Osborne

Printed in the United States of America

Perspectives on Contemporary Issues: Readings Across the Disciplines, Sixth Edition
Katherine Anne Ackley

The Brief Wadsworth Handbook, Fourth Edition
Laurie G. Kirszner | Stephen R. Mandell

ISBN-13: 978-1-285-13967-8

ISBN-10: 1-285-13967-4

Cengage Learning
5191 Natorp Boulevard
Mason, Ohio 45040
USA

Cengage Learning is a leading provider of customized learning solutions with office locations around the globe, including Singapore, the United Kingdom, Australia, Mexico, Brazil, and Japan. Locate your local office at:
international.cengage.com/region.

Cengage Learning products are represented in Canada by Nelson Education, Ltd.
For your lifelong learning solutions, visit **www.cengage.com/custom.**
Visit our corporate website at **www.cengage.com.**

CONTENTS

Perspectives on Contemporary Issues: Readings Across the Disciplines, Sixth Edition, presents an approach to thinking, reading, and writing that views learning as the interconnectedness of ideas and disciplinary perspectives. Contemporary issues engage the students, while the readings provide rich material for class discussion and writing topics. The essays by authors from a variety of disciplines and professions focus on individual, national, and global issues. Regardless of their majors, students will enhance their skills through the writing assignments.

The goals of *Perspectives on Contemporary Issues: Readings Across the Disciplines* are as follows:

- To sharpen students' thinking skills by presenting them with a variety of perspectives on current issues
- To give students practice in both oral and verbal expression by providing questions for discussion and writing after each selection
- To provide students with a variety of writing assignments representing the kinds of writing they will be asked to do in courses across the curriculum
- To encourage students to view issues and ideas in terms of connections with other people, other disciplines, or other contexts

The questions for discussion and writing encourage critical thinking by asking students to go well beyond simple recall of the readings and to use higher-order skills such as integration, synthesis, or analysis of what they have read. Most of the questions are suitable for work in small groups, as well as for class discussion.

NEW TO THIS EDITION

New Chapters. Two new chapter titles reflect the merging of several chapters that were in the fifth edition. Chapter 16, "American Foreign Policy," incorporates both the subject of America's fight against terrorism and America's image abroad, and Chapter 23, "American Business in the Global Marketplace," has readings on outsourcing and America's position in the very competitive global marketplace.

New Readings. There are twenty-six new readings in this edition, almost all of them published in the last couple of years. These new readings cover topics of contemporary interest, and their writers sometimes take controversial positions on the issues under discussion.

Updated MLA Guidelines. The Modern Language Association (MLA) has updated and revised its guidelines for citing and documenting sources, particularly Internet and electronic sources. All discussions of MLA style in Part I, particularly Chapters 6 and 7, reflect revised style recommendations of the *MLA Handbook for Writers of Research Papers*, Seventh Edition, published in 2010.

Fewer Readings. This new edition has a reduced number of readings, on the recommendation of reviewers and users of the fifth edition. Although instructors like the breadth of coverage in the disciplines, many felt that there were too many readings to cover in a semester. As a result, the total number of readings in the textbook has been reduced from eighty-five in the fifth edition to seventy in the sixth edition, and there are twenty-three chapters instead of twenty-six.

READING SELECTIONS

The book has five parts, and the reading selections are organized by four broad disciplinary areas:

- Part Two, Media Studies, Popular Culture, and the Arts (Chapters 8–11), contains chapters with readings on music and video games, media violence, advertising, Hollywood films, television, and the visual arts.
- Part Three, Social and Behavioral Sciences (Chapters 12–16), addresses such matters as education, poverty and homelessness, gender and sex roles, race and ethnicity, and American foreign policy.
- In Part Four, Science and Technology (Chapters 17–20), writers from a variety of disciplines explore such subjects as the relationships among science, technology, and society; public health; computers and digital technology; and the ethical implications of technology and human genetic experimentation.
- Part Five, Business and Economics (Chapters 21–23), addresses marketing and the American consumer, the workplace, and American business in the global marketplace.

The selections in each chapter encourage students to consider issues from different perspectives because their authors come from a wide range of disciplinary backgrounds and training. Sometimes the writers cross disciplinary lines in their essays. For example, a historian extols the virtues of reading. The individual perspectives of the writers may differ markedly from students' own perspectives, thus generating discussion and writing topics.

ACTIVITIES AND ASSIGNMENTS

After each selection,

- Students can make a **Personal Response** to some aspect of the reading.
- Each reading is also followed by several **Questions for Class or Small-Group Discussion**. These questions invite students to consider rhetorical strategies of the piece, think of larger implications, discuss related issues, or make connections between the readings and their own experiences. Many of these questions are appropriate for writing topics as well, and many others will prompt students to discover related topics on which to write.

Toward the end of each chapter, a section called **Perspectives on . . .** provides writing topics based on ideas generated by the collected readings in that chapter. These writing assignments are arranged in two categories:

- **Suggested Writing Topics** are suitable for synthesis, argumentation, and other modes of writing such as the report, the letter, the personal essay, and the comparison and contrast essay.
- **Research Topics** are suitable for development into research papers.

Finally, each chapter in Parts Two through Five concludes with a section called **Responding to Visuals**, which features two photographs or other visual images. These images relate to the thematic focus of the chapter and are accompanied by questions on rhetorical strategies and other relevant matters.

A DEFINITION OF ISSUES

Given the title of this textbook, a definition of *issues* is in order. An issue is usually taken to mean a topic that is controversial, that prompts differences of opinion, or that can be seen from different perspectives. It often raises questions or requires taking a close look at a problem. Although this is not primarily an argument textbook, the inclusion of topics and essays guaranteed to spark controversy is deliberate. Many of the readings will prompt students to take opposing positions. Some of the readings are provocative; others may anger students. Such differences of opinion generate lively class discussions and result in writing opportunities that engage students.

ACKNOWLEDGMENTS

I would like to thank the following reviewers for their helpful suggestions on this new edition:

Sinceree R. Gunn, *University of Alabama, Huntsville*
Linda Lawless, *College of the Desert*

Bronwyn Lepore, *Community College of Philadelphia*
Michael Mangan, *Orange Coast College*
Elaine Minamide, *Palomar College*
Stephanie Richardson, *Genesee Community College*
Kelly Ryan Schendel, *Long Beach City College/Cerritos College*
Lynne M. Smelser, *Baker College*
Sandra Archer Young, *Columbia College.*

Also, thanks to these reviewers from previous editions:
Lynn Alexander, *University of Tennessee*
Valerie K. Anderson, *York College, The City University of New York*
Bim Angst, *Penn State Schuykill*
M. Susan Bonifer, *Mountain State University*
Robert Brown, *Champlain College*
Charlene Bunnell, *University of Delaware*
Joan Canty, *Columbia College*
Edward Carmien, *Westminster Choir College of Rider University*
Jo Cavins, *North Dakota State University*
N. Bradley Christie, *Erskine College*
Judith Cortelloni, *Lincoln College*
Robert Con Davis-Undiano, *University of Oklahoma*
Stacey Donohue, *Central Oregon Community College*
Clark L. Draney, *Idaho State University*
Sarah Duerden, *Arizona State University*
David Elias, *Eastern Kentucky University*
Virginia Fambrough, *Baker University*
James Gifford, *Mohawk Valley Community College*
Fatin Morris Guirguis, *Polk Community College*
Keith Hale, *South Texas Community College*
Letitia Harding, *University of the Incarnate Word*
M. Hunter Hayes, *University of Southern Mississippi*
Kathy Henkins, *Mt. San Antonio College*
Hyo-Chang Hong, *Marshall University*
Elizabeth Huston, *Eastfield College*
William T. Hyndman, III, *Rosemont College*
Karen R. Jacobs, *Louisiana Tech University*
Margaret Johnson, *Idaho State University*
Howard Kerner, *Polk Community College*
Joyce Kessel, *Villa Maria College*
James Kirpatrick, *Central Piedmont Community College*
Mary Kramer, *University of Massachusetts, Lowell*
Lindsay Lewan, *Arapahoe Community College*
Jun Liu, *California State University, Los Angeles*
Jeanette Lugo, *Valdosta State University*

Christopher Mattson, *Keene State College*
James McNamara, *Alverno College*
Brett J. Millan, *South Texas Community College*
Deborah Montuori, *Shippensburg University*
Rosemary Moore, *Iowa Western Community College*
Sean Nighbert, *St. Philip's College*
Debbie Ockey, *Fresno City College*
Debbie Olson, *Central Washington University*
Marc Prinz, *Hofstra University*
Louise Rosenberg, *University of Hartford*
Kiki Leigh Rydell, *Montana State University*
Daniel Schenker, *University of Alabama in Huntsville*
Judith Schmitt, *Macon State College*
Marilyn Schultz, *Delta State University*
Allison D. Smith, *Middle Tennessee State University*
Harvey Solganick, *LeTourneau University*
Shannon C. Stewart, *Coastal Carolina University*
Rosalee Stilwell, *Indiana University of Pennsylvania*
Steve Street, *The State University of New York*
William Tashman, *Baruch College, The City University of New York*
Tiffany Trent, *Virginia Polytechnic Institute and State University*
Sandi Ward, *West Virginia University*
Gwen Wilkinson, *University of Texas at San Antonio.*

As always, I thank my husband, Rich, and my family: Heather, Brian, Elizabeth, and Lucas Schilling; Laurel, Gianni, Zack, and Celia Yahi; and Jeremy, Jenni, and Che White; Robin Ackley-Fay, Terry Fay and Jon Ackley.

I am grateful to my colleagues in the English Department at the University of Wisconsin at Stevens Point. In particular, Tom Bloom and Ann Bloom shared their suggestions on writing an opinion paper, which I have incorporated into the discussion of the research paper, and Don Pattow, former director of Freshman English, gave me materials on writing across the curriculum. I also want to thank the following students who gave permission to use material from their course papers: Erin Anderson, Josanne Begley, Margo Borden, Morris Boyd, Sam Cox, Rita Fleming, Nathan Hayes, Missy Heiman, Linda Kay Jeske, Kelley Kassien, Kari Kolb, Steph Niedermair, Barbara Novak, Shawn Ryan, Lauren Shimulunas, Jodi Simon, Jennifer Sturm, Cory L. Vandertie, Melinda Vang, and Laurel Yahi.

Finally, I owe special thanks and gratitude to my editor, Kathy Sands-Boehmer, who has been a joy to work with.

PERSPECTIVES
on Contemporary Issues

PART • ONE

Writing Critically and Conducting Research

Reading Critically

READING CRITICALLY IN PREPARATION FOR WRITING CRITICALLY

Reading critically does not necessarily mean that you object to what someone has written or that you view it negatively. Rather, it means that you read something carefully, thoughtfully, and thoroughly for two reasons: first, to understand it, and second, to assess it. You read for meaning first because, obviously, you must understand what you read before it can be examined. Once you develop a clear understanding of a piece of writing, you have a solid basis for moving beyond comprehension to evaluation.

Reading critically involves examining an author's ideas and the evidence the author has supplied in support of those ideas. It means that you try to recognize the difference between reasonable, logical assertions and those that are unreasonable or lack credibility. It requires you to distinguish between fact and opinion, to sort out the evidence an author cites, and to evaluate that evidence in terms of its relevance, accuracy, and importance. Thus, reading critically means that you actively engage in what you read, you analyze it, and you evaluate it. Learning to be a critical reader also helps to make you a better writer. If you pay attention to the ways in which professional writers and scholars use language, structure their essays, and develop their ideas, you will learn some valuable lessons for your own writing.

The following guidelines are not ironclad rules for reading critically, but they are useful suggestions to help you get the most from your reading. These guidelines for reading will also be very helpful for any kind of writing required in your college courses, especially the one for which you are using this textbook. If you read the assigned selections carefully, you will very likely be fully prepared to write on one of the topics that end each chapter. Certainly, reading critically is a necessity for any of the varieties of writing and strategies discussed in Part One: summary, critique, argument, synthesis, and the research paper.

Read the Title. Before you read, consider the title. A title often not only reveals the subject of the piece, but it can also tell you something about the way in which the subject will be treated. It may indicate the position the author takes on the subject or reflect the tone of the piece. (*Tone* refers to the writer's attitude toward the subject and audience, which is conveyed largely through word choice and level of language usage, such as informal or formal, colloquial, or slang.) A number of essays in this textbook have revealing titles. For instance, the title "Violent Media is Good for Kids" in Chapter 9 clearly indicates the position of its author, Gerard Jones, on the subject of violent media. You cannot tell from the title alone what his arguments are, but you can expect him to argue that violence in media has benefits for children. Similarly, the title "Stop Blaming Kids and TV" in Chapter 10 indicates that the subject will be young people and television viewing and that the author, Mike Males, believes they are being unfairly blamed for something—though what that is will not be clear until you read the essay. Sometimes authors ask questions in their titles, as in "Sacred Rite or Civil Right?" As readers, we assume that the author of that essay in Chapter 14, Howard Moody, answers the question he poses in his title. There is no indication in that title, however, of how he answers it.

Find Out About the Author. If information about the author is provided, read it. Knowing who the author is, what his or her publications are, and what his or her profession is, for example, gives you an idea of the authority from which the author writes. In magazines, journals, and collections of essays, such as those you will use in many of your college courses, the headnote often tells you about the author. The headnote is the information located between the title and the beginning of the essay, usually highlighted or set off from the body of the essay itself. Here is the headnote for Karen Sternheimer's "Do Video Games Kill?" (Chapter 8):

> *Karen Sternheimer, whose work focuses on youth and popular culture, teaches in the sociology department at the University of Southern California. She is author of* It's Not the Media: The Truth about Pop Culture's Influence on Children *(2003)*; Kids These Days: Facts and Fictions about Today's Youth (2006); *and* Connecting Popular Culture and Social Problems: Why the Media is Not the Answer *(2009). Her commentary has been published in several newspapers, and she has appeared on numerous television and radio programs. This article appeared in the Winter 2007 issue of* Contexts, *the journal of the American Sociological Association.*

The information about Sternheimer's professional interests as an instructor in the sociology department at the University of Southern California, the titles of her books, and the fact that she is invited to write and speak on her research interests all indicate that she is qualified to write on the subject of the relative harm of video games. The place of publication is also important in establishing Sternheimer's credentials as an authority on her subject: journals of professional associations are usually juried (indicating that not everyone who submits an article will be published), and publication in professional journals enhance their authors' scholarly reputations.

Determine the Purpose. Good writers have clear purposes in mind as they plan and draft their work. Most nonfiction writing falls into the categories of persuasive, expository, and expressive writing. These forms of writing are used to achieve different goals, and they adopt different strategies for achieving those goals. In persuasive writing, the emphasis is on the reader: the writer's purpose is to convince the reader of the validity of his or her position on an issue and sometimes even to move the reader to action. In expository writing, the goal is to inform or present an objective explanation. The emphasis is on ideas, events, or objects themselves, not on how the writer feels about them. Much of the writing in college textbooks is expository, as are newspaper, magazine, and professional journal articles, and nonfiction books. Expository writing can take many forms, including cause–effect analysis, comparison–contrast, definition, and classification. Expressive writing emphasizes the writer's feelings and subjective view of the world. The writer's focus is on personal feelings about, or attitude toward, the subject. A journal or diary includes expressive writing. Persuasive, expository, and expressive writing often overlap, but usually a writer has one main purpose. From the opening paragraphs of a written work, you should be able to determine its general purpose or aim. A clearly implied or stated purpose helps the writer to shape the writing, and it helps the reader to understand and evaluate the work.

Try to Determine the Intended Audience. Writers make assumptions about the people they are writing for, including whether their audience will be sympathetic or opposed to their positions, how informed their readers are about the subjects they are writing on, what their education level is, and similar considerations. These assumptions that writers make about their readers directly influence the tone they use, the evidence they select, the way in which they organize and develop their writing, and even their sentence structure, word choice, and diction level. Knowing whom the writer is addressing helps you to understand the writer's point of view and to explain the choices the writer has made in writing the piece. In writing for college courses, students usually assume a general audience of people like themselves who are reasonably intelligent and interested in what they have to say. However, professional writers or scholars often write for specific audiences, depending on the publications in which their writing appears. Knowing whether an audience is familiar with a subject or whether the audience is specialized or general also governs what kinds of evidence to offer and how much to include. Where the writing is published gives you a good idea of who the audience is. Take, for instance, the essays by Mike Males in Chapter 10 and Aaron Sachs in Chapter 20. You know from the headnote that accompanies "Stop Blaming Kids and TV" that it was first published in the *Progressive.* It is fair to assume that readers of the magazine approve of the magazine's mission, which is, according to its website (www.progressive.org), to be "a journalistic voice for peace and social justice at home and abroad." From the word *progressive* and the stated mission, it is reasonable to assume that Males anticipated an audience that is likely to be liberal in its political, social, and philosophical views. On the other hand, it is not immediately clear whether the audience is liberal or conservative for "Humboldt's Legacy and the Restoration of Science," which first appeared in *World Watch,* a publication of the World Watch Institute that features articles on the relationship between people and their environment. According to the World Watch Institute website (www.worldwatch.org), its award-winning, bi-monthly magazine provides a forum for those with a strong interest in environmental issues such as energy, population, biodiversity, climate change, and similar topics. This publication differs from a popular magazine or professional journal in that it offers "concise, cutting-edge analysis from a holistic perspective. Th[e] . . . periodical connects the dots between our natural world and the people who inhabit it." Thus, the target audience has a special interest but includes those with both general interest and specialized expertise in environmental studies.

Locate the Thesis Statement or Main Idea. The thesis states the main idea of the entire essay. Sometimes it is embodied in a single sentence—the thesis statement—and sometimes it is stated in several sentences. If the main idea is not explicitly stated, it should be clearly implied. Whether the thesis is explicit or implicit, it is a necessary component of a clearly written work. A thesis helps the writer to focus the writing and guides the organization and development of key ideas. It also helps to provide direction to the reader by making clear what the point of the essay is, thereby assisting the reader's understanding of the piece.

Locate Key Ideas and Supporting Evidence or Details. For this step in your critical reading, you should underline or highlight the major points of the essay. One important tool for an active, critical reader is a pen or pencil. As you read, underline, star, or in some way highlight major points of development. Look for topic sentences of paragraphs. Although the thesis statement answers the question, What is this essay about? the topic sentence answers the question, What is this paragraph about? If a topic sentence is not clearly stated, it should be clearly implied.

Make Marginal Notes as You Read. In the margins, write your response to a passage or make note of words, phrases, or entire passages you think are important to the piece. Make notes about the evidence or details that support major points. If you have a question about something the author says, write it in the margin for later consideration. If you are not sure of the meaning of a word, circle it and look it up in a dictionary after you have finished reading. Finally, if you are struck by the beauty, logic, or peculiarity of a passage, note marginal comments on that as well.

Summarize What You Have Read. This is the point at which you test your understanding of what you have read. Go back now and look at your underlining and notations. Then try to state in your own words what the writing is about and the main points the writer makes. If you can accurately summarize a piece of writing, then you probably have a good idea of its meaning. Summarizing also helps you to recall the piece later, perhaps in class or in small-group discussions. Incidentally, summarizing is also a good strategy for your own study habits. After reading an assignment for any of your courses, try to write or tell someone a summary of your reading. If you cannot express in your own words the major ideas of what you have just read, it should be reread. For a more detailed discussion of writing a summary, see Chapter 3.

Evaluate What You Have Read. When you are sure that you understand what you have read and can summarize it objectively, you are ready to respond. You can evaluate something in a number of ways, depending on its purpose. First, consider whether the author achieves the stated or implied purpose and whether the thesis or main idea is thoroughly explained, developed, or argued. Has the writer supplied enough details, examples, or other evidence? If you are evaluating an argument or persuasion essay, is the evidence convincing to you? Does the piece make a logical and reasonable argument? Are you persuaded to the writer's position? What questions do you have about any of the writer's assertions? Do you wish to challenge her or him on any points? If the purpose of the essay is to describe, has the writer conveyed to you the essence of the subject with appropriately vivid language? For any piece of writing, you can assess how well written it is. Is it organized? Is the writing clear to you? Does the introduction give you enough information to get you easily into the essay, and does the conclusion leave you satisfied that the writer has accomplished the purpose for the essay? In Chapter 4, Writing a Critique, you will find a more detailed discussion of how to evaluate a passage or entire essay.

GUIDELINES FOR READING CRITICALLY

- Consider what the title tells you about the essay.
- Try to learn something about the author.
- Determine the purpose of the writing.
- Determine the audience for whom the piece was written.
- Locate the thesis statement or main idea.
- Locate key ideas and supporting evidence or details.
- Make marginal notes as you read, including not only a summary of key ideas but also your questions about the content.
- Summarize what you have read.
- Evaluate what you have read.

ILLUSTRATION: READING CRITICALLY

A demonstration of how a reader might apply the guidelines for critical reading accompanies the following essay, "What's in a Name? More than You Think," by Joe Saltzman. Read the essay first, noticing words and passages that are underlined and addressed in the marginal comments. Then read the discussion following it and consider the ways in which your own critical reading might differ from the comments there. Would you add anything? What other words or passages would you underline or highlight? What other marginal comments would you make?

WHAT'S IN A NAME? MORE THAN YOU THINK

JOE SALTZMAN

Academic and professional credentials.

Joe Saltzman is associate mass media editor of USA Today; *associate dean and professor of journalism, University of Southern California Annenberg School for Communication, Los Angeles; and director of the Image of the Journalist in Popular Culture, a project of the Norman Lear Center. He is author of* Frank Capra and the Image of the Journalist in American Film. *Recipient of more than fifty awards, Saltzman produces medical documentaries, acts as a senior investigative producer for* Entertainment Tonight, *and writes articles, reviews, columns, and opinion pieces for hundreds of magazines and newspapers. In this piece, which first appeared in the July 2003 issue of* USA Today Magazine, *Saltzman's use of the phrase "the war in Iraq" refers to the period between the invasion of Iraq by a coalition of American, British, and Australian forces on March 20, 2003, and President George W. Bush's declaration on May 1, 2003, that combat operations in Iraq were over. "The aftermath" is that period immediately following President Bush's declaration.*

His subject. His thesis—note word choice.

Television coverage of the Iraqi war and postwar illustrates once again how American television news is obsessed with show business terminology that at the very least is poor journalism and at its worst corrupts and ignores a basic rule of journalism: fairness and accuracy in all reporting.

Restates thesis.

With the government's public relations arm pushing hard, phrases to describe the war and postwar stories moved from a fair account of what was going on to an oppressive vocabulary that gave a spin to the coverage. Colorful phrases, sometimes patriotic, sometimes just plain wrong, gave much of the TV news coverage a convenient anti-Iraqi/pro-American stance. Some examples:

1st example: "Operation Iraqi Freedom"—sounds noble and heroic.

"Operation Iraqi Freedom" was used constantly by Fox and MSNBC as a banner for summing up the coverage of the war in the Middle East. Few would dispute that "Operation Iraqi Freedom" sounded noble and gave a heroic and honorable reason for going to war as opposed to the accurate and more evenhanded "The War in Iraq" or "The Iraqi Conflict." Fighting for a country's freedom brings images of the American and French revolutions, of World War II soldiers fighting against Hitler and the Japanese, and of friendly, grateful citizens waving American flags to greet soldiers who had liberated their country. These images neatly fit with a title like "Operation Iraqi Freedom." "The War in Iraq" conjures up destruction and death. It is one thing for the Administration to use favorable phrases to win support for its policies, quite another for the American media to use such phrases in trying to describe what is going on in a Middle East war.

2nd example: "coalition forces"—says there was no coalition, just American soldiers.

"Coalition forces" sounds as if a worldwide coalition of military force is being used to fight the war. It's certainly the Bush-approved term for the American and British forces fighting in Iraq. News organizations, however, shouldn't use phrases that do not adequately describe the situation. It was American soldiers in Baghdad, not coalition forces, but most of the news media used the phrase "coalition forces" throughout the coverage of the war.

3rd example: "weapons of mass destruction"—sound fearsome.

Going into a foreign country to get rid of "weapons of mass destruction" makes sense. As *Time* magazine put it, "they sound so much more fearsome than chemical or biological weapons. A few papers, like *the New York Times,* have been careful to use 'unconventional weapons' or other terms instead."

Restates main point.

If you were trying to figure out whether the war in Iraq was justified, see which sentence would convince you: "Operation Iraqi Freedom was underway as coalition forces went into Iraq to discover and destroy weapons of mass destruction"; or "The war in Iraq was underway as American and British forces went into Iraq to discover and destroy unconventional weapons."

4th example: "collateral damage"—softens the reality.

"Collateral damage" doesn't sound as horrific as civilian casualties or, even more accurately, civilians who were wounded, maimed, or killed by American bombs and ground fire.

Reaffirms his position: using catchphrases is demeaning.

Certain phrases make a difference in our perception of what goes on in our world. Catchphrases that make unpopular events less difficult to accept should not be a part of daily news media coverage. It demeans both the journalist and the viewer.

Shifts focus to visual images. Says "embedded journalists" give distorted view of war.

Many watching the television war coverage were impressed with the pictures sent back by "embedded" journalists traveling with various military units in the field. And many of the images and reports were spectacular, but at what cost? No one would deny that reporters embedded with individual units would be partial to the people around them saving their lives.

No one would deny that this kind of coverage simply gives the viewer a glimpse at specific moments in war. No embedded reporter has the chance or the ability to interview the other side during a battle. In many ways, this coverage, while unique in the history of war reporting, gave an even more-distorted view of what was going on in the field than battle reports issued by reporters safely away from the sounds and sights of immediate warfare.

Not opposed to embedded reporters, but there should be a broader perspective of what's going on.

None of this is to say that we shouldn't have reports from embedded reporters. It is one more attempt to figure out what is going on during wartime. It must be put into proper perspective, however. The British broadcasters and the Middle East press did an effective job in showing other sides of the war, other sides that were either not reported by the American news media or given short shrift next to the action-packed, myopic reports from embedded correspondents in the field.

Look up definition of "myopic."

Journalists guilty of censorship—kept pictures of POWs and wounded civilians out of media.

Perhaps even more damaging was the news media's attempt to "censor" unpleasant sights and sounds from the battlefield because they were worried about offending American sensibilities. The most-grievous example was the failure of U.S. news media to show the footage of the American prisoners of war when the entire world was watching what was happening to them. Moreover, other pictures of wounded Iraqi civilians were also missing in much of the American news media coverage. Many viewers turned to other sources for news of the war—newspapers, magazines, the Internet, the BBC, and cable stations showing some of the foreign coverage.

Showing "offensive" pictures might balance the picture of war. TV news media need to change approach to reporting war.

The TV news media never should assume the role of a parent deciding what images and sounds the American people should be allowed to see. While it is true that pictures of wounded Iraqi civilians and abused POWs do not give viewers an accurate and complete picture of the war by themselves, they would have been an important addition to the embedded war coverage of bullets and sand-clouded battles. One wonders what the news media would have shown, however, if an embedded reporter was suddenly blown to bits on camera.

War is always brutal and the images always horrible and hard to watch. If the American TV news media want to cover modern warfare, they will have to do far more than give us fancy showbiz titles and only the sounds and images that they deem suitable for G-rated TV news.

DISCUSSION OF "WHAT'S IN A NAME? MORE THAN YOU THINK"

Title. The title tells readers the subject of the article—names and their connotations—but not what kinds of names. The title does suggest that the author is going to be critical of whatever sort of naming he discusses in the paper (names mean "more than you think").

Author. The information in the headnote suggests that the author seems well qualified to write critically of news reporting. He is a mass media editor of a major news magazine and a professor of journalism. He is active in his discipline, has published a book on the image of journalists in film, and has received numerous awards for his professional work.

Audience. The headnote also says that "What's in a Name? More than You Think" was first published in *USA Today Magazine,* a publication for a general audience of urban readers who like to get the essentials of news stories quickly. Saltzman likely assumed an audience of educated readers who want analyses of important national and international developments but who do not necessarily have the time to read lengthy articles on those topics. Saltzman therefore writes in a style appropriate to newspapers and news magazines—that is, he avoids informal language such as slang or colloquialisms as well as specialized terms or difficult vocabulary. He uses words and terms that would be familiar to an audience of readers who keep up on America's involvement in Iraq. His word choice and sentence structure are appropriate for educated adults who take an interest in the news.

Purpose and Main Idea. Saltzman states his subject and main idea in his first sentence: he believes that television coverage of the Iraqi war and postwar is unfair and inaccurate. He elaborates in the second paragraph by suggesting that TV reporters gave in to pressure from the government and adopted "an oppressive vocabulary" to give "spin" to their coverage of the war. We know from the headnote that Saltzman was writing not long after President Bush declared that the coalition invasion of Iraq was over, so his use of present tense is appropriate for reporting what was going on at the time he wrote his piece. [A further comment on verb tenses: when you are writing about another piece of writing, whether fiction or nonfiction, use present tense to discuss what the writer says in the piece.] He uses language that makes his view of such reporting quite clear when he accuses television news of being "obsessed with show business terminology," which "corrupts and ignores" the basic rule of journalism to be fair and accurate in its reporting. It is clear from those opening paragraphs that his purpose is to argue that American television news reporters have been unfair, inaccurate, and demeaning in their reporting of the war in Iraq and its aftermath.

Key Ideas and Supporting Evidence. Saltzman primarily uses **exemplification** to develop his **argument.** In paragraphs 3–6, he gives examples of the phrases that he finds offensive in American television news reporting, along with his explanation of why their use is bad journalism. He believes that the phrase "Operation Iraqi Freedom," with its associations of patriotism and nobility, is appropriate for the administration, but not for reporters, who are supposed to remain neutral and unbiased. His preferred phrase would be "The War in Iraq." Next he cites the phrase "coalition forces," which suggests a worldwide joining of military forces, when, he asserts, it was only British and American soldiers who were fighting in Baghdad. He goes on to "weapons of mass destruction," a phrase that suggests something quite fearsome, as opposed to a more neutral phrase like "unconventional weapons." His last example is "collateral damage," which he says downplays or helps soften the reality that the phrase refers to "civilian casualties" or "civilians who were wounded, maimed, or killed by American bombs and ground fire" (paragraph 6).

After arguing that the language of American television news reporters is unfair and biased, he goes on to discuss the images that were broadcast on television. He believes that using "'embedded' journalists" gave a narrow, distorted view of the battlefield and that viewers did not get a proper perspective of what was going on in the war. His last example is the "even more damaging" attempts by the media to "'censor' unpleasant sights and sounds from the battlefield" because they did not want to offend "American sensibilities." His point about both embedded journalists and attempts to withhold disturbing images is that reporters give a narrow and distorted perspective of what was happening during the war and what has been going on after it. He argues for a broader picture of the realities of war. Saltzman concludes by asserting that if American television news media want to cover modern warfare, they must drop the "fancy showbiz titles" and stop "censoring" images they believe Americans would find disturbing.

Summary. In "What's in a Name? More than You Think," Joe Saltzman argues that American television news reporters violate the basic rules of reporting by using language and making choices that give an unfair, inaccurate, and distorted view of the war in Iraq and its aftermath. He gives a number of examples of language to make his point. He cites the phrase "Operation Iraqi Freedom," which stirs up patriotic feelings, more appropriately the business of the government's public relations people than reporters. Saltzman then asserts that "coalition forces" is a misleading and inaccurate phrase because there were only American soldiers in Baghdad, not an alliance of many forces from around the world. His remaining two examples are "weapons of mass destruction," with its connotations of terror, and "collateral damage," which softens the reality of what the term actually denotes. From language, Saltzman moves to the images that were broadcast on television. The use of embedded reporters to cover the war was not a bad idea, he says, but it narrowed the view of the war rather than helped present a broad perspective of what was going on. Worse, he argues, was the decision not to show images of the abuses of prisoners of war and wounded Iraqi citizens. Such a failure amounts to censorship. He concludes by reasserting his major point that American television journalists failed in their coverage of the war in Iraq and the period after the war, and he suggests that they change their ways if they want to report modern warfare accurately and fairly.

Evaluation. Saltzman's essay is organized sensibly and logically written in clear, straightforward prose. His use of specific examples and his reasons why they are inappropriate make a convincing case for his argument that American television journalists were inaccurate and unfair in their reporting of the Iraq war. The repetition of "no one would deny" in paragraph 8 lends emphasis to the point he is making about the limited perspective of embedded reporters. Furthermore, the disclaimer in the first sentence of paragraph 9 is his concession, in a way, to readers who may think that he is being overly critical of embedded reporters, and it leads to his repeating—and emphasizing—his opinion. Despite Saltzman's excellent use of examples to support and develop his central idea, he does not go into real depth in his analysis of any of them. It is quite possible that space limitations imposed by the magazine kept him from a fuller discussion. The fact that many of his paragraphs are short—one or two sentences in several cases—may reflect his training in journalism: the physical space of newspaper and in some cases magazine columns requires shorter paragraphs.

Saltzman is an accomplished writer who is not afraid to express opinions that may not be popular with the general public, and these opinions raise questions that bear further exploration and thought. His assertion that American television news reporting of war should give a broader picture, showing if possible the perspective of the enemy and the effects of war on the people we are fighting, is fair. On the other hand, is it the place of the press to be critical of the administration or to challenge the decisions of its country's leaders in time of war? Is it not important to keep up morale on the home front as well as on the battlefield? What is gained by a press hostile to or even subversive of its government in a time when patriotism and public support of its military are crucial to the war effort? These are tough questions that both the press and its critics have been struggling with, and Saltzman's essay is a good starting place for an open discussion of the issues he raises.

RHETORICAL ANALYSIS OF VISUALS

Rhetorical considerations apply to visual images as well as to written forms of communication. "Analysis" as a process involves taking something that is whole and complex and breaking it into its individual components to better understand it. Thus, a rhetorical analysis is a close examination of not just what a work says but, just as importantly, how it says it. Whether you are critiquing an essay in a book or periodical, a visual art form, or an Internet website, questions of audience, tone, purpose, organization, content, and meaning apply. With visuals, as with written works, you must consider perspective or point of view, context, and connotation. Connotation—the emotional associations of a thing—is perhaps even more important when viewing visuals than in reading words. Just as words have associations that go beyond the literal term or add layers of meaning to what they denote ("the dictionary definition"), so images have powerful associations. Images often have the ability to express things—emotions, nuances, insights—in a way that words cannot. They can reveal what is difficult to put into words by conveying impressions or depicting in sharp detail what it would take a great many words to describe or explain, including subtleties of meaning that emerge only after thoughtful consideration and careful perusal of the image. Visuals also have the potential to argue a viewpoint or persuade an audience; their authors use strategies to present a viewpoint or make a statement that is similar to those used by authors of written text.

We see images daily in a variety of forms—in photographs, drawings, paintings, pictures, brochures, advertisements, CD album covers, posters, and Internet web pages, and of course on television and in film. Most of these images go unexamined because we see so many images in our lives that we simply do not have time to analyze them all. But when we find it useful to consider an image closely, how do we analyze it? What can we say about it? How can we express in words what an image means or implies? The answer to these questions is that analyzing images critically requires skills that are quite similar to those for analyzing a piece of writing critically. Just as writers select details and organize essays to make specific points, so too do artists shooting a scene or painting a picture select details and arrange them in order to convey specific ideas or impressions. Writers and artists alike make judgments that in turn shape how readers or viewers perceive their work.

Analyzing a visual involves doing a close "reading" of the image and asking a series of questions about it. In looking critically at a visual image, you want to consider many aspects of it: What do you see when you first look at it? How do you respond initially? What details does the image highlight? What other details are included and what might have been excluded? How does the positioning of various elements of the image emphasize its meaning? The following list of questions will help you analyze the visual images that are located throughout the textbook in each of the chapters of Parts Two through Five. The answers you get when you ask these questions can give you a greater understanding of the images you are scrutinizing. Most of the visual images reproduced in this textbook are photographs or drawings, so the first set of questions is designed to help you in your analysis of them. However, the questions can easily be adapted to other kinds of images, such as advertisements, newspaper page layouts, and Internet web pages. Furthermore, television, film, music videos, and documentaries also convey messages through images that can be analyzed rhetorically in much the same way as the other forms of visual communication can be.

Questions to Ask About a Visual Image.

- **What is your overall immediate impression of the image?** First impressions often linger even after rethinking one's initial response, so what strikes you immediately about an image is particularly important.

- **What detail first catches your attention?** After noting your immediate overall response, consider what detail or details first attract you. Is it the prominence, size, or positioning of the subject? Is it the colors or absence of them? Is it the size, the physical space it occupies? More than likely, the artist wanted you to notice that detail first, and very likely it is an integral part of the "message" or "statement" the image makes.
- **What details emerge after you have studied the image for a while?** Do you detect any pattern in the arrangement of details? If so, how does the arrangement of details function to convey the overall impression?
- **How does the arrangement of objects or people in the picture help draw your attention to the central image, the one you are initially drawn to?** Are some things placed prominently in the center or made larger than others? If so, what is the effect of that arrangement? How does the background function in relation to what is placed in the foreground?
- **If the image is in color, how does the artist use color?** Are the colors selected to represent certain emotions, moods, or other qualities? If it is in black and white, what use does the artist make of the absence of color? Does the artist use degrees of shading and brightness? If so, to what effect?
- **From what perspective is the artist viewing the subject?** Is it close to or far away from the subject? Is the subject viewed straight-on or from the side? Why do you think the artist selected this particular perspective? How might a shift in perspective alter the view of the subject, not just physically but on the level of meaning as well?
- **What emotions does the image evoke in you?** Why? Which details of the image convey the strongest emotion?
- **Has anything important been left out of the image?** What might have been included, and why do you think it was left out?
- **What is happening in the picture?** Does it tell a story or give a single impression?
- **What does the picture tell you about its subject?** How does it convey that message?
- **If there are people in the image, what can you tell about them?** What details tell you those things? Is it the way they are dressed? Their physical appearance? What they are doing?
- **Does the picture raise any questions?** What would you like to ask about the image, the activity, or the people in it? How would you find the answers to your questions?

EXERCISE

Ask the questions for analyzing visuals listed above as you study the following photograph (Figure 1.1). Then, selecting the details you believe are important, write an analysis of the photograph. Begin your analysis with an introductory paragraph that includes a thesis statement or a statement of the main idea of the photograph. This thesis should reflect your understanding of what the photograph means to you—its message, its story, what it suggests symbolically, or whatever ultimately you decide about the photograph. The rest of the paper should draw on details from your answers to the questions as you explain or support your thesis statement.

Here are some questions specific to this photograph that you might want to think about as you work through the questions listed above:

- Besides showing the tattoo, what effect is achieved by taking the picture from behind the man?
- What does the tattoo suggest to you about the man? Does the earring in his left ear add anything to your image of him?
- Can you tell the race or ethnicity of the man, and if so, does that detail add a layer of meaning or implication to the picture?
- Does the man's stance—the way he is standing, the shape of his shoulders, the position of his arms—tell you anything about what he is thinking or what he is about to do? Is the man anticipating a challenge? Is he preparing to climb the dune?
- Does it make a difference that this is a sand dune and not a mountain or some other challenge?
- What do you anticipate happening if the man tries to climb the dune?
- Do the clouds represent anything? Why is the sunlight hidden by the clouds? Is the sun trying to break through the clouds, or are the clouds preventing the sun from shining?

Questions to Ask About an Advertisement. Advertising is a powerful and pervasive force in our world. Ads have the ability to affect how we think, act, and even feel about ourselves and others. Ads can shape, reflect, or distort both individual perceptions and social values, and they do so by employing some of the classic strategies of argument and persuasion: they have a proposition, they know their audience, they make appeals, they use comparisons and examples, and they particularly want to persuade us to action. In addition to the questions to ask about visual images, the following questions will help you analyze both print and nonprint advertisements:

- **What is the message of the advertisement?** What does it say to potential buyers of the product? That is, what is its argument?
- **Who is the intended audience?** How can you tell?

Figure 1.1 *Tattooed man looking at sand dune.*

- **What strategies does the ad use to convey its message?** What appeals—to logic, to emotion, to ethics, or to shared values—does it use? Does it rely primarily on one appeal only or does it combine them? How do the specific details convey that message?
- **How does the text—the actual words used—convey the message of the advertisement?** How are words arranged or placed in the ad and why are they placed that way? If a non-print ad, how are the voice-overs or dialogue used to convey the message?
- **How would you describe the style and tone of the advertisement?** How do they help convey the message or sell the product?

EXERCISE

1. Select a print advertisement for analysis. Ask the questions noted on the previous page and write an analysis based on your notes, assessing the effectiveness of the ad in achieving its purpose. Attach the advertisement with your analysis when you hand it in to your instructor.
2. Select two advertisements for the same kind of product (for instance, clothing, toothpaste, or laundry detergent). Apply the questions noted on the previous page and choose the one that you think is more effective at selling or promoting the product. Formulate a thesis sentence that states your preference, and use details from your scrutiny of both of them to support that statement.

Questions to Ask About a Newspaper Page. Newspapers can shape reader response in the choices they make about the layout of text and photographs. Although we like to think that newspapers are unbiased in their reporting of news items, reading just two different newspapers on the same subject reveals that the choices a newspaper makes about a news item have a huge influence on the impressions it leaves on readers. Just the visual effect of a page layout alone tells us many things. What page an article or picture appears on and where on the page it is located represent a judgment on the part of the paper about the importance of the article or image and cannot help but shape how readers respond to it. Consider the following list about photographs and news articles when looking at a newspaper page:

- **Where in the paper is the article or photograph placed?** Front-page placement indicates that the newspaper considers it more important as a news item than placement on the inside pages.
- **How are photographs and news articles positioned on the page?** Items that are placed high on the page or in the center of the page are likely to draw the attention more readily than those placed low or off center.
- **How large are the photographs or the headlines?** Visually, larger photographs or headlines are likely to draw attention and interest more quickly than small ones.
- **Are photographs in color or black and white?** Choosing to run a picture in color indicates a value judgment that the paper has made about the interest or newsworthiness of the image.

EXERCISE

1. Select a newspaper page for analysis. Front pages are particularly important in newspapers for attracting reader attention, so perhaps you will want to analyze the front page of the newspaper. Ask the questions listed above and write an analysis based on the answers to your questions. What article(s) does the newspaper think

more important than others? How are photographs used on the page? Attach the page with your analysis when you hand it in to your instructor.

2. Select two different newspapers covering the same news story and compare their treatment of the story. How do the two newspapers compare and contrast in their handling of the story? Is one more effective than the other in reporting it? Formulate a thesis that reflects your ultimate judgment of the two papers' treatment of the news story and support that thesis with details gathered from your comparison of the two.

RHETORICAL ANALYSIS OF WEBSITES

The Internet provides a seemingly endless variety of sites to visit for every taste and interest. Web pages can function rhetorically to influence visitors to the site in much the same way as other forms of discourse. The very way in which the web page is constructed can work to produce a desired effect, especially if the constructor of the site wishes to persuade an audience, sway opinion, or impose a particular point of view. A rhetorical analysis looks at the ways a site achieves its stated or implied purpose. Because websites vary considerably in their reliability and currency, you will find additional information about evaluating them in Chapter 7. Many of the same questions one asks when evaluating a website apply when doing a rhetorical analysis of it. What follows are some of the components of a web page and questions to ask about it as you analyze its rhetorical effectiveness.

Questions to Ask About a Website:

- **Domain. What is the URL (uniform record locator) of the site?** The domain—the logical or geographical location of the site on the Internet, indicated by the very last part of the URL—tells you something about the site. Domains differ according to the entity sponsoring them: *.edu* for educational institutions, *.gov* for government agencies, *.com* or *.net* for commercial or personal enterprises, *.org* for organizations. These broad categories give you the first piece of information about the site. Within the categories, there are countless subcategories.
- **Author.** Who created the web page? Is it an individual, an organization, a government agency, an educational institution, or a corporation? Does the text at the site give you information about the author? If not, why do you think that information is not provided? Does the site tell you how to contact the author?
- **Audience.** What audience does the web page target? How can you tell? Is the intended audience stated or implied? Does it make assumptions about values, beliefs, age, sex, race, national origin, education, or socioeconomic background of its target audience?

- **Purpose.** Does the web page want to inform, entertain, sell, argue a position, or persuade people to change their minds or to take action? If it has more than one purpose, what combination of purposes does it have? Is the implied purpose the same as the stated purpose? Does the text state one purpose while word choice, graphics, and page layout suggest or imply another? For instance, a political candidate's website might state that it has no intention of bringing up an opponent's past wrongdoings, while the very fact of stating that there are past wrongdoings to bring up casts doubt on the character of the opponent.
- **Text.** What rhetorical appeals does the written text of the website make? Does it appeal to logic or reason? Does it appeal to emotions? If emotions, which ones does it appeal to—pity, fear, joy, anger, sympathy?
- **Content.** Does the website cover the topic thoroughly? Does it use language that you understand? Does it offer links and if so, how many links? Are the links still active? What is the quality of the links?
- **Background color.** How does the background color choice affect the mood and tone of the page? Is it a vibrant color or a sober one? Does it intrude on the text or enhance it?
- **Page layout.** Is there space between items on the page or are things cramped together? How does the use of space on the page affect your overall impression of the page and your ability to read it?
- **Loading and positioning of items.** What gets loaded first when you go to the web page? Where is that material positioned? What is loaded later or positioned low on the page? Sometimes certain components of a web page are purposely programmed to load first in order to further emphasize the purpose of the site.
- **Graphics.** Are graphics on the web page static or active? Is the print used for the text large, small, or a mix of both? If a mix, what does larger print emphasize that smaller print doesn't? What font is used? Are bold print, italics, or underlining used, and if so, to what effect? Is there a banner? What purpose does the banner serve?
- **Photographs or drawings.** If photographs or other images are used, what is their function? Do they illustrate or help explain something, give information, or serve to decorate the page?
- **Lighting and contrast.** Does the web page make use of contrasts of light and dark? If so, what is the effect of those contrasts?

EXERCISE

Locate two websites on the same topic and compare and contrast their rhetorical effectiveness by applying the relevant questions listed above. After deciding which one you think is more effective, write an analysis in which your thesis states which site you prefer. Use details from your perusal of both of them as proof or evidence to support your thesis statement.

Forums on the Web: Listservs, Blogs, and Social Networking Sites

In addition to websites that people go to for information, entertainment, or news, the Internet also has available a number of forums for people to participate in, such as chat rooms, newsgroups, discussion lists (listservs), blogs, and social networking sites. Although most websites are fairly dynamic in that they are (or should be) regularly updated, forums typically change throughout the day. Three popular forums are **listservs, blogs, and social networking sites.** All three are capable of influencing people's views or the way they think about the topics being discussed at the sites; they even have the potential to actually bring about changes because of the high degree of involvement that they have generated among visitors to their sites. Another distinguishing characteristic of listservs, blogs, and social networking sites is that people are invited to participate in an ongoing, ever-changing discussion. People who become members of these sites have an opportunity to be not just passive readers but also active writers.

Listservs. Listservs are e-mail based discussion groups linked to specific topics. Listservs function as forums for the exchange of ideas, where members can debate, discuss, post news items, seek or give advice, and share in a community of people who have in common their interest in the topic of the listserv. Although listservs have official websites where people can subscribe, read the guidelines for posting, and locate archived postings, among other things, the real activity takes place through e-mail. Members can elect to receive messages either individually as they are posted, or in digests that are sent daily, or whenever a specific number of messages have posted. Members are usually required to follow certain rules or guidelines, primarily those related to conduct and appropriate content, and often the listserv has a moderator who monitors the content of messages to make sure that posts do not violate those rules. Listservs typically archive messages by date, subject of message, and/or author, and these archives can be viewed by nonmembers as well as members. They vary widely in membership numbers, from just a few people to thousands. For instance, a listserv devoted to British novelist Barbara Pym has a small membership of around 100, and posts to the site are occasional and few. In contrast, DorothyL, a discussion and idea list for lovers of the mystery genre, has almost 3,000 subscribers and 50 to 100 postings each day. Because listservs attract people with at least the subject of the listserv in common, they can create a strong sense of community among subscribers. Although listservs are good for reading what many people have to say on various subjects related to the primary topic of the discussion group, postings are, in general, unedited and may not be completely reliable. On the other hand, a posting that seems wrongheaded or erroneous is likely to be corrected or at least commented on by other members of the group.

Blogs. The term *blog* (web log) describes an activity that people had been doing long before the term was coined: maintaining a website where they record personal thoughts and provide links to other sites. Many of them are essentially personal pages that bloggers (owners of the sites) update daily. They provide a forum for the bloggers themselves to argue, explain, comment on, vent frustrations, air opinions, or just gossip, while visitors to the site can express their own opinions or make observations. Membership is not required; anyone can read and respond to anyone's blog. In addition to online journals, blogs can be news summaries, collections of bits and pieces from other websites, and valuable resources for instant access to the latest news. Thus blogs have been described as a cross between an online diary and a cybermagazine, but one of the key characteristics of the most successful or popular blogs is that they are constantly updated. Although just a few years ago there were only a small number of blogs, today there are millions of them. Many blogs are run by professionals like educators, reporters, researchers, scientists, and political candidates, with visits to the sites numbering in the thousands and in a few cases millions, but the vast majority are run by individuals who see them as chatty, stream-of-consciousness journals and whose readership is very limited.

A few blogs have attracted so many readers that they have achieved or exceeded the kind of readership that large newspapers enjoy. Because of the sheer number of readers and their ability to communicate instantly with other bloggers around the world, a few blogs have been responsible for bringing to light events or issues that mainstream media have ignored by focusing public attention on a current issue. Blogs with the most impact on public affairs appear to be those with large numbers of daily visitors, and they tend to have the most influence in politics. One form of blog is the aggregate news site, such as the Daily Beast, which combines original material with links to numerous news websites. A site composed almost entirely of links to a wide variety of news sources is Drudge Report (www.drudgereport.com), which records 20 to 30 million visits daily. For instance, it has links to the front pages of most of the major newspapers in the world, links to all the wire services, links to the opinion columns of perhaps a hundred columnists who are read in newspapers around the United States, links to constant updates on America's involvement in foreign countries, and many more features that make it an excellent site for keeping up on what is being said, thought, and done around the world. Many other respected sites attract millions of visits daily or weekly.

Blogs have certain common features, including making it convenient for people to post or respond to the blog owner, posting messages in reverse chronological order for others to read, and providing links to other blogs and websites. However, blogs differ greatly in the quality and reliability of the information at the site. Blogs by definition are logs or journals and as such are often unedited, not-very-well-thought-out musings on a variety of topics. Be very careful when choosing blogs to follow and even more careful in accepting as truth what you read on a blog. You can apply the same questions to blogs that you would use for analyzing other websites rhetorically, but keep in mind the special nature of blogs and how their unrestricted, constantly changing content is very likely slanted or biased to fit the viewpoint of the blogger.

Social Networking Websites. There are hundreds of services dedicated to establishing networks among people. Some are fairly limited to certain groups of people, such as those graduating from a particular high school or college or those belonging to certain ethnic, religious, or even family groups. Two worldwide, all-encompassing, and well-established services are Facebook and Twitter. Facebook users can register personal information, communicate with friends and colleagues, post pictures, and establish networks with people all over the world. Twitter is similar in purpose to Facebook but is a micro-blogging site that limits messages to 140 characters. Twitter emerged as a significant service when users began posting what was happening at moments of key social and political unrest or upheaval. As with all websites with countless users of all political, social, economic, and ethnic backgrounds, postings can be extremely biased and inaccurate.

EXERCISE

1. Locate two listservs on topics that interest you and read a few days' worth of posts. How do they compare and contrast? What is your impression of the sense of community among the members? What sorts of posts do people send? Do they stay on topic? Do the listservs have moderators? If you were going to join a listserv, which one would you prefer?
2. Locate several blogs on a topic that interests you—baseball, water skiing, crime prevention, politics, a hobby, your major—and assess their rhetorical effectiveness, using the guidelines discussed.
3. Follow a thread or two on a social networking service and assess the sorts of postings people make. How would you characterize the sense of community among the posters? How would you rate the quality of the comments? What conclusions can you draw about the usefulness or purpose of the service?

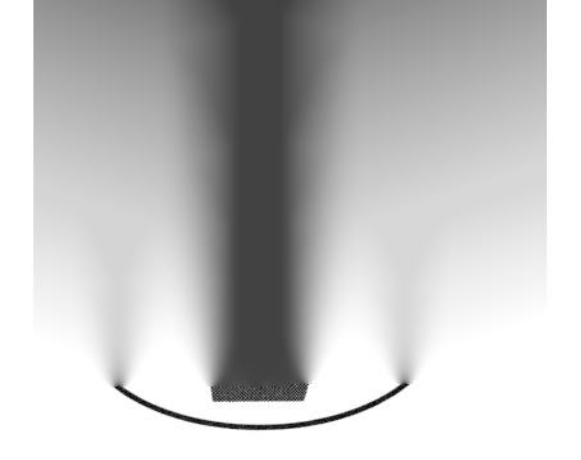

The Writing Process

Writing for any purpose involves a progression of stages, from prewriting, discovery, and planning to composing multiple drafts and then editing and proofreading. This process begins with determining your purpose, then inventing or discovering what you want to say, developing a strategy, planning how to organize your thoughts, writing a rough draft, revising as many times as necessary, proofreading, and then producing and editing the final copy. All writers, not just college students, benefit from treating a written endeavor as a process. Even professional writers plan, draft, revise, and edit before turning in their work. This chapter gives you a brief overview of the writing process. The guidelines presented here assume that you are writing for a college class and that your instructor has given you at least a general or broad subject area to write about and has specified what your purpose is. Often instructors give students a number of choices, but they still outline their expectations for the assignment.

The writing process can be frustrating because it is made up of many components. The key to writing well is to take those components in turn, focusing on each stage rather than worrying about producing a perfect end product right from the beginning of the assignment. It takes time to discover how you are going to approach an assignment, what you have to say about your topic, and how you are going to organize your ideas into a clear, coherent whole. Good writers know that writing often involves false starts, wrong turns, and dead ends; but they also know that giving the writing assignment thought and taking time to prewrite, plan, draft, rewrite, and revise will produce a sense of satisfaction when they hand in their finished paper to the instructor.

PREWRITING

Prewriting is the first stage of any writing project and includes everything you do before you write your first draft. At this stage, you want to think about the best approach to your subject. You want to determine your purpose, identify your audience, and generate ideas before you even begin to write your paper. Whether your instructor has given you a specific assignment or you are to select your own from a variety of possibilities, you need to spend time thinking about the assignment, generating ideas for it, identifying what you already know about it, discovering what you need to know, and narrowing your focus from a general subject to a specific topic. The practices used in prewriting usually spill over into other stages of the writing process as well. Through drafting, revising, editing, and producing the finished product, you are thinking about your topic, discovering new strategies or information, and determining how best to organize, develop, and polish your piece.

Determine Your Purpose. Your first step in the writing process is to determine your purpose, or your reason, for writing. As mentioned in Chapter 1, most writing can be classified as one of several types: argumentative, expository, or expressive. These types take many forms and have differing purposes. Are you to argue a position, persuade an audience to take action, explain a phenomenon, analyze an event, come to a conclusion about something, or describe or narrate an experience? Are you to write a summary or a critique? Perhaps you are to examine the ideas of several people on a specific topic, arrive at your own conclusions, and then incorporate the comments of those people into your own argument or explanation. It is crucial that you know what you hope to accomplish with the piece of writing at the beginning of each written assignment. Knowing your purpose puts you on the right track for the other stages of the process.

Identify Your Audience. For college work, your audience may be your instructor alone, but more often it includes your writing group or your classmates. For college writing classes where your work is not likely to be read outside of the classroom context, your instructor may ask you to imagine an audience or even suggest a specific audience to write for. Whether your instructor tells you what audience to write for or leaves the selection of an audience up to you, knowing whom you are writing to or for will help you determine what details you need to include in your paper.

Ask yourself who is going to read your work and what you know about the people in that audience. If you are writing an argument, anticipating readers who are not already convinced will help sharpen your argument. If your purpose is to explain, illustrate, or analyze, your audience is likely to be informed in general, but not have a deep understanding of your subject. Unless instructed otherwise, assume an intelligent audience of nonspecialists who are interested in learning more about the topic of your paper. Imagining this audience will keep you from having to define or explain every term or concept and will give you room for interesting, informative, and/or intriguing material about the topic.

Generate Ideas and Discover Your Subject. After establishing your purpose and audience, it is time to concentrate on how best to narrow your focus and develop your central idea. A number of useful exercises will help you discover what you know about your subject, generate ideas for your paper, and open up ways for you to narrow your subject to a workable topic. These include the following:

- **Brainstorming or freewriting.** This act involves simply writing without stopping for a set time, putting on paper everything that occurs to you as you think about your subject. To brainstorm or freewrite, time yourself for five or ten minutes while you write on a blank sheet of paper everything that occurs to you about your topic. Do not think too hard about what you are doing. Do not stop to check grammar or spelling. When your time is up, read through everything that you have written. Look for ideas that you think are promising for your assignment, and if you need to explore them further, brainstorm or freewrite on those, or try one of the other exercises for generating ideas. Although you can do this process in your head, it is much more effective if you put words on paper or the computer screen. Then you have something concrete to look at and pursue further.
- **Asking questions.** A good way to find out more about your subject is to simply ask questions about it. The most obvious questions are those that journalists routinely use: Who? What? When? Where? Why? How? Depending on your initial broad subject area, any of the following may help you generate ideas for your paper: Who is affected? Who is responsible? What does it mean? When did it happen or take place? How is it done? Why does it matter? How does it work? What are its components? What happened? Where did it happen? Why did it happen? What does it mean? As you can tell, not every question is relevant for a subject, but asking some of them about your subject when appropriate alerts you to areas that you may need to explore and helps anticipate the kinds of questions readers may have when reading your paper.
- **Making lists.** List everything you know or are curious about for the subject you are working on. Listing is similar to brainstorming but involves just making a simple list of ideas, thoughts, or information related to your subject. Sometimes seeing ideas, concepts, or key words in a list leads to further development of those things.
- **Clustering around a central idea.** Clustering involves placing a key word or central idea in the center of your page and writing related words, phrases, or ideas around this central idea. As you move out from the central point by creating related ideas, you may see patterns emerge or recognize ways to develop your topic.
- **Talking to others.** Discussing your subject with other people can be enormously helpful, whether it be friends, classmates, or your instructor. Oftentimes discussing a subject out loud with someone else helps you to clarify thoughts or to discover new ideas or approaches.
- **Researching.** Reading about or researching your subject will give you information, details, or arguments that you can use in the essay. If you use the

Internet to locate information, be cautious about which sources you accept. Keeping in mind the guidelines in Chapter 1 on evaluating Internet sources, choose your search engine from among the best known or most used; they are likely to be the most reliable. The following search engines and databases, which will be particularly useful for researched writing, are well-known, quite reliable, and likely to give you the results you seek in your search:

- **Gale (www.gale.cengage.com)** has links to full-text magazine and newspaper articles in more than 600 databases that are published online, in print, as eBooks, and in microform. You can link to numerous historical archives, special collection archives, various national libraries, and many databases on specific subjects. This is a subscription service, though some information is available for no fee.
- **Bing (www.bing.com)** is a Microsoft search engine similar to Google but with an added feature that the company calls a "decision engine," designed not only to search but to help users decide among choices.
- **Ask.com (www.ask.com)** has over 2 billion fully indexed, searchable pages. Formerly known as Ask Jeeves and powered by ExpertRank algorithm, it is a good resource for locating articles on a variety of subjects.
- **Alta Vista (www.altavista.com)** at one time had the largest index in the industry, but attempts to change its nature caused it to fall behind the larger Google and Yahoo. Alta Vista is still a good, reliable source of information and, in addition to the usual links like news, images, and shopping, lets you find MP3/audio, video, and human category results.
- **InfoTrac College Edition (http://infotrac.cengage.com)** provides a searchable database of some 20 million periodical articles from over 6,000 journals, newspapers, and magazines covering the last 20 years. It is a rich resource of readings on just about any topic. InfoTrac College Edition is a subscription service that requires a pass code to access the database.
- **LookSmart (www.looksmart.com)** is a human-compiled directory of websites. Its best feature is likely its index of articles, which provides access to the contents of thousands of periodicals. You can search by subject, author, or title in your choice of all periodicals, certain categories of periodicals, or a specific periodical.
- **Search.com (www.search.com)** is a collection of tools designed to find all kinds of information, from World Wide Web sites, to phone numbers, movies, and stock quotes. It searches Google, Ask.com, LookSmart, and dozens of other search engines to give you a broad range of responses to your queries.

Narrow Your Focus. Along with discovering your subject, look for ways to narrow your focus to a specific topic. Keep in mind the distinction between **subject** and **topic:** Subject is the general area of investigation or thought, whereas topic is one narrow aspect of that subject. Here again the techniques for generating ideas will prove helpful. As you brainstorm, freewrite, ask questions, list, cluster, discuss with others, and research, you may come up with narrow aspects of the general subject; but if not, go through the process again. For instance, "organ donation" is a general subject with complex issues. Many articles and books have been written about various aspects of it, including both legal and illegal practices associated with it. A suitable topic on this broad subject would explore one narrow aspect, as Sally Satel does in "About That New Jersey Organ Scandal" in Chapter 18.

DRAFTING YOUR ESSAY

The first draft will likely be your unpolished first effort to create the entire essay, to put all of your ideas about your topic into an organized, coherent whole. Fashion a title that best reflects what you plan to do in the paper. Then begin with a paragraph that introduces your topic by providing a context or background for it and that leads to a **thesis statement.** In the body of your paper, the paragraphs between your introductory and concluding paragraphs, construct **fully developed paragraphs,** each of which is focused on one specific topic—often stated in a **topic sentence**—that is related to your thesis. Bring your paper to an end by writing an appropriate **conclusion.**

Draft Your Working Title. The title is the first thing that your readers see. In the draft stage, do the best you can to create a working title, one that best reflects what you think you are going to do in your paper. You will almost surely change your title as your paper goes through various drafts, and you may even want to wait until you have written a draft or two before you create your title. However, many writers find it helpful to have a title in mind as one more aid in focusing the direction of the paper. If you knew nothing but the title of Kevin Fagan's "Homeless, Mike Dick Was 51, Looked 66" (Chapter 13) you would have a fairly good idea of what his article is about. On the other hand, a colorful title may serve to capture or reflect what the paper is about, but in an intriguing way. For instance, student Nate Hayes's paper (Chapter 6) arguing against human cloning is entitled "Hello, Dolly," a reference to the first cloned animal, a sheep named Dolly, but also a fun play on the title of the musical *Hello, Dolly.*

Draft Your Working Introduction. After your title, your audience reads the first paragraph of your paper. This paragraph serves the important function of introducing the subject of your paper and leading to the specific aspect of that subject that the paper focuses on. Writers are often advised to begin with a general statement that serves to intrigue readers or catch their attention. That general sentence leads to more specific sentences, which in turn lead to an even more specific one, the thesis statement. The first paragraph not only introduces readers to the specific focus of the paper but also sets the tone, prepares readers for what is to follow, and engages their interest. As with your title, you may not be satisfied with your introduction in the first draft or two. You may not know exactly how to introduce your paper until you have organized your thoughts and written at least one complete draft of your paper. Do not get frustrated if you cannot think of a good introduction as you begin writing your first draft. Because of its importance, you will want a working introduction, but most likely your finished version of the introduction will come only after you are fully satisfied with the body of your paper.

When you do get to the stage of drafting your introduction, keep in mind that one of the goals of the introduction is to entice readers or capture their attention. Writers achieve that goal in a variety of ways. You might try a memorable or catchy statement, a colorful example or anecdote, a startling fact, or a dramatic illustration. For instance, here are the first several sentences of the introduction to Nate's paper "Hello, Dolly":

> Little Bo Peep has lost her sheep, but now she can clone a whole new flock! When Dr. Ian Wilmut and his team successfully cloned Dolly the sheep, the world was mystified, amazed, and scared. Immediately, members of the shocked public began to imagine worst case scenarios of reincarnated Hitlers.

The references to Little Bo Peep, Dolly the sheep, and Adolf Hitler all serve as lures to intrigue readers. Nate goes on with his introduction in this way:

> The medical field, however, relished the possibilities of cloning in curing patients with debilitating or terminal illnesses. The controversy over human cloning is part of the larger debate about the potential capabilities of scientists to alter or enhance the biological makeup of humans. This debate over how far "homo sapiens [should] be allowed to go" has grown increasingly heated with developments such as the successful cloning of sheep (Pethokoukis 559).

After his initial startling and colorful language, Nate becomes more focused on his real topic, the possibilities of human cloning as an answer to crippling and deadly illnesses. Note his use of MLA style to cite his source for the quotation and paraphrase in the last sentence.

Draft Your Thesis Statement. Remember that your thesis indicates the central idea of your paper, suggests the direction you will take with that idea, states your position on a topic, or asks a question that you will answer in the course of your paper. Nate's opening sentences in the previous examples lead him to this position statement: *To many people, human cloning makes sense as the next major breakthrough in medical science, but until the troubling issues associated with the procedure are resolved, human cloning must not be allowed to happen.* From his introductory sentences to his increasingly more focused sentences and finally his thesis, readers know what to expect in the rest of his paper: details of the "troubling issues" to argue his position in opposition to attempts at human cloning at this time.

An example of an effective introduction by a professional writer is Anna Quindlen's introduction to "Our Tired, Our Poor, Our Kids" (Chapter 13):

> Six people live here, in a room the size of the master bedroom in a modest suburban house. Trundles, bunk beds, dressers side by side stacked with toys, clothes, boxes, in tidy claustrophobic clutter. One woman, five children. The baby was born in a shelter. The older kids can't wait to get out of this one. Everyone gets up at 6 A.M., the little ones to go to day care, the others to school. Their mother goes out

> to look for an apartment when she's not going to drug-treatment meetings. "For what they pay for me to stay in a shelter I could have lived in the Hamptons," Sharanda says.
>
> Here is the parallel universe that has flourished while the more fortunate were rewarding themselves for the stock split with SUVs and home additions. There is a boom market in homelessness. But these are not the men on the streets of San Francisco holding out cardboard signs to the tourists. They are children, hundreds of thousands of them, twice as likely to repeat a grade or be hospitalized and four times as likely to go hungry as the kids with a roof over their heads. Twenty years ago New York City provided emergency shelter for just under a thousand families a day; last month it had to find spaces for 10,000 children on a given night. Not since the Great Depression have this many babies, toddlers and kids had no place like home.

Quindlen opens with a disturbing description of six people, five of them children, sleeping in one crowded room. This first paragraph serves to gain readers' attention by dramatically illustrating what she goes on to state in her second paragraph: that the population of homeless people is increasingly made up of children. Her language and the tone of these opening paragraphs suggest that she is sympathetic to the plight of homeless children. On the basis of these first two paragraphs, readers can reasonably expect to read in the rest of the article a plea for better housing and living conditions for children without homes.

Not every kind of writing requires a thesis, but most do, especially the kinds of writing that you will do for your college courses. Not every thesis needs to be stated explicitly either, but there must almost always be some clearly implied central point to your writing. The opening paragraphs of Quindlan's "Our Tired, Our Poor, Our Kids" do not have an explicitly worded thesis, but her central purpose is clearly implied. Further, you want to state your thesis early in your paper so that your readers know fairly quickly what your central purpose is. Often a thesis statement works best in the first paragraph, especially for shorter writing assignments. Your thesis might need two sentences to completely state it or be better situated in the second paragraph, especially for longer papers. In the draft stage, you may not know the exact wording of your thesis, but you will want to have a good idea of what it includes. As with a working title, a working thesis helps focus your thoughts as you draft your essay. As you work through drafts of your paper, you will very likely be refining and polishing your thesis. An ideal thesis statement will indicate the specific topic of the paper, suggest how you will approach it, and may even hint at how you will support or develop it.

Develop an Effective Strategy. When you are satisfied that you have a clear understanding of your purpose, your audience, your topic, and your working thesis, it is time to plan the rest of your paper. How will you organize your essay? What strategies will you use to develop and support your thesis? It is helpful in both your own writing and in evaluating the writing of others to be familiar with common kinds of writing and the strategies writers use for organizing and developing their ideas. If you understand what strategies are available to a writer and what elements make those strategies work, you can better evaluate how well a selection is written.

Writers use many different **strategies** or **rhetorical methods** to organize and develop their ideas, depending on their purposes and their audience. Whether they pursue persuasive, expository, or expressive purposes, writers must be focused and clear if they want to engage their readers. They can achieve clarity or coherence with good organization and logical development of ideas. Writers seldom use any one method exclusively or even think about any particular pattern or mode of development. Instead, they first decide what their purpose for writing is, and then they use whatever combination of patterns best achieves their purpose. In your college courses, you will often be given written assignments. No matter what the course, whether it is art history, communications, science, anthropology, or business, the instructor may require a paper on a subject relevant to the course. Furthermore, students are very likely to encounter essay questions on exams, for instructors in courses across the curriculum seem to agree that one of the best tests of understanding is to ask students to write in some detail on quizzes or exams about important course material. Whether it is biology or English, students may be asked to argue a position on a controversial issue. An art professor may ask students to write a description of a painting, or a math professor may test understanding by asking students to explain in writing how to solve a problem. Whatever a writer's purpose, some fairly standard models can help to organize written work. But remember: seldom will a writer use just one of these rhetorical modes in isolation; they are almost always used in combinations of two or more. The important consideration is how a writer can best organize and develop the material for the best effect, that best suits the purpose of the assignment.

Here are common rhetorical strategies for organizing thoughts and developing ideas:

- **Argument/Persuasion.** Argument is a mode of persuasion in which the goal is either to convince readers of the validity of the writer's position (**argument**) or move readers to accept the author's view and even act on it (persuasion). In argument, writers set forth an assertion (often called a **proposition**) about a debatable topic and offer proof intended to convince readers that the assertion is a valid or true one. In persuasion, a writer goes a step further and offers a course of action, with the ultimate goal of making readers take action. The supporting evidence or proof must be so convincing that readers cannot help but agree with the validity of the author's position. The reasoning process must be so logical that readers inevitably draw the same conclusions that the author does from the evidence. Many of the readings in this textbook are arguments, including some that are paired because their authors hold differing viewpoints on an issue. For instance, in Chapter 19 on public health, you will find two articles on the issue of mandatory HPV vaccination. Mike Adams, in "HPV Vaccine Texas Tyranny," opposes mandatory vaccination and argues that the interests of pharmaceutical companies overshadow any concern for the health of women, whereas Arthur Allen, in "The HPV Debate Needs an Injection of Reality," sees vaccination of school girls against the HPV virus as potentially beneficial but advises caution in making it mandatory at this time. You will find readings whose primary purpose is argument or persuasion located throughout the textbook. For a fuller discussion of argumentation, see Chapter 5.

- **Cause–Effect Analysis.** A writer who wants to explain why something happened or show what happened as a result of something—or perhaps both—is doing cause-and-effect analysis. This type of analysis is used frequently in news broadcasts and magazine and newspaper articles to explain phenomena, such as the chain of events that led to a particular action, the effects of a particular event or crisis, or both causes and effects of a specific situation. Cause-and-effect analysis is also used frequently to argue. A writer might use the strategy of causal analysis in arguing that offering sex education in schools or making contraceptives readily available to high school students would be more effective in reducing the number of teenage pregnancies than prohibiting explicit sex scenes on prime time television. The writer would have to sort out possible causes to explain the high rate of teenage pregnancies, determine which likely are most responsible and which are contributing factors, and then conjecture likely results if the recommendation were followed. Many argumentative essays use causal analysis to develop their argument. Indeed, any argument on the effects of an activity—viewing television, playing video games, listening to violent music—of necessity is a causal analysis. Sissela Bok undertakes a causal analysis in her look at opposing sides on the issue of media violence in "Aggression: The Impact of Media Violence" (Chapter 9). Similarly, Elinor Nauen in "A Sporting Chance: Title IX and the Seismic Shift in Women's Sports" (Chapter 14) uses causal analysis to explore the impact of Title IX on women's increased participation in sports.
- **Comparison–Contrast.** Another purpose for writing is to show similarities and differences between two elements in order to make a point. Comparison and contrast can be useful in an argument piece in which the writer supports one of two possible choices and has to explain reasons for that choice. In an expository essay—that is, one with the purpose of explaining something—comparison and contrast can be useful to demonstrate a thorough understanding of the subject. Comparing or contrasting usually promotes one of two purposes: to show each of two subjects distinctly by considering both side-by-side, or to evaluate or judge two things. An analogy is a useful kind of comparison when seeking to explain a complicated or unfamiliar subject by showing its similarities to a less complicated or more familiar subject. An example of a writer using comparison–contrast to make a point is Morris Dickstein in "How Song, Dance and Movies Bailed Us Out of the Depression" (Chapter 11). He compares the economic situation at the end of the first decade of the twenty-first century with the Great Depression of the 1930s and suggests that, just as the arts improved morale during the Depression, so they can today.
- **Classification–Division.** Classification is the process of sorting information and ideas into categories or groups; division is the act of breaking information, ideas, or concepts into parts in order to better understand them. A writer may use classification to explain how a particular class of people, things, or ideas can be separated into groups and labeled according to common characteristics

that distinguish them from other groups. A writer may use division to make a large, complex subject easier to understand by dividing it into smaller, more manageable parts. Thus, Robyn S. Shapiro in "Bioethics and the Stem Cell Research Debate" (Chapter 18) sorts the issues involved in the complex bioethical subject of stem cell research into manageable categories.

- **Definition.** Writers often need to define as they inform or argue. Definition is the process of making clear a precise meaning or significance. In definition, a writer conveys the essential characteristics of something by distinguishing it from all other things in its class. You are familiar with dictionary definitions, or denotations, of words. Writers employ a similar technique to clarify or to explain, but usually in more detail than dictionaries or other sources of definitions give. In addition to providing brief definitions of terms, a writer may provide an extended definition, that is, take the meaning of a word beyond the limits of a simple definition. An extended definition may go for a paragraph or two or even for the length of an entire essay. A writer using abstract terms or concepts unfamiliar to an audience will find the extended definition a useful tool. Howard Moody, in "Sacred Rite or Civil Right?" (Chapter 14), draws distinctions between the state's definition and the church's definition of marriage. These definitions are key components in Moody's argument and help him achieve his central purpose.
- **Narration.** Narration is the re-creation of an experience for a specific purpose. It may be a brief anecdote, a story, or a case history. Writers use narration for a variety of purposes: to explain, illustrate a particular point, report information, entertain, or persuade. Often a narrative is only one part of a written work, but occasionally it may be the entire means of development. Journalists are accustomed to asking themselves a series of questions when they write their stories, to ensure that they give complete narratives: What happened? To whom did it happen? When did it happen? Where did it happen? Why did it happen? How did it happen; that is, under what circumstances or in what way did it happen? Narration is often combined with description. In making his argument that Americans should donate to world charities that aid impoverished children, Peter Singer in "The Singer Solution to World Poverty" narrates hypothetical examples in order to forcefully and vividly persuade readers to act (Chapter 13).
- **Description.** Description depicts in words a person, place, or thing by appealing to the senses, that is, by evoking through words certain sights, smells, sounds, or tactile sensations. Description is an almost indispensable part of writing; it is certainly inextricably linked with narration. As with narration and all other kinds of writing, description has a purpose. The purpose of description may be objective—to convey information without bias—or it may be subjective—to express feelings, impressions, or attitudes about a person, place, or thing. Almost all of the readings in this book have description in one form or another, and often description goes hand in hand with narration. A good example of this combination is the excerpt titled "A Student in a Community College Basic Skills Program" from Mike Rose's book *Why School?* (Chapter 12).

Keep in mind that these various rhetorical methods—ways of organizing and developing ideas—are almost never used in isolation. Seldom will you find a piece of writing that does not combine two or more of these strategies, and they are all equally useful, depending on your purpose for writing, the audience you are writing to, and the context you are writing in. You will notice as you read the essays in this textbook that all of the writers employ a variety of strategies to achieve their purpose.

Draft the Body of Your Paper. The body of your paper will consist of a number of paragraphs that explain, defend, or develop your thesis. Each paragraph must contain key ideas, supporting evidence, detailed explanation, or other information that directly advances your purpose. A typical paragraph focuses on one topic related to the thesis of the paper; has a topic sentence that expresses that single topic; contains perhaps seven to ten supporting sentences; and has a concluding sentence that leads to the next paragraph.

- **Topic Sentence.** Each of the paragraphs in the body of the paper should have a topic sentence. Remember that the thesis statement answers the question "What is this essay about?" In the same way, the topic sentence answers the question "What is this paragraph about?" If your topic sentence is not clearly stated, it should be clearly implied.
- **Supporting sentences.** Sentences in the paragraph should be organized logically, should support only the topic of that paragraph, and should lead clearly and smoothly from one to another. They are used to support the topic sentence, that is, to explain it, illustrate it, or amplify or expand on it. Paragraphs contain details related to and supportive of the focus of the paragraph. They include a mix of both general and specific or detailed statements.
- **Concluding sentence(s).** The final sentence or sentences summarize the connections between the sentences and bring the paragraph to closure. Sometimes the final sentence points to the subject of the next paragraph.
- **Transition.** Provide effective transition to move from thought to thought and point to point as well as from sentence to sentence and paragraph to paragraph. In any kind of writing, you want to strive to be as coherent as possible, and you go a long way in achieving that goal when you provide clear markers to help your readers follow the development of your paper and see connections between ideas and points. We have many tools with which to link or show the connection between thoughts and ideas. Repeating key words, using pronouns to refer to nouns, and using transitional words all help achieve clarity or coherence. The following are just a few examples of the many words we have to make transitions clear:
    - **To show addition:** furthermore, in addition, also, again, too, as well as, another
    - **To show consequence:** therefore, as a result, because, consequently, thus, then, hence, so that, for this reason, because
    - **To show contrast:** on the other hand, however, in contrast, instead, conversely, on the contrary, but, yet, compared to

- **To show similarity:** likewise, similarly, in the same way, moreover, analogous to
- **To illustrate:** for example, such as, in particular, to illustrate, for instance, for one thing, to explain, namely, that is, in this case
- **To show time relationship:** later, earlier, afterward, before, next, eventually, at length, before long, meanwhile, subsequently
- **To make a concession:** although, even though, still, of course, while it may be true, in spite of, at any rate
- **To emphasize:** importantly, unquestionably, without a doubt, of prime importance, certainly, undeniably
- **To summarize:** in brief, in summary, in essence, in other words, to conclude, generally, in any event, on the whole, as I have shown

Use Examples. One feature of a well-developed paper is the use of exemplification. Examples and illustrations are crucial to writing, no matter what the primary purpose. Without examples, writing stays at the general or abstract level and leaves readers only vaguely understanding what the writer means. Examples make meaning clear and help make writing more interesting, livelier, and more engaging than an essay without details. Examples may be brief and numerous or extended and limited in number, and they may take the form of narratives. Most of the readings in this textbook contain examples of one kind or another to both illustrate and argue their theses. It would be difficult to find an effective piece of writing that does not use examples of some sort.

Draft Your Concluding Paragraph. This final paragraph brings the paper to a satisfying conclusion. You may not be ready to write your conclusion when you write the first draft of your paper because the conclusion should come logically from all that has gone before. Sometimes you need to write several drafts before you can write your conclusion. When you are ready to write it, you have a number of approaches to choose from. Sometimes writers simply restate their introductions but try to be more imaginative. You don't have to restate major points, as they should be clear in readers' minds, but referring to them or highlighting them lends emphasis to what you have written and stresses its significance. Try to leave your readers with something to think about: stress the importance of what you have written, suggest a course of action, or point to questions raised by your paper that need further study or exploration. You might refer back to your introduction by mentioning a detail or image from it, or end with an amusing anecdote or humorous or striking comment.

Here is the conclusion from Nate's paper, "Hello, Dolly":

> There are just far too many unanswered questions, and who knows how many remain unasked? It is not easy to anticipate all the possible ramifications for mankind of human cloning. The bottom line is that ethical, psychological, social, and religion questions need to be explored, discussed, and resolved before research in genetic engineering that aims to create new life or significantly alter existing life can be allowed to continue.

Nate reiterates his position and suggests several things that must be done before he would change his mind about scientists pursuing human cloning. Anna Quindlen's conclusion reinforces her central point by using emotionally charged language to move her readers to sympathy and perhaps action to help "Our Tired, Our Poor, Our Kids":

> But these organizations are rafts in a rising river of need that has roared through this country without most of us ever even knowing. So now you know. There are hundreds of thousands of little nomads in America, sleeping in the back of cars, on floors in welfare offices or in shelters five to a room. What would it mean, to spend your childhood drifting from one strange bed to another, waking in the morning to try to figure out where you'd landed today, without those things that confer security and happiness: a familiar picture on the wall, a certain slant of light through a curtained window? "Give me your tired, your poor," it says on the base of the Statue of Liberty, to welcome foreigners. Oh, but they are already here, the small refugees from the ruin of the American dream, even if you cannot see them.

No matter what strategy you choose for concluding your paper, readers should feel that they have come to a satisfactory end.

CHECKLIST FOR REVISING AND EDITING YOUR PAPER

Writers use many techniques to make the revision process meaningful. You truly want to revise, not simply rewrite, your paper, so leave some time between drafts to give yourself a fresh perspective on what you have written. Obviously that means not starting any writing project at the last minute. You will find that it works to your advantage to begin writing as soon as possible after getting an assignment. The more time you have to draft and revise, the more satisfied you are likely to be with your final effort.

When revising, read each sentence and paragraph carefully. Try reading your paper out loud and listen to how it sounds, or read it to someone else to get feedback from a (presumably) objective audience. Rewrite passages that sound awkward or seem to lead nowhere; move things around if the paper seems disorganized; and look for ways to improve the development of every point you make. If you have trouble with certain grammatical structures or misspell the same words all the time, make a conscientious effort to look for those trouble spots. Although the most important aspect of your writing is your content—what you say, how well you say it, and how well you present it—you also want to pay attention to sentence-level skills. Errors at this level distract your reader from what you are saying, and too many such errors weaken your effectiveness as a writer.

It is not uncommon for successful writers to produce several drafts before they are satisfied with their work. As you revise and write new drafts, ask yourself the following questions to help you in the process:

Revision Checklist. When revising your paper, apply the same questions to your own writing that you ask when evaluating the writing of others, as detailed in

Chapter 1 on critical reading. Ask yourself whether you have a clearly stated central idea; your paragraphs are fully developed with specific and detailed statements; your overall organizing pattern is clear; your writing is understandable and intelligent; and the language you have used is appropriate and idiomatic. Here is a list of questions to ask yourself as you evaluate your own work:

- Does your title accurately reflect what the essay is about?
- Does your introduction provide enough information for your audience to understand what you plan to do in the essay? Does it create interest or otherwise pique reader curiosity?
- Does your essay have a clearly stated or implied thesis? Is the purpose of the essay clear, and do you achieve that purpose in the course of the essay? For instance, if the purpose of the essay is to describe, have you conveyed the essence of the thing with appropriately vivid words? If your purpose is to argue or persuade, is your evidence convincing? Is the argument logical and reasonable? Have you avoided fallacies in the logic of your argument?
- Does your essay have a clear plan or organizing principle?
- Have you supplied enough details, examples, or other evidence to fully support, develop, or illustrate your central point?
- Have you anticipated questions that your readers might have or challenges they might make about any of your assertions? If so, have you addressed those potential questions or challenges?
- Does your final paragraph bring your paper to a satisfactory conclusion?
- Is your writing clear?
- Have you used colorful, engaging, and/or lively language?
- Is your tone appropriate for your subject and audience?
- Have you constructed effective sentences that are varied in structure and length?
- Are your words spelled correctly?
- Are sentences punctuated according to standard conventions?

PROOFREADING

After you have revised your paper to the best of your ability, write the final draft. Most instructors require papers to be typewritten or done on a word processor, but follow whatever guidelines your instructor sets for written assignments. See Appendix 2 for formatting guidelines unless your instructor provides different ones for you. Leave time to proofread your final version and make any last minute corrections, preferably on the word processor, but if necessary, written neatly in ink. At this final stage, you are looking for careless or previously undiscovered errors that you can fix easily. If you have given yourself time to write several drafts, edit, and revise, the proofreading stage should just be a final check of work well done.

EXERCISE

The student paper below is five paragraphs and approximately 800 words long. The assignment was to select a historical document and assess its relevance to some aspect of today's culture. Josanne selected the November 19, 1863, address by President Abraham Lincoln at Gettysburg and wrote her essay on its relevance to today's battle against terrorism. As you read the essay, note what you think are its strengths and weaknesses, and be prepared to discuss your responses in class.

Begley 1

Josanne Begley

Professor Schilling

English 101-8

9 November 2010

Josanne's introduction begins with a general statement and becomes more specific as she moves toward her thesis. Josanne frames her thesis in the form of a question.

The Gettysburg Address and the War Against Terrorism

Time alters everything in the physical world: people are born and die, structures are built and destroyed, civilizations rise and fall. But does it follow that the passage of time alters the relevance of the ideas of great thinkers and leaders of the past? Can the words of a speech that is over 140 years old have any significance to today's world? What can the "Gettysburg Address" possibly say to a nation at war with terrorism?

The paragraph focuses on trials that America has survived, connecting the Civil War with the war on terrorism.

Ever since the American founders established a nation based on the principle that all men and women are created equal and are entitled to be free, its enemies have tried its ability to survive. At war internally, the United States even put itself to the test during the Civil War over the issue of slavery. Many people gave their lives in that long fight to preserve the freedom for all people that is a

Josanne discusses the Gettysburg Address and quotes a passage whose words she will refer to later in her paper.

Begley 2

hallmark of this country. More recently, terrorists put America to the test when they used its own airplanes as flying bombs and crashed three of them into the World Trade Center and the Pentagon, along with another one that was diverted into a field in Pennsylvania. That trial, too, was not without sacrifices.

After a bloody battle at Gettysburg during the Civil War, President Abraham Lincoln delivered his famous address to dedicate a cemetery at the site of the battle. The Confederacy was fighting for the right to own and use slaves, but President Lincoln knew that slavery went against the principles of freedom and equality that the nation was built upon. In his speech, Lincoln charged the people of the Union to carry on the fight for which so many lives had already been given:

> The world will little note nor long remember what we say here, but it can never forget what they did here. It is for us the living, rather, to be dedicated here to the unfinished work which they who fought here have thus far so nobly advanced. It is rather for us to be here dedicated to the great task remaining before us—that from these honored dead we take increased devotion to that cause for which they gave the last full measure of devotion—that we here highly resolve that these dead shall not have died in vain.

Note how the first sentence makes the transition into the new paragraph and shifts the focus to the war on terrorism. Josanne contrasts the Civil War with the war on terrorism but then highlights the relevance of Lincoln's words at Gettysburg to the events of September 11.

Begley 3

Lincoln realized that those who gave their lives at the battle of Gettysburg died for a cause they believed in, and his speech to those assembled for the dedication of the cemetery reiterated the need for the living to carry on the battle with renewed and even stronger commitment.

After the terrorist attacks on September 11, 2001, America began once again fighting for freedom, this time not only for the right of each human being to live his or her life as he or she sees fit but also to live that life without the constant fear of a terrorist attack. Obviously the war against terrorism is different from the Civil War. This war has a nebulous and widespread enemy; there is no one specific country to target, but rather persons and their followers whose goal it is to destroy the United States. The war on terrorism has already gone beyond the number of years it took to fight the Civil War and is likely to be protracted for many more years. The goal of this war—eradicating terrorism—is not easy to achieve, but that does not mean that the country will not fight for it. We must not and will not allow the thousands of people who lost their lives on that eleventh day of September to "have died in vain." As buildings were burning and crumbling into rubble, brave police officers and courageous firemen "gave the last full measure of devotion" as they tried to save the lives of innocent people trapped in those buildings.

Josanne's conclusion answers the question posed in her thesis and continues to emphasize the relevance of Lincoln's words to today's battle.

Begley 4

Hearing the horrendous news about the attacks in New York and the Pentagon, people on another hijacked plane rallied together and saved untold numbers of lives by giving up their own. Like the dead at Gettysburg, these people in New York; Washington, D.C.; and Pennsylvania died heroic deaths.

Lincoln's words at Gettysburg do indeed have strong relevance for us today. As a nation, we "can never forget" what those who died on September 11, 2001, did. We must commit ourselves "to the task remaining before us." We must complete "the unfinished work" of preserving our basic liberties and of eliminating terrorism. We must resolve, as Lincoln put it to his audience over 140 years ago, "that this nation under God shall have a new birth of freedom, and that government of the people, by the people, for the people, shall not perish from the earth."

Writing a Summary

Students often must write both informal exercises and formal papers based on readings in their textbooks. In writing assignments for the course using this textbook, for instance, you will find frequent use for information or ideas discussed in the readings. For formal writing assignments, you may be instructed to choose among the writing topics that end each chapter in Parts Two through Five, or you may be asked to suggest your own topic for a paper on a reading or readings. You may choose to argue in favor of or against a position another author takes; you may use information from one or more of the readings to write an essay suggested by a particular chapter; you may decide to compare and contrast two or more essays in a chapter or explain various perspectives on an issue. At some point, you may want to use some of the readings from this or another textbook in combination with other print and Internet resources in a research paper.

This chapter and the next three introduce several specific types of assignments that you may be asked to write, and provide guidelines for writing them. This chapter focuses on the summary, Chapter 4 on writing a critique, Chapter 5 on writing an argument, and Chapter 6 on writing a synthesis with documentation. In all of these assignments, you may be called on to paraphrase, quote, and document material on which you are writing. The guidelines for paraphrasing, quoting, and documenting sources are explained in Chapter 6. All illustrations of handling source material follow MLA (Modern Language Association) documentation style. If your instructor prefers that you use APA (American Psychological Society) documentation style, see Chapter 7 for guidelines.

WRITING A SUMMARY

Summarizing produces an objective restatement of a written passage in your own words, in a much shorter version than the original. The purpose of a summary is to highlight both the central idea or ideas and the major points of a work. A summary does not attempt to restate the entire reading. You might summarize an entire book in the space of a paragraph or perhaps even a sentence, although you will not do full justice to a lengthy work that way.

Many writing assignments call for summarizing. Your instructor may ask you to write a summary of an essay, or a passage from one, to gauge your understanding. Such an assignment may be informal, something that you write in class as a quiz or an ungraded journal entry, or you may be assigned a formal summary, a longer piece that you write out of class in detail and with care. Many kinds of writing include summaries as part of the development of their main ideas. For instance, if you are asked to report on an individual or group research project for a science class, you will probably summarize your purpose, methodology, data, and conclusions. If you write an argumentative paper, you may need to summarize either opposing viewpoints or your own supporting evidence. A research paper often includes summaries of information from source materials, and the research process itself necessitates summarizing portions of what you read. Reviews of books or articles almost always include summaries of the works under discussion, and essay questions on an examination often require summaries of information or data. Across the curriculum, no matter what course you are taking, you will probably be asked to summarize.

Summaries serve useful purposes. Professors summarize as they lecture in order to convey information in a condensed way when a detailed review would take far too much time. Textbook chapters often present summaries of chapter contents as part of chapter introductions (as in Parts Two through Five of this textbook). In this textbook, some of the questions for small-group and class discussion following the readings ask you to summarize major points or portions of readings in order to facilitate your understanding of the text. That process, in turn, enhances the quality of your classroom experience and develops your abilities to follow the discussion intelligently and to make useful contributions to the discussion yourself. Your instructor may ask you to write a summary of a piece you have read as a formal assignment. Summarizing is also an excellent strategy to enhance your own study habits. After reading an assignment for any of your courses, try to write a summary of the reading. If you cannot put into your own words the major ideas of what you have just read, you may need to go back and reread the material.

Outside the classroom and the academic environment, summaries routinely give brief introductions, overviews, and conclusions of subjects at hand. In business, industry, law, medicine, scientific research, government, or any other field, both managers and workers often need quick summaries to familiarize themselves with the high points or essence of information. Knowing how to summarize accurately is a skill that you will find useful in both your academic writing and in your profession or job.

A Summary Is Not a Substitute for Analysis. Do not mistakenly assume that putting another person's words into your own words is an analysis. Instead, **a summary is a brief, concise, objective restatement of the important elements of a piece of writing of any length,** from a paragraph to an entire book. A summary may be brief, as in a one-paragraph abstract that precedes a report or long paper and gives a very short overview of it, or it may be several paragraphs or even pages in length, depending on the length of the writing or writings being summarized. You may summarize as an informal exercise for your own purposes or as a formal assignment that you hand in to your instructor for evaluation.

Abstract. An abstract, like all summaries, is a condensed, objective restatement of the essential points of a text. Its distinguishing characteristic is its brevity. Abstracts are usually quite short, perhaps 100 to 200 words, whereas summaries may be much longer, depending on the length of what is being summarized. As with all summaries, an abstract helps readers determine quickly whether an article or book will be of interest or use. It can also serve as a brief guide to the key points before reading an article or as an aid in recalling the contents of the piece after reading it. Below is an example of an abstract of Henry Jenkins' "Art Form for the Digital Age" (Chapter 8). This abstract provides a broad overview of Jenkins' article, including his major points and conclusions. In his essay, he discusses or develops each of these components at length, providing examples and supporting evidence where necessary. In 123 words, the abstract condenses an article of more than 2,000 words to its most essential points. You can see how an abstract, like summaries of other lengths, is useful for getting a quick overview of a report or essay.

ART FORM FOR THE DIGITAL AGE

Henry Jenkins

Abstract

The cultural impact of video games is underrated despite their widespread use. They have been described as a waste of time and money, and experts warn that games are teaching children to kill. Computer games are nevertheless an emerging form of popular art and should be recognized as such. They have evolved from being primitive ball-bouncers to sophisticated participatory tales with cinema-quality graphics. Games also influence contemporary cinema, whose history can be compared to that of video games. Gilbert Seldes was one of the first academics to treat film as an art form. Games have the potential to follow the same path as cinema, but they need innovation, creativity, and intelligence to make them richer and more emotionally engaging than they are now.

Formal and Informal Summaries. Informal summaries are primarily for personal use and are usually not handed in for evaluation by an instructor. Formal summaries are those that others will read and are sometimes graded assignments. In either case, the process for writing a summary is virtually the same. For an example of an informal summary that would help a student prepare for a class discussion or recall key elements of an article, see the summary of Joe Saltzman's "What's in a Name? More than You Think," located in the discussion that follows that reading in Chapter 1. An example of a formal summary follows Charles Krauthammer's "The Moon We Left Behind," later in this chapter. The summaries of both Saltzman's and Krauthammer's articles underscore the need for a close, critical reading of the text to fairly represent what a writer says.

Although the process is the same for both an assignment that you will hand in to your instructor and a summary for your own use, a formal summary requires the kind of care that you give to longer writing assignments. The following directions will help you prepare and draft your formal summary:

Prewriting.

1. Begin by carefully reading the work. Make a mental note of its thesis or main idea, but do not write anything in the margins yet. If you try to highlight for a summary on your first reading, you might end up underlining or noting too many things. Wait until you have read the entire selection through once before writing anything.
2. After your first reading, write in your own words the thesis or central idea as you understand it. Then go back to the article, locate the thesis or main idea, underline it, and compare it with the sentence you wrote. If your sentence differs from the sentence(s) you underlined, rephrase your own sentence.
3. Next, read the article again, this time looking for major points of development or illustration of the thesis. As you reread, make marginal notes and underline, circle, or in some way mark the key supporting points or major ideas in the development of the thesis.
4. After you have finished reading, look at your notes and state in one sentence, in your own words, the thesis and each major point. Do not include details or minor supporting evidence unless leaving them out would misrepresent or unfairly represent what you are summarizing. If the writing you are summarizing comes to any important conclusions, note them as well in one sentence in your own words.
5. If you are still unclear about which are major and which are minor points, give the piece another reading. The more you read it, the better you understand its purpose, method of development, and major points.

Writing Your Summary.

6. In your opening sentence, state the author's full name, the title of the work, and the thesis or main idea. Write in complete sentences, whether your summary is 100 words or 500 words long.
7. Use the author's last name when referring to what he or she says in the article or when quoting the author directly.
8. Use attributive tags throughout; that is, use words and phrases that attribute or point to your source. Such tags serve the purpose of reminding your readers who you are quoting or summarizing. They may take the form of the author's last name or pronouns referring to the author, credentials of the

author, published source of the material, or other information that identifies the author (for example, "Krauthammer, in a recent article from the *New York Times*, observes that" or "he argues").

9. Do not use the exact words of the author unless you use quotation marks around those words. The summary must use your own wording. Use direct quotations sparingly, and only for a significant word, phrase, or sentence, and make sure that anything you put in quotation marks uses the exact wording of the article.
10. Use present tense to describe or explain what the author has written ("Krauthammer explains" or "Krauthammer concludes").
11. Provide clear transitions from point to point, just as you would in a longer assignment, and write in clear, coherent language.
12. Edit what you have written before turning it in to your instructor.

The key to summarizing accurately is knowing what is important and therefore must be included, and what is secondary and therefore should be omitted. Here you see the usefulness of the guidelines for critical reading. When you read critically, you identify the main idea or thesis of the selection, and you highlight or in some way mark major points. A summary must include the main idea of what you are summarizing, and it should include major points, and only major points. Thus, if you learn to read critically, you can write a summary.

GUIDELINES FOR WRITING A SUMMARY

- On your first reading, mentally note the thesis or central idea of the work or passage you are summarizing without writing anything down.
- After your first reading, write down your understanding of the thesis, locate the thesis in the work, underline it, check what you have written against it, and adjust your own sentence if necessary.
- Now reread the work, noting key points, either in the margin, by highlighting, or on a separate piece of paper.
- When you have finished your second reading, once again write in your own words a one-sentence summary of the thesis or central idea. Use the author's name and title of the reading in that sentence.
- Write in your own words a one-sentence summary of each major point the author has used to develop, illustrate, or support the thesis or central idea. State only essential details related to each major point.
- Do not include minor points unless you believe their omission would give an unfair representation of what you are summarizing.
- Where appropriate, write in your own words a one-sentence summary of any conclusion from the piece.
- Use attributive tags throughout your summary.
- Keep your summary short, succinct, and focused on the central idea and major points of the piece you are summarizing.
- Edit for grammar, punctuation, and spelling before handing in your assignment.

ILLUSTRATION: MAKING MARGINAL NOTES AND SUMMARIZING

Charles Krauthammer's opinion piece "The Moon We Left Behind" is reprinted here along with examples of the kinds of marginal notes a student might make after a first reading of the essay when preparing to write a formal summary of it. The notes highlight the central idea and major points of the selection so that when the student is ready to write a summary, he or she will already have marked the important points to include. A sample summary of the essay follows it.

THE MOON WE LEFT BEHIND

CHARLES KRAUTHAMMER

Charles Krauthammer, contributing editor to the New Republic *and* Time *magazine, writes a weekly syndicated column for the* Washington Post. *A political scientist, psychiatrist, journalist, and speech writer, Krauthammer won a Pulitzer Prize in 1987 for his commentary on politics and society and was the 2004 winner of the first $250,000 Bradley Prize, awarded to individuals of extraordinary talent who have made contributions of excellence in their field. He is author of the book* Cutting Edges: Making Sense of the Eighties *(1985). This essay appeared in the July 17, 2009, issue of the* Washington Post.

Opening quotation leads to his central point: dismay that we have stopped exploring the moon.

Michael Crichton once wrote that if you told a physicist in 1899 that within a hundred years humankind would, among other wonders (nukes, commercial airlines), "travel to the moon, and then lose interest . . . the physicist would almost certainly pronounce you mad." In 2000, I quoted these lines expressing Crichton's incredulity at America's abandonment of the moon. It is now 2009 and the moon recedes ever further.

His thesis—note word choice. Does not believe we will return to moon in 2020 as promised.

Next week marks the 40th anniversary of the first moon landing. We say we will return in 2020. But that promise was made by a previous president, and this president has defined himself as the antimatter to George Bush. Moreover, for all of Barack Obama's Kennedyesque qualities, he has expressed none of Kennedy's enthusiasm for human space exploration.

Astonished by "retreat" from the space program.

So with the Apollo moon program long gone, and with Constellation, its supposed successor, still little more than a hope, we remain in retreat from space. Astonishing. After countless millennia of gazing and dreaming, we finally got off the ground at Kitty Hawk in 1903. Within 66 years, a nanosecond in human history, we'd landed on the moon. Then five more landings, 10 more moonwalkers and, in the decades since, nothing.

Note loaded words: "magnificent bird" now a "truck" for "hauling." Is dismissive of "tinkertoy" space station.

4 To be more precise: almost 40 years spent in low Earth orbit studying, well, zero-G nausea and sundry cosmic mysteries. We've done it with the most beautiful, intricate, complicated—and ultimately, hopelessly impractical—machine ever built by man: the space shuttle. We turned this magnificent bird into a truck for hauling goods and people to a tinkertoy we call the international space station, itself created in a fit of post–Cold War internationalist absentmindedness as a place where people of differing nationality can sing "Kumbaya" while weightless.

Look up references to Spruce Goose and Concorde.

The shuttle is now too dangerous, too fragile and too expensive. Seven more flights and then it is retired, going—like the Spruce Goose and the Concorde—into the Museum of Things Too Beautiful and Complicated to Survive.

America's manned space program is in shambles. Fourteen months from today, for the first time since 1962, the United States will be incapable not just of sending a man to the moon but of sending anyone into Earth orbit. We'll be totally grounded. We'll have to beg a ride from the Russians or perhaps even the Chinese.

Says we'll never fix problems on Earth, so no need to wait to go back to moon.

So what, you say? Don't we have problems here on Earth? Oh, please. Poverty and disease and social ills will always be with us. If we'd waited for them to be rectified before venturing out, we'd still be living in caves.

Says we have enough money to return to moon. Look up "Manhattan Project."

8 Yes, we have a financial crisis. No one's asking for a crash Manhattan Project. All we need is sufficient funding from the hundreds of billions being showered from Washington—"stimulus" monies that, unlike Eisenhower's interstate highway system or Kennedy's Apollo program, will leave behind not a trace on our country or our consciousness—to build Constellation and get us back to Earth orbit and the moon a half-century after the original landing.

Says we must explore the moon for its "immense possibilities."

Why do it? It's not for practicality. We didn't go to the moon to spin off cooling suits and freeze-dried fruit. Any technological return is a bonus, not a reason. We go for the wonder and glory of it. Or, to put it less grandly, for its immense possibilities. We choose to do such things, said JFK, "not because they are easy, but because they are hard." And when you do such magnificently hard things—send sailing a Ferdinand Magellan or a Neil Armstrong—you open new human possibility in ways utterly unpredictable.

Blue Planet icon of environmentalism came from trip to moon.

The greatest example? Who could have predicted that the moon voyages would create the most potent impetus to—and symbol of—environmental consciousness here on Earth: Earthrise, the now iconic Blue Planet photograph brought back by Apollo 8?

Ironically, that new consciousness about the uniqueness and fragility of Earth focused contemporary imagination away from space and back to Earth. We are now deep into that hyper-terrestrial phase, the age of iPod and Facebook, of social networking and eco-consciousness.

Urges readers to look at the moon—a "nightly rebuke" for retreating from it.

12 But look up from your BlackBerry one night. That is the moon. On it are exactly 12 sets of human footprints—untouched, unchanged, abandoned. For the first time in history, the moon is not just a mystery and a muse, but a nightly rebuke. A vigorous young president once summoned us to this new frontier, calling the voyage "the most hazardous and dangerous and greatest adventure on which man has ever embarked." And so we did it. We came. We saw. Then we retreated.

How could we?

THE MOON WE LEFT BEHIND

Charles Krauthammer

Summary

In a recent *New York Times* column, "The Moon We Left Behind," Charles Krauthammer laments the decision by the United States to further postpone exploration of the moon for at least another decade. Declaring that he finds this "retreat from space . . . astonishing," Krauthammer extols the beauty of the space shuttle, calls it an "intricate, complicated . . . magnificent bird," and bemoans its use as little more than "a truck for hauling goods" to the international space station. Describing the manned space program as being in "shambles" and dismissing the argument that we need to pay more attention to problems on Earth, Krauthammer answers the question "Why do it?" by affirming that undertaking difficult journeys have wonderfully unpredictable, glorious results. The moon, he writes, serves as "a nightly rebuke" for our retreat from lunar exploration.

EXERCISE

Select one reading in Parts Two through Five that interests you. Read it, take notes, and write a brief summary of it. Your instructor may want you to hand in your work or use it as part of a class or small-group discussion on summarizing effectively.

CHAPTER 4

Writing a Critique

THE CONNECTION BETWEEN READING CRITICALLY AND WRITING A CRITIQUE

Recall the guidelines for reading critically outlined in Chapter 1. The final step is to evaluate what you have read. **A critique is the written form of an evaluation of a passage or an entire work.** Reading critically is the biggest aid to writing a critique; applying the guidelines for reading critically is a crucial part of preparing to write a critique. You will need to understand not only the purpose of the piece and its central idea but also the writer's main points. Reading critically enriches your understanding of a work and its components, enabling you to focus your critique. So the first step in writing a critique is to read critically and, in the process, to determine your opinion of the piece.

Apply the guidelines detailed in Chapter 1, but especially look for the following: thesis and purpose of the writing, who the likely intended audience is, key ideas or supporting evidence for the thesis, the author's use of language, how well the piece is organized, and how successfully the piece has achieved its stated or implied goal. You may need to read the piece several times before you are clear on your own viewpoint and therefore prepared to write.

WRITING A CRITIQUE

When you write a critique, your goal is to make a formal analysis of and response to a piece of writing, whether a selected passage or an entire essay. Your purpose encompasses both explaining and evaluating a piece of writing. **A critique differs from a summary, which is an objective restatement in your own words of the original material. When you summarize, you leave out your personal or subjective viewpoint. In a critique, you begin objectively but then add your own subjective response to the work.** The components of your critique paper are as follows: introduction, summary, analysis, personal response, and conclusion. Before you begin to draft your critique, you will need to think about each of these components. Prewriting exercises are excellent preparation for the draft stage.

Prewriting

Determine Your Position. To convince an audience that your analysis and response are reasonable or valid, you must convey your views confidently. Thus, before you even begin writing your critique, you must have a clear idea of your own viewpoint on the work. A firm conviction of your own position will help persuade an audience that your critique is sensible and fair.

How do you arrive at your position? You do so by carefully reading and rereading the piece that you are to critique, by thinking seriously about what the piece says and how it says it, and by assessing how persuaded you are as a reader by what the author has said. This stage in the writing process is crucial for helping you formulate and make concrete the points you want to make in the formal assignment.

As with other kinds of writing, any number of tools for generating writing ideas can be used to help you arrive at your position when writing a critique. The following suggestions are variations on those mentioned in Chapter 2, but here they are worded specifically to help you discover your response to a piece of writing that you are to critique.

- **Freewriting.** As soon as you have read the work, write for five to ten minutes on any impressions of any aspect of the piece that occur to you. Write down everything that comes to mind, no matter how jumbled. When your time is up, select a phrase or word that seems important to your purpose, no matter how vaguely, and write a sentence with the phrase or word in it. Put that sentence at the top of another blank piece of paper and repeat the process of writing for another five or ten minutes without thinking very deeply or long about what you are writing. If you do this several times, you should end up with a fairly good idea of the position you want to take in the analysis/assessment part of your paper. If you find that you cannot write very much, go back and reread the piece. It may be that you missed some important points on your first read-through and that a second or even a third reading will greatly clarify your position or view on the work.
- **Summarizing.** A summary of the piece is the first main part of your critique, but the act of summarizing can be a key part of your prewriting efforts. If you get stuck on generating ideas by brainstorming, perhaps you do not completely understand the work. This may be the writer's fault, and that criticism may become a part of your critique, but assuming that the piece itself is clearly written, it may be helpful for you to put in your own words what the author says. Doing that may help you discover the position you will take in your critique of the piece.
- **Listing.** Another way to discover your viewpoint is to simply list terms or phrases describing your response to the piece you are critiquing. Then study your list and group related ideas together. Do you see a pattern? Does one dominant viewpoint emerge from these groupings? If so, write a statement reflecting that pattern or viewpoint. That should give you a sense of your position when it comes to writing your assessment of and response to the work.

- **Asking Questions.** Asking questions is a very useful tool for generating ideas, perhaps most useful when thinking about and drafting your response to a piece of writing. The discussion on analysis that follows suggests a number of useful points to consider when assessing the success of a writer's argument, language, evidence, and logic. Turning them into questions in the prewriting stage can help you arrive at your overall response to the work and to discover your own position in relation to that of the writer whose work you are critiquing. Because the response section of a critique expresses your personal, subjective reaction to the work, you will want to ask yourself these questions:
    - Do you agree with the writer's position on the subject? Why or why not?
    - What reasons can you give for supporting or disagreeing with the writer?
    - Are you convinced by the writer's logic, evidence, and language? Why or why not?
    - If you are not convinced, can you give other evidence to counter the arguments or evidence of the writer?

You do not need to go into great detail in the response section of your paper, but you do need to explain your reasons for your response. **Give careful thought, then, not only to *what* you think of the piece of writing but also to *why* you think that way.** What specific elements of the work influence your reaction to the work? As with freewriting, summarizing, and listing, write out your questions and answers, either on paper or on your computer. Review what you have written and consider whether you have left anything unasked or unanswered.

WRITING A CRITIQUE: PREPARATION AND PREWRITING

- First read the text carefully, applying the guidelines for reading critically (Chapter 1).
- Brainstorm, summarize, list, and/or ask questions.
- Determine the main points, the chief purpose, and the intended audience.
- Identify arguments that support or develop the main point.
- Locate evidence used to support the arguments.
- Determine any underlying biases or unexamined assumptions.

Drafting Your Critique

When you are satisfied with your prewriting activities and feel that you have generated enough ideas to write your critique confidently, you are ready to write your first draft. As with all writing assignments, you will likely write several drafts of a paper before you reach the final version.

Verb Tenses, Quoting, and Paraphrasing. As you write your first draft, keep in mind the following notes about verb tense and handling source material:

Verb Tense. Whenever you write about or refer to another person's work, use the present tense: "Robert Sollod argues . . ." or "Sollod asserts that. . . ." Use the past tense only to refer to something that happened before the time span of the essay: "Sollod says that this omission is not a new development, recalling that his own undergraduate career over thirty years earlier lacked any real information on religion and spirituality."

- **Handling Quotations and Paraphrases.** When writing a critique, you will often want to quote a passage directly or paraphrase it. In either case, you must cite the source where the original appears and use attributive tags (words that identify the source) to give credit to the source. Full details about handling source material appear in Chapter 6, with further examples in Chapter 7, but here are examples from the student paper, written by Kari Kolb, that follows "The Hollow Curriculum":

Kari quotes part of a sentence in this way:

> Sollod continues by warning that a lack of religious studies has resulted in "the loss of ethics, a sense of decency, moderation, and fair play in American society" (45).

Kari attributes the material to Sollod, uses quotation marks around words that she has taken directly from the source, and gives the page number where the material appears in parentheses after the closing quotation mark but before the period.

Kari's sources are listed alphabetically at the end of her paper in a section labeled "Works Cited." Because it is alphabetical by author (or title if no author is named), readers know that the parenthetical number refers to the specific page in the work by Sollod where the quoted words appear.

Here Kari quotes material but leaves some of the words out:

> This wide-ranging analysis enables Sollod to reach his large and somewhat diverse audience. He bases much of his reasoning upon the idea that "religious and spiritually based concepts . . . are the backbone upon which entire cultures have been based" (43).

The **three spaced periods (ellipsis points)** indicate where words appear in the original.

In this next example, **Kari paraphrases (puts in her own words)** some of Sollod's main points, which are made in the order in which Kari paraphrases them. In this case, she must still give a page number, even when they are not Sollod's exact words:

> His proposed solution includes a curriculum assessment of current course offerings in religion and spirituality, active leadership of faculty and administrators across the university to initiate curriculum change, and the involvement of students in the form of debates and committees (45).

Note that Kari uses the author's name (or a pronoun when the antecedent is clear) throughout the paper whenever she refers to his work. When she quotes from other sources, as she does with the Beckman and Jaschik pieces listed in her Works Cited page, she makes it absolutely clear in her paper that she is referring to those sources.

In fact, as Joanne Beckman of Duke University explains . . .

> The study, "God and Majors," concludes that students' religiosity is not necessarily affected negatively by attending colleges that do not stress religion (Jaschik).

One of your primary obligations in any writing that incorporates the words or ideas of other authors is fairness to those you borrow from. Along with that is the obligation to be as clear and accurate as possible for your readers. Quoting and paraphrasing your sources and using attributive tags helps you realize those obligations.

HANDLING SOURCE MATERIAL IN A CRITIQUE

- Use present tense when referring to what the writer says in the work.
- When quoting directly, use exact words and cite source of material.
- When paraphrasing, use your own words and cite source of material.

The following section lists the components of a formal critique and gives directions for writing each of those components. In general, a written critique includes these components: (1) an introduction; (2) an objective, concise summary of the work or passage; (3) an objective analysis of the author's presentation; (4) a subjective response detailing your opinion of the author's views; and (5) a conclusion.

1. Introduction. The first paragraph of your critique should name the author and title of the work that you are critiquing. Do not neglect this information, as it immediately tells readers the subject of your critique. Then give a very brief overview of the piece in two to four sentences. Your intent in the introduction is not to summarize the piece but to tell readers its purpose. Generally, stating the thesis or central idea of the piece along with a highlight or two and/or its major conclusion(s) will be enough to convey its essence and provide background for the rest of your paper. Finally, your introduction should state your own thesis. In one sentence, indicate your assessment of the passage or work that you examined. Your thesis statement should be worded to reveal your position to readers before they begin reading the body of your paper.

2. Summary. The first section in the body of your critique should offer an objective summary of the piece. This summary states the original author's purpose and includes key ideas and major points. Where appropriate, include direct quotations that are particularly important to the development of the piece, but quote sparingly: the summary should be largely in your own words. Use direct quotations only when absolutely necessary when your own words would not do justice to the original. Do not write anything evaluative or subjective at this point. Your purpose here is to give a fair and accurate summary of the intent and main points of the work you are analyzing.

3. Analysis. Once you have summarized the work by stating its purpose and key points, begin to analyze the work. Your goal is to examine how well the author has achieved the purpose and consider the validity or significance of the author's information. Do not try to look at every point the author makes; rather, limit your focus to several important aspects of the piece. Remain as objective as possible in this section, saving your personal opinion of the author's position for the response section of your critique. Different purposes for writing—persuasive, expository, and expressive—require application of different criteria to judge a writer's success in achieving the intended purpose. In general, however, certain considerations help in the assessment of any piece of writing. **Questions about validity, accuracy, significance, and fairness help you to evaluate any author's success or failure.**

Assess Persuasive Writing. Recall that in Chapter 2 argumentative writing is defined as a mode of persuasion in which the goal is either to convince readers of the validity of the writer's position (argument) or to move readers to accept the author's view and perhaps even act on it (persuasion). This means that the writer must supply evidence or proof to support his or her position in such a way as to convince readers that the position is valid, whether they agree with the position or not. If the purpose is to persuade, the supporting evidence or proof must be so convincing that readers adopt the position themselves. Chapter 5 is devoted to a fuller discussion of writing an argument, so you may want to look at that chapter. In any event, when assessing the success of another writer's argument, you should gauge how well that writer has used the standard strategies for argumentation. Furthermore, pay attention to the writer's use of language. Finally, assess the validity of the argument by examining the evidence the writer presents to support his position and the logic of his conclusions.

Look Closely at a Writer's Language. In particular, make sure that the writer defines any words or terms that may be unclear, abstract, or ambiguous. Ask yourself whether the writer's language seems intended to intimidate or confuse readers or whether the writer attempts to manipulate readers by relying on emotionally loaded words. Does the writer make sarcastic remarks or personal attacks? Ultimately, examine a writer's evidence to evaluate credibility and fairness. Good writers do not rely on manipulative language, unclear terms, or loaded or sarcastic words to achieve their purposes.

Examine a Writer's Use of Appeals. Appeals are persuasive strategies that support claims or assertion or that respond to opposing arguments. They call upon logic, ethical considerations, or emotion to convince. An appeal to reason or logic uses statistics, facts, credible authority, expert testimony, or verifiable evidence to support claims in a reasoned, nonemotional way. Karen Sternheimer in "Do Video Games Kill?" (Chapter 8) relies on statistics to counter the claim that there is a causal relation between video games and the impulse to commit murder. Ethical appeals call upon shared values or beliefs to sway readers or motivate them to act. Jeff Corwin in "The Sixth Extinction" (Chapter 20) calls upon shared beliefs and the common good to urge individuals to become socially responsible to ultimately ensure the future of mankind by taking care of all living creatures on Earth, not just humans. Emotional appeals use heavily charged language to evoke feelings of pity, awe, sympathy, or shock, for instance, rather than intellectual responses not tied to the feelings. Joe Saltzman in "What's in a Name?" (Chapter 1) discusses ways that reporters can sway emotions by the words they choose to describe the war in Iraq, whereas Jean Kilbourne in "Advertising's Influence on Media Content" (Chapter 9) looks at some of the ways in which advertisers use loaded words and images to manipulate people to buy their products. A balance of these three kinds of appeals makes the best arguments. As you examine a writing for the appeals used, determine how balanced they are. If a writer relies heavily on one kind of appeal to the exclusion of the others, especially if the main appeal is to emotion, the argument is probably weak.

Evaluate a Writer's Evidence. A writer should support any generalizations or claims with ample, relevant evidence. As a critical reader, consider the kinds of evidence used and the value or significance of that evidence. Evidence may take many forms, including hard fact, personal observation, surveys, experiments, and even personal experience. In evaluating evidence, ask how well the writer provides a context or explanation for the evidence used. Consider whether the writer establishes the significance of the evidence and how it is relevant to the thesis or central point. For instance, factual evidence may be supplied in the form of statistics, facts, examples, or appeals to authorities. Statistics can be manipulated to conform to the needs of the person using them, so make sure that they are based on a large and representative sample; the method of gathering the statistics yields accurate results; and the statistics come from reliable sources. Look closely at statements of facts as well; they should give accurate, complete, and trustworthy information. Examples are specific instances or illustrations that reveal a whole type, and they should give believable, relevant, reliable, and representative support for an author's thesis. Finally, authorities are people who have the training or experience needed to make trustworthy and reliable observations on matters relating to their areas of expertise. In completing a critique, make sure, as far as possible, that the piece under study appeals to believable and credible authorities.

Judge a Writer's Logic. Argumentative or persuasive writing must portray a logical, reasonable, and accurate reasoning process supplemented by relevant, sensible supporting proofs. You will be in a good position to evaluate a writer's reasoning process if you are mindful of any pitfalls that undermine the success of the argument. Evaluating the writer's logic is part of the process of critiquing a work. *For a fuller discussion and more examples of common flaws or fallacies, see the section on assessing evidence in Chapter 5.* The following list is a summary of some of these **flaws in logic** that you should look for when writing your critique:

- **Hasty or faulty generalization.** The drawing of a broad conclusion on the basis of very little evidence. **Example:** Assuming that all rock musicians use hard drugs before performances because of the highly publicized behavior of one or two musicians is an example of faulty generalization.

- **Oversimplification.** Offering a solution or an explanation that is too simple for the problem or issue being argued. This fault in logic overlooks the complexity of an issue. **Example:** Arguing that the crime rate will go down if we just outlaw handguns overlooks such important considerations as crimes committed with weapons other than handguns and the likely probability that the criminal underworld would continue to have access to guns, illegal or not.
- **Stereotyping.** A form of generalization or oversimplification in which an entire group is narrowly labeled or perceived on the basis of a few in the group. **Example:** Arguing that women are not suited for combat because women are weaker than men is a stereotype based on the fact that the average woman is weaker than the average man. Not all women are weaker than men.
- **False analogy.** Falsely claiming that, because something resembles something else in one way, it resembles it in all ways. **Example:** Arguing that antiabortionists cannot favor the death penalty because they view abortion as murder is a false analogy.
- ***Non sequitur.*** Drawing inferences or conclusions that do not follow logically from available evidence. **Example:** Reminding a child who will not eat her food of all the starving children in the world is a line of reasoning that does not follow: If the child eats her food, will that lessen the starvation of other children? If the child does not eat the food, can the food itself somehow aid those starving children?
- ***Ad hominem* arguments.** Attacking the character of the arguer rather than the argument itself. **Example:** Arguing that because someone has been in prison, you shouldn't believe anything she says is an *ad hominem* attack.
- **Circular reasoning or begging the question.** Making a claim that simply rephrases another claim in other words. It assumes as proof the very claim it is meant to support. **Example:** A parent replying "because I said so" when a child asks why he must do something.
- **Emotionally charged language.** Relying on language guaranteed to appeal to their audiences on an emotional rather than an intellectual level. **Example:** Invoking images of dirty homeless children in rags living on dangerous streets and eating scraps of garbage when arguing for increased funds for child services is an appeal to the emotions. This appeal is all right to use sparingly, but it becomes a fault in logic when the argument is based entirely on such language.
- **Either–or reasoning.** Admitting only two sides to an issue and asserting that the writer's is the only possible correct one. **Example:** Arguing that if a fellow citizen does not support your country's involvement in war as you do, he is not patriotic. The implication is that "either you are for your country or you are against it, and the right way is my way."
- **Red herring.** Diverting the audience's attention from the main issue at hand to an irrelevant issue. **Example:** Calling attention to the suffering of a victim's family when arguing for the death penalty shifts focus away from the relevant reasons for capital punishment.

- ***Post hoc, ergo propter hoc* reasoning.** Assuming that something happened simply because it followed something else without evidence of a causal relationship. **Example:** Arguing that an airline is faulty because of flight delays at an airport assumes that the airline caused the delays, when a more important factor might be weather conditions that prevented airplanes from flying.

WRITING A CRITIQUE: QUESTIONS FOR ANALYSIS AND EVALUATION

- Has the author clearly stated or implied a thesis, main idea, or position?
- Has the author written to a clearly identifiable audience?
- What rhetorical strategies in the development and organization of the essay does the writer use? Is the development appropriate to the purpose? Is the essay logically and clearly organized?
- If the writing is an argument, does the author use verifiable facts or convincing evidence?
- If the essay seeks to explain, define, describe, or accomplish some other purpose, has the writer supplied enough details to clearly achieve the stated or implied purpose?
- Are language and word choice accurate, imaginative, correct, and/or appropriate?
- Does the text leave any unanswered questions?

4. Response. In this part of your critique, express your own position relative to that of the writer of the piece and give reasons why you believe as you do. You may find yourself in total agreement or absolutely opposed to the author's position, or you may place yourself somewhere in between. You may agree with some points the author makes but disagree with others. No matter what position you take, you must state your viewpoint clearly and provide reasons for your position. These reasons may be closely linked to your assessment of key elements of the paper, as laid out in your assessment section, or they may spring from ideas that you generated in your prewriting activities.

5. Conclusion. The final paragraph of your critique should reiterate in several sentences your overall assessment of the piece, the conclusions you have drawn from your analysis, and your personal response to the work. This section is not the place to introduce new material; rather, it is an opportunity to provide an overall summary of your paper. You want your readers to feel that you have given them a thorough and thoughtful analysis of the work under consideration and that you have brought your comments to a satisfying close.

GUIDELINES FOR WRITING A CRITIQUE

- **Begin with an Introduction.** The introduction familiarizes readers with the work under discussion, provides a context for the piece, and states your thesis.
- **Summarize main points.** The summary tells readers what major points the writer makes to support her or his position.

- **Analyze how well the writer has achieved the purpose of the piece.** The analysis tells readers what aspects of the work you have examined. In general, assess the overall presentation of evidence, judging its validity, accuracy, significance, and fairness.
- **Explain your response to the piece.** The response section tells readers your personal viewpoint by explaining the extent to which you agree or disagree with the author and why.
- **Conclude with your observations of the overall effectiveness** of the piece and your personal views on the subject. The conclusion summarizes for readers the results of your analysis and your overall judgment of the piece.

EXERCISE

Read Robert N. Sollod's "The Hollow Curriculum" and the sample critique that follows it. Prepare for class discussion by answering the questions for response and discussion after the essay and considering how your response to the piece compares to that of the student writer Kari Kolb.

THE HOLLOW CURRICULUM

ROBERT N. SOLLOD

Robert N. Sollod (1942–2005) was a professor of clinical psychology at Cleveland State University. He was author of many articles on spirituality, psychology, and related topics, and coauthor of a textbook, Beneath the Mask: Introduction to Theories of Personality *(2003). Sollod was a member of the Task Force on Religious Issues in Graduate Education and Training for the American Psychological Association when he wrote this essay for the* Chronicle of Higher Education, *a professional publication for faculty, staff, and administrators in colleges and universities.*

The past decade in academe has seen widespread controversy over curricular reform. We have explored many of the deeply rooted, core assumptions that have guided past decisions about which subjects should be emphasized in the curriculum and how they should be approached. Yet I have found myself repeatedly disappointed by the lack of significant discussion concerning the place of religion and spirituality in colleges' curricula and in the lives of educated persons.

I do not mean to suggest that universities should indoctrinate students with specific viewpoints or approaches to life; that is not their proper function. But American universities now largely ignore religion and spirituality, rather than considering what aspects of religious and spiritual teachings should enter the curriculum and how those subjects should be taught. The curricula that most undergraduates study do little to rectify the fact that many Americans are ignorant of religious and spiritual teachings, of their significance in the history of this and other civilizations, and of their significance in contemporary society. Omitting this major facet of human experience and thought contributes to a continuing shallowness and imbalance in much of university life today.

Let us take the current discussions of multiculturalism as one example. It is hardly arguable that an educated person should approach life with knowledge of several cultures or patterns of experience. Appreciation and understanding of human diversity are worthy educational ideals. Should such an appreciation exclude the religious and spiritually based concepts of reality that are the backbone upon which entire cultures have been based?

4 Multiculturalism that does not include appreciation of the deepest visions of reality reminds me of the travelogues that I saw in the cinema as a child—full of details of quaint and somewhat mysterious behavior that evoked some superficial empathy but no real, in-depth understanding. Implicit in a multicultural approach that ignores spiritual factors is a kind of critical and patronizing attitude. It assumes that we can understand and evaluate the experiences of other cultures without comprehension of their deepest beliefs.

Incomprehensibly, traditionalists who oppose adding multicultural content to the curriculum also ignore the religious and theological bases of the Western civilization that they seek to defend. Today's advocates of Western traditionalism focus, for the most part, on conveying a type of rationalism that is only a single strain in Western thought. Their approach does not demonstrate sufficient awareness of the contributions of Western religions and spirituality to philosophy and literature, to moral and legal codes, to the development of governmental and political institutions, and to the mores of our society.

Nor is the lack of attention to religion and spirituality new. I recall taking undergraduate philosophy classes in the 1960s in which Plato and Socrates were taught without reference to the fact that they were contemplative mystics who believed in immortality and reincarnation. Everything that I learned in my formal undergraduate education about Christianity came through studying a little Thomas Aquinas in a philosophy course, and even there we focused more on the logical sequence of his arguments than on the fundamentals of the Christian doctrine that he espoused. I recall that Dostoyevsky was presented as an existentialist with hardly a nod given to the fervent Christian beliefs so clearly apparent in his writings. I even recall my professors referring to their Christian colleagues, somewhat disparagingly, as "Christers." I learned about mystical and spiritual interpretations of Shakespeare's sonnets and plays many years after taking college English courses.

We can see the significance of omitting teaching about religion and spirituality in the discipline of psychology and, in particular, in my own field of clinical psychology. I am a member of the Task Force on Religious Issues in Graduate Education and Training in Division 36 of the American Psychological Association, a panel chaired by Edward Shafranske of Pepperdine University. In this work, I have discovered that graduate programs generally do not require students to learn anything about the role of religion in people's lives.

8

Almost no courses are available to teach psychologists how to deal with the religious values or concerns expressed by their clients. Nor are such courses required or generally available at the undergraduate level for psychology majors. Allusions to religion and spirituality often are completely missing in textbooks on introductory psychology, personality theory, concepts of psychotherapy, and developmental psychology.

Recent attempts to add a multicultural perspective to clinical training almost completely ignore the role of religion and spirituality as core elements of many racial, ethnic, and national identities. Prayer is widely practiced, yet poorly understood and rarely studied by psychologists. When presented, religious ideas are usually found in case histories of patients manifesting severe psychopathology.

Yet spiritual and mystical experiences are not unusual in our culture. And research has shown that religion is an important factor in the lives of many Americans; some studies have suggested that a client's religious identification may affect the psychotherapeutic relationship, as well as the course and outcome of therapy. Some patterns of religious commitment have been found to be associated with high levels of mental health and ego strength. A small number of psychologists are beginning to actively challenge the field's inertia and indifference by researching and writing on topics related to religion and spirituality. Their efforts have not as yet, however, markedly affected the climate or curricula in most psychology departments.

Is it any wonder that religion for the typical psychotherapist is a mysterious and taboo topic? It should not be surprising that therapists are not equipped even to ask the appropriate questions regarding a person's religious or spiritual life—much less deal with psychological aspects of spiritual crises.

12 Or consider the field of political science. Our scholars and policy makers have been unable to predict or understand the major social and political movements that produced upheavals around the world during the last decade. That is at least partly because many significant events—the remarkable rise of Islamic fundamentalism, the victory of Afghanistan over the Soviet Union, the unanticipated velvet revolutions in Eastern Europe and in the Soviet Union, and the continuing conflicts in Cyprus, Israel, Lebanon, Northern Ireland, Pakistan, Sri Lanka, Tibet, and Yugoslavia—can hardly be appreciated without a deep understanding of the religious views of those involved. The tender wisdom of our contemporary political scientists cannot seem to comprehend the deep spirituality inherent in many of today's important social movements.

Far from being an anachronism, religious conviction has proved to be a more potent contemporary force than most, if not all, secular ideologies. Too often, however, people with strong religious sentiments are simply dismissed as "zealots" or "fanatics"—whether they be Jewish settlers on the West Bank, Iranian demonstrators, Russian Baptists, Shiite leaders, anti-abortion activists, or evangelical Christians.

Most sadly, the continuing neglect of spirituality and religion by colleges and universities also results in a kind of segregation of the life of the spirit from the life of the mind in American culture. This situation is far from the ideals of Thoreau, Emerson, or William James. Spirituality in our society too often represents a retreat from the world of intellectual discourse, and spiritual pursuits are often cloaked in a reflexive anti-intellectualism, which mirrors the view in academe of spirituality as an irrational cultural residue. Students with spiritual interests and concerns learn that the university will not validate or feed their interests. They learn either to suppress their spiritual life or to split their spiritual life apart from their formal education.

Much has been written about the loss of ethics, a sense of decency, moderation, and fair play in American society. I would submit that much of this loss is a result of the increasing ignorance, in circles of presumably educated people, of religious and spiritual world views. It is difficult to imagine, for example, how ethical issues can be intelligently approached and discussed or how wise ethical decisions can be reached without either knowledge or reference to those religious and spiritual principles that underlie our legal system and moral codes.

16 Our colleges and universities should reclaim one of their earliest purposes—to educate and inform students concerning the spiritual and religious underpinnings of thought and society. To the extent that such education is lacking, our colleges and universities are presenting a narrow and fragmented view of human experience.

Both core curricula and more advanced courses in the humanities and social sciences should be evaluated for their coverage of religious topics. Active leadership at the university, college, and departmental levels is needed to encourage and carry out needed additions and changes in course content. Campus organizations should develop forums and committees to examine the issue, exchange information, and develop specific proposals.

National debate and discussion about the best way to educate students concerning religion and spirituality are long overdue.

PERSONAL RESPONSE

Describe the degree to which you are spiritual or religious. How important is religion in your life?

QUESTIONS FOR CLASS OR SMALL-GROUP DISCUSSION

1. Sollod gives examples of how an understanding of religion and spirituality would help someone trained in his field, psychology, and how it would help political scientists. In what other disciplines or fields do you think such training would be important? Explain how it would enhance the understanding of people trained in those fields.
2. Discuss whether you agree with Sollod that religion and spirituality have a place in the college curriculum.
3. Sollod calls for campus organizations to develop forums and committees to examine the place of religion and spirituality on the college campus and to develop specific proposals on the issue (paragraph 18). Conduct your own class forum or create a class committee to consider the issues that Sollod raises. Where do people learn about spirituality? How do you think a person could benefit from learning about religion and spirituality in college courses?

SAMPLE STUDENT PAPER: CRITIQUE

Kolb 1

Kari Kolb

Dr. Aaron

English 150-4

15 November 2010

A Critique of "The Hollow Curriculum"

In his essay "The Hollow Curriculum," Robert N. Sollod addresses the controversial subject of religion in the public school system, particularly at the college level. Sollod believes that by failing to acknowledge religious histories and teachings, universities contribute to the declining morality of society. He recommends an evaluation of course offerings in terms of ways in which courses on religion or spirituality can be integrated into higher education curriculum. Such a project would involve not only university faculty and administrators but also American citizens nationwide. While it may be true that recent years have seen a moral or ethical decline in the general public, Sollod's assertion that this decline is a result of religious ignorance is not only unfounded but also untrue.

Sollod begins his piece by noting the lack of religious and spiritual emphasis in the national curriculum and in the lives of most Americans (67). Noting that much of multicultural appreciation depends on a full understanding of others' cultures, Sollod points out that many other cultures are built on a foundation of religious and spiritual beliefs and suggests that all-inclusive religious studies would enrich the lives and careers of college students (67-68). Sollod continues by warning that a lack of religious studies has resulted in "the loss of ethics, a sense of decency, moderation, and fair play in American society" (69). His proposed solution includes a curriculum assessment of current course offerings in religion and spirituality, active leadership of faculty and administrators across the university to initiate curriculum change, and the involvement of students in the form of debates and committees (69).

Sollod has a solid sense of his audience, made up primarily of faculty and staff in higher education. By implication, what he proposes is of interest to students as well. Sollod draws readers into his argument with a series of questions and then offers information in a simple yet authoritative manner. He provides detailed examples, explaining how religious understanding would enhance all areas of study, ranging from the broad fields of political science and psychology to the ideas of Shakespeare and Socrates. This wide-ranging analysis enables Sollod to reach his large and somewhat diverse audience. He bases much of his reasoning upon the idea that "religious and spiritually based concepts . . . are the backbone upon which entire cultures have been based" (67), a point that informs his argument throughout. Sollod's valid argument is made even more credible when he extends it to include familiar examples,

Kolb 3

such as conflicts in the former Soviet Union, Ireland, and the Middle East. At times, Sollod relies on emotional appeals, seen most often in his occasional use of loaded words and phrases such as "continuing shallowness and imbalance" (67) and "mysterious and taboo" (68). In general, though, he makes a fair and logical argument, and he concludes with a rational solution to what he sees as a serious problem.

Sollod is correct when he states that the college curriculum would be greatly enhanced by the addition of courses in religion and spirituality or the incorporation of such material in traditional courses. Such courses would provide a solid grounding for most professions and promote a greater cultural understanding in general. However, Sollod exaggerates in his statement that the loss of ethics in American society is "a result of the increasing ignorance, in circles of presumably educated people, of religious and spiritual world views" (69). Here, Sollod makes an inaccurate generalization, with no evidence or clear reasoning to back up his position. On the contrary, statistics show that in the past thirty years, religion has not only sustained itself, but it has also diversified. According to a recent survey, "Some 375 ethnic or multiethnic religious groups have already formed in the United States in the last three decades. Sociologists of religion believe the numbers will only increase in the coming years" (Beckman). These religious groups are not only the creations of immigrants, but they also reflect America's growing diversity. In fact, as Joanne Beckman of Duke University explains, almost half of the baby boomer generation has dropped out of their traditional churches and are "just as willing to sample Eastern religions, New Age spiritualism, or quasi-religious self-help groups. . . . [F] or [these] seekers, spirituality is a means of individual expression, self-discovery, inner healing, and personal growth." Although the deterioration of moral values is a frustrating problem in our society, it cannot, as Sollod suggests, be attributed entirely to a lack of religious appreciation and diversity.

Furthermore, while a recent national study of the effects of attending a secular college on students' religiosity has determined that some students' beliefs are shaken, the study also discovered that high school students who attend religious services regularly are more likely to attend college than those who do not and that, once in college, students' religious attendance "is positively associated with staying in majors in the social sciences, biological sciences, and business" (Jaschik). The study, "God and Majors," concludes that students' religiosity is not necessarily affected negatively by attending colleges that do not stress religion (Jaschik). This result seems to counter Sollod's assertion that colleges contribute to the decline of morality by not stressing religion and spirituality. "The Hollow Curriculum" endorses

Kolb 5

a controversial proposal that has prompted much deliberation: the addition of, or increase in, religious and spiritual studies in our national curriculum. Although Sollod does well in arguing his position on the subject, he assumes, without proof, that much of university life is shallow and that university curricula is unbalanced. Further, he makes a hasty generalization when he places the blame of America's ethical undoing on the lack of "knowledge or reference to those religious and spiritual principles that underline our legal system and moral codes" (69). In this generalization, he neglects to recognize the growing religious and spiritual diversity of the American people. This omission weakens the foundation of his argument—that an increase in religious studies will benefit all areas of life—by overlooking evidence showing that, despite an increase in spiritual awareness, the loss of ethics remains a problem in our society. Sollod thus undermines his own position and leaves his readers, though inspired by his zeal, understandably skeptical.

Kolb 6

Works Cited

Beckman, Joanne. "Religion in Post-World War II in America." *Divining America.* The National Humanities Center. September 2005. Web. 8 Nov. 2010.

Jaschik, Scott. "God and Majors." *Inside Higher Ed.* 28 July 2009. Web. 8 Nov. 2010.

Sollod, Robert. "The Hollow Curriculum." *Perspectives on Contemporary Issues: Readings Across the Disciplines.* 5th ed. Ed. Katherine Anne Ackley. Boston: Wadsworth/ Cengage Learning, 2009. 66-69. Print.

EXERCISE

Select one reading in Parts Two through Five that interests you. Read it, take notes, and write a critique of it. Your instructor may want you to hand in your work or use it as part of a class or small-group discussion on summarizing effectively.

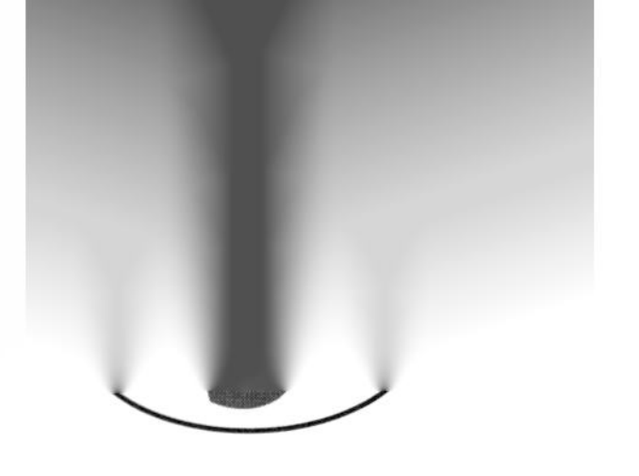

Writing an Argument

Much of the writing that you do for your college classes is argumentation. It may not be called that formally, but any writing exercise that asks you to state a position and defend it with evidence that is true or reasonable is a form of argument. Whenever you state your opinion or make an assertion and back it with proof, you are making an argument. As you can see, just about any writing that has a thesis or implicit central idea that requires evidence or proof is a form of argument. Whether you provide evidence to explain, illustrate what you know, inform, prove a point, or persuade, if you take a position on a subject and support or develop it with evidence to demonstrate that it is valid or sound, you are making an argument.

However, oftentimes students are specifically assigned the rhetorical mode of argumentation, a reasoning process that seeks to provide evidence or proof that a proposition is valid or true. **An argument sets forth a claim in the form of a thesis statement, refutes the arguments of the opposition—sometimes giving in or conceding to certain points—and presents a coherent, organized set of reasons why the claim is reasonable. To demonstrate that your position is logical or right, you must offer reasons why you believe that way in order to convince your audience**. An argument may have several goals or purposes, either singly or in combination, such as to show relationships between things (causal argument), to explain or define something (definition argument), to evaluate something or support a position on it (evaluative argument), to inform (informative argument), or to sway an audience to change a position or take action on something (persuasive argument). Argumentation is a useful tool for developing critical thinking because doing it well requires close analysis of your own ideas as well as those of others. Writing an argument involves the same general procedure as that detailed in Chapter 2 on the writing process: prewriting or planning, drafting, revising, and editing.

NARROWING YOUR FOCUS AND DISCOVERING YOUR POSITION

All arguments begin with a position, claim, or proposition that is debatable and that has opposing viewpoints. Statements of fact are not debatable; abstract generalizations are too vague. If your position is not debatable, there is no argument. Furthermore, in an argument, your goal is to convince those opposed to your position or who are skeptical of it that yours is valid or true. You might even want to persuade your audience to abandon their position and adopt yours or go beyond that and perform some action. Your first step, then, is to select a controversial subject or issue in which you have a strong interest. That begins the process that will ultimately lead you to the position that you want to argue.

A good starting point for discovering a topic to argue is to make a list of controversial issues currently in the news or being discussed and debated publicly or among your friends or family. ***Remember that this is only a starting point.*** These general topics are far too broad for a short paper, but they give you a beginning from which to start narrowing your focus. From your list, select the subjects that interest you most or that you feel strongly about and develop a series of questions that you might ask about them. This process of considering a variety of views when contemplating a topic you would like to argue helps you solidify your position. For instance, you might ask the following: Should bilingual education be offered in public schools? Should the Electoral College be abolished? Is affirmative action a fair policy? Should gay couples be allowed to marry? Although such questions seldom have absolutely right or wrong answers, it is useful to frame your position by saying (or implying), "Yes, bilingual education should be offered in public schools," or, "No, affirmative action is not a fair policy." But making up your mind about how you feel about an issue is only the beginning. You must also convince others that your position is logical, reasonable, or valid. You do that by providing strong evidence or reasons to support your position and by anticipating and addressing the arguments of those who do not agree with you.

Examples.

1. Suppose you are interested in the subject of downloading copyrighted music from the Internet without paying for it, currently illegal but still being done all over the world. Should those who download music from the Internet be charged with a crime? Should those who wish to download music from the Internet have to pay for that service? People will disagree on how these questions should be answered; thus, they are legitimate subjects for argumentation. Suppose you believe that, no, downloading music from the Internet should not be regarded as a criminal act. What other questions does that position lead to, then? Should downloading music be free and open to anyone who wants to do it? If so, what is the fairest way to treat artists whose copyrighted music is being downloaded from the Internet? Do they not have the right to profit from the use of their music?

2. Consider the suggestion that the grading system at the college level be abolished. You might wonder: Should the grading system be abolished? Who would benefit from abolishing the grading system? Why should the grading system be abolished? Why should the grading system not be abolished? What would replace the grading system were it abolished? How would abolishing the grading system affect students and instructors? Would it change the dynamics of the learning process?
3. Imagine that the office in charge of programming at your campus wants to bring a controversial person for its speaker series. Suppose you are a student at a private faith-based liberal arts college and the speaker is an avowed atheist, or suppose you are a state-funded liberal arts university and the speaker is a religious-right fundamentalist. Who would support bringing this speaker to campus? Who would oppose it? What reasons might both those in favor of and against bringing the speaker to campus give to support their positions? Are there contexts or situations where it might be appropriate and others where it would not? Which side would you support in such a controversy?

The following list of potentially controversial subjects may give you an idea of the kinds of general topics that can be narrowed for an argumentative paper. To this list, add others that appeal to you as potential topics for an argument. Then, select those subjects that you have the strongest interest in or hold opinions about and, taking each in turn, spend some time writing down questions that come to mind about that subject, issues related to it that you are aware of, and/or what your preliminary position on the subject is: What is the controversy? Who is affected by it? Why is it controversial? What is the context or situation? What is your position on that controversy? Why do you believe as you do? What evidence or proof do you have to support your position? What do those opposed to your position argue?

At this stage, you are simply **brainstorming or freewriting** to see what you know about certain self-selected subjects that you would be comfortable with developing into an argument paper. When you have finished, examine the results of your brainstorming session and narrow your list to the one or two that you have the most to say about or feel most strongly about. Brainstorm further on those issues by framing questions about the subject or trying to identify the problem associated with it. Keep in mind that you not only want to find an issue or issues that you have a strong interest in, you must also consider the implications of the position you take on that issue. How will you convince your audience that your position is reasonable or logical? How can you best defend your position? How can you best meet the arguments of those opposed to you?

You are looking for a topic that poses a question or problem you believe that you know the answer or solution to. This is your position. Once you know your position, you are ready to commit time to thinking about and researching the best evidence or proof to support your position.

POSSIBLE SUBJECTS FOR ARGUMENTATION

- Adolescents tried as adults
- Advertising images
- AIDS treatment or prevention
- Airline security
- Animal rights
- Arts funding
- Banning smoking in public places
- Bilingual education
- Binge drinking
- Censorship
- Civil rights
- College—is it for everyone?
- Compensation for organ donors
- Controversial speakers on campus
- Cyber bullying
- Cyber stalking
- Data mining of social networking sites
- Date rape
- Downloading music from the Internet
- Drugs and drug abuse
- Drunken driving or DUI punishment
- Eating disorders
- Education costs
- Electoral College
- Eliminating the grading system
- Embryo or stem-cell research
- English-only movement
- The environment
- Free agency in sports
- Free trade agreements
- Gays in the military
- Gender issues
- Gender roles
- Genetic engineering
- Global warming
- Government-sponsored child day care
- Gun control/gun rights
- Hate groups
- Homelessness
- Home schooling
- Human cloning
- Human rights
- Illegal aliens
- Immigration
- Inoculation against HPV
- Intellectual freedom
- Intellectual property rights
- Internet: government control
- Minimum-wage jobs
- Monitoring Internet social networking sites
- Mudslinging in political campaigns
- National image of America abroad
- National security
- Nuclear energy
- Nuclear proliferation
- Nuclear waste Ozone layer depletion
- Outsourcing
- The Patriot Act
- Pay inequity
- Pollution
- Poverty
- Publishing images of war
- Racial profiling
- Regulating toxic emissions
- Reparations for slavery
- Runaway teens
- Same-sex marriages
- School prayer
- Space exploration
- Special interest groups
- Standardized exams
- Steroids and athletes
- Sports violence
- Stereotypes in mass media
- Sweatshops
- Terrorism in America
- Tobacco use
- Violence in film
- Violence in rock lyrics
- Violence in schools
- Violence on television
- Workplace discrimination

Example. Erin was intrigued by an essay she read on advertising images of women, so she began the process of discovering her position on that topic by thinking about the very general subject "advertising images." Here are the questions she asked and the thoughts that she jotted down:

- Do advertising images affect behavior?
- Isn't it the purpose of an ad to influence behavior?
- So what if advertisements do affect behavior? What's the harm?
- Such power might influence behavior the wrong way.
- What is the wrong way? Affects self-esteem. Makes people feel inadequate. Reduces women to objects.
- What about men? Ads affect them too.
- Some ads set up unrealistic, even impossible-to-attain, images of men and women. Young or old, male or female.
- Ads present false images of relationships between men and women. Ads focus a lot on sex and on attacking people's vulnerabilities.
- Who bears responsibility? Advertisers. They need to consider the effects of their ads.
- What should they do? Modify images that attack and weaken self-esteem.
- Topic: advertisers' responsibility for their ads.

Her questions, answers, and ideas may look rambling, but they ultimately led her to her topic, which she refined by focusing specifically on ads featuring women that have the potential to affect self-esteem and body image.

GUIDELINES FOR NARROWING YOUR FOCUS AND DISCOVERING YOUR POSITION

- Make a list of controversial or arguable subjects that you have a strong interest in or about which you have an opinion.
- Ask questions about each subject from as many angles as you can think of.
- Keep narrowing your focus as often as possible.
- Write down ideas that occur to you as you ask questions.
- Select one or two topics that seem most promising to you.
- Repeat the brainstorming process by asking more questions and writing more thoughts as they occur. At this stage you are working toward a defensible position on a fairly narrow topic.
- Consider how you might defend your position, how you would counter arguments against it, and what evidence you might need.
- Select the topic that emerges as your strongest and begin the process of thinking about, researching, and writing your paper on that narrow topic.

STRUCTURING AN ARGUMENT

Structuring an argument is similar to structuring most other kinds of writing. Recall that in Chapter 2, the typical essay has certain components: a title, an opening paragraph that introduces the topic by providing a context or background for it and that leads to a **thesis statement**; fully developed paragraphs in the body of the paper that advance, support, illustrate, or otherwise relate to the thesis; and a **conclusion**. Effective arguments follow that pattern, with some additions or variations. In formal argumentation, these parts of your essay might be labeled differently, but they are essentially the same. For instance, a thesis might be called a proposition or position statement but it is still the central idea of the paper. Development might be referred to as offering supporting proof by refuting the opposition, making concessions where necessary, and offering evidence in a logical, well-reasoned way.

What follows are various components of a well-organized and well-developed argument. The discussion in general assumes a traditional, formal Aristotelian mode of argument, with the goal of proving one's proposition or thesis while countering or refuting the opposition, but there are other approaches that use different lines of reasoning. Two of the most prominent are the informal approach of Toulmin and Rogers. The Toulmin approach, like the Aristotelian, views argument as oppositional, with a goal to proving one's position; the Rogerian, on the other hand, uses conflict-resolution based on compromise, a goal that searches for common ground or mutual agreement rather than refuting the opposition. These three approaches are discussed in more detail in the section labeled "Strategies for Arguing Effectively," under the heading "Follow a Logical Line of Reasoning."

Introduction. The opening of your argument lays the groundwork for the rest of the paper by establishing the tone you will take, providing any clarification or preliminary information necessary and/or giving a statement of your own qualifications for asserting a position on the topic. Here is an opportunity to provide a context for your argument, establish your initial credibility, and connect with your audience. Credibility is the level of trustworthiness your audience perceives in you. If you can convey an impression that you are credible early in your paper, your audience may be more willing to think of you as reliable or trustworthy and therefore be more receptive to your argument. Otherwise, they may dismiss your evidence, question your motive, or simply refuse to accept what you are saying.

Context. When explaining background or situation, you establish a context within which your audience is to consider your argument. Establishing tone is part of the context. You might provide a striking quotation, cite statistics, or define the problem or controversy in terms that everyone agrees on. For instance Peter Singer's opening in "The Singer Solution to World Poverty" provides a context when he recounts the plot of a film about a Brazilian woman who sells a homeless child to organ peddlers. From there, he moves to his real point when he asks what the difference is between the immoral act of that fictional woman and "an American who already has a TV and upgrades to a better one—knowing that the money could be donated to an organization that would use it to save the lives of kids in need?" He goes on to discuss reasons why moral judgments of the two situations might not be the same, but he establishes a sympathetic bond with readers in his opening that leads smoothly to his focus on the ethics of our actions.

When an issue is particularly controversial, writers may not be able to establish sympathy with readers. Nevertheless, some sort of context or reason for writing needs to be established early in the essay. We see this in Cathleen Rountree's "In Defense of Hip-Hop" (Chapter 8). The title reveals her position on a highly charged issue, the sexually explicit and often violent nature of hip-hop lyrics. Rountree begins with a reference to a controversy current at the time that she wrote her opinion piece. This reference gives the reader a context for her defense of hip-hop music by mentioning critics of the music and then "the Don Imus escapade in April," the incident that led to her writing the essay. Reading her essay a few years after it was first published, readers may not recognize the reference, but her next paragraph explains it:

> Yes, those sleazy words, "nappy-headed hos," that Slimy Imus regurgitated during his live radio broadcast in reference to the Rutgers University women's basketball team, inadvertently returned social critics [including Al Sharpton] to the comfort zone of blaming hip-hop for all that ails contemporary pop culture. The fact that Imus used hip-hop as an excuse for his long-standing and well-documented proclivity for racial epithets seemed especially smarmy.

Note that writers are not required to explain every reference they make. Writers must make certain assumptions about their audiences—that they are reasonably well educated and aware of current happenings in most aspects of everyday life, and that if they do not recognize a reference, they are capable of finding out what the references mean on their own. Rountree's first reference to Al Sharpton, for example, identifies him as a social critic, but she also uses his name in the conclusion of her essay without any further explanation. His name may not mean anything to some readers, but an Internet search quickly reveals that he is a political and civil rights activist, known for his outspokenness and sometimes flamboyant personality, who was a vocal and high-profile critic of Don Imus in the days following Imus's sexist and racist remarks.

Credibility. Any number of strategies help to establish credibility in an argument. Beginning with your introduction and continuing throughout your argument, demonstrating to your readers that you are fully informed, reasonable, and fair establishes credibility and makes your audience more receptive to your position. Using trustworthy outside sources to support, explain, defend, or back general statements demonstrates that your position is based on more than just your personal opinion. To show that others, perhaps professionals with more experience than you, have done research or hold similar views reflects well on your own credibility. Furthermore, citing sources or statistics shows that you have done your homework, that you are so familiar with or knowledgeable about your subject that you know what others have to say about it. These things go to your credibility as a writer. Using hard data such as facts or statistics also helps, as does acknowledging and countering viewpoints opposed to yours.

Statement of the Case. As clearly as possible in your opening paragraph(s), provide a rationale or need for what you are arguing. Provide a context for the argument, give relevant background material, or explain why you believe as you do. Establishing need helps to convey your credibility by showing that you are knowledgeable about your subject. It is also a good strategy for connecting with your audience. In stating the case for the argument, you might explain that it is worth upholding or endorsing because it has some bearing on the lives of readers or the common good of a community or society. You may also want to indicate the degree to which a particular issue or policy is controversial. Take, for instance, Michael Crichton's opening in "Patenting Life" (Chapter 18): "You, or someone you love, may die because of a gene patent that should never have been granted in the first place. Sound far-fetched? Unfortunately, it's only too real." His next sentences elaborate on that opening, but the compelling first few sentences strongly suggest a need to look at the issue of gene patents.

Proposition. The proposition is an assertion or claim about the issue. It is virtually the same as a thesis or position statement and should be stated clearly near the beginning of the essay. In most arguments, you must make your position clear very early in the argument and then devote the rest of your paper to providing supporting evidence, details, or facts to "prove" that your position is a logical or reasonable one. The strength of your argument will come from your skill at refuting or challenging opposing claims or viewpoints, giving in or conceding on some points, and then presenting your own claims, evidence, or other details that support your position.

Refutation of Opposing Arguments. It is not enough to find facts or evidence that argue your own position and therefore prove its validity; you must also realize that those opposed to your position will have their own facts or evidence. You must try to project what you think others may say or even try to put yourself into their position. An excellent strategy for argumentation, therefore, is to first look at the claims of others and challenge or dispute them. One of the chief strengths of a good argument is its ability to counter evidence produced by the opposing side. In fact, you must imagine more than one opposing side. Rarely is an issue represented by just two equal and opposing arguments. Often it is represented by multiple viewpoints. Obviously you cannot present every aspect and every position of an issue, but you must demonstrate that you are aware of the major viewpoints on your subject and that the position you have taken is a reasonable one. The preparatory step of anticipating or imagining the opposing position(s) will be a huge help in developing your own argument. Ask yourself what you think will be the strategy of those opposed to your position and how you can best address that opposition and counter it with your own logical reasoning. Ignoring an opposing opinion is a major fault in argumentation because it suggests that you have not explored enough aspects of the topic to warrant the position you are taking. For more on refutation, see the section on anticipating the opposition in the section on strategies for effective argumentation later.

Concessions to Opposing Arguments. Oftentimes, some of what those opposed to your position argue is valid or irrefutable. A very effective, necessary, and wise strategy is to make concessions to the opposition. It helps establish your reliability as a fair-minded person. The act of acknowledging limitations or exceptions to your own argument and accepting them actually strengthens your argument. It indicates your commitment to your position despite its flaws, or suggests that, even flawed, your position is stronger than the positions of those opposed to it. It is best to make these concessions or acknowledgements early in your paper rather than later. For more on making concessions, see the section on conceding to the opposition in the section on strategies for effective argumentation.

Development of Your Argument. In this stage of the process, you present evidence or proof to persuade your audience of the validity of your position. The argument will be most effective if it is organized with the least convincing or least important point first, building to its strongest point. This pattern lends emphasis to the most important points and engages readers in the unfolding process of the argument as the writer moves through increasingly compelling proofs. A successful argument also gives evidence of some sort for every important point. Evidence may include statistics, observations or testimony of experts, personal narratives, or other supporting proof. A writer needs to convince readers by taking them from some initial position on an issue to the writer's position, which readers will share if the argument succeeds. The only way to do this is to provide evidence that convinces readers that the position is a right or valid one.

Conclusion. In the closing paragraph(s) of your paper, you have a final opportunity to convince your audience that the evidence you have presented in the body of your paper successfully demonstrates why your proposition is valid. You may want to summarize your strongest arguments or restate your position. You may want to suggest action, solutions, or resolutions to the conflict. This final part of your paper must leave your audience with a feeling that you have presented them with all the essential information they need to know to make an intelligent assessment of your success at defending your position and possibly persuading them to believe as you do.

GUIDELINES: STRUCTURE OF AN ARGUMENT

- **Introduction**—Familiarizes audience with subject, provides background or context, conveys your credibility, and establishes tone.
- **Statement of the case**—Provides rationale or need for the argument.
- **Proposition**—Asserts a position or claim that will be supported, demonstrated, or proved in the course of the paper.
- **Refutation of opposing arguments**—Mentions and counters potential evidence or objections of opposing arguments.
- **Concession**—Acknowledges validity of some opposing arguments or evidence.
- **Development of the argument**—Offers convincing, creditable, evidence in support of proposition.
- **Conclusion**—Brings paper to a satisfactory end.

STRATEGIES FOR ARGUING EFFECTIVELY

Whereas the previous section outlines the essential structure of an argument, the following comments will also help you write an effective argument.

Know Your Audience. A consideration of who your audience is will help you anticipate the arguments of those opposed to you. Many instructors tell students to imagine an audience who disagrees with them. After all, there really is no argument if you address an audience of people who believe exactly as you do. Knowing your audience will help you figure out what strategies you must use to make your position convincing. Imagine that you are addressing an audience who is either indifferent to or opposed to your position. This will help direct the shape of your argument because such an audience will require solid evidence or persuasive illustrations to sway its opinion.

Establish an Appropriate Tone. Tone refers to the writer's attitude toward his or her subject. As a writer of argument, you want your audience to take you seriously; weigh what you have to say in defense of your position; and, ideally, not only agree that your reasoning is sound but also agree with your position. Therefore, try to keep your tone sincere, engaging, and balanced. You do not want to take a hostile, sarcastic, or antagonistic tone because then you risk alienating your audience. If you are too light, flippant, or humorous, your audience might believe you to be insincere or not truly interested in your topic.

Anticipate the Arguments of the Opposition. As mentioned above, one key aspect of argumentation is refuting arguments of those who hold opposing opinions. How do you anticipate what those opposed to your position believe? Perhaps you are already familiar with opposing positions from your own observations or discussions with others, but a good step in your preparation is to look for articles or books that express an opinion or position that you do not share. Read the arguments, determine the authors' positions, and note the evidence they produce to support their positions. How can you refute them? What evidence of your own contradicts them and supports your own position? Sometimes students find themselves being convinced by the arguments of others and switch their positions. Do not worry if that happens to you. In fact, it will probably aid you in your own argument because you are already familiar with the reasoning of that position and can use the new evidence that persuaded you to find fault with your old position.

Keep in mind that this strategy of refuting an opposing argument does not always require disproving the point. You may also question its credibility, challenge the point, identify faulty logic, or otherwise cast doubt on it. Take care when challenging the opposition that you are on solid ground and can back up your own claims with proof. To attack a point by simply declaring it wrongheaded or insubstantial without having your own solid evidence is to considerably weaken your argument. So look for any of the following ways to challenge the opposition:

- Question the validity of data or evidence: Are statistics accurate? What is the source of data? Does the opposition skew or slant data to fit its own needs?
- Question authority: What are the credentials of authorities cited in arguments? Do their credentials qualify them to have informed opinions on the topic? Do they have questionable motives?
- Challenge the logic of the opposition: What fallacies do you find? What flaws in the reasoning process are there?

Make Concessions. Sometimes it is necessary to concede a point to the opposition—that is, to acknowledge that the opposition has made a reasonable assertion. Making a concession or two is inevitable in arguments of complex issues. Conceding to the opposition is actually a good strategy as long as you follow such a concession with even stronger evidence that your position is the reasonable one. You agree that the opposition makes a good point, but you follow that agreement with an even more persuasive point.

Follow a Logical Line of Reasoning.

Aristotelian Logic. Formal, classic argumentation typically follows one of two common lines of reasoning, deductive and inductive reasoning. In deductive reasoning, you move from a general principle, or shared premise, to a conclusion about a specific instance. Premises are assumptions that people share, and the conclusion will be implied in the premises or assumptions. The traditional form of deductive reasoning is the syllogism, which has two premises and a conclusion. A premise is defined as an assumption or a proposition on which an argument is based or from which a conclusion is drawn. The premises are often referred to as major and minor, with the major premise being the general truth and the minor premise a specific instance. The classic syllogism, offered by Aristotle (384–322 BCE), a Greek mathematician and logician, is the following:

Major premise: All men are mortal.
Minor premise: Socrates is a man.
Conclusion: Socrates is mortal.

This simple example of syllogism indicates the basic formula: A is B. C is B. Therefore A is C. Arguments are described as valid when the premises lead logically to the conclusion. If they do not, the argument is invalid. Similarly, an argument is said to be sound if the argument is valid and leads to the conclusion; it is unsound if the argument is valid but does not lead to the conclusion or if the conclusion is valid but the argument is not. Here is another example:

Major premise: Driving while drunk is illegal.
Minor premise: Joe was drunk when he drove home from the party.
Conclusion: Joe committed a crime.

In contrast, inductive reasoning moves from a number of specific instances to a general principle. Rather than begin with a shared assumption or generalization, you must provide sufficient data or evidence that the generalization is warranted. Your intent is to show the general pattern by presenting relevant specific instances as evidence. To avoid being accused of overgeneralizing or making a hasty generalization, you must provide enough data, examples, or specific instances to ensure that your audience is satisfied with your conclusion. In contrast to deductive reasoning, which rests on certainties (shared or commonly acknowledged truths), inductive reasoning relies on probability (the likelihood that something is true).

Example.

Observation one: Students entering the classroom have wet hair and damp clothes.
Observation two: Students typically come from outside the building to class.
Conclusion: It must be raining outside.

With induction, you must be very careful that your data do indeed warrant your conclusion. For instance, consider the following example of **hasty generalization:**

Observation one: The daily high temperatures for the last several days have been unusually high.
Observation two: I don't remember it ever being this hot during the summer.
Conclusion: We must be experiencing global warming.

Obviously there is not enough evidence in either of the observations to establish that global warming accounts for the recent high temperatures.

Although formal argumentation is useful when arguing in abstract or ideal disciplines, such as mathematics, it is less effective in complex, real-world situations—that is, the kinds of arguments in which you are likely to be engaged. Aristotle himself realized that syllogistic reasoning, which deals in absolutes, was not suited to all arguments and that many arguments depended on an informal logic of probabilities or uncertainties. His study of this system of reasoning was known as **rhetoric**, which he defined as "the faculty of discovering in any particular case all of the available means of persuasion." Formal syllogistic logic typically leads to one correct and incontrovertible conclusion, while informal or rhetorical logic allows for probable or possible conclusions. As in syllogistic logic, the reasoning process must be rational and practical.

The Toulmin Model of Reasoning. A model of informal argumentation, or practical reasoning, is that described by Stephen Toulmin, a twentieth-century philosopher, mathematician, and physicist. This method is not as constrictive as formal syllogistic reasoning because it allows for probable causes and reasonable evidence. With this method, an argument is broken down into its individual parts and examined: each stage of the argument leads to the next. Toulmin defined argumentation as a process or logical progression from **data** or **grounds** (evidence or reasons that support a claim), to the **claim** (the proposition, a debatable or controversial assertion, drawn from the data or grounds) based on the **warrant** (the underlying assumption). The ***claim*** is the point your paper is making, your thesis or arguable position statement. ***Data*** or ***grounds*** constitute your proof and demonstrate how you know the claim is true or the basis of your claim. ***Warrants*** are the underlying assumptions or inferences that are taken for granted and that connect the claim to the data. They are typically unstated or implied and can be based on any of several types of appeals: logic, ethics, emotion, and/or shared values.

This view of argumentation as a logical progression has similarities to formal argumentation but does not rely on inductive or deductive reasoning that leads inevitably to one true conclusion. Rather, it relies on establishing the relationship between data and the claim by offering evidence that supports the warrant and leads to the best possible, the most probable, or the most likely conclusion. In such reasoning, the argument often attempts to defuse opposing arguments with the use of **qualifiers** such as *some, many, most, usually, probably, possibly, might,* or *could.* Qualifiers indicate awareness that the claim is not absolute but reasonable in the specific instance. This step reveals how sure you are of your claim.

The argument should also recognize any **conditions of rebuttal**—that is, exceptions to the rule. Rebuttals address potential opposing arguments, usually by showing flaws in logic or weakness of supporting evidence. An argument will also, if necessary, make **concessions** or acknowledgments that certain opposing arguments cannot be refuted. Often **backing**—additional justification or support for the warrant—is supplied as a secondary argument to justify the warrant. To succeed, an argument following the Toulmin model depends heavily on the strength of its warrants or assumptions, which in turn means having a full awareness of any exceptions, qualifications, or possible reservations.

Rogerian Argument. Based on the work of the American psychologist Carl R. Rogers, this approach adopts the stance of listening to arguments opposed to your own with an open mind, making concessions, and attempting to find a common ground. Thus it attempts to compromise rather than assume confrontational or adversarial opposition. The Rogerian approach is well suited to subjects that are particularly explosive or controversial, when the writer knows that the audience will be hostile or hold opinions and beliefs different from her own. This approach to argumentation differs from both the Aristotelian and Toulmin methods by focusing on conflict resolution, with both sides finding aspects of the issue that they can agree on. An argumentative essay using the Rogerian method will usually begin with a statement of common beliefs or goals and then proceed in the body of the paper to give as reasonable an explanation of the writer's position as possible without being overtly defensive or aggressive. The conclusion will present a position that encompasses the concessions the writer has made.

Use Appeals Effectively. An appeal is a rhetorical strategy whose object is to persuade. Appeals go beyond fact or logic to engage the audience's sympathy, sense of authority or higher power, or reason. Aristotle maintained that effective persuasion is achieved by a balanced use of three appeals to an audience: *logos* (logic), *ethos* (ethics), and *pathos* (emotion, related to the words pathetic, sympathy, and empathy). Other appeals may be used, such as shared values. In the Toulmin method, appeals support warrants. The appeal to ethos is a strong characteristic of Rogerian argumentation, with its emphasis on finding a common ground and its genuine attempts to understand opposing arguments and resolve conflicts. But a good argument does not rest solely on any one appeal. Thus, a good argument will use sound reasoning or apply inductive or deductive reasoning (logic), it will call upon recognized authority or establish the credibility of its sources (ethics), and it will reach audience members on an affecting, disturbing, touching, or other poignant level (emotion). An argument may also make appeals to the audience on the basis of shared values, such as human dignity, free speech, fairness, and the like.

Logical appeals offer clear, reasonable, well-substantiated proofs, including such things as data, statistics, case studies, or authoritative testimony or evidence, and they acknowledge and refute the claims of the opposition. We see such a logical appeal in Jessica Reaves' "What the Rest of Africa Could Learn about AIDS" (Chapter 19) when she cites statistics that demonstrate Senegal's success in combating and preventing AIDS, in sharp contrast to other African countries.

Ethical appeals are often made in the introduction and conclusion because they are not based on statistics or hard data. Rather, they take advantage of the beliefs or values held by the audience and often help establish context. In "The Sixth Extinction," an essay about the potential for half of the Earth's species to disappear by the end of the century (Chapter 20), Jeff Corwin cites the work of scientists around the world who are helping to reverse the trend, and then he concludes with an ethical appeal: "These committed scientists bring great generosity and devotion to their respective efforts to stop the sixth extinction. But if we don't all rise to the cause and join them in action, they cannot succeed. The hour is near, but it's not too late." Corwin calls on the shared interests and values of his audience to take action to help prevent global disaster.

Emotional appeals can be quite effective but must not be overdone, certainly not to the exclusion of logical appeals. Anna Quindlen in "Our Tired, Our Poor, Our Kids" (Chapter 13) makes a strong emotional appeal in her opening paragraph with a striking and startling description: "Six people live here, in a room the size of the master bedroom in a modern suburban house. . . . One woman, five children. The baby was born in a shelter." Her opening touches readers on an emotional level and sets the tone for what she argues in the rest of her article.

Use Analogy. An analogy is a comparison of two things in order to show their similarities. Often the comparison is of a difficult or unfamiliar concept to a simpler or more familiar one, an excellent way to advance your argument. As a strategy in argumentation, you want to make the point that if the situation in the example is true or valid, it will be true or valid in the situation you are arguing. Paul Johnson in "American Idealism and Realpolitik" (Chapter 16) uses an extended analogy when he compares the concept of life without America's taking responsibility for enforcing law abroad to "the bestial existence described in Thomas Hobbes' great work, *Leviathan*." You must choose your comparisons wisely and avoid making false comparisons: if the argument is weak for your example, it will be weak for the argument you are making.

Assess the Evidence. Reading critically is important in argumentation. You can build your own argument by trying to keep an open mind when analyzing the arguments of those opposed to your position as you read in search of evidence to support your position. What questions should you ask when analyzing the positions of those opposed to you? Consider the following: What is the author's purpose? How well does he or she achieve that purpose? What evidence does the writer give in support of that purpose? How does the author know the evidence is true? What is the argument based on? Has the writer omitted or ignored important evidence? Does the author's argument lead to a logical conclusion? Sometimes something that seems to be logical or reasonable turns out to be false. Are you convinced that the author's sources are trustworthy? What sort of language does the writer use? Is it clear and fair? Does the writer use words that are heavily charged or "loaded" and therefore likely to play on emotions rather than appeal to reason? Does the writer make any of the common fallacies (errors of reasoning) associated with attempts to be logical and fair?

Avoid Common Rhetorical Fallacies. Part of your strategy in writing a good argument is to evaluate your own reasoning process as well as that of other writers, especially those whose works you may use in support of your own argument. A fallacy is a flaw or error in reasoning that makes an argument invalid or, at best, weak. Look for these **common flaws** or **fallacies** in your own writing or in that of any writing you analyze:

- ***Ad hominem* arguments.** This Latin term means "against the man" or "toward the person" and applies to arguments that attack the character of the arguer rather than the argument itself. *Ad hominem* arguments often occur in politics, for instance, when opponents of a candidate refer to personal characteristics or aspects of the candidate's private life as evidence of her or his unsuitability to hold office. **Example:** Arguing that a candidate would not make a good senator because she is a single parent or that a candidate would not be effective as mayor because he is homosexual ignores the more important questions of qualifications for the office, the candidate's stand on issues relevant to the position, the candidate's experience in political office, and similar substantive considerations.
- **Circular reasoning or begging the question.** This error makes a claim that simply rephrases another claim in other words. It assumes as proof the very claim it is meant to support. **Examples:** This sort of logic occurs in statements such as "We do it because that's the way we've always done it," which assumes the validity of a particular way of doing things without questioning or examining its importance or relevance. Another example is stating that your candidate is the best person for an office because he is better than the other candidates.
- **Either–or reasoning.** If a writer admits only two sides to an issue and asserts that his is the only possible correct one, the writer has probably not given full thought to the subject or is unaware of the complexity of the issue. Most arguable topics are probably complex, and few are limited to either one or

another right viewpoint. Be wary of a writer who argues that there is only one valid position to take on an issue.

- **Emotionally charged language.** Writers may rely on language guaranteed to appeal to their audiences on an emotional level rather than an intellectual level. Writers do not have to avoid appeals to the emotions entirely, but they should limit their use of such appeals. Arguments on ethical or moral issues such as abortion or capital punishment lend themselves to emotional appeals, but arguments on just about any subject may be charged with emotion. This fallacy can appeal to any number of emotions, such as fear, pity, hatred, sympathy, or compassion. Emotionally charged language also includes **loaded words**, those whose meanings or emotional associations vary from person to person or group to group, and **slanted words**, those whose connotations (suggestive meaning as opposed to actual meaning) are selected for their emotional association. **Examples:** Abstract words are usually loaded, such as democracy, freedom, justice, or loyalty. Words may be slanted to convey a good association, such as those used in advertisements—cool, refreshing, or smooth—or to convey a bad association—sweltering, noisy, or stuffy. In argumentative writing, loaded or slanted language becomes problematic when it is used to deceive or manipulate.
- **False analogy.** A writer may falsely claim that, because something resembles something else in one way, it resembles it in all ways. This warning does not deny that analogy has a place in argument. It can be an extremely useful technique by emphasizing a comparison that furthers an argument, especially for a difficult point. Explaining a difficult concept in terms of a simpler, more familiar one can give helpful support to readers. However, make sure that the analogy is true and holds up under close scrutiny. **Example:** A controversial analogy that is sometimes used is the comparison of America's internment of American citizens of Japanese descent during World War II to Hitler's concentration camps. On some levels the comparison is justified: people in the U.S. internment camps were held against their will in confined areas guarded by armed soldiers, they often lost all of their property, and some were even killed in the camps. On the other hand, they were not starved to death, exterminated, or used as subjects of medical experiments. The analogy is useful for making a point about the unfair treatment of American citizens during wartime, but many would argue that the analogy breaks down on some very important points.
- **Faulty appeal to authority.** Stating that a claim is true because an authority says it is true may be faulty if the authority is not an expert in the area being discussed, the subject is especially controversial with much disagreement over it, or the expert is biased. Such false appeals appear often in advertisement, as when an actor who portrays a lawyer on television appears in an ad for a real-life law firm. Similarly, actors who portray doctors on medical television shows are often used in health and beauty products to present an appearance of authority. The underlying assumption seems to be that audience members will equate the fictional lawyer's or doctor's words with those of an actual lawyer or physician.

- **Hasty generalization.** A writer makes a hasty generalization if she draws a broad conclusion on the basis of very little evidence. Such a writer probably has not explored enough evidence and has jumped too quickly to conclusions. **Examples:** Assuming that all politicians are corrupt because of the bad behavior of one is an example of making a hasty generalization. Condemning all films with violent content because of one film that has received widespread criticism for its graphic violence is another example.
- **Oversimplification.** In oversimplification, the arguer offers a solution that is too simple for the problem or issue being argued. **Example:** For instance, arguing that the problem of homelessness could be solved by giving jobs to homeless people overlooks the complexity of the issue. Such a suggestion does not take into account such matters as drug or alcohol dependency that sometimes accompanies life on the streets or a range of other problems faced by people who have lost their homes and learned to live outdoors.
- ***Non sequitur.*** This Latin term, meaning "does not follow," refers to inferences or conclusions that do not follow logically from available evidence. *Non sequiturs* also occur when a person making an argument suddenly shifts course and brings up an entirely new point. **Example:** The following demonstrates a *non sequitur*: "My friend Joan broke her arm during a gymnastics team practice after school. After-school activities are dangerous and should be banned."
- ***Post hoc, ergo propter hoc* reasoning.** This Latin term means "after this, therefore because of this." It applies to reasoning that assumes that Y happened to X simply because it came after X. **Example:** Accusing a rock group of causing the suicide of a fan because the fan listened to the group's music just before committing suicide is an example of such reasoning. Although the music might be a small factor, other factors are more likely to account for the suicide, such as a failed love relationship, feelings of low self-worth, or personal despair for a variety of reasons.
- **Red herring.** A red herring diverts the audience's attention from the main issue at hand to an irrelevant issue. The fallacy is to discuss an issue or topic as if it were the real issue when it is not. Writers of mystery fiction often use red herrings to distract readers from identifying the stories' criminals. That is part of the fun of reading a mystery. But an argumentative writer who tries to use red herrings probably does not have enough relevant supporting evidence or does not recognize the irrelevance of the evidence. **Example:** Arguing against the death penalty on the grounds that innocent people have been executed avoids the issue of why the death penalty is wrong. Citing the execution of innocent people is a red herring.
- **Stereotyping.** Another form of generalization is stereotyping—that is, falsely applying the traits of a few individuals to their entire group or falsely drawing a conclusion about a group on the basis of the behavior or actions of a few in that group. Stereotyping is also oversimplification because it ignores the complexity of humans by reducing them to a few narrow characteristics.

Stereotyping produces a false image or impression of a large number of people who have a certain thing in common—most frequently race, ethnicity, gender, or sexual preference—but also such widely differing things as occupation, hair color, speech habits, or educational level. **Example:** Any assertion about an entire group of people on the basis of a few in that group is stereotyping.

STRATEGIES FOR CONSTRUCTING A CONVINCING ARGUMENT

- **Know your audience.** This helps you understand what evidence you need to make your argument convincing.
- **Establish appropriate tone**. Your attitude toward your subject is important in making your argument convincing. Using the appropriate tone strengthens your argument.
- **Anticipate the arguments of those opposed to you.** Anticipating and countering others' arguments strengthens your own position.
- **Make concessions where necessary**. Acknowledging truths in the arguments of others reveals that you are aware of those truths but are still committed to your own position. Follow such concessions with your own even stronger evidence, proof, or support.
- **Follow a logical line of reasoning**. Whether formal or informal, inductive or deductive, or some other method recommended by your instructor, your argument must be reasonable and sound.
- **Use appeals effectively**. Appeals to logic, ethics, emotions, or shared values all help develop your argument. Be cautious when appealing to emotions; such appeals are all right in small measure, but your main appeals should be to logic and/or ethics.
- **Assess the evidence.** Examine carefully the evidence you use for your argument. Weak or flawed evidence weakens your own argument.
- **Look for flaws in your own and others' reasoning process.** Avoid fallacies or errors in reasoning in your own writing and examine the arguments of others for such flaws.

SAMPLE STUDENT PAPERS

You can see examples of argumentative papers in Chapter 6 with Nate Hayes's "Hello, Dolly" and in Chapter 7 with Nate's research paper that grew out of his shorter paper on cloning, "A Positive Alternative to Cloning." In the following pages you will find Rita's argumentative paper annotated with marginal comments on her strategies. In addition to noting Rita's argumentative strategies, pay attention to the ways in which she uses sources to bolster her argument. **Note that she follows MLA style guidelines for handling source material as outlined in Chapters 6 and 7.**

In her introductory women's studies and sociology classes, Rita became interested in the status of women in the workforce. She learned about federal legislation that made it illegal to discriminate in the workplace on the basis of sex, among other things. She also knew that when her mother and grandmother were growing up, the women's movement had done much to address inequities in women's lives. So she was surprised by some of the facts that she learned in her classes about women's work force participation and earnings. On the other hand, Rita had often heard people comment that women have now achieved equity, even arguing that there was no longer job discrimination or discrepancies between what men and women earn for the same work. Furthermore, several class-action sex-discrimination lawsuits brought by female employees against large corporations had been in the news recently, with the corporations hotly denying any form of sex discrimination. Therefore, when her English instructor assigned an argumentative paper using source materials, Rita decided to research this controversial subject.

Rita's question was, Have women really achieved equality in the workplace? Her reading in this area led her to the conclusion that, no, despite everything that has been done to make women equal to men in employment, they have not yet achieved that goal. Although she found that there are differences not only in earnings but also in rates of promotion and representation at higher, managerial ranks, she decided to focus her paper on just the issue of the wage gap. The proposition she formulated for her paper is the following: Despite decades of struggling for women's equality in the workplace, the wage gap between men and women remains unacceptably wide.

Fleming 1

Rita Fleming

English 102-2

Professor White

21 Oct. 2010

Women in the Workforce: Still Not Equal

Rita begins with background information and establishes importance of the issue by appealing to the common good. Her proposition states clearly what her position is.

Nearly seventy-one million American women, over half of those over the age of 16, are in the civilian labor force, and over half of those women work full time, year round. Many people have the perception that women's large presence in the workforce in combination with federal laws that prohibit job discrimination means that women enjoy equality with men in the workplace. However, recent class-action sex-discrimination suits brought by women workers against large corporations suggest that millions of

Rita acknowledges the opposition, makes concessions, and reaffirms her position.

Fleming 2

women feel discriminated against in the workplace. Furthermore, a look at labor statistics compiled by the federal government, such as those from the U.S. Census Bureau, reveals that women on average are still paid significantly less than men. Despite decades of struggling for women's equality in the workplace, the wage gap between men and women remains unacceptably wide.

Some argue that workplace inequity has disappeared as a result of federal legislation that makes discrimination in employment illegal. It is true that efforts to correct disparities between men's and women's wages have a long history. Executive Orders have been legislated to fight discrimination in employment, beginning in 1961 with President John F. Kennedy's Executive Order 10925 creating a President's Committee on Equal Employment Opportunity prohibiting discrimination on the basis of sex, race, religious belief, or national origin. The Equal Pay Act of 1963 prohibits paying women less than men working in the same establishment and performing the same jobs, and Title VII of the 1964 Civil Rights Act prohibits job discrimination on the basis of not only race, color, religion, and national origin but also sex. It is also true that when the Equal Pay Act was signed, women working full-time, year round made only 59 cents on average for every dollar a man made and that the figure had increased to 82 cents by 2005 (Brunner). Yes, women have made gains over the past decades, but is 82 cents for every dollar a man makes acceptable? If women

Fleming 3

are acceptable? If women are truly equal to men in this society, why are their average earnings not equal? Finally, if there is true pay equity in the workplace, why does the number of workplace suits charging discrimination of all kinds, including wage inequities, continue to rise ("Class Action Suits in the Workplace" 84)?

Rita offers explanations for the inequity by citing data supporting her position.

There are many reasons for this inequity. One reason is that most women work in service and clerical jobs, including such occupations as secretaries, teachers, cashiers, and nurses. For instance, in 2006, 92.3% of registered nurses and 82.2% of elementary and middle school teachers were women (BLS). In 2006, 97.7% of preschool and kindergarten teachers, 97.1% of dental hygienist, and 97.3% of secretaries were (BLS). In 1999, 97.3% of preschool and kindergarten teachers as well as dental assistants were female, and 96.7% of secretaries were (Weinberg 11). Women also tend to work at jobs that pay less than the jobs that men typically work at. Eitzen and Zinn point out that, as the economy shifted in recent times from being manufacturing-based to being more service oriented, a dual labor market emerged. In a dual labor market, there are two main types of jobs, primary and secondary. Primary jobs are usually stable, full-time jobs with high wages, good benefits, and the opportunity to move up the promotion ladder, whereas secondary jobs are the opposite. Secondary occupations are unstable, normally part time, with few benefits and little opportunity for advancement (218). Unfortunately, large corporations have been eliminating many primary jobs and creating new,

Rita continues to explain, backing assertions with supporting proof.

As she offers more reason to account for the wage gap, Rita reinforces her position that the gap is unacceptable.

Fleming 4

secondary jobs to take their places, and it is mostly women who are hired to fill these secondary positions.

The term "occupational segregation" is used to describe the phenomenon of women workers being clustered in secondary or low-paying jobs (Andersen and Collins 238). This segregation is particularly startling when you consider such statistics as the following: "Since 1980, women have taken 80 percent of the new jobs created in the economy, but the overall degree of gender segregation has not changed much since 1900" (Andersen and Collins 236). Fully 60% of women workers are in clerical and service occupations, while only 30% are managers and professionals ("USA" 68). In the very few occupations where the median earnings for women are at least 95% of those for men, only one—meeting and convention planners—employs a higher percentage of female workers than male (Weinberg 13). Women are simply not crossing over into traditionally male-dominated occupations at a very high rate. This does not mean that women do not have opportunities or are not educated. It could mean, however, that the workplace is still plagued by old, outdated stereotypes about gender-based occupations.

Another explanation for the wage gap is that women earn less because of the differences in years of experience on the job. Collectively, women earn less because they haven't worked as many years as men have in certain professions (Robinson 183-84). Women often drop out of the job market to have their families, for instance, while men stay at their jobs when they have families. Yet another reason for the wage gap, offered by Borgna Brunner, is that older women may be working largely in jobs that are "still subject to the attitudes and conditions of the past." Brunner points out: "In contrast, the rates for young women coming of age in the 1990s reflect women's social and legal advances. In 1997, for example, women under 25 working full-time earned 92.1% of men's salaries compared to older women (25-54), who earned 74.4% of what men made." This is great news for young women but a dismal reality for the significantly large number of working women who fall into the 25-54 age group.

Reasons to account for the persistence of a wage gap are many, but sometimes there is no explanation at all. Analysts have tried to determine why, as the U.S. Census Bureau figures for 1999 reveal, "Men earn more than women at each education level," taking into account all year-round, full-time workers over age 25 (Day and Newburger 4). Surprisingly, the wage gap is greater than one might expect at the professional level: female professionals (doctors, lawyers, dentists) make substantially less than what male professionals make. Female physicians and surgeons aged 35-54, for instance, earned 69% of what male physicians and surgeons made (Weinberg 21). How can such a wage gap be explained? The reality is, according to the Women's International Network News, "Between one-third and one-half of the wage difference between men and women cannot be explained by differences in experience, education, or other legitimate qualifications" ("USA" 68). Even the U. S. Census Bureau concludes: "There is a substantial gap in

Rita suggests actions to address the problem she has substantiated in her paper.

Fleming 6

median earnings between men and women that is unexplained, even after controlling for work experience . . . education, and occupation" (Weinberg 21). Given this statement, it is likely that the most unfair reason of all to explain why women are paid less than men for the same or equal work is simply discrimination. This situation is intolerable.

What can be done to correct the wage differential between men's and women's earnings? Laws have failed to produce ideal results, but they have done much to further women's chances in the workplace and they give women legal recourse when they feel that discrimination has taken place. Therefore, better vigilance and stricter enforcement of existing laws should help in the battle for equal wages. Young women should be encouraged to train for primary jobs, while those who work in secondary jobs should lobby their legislators or form support groups to work for better wages and benefits. Working women can join or support the efforts of such organizations as 9to5, the National Association of Working Women. Women's position in the workforce has gradually improved over time, but given the statistics revealing gross differences between their wages and those of men, much remains to be done.

Fleming 7

Works Cited

Andersen, Margaret L., and Patricia Hill Collins, eds. *Race, Class and Gender: An Anthology.* 3rd ed. Belmont, CA: Wadsworth, 1998. Print.

Brunner, Borgna. "The Wage Gap: A History of Pay Inequity and the Equal Pay Act." *Infoplease.* March 2005. PDF file.

"Class Action Suits in the Workplace are on the Rise." *HR Focus* April 2007: 84-85. Print.

Day, Jennifer Cheeseman, and Eric C. Newburger. *The Big Payoff: Educational Attainment and Synthetic Estimates of Work-Life Earnings.* United States Census Bureau, July 2002. Web. 15 Oct. 2010.

Eitzen, Stanley D., and Maxine Baca Zinn. *Social Problems.* 7th ed. Needham Heights, MA: Allyn and Bacon, 1997. Print.

"101 Facts on the Status of Working Women." Business and Professional Women October 2007. Web. 12 October 2010.

Robinson, Derek. "Differences in Occupational Earnings by Sex." In *Women, Gender, and Work.* Ed. Martha Fetherolf Loutfi. Geneva: International Labor Office, 2001. Print.

United States. Department of Labor Bureau of Labor Statistics (BLS) *Women in the Labor Force: A Databook (2006 Edition).* 20 Nov. 2006. Web. 12 Oct. 2010.

Weinberg, Daniel H. *Evidence from Census 2000 about Earnings by Detailed Occupation for Men and Women.* United States Census Bureau, May 2004. Web. 15 Oct. 2010.

Synthesizing Material and Documenting Sources Using MLA Style

WRITING A SYNTHESIS

A synthesis draws conclusions from, makes observations on, or shows connections between two or more sources. In writing a synthesis, you attempt to make sense of the ideas of two or more sources by extracting information that is relevant to your purpose. The ability to synthesize is an important skill, for people are continuously bombarded with a dizzying variety of information and opinions that need sorting out and assessment. To understand your own thinking on a subject, it is always useful to know what others have to say about it. You can see the importance of reading and thinking critically when synthesizing the ideas of others. The sources for a synthesis may be essays, books, editorials, lectures, movies, group discussions, or any of the myriad forms of communication that inform academic and personal lives. At minimum, you will be required in a synthesis to reflect on the ideas of two writers or other sources, assess them, make connections between them, and arrive at your own conclusions on the basis of your analysis. Often you will work with more than two sources; certainly you will do so in a research paper.

Your purpose for writing a synthesis will be determined by the nature of your assignment, although syntheses are most commonly used to either explain or argue. Perhaps you want to explain how something works or show the causes or effects of a particular event. You may argue a particular point, using the arguments of others as supporting evidence or as subjects for disagreement in your own argument. You may want to compare or contrast the positions of other writers for the purpose of stating your own opinion on the subject. When you write a research paper, you most certainly must synthesize the ideas and words of others. Whether your synthesis paper is a report or an argument, you must sort through and make sense of what your sources say. Sometimes you will want to read many sources to find out what a number of people have to say about a particular subject in order to discover your own position on it.

Synthesis, then, involves not only understanding what others have to say on a given subject but also making connections between them, analyzing their arguments or examples, and/or drawing conclusions from them. These are processes you routinely employ in both your everyday life and in your courses whenever you consider the words, ideas, or opinions of two or more people or writers on a topic. Beginning with Chapter 8, each chapter in Parts Two through Five ends with a list of suggestions for writing. Many of the topics require that you synthesize material in the readings in that chapter. These topics ask you to argue, to compare and contrast, to explore reasons, to explain something, to describe, or to report on something, using at least two of the essays in the chapter.

In all cases, no matter what your purpose for writing the synthesis, you will need to state your own central idea or **thesis** early in your paper. In preparation for writing your essay, you will complete a very helpful step if you locate the central idea or thesis of each of the works under analysis and summarize their main points. The summary is itself a kind of synthesis, in that you locate the key ideas in an essay, state them in your own words, and then put the ideas back together again in a shortened form. This process helps you understand what the authors believe and why they believe it. Furthermore, your own readers benefit from a summary of the central idea or chief points of the articles you are assessing. As you write your essay, you will not only be explaining your own view, opinion, or position, but you will also be using the ideas or words of the authors whose works you are synthesizing. These will have to be documented, using the appropriate formatting for documenting sources illustrated in this chapter. See the box "Guidelines for Writing a Synthesis" for step-by-step directions on writing your synthesis.

GUIDELINES FOR WRITING A SYNTHESIS

- **Determine your purpose for writing by asking yourself what you want to do in your essay.** Without a clear purpose, your synthesis will be a loosely organized jumble of words. Although your purpose is often governed by the way in which the assignment is worded, make sure you understand exactly what you intend to do.
- **Consider how best to accomplish your purpose.** Will you argue, explain, compare and contrast, illustrate, show causes and effects, describe, or narrate? How will you use your sources to accomplish your purpose?
- **Read each source carefully and understand its central purpose and major points.** If you are unclear about the meaning of an essay, reread it carefully, noting passages that give you trouble. Discuss these passages with a classmate or with your instructor if you still lack a clear understanding.
- **Write a one-sentence statement of the central idea or thesis and a brief summary of each source you will use in your paper.** This process will help clarify your understanding of your sources and assist you in formulating your own central idea. These statements or summaries can then be incorporated appropriately into your synthesis.
- **Write a one-sentence statement of your own thesis or central purpose for writing the synthesis.** This statement should be a complete sentence, usually in the first paragraph of your essay. The thesis statement helps you focus your thoughts as you plan your essay by limiting the nature and scope of what you intend to accomplish. It is also a crucial aid to your readers, because it is essentially a succinct summary of what you intend to do.
- **Develop or illustrate your thesis by incorporating the ideas of your sources into the body of your paper, either by paraphrasing or directly quoting.** Part of your purpose in writing a synthesis is to demonstrate familiarity with your sources and to draw on them in your own essay. This goal requires that you make reference to key ideas of the sources.
- **Document your sources.** Keep in mind the guidelines for documenting all borrowed material.

CITING AND DOCUMENTING SOURCES

No matter what your purpose or pattern of development, if you draw on the writing of someone else, you must be fair to the author of the material you borrow. If you paraphrase an author's words or, occasionally, quote them exactly as they appear in the original text, you must cite your source. In any case, when you are using the ideas or words of another, you must give credit to your source. In academic writing, credit is given by naming the author of the borrowed material, its title, the place and date of publication, and the page number or numbers where the information is located.

The rest of this chapter introduces some basic skills needed to incorporate the words and ideas of others into your own written work. It begins with a discussion of documenting sources, goes on to provide guidelines and examples for paraphrasing and quoting, illustrates some useful tools for handling source material and integrating source materials, and ends with directions for documenting sources from collections of essays, such as this textbook. The guidelines in this chapter follow MLA (Modern Language Association) documentation style. (*Note:* If your instructor prefers that you use APA style or gives you a choice of styles, guidelines for APA documentation style appear in Chapter 7.) MLA style is used primarily in the humanities disciplines, such as English and philosophy, whereas other disciplines have their own guidelines. If you learn the skills necessary for paraphrasing, quoting, and documenting the material located in this textbook, you will be prepared to incorporate library and Internet resources, as well as other materials, into long, complex research papers. For more discussion of MLA style, with sample works-cited entries for a broad range of both print and nonprint sources, including the Internet, see Chapter 7.

IN-TEXT CITATIONS AND LIST OF WORKS CITED

The MLA style of documentation requires that you give a brief reference to the source of any borrowed material in a parenthetical note that follows the material. This parenthetical note contains only the last name of the authority and the page number or numbers on which the material appears, or only the page number or numbers if you mention the author's name in the text. This in-text citation refers to specific information or ideas from a source for which you give complete bibliographic information at the end of the paper in the works-cited list. With the author (or title, if no author) given in the paper itself, your readers can quickly locate full details of your source by looking at the alphabetical list of all the works you drew upon in your paper.

The parenthetical citation is placed within the sentence, after the quotation or paraphrase, and before the period. If punctuation appears at the end of the words you are quoting, ignore a comma, period, or semicolon but include a question mark or exclamation mark. In all cases, the period for your sentence follows the parenthetical citation.

The name or title that appears in the parenthetical citation in your text corresponds to an entry in the works-cited list at the end of your paper. This list is labeled "Works Cited." Individual entries in this list contain complete bibliographic information about the location of the works you reference, including the full name of the author (if known), the complete title, the place of publication, and the date of publication (if known).

Treat World Wide Web and other electronic sources as you do printed works, that is, name the author, if known, or the title if no author is named. If you use a source with no page numbers, such as a Web site or a film, you cannot give a page number in the parenthetical citation.

Illustration: In-Text Citations and Works-Cited Entries. The following examples show formats for citing sources in the text of your paper. The works-cited formats for many of the references are included here. You can find more examples in Chapter 7.

- **Book or article with one author.** Name of author followed by the page number: (Sollod 67)
  Source as it appears on the list of works cited: Sollod, Robert. "The Hollow Curriculum." *Perspectives on Contemporary Issues: Readings Across the Disciplines.* 5th ed. Ed. Katherine Anne Ackley. Boston: Wadsworth, Cengage Learning, 2009. 66–69. Print.
- **Book or article with two or three authors.** Name of authors followed by the page number: (Gilbert and Gubar 78), (Fletcher, Miller, and Caplan 78)
  Sources as they appears on the list of works cited: Gilbert, Sandra M., and Susan Gubar. *The Madwoman in the Attic: The Woman Writer and the Nineteenth-Century Literary Imagination.* 2nd ed. New Haven: Yale UP, 2000. Print.

  Fletcher, John C., Franklin G. Miller, and Arthur L. Caplan. "Facing Up to Bioethical Decisions." *Issues in Science and Technology.* Fall 1994: 75–80. Print.
- **Book or article with more than three authors.** Name just the first author followed by "et al." (Latin for "and others") and then the page number: (Mitchell et al. 29)
  Source as it appears on the list of works cited: Mitchell, James, Jane Smith, and Al Young. *Herbal Supplements: Benefits and Dangers.* Los Angeles: Global Health Press, 2009. Print.

Note: Reproduce the names in the order in which they appear on the title page. If they are not listed alphabetically, do not change their order.

- **Article or other publication with no author named.** Give a short title followed by the page number, if available: ("New Year's Resolutions" 1), ("44 Ways")
  Sources as they appear on the list of works cited: "New Year's Resolutions." *Columbia City Post and Mail* [Indiana] 2 Jan. 2010: 1+. Print.
  "44 Ways to Kick-Start Your New Year." *Success.Com.* Success Media, 30 Nov. 2009. Web. 12 October 2010.

Note: If you cite two anonymous articles beginning with the same word, use the full title of each to distinguish one from the other: ("Classrooms without Walls" 45), ("Classrooms in the 21st Century" 96)

- **Two works by the same author.** Give the author's name followed by a comma, a short title and the page number: (Heilbrun, *Hamlet's Mother* 123), (Heilbrun, *Writing a Woman's Life* 35)
  Sources as they appear in the list of works cited: Heilbrun, Carolyn. *Hamlet's Mother and Other Women*. 2nd ed. New York: Columbia UP, 2002. Print.
  ______. *Writing a Woman's Life*. 1988. New York: Norton, 2008. Print.

Note: A reprint differs from a new edition of the work, so the entry for *Hamlet's Mother and Other Women* names the edition and date of its publication. However, *Writing a Woman's Life* was a reprint, not a new edition, so the entry includes the date of first printing (1988) as well as the date of the work being referenced (2008).

- **An Internet work.** Use author's last name or short title: (Fletcher)
  Source as it appears on the list of works cited: Fletcher, Dan. "Say No More: The Banned Words of 2010." *Time.Com*. Time Magazine, 02 Jan. 2010. Web. 21 Sept. 2010.
- **An article from an electronic database.** Use author's last name and page number: (Harvey and Delfabbro 4)
  Source as it appears on the list of works cited: Harvey, J., and P. H. Delfabbro. "Psychological Resilience in Disadvantaged Youth." *Australian Psychologist* 39.1 (Mar. 2004): 3–13. Academic Search Premier. Web. 12 Nov. 2010.

GUIDELINES FOR DOCUMENTING SOURCES

- Provide a citation every time you paraphrase or quote directly from a source.
- Give the citation in parentheses following the quotation or paraphrase.
- In the parentheses, give the author's last name and the page number or numbers from which you took the words or ideas, if available. Do not put any punctuation between the author's last name and the page number.
- If you name the author as you introduce the words or ideas, the parentheses will include only the page number or numbers. If source is from a Web site with no page numbers and you name the author in your text, no parentheses are needed.
- At the end of your paper, provide an alphabetical list of the authors you quoted or paraphrased and give complete bibliographic information, including not only author and title but also where you found the material. This element is the Works Cited page.

PARAPHRASING

Paraphrasing is similar to summarizing in that you restate in your own words something someone else has written, but a paraphrase restates everything in the passage rather than highlighting just the key points. Summaries give useful presentations of the major points or ideas of long passages or entire works, whereas paraphrases are most useful in clarifying or emphasizing the main points of short passages.

To paraphrase, express the ideas of the author in your own words, being careful not to use phrases or key words of the original. Paraphrases are sometimes as long as the original passages, though often they are slightly shorter. The purpose of paraphrasing is to convey the essence of a sentence or passage in an accurate, fair manner and without the distraction of quotation marks. If your paraphrase repeats the exact words of the original, then you are quoting, and you must put quotation marks around those words. **A paper will be more interesting and more readable if you paraphrase more often than you quote.** Think of your own response when you read something that contains quotations. Perhaps, like many readers, you will read with interest a paraphrase or short quotation, but you may skip over or skim quickly long passages set off by quotation marks. Readers generally are more interested in the ideas of the author than in his or her skill at quoting other authors.

GUIDELINES FOR PARAPHRASING

- Restate in your own words the important ideas or essence of a passage.
- Do not repeat more than two or three exact words of any part of the original, unless you enclose them in quotation marks.
- If you must repeat a phrase, clause, or sentence exactly as it appears in the original, put quotation marks around those words.
- Keep the paraphrase about the same length as the original source, or slightly shorter.
- Give the source of the paraphrased information either in your text or in parentheses immediately after the paraphrase.
- Try to paraphrase rather than quote as often as possible, saving direct quotations for truly remarkable language, startling or unusual information, or otherwise original or crucial wording.

Illustration: Paraphrasing. This section provides examples of paraphrases using selected passages from the sources indicated.

1. **Source:** Isaacson, Walter. *Einstein: His Life and Universe*. New York: Simon, 2007. Print.

> **Original** (page 54): Among the many surprising things about the life of Albert Einstein was the trouble he had getting an academic job. Indeed, it would be an astonishing nine years after his graduation from the Zurich Polytechnic in 1900—and four years after the miracle year in which he not only upended physics but also finally got a doctoral dissertation accepted—before he would be offered a job as a junior professor.
>
> **Paraphrase:** In his biography of Albert Einstein, Walter Isaacson notes the rather surprising fact that Einstein not only had trouble finding a teaching job after college graduation, but it took nine years to do so (54).

COMMENT

Even when you put the material into your own words, you must cite the source and give a page number where the paraphrased material is located.

2. **Source:** Gibbs, Nancy. "The End of Helicopter Parents." *Time* 30 Nov. 2009: 52–57. Print.

Original (page 54): The insanity crept up on us slowly; we just wanted what was best for our kids. We bought macrobiotic cupcakes and hypoallergenic socks, hired tutors to correct a 5-year-old's "pencil-holding deficiency," hooked up broadband connections in the treehouse but took down the swing set after the second skinned knee. We hovered over every school, playground and practice field—"helicopter parents," teachers christened us, a phenomenon that spread to parents of all ages, races, and religions.

Paraphrase: In a cover story for *Time* magazine, Nancy Gibbs discusses the trend that has developed among parents to do everything they can think of to protect and provide for their children. Teachers have coined the term "'helicopter parents'" to describe the moms and dads who stay close to their children, "hover[ing]" over them in their efforts to protect them (54).

COMMENT

When it is clear that you are paraphrasing from the same source in two or more consecutive sentences *and* you have named the author or source in the first sentence, you need give only one parenthetical citation at the end of the series of sentences.

Note also that key terms from the original are placed in quotation marks to indicate that they are not the student's own words.

3. **Source:** Camarota, Steven A. *The High Cost of Cheap Labor: Illegal Immigration and the Federal Budget*. Center for Immigration Studies. August 2004. Web. 12 Oct. 2010.

Original: Our findings show that many of the preconceived notions about the fiscal impact of illegal households turn out to be inaccurate. In terms of welfare use, receipt of cash assistance programs tends to be very low, while Medicaid use, though significant, is still less than for other households. Only use of food assistance programs is significantly higher than that of the rest of the population. Also, contrary to the perceptions that illegal aliens don't pay payroll taxes, we estimate that more than half of illegals work "on the books." On average, illegal households pay more than $4,200 a year in all forms of federal taxes. Unfortunately, they impose costs of $6,950 per household.

Paraphrase: According to a 2004 study by the Center for Immigration Studies of the impact of illegal immigration on the federal budget, many of the notions about illegal immigrants are incorrect. Although they do receive more food aid than the general population, they receive less welfare and Medicaid benefits. Furthermore, most illegal immigrants pay federal taxes (Camarota).

COMMENT

For Internet or other electronic sources without pagination, many instructors recommend that you repeat the author's name in parentheses after all paraphrases and direct quotations, even if the name is already included in the text.

QUOTING

When you want to include the words of another writer, but it is not appropriate to either paraphrase or summarize, you will want to quote. Quoting requires that you repeat the exact words of another, placing quotation marks before and after the material being quoted. **A crucial guideline requires that you copy the words exactly as they appear in the original text.** To omit words or approximate the original within quotation marks is sloppy or careless handling of your source material.

Be selective in the material you choose to quote directly, however. You should usually paraphrase the words of another, restating them in your own language, rather than relying on exactly copying the words. How do you know when to quote rather than paraphrase? You should quote only words, phrases, or sentences that are particularly striking or that must be reproduced exactly because you cannot convey them in your own words without weakening their effect or changing their intent. Quote passages or parts of passages that are original, dramatically worded, or in some way essential to your paper. Otherwise, rely on paraphrasing to refer to the ideas of others. In either case, document your source by identifying the original source and the location of your information within that source.

GUIDELINES FOR QUOTING

- Be selective: Quote directly only words, phrases, or sentences that are particularly striking and whose beauty, originality, or drama would be lost in a paraphrase.
- Quote directly passages that are so succinct that paraphrasing them would be more complicated or take more words than a direct quotation would require.
- Enclose the exact words you are quoting between quotation marks.
- Do not change one word of the original unless you indicate with brackets, ellipses, or other conventions that you have done so.
- Provide the source of your quoted material either in your text or in parentheses following the material.

Illustration: Quoting. This section provides examples of quotations using selected passages from Gerald Graff's "Ships in the Night." The source for all examples in this section is the following:

Source: Graff, Gerald. *Beyond the Culture Wars: How Teaching the Conflicts Can Revitalize American Education*. New York: Norton, 1992. Print.

1. **Original** (page 106): To some of us these days, the moral of these stories would be that students have become cynical relativists who care less about convictions than about grades and careers.

   Quotation: Gerald Graff suggests that some people see students as "cynical relativists who care less about convictions than about grades and careers" (106).

COMMENTS

- Place double quotation marks before and after words taken directly from the original.
- When the quoted material is an integral part of your sentence, especially when preceded by the word "that," do not capitalize the first letter of the first word.
- Where possible, name the author whose ideas or words you are quoting or paraphrasing.
- In parentheses after the quotation, give the page number in the source where the quotation is located (hence the phrase "parenthetical citation"). This example contains only the page number because the author's name is mentioned in the text. If the text had not given the author's name, it would be included in the parenthetical citation.

2. **Original** (page 118): The more fundamental question we should be asking in most cases is not how *much time* teachers are spending in the classroom but *under what conditions*.

   Quotation: Gerald Graff believes that "the more fundamental question . . . is not *how much* time teachers are spending in the classroom but *under what conditions*" (118).

COMMENTS

- When a quotation preceded by *that* forms an integral part of your sentence, do not capitalize the first word in the quotation, even when it is capitalized in the original. Use the ellipsis (three spaced periods) to indicate the omission of text from the original.
- If some text is italicized in the original, you must italicize it in your quotation.

3. **Original** (page 109): Among the factors that make academic culture more confusing today than in the past is not only that there is more controversy but that there is even controversy about what can legitimately be considered

controversial. Traditionalists are often angry that there should even be a debate over the canon, while revisionists are often angry that there should even be a debate over "political correctness," or the relevance of ideology and politics to their subjects.

Quotation: In discussing the factors that confuse people about college curricula today, Gerald Graff notes: "Traditionalists are often angry that there should even be a debate over the canon, while revisionists are often angry that there should even be a debate over 'political correctness'..." (109).

COMMENTS

- If your direct quotation is preceded by introductory text and a colon or comma, capitalize the first letter of the first word of the quotation.
- If you quote something that appears in quotation marks in the original source, use single marks within the double quotes.
- If your quotation appears to be a complete sentence but the actual sentence continues in the original, you must use the ellipsis at the end of your quotation to indicate that.
- If an ellipsis comes at the end of a quotation, the closing quotation mark follows the third period, with no space between the period and quotation mark. The parenthetical citation follows as usual.

Combination of Paraphrase and Direct Quotation. The following example illustrates how one can combine paraphrasing and quoting for a balanced handling of source material.

4. **Original** (page 118): But the most familiar representation of the sentimental image of the course as a scene of conflict-free community is the one presented on untold numbers of college catalog covers: A small, intimate class is sprawled informally on the gently sloping campus greensward, shady trees overhead and ivy-covered buildings in the background. Ringed in a casual semicircle, the students gaze with rapt attention at a teacher who is reading aloud from a small book—a volume of poetry, we inevitably assume, probably Keats or Dickinson or Whitman. The classroom, in these images, is a garden occupying a redemptive space inside the bureaucratic and professional *machine*.

   Paraphrase and Quotation: Gerald Graff thinks that colleges project an image different from the realities of academic life. College catalog covers, he says, foster "the sentimental image of the course as a scene of conflict-free community" when they portray students sitting outside on a sunny day, mesmerized by the instructor who stands before them, reading someone's words of insight or wisdom. According to him, the classroom becomes "a garden occupying a redemptive space inside the bureaucratic and professional machine" (118).

More Examples of Correctly Handled Direct Quotations.

5. Jack Santino in "Rock and Roll as Music; Rock and Roll as Culture" maintains that "such things as suicide, drugs, sex, and violence *are* teenage concerns" and that, "while artists have a responsibility not to glamorize them, that does not mean these themes should not be explored" (196).

6. In "Rock and Roll as Music; Rock and Roll as Culture," Jack Santino observes: "Furthermore, such things as suicide, drugs, sex, and violence *are* teenage concerns. While artists have a responsibility not to glamorize them, that does not mean these themes should not be explored" (196).

COMMENTS

- Notice the difference between examples 5 and 6. The first integrates the quoted material into the sentence with the word *that,* so the first words in each of the quoted passages do not require a capital first letter.
- In the second example, the quotation is introduced and set off as a separate sentence, so the first word after the quotation mark begins with a capital letter.

INTEGRATING SOURCE MATERIALS INTO YOUR PAPER

When quoting or paraphrasing material, pay special attention to your treatment of source materials. Authors have developed many ways of skillfully integrating the words and ideas of other people with their own words. Your paper should not read as if you simply cut out the words of someone else and pasted them in your paper. You can achieve smooth integration of source materials into your text if you keep the following suggestions in mind:

- **Mention the cited author's name in the text of your paper to signal the beginning of a paraphrase or quotation.** The first time you mention the name, give both first and last names. After the first mention, give only the last name:

  Robert Sollod points out in "The Hollow Curriculum" that colleges would not think of excluding courses on multiculturalism from today's curriculum, given the importance of "appreciation and understanding of human diversity." **Sollod** asks, "Should such an appreciation exclude the religious and spiritually based concepts of reality that are the backbone upon which entire cultures have been based?" (A60).

- **Mention the source if no author is named.** This practice gives credit to the source while providing an introduction to the borrowed material:

  A *U.S. News & World Report* article notes that, although no genes determine what occupation one will go into, groups of genes produce certain tendencies—risk-taking, for instance—that might predispose one to select a particular kind of work ("How Genes Shape Personality" 64).

CAUTION—AVOID DROPPED QUOTATIONS

Never incorporate a quotation without in some way introducing or commenting on it. A quotation that is not introduced or followed by some concluding comment, referred to as a "dropped" quotation, detracts from the smooth flow of your paper.

- **Give citations for all borrowed material.** State the authority's name, use quotation marks as appropriate, give the source and page number in a parenthetical citation, give some sort of general information, and/or use a pronoun to refer to the authority mentioned in the previous sentence. **Do not rely on one parenthetical citation at the end of several sentences or an entire paragraph:**

  Regna Lee Wood has also researched the use of phonics in teaching children to read. **She** believes that the horrible failure of our schools began years ago. Wood notes that "it all began in 1929 and 1930 when hundreds of primary teachers, guided by college reading professors, stopped teaching beginners to read by "matching sounds with letters that spell sounds" (52). **She** adds that since 1950, when most reading teachers switched to teaching children to sight words rather than sound them by syllable, "fifty million children with poor sight memories have reached the fourth grade still unable to read" (52).

- **Vary introductory phrases and clauses.** Avoid excessive reliance on such standard introductory clauses as "Smith says," or "Jones writes." For instance, vary your verbs and/or provide explanatory information about sources, as in the following examples:

  Michael Liu notes the following:
  Professor Xavier argues this point convincingly:
  According to Dr. Carroll, chief of staff at a major health center:
  As Marcia Smith points out,

- **The first mention of an authority in your text (as opposed to the parenthetical citation) should include the author's first name as well as last name.** The second and subsequent references should give the last name only (never the first name alone).

  First use of author's name in your paper: Susan Jaspers correctly observes that . . .

  Second and subsequent mentions of that author: Jaspers contends elsewhere that . . .

- **Combine quotations and paraphrases.** A combination provides a smoother style than quoting directly all of the time:

  W. H. Hanson's 2008 survey of college students reveals that today's generation of young people differs from those he surveyed in 2003.

> Hanson discovered that today's college students "are living through a period of profound demographic, economic, global, and technological change." Since these students of the 00s see themselves living in a "deeply troubled nation," they have only guarded optimism about the future (32–33).

- **For long quotations (more than four typed lines), set the quoted material off from the text (referred to as a block quotation).** Write your introduction to the quotation, generally followed by a colon. Then begin a new line indented ten spaces from the left margin, and type the quotation, double spaced as usual.
- **Do not add quotation marks for block quotations indented and set off from the text. If quotation marks appear in the original, use double quotation marks, not single.** If you quote a single paragraph or part of one, do not indent the first line any more than the rest of the quotation.
- **For block quotations, place the parenthetical citation after the final punctuation of the quotation.** See the following example of a block quotation:

> In her article exploring the kind of workforce required by a high-tech economy, Joanne Jacobs suggests that many of today's high school graduates lack crucial skills necessary for jobs in the rapidly growing technical and computer industries. For instance, a number of corporations agreed on the following prerequisites for telecommunications jobs:
>
> - Technical reading skills (familiarity with circuit diagrams, online documentation, and specialized reference materials).
> - Advanced mathematical skills (understanding of binary, octal, and hexadecimal number systems as well as mathematical logic systems).
> - Design knowledge (ability to use computer-aided design to produce drawings) (39–40).

USING ELLIPSIS POINTS, SQUARE BRACKETS, SINGLE QUOTATION MARKS, AND "QTD. IN"

This section offers some additional guidelines on the mechanics of handling source materials and incorporating them into your paper.

Ellipsis Points.

- **If you want to omit original words, phrases, or sentences from your quotation of source material, use ellipsis points to indicate the omission.** Ellipsis points consist of three spaced periods, with spaces before, between, and after the periods. In quotations, ellipses are most frequently used within sentences, almost never at the beginning, but sometimes at the end. In every case, the quoted material must form a grammatically complete sentence, either by itself or in combination with your own words.

Original: The momentous occurrences of an era—from war and economics to politics and inventions—give meaning to lives of the individuals who live through them.

Quotation with an ellipsis in the middle: Arthur Levine argues, "The momentous occurrences of an era . . . give meaning to lives of the individuals who live through them" (26).

Use ellipsis marks at the end of a quotation only if you have not used some words from the end of the final sentence quoted. In that case, include four periods. When the ellipsis coincides with the end of your own sentence, use four periods with no space before the first nor after the last.

Quotation with an ellipsis at the end: You know the old saying, "Eat, drink, and be merry. . . ."

If a parenthetical reference follows the ellipsis at the end of your sentence, use a space before each period and place the sentence period after the final parenthesis:

According to recent studies, "Statistics show that Chinese women's status has improved . . ." (*Chinese Women* 46).

- **Ellipsis points are not necessary** if you are quoting a fragment of a sentence, that is, a few words or a subordinate clause, because context will clearly indicate the omission of some of the original sentence.

Sociobiologists add that social and nurturing experiences can "intensify, diminish, or modify" personality traits (Wood and Wood 272).

Square Brackets.

- ***The MLA Handbook for Writers of Research Papers*, 7th ed., says that "unless indicated in brackets or parentheses . . . , changes must not be made in the spelling, capitalization, or interior punctuation of the source" (3.7.1).** Although you should look for ways to integrate source material into your text that avoid overuse of square brackets, the following guidelines apply when changing source material is unavoidable.
- **If you want to change a word or phrase to conform to your own sentence or add words to make your sentence grammatically correct, use square brackets to indicate the change.** The square brackets enclose only the changed portion of the original.

Original: They were additional casualties of our time of plague, demoralized reminders that although this country holds only two percent of the world's population, it consumes 65 percent of the world's supply of hard drugs.

Quotation: According to Pete Hamill in his essay "Crack and the Box," America "holds only two percent of the world's population, [yet] it consumes 65 percent of the world's supply of hard drugs" (267).

Original: In a miasma of Walt Disney images, Bambi burning, and Snow White asleep, the most memorable is "Cinderella."

Quotation: Louise Bernikow recalls spending Saturday afternoons at the theatre when she was growing up "in a miasma of Walt Disney images, . . . the most memorable [of which] is 'Cinderella'" (17).

Note: This example illustrates the use not only of square brackets but also of ellipsis points and single and double quotation marks.

- **Use square brackets if you add some explanatory information or editorial comment.**

Original: Then, magically, the fairy godmother appears. She comes from nowhere, summoned, we suppose, by Cinderella's wishes.

Quotation: Louise Bernikow points out that "she [the fairy godmother] comes from nowhere, summoned . . . by Cinderella's wishes" (19).

- **If the passage you quote itself contains an ellipsis, place square brackets around your own ellipsis.** The brackets tell readers that the ellipsis without brackets is in the original and that the ellipsis in brackets is your addition. MLA notes that, alternatively, you can add an explanatory note in parentheses after the quotation, if you prefer.

Source: Du Maurier, Daphne. "Don't Look Now." *Don't Look Now: Stories*. Ed. Patrick Mc Grath. New York: New York Review Books, 2008. 3–58. Print.

Original (page 10): She seemed normal, herself again. She wasn't trembling. And if this sudden belief was going to keep her happy he couldn't possibly begrudge it. But . . . but . . . he wished, all the same, it hadn't happened. There was something uncanny about thought-reading, about telepathy.

Quotation with an added ellipsis: The husband in "Don't Look Now" is disturbed after an encounter that his wife has just described: "He couldn't possibly begrudge it. But . . . but . . . he wished, all the same, it hadn't happened. There was something uncanny about [. . .] telepathy" (Du Maurier 10).

Alternative handling of added ellipsis: The husband in "Don't Look Now" is disturbed after an encounter that his wife has just described: "He couldn't possibly begrudge it. But . . . but . . . he wished, all the same, it hadn't happened. There was something uncanny about . . . telepathy" (Du Maurier 10; 1st ellipsis in orig.).

- **The Latin word *sic* (meaning "thus") in square brackets indicates that an error occurs in the original source of a passage you are quoting.** Because you are not at liberty to change words when quoting word for word, reproduce the error but use [*sic*] to indicate that the error is not yours.

Original: Thrills have less to do with speed then changes in speed.

Quotation: Dahl makes this observation: "Thrills have less to do with speed then [*sic*] changes in speed" (18).

Single Quotation Marks.

- **If you quote text that itself appears in quotation marks in the original, use single marks within the double that enclose your own quotation.**

Original: This set me pondering the obvious question: "How can it be so hard for kids to find something to do when there's never been such a range of stimulating entertainment available to them?"

Quotation: Dahl is led to ask this question: "'How can it be so hard for kids to find something to do when there's never been such a range of stimulating entertainment available to them?'" (18–19).

Qtd. in.

- **If you quote or paraphrase material that is quoted in an indirect source, use the abbreviation "qtd." with the word "in."** An indirect source is a second-hand one that quotes or paraphrases another's words, unlike a primary source, which is the writer's own work. In college research papers, you want to use primary sources as often as possible, but you are likely to have occasion to use secondary sources as well. Use "qtd. in" whenever you quote or paraphrase the published account of someone else's words or ideas. The works-cited list will include not the original source of the material you quoted or paraphrased but rather the indirect source, the one where you found the material. You will likely be using the single quotation marks within the double because you are quoting what someone else has quoted.

Original: Printed in bold letters at the entrance of the show is a startling claim by Degas' fellow painter Auguste Renoir: "If Degas had died at 50, he would have been remembered as an excellent painter, no more; it is after his 50th year that his work broadened out and that he really becomes Degas."

Quotation: Impressionist painter Auguste Renoir observed of Degas: "'If Degas had died at 50, he would have been remembered as an excellent painter, no more; it is after his 50th year that his work broadened out and that he really becomes Degas'" (qtd. in Benfey).

GUIDELINES FOR INTEGRATING SOURCE MATERIALS INTO YOUR PAPER

- Avoid "dropped" quotations by introducing all direct quotations.
- Use the author's name, where appropriate, to signal the beginning of a paraphrase or quotation.
- Cite sources for all borrowed material.
- Name a source title, if the article does not list an author's name.
- Vary the way you introduce source material.
- Try combining direct quotations and paraphrases in the same sentence.
- Become familiar with appropriate uses of ellipsis points, brackets, single quotation marks, and "qtd. in."

DOCUMENTING SOURCES IN A COLLECTION OF ESSAYS

You have been reading about and looking at examples of one important component of source documentation: in-text citations. The other component is the alphabetical list, appearing on a separate page at the end of your paper, of all the works that you quoted from or paraphrased. This is the list of works cited. Each entry in the list begins with the author's name, last name first, followed by the title of the article, book, or other source and information about its place and date of publication. The author's name (or title of the work, if it is published anonymously) in the text's parenthetical citation refers to one item in this list at the end of the paper.

You will find more discussion of documenting sources in Chapter 7, but the brief treatment here gives useful guidelines for short papers using materials reprinted in a collection of essays, such as this textbook. Although the examples in this section illustrate how to document materials reprinted in the fifth edition of this textbook, the guidelines apply to any collection of essays. Because much of *Perspectives on Contemporary Issues* is a collection of other people's works, not the editor's, you will probably not have occasion to use the words or ideas of Ackley herself. However, because you are not reading the essays in their original source, you must indicate that you have read them in her book.

Citing One Source in a Collection. Suppose your paper quotes or paraphrases a statement from a reading in the 5th edition of Perspectives on Contemporary Issues, Deborah Tannen's "We Need a Higher Quality Outrage," After you write either the exact words of Tannen or your paraphrase of her words, put a parenthesis, then give her last name and the page number where you read the words with no punctuation between them, and then close the parenthesis: (Tannnen 55). Do not write the word "page" or "pages" nor insert a comma between the author's name and the number of the page. If Tannen's piece is the only one you use in your paper, write "Work Cited" (note the singular form of "Work") at the end of your paper and enter complete bibliographic information for the article:

Work Cited

Tannen, Deborah. "We Need a Higher Quality Outrage." *Perspectives on Contemporary Issues: Readings Across the Disciplines*. 5th ed. Ed. Katherine Anne Ackley. Boston: Wadsworth Cengage, 2009. 54-57. Print.

Citing Two or More Sources in a Collection. If you draw material from two or more works in a collection, MLA style recommends that you create an entry for the collection and then cross-reference each work to that collection. That is, you do not need to repeat the full information for the collection with the citation for each essay. Instead, list the collection by the editor's name, giving full bibliographic information. Then list separately each article you use by author and title, but after each essay title, give only the collection editor's name and the inclusive page numbers of the essay.

For example, suppose you write a paper on the power of words and images to affect perception. In your essay, you use information from several essays in the 5th edition of this textbook. Here is how your Works Cited page might look:

Work Cited

Ackley, Katherine Anne, ed. *Perspectives on Contemporary Issues: Readings Across the Disciplines.* 5th ed. Boston: Wadsworth Cengage 2009. Print.

Krauthammer, Charles. "The War and the Words." Ackley 14-15.

Magubane, Zine. "Why 'Nappy' is Offensive." Ackley 43-44.

Saltzman, Joe. "What's in a Name? More than You Think." Ackley 8-11.

STUDENT PAPER DEMONSTRATING SYNTHESIS WITH IN-TEXT CITATIONS USING MLA STYLE

Following is a student paper that synthesizes material from several works in one collection and follows MLA guidelines for paraphrasing and quoting. Nate Hayes's "Hello Dolly" uses sources located in the 5th edition of this textbook, and his works-cited list may be used as a model for papers that you are asked to write using readings from this textbook (using information for the current edition, of course). The marginal comments call attention to various strategies of writing an effective synthesis. Note that a works-cited list appears on a separate page at the end. The works-cited list gives full bibliographic information for the collection and cross-references the individual works to the collection. Notice that works are listed alphabetically and that each citation conforms in punctuation and spacing to the MLA style of documentation (Chapter 7).

MLA formatting guidelines for papers call for the author's last name to appear in the running head before the page number, even on the first page. Note also that the student's name, class, instructor's name, and date appear on the left-hand side above the title of the paper. MLA style recommends using the day/month/year format for the date. Double-space between all lines of your paper, including between the date and your title and between your title and the first line of your paper. For more on using MLA style in writing that uses sources, including guidelines for formatting the works-cited list, see Chapter 7.

The opening paragraph introduces readers to the controversial issue that is the subject of the paper.

Hayes 1

Nate Hayes

English 102-2

1 October 2010

Hello, Dolly

(1) Little Bo Peep has lost her sheep, but now she can clone a whole new flock. When Dr. Ian Wilmut and his team successfully cloned Dolly the sheep, the world was mystified, amazed, and scared. Immediately, members of the shocked public began to imagine worst case scenarios of reincarnated Hitlers. The medical field, however, relished the possibilities of cloning in curing patients with debilitating or terminal illnesses. The controversy over human cloning is part of the larger debate about the potential capabilities of scientists to alter or enhance the biological makeup of humans. This debate over how far scientists should go has grown increasingly heated with developments such as the successful cloning of sheep To many people, human cloning makes sense as the next major breakthrough in medical science, but until the troubling issues associated with the procedure are resolved, human cloning must not be allowed to happen.

Nate's thesis is a straightforward declarative sentence that makes his position on the subject clear.

Nate briefly indicates the views of two scientists holding differing opinions on the subject of the paper.

Only page number is given in the citation because the author's name is mentioned in the text. Note that last names only are used because Nate has already given their full names.

Nate uses single quotation marks within the double because the word "superpersons" is in quotation marks in Watson's article.

Nate continues to draw on Wilmut's comments because Nate shares his viewpoint.

Hayes 2

Scientists, politicians, and the general public all have mixed feelings about the developments in medical science. Even people like Ian Wilmut, the Scottish embryologist whose team of researchers was responsible for cloning Dolly, and James D. Watson, Nobel-Prize-winning co-discoverer of the double helix configuration of DNA, hold different views on the issue. Despite his previous work on cloning, Wilmut is very cautious, especially about whole-being cloning. He raises a number of questions about the wisdom of carrying on full speed with cloning research, suggesting: "Even if the technique were perfected, however, we must ask ourselves what practical value whole-being cloning might have" (535). On the other hand, Watson urges: "You should never put off doing something useful for fear of evil that may never arise" (534). Although he does not directly address the issue of cloning in his article "All for the Good," Watson touches on the subject when he states his strong support of research on germ-line genetic manipulations in pursuit of what he calls "'superpersons'" or "gene-bettered children" (536). The controversy has divided people and spurred ongoing discussions—or arguments—about the extent to which human genetic makeup should be modified or amended.

The populations that might benefit most if human cloning were to become a reality are infertile couples, homosexual couples, or single people wanting children. In commenting on this possible use for cloning, Wilmut suggests that having an identical version of yourself or someone you

Hayes 3

love would be unsettling and difficult to handle emotionally (536). Cloning has even been suggested as a possibility for grieving parents to replace—or bring back to life—a child who has died tragically or violently by using cells to clone a new, identical person. On this point, Wilmut wonders how the cloned child would feel when he learns that he exists to replace another child. Wilmut's cautious approach to the issue of cloning is sensible. Many potential problems associated with human cloning need close examination. For instance, it is commonly believed that an infant would be exactly the same as the parent it is cloned from. This cannot be true. The infant would look the same, of course, but mentally and emotionally he or she would be an entirely new person. This new child would have feelings, thoughts, and experiences completely different from those of the person he or she was cloned from. The same would be true in the case of cloning a child that had died. Even were the parents to attempt replicating an environment identical to that of the original child, it would be an impossible task. Furthermore, a clone would surely have problems with individuality. How could a carbon copy of another human being feel unique? Cloning thus poses the risk of serious psychological harm.

Nate expresses his own views on the points that Wilmut raises in opposition to human cloning.

An alternative to cloning a whole person is to clone an entity for making spare human parts. The idea is that a brainless clone might be produced that could supply crucial body parts, such as a heart, a liver, kidneys, and eyes. However, this possibility still lies in the realm of science

Nate mentions an alternative use of cloning but rejects it.

Hayes 4

fiction. No one has figured out how to do such a thing in the first place, let alone suggest ways to deal with all the potential problems of dealing with such a creature. Such a step is obviously not the best use of human cloning.

Nate suggests a possible alternative to human cloning, stem cell research, but notes that it is controversial as well.

(5) A potentially beneficial use of genetic manipulation lies in stem cell research. Stem cells are those that have not yet specialized. Scientists have learned that such cells can be isolated and grown into healthy tissue that can then be used in humans to cure just about any ailment known to humans. Research in this area holds far more promise than research into cloning whole humans, although this research has its detractors and critics also. Michael Crichton, for instance, worries that a "mistake" by the U.S. Patent Office allowing genes to be patented will cause hardships for patients who could benefit by gene therapy (538), and bioethics specialists like Robyn S. Shapiro have identified a number of "key ethical and legal/regulatory issues that surround embryonic stem cell research" (541). Despite these issues, the potential of stem cell research to identify, prevent, and/or cure diseases is exciting and very promising.

Nate's conclusion rephrases and emphasizes his thesis statement.

(6) There are just far too many unanswered questions, and who knows how many remain unasked? It is not easy to anticipate all the possible ramifications for mankind of human cloning. The bottom line is that ethical, psychological, social, and religion questions need to be explored, discussed, and resolved before research in genetic engineering that aims to create new life or significantly alter existing life can be allowed to continue.

Hayes 5

Work Cited

Ackley, Katherine Anne, ed. *Perspectives on Contemporary Issues: Readings Across the Disciplines.* 5th ed. Boston: Wadsworth, Cengage Learning, 2009. Print.

Crichton, Michael. "Patenting Life." Ackley 538-40.

Shapiro, Robyn S. "Bioethics and the Stem Cell Research Debate." Ackley 540-45.

Watson, James D. "All for the Good." Ackley 532-35.

Wilmut, Ian. "Dolly's False Legacy." Ackley 535-38.

CHAPTER 7

Writing a Research Paper

When you are asked to write a paper using sources, no matter what course it is for, your goal is the same: to skillfully support a carefully formulated thesis with documented evidence. Writing such a paper can seem both overwhelming and exciting, especially if you have never written one before. This chapter presents a brief overview of the key steps in discovering a topic, researching it, and writing a paper incorporating the sources you have used. Keep in mind the discussion in Chapter 6 on paraphrasing, quoting, and documenting sources. A research paper is likely to be much longer than a writing assignment generated from readings in this book, but otherwise little difference separates the processes of using materials from this textbook and using materials from other sources in terms of accuracy and fairness to your sources. Furthermore, the process of writing a research paper is not much different from the process of writing any other paper, as explained in Chapter 2. To do your best work, you will go through the prewriting, drafting, revising, editing, and proofreading stages.

DEFINING YOUR PURPOSE

Your instructor will tell you whether your purpose in the research paper is to argue, explain, analyze, or come to some conclusion about something. Many instructors prefer that students write argumentative papers. In that case, you will make a judgment about your topic on the basis of what you find in your research. Recall the discussion in Chapter 5 on writing an argument. The same guidelines apply whether you are writing a researched argument or one without sources. You will begin your research with an idea of what your position is, then research your subject extensively, arrive at an informed opinion, and finally defend that position by presenting evidence that seems valid (that is, logical and convincing) to you. If you want to go a step further and convince your audience to adopt your position or to act on suggestions you propose, then your purpose is persuasion. The subjects for argumentative papers are virtually unlimited, but they often include controversial issues, such as those addressed in this textbook, topics on which people hold widely varying opinions.

On the other hand, some instructors direct students to explain or analyze something in their research papers. An informative paper does not necessarily address a controversial subject. If you are to write an explanatory paper, you will gather information about your topic and present it in such a way that your reader fully understands it. You will explain, describe, illustrate, or narrate something in full detail, such as what a black hole is, how photosynthesis works, the circumstances surrounding a historical event, significant events in the life of a famous person, and the like.

Audience. Having a clear sense of your audience will direct your research and help you write your paper. If you are writing an argument, the most useful audience to address is one that is opposed to your position or, at best, uncertain about where they stand on the issue. A good argument seeks to persuade or convince an audience, so anticipating readers who are not already convinced will help sharpen your argument. If your purpose is to explain, illustrate, or analyze, your audience is likely to be informed in general about the particular subject of your paper, but not in great depth. Unless instructed otherwise, assume an intelligent audience of nonspecialists who are interested in learning more about the topic of your paper. Imagining this audience will keep you from having to define or explain every term or concept and give you room for interesting, informative, and/or intriguing material about the topic.

DISCOVERING A TOPIC

Once you know your purpose and audience, the next step in writing a research paper is to find a subject that you will be comfortable working with for many weeks and then narrow it to a specific topic. Some instructors assign topics, but most leave the choice to students. The freedom to choose your own research paper topic can be intimidating because so much depends on selecting the right topic. You want a topic that not only holds your interest but that also offers you an opportunity to investigate it in depth.

The process of discovering what you will write about involves first determining the broad subject you are particularly interested in pursuing. Once you have settled on the subject, you will need to narrow it to one specific aspect of that subject. For many research paper assignments, that topic will have to be arguable, one that requires you to investigate from several angles and arrive at and defend your own position. This position will be worded in the form of a hypothesis or thesis, stated most often as a declarative statement but sometimes as a question. Discovering your final topic takes time, so do some serious thinking about this important step as soon as the paper is assigned. You will be reshaping, narrowing, and refining your topic for much of the research process, so you do not want to switch subjects halfway through.

Any or all of the suggestions for generating ideas in the prewriting stage that are discussed in Chapter 2 would be useful when trying to discover a topic for your research paper. Brainstorming, making lists, clustering, even researching in a preliminary way and talking with others can be of use. Asking questions, thinking about your personal interests or personal opinion, considering commonly held opinions, and thinking about controversial topics can all be quite helpful in the process of discovering a research topic.

Asking Questions. One of the best ways to approach the research project is to ask questions about a subject that interests you and that seems worth investigating. As you read through the suggestions for discovering a topic that follow, think in terms of questions that you might ask about the initial subjects you come up with. Try to think in terms of questions that can be answered in a research paper as opposed to a short essay. As you narrow your field of potential topics, look for those about which you can ask questions whose answers are neither too broad nor too narrow. You want the topic that you ultimately select to be challenging enough that your paper will be interesting to you as well as to your audience. Avoid topics about which questions are unanswerable or highly speculative. Your goal in the research process will be to arrive at an answer, insofar as that is possible, to your question.

Any of the topics listed as possible subjects of argumentation in Chapter 5 are appropriate for researched writing. Here are examples of questions that one might ask about various argumentative subjects when trying to generate ideas for a research paper:

- Under what conditions, if any, is censorship justifiable?
- Should research into human cloning continue?
- Do advertising images of women set up impossible standards of femininity?
- What is the appropriate punishment for steroid use in athletes?
- Which plays a more prominent role in determining behavior, genes or environment?
- What role does phonics education play in the teaching of reading?
- How dangerous is secondhand smoke?
- Should cities be allowed to ban smoking in public places such as bars, restaurants, and private clubs?
- Should sex education be taught by parents or by schools?
- Was King Arthur a real person?
- What is the best strategy for combating terrorism?
- Are restrictions on freedom of speech necessary in time of war?
- How far should Homeland Security go to protect Americans from terrorists?
- Is there still a "glass ceiling" for women in the work force?
- Should the government provide child day care for all workers?
- Does watching too much television have a harmful effect on preschool children?
- What factors affect academic success in females versus males?
- Should the Electoral College be abolished?
- Does America need an official language?
- Is hormone replacement therapy a safe choice for women?
- Do women do better academically in all-female schools?

- Should prostitution be legalized?
- Should there be a formal apology from the government for slavery?
- Should there be reparations for slavery, as there has been for Japanese interned in camps during WWII?
- Should grades be abolished?
- Should the HPV vaccination be mandatory?
- What should be done about illegal immigrants in the United States?

Generating Topics from Personal Interest. One way to find a topic for your research paper is to begin with subjects you already know well, are interested in, or think you would like to improve your knowledge of. Begin by writing down such things as hobbies, sports, issues in your major, contemporary social issues, or topics in classes you are taking. Consider topics that attracted your interest in high school or in previous college classes, any reading you have already done on subjects that appeal to you, or the kinds of things that capture your attention when you watch television news, read news magazines or newspapers, or select nonfiction books for leisure-time reading.

Generating Topics from Personal Opinions. Virtually any topic can be turned into an argument, but opinions are always subject to debate. Therefore, one way to generate a research paper topic is to begin with your own strongly held opinions.

Caution: Avoid a topic that is based entirely on opinion. Evaluative statements are especially good for argumentative papers because they are likely to have differing opinions. Once you say that something is the best, the most significant, the most important, or the greatest, for instance, you have put yourself in the position of defending that statement. You will have to establish your criteria for making your judgment and defend your choice against what others might think. Here are some ideas for this particular approach:

- The most influential person in the twentieth century (or in America, in the world, in a particular field such as education, government, politics, arts, entertainment, or the like)
- The most significant battle in the Civil War (or World War I, World War II, the Korean War, the Vietnam War, the Gulf War, the war in Afghanistan, the war in Iraq)
- The greatest basketball (or football, tennis, soccer, baseball) player (either now playing or of all time)
- The greatest or worst president
- The best movie, book, or album of all time
- The business or industry with the greatest impact on American life in the last decade (or last twenty years, last fifty years, or last century)

Because your conclusion on any of these or similar topics is your opinion, you need to establish criteria for your conclusion, clearly describe the process you used to make it, and explain the logical basis for that process.

Generating Topics from Commonly Held Opinions. Another possibility for a research paper topic is to take a commonly held opinion (though not necessarily one that you share), especially one based on stereotyped assumptions about a group or class of people, and explore the validity of that belief. Your goal is to determine whether the commonly held opinion is a valid, partially valid, or invalid position. Even if you cannot arrive at a definitive evaluation of the validity of the statement, you can still present the evidence you find and explain why your research does not reach a conclusion. Here are examples of commonly held beliefs:

- Watching violence on television produces violent behavior.
- People who were abused as children often grow up to be abusers themselves.
- Men naturally perform mechanical tasks better than women do.
- Women naturally perform better at nurturing children than men do.
- Young people do not have much hope for a bright future.
- Women are more emotional than men.
- People stay on welfare because they are too lazy to work.
- Homosexuals could become "straight" if they wanted to.
- Homeless people could get off the streets if they really tried.

When determining the validity of a commonly held opinion or belief, your research focuses on gathering evidence without bias. Although you may want to interview people about their opinions on a particular belief, the basis of your conclusion must rest on clearly reliable evidence.

Generating Topics from Controversy. Yet another way to discover a topic you find intriguing enough to commit many hours of time to is to think of controversial issues that always generate heated debate. These topics may be frequently discussed in newspapers, news magazines, and on television news programs and talk shows. They may be issues on which candidates for public office, from local county board members to state and federal officials, are pressed to take stands. Here are some examples of controversial statements:

- Affirmative action laws are unfair to white males and should be repealed.
- Media coverage of celebrity trials should be banned.
- Birth parents should always have a legal right to take back children they have given up for adoption.
- Children whose parents are on welfare should be placed in state-run orphanages.
- Women should be barred from participating in combat duty.
- Graphic violence in the movies (or in video games or MTV videos) poses a serious threat to the nation's moral values.
- The federal government should stop funding projects in the arts and the humanities.
- The federal government should provide unlimited funds to support research to find a cure for AIDS.
- Children who commit murder should be tried as adults no matter what their age.
- Illegal aliens should be forced to return to their country of origin.

Narrowing Your Subject to a Specific Topic. Most research paper assignments are short enough that you simply must narrow your focus to avoid a too shallow or too hopelessly general treatment of your topic. Keep in mind the distinction between subject and topic: Subject is the general area under investigation, whereas topic is the narrow aspect of that subject that you are investigating. For example, Jack the Ripper is a subject, but entire books have been written on the notorious 1888 murders in the Whitechapel area of London. A suitable topic on the subject would be to explore the controversy surrounding the alleged links of the Duke of Clarence with the murders, taking a position in favor of the theory most plausible to you.

One way to get a sense of how a general topic can be narrowed is to look at the table of contents of a book on a subject that interests you. Notice the chapter headings, which are themselves subtopics of the broad subject. Chapters themselves are often further subdivided. You want to find a topic that is narrow enough that you can fully explore it without leaving unanswered questions, yet broad enough that you can say enough about it in a reasonably long paper.

To narrow your subject to a topic, take a general subject and go through the brainstorming process again, this time listing everything that comes to mind about that particular subject. What subtopics does your subject have? What questions can you ask about your general subject? How might you narrow your focus on that subject? Ultimately, you want to generate an idea that gives focus to your preliminary library search.

FORMING A PRELIMINARY THESIS AND A WORKING BIBLIOGRAPHY

No matter what your purpose or who your audience is, you will have one central idea, most often articulated early in the paper in the form of a single thesis statement. You will take a position on your topic and defend or illustrate it convincingly with evidence from your source materials.

When you believe that you have narrowed your topic sufficiently, you are ready to form your preliminary thesis. This is the position that you believe you want to take on your topic, based on your early thinking about and narrowing down of a subject. Your preliminary or working thesis can be in the form of either a question or a statement. In much the same way as your final thesis gives direction and focus to your paper, your preliminary thesis gives you direction and focus in the research process. As you review potential sources and read about your topic, you may find yourself changing your preliminary thesis for any number of reasons. Perhaps your topic is too narrow or too new and you simply cannot find enough sources with which to write a fair and balanced research paper. Or you may discover that your topic is too broad to cover in a research paper and that you need to narrow your focus even more.

A common reason for changing a preliminary thesis is that, once you actually start reading sources, you discover that you want to change your initial position. You may discover that you were wrong in your assumption or opinion about your topic and that you are persuaded to change your position. Part of the pleasure in researching a topic is discovering new ideas or information, so it makes sense that your early views on your topic may shift as you learn more about it. More than likely, your final thesis will differ in some way from your preliminary thesis.

With your preliminary thesis in mind, you are ready to start the actual research process. First, you need to locate potential sources. A working bibliography is a list of the sources you **might** use in your research paper, those that look particularly promising during a preliminary search. At this point, you will not have had time to read or even carefully skim all potential sources, let alone imagine how they fit together to support your working thesis. Your goal is to find the sources that bear most directly on your topic and select from them the most useful ones to read carefully, taking notes as you read. One obvious place to start looking for sources is the library; another source is the Internet.

GUIDELINES FOR DEVELOPING A WORKING BIBLIOGRAPHY

- List sources that sound promising for your research, recording titles and locations as you discover them.
- If the source is a library book, record the title, author, and call number.
- If the source is an article from your library, write the title of the piece, the name of its author, the title of the magazine or journal where it appears, the date of the issue, and the inclusive pages numbers. You will need all this information to find the article.
- For other sources in the library, such as videotapes, audiotapes, government documents, or pamphlets, write down as much information as you can find to help locate them. Write the location of any source, such as a special collection, government document, stack, periodical, and so on.
- For an Internet site, record the URL (Uniform Resource Locator) or bookmark it on your computer. Record the title; the author, if known; the name of the site; the name of its creator, if available; and the date the site was created, if available. If you use the source in your paper, you will add the date that you accessed the material in the works-cited entry, so include that as well.
- You may want to retrieve the full text files of Internet sites that seem promising, as you discover them, to ensure their availability when you are ready to begin reading and taking notes.

USING THE LIBRARY

Your library has a good number of valuable resources to help you in your search for materials on your research topic. Although the Internet has made searching for reference materials easy and quick, libraries house books, periodicals, and other materials that you can hold, leaf through, check out, and read. Furthermore, many libraries have special collections on specific subjects and offer access to online databases that they subscribe to. Increasingly, libraries are working to connect their own digital resources stored in databases to Internet search engines. In the meantime, do not overlook the potential for excellent sources available on your own campus or through your university library's online catalog. Your library may have print copies of sources that you cannot find on the Internet.

Online Catalog. Begin your library search for sources on your general subject or topic (if you have sufficiently narrowed your focus) by reviewing the online catalog for titles of potential sources. The catalog cross-references sources by (1) name of author, (2) title, and (3) subject matter. In this searching stage, you probably will not know titles of works or authors, so you will begin by looking under subject headings for titles that sound relevant to your research subject. The catalog gives titles of books, audio-visual materials, and government documents housed in the library. Jot down the titles and call numbers of materials that look promising and then locate them. One advantage of using your library is that you can physically examine a book, flip through its table of contents, check its index, read the author's credentials, and skim some of the text. If it seems to suit your purpose, you can check it out and take it home with you.

Electronic Databases. Most libraries provide access to electronic indexes or databases and often have CD-ROMs or DVD-ROMS that have full-text copies of periodical articles or bibliographies of books and periodical articles related to particular subject areas. CD- and DVD-ROMs have a disadvantage that the Internet does not have in that, once it is produced, it cannot be updated. Still, they can be very useful for locating articles for research. You can search all of these resources by subject, author, title, or keywords. Generally, such a listing provides the full name of the author, the title, and complete bibliographic information (publisher and year for books; title of magazine or journal; month and year of issue; and page numbers for articles). Often, computer services provide abstracts of articles and sometimes entire texts that you can download and print out or send for via mail or fax for a fee.

Your library may subscribe to one of the following frequently used databases. All are subscription services that require a passcode to access the database:

1. **InfoTrac College Edition** provides a searchable database of some 15 million periodical articles from over 5,000 journals, newspapers, and magazines covering the last twenty years. It is a rich resource of readings on just about any topic you are interested in searching. InfoTrac College Edition offers specialized databases to which your library can subscribe, including *Custom Newspapers*, which contains articles from well-known newspapers like the *Wall Street Journal* and *The New York Times*; Health Reference Center, with articles on topics such as medicine, disease, public health, and other health-related topics; and *General Reference Center*, which has articles from publications of general interest.
2. **Gale** has links to full-text magazine and newspaper articles in more than 600 databases that are published online, in print, as eBooks, and in microform. You can link to numerous historical archives, special collection archives, various national libraries, and many databases on specific subjects.
3. **EBSCO** offers databases similar to InfoTrac College Edition, that is, specialized databases with links to periodical articles in such areas as business,

education, and health. It also offers full-text databases and provides online access to more that 150 databases and thousands of e-journals.

4. **LexisNexis Academic Universe** provides the full text of more than 350 newspapers from the United States and abroad, updated daily, and texts of more than 300 magazine and journals and over 600 newsletters. It also supplies broadcast transcripts from the major television and radio networks as well as political transcripts covering Congressional committee hearings; press briefings from the State, Justice, and Defense departments; and presidential news conferences.

Indexes. In addition to the services mentioned above, there are many other general and specialized indexes for additional titles of sources. These resources are all are available online, usually through a service such as WilsonWeb, Gale, or ProQuest that your library subscribes to. Here are titles of some **general indexes:**

- ***Bibliographic IndexPlus: A Cumulative Bibliography of Bibliographies*** lists by subject bibliographies that appear in books, pamphlets, and periodical articles.
- ***Biography Index: Past to Present*** lists articles and books on important people; it also lists the people included in the index by profession or occupation.
- ***Essay and General Literature Index***, a guide to over 86,000 essays in anthologies and collections, focuses on material in the social sciences and humanities, organized according to author, subject, and title. It lists periodical articles, individual essays, and book chapters on particular subjects.
- ***Catalog of United States Government Publications***, available at http://catalog.gpo.gov/F, indexes all government-generated materials.
- ***General Science Index*** is a bibliographic database arranged by subject and lists articles of one column length or more in all general science periodicals published in the United States and Great Britain.
- ***Periodical Abstracts*** provides abstracts of articles from over 1,600 periodicals, covering the humanities, social sciences, general science, and general interest.
- ***Reader's Guide to Periodical Literature*** is a standard reference tool for locating articles in popular magazines. Organized by both subject and author, it provides titles of articles, authors, names of publications, and dates of publication.

Specialized Indexes. These list articles on particular subjects or areas that appear in professional journals, written by and published for specialists in those areas. Specialized indexes cover specific areas of interest in the humanities, fine arts, social sciences, and natural and applied sciences. A look at just a few of the titles of specialized indexes gives you an idea of the resources available. Like general indexes, specialized indexes are available by subscription, usually through your library:

- ***Art Index*** collects titles of articles on archaeology, art history, architecture, and the fine arts.
- ***Biological Abstracts*** gives brief summaries of articles on biology and biomedicine.
- ***Business Index*** is a good source for current material on business topics.
- ***The Directory of Online Databases*** provides a current listing of databases in all fields.

- ***Historical Abstracts*** contains abstracts of articles on world history.
- ***Humanities Index*** lists titles of periodical articles on a broad range of topics in the social sciences and humanities.
- ***MLA International Bibliography of Books and Articles on the Modern Languages and Literatures*** provides titles of articles on languages and literature, arranged by nationality and literary period.
- ***Philosopher's Guide to Sources, Research Tools, Professional Life, and Related Fields*** is useful for all sorts of information on philosophical topics.
- ***Psychological Abstracts*** presents abstracts of articles and books in all areas of the social sciences.
- ***Political Science: A Guide to Reference and Information Sources*** cites current sources on a range of topics in political science.

Locating Material on the Internet. To find Internet materials, you can use any of a number of equally good search engines available on the Web. Search engines collect many sites in their databanks; they return sites that match the keywords you type to begin your search. Search engines get their information in one of two major ways, either by crawler-based technology or human-powered directories, but increasingly they use a combination of both. Crawler-based search engines gather their information automatically by "crawling" or sending "spiders" out to the Web, searching the contents of other systems and creating a database of the results. Human-powered directories depend on humans for the listings you get in response to a search; they manually approve material for inclusion in a database. You can find more about these terms and others related to the Internet by going to www.Webopedia.com, an online dictionary and search engine for definitions of computer and Internet terms.

Be very careful when searching for sources on the Internet: keep in mind the guidelines in Chapter 1 on evaluating Internet sources. Begin by choosing your search engine from among the best known or most used; they are likely to be the most reliable. Commercially-backed search engines are usually well maintained and frequently upgraded, thus ensuring reliable results. Chapter 1 has a list of well-known search engines that are quite reliable, and likely to give you the results you seek in your search.

USING OTHER SOURCES

Do not overlook other excellent sources of information, such as personal interviews, surveys, lectures, taped television programs, films, documentaries, and government publications. For example, if you research the human genome project, you will likely find a number of books, periodical articles, and government documents on the subject. A search of the World Wide Web will turn up hundreds of thousands of site matches. You could easily become overwhelmed by the mass of materials available on your subject. Your task is to select the sources that seem most relevant to your project and to narrow your research topic as quickly as possible to avoid wasting time gathering materials you ultimately cannot use. To clarify and focus your own approach to the subject, you may want to interview a biology professor for information about the scientific aspects of the project and a philosophy professor for an opinion on its ethical implications. In addition to such interviews, you may use material from a lecture, a television documentary, a film, or your own survey.

The Difference Between Primary and Secondary Sources. "Primary" refers to original sources, actual data, or first-hand witnesses, such as interviews, surveys, speeches, diaries, letters, unpublished manuscripts, photographs, memoirs or autobiographies, published material written at the time of the event such as newspaper articles, and similar items. They are actual recorded accounts or documentary evidence of events. "Secondary" refers to sources like books and articles that discuss, explain, or interpret events or that are seen second-hand. They are written or recorded after the fact and represent processed information: interpretations of or commentary on events.

For instance, suppose you are interested in the controversy over a film like Mel Gibson's *The Passion of the Christ* (2004). (See a still image from the film in the "Responding to Visuals" section at the end of Chapter 10.) Literally hundreds of articles have been written about the film, ranging from harsh criticism of it to high praise. These articles represent secondary sources, while the film itself is the primary source. For a paper on the film, you would view the movie and undoubtedly include details of it in your paper, but you would also offer the commentary and opinions of others who reacted to, analyzed, and wrote about it.

Another example is student Sam Cox's paper "Proving Their Loyalty During World War I: German Americans Confronted with Anti-German Fervor and Suspicion." (See introduction and conclusion to his paper later in the chapter.) Sam was interested in the subject of the loyalty of German Americans living in the United States during WWI. To find out about it, he read numerous newspaper accounts of and by German Americans as reported in two newspapers and written in both German and English. To help him come to his conclusion that German Americans were loyal to America at the time that America was at war with Germany, Sam read dozens of both primary and secondary sources. These are listed together in his Works Cited page at the end of his paper. A selection of his sources appear later in this chapter, as do his opening paragraphs.

Reporting the Results of a Survey Using Tables and Graphs. Surveys are another good primary source. For instance, in a group-written paper, four students were interested in the question of the influence of gender on academic success on their college campus. They prepared a survey that they distributed to classmates. Their paper reports the results of their findings based on 103 surveys and includes four charts and graphs that represent these findings. One of these is reproduced in the guidelines for putting all of the parts of a paper together later in this chapter. You can also find examples in Chapter 23 in Benjamin Powell's article, "In Defense of 'Sweatshops.'"

CREATING A PRELIMINARY BIBLIOGRAPHY

Once you complete a list of sources to investigate, you need to evaluate them as potential references for your research paper. If you discover that you cannot use a source, cross it off your list or delete it from your bookmarked sites. When you find a source that definitely looks promising for your research topic, make sure that you have recorded all pertinent bibliographic information, preferably in the form in which it will appear on your Works Cited page. The section in this chapter entitled "Documenting Sources" lists appropriate formats for various kinds of sources. Note the following sample work-cited formats for some common types of sources:

Book with One Author.

Connolly-Smith, Peter. *Translating America: An Immigrant Press Visualizes American Popular Culture, 1895-1918.* Washington: Smithsonian, 2004. Print.

Journal Article with One Author.

Capozzola, Christopher. "The Only Badge Needed Is Your Patriotic Fervor: Vigilance, Coercion, and the Law in World War I America." *Journal of American History* 88 (2002): 1354-82. Print.

Journal Article with Two Authors.

Cusimano, Michael, and Judith Kwok. "Skiers, Snowboarders, and Safety Helmets." *JAMA* 303.7 (2010): 661-62. Print.

Journal Article with No Author Named.

"Class Action Suits in the Workplace Are on the Rise." *HR Focus* April 2007: 84-85. Print.

Newspaper Article with Author Named.

Fagan, Kevin. "Homeless, Mike Dick Was 51, Looked 66." *San Francisco Chronicle* 2 Mar. 2008: G1+. Print.

Newspaper Article, Online.

Wilford, John Noble. "Malaria Most Likely Killed King Tut, Scientists Say." *New York Times*. New York Times, 16 Feb. 2010. Web. 12 Oct. 2010.

Magazine Article with Author Named.

Gibbs, Nancy. "The End of Helicopter Parents." *Time* 30 Nov. 2009: 52-57. Print.

Magazine Article with Author Named, Online.

Krauthammer, Charles. "The Moon We Left Behind." *Washington Post*. Washington Post, 17 July 2009. Web. 21 Oct. 2010.

Magazine Article with No Author Named.

"Inside Geographic." *National Geographic* Dec. 2009: 150. Print.

Chapter from a Collection of Essays.

Smiley, Jane. "You Can Never Have Too Many." *The Barbie Chronicles: A Living Doll Turns Forty*. Ed. Yona Zeldis McDonough. New York: Touchstone/Simon, 1999. 189-92. Print.

Government Document.

United States. Cong. House. Committee on Armed Services. *Women in the Military: Hearing before the Military Personnel and Compensation Subcommittee*. 101st Cong., 2nd sess. 20 Mar. 1990: 14-56. Print.

Internet Website.

"Americans See Life Through Rosiest Lenses in Two Years." *Gallup-Healthways Well-Being Index*. 11 Feb. 2010. Web. 21 Sept. 2010.

A Translation.

Witten, Johann. "Letters to Christoph Witten, 3 December 1914, 5 December 1915, 9 September 1919, 18 September 1920." *News from the Land of Freedom: German Immigrants Write Home*. Trans. Susan Vogel. Eds. Walter Kamphoefner, Wolfgang Helbich, and Ulrike Sommer. Ithaca, NY: Cornell UP, 1991. 278-83. Print.

Following the formatting guidelines for the Works Cited page will save time later in the process when you put your paper in its final form. As you record information in the proper format, alphabetize your list, placing new items in the appropriate alphabetical position. Then, when you need to assemble the Works Cited page, just move the list to the file where you store your paper (or keep the list in the same file). As you evaluate sources to determine whether they are appropriate for your paper, delete those that you decide not to pursue further. Here is how a list of the works on the previous sample bibliography entries would look in a computer file:

Works Cited

"Americans See Life Through Rosiest Lenses in Two Years." *Gallup-Healthways Well-Being Index*. 11 Feb. 2010. Web. 21 Sept. 2010.

Capazzola, Christopher. "The Only Badge Needed Is Your Patriotic Fervor: Vigilance, Coercion, and the Law in World War I America." *Journal of American History* 88 (2002): 1354-82. Print.

"Class Action Suits in the Workplace Are on the Rise." *HR Focus* April 2007: 84-85. Print.

Connolly-Smith, Peter. *Translating America: An Immigrant Press Visualizes American Popular Culture, 1895-1918*. Washington: Smithsonian, 2004. Print.

Cusimano, Michael, and Judith Kwok. "Skiers, Snowboarders, and Safety Helmets." *JAMA* 303.7 (2010): 661-62. Print.

Fagan, Kevin. "Homeless, Mike Dick Was 51, Looked 66." *San Francisco Chronicle* 2 Mar. 2008: G1+. Print.

Gibbs, Nancy. "The End of Helicopter Parents." *Time* 30 Nov. 2009: 52-57. Print.

Krauthammer, Charles. "The Moon We Left Behind." *Washington Post*. Washington Post, 17 July 2009. Web. 21 Oct. 2010.

Smiley, Jane. "You Can Never Have Too Many." *The Barbie Chronicles: A Living Doll Turns Forty*. Ed. Yona Zeldis McDonough. New York: Touchstone/Simon, 1999. 189-92. Print.

United States. Cong. House. Committee on Armed Services. *Women in the Military: Hearing before the Military Personnel and Compensation Subcommittee*. 101st Cong., 2nd sess. 20 Mar. 1990: 14-56. Print.

Wilford, John Noble. "Malaria Most Likely Killed King Tut, Scientists Say." *New York Times*. New York Times, 16 Feb. 2010. Web. 12 Oct. 2010.

Witten, Johann. "Letters to Christoph Witten, 3 December 1914, 5 December 1915, 9 September 1919, 18 September 1920." *News from the Land of Freedom: German Immigrants Write Home*. Trans. Susan Vogel. Eds. Walter Kamphoefner, Wolfgang Helbich, and Ulrike Sommer. Ithaca, NY: Cornell UP, 1991. 278-83. Print.

EVALUATING PRINT SOURCES

Before you begin taking notes from any source, carefully assess its reliability. Ideally, your research should rely on unbiased, current, well-documented sources written by people with the authority to discuss the subject. However, you are likely to find a great number of sources that are written from particular perspectives that are out of date or incomplete, that are written by people with no authority whatsoever, or that do not document their own sources. Part of your job as a researcher is to try to discover these aspects of your sources, to reject those that are completely unreliable, and to use caution with sources when you lack complete confidence in them. Although you may never know for sure how much to trust a particular source, you can check certain things to help in your assessment.

Check for Bias. Try to find out whether the author, publication, organization, or person being interviewed is known to give fair coverage. People, organizations, and publications often promote particular perspectives, which you should recognize and take into account. You need not reject sources outright if you know they take particular positions on subjects, especially controversial issues. However, your own paper should be as unbiased as possible, which requires acknowledgment of the known biases of your sources.

Check the Date of Publication. In general, an increasingly recent publication or update of a website provides an increasingly reliable source. For many subjects, current information is crucial to accurate analysis. If you are researching issues such as global warming, morality at high governmental levels, or controversial treatments for AIDS victims, for instance, you need the most recent available information. However, if you are examining a historical matter, such as the question of Richard III's guilt in his two young cousins' deaths or whether King Arthur of Britain is an entirely mythical figure, you can rely in part on older materials. You still want to look for the latest theories, information, or opinions on any subject you research, though.

Check the Author's Credentials. Find out whether the author has sufficient education, experience, or expertise to write or speak about your subject. You can do this in a number of ways. Any book usually gives information about an author, from a sentence or two to several paragraphs, either on the dust jacket or at the beginning or end of the book. This information reveals the author's professional status, other books she has published, and similar information that helps to establish her authority. You can also look up an author in sources like *Contemporary Authors*, *Current Biography*, and *Who's Who*, Other checks on an author's reliability might review what professionals in other sources say about her or note how often her name shows up on reference lists or bibliographies on your subject.

Check the Reliability of Your Source. In evaluating a book, determine whether the publishing house is a respectable one. For a magazine, find out whether it is published by a particular interest group. Evaluation of a book could include reading some representative reviews to see how it was received when first published. Both the *Book Review Digest* and *Book Review Index* will help you locate reviews.

Check the Thoroughness of Research and Documentation of Sources. If your source purports to be scholarly, well informed, or otherwise reliable, check to see how the evidence was gathered. Determine whether the source reports original research or other people's work and what facts or data support its conclusions. Look for references either at the ends of chapters or in a separate section at the end of a book. Almost all journal articles and scholarly books document sources, whereas few magazine articles and personal accounts do. Also, consider how statistics and other data are used. Statistics are notoriously easy to manipulate, so check how the author uses them and confirm his fair interpretation.

EVALUATING INTERNET SOURCES

As with print sources, you must take care to evaluate any material you locate on the Internet before you use it in your paper. The Internet may pose more difficulty because its resources may offer fewer clues than a book or journal article might give. However, searching the Internet will turn up many useful sources, such as scholarly projects, reference databases, text files of books, articles in periodicals, and professional sites. You must use your judgment when selecting sources for your research paper. Remember that anyone with some knowledge of the Internet can create a website, so be very cautious about accepting the authority of anything you find on the Internet. In general, personal sites are probably not as reliable as professional sites and those of scholarly projects. Reference databases can be extremely useful tools for locating source materials.

You must apply the same sort of skills that you bring to critical reading when looking at an Internet website, particularly when searching for materials for a class assignment. You must ask a number of questions about the site before accepting and using materials that you locate on the Internet. Some key areas to consider are the authority or credentials of the person or persons responsible for the site, the scope, accuracy, timeliness, and nature of the information at the site, and the presentation of the information at the site. Here is a list of questions that will help you evaluate Internet websites:

- **What can you tell about the site from its URL?** Websites exist for a variety of purposes, including the following: to sell a product, to advocate a position, to influence readers, and to inform. They may be sponsored by individuals for personal reasons, by professionals to impart information, by corporations to sell products, or by agencies or groups to influence opinion or advocate a specific position. Knowing what domain the abbreviation at the end of the URL represents can give you your first clue about a website's purpose. The domain is the system for indicating the logical or geographical location of a web page from the Internet. Outside the United States, domains indicate country, such as ca (Canada), uk (United Kingdom), or au (Australia). In the United States, the following are common domains:
  - **Educational** websites exist to provide information about educational institutions, including elementary, secondary, and university levels. Their Internet addresses end in **.edu**.
  - **Government** websites provide information about governmental departments, agencies, and policies at all levels of government, including city,

county, state, and federal governments. Their Internet addresses end in **.gov**.
  - **Organizational** websites advocate the viewpoint of particular groups. The URL for organizational websites typically end in **.org**.
  - **Commercial** websites aim to sell products or services. Their URLs usually end in **.com**.
  - **Military** websites provide information about the military. Their Internet addresses end in **.mil**.
  - **News** websites exist to provide information about current events. Their Internet addresses usually end in **.com**.
  - **Personal** websites are constructed by individuals about themselves. The address or personal sites end in various ways, probably most typically **.com**.
  - **Entertainment** websites exist to amuse, entertain, and provide information about the entertainment industry. Their Internet addresses usually end in **.com**.
  - **Internet service provider** websites exist to provide information about companies and services related to the Internet. Their website addresses end in **.net**.
- **What do you know about the author of the site?** Is the author of the website qualified to give information on the subject? Does the site give information about the author's qualifications? Are the author's credentials, such as academic affiliation, professional association, or publications, easily verified? Because anyone can create a web page, you want to determine whether the author of the website you are looking at is qualified to give the information you are seeking.
- **Is the material on the website presented objectively, or do biases or prejudices reveal themselves?** The language used may be a clue, but probably the best way to discover a particular bias is to look at a great many sites (and other sources) on the same topic. When you understand the complexity of your topic and the variety of viewpoints on it, you should be able to determine whether a site is objective or subjective.
- **Is the information reliable?** Can you verify it? How does it compare with information you have learned from other sources? How well does the website compare with other sites on the same topic? Does the site offer unique information, or does it repeat information that you can find at other sites?
- **How thoroughly does the website cover its topic?** Does it provide links to other sites for additional information? Does the site have links to related topics, and do those links work?
- **How accurate is the information?** This may be difficult to assess when you first begin your research, but the more you read about your topic and examine a variety of sources, the better able you will be to evaluate information accuracy.
- **When was the website last updated?** Is the information at the site current?
- **What is your impression of the visual effect of the site?** Are the graphics helpful or distracting, clear or confusing? Are words spelled correctly? Is the page organized well?

ILLUSTRATION: SEEKING PROMISING WEBSITES

Suppose, for example, that student Shawn Ryan is interested in finding information on the Internet for his paper on King Arthur. When he first enters the keywords "Arthurian legend," a search engine returns almost half a million hits. Obviously, he cannot look at every site in the list , but he can begin his search by scrolling through the first page of hits, picking a site that sounds promising and going to that site. The list shows several entries that appear to be newsgroups or personal sites, whereas two will take him to the sites of a scholarly society and a scholarly project associated with a university. Because he is looking for sources for a research paper, as opposed to satisfying general curiosity, Shawn prefers the scholarly sites.

Both of the scholarly sites provide enormously useful information. One takes him to the home page of the North American branch of the International Arthurian Society, whose journal, *Arthuriana*, Shawn can read on the Web. Furthermore, the site offers manuscripts, reviews, and scholarly essays, including the titles of over 200 sources listed under the heading "Nonfiction and Research." In addition, the site offers links to other Arthurian sites. As with print sources, Shawn has to judge the trustworthiness and reliability of an Internet source on the basis of who created the site, the credentials of the authorities, and the kind of information it gives. For instance, he particularly likes the information available at the website for the Camelot Project at the University of Rochester. Shawn determines that this site is a reliable source for several reasons. According to its home page, the Camelot Project aims to create a database of Arthurian texts, bibliographies, and other information. This goal tells Shawn that the site is not devoted to one person's opinions or to an informal collection of materials. Rather, it has a legitimate, scholarly aim, making it a valuable source of relevant materials for his paper. The Camelot Project itself is sponsored by the University of Rochester and the Robbins Library, associations that assure a certain level of reliability and scholarly appropriateness.

Finally, the material at the site is continually updated, the most recent change occurring just one month before Shawn visited the site. Thus, Shawn has found a source that he is confident he can trust and that is sure to lead him to other reliable sources.

QUESTIONS TO ASK WHEN EVALUATING SOURCES

- Is the publication or site known to be fair, or does it have a bias or slant?
- Does the source seem one-sided, or does it try to cover all perspectives on an issue?
- Is the information current or outdated?
- Does the authority have respectable credentials?
- How reliable is the source?
- How thoroughly does the source cover its subject?
- Does the source offer adequate documentation for its information?
- If the source relies on research data, how was evidence gathered? Are statistics used fairly, or are they misrepresented?

TAKING NOTES

When you find an article, book, pamphlet, website, or other source you believe will be important or informative in your research, take notes from that source. There are several kinds of notes that you will take:

Summary. A summary produces an objective restatement of a written passage in your own words. A summary is much shorter than the original work. Because its purpose is to highlight the central idea or ideas and major points of a work, make summary notes to record general ideas or main points of a large piece of writing—perhaps several pages, a chapter, or an entire article.

Paraphrase. A paraphrase is a restatement of the words of someone else in your own words. Use paraphrasing when you want to use another writer's ideas but not the exact words, or to explain difficult material more clearly. Your own version of someone else's words must be almost entirely your own words. When incorporating paraphrased material into your research paper, you must be clear about when the paraphrased material begins and ends.

Direct Quotation. A direct quotation is a record of the exact words of someone else. You will want to quote directly when the words are unique, colorful, or so well stated that you cannot fairly or accurately paraphrase them. Use direct quotations when you do not want to misrepresent what an author says or when the author makes a statement that you wish to stress or comment on. You may want to quote directly in order to analyze or discuss a particular passage. Use direct quotations sparingly and integrate them smoothly into your paper. Too many direct quotations in your paper will interrupt the flow of your own words.

Recording Source and Page Numbers. Note taking is crucial to the success of your paper. You must take accurate and careful notes, reproducing an author's words exactly as they appear if you quote, completely restating the author's words if you paraphrase, and accurately capturing the essence of the material if you summarize. In any case, you will give a citation in your paper, so ***you must record the source and page number for any notes.***

Caution: When taking notes, some students are tempted to write every detail as it appears in the original, thinking that they will paraphrase the material at some later time. They must then spend valuable time later rephrasing material when they should be concentrating on writing their papers, or else they take the easier route and use the direct quotations. The result may be a paper that is too full of direct quotations and lacking in effective paraphrases. Remember that you should quote directly only language that is particularly well expressed or material that you do not feel you can adequately restate in your own words. Your final paper should have far more paraphrases than direct quotations.

Where you record your notes does not matter, as long as you develop an efficient system. The important consideration is the accuracy and fairness of your notes. Traditionally, researchers used 436-inch cards because they are large enough to record ideas, summaries, quotations, or major points. When the note-taking part of the research ends, the researcher can shuffle the cards about, arranging them in the order that makes sense for the research paper. Some people like the note card system and work well with it, but most now prefer to use a computer as a more convenient way to record and store notes.

A computer can be very helpful for organizing and sorting notes. Most programs allow you to arrange your notes in numerical order. However, make sure to develop a filing system for your notes. If your program lets you create folders, you can keep your notes from different sources under specific headings, each with its own subheadings.

Place the subject heading at the beginning of your notes, and put the page number at the end. ***Make sure that your notes clearly identify sources for all information.***

GUIDELINES FOR TAKING NOTES

- **Write both the author's last name and the page number from which the information is taken.** That is all the information you need, as long as you have a bibliography card or file for the source that lists complete bibliographic information.
- **Use subject headings as you take notes.** This labeling system will help you sort and arrange your notes when you write your paper.
- **Record only one idea or several small, related ones in each note.** This practice will help you to organize your notes when you begin writing.
- **Place quotation marks before and after the material taken directly from a source.**
- **Don't rely on memory to determine whether words are identical to the original or paraphrased.**
- **Use notes to summarize.** A note may refer to an entire passage, an article, or a book, without giving specific details. Make a note to remind you that the information is a summary.
- **Use notes to record original ideas that occur to you while you are reading.** Make sure you identify your own ideas.

HANDLING SOURCE MATERIAL

Handling source material fairly, accurately, and smoothly is one of your main tasks in writing a successful research paper. More than likely, your instructor will evaluate your research project not only on how successfully you argue, explain, examine, or illustrate your topic but also on how skillfully you handle source materials. This means that you must take great care not only when you take notes but also when you transfer those notes into your paper. Always keep in mind—as you are taking notes, when drafting your paper, and when writing its final version—that you must acknowledge the source for all borrowed material. Any information that you take from a source must be properly attributed to its author or, if no author, to its title.

At the same time, you must not simply drop material into your text but be mindful of providing smooth integration of your source material into your own text. After all, the text is your work: the thesis of the paper, the overall organization and development, transitions from point to point, general observations, and the conclusions are all yours. Your source materials serve to support, illustrate, develop, or exemplify your own words. Source materials must not interrupt the flow of your words or call attention to themselves. They are an important and integral part of your own paper.

Illustration: Summarizing, Paraphrasing, and Quoting. Chapter 6 has detailed directions and summary guidelines for both paraphrasing source material and quoting directly. Chapter 6 also discusses some common tools for handling source material: ellipsis points, brackets, single quotation marks, and "qtd. in." Sample research papers located later in this chapter also give examples of the correct handling of source material. Here is another illustration that shows how to handle source material based on this opening paragraph from Ian Wilmut's "Dolly's False Legacy":

> Overlooked in the arguments about the mortality of artificially reproducing life is the fact that, at present, cloning is a very inefficient procedure. The incidence of death among fetuses and offspring produced by cloning is much higher than it is through natural reproduction—roughly 10 times as high as normal before birth and three times as high after birth in our studies at Roslin. Distressing enough for those working with animals, these failure rates surely render unthinkable the notion of applying such treatment to humans.

In the following passage from Nate Hayes' research paper, "A Positive Alternative to Cloning" (located later in this chapter), he combines summary, paraphrase, and direct quotation. Nate begins by summarizing and then paraphrases and quotes from the introductory paragraph:

> One big question has to do with the high failure rate of cloning. Despite having been responsible for the first cloned mammal, Dr. Wilmut is very conservative in his views of the wisdom of carrying on full speed with cloning research because of its unreliability. In "Dolly's False Legacy," he identifies some of the likely problems a cloned human might have. For instance, Wilmut warns of the inefficiency of cloning, noting the high death rate in fetuses and live births when cloning is used in animal tests. This fact leads him to suggest that "these failure rates surely render unthinkable the notion of applying such treatment to humans" (535).

Nate first identifies the author and title of his source and summarizes a key point of Wilmut's essay. Then he paraphrases the reference to death rates in animals produced by cloning versus those produced naturally. Finally, Nate quotes directly a passage that he believes is forcefully worded.

GUIDELINES FOR HANDLING SOURCE MATERIAL

- **Introduce or provide a context for quoted material.** "Dropped" quotations occur when you fail to integrate quotations smoothly into your text. The abrupt dropping of a quotation disrupts the flow of your text.
- **Name your authority or, when no author is named, use the title of the source.** Provide this information either in the text itself or in the parenthetical citation. Rely on standard phrases such as "one writer claims," "according to one expert," and the like to introduce quotations or paraphrases.
- **Use both first and last names of author at the first mention in your text.** After that, use just the last name. Always use last name only in parenthetical citations (unless you have sources by two authors with the same last name).
- **Acknowledge source material when you first begin paraphrasing.** Make sure you give some kind of signal to your reader when you begin paraphrasing borrowed material. This is particularly important if you paraphrase more than one sentence from a source. Otherwise, your reader will not know how far back the citation applies.
- **Quote sparingly**. Quote directly only those passages that are vividly or memorably phrased, so that you could not do justice to them by rewording them; those that require exact wording for accuracy; or those that need the authority of your source to lend credibility to what you are saying.
- **Intermingle source material with our own words.** Avoid a "cut-and-paste" approach to the research process. Remember that source materials serve primarily to support your generalizations. Never run two quotations together without some comment or transitional remark from you.
- **Make sure that direct quotations are exact.** Do not change words unless you use brackets or ellipses to indicate changes. Otherwise, be exact. For instance, if your source says "$2 million," do not write "two million dollars."
- **Make sure that paraphrases are truly your own words.** Do not inadvertently commit plagiarism by failing to paraphrase fairly.

AVOIDING PLAGIARISM

Giving proper credit to your sources is a crucial component of the research process. It is also one of the trickiest aspects of the process because it requires absolute accuracy in note taking. Many students have been disheartened by low grades on papers that took weeks to prepare, because they were careless or inaccurate in handling and documenting source materials.

Simply defined, **plagiarism** is borrowing another person's words without giving proper credit. The worst form of plagiarism is deliberately using the words or important ideas of someone else without giving any credit to that source. Handing in a paper someone else has written or copying someone else's paper and pretending it is yours are the most blatant and inexcusable forms of plagiarism, crimes that on some campuses carry penalties like automatic failure in the course or even immediate expulsion from school. Most student plagiarism is not deliberate, but rather results from carelessness either in the research process, when notes are taken, or in the writing process, when notes are incorporated into the student's own text. Even this unintentional plagiarism can result in a failing grade, however, especially if it appears repeatedly in a paper.

Keep the following standards in mind when you take notes on your source materials and when you write your research paper:

- **You commit plagiarism if you use the exact words or ideas of another writer without putting quotation marks around the words or citing a source.** The reader of your paper assumes that words without quotation marks or a source citation are your own words. To use the words of another without proper documentation suggests that you are trying to pass the words off as your own without giving credit to the writer.
- **You commit plagiarism if you use the exact words of another writer without putting quotation marks around those words, even if the paper cites the source of the material.** Readers assume that words followed by a parenthetical citation are paraphrased from the original—that is, that they are your own words and that the general idea was expressed by the author of the source material. Be especially carefully when you copy and paste from an Internet site: always use quotation marks around such material to remind yourself that they are the exact words.
- **You commit plagiarism if you paraphrase by changing only a few words of the original or by using the identical sentence structure of the original, with or without a source.** Again, readers assume that words without quotation marks followed by a parenthetical citation are your own words, not those of someone else. In a paraphrase, the idea is that of another; the words are your own.
- **You inaccurately handle source material when you use quotation marks around words that are not exactly as they appear in the original.** Readers assume that all words within quotation marks are identical to the original.

Obviously, accuracy and fairness in note taking are essential standards. Great care must be taken when you read your source materials and again when you transfer your notes to your final paper.

ILLUSTRATION: PLAGIARISM, INACCURATE DOCUMENTATION, AND CORRECT HANDLING OF SOURCE MATERIAL

The passage that follows is from an opinion column by Anna Quindlen. Complete bibliographic information follows, as it would appear on your bibliography list and on the Works Cited page of a research paper:

Quindlen, Anna. "A Teachable Moment." *Newsweek*
27 April 2009: 64. Print.

Here is the passage:

> Several years ago a psychologist named Laurie Miller Brotman spearheaded a study of young children that yielded stunning results. The kids were from poor and troubled families, the preschool-age siblings of older children who were already acquainted with the criminal-justice system. Brotman's team tested levels of cortisol, a hormone that usually spikes when human beings are under stress. On average, these kids had flattened cortisol in stressful situations; so do many who have been maltreated or have behavior problems.
>
> So far, so bad. But here's what happened to half the children in this study: their parents were enrolled in a program that helped them learn the kind of child rearing that Dr. Spock made popular. Consistent discipline without corporal punishment. Positive reinforcement for good behavior. Even how to get down on the floor and play.
>
> And their kids' cortisol levels changed. Or, as the study itself says in science-speak, "family-based intervention affects the stress response in preschoolers at high risk." By the time those same kids were 11, both boys and girls were less aggressive, and the girls less obese, than the kids in a control group. Having their parents learn the basics of good child rearing had actually shifted the biology of these kids, so that it became similar to that of "normally developing, low-risk children."

Now look at each of these sentences from a hypothetical research paper using information from the Quindlen article. The commentary that follows identifies plagiarism, inaccurate handling of the original source material, or correct handling of source material:

1. Having their parents learn the basics of good child rearing actually shifted the biology of kids from poor and troubled families, the preschool-age siblings of older children who were already acquainted with the criminal-justice system.
   [This is **plagiarism**: Quotation marks are needed around words identical to the original, and a source must be cited.]
2. Having their parents learn the basics of good child rearing actually shifted the biology of kids (Quindlen 64).
   [This is **plagiarism:** Quotation marks are needed around words taken directly from the original.]
3. Parents were taught the approach to child-rearing that Dr. Spock made popular, consistent discipline without corporal punishment and positive reinforcement for being good (Quindlen 64).
   [This is **plagiarism:** Original words are changed only slightly and the original sentence structure is retained.]
4. Quindlen cites the study's conclusion that "family-based intervention affects the stress response in preschoolers at high risk" (64).
   [This is **inaccurate documentation:** Single quotation marks are needed within the double marks to indicate that quotation marks are in the original.]
5. Writer Anna Quindlen notes the results of a recent study on the effects of good parenting on children's well-being. The study suggests that when parents of children who have been in trouble with the law are taught non-violent forms of punishment and other positive parenting skills, the effects

on their children are profound. The study concluded that "the basics of good child rearing had actually shifted the biology of these kids" (64).
[This is **correct:** The text acknowledges the author, and the general idea of the article is adequately summarized. Quotation marks enclose material taken directly from the original.]

Students are sometimes frustrated by these guidelines governing note taking and plagiarism, arguing that virtually everything in the final paper will be in quotation marks or followed by citations. But keep in mind that your final paper is a synthesis of information you have discovered in your research with your own thoughts on your topic, thoughts that naturally undergo modification, expansion, and/or revision as you read and think about your topic.

Probably half of the paper will be your own words. These words will usually include all of the introductory and concluding paragraphs, all topic sentences and transitional sentences within and between paragraphs, and all introductions to direct quotations. Furthermore, you need give no citation for statements of general or common knowledge, such as facts about well-known historical or current events. If you keep running across the same information in all of your sources, you can assume it is general knowledge.

GUIDELINES FOR AVOIDING PLAGIARISM

- **For direct quotations, write the words exactly as they appear in the original.** Put quotation marks before and after the words. Do not change anything.
- **For paraphrased material, restate the original thought in your own words, using your own writing style.** Do not use the exact sentence pattern of the original, and do not simply rearrange words. You have to retain the central idea of the paraphrased material, but do so in your own words.
- **When using borrowed material in your paper, whether direct quotations or paraphrases, acknowledge the source by naming the author or work as you introduce the material.** Doing so not only tells your reader that you are using borrowed material but also often provides a clear transition from your own words and ideas to the borrowed material that illustrates or expands on your ideas.
- **Provide a parenthetical, in-text citation for any borrowed material.** Give the author's last name if it is not mentioned in the text of the paper, followed by page number(s). If the source material is anonymous, use a shortened version of the title in place of a name.
- **Assemble all sources cited in your paper in an alphabetical list at the end of the paper.** This is your list of works cited, containing only those works actually used in the paper.

DOCUMENTING SOURCES

Follow the Appropriate Style Guidelines. The examples of documentation and sample research papers that appear in this chapter all follow MLA (Modern Language Association) documentation style. That style governs because this textbook is often used in English courses, and English is located within the discipline of the humanities. However, your instructor may permit you to choose the style appropriate to the major field you intend to study. A section later in this chapter provides guidelines for writing a research paper using APA (American Psychological Association) style. That style is probably as commonly used as MLA in undergraduate course papers. In addition to MLA and APA, other frequently used documentation styles are CBE (Council of Biology Editors) and CMS (Chicago Manual of Style). Following this summary of the chief differences among those four styles, the chapter lists stylebooks that give additional guidelines.

Style Guides. To find full details on a particular documentation style, consult the following style guides:

MLA

Modern Language Association of America. *MLA Handbook for Writers of Research Papers*. 7th ed. New York: MLA, 2009.

APA

American Psychological Association. *Publication Manual of the American Psychological Association*. 6th ed. Washington: APA, 2010.

CBE

CBE Style Manual Committee. *Scientific Style and Format: The CBE Manual for Authors, Editors, and Publishers*. 7th ed. Chicago: Council of Science Editors, 2006.

CMS

Turabian Kate L. *A Manual for Writers of Term Papers, Theses, and Dissertations*. 7th ed. Rev. by Wayne C. Booth et al. Chicago: U of Chicago P, 2007.

——. *Student's Guide to Writing College Papers*. 4th ed. Rev. by Gregory G. Colomb, Joseph M. Williams, and Chicago UP Editorial Staff. Chicago: U of Chicago P, 2010.

University of Chicago Press Staff. *The Chicago Manual of Style*. 15th ed. Chicago: U of Chicago P, 2003.

SUMMARY OF DIFFERENCES AMONG DOCUMENTATION STYLES

- **MLA:** Used by writers in the many areas of the humanities (English, foreign languages, history, and philosophy); requires parenthetical in-text citations of author and page number that refer to an alphabetical list of works cited at the end of the paper.
- **APA:** Used by writers in the behavioral and social sciences (education, psychology, and sociology); requires parenthetical in-text citations of author and date of publication that refer to an alphabetical list of references at the end of the paper.
- **CBE:** Used by writers in technical fields and the sciences (engineering, biology, physics, geography, chemistry, computer science, and mathematics); requires either a

name–year format or a citation–sequence format. The name–year format places the author's last name and the year of publication in parentheses, referring to an alphabetical list of references at the end of the paper.

- **CMS**: Used by some areas of the humanities, notably history, art, music, and theatre; requires a superscript number (e.g., 1) for each citation, all of which are numbered sequentially throughout the paper; no number is repeated. Numbers correspond either to footnotes at the bottoms of pages or a list of notes at the end of the paper. The first note gives complete information about the source, with shortened information for each subsequent reference to that source. A bibliography follows the notes, giving the same information, except for the page number, as in the first citation of each source. The information is also punctuated and arranged differently from the note copy.

Internet Citation Guides. Many research resources are available on the Internet, including guides for citing such sources. Your university librarian may have created a website where you will find the names of sites that give directions for citing electronic sources. Because Internet sites constantly change, URLs are not provided in the list below. You can locate the website by searching for the name. The ease of changing and updating Internet sites often means that they may have more current information than print guides offer. If you doubt the reliability and currency of a website, consult with your instructor about the advisability of using the site. Here are a few reliable sites that provide guidelines and models for finding and documenting sources. Many university libraries offer such services online:

- *How to Cite Electronic Sources*, Library of Congress. Explains how to cite media available online, such as films, music, maps, photographs, and texts Covers MLA and Chicago styles.
- *How to Cite Electronic Sources*, Indiana University. Covers MLA and APA.
- *MLA Style*, Modern Language Association of America. Includes list of frequently asked questions about MLA style.
- *MLA Formatting and Style Guide*. Purdue University's Online Writing Lab (OWL). Covers both MLA and APA styles.
- *Research Guide to Documentation Online* by Diana Hacker. Covers MLA, APA, and Chicago styles.
- *Style Sheet for Citing Resources (Print & Electronic)*. UC–Berkeley Library. Provides examples and rules for MLA, APA, Chicago, and Turabian.

PARENTHETICAL DOCUMENTATION—CITING SOURCES IN THE TEXT

Recall from the discussion in Chapter 6 on documenting sources with in-text citations and the discussion in this chapter on taking notes that a crucial task of the researcher is to identify accurately sources for all borrowed material. This section expands the discussion from Chapter 6 with illustrations of treatments for several types of sources. It also includes guidelines for creating a list of works cited that incorporates a variety of sources, including electronic sources. These examples follow MLA guidelines as they appear in the *MLA Handbook for Writers of Research Papers*, 7th edition.

Parenthetical, In-Text Citations

Remember that you must name your source for any borrowed material. The parenthetical citation must give enough information to identify the source by directing your reader to the alphabetized list of works cited at the end of your paper. The citation should also give the page number or numbers, if available, on which the material appears.

Author–Page Format

MLA guidelines call for the author–page format when acknowledging borrowed material in the text of your paper. You must name the author (or source, if no author is named) and give a page number or numbers where the borrowed material appears in the source. The author's name or title that you give in your text directs readers to the correct entry in the works-cited list, so the reference must correspond to its entry on that list. Here are some examples:

Book or Article with One Author. Author's last name and page number, without punctuation.

(Sollod 67)

Book or Article with Two or Three Authors. Both or all three authors' last names followed by the page number.

(Barrett and Rowe 78) (Fletcher, Miller, and Caplan 78)

Note: Reproduce the names in the order in which they appear on the title page. If they are not listed alphabetically, do not change their order.

Book or Article with More Than Three Authors. First author's last name followed by et al. and page number.

(Leitch et al. 29)

Article or Other Publication with No Author Named. Short title followed by page number.

("Teaching" 10)

Note: When citing any source in a parenthetical reference in your text that appears on your works-cited list, use the full title if short or a shortened version. When using a shortened version, begin with the word by which the source is alphabetized.

Two Anonymous Articles Beginning with the Same Word. Use the full title of each to distinguish one from the other.

("Classrooms without Walls" 45) ("Classrooms in the 21st Century" 96)

Two Works by the Same Author. Author's name followed by a comma, a short title, and the page number.

(Heilbrun, *Hamlet's Mother* 123) (Heilbrun, *Writing a Woman's Life* 35)

Works by People with the Same Last Name. First and last names of author and page number.

(Elizabeth Schilling 16)

Sources as they appear on the list of works cited:

Schilling, Elizabeth. "The Groundbreaking Musical *Rent*." *Review of Contemporary Theatre* 1.1 (2010): 12–16. Print.

Schilling, Lucas. *Card Games You Never Knew Existed.* Chicago: Leisure Games, 2010. Print.

Exceptions to Author–Page Format Such as a Lecture or Television Program. Many papers must accommodate some exceptions to the basic author–page parenthetical citation. For instance, for nonprint sources such as an Internet website, a lecture, a telephone conversation, a television documentary, or a recording, name the source in parentheses after the material without giving a page number:

("U.S. Technology in Iran")

Source as it appears on the list of works cited:

"U.S. Technology in Iran." Narr. Lesley Stahl. *Sixty Minutes.* CBS. WPTA, Fort Wayne, 21 Feb. 2010. Television.

Citing an Entire Work. You may want to refer to an entire work rather than just part of it. In that case, name the work and the author in the text of your paper, without a parenthetical citation:

Sir Arthur Conan Doyle's *Hound of the Baskervilles* features Watson to a much greater degree than do the earlier Holmes stories.

MLA suggests that this approach might be appropriate for Web publications with no pagination, television broadcast, movies, and similar works.

Citing Volume and Page Number of a Multivolume Work. If you refer to material from more than one volume of a multivolume work, state the volume number, followed by a colon, and then the page number. Do not use the words or abbreviations for *volume* or *page*. The two numbers separated by a colon explicitly indicate volume and page. Your works-cited entry will state the number of volumes in the work.

> Edgar Johnson's critical biography of Charles Dickens concludes with a rousing tribute to the author's creative imagination: "The world he [Dickens] created shines with undying life, and the hearts of men still vibrate to his indignant anger, his love, his tears, his glorious laughter, and his triumphant faith in the dignity of man" (2: 1158).
>
> Source as it appears on the list of works cited:
>
> Johnson, Edgar. *Charles Dickens: His Tragedy and Triumph.* 2 vols. New York: Simon, 1952.

If you draw material from just one volume of a multivolume work, your works-cited entry states which volume, and your in-text citation gives only the page number:

> The works of Charles Dickens fervently proclaim "his triumphant faith in the dignity of man" (Johnson 1158).
>
> Source as it appears on the list of works cited:
>
> Johnson, Edgar. *Charles Dickens: His Tragedy and Triumph.* Vol. 2. New York: Simon, 1952.

Citing a Work by a Corporate Author or Government Agency. Cite the author's or agency's name, followed by a page reference, just as you would for a book or periodical article. However, if the title of the corporate author is long, put it in the body of the text to avoid an extensive parenthetical reference:

> Testifying before a subcommittee of the U.S. House Committee on Public Works and Transportation, a representative of the Environmental Protection Agency argued that pollution from second-hand smoke within buildings is a widespread and dangerous threat (173–74).

Citing Internet Sources. According to the MLA guidelines, works on the World Wide Web are cited just like printed works when citing sources in your text, that is, with author's name or short title if there is no author listed. A special consideration with Web documents is that they generally do not have fixed page numbers or any kind of section numbering. If your source lacks numbering, there your parenthetical citation will give the author's last name if known, e.g., (Plonsky), or the title if the original gives no author's name, e.g., ("Psychology with Style"). If an author incorporates page numbers, section numbers, or paragraph numbers, you may cite the relevant numbers. Give the appropriate abbreviation before the numbers: (Plonsky, pars. 5–6). (*Pars.* is the abbreviation for *paragraphs.*) For a document on the World Wide Web, the page numbers of a printout should normally not be cited, because the pagination may vary in different printouts.

Remember that the purpose of the parenthetical citation is to indicate the location of the quotation or paraphrase in the referenced work and to point to the referenced work in the list of works cited. The entry that begins the reference in the works-cited list (i.e., author's last name or title of work) is the same entry that should also appear in the parenthetical reference or in the body of the text.

GUIDELINES FOR PARENTHETICAL DOCUMENTATION

- **Name the source for all borrowed material,** including both direct quotations and paraphrases, either in your text or in parentheses following the borrowed material.
- **Give the citation in parentheses at the end of the sentence** containing the quotation or paraphrase.
- **In the parentheses, state the author's last name and the page number** or numbers from which you took the words or ideas, with no punctuation between the name and the page number.
- **When citing Internet or other sources such as television broadcasts, movies, or lectures that have no page numbers, use the author's last name in parentheses.** If you mention the author's name in your text, it is helpful to repeat it in the parenthetical citation as well, to indicate where the borrowed material ends, though MLA style does not require it.
- **For smooth transition to borrowed material, name the author or source as you introduce the words or ideas.** In that case, the parentheses will include only the page number or numbers.
- **At the first mention of an author in your text, use the author's full name.** Thereafter, use the last name only.
- **Create a page titled "Works Cited" at the end of your paper** that lists all sources quoted or paraphrased in the paper. Do not include any works that you consulted but did not directly use in your paper.

CREATING A WORKS CITED PAGE USING MLA STYLE

The Works Cited page of a research report lists in alphabetical order all the sources you cite in your paper. It comes at the end of your paper, beginning on a separate page.

Include an entry for every work quoted from, paraphrased, summarized, or otherwise alluded to in your paper. ***Do not include on your list of works cited any sources you read but did not use in the paper.*** You may want to include a list of useful works that informed your understanding of the topic but that you did not quote or paraphrase from in your final paper; to do so, create a separate page entitled "Works Consulted."

GENERAL GUIDELINES FOR CREATING A LIST OF WORKS CITED

- **Begin your list of cited works on a new page after the conclusion of your paper.**
- **Center the title "Works Cited" one inch from the top of the page.**
- **Continue the page numbers of the text, with a separate number for each of the Works Cited pages.**
- **Alphabetize the list of sources.**
- **Begin the first line of each entry flush with the left margin.** Indent the second and subsequent lines within each entry five spaces.

- **Begin with the author's last name, followed by a comma and then the first name.** For a source with two or more authors, invert only the first name. List the other name or names in normal order.
- **Italicize the titles of books, journals, magazines, newspapers, and websites.** Do not use quotation marks.
- **Double-space within and between all entries.**
- **Place a period at the end of each entire entry.**

The remainder of this section gives guidelines for creating works-cited entries for books, periodicals, and electronic sources, supplemented by models for miscellaneous types of entries. The numbers on this list correspond to the numbered illustrations in each section (books, periodicals, electronic sources, miscellaneous) in the following pages:

Print Sources.

1. Book with a single author
2. Collection or anthology
3. Article in a collection or anthology
4. Book by two or three authors or editors
5. Book by more than three authors or editors
6. Two works by the same author
7. Reprint of a book
8. Preface, foreword, introduction, or afterword to a book
9. Edition of a book
10. Multivolume work
11. Article in a journal with continuous pagination
12. Article in a journal with separate pagination
13. Article in a weekly or biweekly magazine
14. Article in a monthly or bimonthly magazine
15. Article in a quarterly magazine
16. Magazine article with no author
17. Newspaper article
18. Periodical article that does not appear on consecutive pages

Creating a Works-Cited List for Electronic Sources.

19. Scholarly project
20. Professional site
21. Article in a reference database
22. Online article

Online Sources of Full-Text Articles.

23. Article with author named, scholarly journal
24. Article in magazine
25. Article with no author named
26. Article in magazine from personally subscribed service

Miscellaneous Electronic Sources.

27. Posting to a discussion group
28. E-mail message
29. Government document

Works-Cited Formats for Sources Other Than Books, Periodicals, and Electronic Sources.

30. Congressional record
31. Government publication
32. Lecture
33. Letter
34. PDF file
35. Personal interview
36. Telephone interview
37. Pamphlet
38. Television or radio program
39. Sound recording
40. Article in a reference book

Books in a Work-Cited List. Citations for books have several main parts: author's name, title of book, and publication information, including place of publication, publisher, and date the book was published. Often a book has more than one author or an editor, and often books are collections of a number of essays with individual authors.

GUIDELINES FOR CITING BOOKS ON THE WORKS-CITED LIST

- **Begin with the author's last name, followed by a comma, and then the first name, followed by a period.** For a source with two or more authors, invert the first author's name with a comma before and after the first name, then write the word *and* and put the other author's name in normal order.
- **Italicize the title of the book.**
- **State the city of publication, the publisher, and the date the book was published:** City: Publisher, date. Note that only the city name is given unless it is not unclear which city it is. For cities like Boston, New York, Los Angeles, and London, for instance, you would not need to add state or country. For a city like Athens, it is necessary to add

the state to avoid ambiguity: Athens, OH. Use the same state abbreviation system as for zip codes.

- **Separate each item in an entry by a period:** Author. Title. Publication information and date. Note that each period is followed by one space. MLA guidelines recommend using only one space after a concluding punctuation mark unless your instructor requests that you use two.
- **For essays in collections, begin by listing the author of the essay, then the title within quotation marks, the book it appears in, the editor's name, and publication information for the book.** Put the inclusive page numbers of the essay at the end of the entry.
- **Shorten publishers' names and drop such words as *Inc., Co.,* and *Press.*** Abbreviate *University* and *Press* for university presses, as "U of Wisconsin P" for University of Wisconsin Press or "Oxford UP" for Oxford University Press.
- **State the medium of publication (Print).**

The following section provides guidelines for documenting the most common kinds of books that you are likely to come across in your research.

1. **Book with a Single Author**

Author's name. *Title of Book.* City of publication: Publisher, date of publication. Print.

Cummings, Claire Hope. *Uncertain Peril: Genetic Engineering and the Future of Seeds.* Boston: Beacon, 2008. Print.

2. **Collection or Anthology**

Use this format when you cite the ideas of the editor(s) or when you refer to the entire collection. Name the editor, followed by the abbreviation "ed." Treat the rest of the entry as you would for a book.

Editor's name, ed. *Title of Collection.* City of publication: Publisher, date of publication. Print.

Taylor, Helen, ed. *The Daphne Du Maurier Companion.* London: Virago, 2007. Print.

For two or more editors, list the first editor's name in inverted order, followed by a comma, the word *and*, and the second editor's name in normal order.

Schofield, Mary Anne, and Cecilia Macheski, eds. *Fetter'd or Free? British Women Novelists, 1670–1815.* Athens, OH: Ohio UP, 1986. Print.

Article in a Collection or Anthology

Name the author, the title of the article, the title of the collection, the editor or coeditors of the collection, publication information, and the **inclusive page numbers** of the entire article. Follow this format:

Author's name. "Title of Article." *Title of Collection.* The abbreviation "Ed." Editor's name in normal order. City of publication: Name of publisher, date of publication. Inclusive page numbers on which the article appears. Print.

Munford, Rebecca. "Spectres of Authorship: Daphne du Maurier's Gothic Legacy." *The Daphne Du Maurier Companion*. Ed. Helen Taylor. London: Virago, 2007. 68–74. Print.

If the edition has two or more editors, use the abbreviation "Eds." followed by both editors' names:

Spacks, Patricia Meyer. "Sisters." *Fetter'd or Free? British Women Novelists, 1670–1815*. Eds. Mary Anne Schofield and Cecilia Macheski. Athens, OH: Ohio UP, 1986. 136–51. Print.

4. Book by Two or Three Authors or Editors

List the names of the authors in the same order as they are listed on the title page, even if they are not in alphabetical order.

First author's name in inverted order, and second author's name in normal order. *Name of Book*. City of publication: Publisher, date of publication. Print.

Gilbert, Sandra M., and Susan Gubar. *The Madwoman in the Attic: The Woman Writer and the Nineteenth-Century Literary Imagination*. New Haven: Yale UP, 1979. Print.

5. Book by More Than Three Authors or Editors

List the names of the authors in the same order as they are listed on the title page, even if they are not in alphabetical order. MLA style gives you the option of listing all of the authors or editors or just the first one, followed by *et al.* ("and others").

Leitch, Vincent B., William E. Cain, Laurie Finke, Barbara Johnson, John McGowan, T. Denean Sharpley-Whiting, and Jeffrey T. Williams, eds. *The Norton Anthology of Theory and Criticism*. 2nd ed. New York: Norton, 2010. Print.

OR

Leitch, Vincent B., et al., eds. *The Norton Anthology of Theory and Criticism*. 2nd ed. New York: Norton, 2010. Print.

6. Two Works by the Same Author

List the books in alphabetical order by title. For the second and subsequent books by the same author, type three hyphens followed by a period in place of the name.

Chabon, Michael. *Motherhood for Amateurs: The Pleasures and Regrets of a Husband, Son, and Father*. New York: Harper, 2009. Print.

———. *The Amazing Adventures of Kavalier and Clay*. New York: Ballantine, 2000. Print.

7. Reprint of a Book

Follow the same format as for books, but add the date of the first publication after the title.

Author's name. *Title of Book*. First date of publication. City of publication of this edition: Publisher, date of publication. Print.

Symons, Julian. *Bloody Murder: From the Detective Story to the Crime Novel: A History*. 1972. 1985. London: Pan Macmillan, 1992. Print.

If a different publisher produced earlier editions, you have the option of naming the place of publication and publisher for the other editions as well as for the current one.

Symons, Julian. *Bloody Murder: From the Detective Story to the Crime Novel: A History*. London: Faber, 1972. London: Viking, 1985. London: Pan Macmillan, 1992. Print.

8. Preface, Foreword, Introduction, or Afterword to a Book

If you use material *only* from the preface, foreword, introduction, or afterword of a book, your works-cited entry begins with the name of the person who wrote the selection you use, not necessarily with the author of the book (though sometimes they are the same person). You will need to indicate what part of the book you cite (preface, foreword, introduction, or afterword), then name the book and author and give complete bibliographic information. Finally, give the inclusive page numbers of the preface, foreword, introduction, or afterword. Follow this model:

Author of introduction. Introduction. *Title of Book*. By author's name in normal order. Place of publication: Publisher, date of publication. Inclusive page numbers on which the introduction appears. Print.

Green, Richard Lancelyn. Introduction. *The Adventures of Sherlock Holmes*. By Arthur Conan Doyle. 1892. Oxford: Oxford UP, 1993. xi–xxxv. Print.

9. Edition of a Book

Use this format for a book prepared for publication by someone other than the author if you refer primarily to the text itself:

Doyle, Arthur Conan. *The Adventures of Sherlock Holmes*. Ed. Richard Lancelyn Green. Oxford: Oxford UP, 1994. Print.

If you refer primarily to the work of the editor, for instance, material from the introduction or notes to the text, begin with the editor's name:

Green, Richard Lancelyn, ed. *The Adventures of Sherlock Holmes*. By Arthur Conan Doyle. 1892. Oxford: Oxford UP, 1993. Print.

10. Multivolume Work

If you draw material from two or more volumes of a work, cite the total number of volumes in the entire work. When you refer to the work in the text of your paper, your parenthetical reference gives the volume number and page number.

Johnson, Edgar. *Charles Dickens: His Tragedy and Triumph.* 2 vols. New York: Simon, 1952. Print.

If you refer to only one volume of a multivolume work, state the number of that volume in the works-cited entry. Your parenthetical in-text citation supplies page number only, not volume and page.

Johnson, Edgar. *Charles Dickens: His Tragedy and Triumph.* Vol. 2. New York: Simon, 1952. Print.

Periodicals in a Works-Cited List. Periodicals are magazines or journals that are published frequently and at fixed intervals. Distinguish between journals and magazines by considering audience, subject matter, and frequency of publication. Journals are fairly specialized, usually written for people in a specific profession, and more technical and research oriented than magazines; they generally appear much less frequently than magazines, perhaps bimonthly or four times a year. Magazines, on the other hand, are intended for general audiences, are not heavily research-oriented, and usually appear in monthly or even weekly editions. As with books, works-cited entries for periodicals have three main divisions: the author's name, the title of the article, and publication information, including the name of the periodical, the date the article was published, and the inclusive page numbers on which it appears.

GUIDELINES FOR CREATING WORKS-CITED ENTRIES FOR PERIODICALS

- **Place the author's name first, in inverted order, followed by a period.**
- **If the article is published anonymously, begin the entry with the title.** For placing the entries in alphabetical order on the list, ignore *The*, *A*, *And*, and numbers at the beginnings of titles.
- **State the title of the article, enclosing it in quotation marks, ending with a period.**
- **State the name of the periodical, italicized, followed by no punctuation.**
- **State series number, volume number, and/or issue number, if relevant.**
- **State the date of publication. For publications with a specific day and month named, use this format: day month year.** For scholarly journals, include volume number and issue number, if given, and enclose the date in parentheses. Abbreviate the names of all months except May, June, and July.
- **Follow the date with a colon and the inclusive page numbers of the article. Put a period after the page numbers.**
- **Do not use the abbreviations "p." or "pp." for pages.**
- **State the medium of the publication (Print) followed by a period.**

11. Article in a Journal with Continuous Pagination

Use this format for journals that continue pagination throughout the year.

Author's name. "Title of Article." *Name of Periodical* volume number. issue number (date): inclusive page numbers of article. Print.

Allen, Paul. "Dickens in Composition Classrooms." *College English* 92.4 (Mar. 2011): 325–33. Print.

12. Article in a Journal with Separate Pagination

Use this format for journals that begin each issue with page 1. Give the issue number as well as the volume number.

Author's name. "Title of Article." *Name of Periodical* volume number.issue number (date): inclusive page numbers of article. Print.

Annan, Kofi. "Development Without Borders." *Harvard International Review* 23.2 (Summer 2001): 84. Print.

13. Article in a Weekly or Biweekly Magazine

Author's name. "Title of Article." *Name of Magazine* complete date, beginning with the day and abbreviating the month, page number(s). Print.

Gibbs, Nancy. "The End of Helicopter Parents." *Time* 30 Nov. 2009: 52–57. Print.

14. Article in a Monthly or Bimonthly Magazine

Author's name. "Title of Article." *Name of Magazine* date, including month and year: page number(s). Print.

Bowden, Mark. "The Lessons of Abu Ghraib." *Atlantic Monthly* July–Aug. 2004: 33–36. Print.

15. Article in a Quarterly Magazine

Fletcher, John C., Franklin G. Miller, and Arthur L. Caplan. "Facing Up to Bioethical Decisions." *Issues in Science and Technology* Fall 2004: 75–80. Print.

16. Magazine Article with No Author

"44 Ways to Kick-Start Your New Year." *success.com. Success Media*, 30 Nov. 2009. Web. 12 October 2010. Print.

17. Newspaper Article

Supply the following, in this order:

a) author's name, if known;

b) article title;

c) name of the newspaper, italicized;

d) city where the newspaper is published, if not included in its name, in brackets after the name;

e) the date, beginning with the day, abbreviating the month, and the year, followed by a colon;

f) page number(s) where the article appears. If the newspaper has more than one section and each section is paginated separately, give both section and page number. If you gather material from a special edition of the newspaper, indicate that fact, as well.

Kingsolver, Barbara. "A Pure, High Note of Anguish." *Los Angeles Times* 23 Sept. 2001: M1. Print.

18. Periodical Article That Does Not Appear on Consecutive Pages
Give only the first page number, followed by a plus sign:

Nye, Joseph S. Jr. "The Decline of America's Soft Power." *Foreign Affairs* May–June 2004: 16+. Print.

Creating a Works-Cited List for Electronic Sources. As with other types of sources you cite in your research paper, your works-cited entries for electronic sources should provide enough information that your reader can locate them. These sources pose a particular problem that books, periodicals, and other print media do not: they change frequently, are updated, move to new sites, or are even removed from the Internet. References to electronic works require slightly more and certainly different information than print sources require. Supply as much of the following information as is available, in this order:

a) author's name;

b) title of the work;

c) title of the site;

d) publisher or sponsor of the site; N. p. if not available;

e) date the site was created or updated;

f) the medium of publication (Web); and

g) date that you accessed the material.

See the guidelines that follow for additional details. Keep in mind that electronic sources are not uniform in the amount of information they provide. A site may not incorporate page numbers, an author's name, reference markers such as paragraph or page breaks, or other conventional print references. You can supply only the information that is available at any particular site. Use common sense: include as much information as you have available to you.

GUIDELINES FOR CREATING A WORKS-CITED LIST FOR ELECTRONIC SOURCES

- Name the author, editor, narrator, or compiler, if known, last name first, followed by a period.
- State the title of the work, if part of a larger work, in quotation marks. If independent, italicize it. Follow with a period.
- State the title of the site, italicized, followed by a period.
- If a scholarly project or database, name the editor, if known.
- Supply any identifying information, such as version, volume, or issue number.
- For a posting to a newsgroup, discussion group, or forum, give the date of the posting.
- For a periodical article that also appears in print form, include page numbers if provided or the abbreviation *n. pag.* if no pagination is provided.
- For a posting to a discussion list or forum, give the name of the list or forum.
- Supply the name of any institution or organization sponsoring or associated with the site, followed by a comma.
- State the date of publication, followed by a period. If no date is given, use *n.d.*
- State the medium of publication (Web), followed by a period.
- State the date you visited the site, followed by a period.

19. Scholarly Project

Virtual London: Monuments and Dust. Codirectors Michael Levenson, David Trotter, and Anthony Wohl. U of Virginia. 4 Sept. 2008. Web. 12 Nov. 2010.

20. Professional Site

The Camelot Project. Ed. Alan Lupack and Barbara Tepa Lupack. 3 Sept. 2004. U of Rochester. Web. 4 Dec. 2010.

21. Article in a Reference Database

"Susan Brownell Anthony." *The Columbia Encyclopedia*, 6th ed. Columbia UP. 2003. Web. 12 Apr. 2010.

22. Online Article

Benfey, Christopher. "Better Late Than Ever." *Slate* 19 Dec. 2006. n. pag. Web. 28 Nov. 2010.

Online Sources of Full-Text Articles. Examples 22–25 illustrate citations from online services offering full-text articles, such as EBSCO, Gale, InfoTrac College Edition, Proquest, and Periodicals Abstract. The format remains essentially the same as for other electronic sources:

a) name of author (if given);

b) title of article;

c) title of journal or magazine; volume and issue number if a journal;

d) date of publication;

e) page number(s) if given or *n. pag.* (for no pagination);

f) name of the service, such as EBSCO, InfoTrac College Edition, or Lexis-Nexis Academic;

g) Medium of publication (Web); and

h) date that you read the material.

23. Article with Author Named, Scholarly Journal

Taylor, Susan Lee. "Music Piracy: Differences in the Ethical Perceptions of Business Majors and Music Business Majors." *Journal of Education for Business* 79.5 (May–June 2004): 306. InfoTrac College Edition. Web. 14 Nov 2010.

24. Article in Magazine

Murphy, Victoria. "The Enemy Strikes Back." *Forbes* 24 Nov. 2003: 218. LexisNexis Academic. Web. 6 Nov. 2010.

25. Article with No Author Named

"Yelling 'Fire.'" *New Republic* 3 April 2000: 9. EBSCO. Web. 12 Oct. 2010.

26. Article in Magazine from Personally Subscribed Service

If you access an article through a service that you subscribe to, such as America Online, give the information as usual, followed by the name of the service, the date you accessed it, and the keyword you used to retrieve the source.

Kalb, Claudia. "The Life in a Cell; Stem-Cell Researchers Find Fresh Hope for Curing Deadly Diseases—Along with New Controversies." *Newsweek International* 28 June 2004: 50. Web. 12 October 2010.

Miscellaneous Electronic Sources.

27. Posting to a Discussion Group

Walton, Hilary. "New Pym Biography." Online posting. 2 Feb. 2008. Pym-1. Web. 3 Feb. 2010.

28. E-Mail Message

Konrad, Lucas. "Antique Fire Trucks." Message to the author. 11 Nov. 2010. E-mail.

29. Government Document

United States. Dept. of Labor. Bureau of Labor Statistics. *Occupational Outlook Handbook, 2010–2011*. Web. 12 October 2010.

Works-Cited Formats for Sources Other Than Books, Periodicals, and Electronic Sources.

30. Congressional Record

United States. Senate. *Children's Health Care Quality Act*. 111th Cong., 1st sess. S225. Washington: GPO, 2010. Print.

United States. House. Committee on Energy and Commerce. *E-Rate 2.0 Act of 2010*. 111th Cong. 2nd sess. H. R. 4619. Washington: GPO, 2010. Print.

31. Government Publication

United States. Dept. of Justice. *A Guide to Disability Rights*. Washington, DC: DOJ, Sept. 2010. Print.

32. Lecture

Schilling, Brian. "The Role of First Responders in Medical Emergencies." Careers Club. Manchester High School, North Manchester. 22 Dec. 2010. Lecture.

33. Letter

White, Jeremy. Letter to the author. 1 Oct. 2010. MS.

Note that *MS* represents a work prepared by hand. For machine-generated work, use *TS*, for typescript.

34. PDF file

Brunner, Borgna. "The Wage Gap: A History of Pay Inequity and the Equal Pay Act." *Infoplease* March 2005. PDF file.

35. Personal Interview

Yahi, Mourad. Personal interview. 10 Nov. 2010.

36. Telephone Interview

Yahi, Laurel. Telephone interview. 12 Jan. 2010.

37. Pamphlet

Tweddle, Dominic. *The Coppergate Helmet*. York, UK: Cultural Resource Management, 1984.

38. Television or Radio Broadcast

"U.S. Technology in Iran." Narr. Lesley Stahl. *Sixty Minutes*. CBS. WPTA, Fort Wayne, 21 Feb. 2010. Television.

On the Air. WOWO, Fort Wayne, 12 Apr. 2010. Radio.

"Lights Out." *ER*. NBC. 23 Sept. 1999. DVD.

39. Sound Recording

List first the aspect of the recording you want to emphasize: composer, conductor, or performer. Give that name first, then the title of the recording or selection, the manufacturer, the year of issue (write *n.d.* if no date appears on the package or disc), and the medium (compact disc, audiotape, audiocassette). Do not enclose the name of the medium in italics or quotation marks.

Uchida, Mitsuko, pianist. *Piano Sonatas in D*, KV. 284, *Sonata in B flat*, KV. 570, and *Rondo in D*, KV. 485. By Wolfgang Amadeus Mozart. Philips, 1986. CD.

40. Article in a Reference Book

Treat an entry in an encyclopedia or dictionary as you would an article in a collection, but do not cite the book's editor. If the article is signed, begin with the author's name, followed by the title of the entry; otherwise, begin with the title. For familiar reference books such as standard encyclopedias and dictionaries that are frequently updated and reissued, you need not give publication information. Just list the edition (if stated) and year of publication.

Watkins, Calvert. "Indo-Europe and the Indo-Europeans." *American Heritage Dictionary of the English Language*. 3rd ed. 1991. Print.

When citing less familiar books, give full publication information.

Rose-Bond, Sherry, and Scott Bond. "Sherlockiana." *Encyclopedia Mysteriosa: A Comprehensive Guide to the Art of Detection in Print, Film, Radio, and Television*. Ed. William L. DeAndrea. New York: Prentice, 1994. 327–330. Print.

Sample Works Cited Pages. Here is an alphabetized list of sources drawn from the examples on the previous pages, using a hypothetical student's last name.

White 15

Works Cited

Annan, Kofi. "Development Without Borders." *Harvard International Review* 23.2 (Summer 2001): 84. Print.

Benfey, Christopher. "Better Late Than Ever." *Slate* 18 Dec. 2006. n. pag. Web. 28 Nov. 2010.

Bowden, Mark. "The Lessons of Abu Ghraib." *Atlantic Monthly* July-Aug. 2004: 33-36. Print.

White 16

Cummings, Claire Hope. *Uncertain Peril: Genetic Engineering and the Future of Seeds*. Boston: Beacon, 2008. Print.

Kingsolver, Barbara. "A Pure, High Note of Anguish." *Los Angeles Times* 23 Sept. 2001: M1. Print.

Murphy, Victoria. "The Enemy Strikes Back." *Forbes* 24 Nov. 2003: 218. LexisNexis Academic. Web. 6 Nov. 2010.

Nye, Joseph S. Jr. "The Decline of America's Soft Power" *Foreign Affairs* May-June 2004: 16+. Print.

Spacks, Patricia Meyer. "Sisters." *Fetter'd or Free? British Women Novelists*, 1670-1815. Eds. Mary Anne Schofield and Cecilia Macheski. Athens, OH: Ohio UP, 1986. 136-51. Print.

United States. Dept. of Justice. *A Guide to Disability Rights*. Washington, DC: DOJ, Sept. 2010. Print.

"U.S. Technology in Iran." Narr. Lesley Stahl. *Sixty Minutes*. CBS. WPTA, Fort Wayne, 21 Feb. 2010. Television.

Yahi, Mourad. Personal interview. 10 Nov. 2010.

ASSEMBLING THE PARTS OF A RESEARCH PAPER

In general, putting a research paper together is not so different from writing any other kind of paper. Following the guidelines explained in Chapter 2 on the writing process, you will have the same components in a longer paper with sources as you do in a shorter one. You will have an introduction, though it is likely to be longer than in other writing assignments. You must have a thesis statement or clearly evident central idea. Your paper as a whole and individual paragraphs within it must be organized and fully developed. Sentences must be crafted grammatically and imaginatively, and your language should be idiomatic, colorful, and clear. You must provide transitions between points within paragraphs and from paragraph to paragraph throughout the paper, and you must have a conclusion that brings the paper to a satisfactory finish. Of course a major difference between the research paper and other papers you will write for your college classes is that research papers incorporate the works of others. Thus, you will have in-text citations for all references to your sources and a work-cited list of all sources referenced in your paper. Your instructor may also ask you to include an outline of your paper.

The following sections will take you through the process of putting together your final paper. They address the following components:

- First page of paper without a separate title page or title page
- Title page
- First page of a paper with a separate title page
- Pagination and spacing
- Tables, figures, and illustrations
- Outline page
- Introductory paragraph and body of the paper
- Conclusion
- Works Cited page
- The complete research paper

First Page of a Research Paper Without a Separate Title Page. MLA guidelines state that a research paper does not need a separate title page. Follow these guidelines:

- Type your last name and the number 1 in the upper right-hand corner, one-half inch from the top of the page, flush with the right margin.
- Place your name, your instructor's name, the course title and section, and the date in the upper left-hand corner, one inch from the top of the paper and flush with the left margin.
- Double-space between each line.
- Double-space below the date and center your title.
- Do not italicize your title, enclose it in quotation marks, capitalize every letter, or place a period after it.
- Capitalize the first letter of every important word in the title.
- Double-space again and begin the body of your paper.

Hayes 1

Nate Hayes

Professor White

English 102-8

15 April 2008

A Positive Alternative to Cloning

Since Dr. Ian Wilmut's successful cloning

Hayes 2

of a sheep in 1996, the debate over how far medical science should be allowed to go has grown increasingly heated. Some people are completely opposed to any kind of experimentation that involves genetic manipulation or the development of procedures that some consider should be reserved only for God.

Title Page. Although MLA style does not require a separate title page, many instructors ask for it. If your instructor requires a title page, follow these guidelines:

- Center your title about one-third to halfway down the page.
- Do not italicize your title, enclose it in quotation marks, capitalize every letter, or place a period after it.
- Capitalize the first letter of every important word in the title.
- Underneath the title, about halfway down the page, write your name, centered on the line.
- Drop farther down the page and center on separate lines, double spaced, your instructor's name; the course name, number, and section; and the date.

Arthur of Camelot: The Once and Future King

by

Shawn Ryan

Professor Zackary

English 102-21

1 May 2010

First Page of a Research Paper with a Separate Title Page. If your instructor requires a separate title page, follow these guidelines for the first text page of your paper:

- Type your last name and the number 1 in the upper right-hand corner, one-half inch from the top of the page, flush with the right margin.
- Drop down two inches from the top of the page and center your title, exactly as it appears on your title page.
- Do not italicize your title, enclose it in quotation marks, capitalize every letter, or place a period after it.
- Capitalize the first letter of every important word in the title.
- Double-space and begin the body of your paper.

Ryan 1

Arthur of Camelot: The Once and Future King

North and west the wind blew beneath
the morning sun, over endless miles of
rolling grass and far scattered thickets
. . . [and] Dragonmount, where the dragon
had died, and with him, some said, the Age of
Legend—where prophecy said he would be born
again. (Jordan 13)

Pagination and Spacing. The entire paper should be double-spaced, with each page numbered in the upper right-hand corner, one-half inch from the top and flush with the right margin. MLA style requires that pagination begin with page 1 and recommends that you include your last name before the page number.

Tables, Figures, and Illustrations. Place tables, figures, and illustrations close to the parts of the paper that they relate to.

Table. A table is labeled *Table*, given an Arabic number, and captioned. This information is capitalized as you would a title, placed above the table, and typed flush with the left-hand margin on separate lines. Place the name of the source and any additional comments directly below the table, as illustrated here:

Table I Male vs. Females: Free-Time Activities

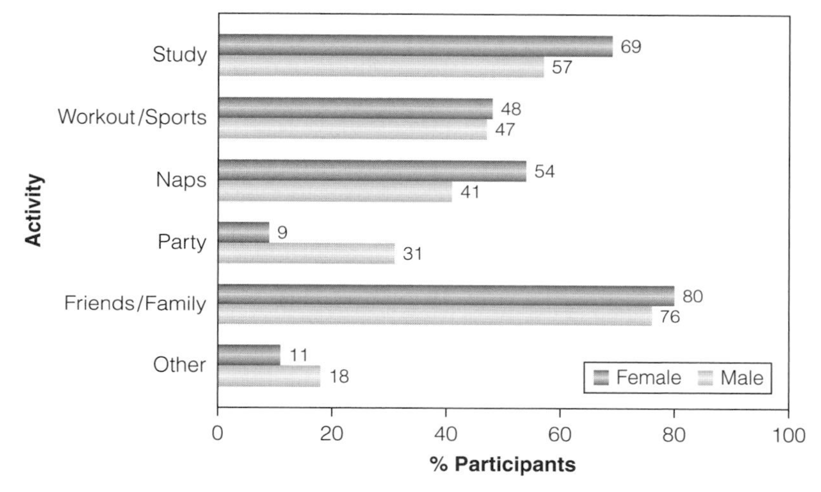

Source: Survey conducted by Margo Borgen, Morris Boyd, Maicha Chang, and Kelly Kassien, University of Wisconsin–Stevens Point, May 2008.

Figures and Illustrations. Visual images such as photographs, charts, maps, and line drawings are labeled *Figure* (usually abbreviated *Fig.*), assigned an Arabic number, and given a title or caption. A label and title or caption are positioned ***below the illustration and have the same margins as the text.*** The following illustrates correct handling of a visual image:

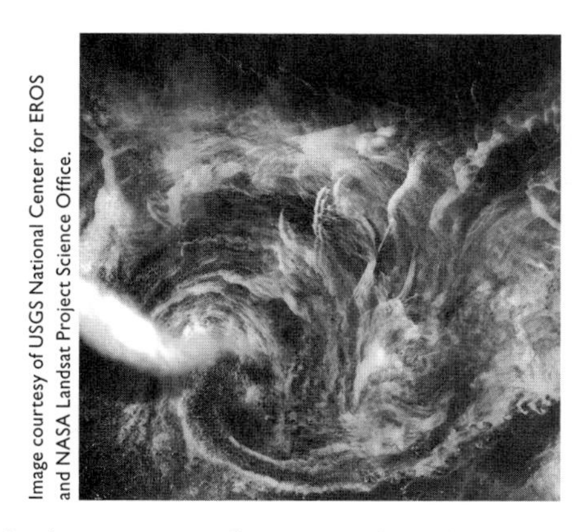

Fig. 1. Whirlpool in the Air: a spinning formation of ice, clouds, and low-lying fog off the eastern coast of Greenland.

Outline Page. If your instructor requires a formal outline, place it immediately after the title page. Your instructor will tell you how detailed your outline should be, but follow these basic directions in most cases:

- Begin your outline with the thesis statement of your paper.
- Double-space between all lines of the outline.
- If your instructor requires a topic outline, use only short phrases or key words. If your instructor requires a sentence outline, write complete sentences.
- Use uppercase roman numerals (I, II, III) for each major division of your outline and capital letters (A, B, C) for each subdivision under each major division.
- If you find it necessary to further subdivide, use Arabic numerals (1, 2, 3) under capital letters and lowercase letters (a, b, c) under Arabic numerals.
- Number the outline page(s) with lowercase roman numerals (i, ii, iii, iv) placed in the upper right-hand corner, one-half inch from the top of the page and flush with the right margin. Include your last name.
- End with a statement summarizing your conclusion.

Here is a sample topic outline page from a student paper.

Ryan i

Outline

Thesis: An examination of some of the research on Arthurian legend suggests that the evidence supports the theory that a man like Arthur did exist.

I. The birth of Arthur
   A. The legend
   B. Evidence of Tintagel
II. The places and people most important to Arthur
   A. Camelot
   B. Glastonbury Abbey
   C. Lancelot and Perceval
III. Arthur's impact on society
   A. His image
   B. The difference between the man and the legend

Conclusion: Arthur's existence as a man is indeterminable, but Arthur's presence in the minds and hearts of people everywhere gives credence to his existence as a leader of nations.

Introductory Paragraphs and Body of the Paper. As for any other kind of writing assignment, begin with an introduction that provides background information that clearly portrays the topic of your paper or the direction your argument will take, or that in some way sets the stage for what follows. State your thesis or central idea early in the paper. If your topic is controversial, explain the nature of the controversy. Once you have introduced your topic sufficiently, begin developing your argument. Here are the opening paragraphs from Sam Cox's paper "Proving Their Loyalty During World War I: German-Americans Confronted with Anti-German Fervor and Suspicion."

Cox 1

Sam Cox

Professor Heather Schilling

Humanities 310-01

12 April 2010

Proving Their Loyalty During World War I:
German-Americans Confronted with Anti-German
Fervor and Suspicion

In May 1915, a *Milwaukee Abendpost* editorial voiced the unsettling feelings that German-Americans were experiencing in the early months of the First World War and that would intensify as the war dragged on. Supportive of the Fatherland in the European conflict, German-Americans found themselves at odds with an English-speaking majority and Anglo-oriented government. After the United States entered the war on the side of the Triple Entente, many German-Americans were faced with the agonizing choice of whom to support. A review of the *Indianapolis Telegraph und Tribüne* and the *Indianapolis Spottvogel* leads to the conclusion that German-Americans unwaveringly supported their new homeland in the war in nearly all instances.

Cox 2

Nevertheless, the loyalty and trustworthiness of German-Americans was questioned by many in the public. The government implemented certain measures intended to track the activity of the German population in the United States and censor their publications. German culture came under popular and official attack throughout the country as German-Americans experienced intense pressure to Americanize. German-Americans responded by trying to prove their loyalty to the United States. They participated in Liberty Loan war bond drives and discontinued the use of the German language. As a result, the influence of Germans on American life faded after World War I. German-Americans were forced to decide whether their loyalties lay with Germany, the land of their heritage, or with the United States, their adopted homeland and enemy of Germany. Finding their loyalty questioned all around them, German-Americans sacrificed their culture, language, and unique identity in the face of overwhelming pressure to become true Americans and prove their dedication to their new homeland.

Conclusion. Recall from Chapter 2 that the conclusion brings the paper to a satisfying end, no matter what its length. Whether the assignment is a 500-word essay or a 5,000-word research paper, readers should not be left with unanswered questions and should have a sense that the writer has fully explained, argued, developed, or illustrated the central idea or thesis. A good conclusion forcefully reiterates the introduction, reinforces the writer's connection with the audience, looks to the future, reemphasizes the central argument, or suggests a course of action. Here is the conclusion to Sam Cox's paper. Notice how his conclusion reinforces points made in the opening paragraphs above but does so without repeating them word for word.

Cox 14

German-Americans bore an unfounded attack on their language and culture during World War I. Efforts to wipe out their language, their cultural establishments, their newspapers, and their ethnic identity were so powerful in that era of suspicion, threats, and violence, that most German-Americans succumbed to the unyielding pressure. They changed the names of clubs, shut down newspapers, bought Liberty Bonds, and stopped speaking German. Done willingly but often reluctantly, these actions demonstrated their loyalty to their new homeland during the time when their loyalty was demanded most. Despite their deep affection for their old Fatherland and the knowledge that they were surrendering much of their cultural identity, German-Americans wanted to prove that they were steadfast patriots of their new homeland of freedom and prosperity.

Works Cited Page. Here is the page listing works cited in Sam Cox's paper "Proving Their Loyalty During World War I: German-Americans Confronted with Anti-German Fervor and Suspicion," which uses both primary and secondary sources.

Cox 15

Works Cited

"The Alarm against Spies." *The Literary Digest* 21 July 1917: 13-14. Print.

Cox 16

"Am Dienstag kommen die deutschen Zeitungen unter den Arm des Censors." *Indianapolis Spottvogel* 14 October 1917: 1. Print.

Brocke, Frank. "'We Had to Be so Careful' A Farmer's Recollections of Anti-German Sentiment in World War I." *History Matters: The U.S. Survey Course on the Web*. 31 March 2006. Web. 30 Oct. 2010.

"A Call to German Americans to 'Organize.'" *The Literary Digest* 50 9 January 1915: 42-43. Print.

"Deutsche Kundgebung in New York." *Indianapolis Spottvogel* 9 August 1914: 4. Print.

"German-American Loyalty." *The Literary Digest 50* 29 May 1915: 1262-64. Print.

Heinrichs, Rudolf. "A Family Letter." *Atlantic Monthly* 120 (1917): 739-45. Print.

"Der Kampf für Erhaltung der persönlichen Freiheit ist der Kampf der Deutschen in Amerika." *Indianapolis Spottvogel* 16 August 1914: 17. Print.

"Malicious Anti-German Attacks." *Indianapolis Spottvogel* 16 August 1914: 9. Print.

Ramsey, Paul. "The War against German-American Culture: The Removal of German Language Instruction from the Indianapolis Schools, 1917-1919." *Indiana Magazine of History* 95.4 (2002): 285-303. Print.

Witten, Johann. Letters to Christoph Witten, 3 December 1914, 5 December 1915, 9 September 1919, 18 September 1920. Trans. Susan Vogel. *News from the Land of Freedom: German Immigrants Write Home*. Eds. Walter Kamphoefner, Wolfgang Helbich, and Ulrike Sommer. Ithaca: Cornell University Press, 1991. 278-83. Print.

STUDENT RESEARCH PAPER USING MLA STYLE

The following student research paper implements MLA style guidelines for incorporating and documenting source material as explained in Chapters 6 and 7. Marginal notes point out various components of the research paper.

Nate's introduction provides a context for his topic and states the nature of the controversy over cloning and stem-cell research.

Complete bibliographic information for the Pethokoukis source is given on Nate's Works Cited page.

Nate's thesis states his position: he is opposed to further research on cloning but believes that stem-cell research should continue.

Hayes 1

Nate Hayes

Professor White

English 102-8

30 May 2010

A Positive Alternative to Cloning

Since Dr. Ian Wilmut's successful cloning of a sheep in 1996, the debate over how far medical science should be allowed to go has grown increasingly heated. Some researchers think that cloning human parts, if not entire humans, is feasible, but a more likely and very promising development lies in stem cell research, which could lead to developments that could "alter mankind in some astounding ways" (Pethokoukis). Such potential has many people worried about the extent to which human genetic makeup should be modified or amended. Some people are completely opposed to any kind of experimentation that involves genetic manipulation or the development of procedures that some consider should be reserved only for God. The controversy centers on the questions of how far science should go and who should control the technology. A review of the arguments for and against stem-cell research leads me to conclude that, although there needs to be a long, serious national debate on the subject, scientists should stop short of cloning humans but be allowed to continue their research on stem cells.

Nate provides the acronym for the long name of the advisory commission and then uses it whenever he quotes from the commission again. Nate gives only the page number because he has mentioned the name of the source in his text.

Nate is using general knowledge here and does not need to document his statements.

The information about James D. Watson establishes his credentials. Nate's combination of both paraphrase and direct quotations serve to smoothly integrate source material into his text.

The single marks within the double indicate that the word is in quotations marks in the original.

Hayes 2

What exactly is cloning? According to the National Bioethics Advisory Commission (NBAC), the word "in its most simple and strict sense . . . refers to a precise genetic copy of a molecule, cell, plant, animal or human being" (13). This technique of cloning used by Dr. Wilmut's team to create Dolly is called somatic cell nuclear transplantation. Sex cells contain only one set of 23 chromosomes, whereas body cells house two sets for a total of 46. When the parent's sperm fertilizes the egg, 46 chromosomes establish a human. During nuclear transfer cloning, the fertilization step is skipped because "the nucleus is removed from an egg and replaced with the diploid nucleus of a somatic [body] cell" (NBAC 15). Therefore, there is only one true parent, and the clone will be the exact genetic copy of that parent. James D. Watson, Nobel-Prize-winning co-discoverer of the double helix configuration of DNA, is a strong supporter of this kind of genetic manipulation in pursuit of what he calls "'superpersons'" or "gene-bettered children" (563).

But as exciting as it sounds, such experimentation must be very carefully approached. The controversy over cloning involves both ethical and religious issues. Should humans "play God"? What if the process were used to create exact copies of evil people? What potential dreadful side effects might develop in cloned humans? What possible reasons can there be for wanting to clone humans? The suggested uses for cloned humans usually focus on replacing loved ones who

Paragraphs 3 and 4 are phrased entirely in Nate's own words. He has done enough reading on his topic to understand some of the questions and to supply his own responses to them. The paragraph consists of general knowledge that Nate has acquired and thus does not require any documentation.

Hayes 3

have died, particularly young children who have died tragically, either from illness or accident. The idea is that cloning the dead child would in effect replace the child that died. However, that new child would be a real person, with thoughts and feelings unique to him or her. The new child would only look like the dead child and have identical genetic material. He or she would grow up in an entirely different environment, even if the parents attempted to recreate the identical conditions in which the dead child was nurtured. It would simply be impossible to recreate those conditions. Furthermore, would the child not be damaged psychologically if she knew that she was replacing another child? There are simply too many unexplored questions associated with cloning.

An alternative to cloning a whole person is to clone an entity for making spare human parts. The idea is that a brainless clone might be produced that could supply crucial body parts, such as a heart, a liver, kidneys, and eyes. No one has figured out how to do such a thing in the first place, let alone suggest ways to deal with all the potential problems of dealing with such a creature. Such a step is obviously not the best use of human cloning.

One big question has to do with the high failure rate of cloning. Despite having been responsible for the first cloned mammal, Dr. Wilmut is very conservative in his views of the wisdom of carrying on full speed with cloning research because of its unreliability. In "Dolly's False Legacy," he

Nate combines a direct quotation and a paraphrase. He names the author and clearly refers to him for several sentences. The parenthetical citation tells the page number on which the quoted and paraphrased material is found.

Nate introduces the quotation by naming his source. The colon is called for because both the introductory statement and the quotation are complete sentences.

Hayes 4

identifies some of the likely problems a cloned human might have. For instance, Wilmut warns of the inefficiency of cloning, noting the high death rate in fetuses and live births when cloning is used in animal tests. This fact leads him to suggest that "these failure rates surely render unthinkable the notion of applying such treatment to humans" (564). Writer Rick Weiss cites one example of this difficulty in his article "Failure in Monkeys Hints at Human Cloning Snags": "Despite having tried 135 times, researchers in Oregon have 'utterly failed' to clone a single monkey" (2). These failures are particularly significant because of the genetic similarity between monkeys and humans. The implications for success in cloning humans are dismal indeed, much to the delight of those who disapprove of it.

A more useful line of inquiry and experimentation may lie in stem-cell research. Scientists and medical researchers, though, are excited about the potential for previously unimaginable achievements in the prevention and cure of debilitating or fatal diseases, such as cystic fibrosis, muscular dystrophy, or amyotropic lateral sclerosis (Lou Gehrig's disease). Embryonic stem cells are those that have not yet specialized. Scientists believe that such cells could be isolated and grown into "healthy replacement tissue" that could then be used in humans to cure just about any ailment known to humans (Lemonick 89). The healthy tissue would be surgically implanted

Hayes 5

into the body, replacing or repairing damaged tissue. Research in this area holds great promises, but, as with cloning, the subject of stem-cell research is riddled with controversy. Here the controversy is aimed at research on embryonic stem cells as opposed to adult stem cell research: "Hailed by some as a cure for deadly disease, derided by others as the destruction of human life, embryonic stem cells are at the center of a heated debate over science, religion and politics around the globe" (Kalb 50). Bioethics specialists like Robyn S. Shapiro have identified a number of "key ethical and legal/regulatory issues that surround embryonic stem cell research" (541). Despite these issues, the potential of stem cell research to identify, prevent, and/or cure diseases is exciting and very promising.

Researchers believe that stem cells hold the promise for curing such dreaded diseases as cancer or blood diseases like sickle-cell anemia. Even a cure for HIV seems not out of the question. While it is possible to cure some diseases with adult stem cells, most people agree that infinitely more promising are embryonic stem cells, "the blank-slate cells that give rise to all organs and tissue types and that (theoretically) can repair all forms of organic damage and disease. These endlessly malleable cells . . . have been touted as the cure for nearly every disease, and even as the antidote to aging and death" (Lenzer). Researchers believe that new, healthy genes can be generated to replace

Nate omits words from his source and uses ellipsis points, three spaced periods, to indicate that.

Hayes 6

those causing disease. Such research seems more feasible and far more preferable than research on cloning.

There are just far too many unanswered questions about cloning, and it is not easy to anticipate all the possible ramifications for mankind were it to be pursued. The bottom line is that ethical, psychological, social, and religion questions need to be explored, discussed, and resolved before research in genetic engineering that aims to create new life or significantly alter existing life can be allowed to continue. Stem-cell research seems far more promising and more practical than human cloning, which must remain in the realm of science fiction.

Hayes 7

Works Cited

Ackley, Katherine Anne, ed. *Perspectives on Contemporary Issues: Readings Across the Disciplines*, 5th ed. Boston: Wadsworth Cengage Learning, 2009. Print.

Kalb, Claudia. "The Life in a Cell; Stem-cell Researchers Find Fresh Hope for Curing Deadly Diseases—Along with New Controversies." *Newsweek International* 28 June 2004: 50. Web. 22 Sept. 2010.

Lemonick, Michael D. "Tomorrow's Tissue Factor." *Time* 11 Jan. 1999: 89. Online. InfoTrac College Edition. Web. 22 Sept. 2010.

Hayes 8

Lenzer, Jeanne. "Have We Entered the Stem-Cell Era?" *Discover*. Discover Magazine, 14 Dec. 2009. Web. 20 May 2010.

National Bioethics Advisory Commission (NBAC). *Cloning Human Beings*. Rockville, MD: NBAC, 1997. Print.

Pethokoukis, James. "Our Biotech Bodies, Ourselves" *U.S. News & World Report*. U.S. News & World Report, 23 May 2004. Web. 12 May 2010.

Shapiro, Robyn S. "Bioethics and the Stem Cell Research Debate." Ackley 540-45.

Watson, James D. "All for the Good." Ackley 561-63.

Weiss, Rick. "Failure in Monkeys Hints at Human Cloning Snags." *Washington Post* 29 Jan. 1999: A02. EBSCO. Web. 22 Sept. 2010.

Wilmut, Ian. "Dolly's False Legacy." Ackley 564-67.

WRITING A RESEARCH PAPER USING APA STYLE

The documentation style of the American Psychological Association (APA), also referred to as the *author–date system*, is used widely in the behavioral and social sciences. It differs from that of the Modern Language Association (MLA), used primarily in the humanities, in some significant ways. APA style cites sources in parenthetical notes in the sentences to which they refer, as does MLA style, but the contents of the notes differ. In the APA system, the year of publication is given in the parenthetical note, and page numbers are given only for quotations, not for paraphrases. Finally, sources are listed at the end of the paper on a page called *References* rather than *Works Cited*, and formatting for that page is quite different from formatting in MLA style. This section gives general guidelines for both parenthetical citations and composing a references page using APA style. The guidelines are accompanied by sample pages from a student research paper using APA documentation style. For complete guidelines on APA Style, consult the following book:

American Psychological Association. *Publication Manual of the American Psychological Association*. 6th ed. Washington: APA, 2010.

For the latest updates on APA Style, go to the official website of the American Psychological Association, located at www.apastyle.org.

PARENTHETICAL CITATIONS USING APA STYLE

Quotations.

- Include the author's last name, a comma, the year the work was published, another comma, and the page number, preceded by the abbreviation "p." or "pp.":

  > Many experts agree that "it is much easier and more comfortable to teach as one learned" (Chall, 2009, p. 21).

- If the source has two authors, name them both, and separate their names with an ampersand (&):

  > President Truman and his advisors were aware that the use of the bomb was no longer required to prevent an invasion of Japan by the Soviets (Alperovitz & Messer, 1991).

- Omit from the parenthetical citation any information given in the text:

  > Samuel E. Wood and Ellen R. Green Wood (2003a) note that sociobiologists believe that social and nurturing experiences can "intensify, diminish, or modify" personality traits (p. 272).

- If the author's name is given in the text, follow it with the year of publication in parentheses:

  > Nancy Paulu (1988) believes that children who are taught phonics "get off to a better start" than those who are not taught phonics (p. 51).

- For works with three to five authors, name all of the authors the first time you refer to the work, but give only the last name of the first author followed by "et al." in subsequent citations. For a work with six or more authors, give only the first author's last name, followed by "et al." for all citations, including the first.
- If the author's name is repeated in the same paragraph, it is not necessary to repeat the year. However, if the author is cited in another paragraph, give the year of the work again.
- For summaries and paraphrases, give author and year, but not the page number where the information appears:

  > Minnesota scientists have concluded that this data shows that genes are more influential than nurture on most personality traits (Bazell, 2007).

- If the source names no author, cite a short form of the title:

The twins were both born with musical abilities, but their unique experiences determined whether they acted on this ability ("How Genes Shape Personality," 2007).

Note: The first letter of each word in the short title is capitalized, but in the references list, only the first letter of the first word is capitalized.

- If you use two or more sources by the same author and they were published in the same year, add lowercase letters to refer to their order on the references page:

  Wood and Wood (2003a) observe that . . .
  Other authorities (Wood & Wood, 2003b) agree, pointing out that . . .

- If one of your sources quotes or refers to another, and you want to use the second source in your paper, use the words "cited in," followed by the source you read and the year the source was published. If you quote directly, give the page number of the source you read on which the quotation appeared:

  Gerald McClearn, a psychologist and twin researcher at Pennsylvania State University, explained personality development realistically when he said: "'A gene can produce a nudge in one direction or another, but it does not directly control behavior. It doesn't take away a person's free will'" (cited in "How Genes Shape Personality," 2007, p. 62).

- To cite electronic material, indicate the page, chapter, figure, table, or equation at the appropriate point in the text. Give page number(s) for quotations, if available. If the source does not provide page numbers, use paragraph number if available, preceded by the paragraph symbol or the abbreviation para. If neither page number or paragraph number is visible, cite the heading and the number of the paragraph so that the reader can locate the material at the website:

  (Merriwether, 2004, p. 27)
  (Johnson, 2009, para. 3)
  (Shaw, 2003, conclusion section, para. 1)

Abstract. Papers written in APA style often have an abstract, which succinctly summarizes its important points, instead of an outline. Here is the abstract of the paper by a group of students who surveyed classmates on various study and leisure-time patterns to discover whether biological sex has an influence on academic achievement:

EFFECT OF BIOLOGICAL SEX ON GRADES 2

Abstract

Can differences in academic achievement be explained on the basis of biological sex? We hypothesized that sex is not the dominating factor influencing the success of University of Wisconsin-Stevens Point (UWSP) students. We conducted a

EFFECT OF BIOLOGICAL SEX ON GRADES 3

survey of 108 college students, investigating their pastimes, study habits, work schedules and housing status in addition to their grade point averages (GPA). The data showed a small difference in GPAs with respect to sex, but not large enough for sex alone to be the deciding factor. Our hypothesis that sex alone does not account for academic success was proved. We found that other factors, such as length of time spent studying, the number of hours of work per week, and time spent partying, all play significant roles as well.

APA-STYLE REFERENCES LIST

- Bibliographic entries for all works cited in a paper are listed in alphabetical order on a page entitled References.
- After the first line of each entry, use a hanging indentation of five spaces.
- Give the last names and only the initials of the first and middle names of authors.
- The year of publication, in parentheses, follows the author's name.
- For a book, capitalize only proper nouns and the first word of the title and subtitle; italicize the title.
- If a book is edited, place the abbreviation "Ed." or "Eds." in parentheses after the name(s) of the editor(s).
- If a citation names two or more authors, each name is reversed and an ampersand (&), not the word *and*, is placed before the last name.
- For an article, book chapter title, or title of an essay in a collection, capitalize as for a book title and do not use quotation marks or italicize.
- Capitalize the first letters of all important words in the name of the periodical and italicize it.
- Use the abbreviations "p." and "pp." for inclusive page numbers of articles in newspapers, but not in magazines and journals. If volume number is given for a periodical, place it after the name of the periodical and italicize it. If an issue number is also given, place it in parentheses after the volume number, but do not italicize it:

Hamby, A. L. (2001, Spring). An American Democrat: A reevaluation of the personality of Harry S Truman. *Political Science Quarterly*, 106, 33–55.

Stephenson, F. (2002, Aug.). The phonics revival. *Florida Trend*, 45 (4), 10–24.

- If two or more works by the same author appear on the references list, put them in chronological order. Repeat the author's name each time, followed by the date in parentheses.
- If you cite two works of one author published in the same year, alphabetize them by title, and give each entry a lowercase letter: (1996a), (1996b).
- Words like "university" and "press" are spelled out, not abbreviated.

Below is the reference list for the group project of four students who used a survey for their primary source and supplemented with several secondary sources retrieved from the Internet.

EFFECT OF BIOLOGICAL SEX ON GRADES 15

References

Burke, P. (1989 June). Gender identity, sex, and school performance. *Social Psychology Quarterly*. Retrieved 2009 April 21, from http://www.jstor.org/pss/2786915

Duckworth, A. L., & Seligman, M. E. P. (2006 February). Self-discipline gives girls the edge: Gender in self-discipline, grades and achievement test scores. *Journal of Education Psychology*. Retrieved April 21, 2009, from www.sas.upenn.edu/~duckwort/images/GenderDifferencesFeb2006.pdf

Pajares, F. (2002). Gender and perceived self-efficacy in self-regulated learning. *Theory into Practice*. Retrieved April 21, 2009, from http://www.jstor.org/pss/1477463

Wang, Y., Arboldea, A., Shelly II, M.C., & Whalen, D.F. (2004). The influence of residence hall community on academic success of male and female undergraduate students. *Journal of College & University Student Housing*, 33 (1), 16-22.

SAMPLE PAGES FROM A STUDENT RESEARCH PAPER USING APA STYLE

Here are sample pages, with marginal comments, of a student research paper illustrating in-text citations using APA style. The first several pages of the paper are given, along with the concluding paragraph and list of references.

Indicate what your running head, or page header, is by writing "Running head: Shortened Version of Title" on title page. Use the running head on every page of your paper, flush left. Number every page, beginning with the cover page, placing the number flush right.

PHONICS 1

The Phonics Controversyby

University of Wisconsin

Cory L. Vandertie

Professor Kathy Mitchell

English 102

19 April 2010

The introductory paragraphs provide background for the research topic.

PHONICS 2

The Phonics Controversy

In recent years, school officials, teachers, and parents have been wrestling with the issue of how best to teach reading, with the controversy often centering on the conflict over the effectiveness of phonics in such instruction. Rudolph Flesch, in his best-selling 1955 book *Why Johnny Can't Read*, was one of the first educators to advocate the use of phonics in reading classes. His book not only brought national attention to the reading problems

Cory read about the Flesch book in Groff's book, hence "as cited in."

of America's children but also endorsed the use of phonics to overcome those problems (as cited in Groff, 2009) Neither the problem of children's inability to read effectively nor the effectiveness of phonics instruction has been satisfactorily addressed in the 50 years since Flesch's book, however. Regna Lee Wood (2003) warned about declining literacy rates. In "That's Right—They're Wrong: Decline in Reading Ability Due to Abandonment of Phonics," she points out that in 1930, only 3 million Americans could not read, but in 1990, 30 to 35 million U.S. citizens could not read and were considered to be truly illiterate. In 2000, the National Assessment of Educational Progress (NAEP) reported that "more than a third (37 percent) of America's fourth grade children (roughly 10 million kids) could not read at even a basic level" and of those 10 million, "up to 40 percent will eventually drop out of high school" (as cited in Stephenson, 2002). Statistics such as these have created tension among educators as they debate how to improve reading skills.

Although only the first letter of the first word in the title of a work is capitalized in the references list, in your paper you must capitalize as you would other titles.

The declining literacy rate is an alarming indicator that something must be done differently in our schools. Wood (2008) discovered that 70 percent of U.S. high school students cannot read ninth-grade assignments and that 30 percent of U.S. twelfth graders cannot read at a fourth-grade level. Educators and parents who are concerned about this dramatic increase in the illiteracy rate and the inability of the majority of students to read at their own grade levels cannot refuse to explore all possible explanations for the failure of our schools to teach reading adequately. One avenue for

Although there are two works by Regna Lee Wood on Cory's list of references, the date of publication indicates the specific work being cited.

PHONICS 4

exploration that may prove fruitful is the phonics controversy. Parents, teachers, and reading experts familiar with phonics all differ sharply in their views, compounding the dilemma of whether phonics instruction should be included in American schools.

What role *does* phonics education play in the teaching of reading?

More than 450 years ago, phonics instruction was introduced to help young readers learn more about the relationship between letters and sound (Groff, 2009). Some researchers think that phonics has been used to teach reading since the time of ancient Greeks. Chall (2009) describes the method "as a tool for helping beginners identify words accurately so that they can read texts with comprehension earlier and more efficiently" (p. 4).

Give the page number on which a direct quotation appears in the source.

Groff (2009) agrees that phonics instruction can be very useful for the development of children's word recognition skills. The problem is how to convince parents and teachers of the benefits of phonics. Wood (2002) believes that the horrible failure of our schools to teach children to read skillfully began years ago. She writes that "[the failure of schools to teach reading] began in 1929 and 1930 when hundreds of primary teachers, guided by college reading professors, stopped teaching beginners to read by matching sounds with letters that spell sounds" (p. 52).

Phonics is not the entire answer to the question of how best to teach children to read, however. Most reading experts agree that "the most the application of phonics can do is help children produce the approximate pronunciation of words" (Groff, 2009,

p. 6). Roberts (2009), writing for *Parents* magazine, reports that phonics may not help all children learn to pronounce words. He explains that anyone who has a visual or auditory handicap will find it harder to read using phonics. For instance, Roberts points out that a child who has suffered from an ear infection that caused temporary hearing loss at an early age may find it difficult to learn to read by using phonics because of missing out on experiencing sound discrimination.

* * * * *

In conclusion, many experts believe that we have the ability and the knowledge to educate our schoolchildren more effectively by using phonics. But while both traditional and experimental evidence supports the use of phonics, the debate continues. Educators who are not familiar with phonics instruction must be enlightened, perhaps with in-service workshops from experts on phonics instruction. Parents, too, may need to be convinced.

Reading experts must be willing to work together to resolve some of the issues in the phonics debate, perhaps by putting together a combination of approaches to the teaching of reading that includes phonics. The bottom line is that we all must work to find a solution to the appalling rate of adult illiteracy in this country and the unsettling inability of students to read at their own grade levels. We must find solutions to these problems, or we risk jeopardizing not only our children's futures but our own.

PHONICS 6

References

Chall, J. S. (2009). *The role of phonics in teaching reading*. Washington, DC: U.S. Department of Education, Office of Educational Research and Improvement.

Groff, P. (2009). *Modern phonics instruction.* Washington, DC: U.S. Department of Education, Office of Educational Research and Improvement.

Johnson, D. (2009). Critical issue: Addressing the literacy needs of emergent and early readers. North Central Regional Educational Laboratory. Retrieved April 7, 2010, from www.ncrel.org/sdrs/areas/issues/content/cntareas/reading/1i100.htm Roberts, F. (2009, January). Does phonics cure reading problems? *Parents*, p. 49.

Stephenson, F. (2002, August). The phonics revival. *Florida Trend*, 45 (4), 10-24.

Wood, R. L. (2002, September 14). That's right—they're wrong: Decline in reading ability due to abandonment of phonics. *National Review*, 49-52.

Wood, R. L. (2003). *Time for a "2 By 1" Core Curriculum*. Oklahoma City: Oklahoma Council of Public Affairs.

STUDENT PAPER, APA STYLE, WITH TITLE PAGE, ABSTRACT, BODY OF PAPER, AND REFERENCES

EFFECTS OF HIS MOTHER'S DEATH ON JOSEPH 1

Effects of His Mother's Death on

Joseph's Social and Emotional Development

Indiana University

Laurel L. Yahi

Ed P240

Professor Jennings

12 May 2010

EFFECTS OF HIS MOTHER'S DEATH ON JOSEPH 2

Abstract

Four-year-old Joseph suddenly lost his mother two years ago. I have observed Joseph in my home daycare for 50 hours a week since his mother's death. With ample opportunity to observe him in this natural setting, I set about determining whether his mother's death might have long-term effects on Joseph's social and emotional development. At play, when working alone, at lunch time, and nap time, Joseph's cognitive abilities, vocabulary skills, willingness to listen to and obey adults, and social interaction skills appear normal for his age. He is well liked by the other children in the daycare. His progress, determination to learn, and intellectual growth all reflect a natural resiliency that lets him grow and mature without serious developmental problems. With a strong support system and a loving family, he should be able to grow into a healthy adult with no lasting negative effects on his ability to form relationships, participate fully in social settings, and enjoy good emotional health.

Effects of His Mother's Death on Joseph's Social and Emotional Development

Two years ago, when Joseph was just 26 months old, his mother died. His world suddenly took a drastic turn. Joseph was embraced by a strong support system, but how would this huge life-altering event affect who he is today and who Joseph will be as an adult? Joseph is Caucasian and his immediate family now includes only his father and a brother who is 13 months younger. He spends 50 hours a week in my home daycare. I've observed Joseph with ecological validity, taking note of the effects of him in and on the naturalistic setting of the daycare as part of his daily routine and interactions with his friends (Bronfenbrenner, 1977). I will theorize what possible effects the death of Joseph's mother may have on his social and emotional development.

Joseph's physical development is average for a four year old. He has lost his rounded babyish appearance, gained boundless physical energy, and acquired fine motor skills (McDevitt and Ormrod, 2007). Joseph's gross motor skills involve rough and tumble play, characterized by good-natured "fighting" (McDevitt and Ormrod, 2007). He frequently uses his imagination to become Superman and fight with swords. Just two months ago, Joseph struggled with knowing how his coloring should look but was unable to create the desired results because of physical developmental limitations. He persevered, however, and made the leap he wanted in his abilities. Part of these changes came with natural growth, part was from instruction, but most was due to his earnest determination. Joseph's accomplishments were the result of desire and consistent, repeated practice (McDevitt and Ormrod, 2007).

Joseph is firmly placed in the preoperational stage of cognitive development. He uses objects to represent the real world (e.g., toy shopping cart as lawn mower) (McDevitt and Ormrod, 2007). His vocabulary and language skills continue to build, as illustrated in the October 3rd anecdotal record, in which he participated in an elaborate imaginary story with Dylan. Their back-and-forth contributions allowed Joseph to build his story in conjunction with Dylan's. Also typical of the preoperational stage is that children are unable to think in logical, adult-like ways (p. 199). Joseph's developing language skills have enabled him to engage in the fantasy and make-believe on which he thrives (McDevitt and Ormrod, 2007). One example of Joseph's fantasy thinking is illustrated in the April 21st interview. When I asked Joseph if he knew why his mother died, he replied, "I know why she died because I want Christmas to come up. Diego can save her and the Credible Hulk can save her." This illogical thinking is typical of the preoperational stage and will change as he begins to make logical inferences and starts to make sense of his reasoning (McDevitt and Ormrod, 2007).

Joseph faced a traumatic loss not experienced by many children his age and the effects on his emotional development are immeasurable. To begin to heal from the emotional devastation of losing his mother, Joseph had to draw on his natural resilience. Everyone deals with stressors in their lives; how they deal with adversity is the result of a correlation of their temperament with personal characteristics (Harvey and Delfabbro, 2004). In addition, resilient children exhibit active problem-solving abilities, gain positive attention from others, and perceive life from a positive perspective (Harvey and Delfabbro, 2004). Joseph is well liked by his friends in the daycare. According to the Social Attributes Checklist taken April 10th, it's clear that Joseph is socially well balanced. This is attributable in part to his inherent natural resiliency that continues to enable him to cope with losing his mother.

Urie Bronfenbrenner (1977) taught us that children are at the center of five social systems which affect and support their lives. These ecosystems are continuously changing, an intertwining influence on each aspect of their lives (Bronfenbrenner, 1977). Not only do Joseph's environment and the events he experiences have an impact on him, but he also has an impact on his environment and those in it. By rereading the anecdotal records, I noticed Joseph's strong sensitivity. When he cries, I run to comfort him. His mother's death affected other ecosystems surrounding him, including mine. I feel deep empathy for him and want to fill the maternal void. Through grieving, Joseph's sensitivity may have become more pronounced which in turn made those around him move to comfort him. Bronfenbrenner (1977) explains that through ecological transition, change "invariably alters the relations between others" (p. 525). The single ecological transitional event of losing his mother already has a rippling effect in shaping the course of Joseph's life.

An infant's early attachment sets the stage for future relationships (McDevitt and Ormrod, 2007). Joseph lost his primary attachment figure, his mother. Some research suggests that this could cause Joseph to be untrusting in future relationships, but other research shows that the maternal bond doesn't firmly decide the strength of trust children will have in others (McDevitt and Ormrod, 2007). Children form "several mental representations of what interpersonal relationships are like" (McDevitt and Ormrod, 2007, p. 415). John Bowlby, one of psychiatry's leading theorist, expanded consideration of childhood experiences of parental death. He argued that healthy mourning depended on certain environmental factors including "the extent of the child's network of support from extended family and others" (as cited in Hurd, 1999, p. 19). To assist Joseph's level of secure attachments, I strive to offer him warm, sensitive care, give positive response to newly developed abilities, and set limits in a gently way for unacceptable behavior (McDevitt and Ormrod, 2007).

Life-changing transitions in ecological environments alter how children develop and interact with others (Bronfenbrenner, 1977). When these changes occur in young children, they can have long-term effects. In Joseph's short lifespan, he has experienced a major transition that has already had a profound effect on him. This is especially evident in his sensitivity to criticism or his feelings of insecurity. The loss of his mother may continue to affect and change him, but I've learned that with nurturing, understanding, and loving care Joseph will hopefully in time lose his fragility and have a fulfilling adulthood with solid relationships.

References

Bronfenbrenner, U. (1977). Toward an experimental ecology of human development. Cornell University: American Psychologist.

Harvey, J., and Delfabbro, P. H. (2004). *Psychological resilience in disadvantaged youth*. University of Adelaide: Australian Psychologist. Retrieved April 29, 2010, from Ebscohost, Academic Search Premier.

Hurd, Russell C. (1999). *Adults view their childhood bereavement experiences*. Canton, Ohio: Kent State University. Retrieved April 29, 2010, from Ebscohost, Academic Search Premier.

McDevitt, T., and Ormrod, J. (2007). *Child development and education* (3rd ed). Upper Saddle River: Pearson Education.

PART • TWO

Media Studies, Popular Culture, and the Arts

Music and Video Games

People's opinions about what expressive forms can be considered works of art change and evolve over time. It is likely that few people would think of video games when asked to name works of arts. However, Henry Jenkins in "Art Form for the Digital Age," written when video games were beginning to get creative in the scope and range of what they offered players, argues that video games are a legitimate art form that must be taken seriously. He writes that they play an important part in "shaping the aesthetic sensibility of the 21st century." As you read what he has to say in defense of his proposition, consider the video games that you, your friends, or your children play. Does Jenkins make a compelling case for viewing them as art?

Certainly video games, if not viewed as works of art, are treated seriously by young people, particularly boys, and many writers have explored the larger issues of whether video games have value and how to account for the fact that they are a "gendered" phenomenon. Critics of video games question whether they have any "redeeming social value" and explore how to account for their wild popularity with boys but girls' almost indifferent attitude toward them. The subject of gender differences is treated in greater length in this book in Chapter 14, but for an intriguing commentary on the effects of playing violent video games on young people in this chapter, read Karen Sternheimer's "Do Video Games Kill?" An academic whose article was published in a sociological journal, Sternheimer argues that blaming youth violence on video games is unfair and inaccurate. Citing newspaper articles and studies done following some high-profile school shootings in the late 1990s, she argues that much more than playing violent video games is to blame for the deviant behavior of a few white middle-class males who murdered their classmates.

Although video games are a very recent development in popular culture, evidence suggests that music has been an integral part of humans' lives from their earliest existence. Song and instrumental music have spoken to, soothed, excited, and otherwise influenced humans of virtually all cultures and time periods in a seemingly endless variety of styles, subject matter, and methods of delivery. Each new musician, composer, or singer hopes to create a style uniquely his or her own, often acknowledging the influence of a previous form or artist. Sometimes a wholly new form of musical expression is created, from which generations of musicians and music lovers in turn take their inspiration.

Among the most controversial forms of contemporary music are certain types of rock, hip-hop, and gangsta rap. Their lyrics generate heated debate, with defenders of the music just as convinced of their legitimacy as their detractors are that that such lyrics are abusive and even dangerous. Like violent video games, sexually explicit and violently graphic music lyrics come under frequent and vocal attack from those who believe they have devastating effects on certain groups of people. Cathleen Rountree and Jennifer McLune hold opposing viewpoints on the subject of hip-hop music, which is often the target of criticism. Rountree's "In Defense of Hip-Hop" calls for a sympathetic understanding of the hip-hop culture. She believes that hip-hop has been a scapegoat and urges readers not to blame hip-hop artists for the violent and misogynistic content of their music because "they're simply reflecting their surrounding environment." In contrast, McLune asserts in "Hip-Hop's Betrayal of Black Women" that "women too are raised in this environment of poverty and violence but have yet to produce the same negative and hateful representation of black men that male rappers are capable of making against women." As you read those two essays, think about your reaction to and understanding of hip-hop and gangsta rap music. With which writer are you more sympathetic? Is one more persuasive than the other?

ART FORM FOR THE DIGITAL AGE

HENRY JENKINS

Henry Jenkins is Provost's Professor of Communication, Journalism, and Cinematic Arts at the University of Southern California. Among his publications are dozens of periodical articles and twelve books on various aspects of the media and popular culture, beginning in 1992 with What Made Pistachio Nuts? Early Sound Comedy and the Vaudeville Aesthetic *and* Textual Poachers: Television Fans and Participatory Culture. *Among his other books are* Classical Hollywood Comedy *(1994), coedited with Kristine Brunovska Karnick;* From Barbie to Mortal Kombat: Gender and Computer Games *(1998), coedited with Justine Cassell;* Hop on Pop: The Politics and Pleasures of Popular Culture *(2003), coedited with Tara McPherson and Jane Shattuc;* Rethinking Media Change: The Aesthetics of Transition *(2003), coedited with David Thorburn;* Convergence Culture: Where Old and New Media Collide *(2006); and* Fans, Bloggers and Gamers: Exploring Participatory Culture *(2006).* His weblog address is www.henryjenkins.org. This article was first published in the September 2000 issue of *Technology Review.*

Video games shape our culture. It's time we took them seriously.

Last year, Americans bought over 215 million computer and video games. That's more than two games per household. The video game industry made almost as much money from gross domestic income as Hollywood. So are video games a massive drain on our income, time and energy? A new form of "cultural pollution," as one U.S. senator described them? The "nightmare before Christmas," in the words of another? Are games teaching our children to kill, as countless op-ed pieces have warned?

No. Computer games are art—a popular art, an emerging art, a largely unrecognized art, but art nevertheless.

4 Over the past 25 years, games have progressed from the primitive two-paddles-and-a-ball Pong to the sophistication of Final Fantasy, a participatory story with cinema-quality graphics that unfolds over nearly 100 hours of play. The computer game has been a killer app for the home PC, increasing consumer demand for vivid graphics, rapid processing, greater memory and better sound. The release this fall of the Sony Playstation 2, coupled with the announcement of next-generation consoles by Nintendo and Microsoft, signals a dramatic increase in the resources available to game designers.

Games increasingly influence contemporary cinema, helping to define the frenetic pace and model the multi-directional plotting of *Run Lola Run*, providing the role-playing metaphor for *Being John Malkovich* and encouraging a fascination with the slippery line between reality and digital illusion in *The Matrix*. At high schools and colleges across the country, students discuss games with the same passions with which earlier generations debated the merits of the New American Cinema. Media studies programs report a growing number of their students want to be game designers rather than filmmakers.

The time has come to take games seriously as an important new popular art shaping the aesthetic sensibility of the 21st century. I will admit that discussing the art of video games conjures up comic images: tuxedo-clad and jewel-bedecked patrons admiring the latest Streetfighter, middle-aged academics pontificating on the impact of Cubism on Tetris, bleeps and zaps disrupting our silent contemplation at the Guggenheim. Such images tell us more about our contemporary notion of art—as arid and stuffy, as the property of an educated and economic elite, as cut off from everyday experience—than they tell us about games.

New York's Whitney Museum found itself at the center of controversy about digital art when it recently included web artists in its prestigious biannual show. Critics didn't believe the computer could adequately express the human spirit. But they're misguided. The computer is simply a tool, one that offers artists new resources and opportunities for reaching the public; it is human creativity that makes art. Still, one can only imagine how the critics would have responded to the idea that something as playful, unpretentious and widely popular as a computer game might be considered art.

In 1925, leading literary and arts critic Gilbert Seldes took a radical approach to the aesthetics of popular culture in a treatise titled *The Seven Lively Arts*. Adopting what was then a controversial position, Seldes argued that America's primary contributions to artistic expression had come through emerging forms of popular culture such as jazz, the Broadway musical, the Hollywood cinema and the comic strip. While these arts have gained cultural respectability over the past 75 years, each was disreputable when Seldes staked out his position.

Readers then were skeptical of Seldes' claims about cinema in particular for many of the same reasons that contemporary critics dismiss games—they were suspicious of cinema's commercial motivations and technological origins, concerned about Hollywood's appeals to violence and eroticism, and insistent that cinema had not yet produced works of lasting value. Seldes, on the other hand, argued that cinema's popularity demanded that we reassess its aesthetic qualities.

Cinema and other popular arts were to be celebrated, Seldes said, because they were so deeply imbedded in everyday life, because they were democratic arts embraced by average citizens. Through streamlined styling and syncopated rhythms, they captured the vitality of contemporary urban experience. They took the very machinery of the industrial age, which many felt dehumanizing, and found within it the resources for expressing individual visions, for reasserting basic human needs, desires and fantasies. And these new forms were still open to experimentation and discovery. They were, in Seldes' words, "lively arts."

Games represent a new lively art, one as appropriate for the digital age as those earlier media were for the machine age. They open up new aesthetic experiences and transform the computer screen into a realm of experimentation and innovation that is broadly accessible. And games have been embraced by a public that has otherwise been unimpressed by much of what passes for digital art. Much as the salon arts of the 1920s seemed sterile alongside the vitality and inventiveness of popular culture, contemporary efforts to create interactive narrative through modernist hypertext or avant-garde installation art seem lifeless and pretentious alongside the creativity that game designers bring to their craft.

12 Much of what Seldes told us about the silent cinema seems remarkably apt for thinking about games. Silent cinema, he argued, was an art of expressive movement. He valued the speed and dynamism of D.W. Griffith's last-minute races to the rescue, the physical grace of Chaplin's pratfalls and the ingenuity of Buster Keaton's engineering feats. Games also depend upon an art of expressive movement, with characters defined through their distinctive ways of propelling themselves through space, and successful products structured around a succession of spectacular stunts and predicaments. Will future generations look back on Lara Croft doing battle with a pack of snarling wolves as the 21st-century equivalent of Lillian Gish making her way across the ice floes in *Way Down East?* The art of silent cinema was also an art of atmospheric design. To watch a silent masterpiece like Fritz Lang's Metropolis is to be drawn into a world where meaning is carried by the placement of shadows, the movement of machinery and the organization of space. If anything, game designers have pushed beyond cinema in terms of developing expressive and fantastic environments that convey a powerful sense of mood, provoke our curiosity and amusement, and motivate us to explore.

Seldes wrote at a moment when cinema was maturing as an expressive medium and filmmakers were striving to enhance the emotional experience of going to the movies—making a move from mere spectacle towards character and consequence. It remains to be seen whether games can make a similar transition. Contemporary games can pump us full of adrenaline, they can make us laugh, but they have not yet provoked us to tears. And many have argued that, since games don't have characters of human complexity or stories that stress the consequences of our actions, they cannot achieve the status of true art. Here, we must be careful not to confuse the current transitional state of an emerging medium with its full potential. As I visit game companies, I see some of the industry's best minds struggling with this question and see strong evidence that the games released over the next few years will bring us closer and closer to the quality of characterization we have come to expect from other forms of popular narrative.

In the March 6 [2000] issue of *Newsweek*, senior editor Jack Kroll argued that audiences will probably never be able to care as deeply about pixels on the computer screen as they care about characters in films: "Moviemakers don't have to simulate human beings; they are right there, to be recorded and orchestrated ... The top-heavy titillation of Tomb Raider's Lara Croft falls flat next to the face of Sharon Stone. ..."

Yet countless viewers cry when Bambi's mother dies, and World War II veterans can tell you they felt real lust for *Esquire*'s Vargas girls. We have learned to care as much about creatures of pigment as we care about images of real people. Why should pixels be different?

In the end, games may not take the same path as cinema. Game designers will almost certainly develop their own aesthetic principles as they confront the challenge of balancing our competing desires for storytelling and interactivity. It remains to be seen whether games can provide players the freedom they want and still provide an emotionally satisfying and thematically meaningful shape to the experience. Some of the best games—Tetris comes to mind—have nothing to do with storytelling. For all we know, the future art of games may look more like architecture or dance than cinema.

16 Such questions warrant close and passionate engagement not only within the game industry or academia, but also by the press and around the dinner table. Even Kroll's grumpy dismissal of games has sparked heated discussion and forced designers to refine their own grasp of the medium's distinctive features. Imagine what a more robust form of criticism could contribute. We need critics who know games the way Pauline Kael knew movies and who write about them with an equal degree of wit and wisdom.

When *The Seven Lively Arts* was published, silent cinema was still an experimental form, each work stretching the medium in new directions. Early film critics played vital functions in documenting innovations and speculating about their potential. Computer games are in a similar phase. We have not had time to codify what experienced game designers know, and we have certainly not yet established a canon of great works that might serve as exemplars. There have been real creative accomplishments in games, but we haven't really sorted out what they are and why they matter.

But games do matter, because they spark the imaginations of our children, taking them on epic quests to strange new worlds. Games matter because our children no longer have access to real-world play spaces at a time when we've paved over the vacant lots to make room for more condos and the streets make parents nervous. If children are going to have opportunities for exploratory play, play that encourages cognitive development and fosters problem-solving skills, they will do so in the virtual environments of games. Multi-player games create opportunities for leadership, competition, teamwork and collaboration—for nerdy kids, not just for high school football players. Games matter because they form the digital equivalent of the Head Start program, getting kids excited about what computers can do.

The problem with most contemporary games isn't that they are violent but that they are banal, formulaic and predictable. Thoughtful criticism can marshal support for innovation and experimentation in the industry, much as good film criticism helps focus attention on neglected independent films. Thoughtful criticism could even contribute to our debates about game violence. So far, the censors and culture warriors have gotten more or less a free ride because we almost take for granted that games are culturally worthless. We should instead look at games as an emerging art form—one that does not simply simulate violence but increasingly offers new ways to understand violence—and talk about how to strike a balance between this form of expression and social responsibility. Moreover, game criticism may provide a means of holding the game industry more accountable for its choices. In the wake of the

Columbine shootings, game designers are struggling with their ethical responsibilities as never before, searching for ways of appealing to empowerment fantasies that don't require exploding heads and gushing organs. A serious public discussion of this medium might constructively influence these debates, helping identify and evaluate alternatives as they emerge.

20 As the art of games matures, progress will be driven by the most creative and forward-thinking minds in the industry, those who know that games can be more than they have been, those who recognize the potential of reaching a broader public, of having a greater cultural impact, of generating more diverse and ethically responsible content and of creating richer and more emotionally engaging stories. But without the support of an informed public and the perspective of thoughtful critics, game developers may never realize that potential.

PERSONAL RESPONSE

Do you find video games aesthetically appealing in any way? If you play video games, explain their appeal, and if you do not play them, explain why not.

QUESTIONS FOR CLASS OR SMALL-GROUP DISCUSSION

1. Jenkins begins by stating, "Video games shape our culture." How does he support that statement? Do you agree with Jenkins on the importance of video games in "shaping the aesthetic sensibility of the 21st century" (paragraph 7)?
2. In paragraph 5, Jenkins gives examples of video games that illustrate his observation that they have progressed over time from a primitive state to sophistication. What criteria does he use to make that judgment? What examples of currently popular video games can you name that illustrate his point? If you do not believe that they have continued to evolve, give examples that disprove his point.
3. What is Jenkins' argumentative strategy? That is, what is his proposition? What is his supporting evidence? Does he acknowledge opposing viewpoints or make any concessions? Does he urge action? How persuasive do you find the essay?
4. Explain Gilbert Seldes' approach to popular culture (paragraph 9 and following) and assess its applicability to the question of video games as a legitimate art form.
5. In several places, Jenkins states that certain things in the development of video games "remain to be seen" (paragraphs 14 and 16). He also writes in his concluding paragraph about the potential of video games. Do you believe that video games have realized the potential that Jenkins thought they had in 2000? Do you consider it necessary or inevitable that video games evolve over time and, if so, what form might that evolution take?

DO VIDEO GAMES KILL?

KAREN STERNHEIMER

Karen Sternheimer, whose work focuses on youth and popular culture, teaches in the sociology department at the University of Southern California and is the author of Connecting Popular Culture and Social Problems: Why the Media Is Not the Answer *(2009),* Kids These Days: Facts and Fictions About Today's Youth *(2006), and* It's Not the Media: The Truth about Pop Culture's Influence on Children *(2003). Her commentary has been published in several newspapers, and she has appeared on numerous television and radio programs. This article appeared in the Winter 2007 issue of* Contexts, *the journal of the American Sociological Association.*

As soon as it was released in 1993, a video game called *Doom* became a target for critics. Not the first, but certainly one of the most popular first-person shooter games, *Doom* galvanized fears that such games would teach kids to kill. In the years after its release, *Doom* helped video gaming grow into a multibillion-dollar industry, surpassing Hollywood box-office revenues and further fanning public anxieties.

Then came the school shootings in Paducah, Kentucky; Springfield, Oregon; and Littleton, Colorado. In all three cases, press accounts emphasized that the shooters loved *Doom*, making it appear that the critics' predictions about video games were coming true.

But in the ten years following *Doom*'s release, homicide arrest rates fell by 77 percent among juveniles. School shootings remain extremely rare; even during the 1990s, when fears of school violence were high, students had less than a 7 in 10 million chance of being killed at school.

4 During that time, video games became a major part of many young people's lives, few of whom will ever become violent, let alone kill. So why is the video game explanation so popular?

Contemporary Folk Devils

In 2000 the FBI issued a report on school rampage shootings, finding that their rarity prohibits the construction of a useful profile of a "typical" shooter. In the absence of a simple explanation, the public symbolically linked these rare and complex events to the shooters' alleged interest in video games, finding in them a catchall explanation for what seemed unexplainable—the white, middle-class school shooter. However, the concern about video games is out of proportion to their actual threat.

Politicians and other moral crusaders frequently create "folk devils," individuals or groups defined as evil and immoral. Folk devils allow us to channel our blame and fear, offering a clear course of action to remedy what many believe to be a growing problem. Video games, those who play them, and those who create them have become contemporary folk devils because they seem to pose a threat to children.

Such games have come to represent a variety of social anxieties: about youth violence, new computer technology, and the apparent decline in the ability of adults to control what young people do and know. Panics about youth and popular culture have emerged with the appearance of many new technologies. Over the past century, politicians have complained that cars, radio, movies, rock music, and even comic books caused youth immorality and crime, calling for control and sometimes censorship.

8 Acting on concerns like these, politicians often engage in battles characterized as between good and evil. The unlikely team of Senators Joseph Lieberman, Sam Brownback, Hillary Rodham Clinton, and Rick Santorum introduced a bill in March 2005 that called for $90 million to fund studies on media effects. Lieberman commented, "America is a media-rich society, but despite the flood of information, we still lack perhaps the most important piece of information—what effect are media having on our children?" Regardless of whether any legislation passes, the senators position themselves as protecting children and benefit from the moral panic they help to create.

Constructing Culpability

Politicians are not the only ones who blame video games. Since 1997, 199 newspaper articles have focused on video games as a central explanation for the Paducah, Springfield, and Littleton shootings. This helped to create a groundswell of fear that schools were no longer safe and that rampage shootings could happen wherever there were video games. The shootings legitimated existing concerns about the new medium and about young people in general. Headlines such as "Virtual Realities Spur School Massacres" (*Denver Post*, July 27, 1999), "Days of Doom" *(Pittsburgh Post-Gazette*, May 14, 1999), "Bloodlust Video Games Put Kids in the Crosshairs" (*Denver Post*, May 30, 1999), and "All Those Who Deny Any Linkage between Violence in Entertainment and Violence in Real Life, Think Again" (*New York Times*, April 26, 1999) insist that video games are the culprit.

These headlines all appeared immediately after the Littleton shooting, which had the highest death toll and inspired most (176) of the news stories alleging a video game connection.

Across the country, the press attributed much of the blame to video games specifically, and to Hollywood more generally. The *Pittsburgh Post-Gazette* article "Days of Doom" noted that "eighteen people have now died at the hands of avid *Doom* players." The *New York Times* article noted above began, "By producing increasingly violent media, the entertainment industry has for decades engaged in a lucrative dance with the devil," evoking imagery of a fight against evil. It went on to construct video games as a central link: "The two boys apparently responsible for the massacre in Littleton, Colo., last week were, among many other things, accomplished players of the ultraviolent video game *Doom*. And Michael Carneal , the 14-year-old boy who opened fire on a prayer group in a Paducah, Ky., school foyer in 1997, was also known to be a video-game expert."

12 Just as many stories insisted that video games deserved at least partial blame, editorial pages around the country made the connection as well:

> President Bill Clinton is right. He said this shooting was no isolated incident, that Kinkel and other teens accused of killing teachers and fellow students reflect a changing culture of violence on television and in movies and video games. (*Cleveland Plain Dealer*, May 30, 1998)

> The campaign to make Hollywood more responsible . . . should proceed full speed ahead. (*Boston Herald*, April 9, 2000)

> Make no mistake, Hollywood is contributing to a culture that feeds on and breeds violence. . . . When entertainment companies craft the most shocking video games and movies they can, peddle their virulent wares to an impressionable audience with abandon, then shrug off responsibility for our culture of violence, they deserve censure. (*St. Louis Post-Dispatch*, April 12, 2000)

The video game connection took precedence in all these news reports. Some stories mentioned other explanations, such as the shooters' social rejection, feelings of alienation at school, and depression, but these were treated mostly as minor factors compared with video games. Reporters gave these other reasons far less attention than violent video games, and frequently discussed them at the end of the articles.

The news reports typically introduce experts early in the stories who support the video game explanation. David Grossman, a former army lieutenant described as a professor of "killology," has claimed that video games are "murder simulators" and serve as an equivalent to military training. Among the 199 newspaper articles published, 17 of them mentioned or quoted Grossman. Additionally, an attorney who has filed several lawsuits against video game producers wrote an article for the *Denver Post* insisting that the games are to blame. By contrast, only seven articles identified sociologists as experts. Writers routinely presented alternative explanations as rebuttals but rarely explored them in depth.

Reporting on Research

By focusing so heavily on video games, news reports downplay the broader social contexts. While a handful of articles note the roles that guns, poverty, families, and the organization of schools may play in youth violence in general, when reporters mention research to explain the shooters' behavior, the vast majority of studies cited concern media effects, suggesting that video games are a central cause.

16 Since the early days of radio and movies, investigators have searched for possible effects—typically negative—that different media may have on audiences, especially children. Such research became more intense following the rise in violent crime in the United States between the 1960s and early 1990s, focusing primarily on television. Several hundred studies asked whether exposure to media violence predicts involvement in actual violence.

Although often accepted as true—one scholar has gone so far as to call the findings about the effects of media violence on behavior a "law"—this body of research has been highly controversial. One such study fostered claims that television had led to more than 10,000 murders in the United States and Canada during the 20th century. This and many other media-effects studies rely on correlation analysis, often finding small but sometimes statistically significant links between exposure to media violence and aggressive behavior.

But such studies do not demonstrate that media violence causes aggressive behavior, only that the two phenomena exist together. Excluding a host of other factors (such as the growing unrest during the civil rights and antiwar movements, and the disappearance of jobs in central cities) may make it seem that a direct link exists between the introduction of television and homicides. In all likelihood any connection is incidental.

It is equally likely that more aggressive people seek out violent entertainment. Aggression includes a broad range of emotions and behaviors, and is not always synonymous with violence. Measures of aggression in media-effects research have varied widely, from observing play between children and inanimate objects to counting the number of speeding tickets a person received. Psychologist Jonathan Freedman reviewed every media-violence study published in English and concluded that "the majority of studies produced evidence that is inconsistent or even contradicts" the claim that exposure to media violence causes real violence.

20 Recently, video games have become a focus of research. Reviews of this growing literature have also been mixed. A 2001 meta-analysis in *Psychological Science* concluded that video games "will increase aggressive behavior," while a similar review published that same year in a different journal found that "it is not possible to determine whether video game violence affects aggressive behavior." A 2005 review found evidence that playing video games improves spatial skills and reaction times, but not that the games increase aggression.

The authors of the *Psychological Science* article advocate the strong-effects hypothesis. Two of their studies were widely reported on in 2000, the year after the Columbine High School shootings, with scant critical analysis. But their research was based on college undergraduates, not troubled teens, and it measured aggression in part by subjects' speed in reading "aggressive" words on a computer screen or blasting opponents with sound after playing a violent video game. These measures do not approximate the conditions the school shooters experienced, nor do they offer much insight as to why they, and not the millions of other players, decided to acquire actual weapons and shoot real people.

Occasionally reporters include challenges like this in stories containing media-effects claims, but news coverage usually refers to this body of research as clear, consistent, and conclusive. "The evidence, say those who study violence in culture, is unassailable: Hundreds of studies in recent decades have revealed a direct correlation between exposure to media violence—now including video games—and increased aggression," said the *New York Times* (April 26, 1999). The *Boston Herald* quoted a clinical psychologist who said, "Studies have already shown that watching television shows with aggressive or violent content makes children more aggressive" (July 30, 2000). The psychologist noted that video game research is newer, but predicted that "in a few years, studies will show that video games increase a child's aggression even more than violent TV shows." News reports do not always use academic sources to assess the conclusiveness of media effects research. A *Pittsburgh Post-Gazette* story included a quote by an attorney, who claimed, "Research on this has been well-established" (May 14, 1999).

It is no accident that media-effects research and individual explanations dominate press attempts to explain the behavior of the school shooters. Although many politicians are happy to take up the cause against video games, popular culture itself suggests an apolitical explanation of violence and discourages a broader examination of structural factors. Focusing on extremely rare and perhaps unpredictable outbursts of violence by young people discourages the public from looking closely at more typical forms of violence against young people, which is usually perpetrated by adults.

24 The biggest problem with media-effects research is that it attempts to decontextualize violence. Poverty, neighborhood instability, unemployment, and even family violence fall by the wayside in most of these studies. Ironically, even mental illness tends to be overlooked in this psychologically oriented research. Young people are seen as passive media consumers, uniquely and uniformly vulnerable to media messages.

Missing Media Studies

News reports of the shootings that focus on video games ignore other research on the meanings that audiences make from media culture. This may be because its qualitative findings are difficult to turn into simple quotations or sound bites. Yet in seeking better understanding of the role of video games in the lives of the shooters and young people more generally, media scholars could have added much to the public debate.

For instance, one study found that British working-class boys boast about how many horror films they have seen as they construct their sense of masculinity by appearing too tough to be scared. Another study examined how younger boys talk about movies and television as a way to manage their anxieties and insecurities regarding their emerging sense of masculinity. Such studies illustrate why violent video games may appeal to many young males.

Media scholars have also examined how and why adults construct concerns about young people and popular culture. One such study concluded that some adults use their condemnation of media as a way to produce cultural distinctions that position them above those who enjoy popular culture. Other researchers have found that people who believe their political knowledge is superior to that of others are more likely to presume that media violence would strongly influence others. They have also found that respondents who enjoy television violence are less likely to believe it has a negative effect.

28 Just as it is too simplistic to assert that video game violence makes players more prone to violence, news coverage alone, however dramatic or repetitive, cannot create consensus among the public that video games cause youth violence. Finger-wagging politicians and other moralizers often alienate as many members of the public as they convert. In an ironic twist, they might even feed the antiauthoritarian appeal that may draw players of all ages to the games.

The lack of consensus does not indicate the absence of a moral panic, but reveals contradictory feelings toward the target group. The intense focus on video games as potential creators of violent killers reflects the hostility that some feel toward popular culture and young people themselves. After adult rampage shootings in the workplace (which happen more often than school shootings), reporters seldom mention whether the shooters played video games. Nor is an entire generation portrayed as potential killers.

Ambivalence about Juvenile Justice

The concern in the late 1990s about video games coincided with a growing ambivalence about the juvenile justice system and young offenders. Fears about juvenile "super-predators," fanned by former Florida Representative Bill McCollom's 1996 warning that we should "brace ourselves" against the coming storm of young killers, made the school shootings appear inevitable. McCollom and other politicians characterized young people as a "new breed," uniquely dangerous and amoral.

These fears were produced partially by the rise in crime during the late 1980s and early 1990s, but also by the so-called echo boom that produced a large generation of teens during the late 1990s. Demographic theories of crime led policymakers to fear that the rise in the number of teen males would bring a parallel rise in crime. In response, virtually every state changed its juvenile justice laws during the decade. They increased penalties, imposed mandatory minimum sentences, blended jurisdiction with criminal courts, and made it easier to transfer juvenile cases to adult criminal courts.

32 So before the first shot was fired in Paducah, politicians warned the public to be on the lookout for killer kids. Rather than being seen as tragic anomalies, these high-profile incidents appeared to support scholarly warnings that all kids posed an increasing threat. Even though juvenile (and adult) crime was in sharp decline by the late nineties, the intense media coverage contributed to the appearance of a new trend.

Blaming video games meant that the shooters were set aside from other violent youth, frequently poor males of color, at whom our get-tough legislation has been targeted. According to the National Center for Juvenile Justice, African-American youth are involved in the juvenile justice system more than twice as often as whites. The video game explanation constructs the white, middle-class shooters as victims of the power of video games, rather than fully culpable criminals. When boys from "good" neighborhoods are violent, they seem to be harbingers of a "new breed" of youth, created by video games rather than by their social circumstances. White, middle-class killers retain their status as children easily influenced by a game, victims of an allegedly dangerous product. African-American boys, apparently, are simply dangerous.

While the news media certainly asked what role the shooters' parents may have played, the press tended to tread lightly on them, particularly the Kinkels of Springfield, Oregon, who were their son's first murder victims. Their middle-class, suburban, or rural environments were given little scrutiny. The white school shooters did more than take the lives of their classmates; their whiteness and middle-class status threatened the idea of the innocence and safety of suburban America.

In an attempt to hold more than just the shooters responsible, the victims' families filed lawsuits against film producers, Internet sites, and video game makers. Around the same time, Congress made it more difficult to sue gun manufacturers for damages. To date, no court has found entertainment producers liable for causing young people to commit acts of violence. In response to a lawsuit following the Paducah shootings, a Kentucky circuit judge ruled that "we are loath to hold that ideas and images can constitute the tools for a criminal act," and that product liability law did not apply because the product did not injure its consumer. The lawsuit was dismissed, as were subsequent suits filed after the other high-profile shootings.

Game Over?

36 Questions about the power of media and the future of the juvenile justice system persist. In March 2005, the U.S. Supreme Court ruled that juvenile executions were unconstitutional. This ruling represents an about-face in the 25-year trend toward toughening penalties for young offenders. While many human rights and children's advocates praised this decision, it was sharply criticized by those who believe that the juvenile justice system is already too lenient. Likewise, critics continue to target video games, as their graphics and plot capabilities grow more complex and at times more disturbing. Meanwhile, youth crime rates continue to decline. If we want to understand why young people, particularly in middle-class or otherwise stable environments, become homicidal, we need to look beyond the games they play. While all forms of media merit critical analysis, so do the supposedly "good" neighborhoods and families that occasionally produce young killers.

Recommended Resources

Ronald Burns and Charles Crawford. "School Shootings, the Media, and Public Fear: Ingredients for a Moral Panic." *Crime, Law, and Social Change* 32 (1999): 147–68. Examines fears about school shootings in the 1990s, paying special attention to the disproportional response compared to the actual threat.

Jonathan L. Freedman. *Media Violence and Its Effect on Aggression: Assessing the Scientific Evidence* (University of Toronto Press, 2002). A thorough analysis of media-effects research, with a critique of methods and interpretation of results.

Erich Goode and Nachman Ben-Yehuda. *Moral Panics: The Social Construction of Deviance* (Blackwell, 1994). A primer on moral panics, with basic definitions as well as several seminal case studies.

40 John Springhall. *Youth, Popular Culture and Moral Panics: Penny Gaffs to Gangsta-Rap, 1830–1996* (St. Martin's, 1998). A history of fears about young people and media.

Franklin E. Zimring. *American Youth Violence* (Oxford University Press, 1998). A comprehensive look at trends in youth crime, juvenile justice, and political discourse about youth violence.

PERSONAL RESPONSE

What is your opinion of violent video games? Are they harmless fun, or do you believe that they may have some effect on behavior? What is your experience with playing such games or watching others play them?

QUESTIONS FOR CLASS OR SMALL-GROUP DISCUSSION

1. Explain in your own words what you understand Sternheimer to mean by the term "folk devils." She suggests that "video games, those who play them, and those who create them have become contemporary folk devils" (paragraph 4). Can you give examples of other such "folk devils?"
2. What criticisms of media-effects research does Sternheimer make? What do you think of her rationale for those criticisms?
3. Discuss the factors besides video games that may account for aggressive behavior in teenagers, according to Sternheimer.
4. What point does Sternheimer make about poor males of color who get in trouble with the law vs. white middle-class males who kill? Do your own observations confirm or contradict her viewpoint?
5. Analyze the structure of Sternheimer's argument. What is her thesis? Where does she make concessions? What evidence does she supply? How convinced are you by her evidence?

IN DEFENSE OF HIP-HOP

CATHLEEN ROUNTREE

Cathleen Rountree is a film journalist, educator, and author, who holds MA, BFA, and PhD degrees. Among her nine books are The Writer's Mentor: A Guide to Putting Passion on Paper *(2002),* The Movie Lovers' Club *(2006), and a five-volume series documenting women's life stages. She lectures frequently on such subjects as artists and the creative process, women's issues, men's issues, and childhood and adolescent issues. This piece appeared in the May 19, 2007, issue of the* Santa Cruz Sentinel. *You can visit her on the blog* Women in World Cinema *at www.womeninworldcinema.com.*

Long under fire from stalwart social regulators, such as the likes of Tipper Gore, members of Congress and those bastions of self-righteousness found on cable news broadcasts, hip-hop music frequently assumes the central role of scapegoat when violent words and deeds erupt among the young—and sometimes the old, as we saw with the Don Imus escapade in April.

Yes, those sleazy words, "nappy-headed hos," that Slimy Imus regurgitated during his live radio broadcast in reference to the Rutgers University women's basketball team, inadvertently returned social critics [including Al Sharpton] to the comfort zone of blaming hip-hop for all that ails contemporary pop culture. The fact that Imus used hip-hop as an excuse for his long-standing and well-documented proclivity for racial epithets seemed especially smarmy.

It was comedian Flip Wilson's cross-dressing character Geraldine who immortalized the excuse: "The Devil made me do it!" Now, it often seems, in many circles hip-hop equals Satan: "Hip-Hop made me do it." If the music is sometimes violent, misogynistic, or materialistic, don't blame hip-hop artists, for they're simply reflecting their surrounding environment.

What elicits my ire is the person who condemns hip-hop without having a basic understanding of it, something I myself had once been guilty of. But, about four years ago, I watched "Tupac Resurrection," a documentary about the life and [as yet unsolved] murder of rap artist Tupac Shakur. The two-hour screening time was for me an epiphany and an entirely new world opened up: a world of beats, words, images, insights, raw expressions that were positively transporting. Like any new convert, I explored, studied, listened to, read about, fell in love with, even proselytized, an art form about which I, too, had once been critical. In fact, it became such a valued part of my life that I eagerly devoted a unit to it in a course I teach at UC Santa Cruz on the Arts in a Multicultural Society.

What had changed? Through "Tupac Resurrection" I found the humanity and powerful social commentary inherent in the entire lexicon of hip-hop culture, and, believe me, it is a unique, fully animated, communicative and consequential culture. The best of hip-hop culture is, in addition to artistic, both political and spiritual, and makes people think. Indeed, hip-hop culture serves as a crossover culture—from music to music videos to movies, from black to white, from urban to suburban, from youth to middle-aged, from deprived to privileged, from street smart to public enemy, from authenticity to false personas and negative stereotypes, from sistahs to "bitches and hos," from bros to "pimps," from freedom to incarceration, from life-affirming to nihilistic, from community to isolation, from politically engaged to apathetic, from principled to morally corrupt, from life to death.

This summer *The Hip Hop Project*, a film produced by Bruce Willis and Queen Latifah, beats its way to movie theaters. *The Hip Hop Project* is the compelling story of Kazi, a formerly homeless teenager who inspired a group of New York City teens to transform their life stories into powerful works of art, using hip-hop as a vehicle for self-development and personal discovery.

Kazi challenges these young people to write music about real issues affecting their lives as they strive to overcome daunting obstacles to produce a collaborative album. Russell Simmons, hip-hop mogul and longtime supporter of the project, partners with Bruce Willis to donate a recording studio to *The Hip Hop Project*. After four years of collaboration, the group produces a powerful and thought-provoking CD filled with moving personal narratives and sharp social commentaries. In contrast to all the negative attention focused on hip-hop and rap music, this is a story of hope, healing and the realization of dreams. It should be required viewing for both Don Imus and Al Sharpton.

PERSONAL RESPONSE QUESTION

Do you listen to and enjoy hip-hop? If so, explain its appeal. If not, explain what kind(s) of music you do listen to and enjoy.

QUESTIONS FOR CLASS OR SMALL-GROUP DISCUSSION

1. In what way (s) does Rountree defend hip-hop music (title)?
2. How might blaming "hip-hop artists for all that ails contemporary pop culture" be a "comfort zone" (paragraph 2)? What do you think are the ailments of pop culture that Rountree has in mind?
3. In paragraph 5, Rountree asserts the ways that she believes the hip-hop culture has an inherent "humanity and powerful social commentary." What do you understand her to mean by that and to what extent do you agree with her?
4. If you have seen either the documentary of Tupac Shakur's life (paragraph 4) or *The Hip-Hop Project* (paragraph 6), explain your assessment of or reaction to it. If you have seen any films or documentaries similar to those that Rountree mentions, what image of the hip-hop culture did they convey?
5. Rountree maintains that the hip-hop culture is a "cross-over culture" (paragraph 5). How doe she define cross-over culture, and to what extent do you agree with her?

HIP-HOP'S BETRAYAL OF BLACK WOMEN

JENNIFER MCLUNE

Jennifer McLune is a librarian, activist, and writer living in Washington, D.C. This piece appeared in Z Magazine Online *in the July/August 2006 issue. According to its mission statement, Z Magazine is "dedicated to resisting injustice, defending against repression, and creating liberty. It sees the racial, gender, class, and political dimensions of personal life as fundamental to understanding and improving contemporary circumstances; and it aims to assist activist efforts for a better future." You can view Z at www.zcommunications.org/zmag .*

Kevin Powell in "Notes of a Hip Hop Head" writes, "Indeed, like rock and roll, hip-hop sometimes makes you think we men don't like women much at all, except to objectify them as trophy pieces or, as contemporary vernacular mandates, as baby mommas, chickenheads, or bitches.

"But just as it was unfair to demonize men of color in the 1960s solely as wild-eyed radicals when what they wanted, amidst their fury, was a little freedom and a little power, today it is wrong to categorically dismiss hip-hop without taking into serious consideration the socioeconomic conditions (and the many record labels that eagerly exploit and benefit from the ignorance of many of these young artists) that have led to the current state of affairs. Or, to paraphrase the late Tupac Shakur, we were given this world, we did not make it."

4 Powell's "socioeconomic" explanation for the sexism in hip-hop is a way to silence feminist critiques of the culture. It is to make an understanding of the misogynistic objectification of black women in hip-hop so elusive that we can't grasp it long enough to wring the neck of its power over us. His argument completely ignores the fact that women, too, are raised in this environment of poverty and violence, but have yet to produce the same negative and hateful representation of black men that male rappers are capable of making against women.

Powell's understanding also lends itself to elitist assumption that somehow poverty breeds sexism, or at least should excuse it. Yet we all know that wealthy white boys can create the same hateful and violent music as poor black boys. As long as the boys can agree that their common enemy is female and that their power resides in their penis, women must not hesitate to name the war they have declared on us.

Hip-hop owes its success to the ideology of woman-hating. It creates, perpetuates, and reaps the rewards of objectification. Sexism and homophobia saturate hip-hop culture and any deviation from these forms of bigotry is made marginal to its most dominant and lucrative expressions. Few artists dare to embody equality and respect between the sexes through their music. Those who do have to fight to be heard above the dominant chorus of misogyny.

The most well known artists who represent an underground and conscious force in hip-hop—like Common, The Roots, Talib Kweli, and others—remain inconsistent, apologetic, and even eager to join the mainstream player's club. Even though fans like me support them because of their moments of decency toward women, they often want to remain on the fence by either playing down their consciousness or by offering props to misogynistic rappers. Most so-called conscious artists appear to care more about their own acceptance by mainstream artists than wanting to make positive changes in the culture.

The Roots, for example, have backed Jay-Z on both his *Unplugged* release and Fade to Black tours. They've publicly declared their admiration for him and have signed on to his new "indie" hip-hop imprint Def Jam Left to produce their next album. Yet Jay-Z is one of the most notoriously sexist and materialistic rappers of his generation.

8 Hip-hop artists like Talib Kweli and Common market themselves as conscious alternatives, yet they remain passive in the face of unrelenting woman-hating bravado from mainstream artists. They are willing to lament in abstract terms the state of

hip-hop, but refuse to name names—unless it's to reassure their mainstream brethren that they have nothing but love for their music.

Talib Kweli has been praised for his song "Black Girl Pain," but clearly he's clueless to how painful it is for a black girl to hear his boy Jay-Z rap, "I pimp hard on a trick, look Fuck if your leg broke bitch, hop up on your good foot."

The misogyny in hip-hop is also given a pass because some of its participants are women. But female hip-hop artists remain marginalized within the industry and culture—except when they are trotted out to defend hip-hop against feminist criticism. But the truth is, all kinds of patriarchal institutions, organizations, and movements have women in their ranks in search of power and meaning. The token presence of individual women changes nothing if women as a group are still scapegoated and degraded.

Unlike men, women in hip-hop don't speak in a collective voice in defense of themselves. The pressure on women to be hyper-feminine and hyper-sexual for the pleasure of men, and the constant threat of being called a bitch, a ho—or worse, a dyke—as a result of being strong, honest, and self-possessed, are real within hip-hop culture and the black community at large. Unless women agree to compromise their truth, self-respect, and unity with other women and instead play dutiful daughter to the phallus that represents hip-hop culture, they will be either targeted, slandered, or ignored altogether. As a result, female rappers are often just as male-identified, violent, materialistic, and ignorant as their male peers.

12 Hip-hop artist Eve, who describes herself as "a pit bull in a skirt," makes an appearance in the Sporty Thieves video for "Pigeons," one of the most hateful misogynistic anthems in hip-hop. Her appearance displays her unity not with the women branded "pigeons," but with the men who label them. This is a heartbreaking example of how hip-hop encourages men to act collectively in the interest of male privilege while dividing women into opposing camps of good and bad or worthy and unworthy of respect.

Lip-service protest against sexism in hip-hop culture is a sly form of public relations to ensure that nobody's money, power, or respect is ever really threatened. Real respect and equality might interfere with hip-hop's commercial appeal. We are asked to dialogue about and ultimately celebrate our "progress"—always predicated on a few rappers and moguls getting rich. Angry young black women are expected to be satisfied with a mere mention that some hip-hop music is sexist and that this sexism of a few rappers is actually, as Powell calls it, "the ghetto blues, urban folk art, a cry out for help." My questions then are: "Whose blues? Whose art? Why won't anybody help the women who are raped in endless rotation by the gaze of the hip-hop camera?"

They expect us to deal with hip-hop's pervasive woman-hating simply by alluding to it, essentially excusing and even celebrating its misogyny, its arrogance, its ignorance. What this angry black woman wants to hear from the apologists is that black women are black people too. That any attack on the women in our community is an attack on us all and that we will no longer be duped by genocidal tendencies in black-face. I want to hear these apologists declare that any black man who makes music perpetuating the hatred of women will be named, shunned, and destroyed, financially and socially, like the traitor of our community he is. That until hip-hop does right by black women, everything hip-hop ever does will fail.

If we accept Powell's explanation for why hip-hop is the way it is—which amounts to an argument for why we should continue to consume and celebrate it—then ultimately we are accepting ourselves as victims who know only how to imitate our victimization while absolving the handful of black folk who benefit from its tragic results. I choose to challenge hip-hop by refusing to reward its commercial aspirations with my money and my attention.

16 I'm tired of the ridiculous excuses and justifications for the unjustifiable pillaring of black women and girls in hip-hop. Are black women the guilty parties behind black men's experience of racism and poverty? Are black women acceptable scapegoats when black men suffer oppression? If black women experience double the oppression as both blacks and women in a racist, patriarchal culture, it is our anger at men and white folks that needs to be heard.

The black men who make excuses for the ideology of woman-hating in hip-hop remind me of those who, a generation ago, supported the attacks on black female writers who went public about the reality of patriarchy in our community. The fact that these black female writers did not create incest, domestic violence, rape, and other patriarchal conditions in the black community did not shield them from being skewered by black men who had their feelings hurt by the exposure of their male privilege and domination of black women. Black women's literature and activism that challenges sexism is often attacked by black men (and many male-identified women) who abhor domination when they are on the losing end, but want to protect it when they think it offers them a good deal.

Black women writers and activists were called traitors for refusing to be silent about the misogynistic order of things and yet women-hating rappers are made heroes by the so-called masses. To be sure, hip-hop is not about keeping it real. Hip-hop lies about the ugly reality that black women were condemned for revealing. Hip-hop is a manipulative narrative that sells because it gets men hard. It is a narrative in which, as a Wu Tang Clan video shows, black women are presented as dancing cave "chicks" in bikinis who get clubbed over the head; or where gang rapes are put to a phat beat; or where working class black women are compared to shit-eating birds.

As a black woman who views sexism as just as much the enemy of my people as racism, I can't buy the apologies and excuses for hip-hop. I will not accept the notion that my sisters deserve to be degraded and humiliated because of the frustrations of black men—all while we suppress our own frustrations, angers, and fears in an effort to be sexy and accommodating. Although Kevin Powell blames the negatives in hip-hop on everything but hip-hop culture itself, he ultimately concludes, "What hip-hop has spawned is a way of winning on our own terms, of us making something out of nothing."

20 If the terms for winning are the objectification of black women and girls, I wonder if any females were at the table when the deal went down. Did we agree to be dehumanized, vilified, made invisible? Rather than pretending to explain away the sexism of hip-hop culture, why doesn't Powell just come clean—in the end it doesn't matter how women are treated. Sexism is the winning ticket to mainstream acceptability and Powell, like Russell Simmons and others, knows this. It's obvious

that if these are the winning terms for our creativity, black women are ultimately the losers. And that's exactly how these self-proclaimed players, thugs, and hip-hop intellectuals want us—on our backs and pledging allegiance to the hip-hop nation.

If we were to condemn woman-hating as an enemy of our community, hip-hop would be forced to look at itself and change radically and consistently. Then it would no longer be marketable in the way that these hip-hop intellectuals celebrate. As things stand, it's all about the Benjamins on every level of the culture and black women are being thugged and rubbed all the way to the bank.

PERSONAL RESPONSE

Write in response to McLune's statement in paragraph 5 that "[h]ip-hop owes its success to the ideology of woman hating."

QUESTIONS FOR CLASS OR SMALL-GROUP DISCUSSION

1. How well do you think that McLune explains her title? In what ways is hip-hop a betrayal of black women, according to her?
2. Explain in your own words McLune's argument against Kevin Powell's explanation for the "misogynistic objectification of black women in hip-hop" (paragraph 3).
3. McLune writes: "Few artists dare to embody equality and respect between the sexes through their music" (paragraph 5). What do you think of her assessment of those few artists she names who "represent an underground and conscious force in hip-hop" (paragraph 6)? Can you name similar artists who resist using sexist and homophobic lyrics?
4. To what extent do you agree with McLune's comments on female hip-hop artists (paragraphs 10–12)?
5. Discuss your opinion of what McLune calls for apologists of black hip-hop music and the artists themselves to do.

✧ PERSPECTIVES ON MUSIC AND VIDEO GAMES ✧

Suggested Writing Topics

1. Argue your position on Henry Jenkins's opening statement in "Art Form for the Digital Age" that video games shape our culture and should be taken seriously.
2. Henry Jenkins in "Art Form for the Digital Age" writes, "It remains to be seen whether games can provide players the freedom they want and still provide an emotionally satisfying and thematically meaningful shape to the experience" (paragraph 16). Using the example of a specific video game (or more than one, if you like), argue whether you believe that games today have achieved that goal.

3. Argue in support of or against the statement that video games have "a socially redeeming value."
4. Rock, hip-hop, rap, and other musical groups have long been able to whip a crowd into an almost hysterical frenzy during their performances. If you have ever seen or experienced such a phenomenon, describe what happened and explore why you think music has that kind of control over people's emotions.
5. Refute or support this statement in Jennifer McLune's "Hip-Hop's Betrayal of Black Women": "Sexism and homophobia saturate hip-hop culture and any deviation from these forms of bigotry is made marginal to its most dominant and lucrative expressions" (paragraph 5). Use examples from song lyrics to support your position.
6. Argue in support of or against Cathleen Rountree's assertion that hip-hop is "a unique, fully animated, communicative and consequential culture" ("In Defense of Hip-Hop," paragraph 5).
7. Do a detailed analysis of a hip-hop, rap, or other song that you are familiar with. What images does it portray? What message, if any, does it send? How do the lyrics work to make the song artistically good?
8. Analyze the lyrics of a song that you believe to be socially responsible or that comments on a current social issue.
9. Analyze your involvement with a video game that you find particularly compelling.
10. Argue for or against extending the First Amendment's guarantee of freedom of speech to include violent or offensive lyrics in hip-hop, rock, or other forms of music. Consider how far you think First Amendment's protection of free speech should be allowed to go.
11. Drawing on any of the readings in this chapter, argue in support of or against the statement that music or video games influence violent behavior in individuals.

Research Topics

1. Henry Jenkins in "Art Form for the Digital Age" notes that a leading critic in the 1920s argued that the important contributions to America's artistic expression came from popular culture, especially "jazz, the Broadway musical, the Hollywood cinema and the comic strip" (paragraph 9). Select one of those forms and research its development as a culturally respectable medium. Consider questions like the following: How long did it take for the form to gain legitimacy? What was the nature of early criticism of it? What contributions does the form make to culture? What are the chief characteristics of its evolution from its primitive beginnings to sophistication?

2. Argue in support of or against the view that rock or hip-hop music is violent or that it is a menace to society.
3. Research the development of hip-hop or gangsta rap music, taking into consideration Jennifer McLune's "Hip-Hop's Betrayal of Black Women" and Cathleen Rountree's "In Defense of Hip-Hop."
4. Research the subject of the influence of violent video games on behavior, drawing on Karen Sternheimer's "Do Video Games Kill?" Note the list of resources that she mentions at the end of her article.
5. Use an approach similar to that of Karen Sternheimer in "Do Video Games Kill?" to analyze newspaper coverage of a school shooting, such as the student massacre at Virginia Tech in April 2007.
6. Research the phenomenon of the physiological and/or psychological effects of music. Look not only for information about scientific research on the subject but also for comments or criticisms of people skeptical of such research. Weigh the evidence and arrive at your own opinion on the subject.
7. Research a particular musician, musical group, or entertainer from an earlier decade, such as the 1950s, 1960s, 1970s, or 1980s. Find out the performer's history, the audience he or she appealed to, what distinguished him or her from others, and what his or her influence seems to have been on popular culture. Formulate your own assessment of the entertainer's significance and make that your thesis or central idea.
8. Research a particular kind of music, such as hip-hop, rap, "grunge," alternative, blues, jazz, or salsa, for the purpose of identifying its chief characteristics, the way it differs from and is influenced by other kinds of music, and its artistic merit or social significance. Include opposing viewpoints and argue your own position on its merits or significance.
9. Examine allegations of racism, sexism, and/or homophobia leveled against a particular video game, song, musician, or group, and draw your own conclusions about the fairness, appropriateness, and/or accuracy of those allegations.
10. Research the history of a popular hand-held video game, taking into consideration marketing strategy, target audience, responses of users, and/or longevity of the game.
11. Research the latest studies and opinion pieces on the cultural impact of video games, and draw your own conclusions about their importance in shaping culture.

Responding to Visuals

Hip Hop musicians performing

1. What do the performers' facial expressions reveal about how they feel about performing?
2. What do the clothes and jewelry of the performers reveal about them? How do the two performers contrast?
3. How does the background function, especially the blurred graffiti on the wall?
4. Vibe awards are presented to outstanding performers in urban music. What impression of urban music might someone who is unfamiliar with it get from this photograph?

RESPONDING TO VISUALS

Youth Express Leader and a member, ages 19 and 13, shooting at a Point Blank video game with red and blue replica 45 caliber plastic pistols in St. Paul, Minnesota.

1. What is the implied message of this photograph? What details of the image contribute to your understanding of that message?
2. What do the looks on the two young men's faces suggest about their enjoyment of the video game?
3. What is the effect of the photographer's perspective? Might a change in perspective alter the implied message of the image?
4. How would the image change were the two young people white or some other ethnic group? Does their age have an effect on your perception of the image?

Media Studies

Because of the pervasiveness of the media in American culture, critics, researchers, and others assume that it affects people in both obvious and subtle ways. Analysts are interested in how newspapers, magazines, film, television, video games, interactive computer programs, music, or the Internet influence behavior, habits, thought, and opinions. There are myriad ways that this wide range of media can influence people of all ages. For example, students of media studies may examine the effects of advertising on people's self image, theirs perceptions of others, what they choose to buy at the market, or which fast food restaurant to eat at. They may be interested in how certain video games, television programs, or comic books influence the behavior of children. Any research on the general topic "media studies" will lead you to dozens of directions that you can go in looking at the ways in which media influence people.

Although the subjects of the other chapters in part 2 are also "media," those chapters look at issues relating to specific media; this chapter considers broader issues relating to "the media" as a whole or several kinds of media. Media analysts often serve as watchdogs against threats to freedom of speech and thought. They concern themselves with social issues such as media violence, censorship in the media, biased reporting, discrimination in programming, and the ways in which the media shape social and political discourse. They analyze the power of the media and the power behind the media.

A look at the goals and purposes of university media studies programs gives an idea of what is involved in "media studies." Such programs examine the social, cultural, political, ethical, aesthetic, legal, and economic effects of the media and are interested in the variety of contexts in which the media have influence in those areas. They cite in their rationales for their programs the proliferation of media, the interconnectedness of media on a global level, and the pervasiveness of media in our lives. Furthermore, large numbers of groups, agencies, and organizations identify themselves as "media watchers" and many are media activists. You will find both conservative and liberal, extremists and moderates on such a list.

One particular aspect of popular culture that media analysts have long been interested in is violence in the media and its influence on people, especially young people. The first reading in this chapter provides an overview of the issue by one of the most well-known contributors in the debate over the role media violence plays in forming children's characters and values. An excerpt from her book *Mayhem: Violence as Public Entertainment* (1998), Sissela Bok's "Aggression: The Impact of Media Violence" discusses a topic that is often quite volatile. As you read what she has to say, consider your own position on this controversial issue. Following Bok, Gerard Jones explains his rather an unusual position on the subject of media violence in "Violent Media is Good for Kids." From the title, it is clear that he not only thinks kids should be allowed to watch violent media but that he also believes it benefits them. Based on his own experiences as a child, he argues his case. As you read his defense of violent media, consider your own childhood experience with it and consider whether you agree with him. Media watchers know that which news stories are reported and how they are reported—what gets emphasized and what gets left out—can shape or destroy someone's reputation or bring an issue to the public's attention. Peter H. Gibbon's "The End of Admiration: The Media and the Loss of Heroes" focuses on the subject of the role that journalists play in building or destroying the reputations of public figures. He suggests that journalists, by encouraging cynicism and celebrity worship, discourage hero worship and idealism. He believes that, with the media's central bias toward bad news, journalists have made it difficult if not impossible for Americans to have heroes. Consider his words carefully as you read his essay. Is he on target with his critique, or does he overgeneralize or ignore positive examples to prove his point? Can you supply examples to either support or refute his argument?

Another issue of concern to media analysts is commercial media's dependence on advertising and their need to make a profit. Jean Kilbourne in "Advertising's Influence on Media Content" argues that advertising has a big influence not only on audiences but also on the media itself. She explains two major ways in which that influence is exerted and gives examples to support her allegations. Kilbourne would argue that the power advertisers hold over commercial media produces a biased media. As you read her examples and her analyses of the influence of advertisers on various kinds of media, see if you can think of other examples to either support or refute what she claims.

AGGRESSION: THE IMPACT OF MEDIA VIOLENCE

SISSELA BOK

Born in Sweden and educated in Switzerland, France, and the United States, Sissela Bok earned a PhD in philosophy from Harvard University. She has been a professor of philosophy at Brandeis University and is currently a Distinguished Fellow at the Harvard Center for Population and Development Studies. Widely known for her writings on topics in bioethics, applied ethics, biography and autobiography, and public affairs, her books include Lying: Moral Choice in Public and Private Life *(1978);* Secrets: On the Ethics of Concealment and Revelation *(1983);* A Strategy for Peace: Human Values and the Threat of War *(1989);* Alva Myrdal: A Daughter's Memoir *(1991);* Common Values *(1995); and* Mayhem: Violence as Public Entertainment *(1998), from which the following is taken.*

Even if media violence were linked to no other debilitating effects, it would remain at the center of public debate so long as the widespread belief persists that it glamorizes aggressive conduct, removes inhibitions toward such conduct, arouses viewers, and invites imitation. It is only natural that the links of media violence to aggression should be of special concern to families and communities. Whereas increased fear, desensitization, and appetite primarily affect the viewers themselves, aggression directly injures others and represents a more clear-cut violation of standards of behavior. From the point of view of public policy, therefore, curbing aggression has priority over alleviating subtler psychological and moral damage.

Public concern about a possible link between media violence and societal violence has further intensified in the past decade, as violent crime reached a peak in the early 1990s, yet has shown no sign of downturn, even after crime rates began dropping in 1992. Media coverage of violence, far from declining, has escalated since then, devoting ever more attention to celebrity homicides and copycat crimes. The latter, explicitly modeled on videos or films and sometimes carried out with meticulous fidelity to detail, are never more relentlessly covered in the media than when they are committed by children and adolescents. Undocumented claims that violent copycat crimes are mounting in number contribute further to the ominous sense of threat that these crimes generate. Their dramatic nature drains away the public's attention from other, more mundane forms of aggression that are much more commonplace, and from . . . other . . . harmful effects of media violence.

Media analyst Ken Auletta reports that, in 1992, a mother in France sued the head of a state TV channel that carried the American series *MacGyver*, claiming that her son was accidentally injured as a result of having copied MacGyver's recipe for making a bomb. At the time, Auletta predicted that similar lawsuits were bound to become a weapon against media violence in America's litigious culture. By 1996, novelist John Grisham had sparked a debate about director Oliver Stone's film *Natural Born Killers*, which is reputedly linked to more copycat assaults and murders than any other movie to date. Grisham wrote in protest against the film after learning that a friend of his, Bill Savage, had been killed by nineteen-year-old Sarah Edmondson and her boyfriend Benjamin Darras, eighteen: after repeated viewings of Stone's film on video, the two had gone on a killing spree with the film's murderous, gleeful heroes expressly in mind. Characterizing the film as "a horrific movie that glamorized casual mayhem and bloodlust," Grisham proposed legal action:

> Think of a film as a product, something created and brought to market, not too dissimilar from breast implants. Though the law has yet to declare movies to be products, it is only a small step away. If something goes wrong with the product, either by design or defect, and injury ensues, then its makers are held responsible. . . . It will take only one large verdict against the like of Oliver Stone, and his production company, and perhaps the screenwriter, and the studio itself, and then the party will be over. The verdict will come from the heartland, far away from Southern California, in some small courtroom with no cameras. A jury will finally say enough is enough; that the demons placed in Sarah Edmondson's mind were not solely of her own making.

4 As a producer of books made into lucrative movies—themselves hardly devoid of violence—and as a veteran of contract negotiations within the entertainment industry, Grisham may have become accustomed to thinking of films in industry

terms as "products." As a seasoned courtroom lawyer, he may have found the analogy between such products and breast implants useful for invoking product liability to pin personal responsibility on movie producers and directors for the lethal consequences that their work might help unleash.

Oliver Stone retorted that Grisham was drawing "upon the superstition about the magical power of pictures to conjure up the undead spectre of censorship." In dismissing concerns about the "magical power of pictures" as merely superstitious, Stone sidestepped the larger question of responsibility fully as much as Grisham had sidestepped that of causation when he attributed liability to filmmakers for anything that "goes wrong" with their products so that "injury ensues." Because aggression is the most prominent effect associated with media violence in the public's mind, it is natural that it should also remain the primary focus of scholars in the field. The "aggressor effect" has been studied both to identify the short term, immediate impact on viewers after exposure to TV violence, and the long-term influences. . . . There is near-unanimity by now among investigators that exposure to media violence contributes to lowering barriers to aggression among some viewers. This lowering of barriers may be assisted by the failure of empathy that comes with growing desensitization, and intensified to the extent that viewers develop an appetite for violence—something that may lead to still greater desire for violent programs and, in turn, even greater desensitization.

When it comes to viewing violent pornography, levels of aggression toward women have been shown to go up among male subjects who view sexualized violence against women. "In explicit depictions of sexual violence," a report by the American Psychological Association's Commission on Youth and Violence concludes after surveying available research data, "it is the message about violence more than the sexual nature of the materials that appears to affect the attitudes of adolescents about rape and violence toward women." Psychologist Edward Donnerstein and colleagues have shown that if investigators tell subjects that aggression is legitimate, then show them violent pornography, their aggression toward women increases. In slasher films, the speed and ease with which "one's feelings can be transformed from sensuality into viciousness may surprise even those quite conversant with the links between sexual and violent urges."

Viewers who become accustomed to seeing violence as an acceptable, common, attractive way of dealing with problems find it easier to identify with aggressors and to suppress any sense of pity or respect for victims of violence. Media violence has been found to have stronger effects of this kind when carried out by heroic, impressive, or otherwise exciting figures, especially when they are shown as invulnerable and are rewarded or not punished for what they do. The same is true when the violence is shown as justifiable, when viewers identify with the aggressors rather than with their victims, when violence is routinely resorted to, and when the programs have links to how viewers perceive their own environment.

8 While the consensus that such influences exist grows among investigators as research accumulates, there is no consensus whatsoever about the size of the correlations involved. Most investigators agree that it will always be difficult to disentangle the precise effects of exposure to media violence from the many other factors contributing to societal violence. No reputable scholar accepts the view

expressed by 21 percent of the American public in 1995, blaming television more than any other factor for teenage violence. Such tentative estimates as have been made suggest that the media account for between 5 and 15 percent of societal violence. Even these estimates are rarely specific enough to indicate whether what is at issue is all violent crime, or such crimes along with bullying and aggression more generally.

One frequently cited investigator proposes a dramatically higher and more specific estimate than others. Psychiatrist Brandon S. Centerwall has concluded from large-scale epidemiological studies of "white homicide" in the United States, Canada, and South Africa in the period from 1945 to 1974, that it escalated in these societies within ten to fifteen years of the introduction of television, and that one can therefore deduce that television has brought a doubling of violent societal crime:

> Of course, there are many factors other than television that influence the amount of violent crime. Every violent act is the result of a variety of forces coming together—poverty, crime, alcohol and drug abuse, stress—of which childhood TV exposure is just one. Nevertheless, the evidence indicates that if hypothetically, television technology had never been developed, there would today be 10,000 fewer homicides each year in the United States, 70,000 fewer rapes, and 700,000 fewer injurious assaults. Violent crime would be half of what it now is.

Centerwall's study, published in 1989, includes controls for such variables as firearm possession and economic growth. But his conclusions have been criticized for not taking into account other factors, such as population changes during the time period studied, that might also play a role in changing crime rates. Shifts in policy and length of prison terms clearly affect these levels as well. By now, the decline in levels of violent crime in the United States since Centerwall's study was conducted, even though television viewing did not decline ten to fifteen years before, does not square with his extrapolations. As for "white homicide" in South Africa under apartheid, each year brings more severe challenges to official statistics from that period.

Even the lower estimates, however, of around 5 to 10 percent of violence as correlated with television exposure, point to substantial numbers of violent crimes in a population as large as America's. But if such estimates are to be used in discussions of policy decisions, more research will be needed to distinguish between the effects of television in general and those of particular types of violent programming, and to indicate specifically what sorts of images increase the aggressor effect and by what means; and throughout to be clearer about the nature of the aggressive acts studied.

12 Media representatives naturally request proof of such effects before they are asked to undertake substantial changes in programming. In considering possible remedies for a problem, inquiring into the reasons for claims about risks is entirely appropriate. It is clearly valid to scrutinize the research designs, sampling methods, and possible biases of studies supporting such claims, and to ask about the reasoning leading from particular research findings to conclusions. But to ask for some demonstrable pinpointing of just when and how exposure to media violence affects levels of aggression sets a dangerously high threshold for establishing risk factors.

We may never be able to trace, retrospectively, the specific set of television programs that contributed to a particular person's aggressive conduct. The same is true when it comes to the links between tobacco smoking and cancer, between drunk driving and automobile accidents, and many other risk factors presenting public health hazards. Only recently have scientists identified the specific channels through which tobacco generates its carcinogenic effects. Both precise causative mechanisms and documented occurrences in individuals remain elusive. Too often, media representatives formulate their requests in what appear to be strictly polemical terms, raising dismissive questions familiar from debates over the effects of tobacco: "How can anyone definitively pinpoint the link between media violence and acts of real-life violence?

If not, how can we know if exposure to media violence constitutes a risk factor in the first place?" Yet the difficulty in carrying out such pinpointing has not stood in the way of discussing and promoting efforts to curtail cigarette smoking and drunk driving. It is not clear, therefore, why a similar difficulty should block such efforts when it comes to media violence. The perspective of "probabilistic causation" . . . is crucial to public debate about the risk factors in media violence. The television industry has already been persuaded to curtail the glamorization of smoking and drunk driving on its programs, despite the lack of conclusive documentation of the correlation between TV viewing and higher incidence of such conduct. Why should the industry not take analogous precautions with respect to violent programming?

Americans have special reasons to inquire into the causes of societal violence. While we are in no sense uniquely violent, we need to ask about all possible reasons why our levels of violent crime are higher than in all other stable industrialized democracies. Our homicide rate would be higher still if we did not imprison more of our citizens than any society in the world, and if emergency medical care had not improved so greatly in recent decades that a larger proportion of shooting victims survive than in the past. Even so, we have seen an unprecedented rise not only in child and adolescent violence, but in levels of rape, child abuse, domestic violence, and every other form of assault.

16 Although America's homicide rate has declined in the 1990s, the rates for suicide, rape, and murder involving children and adolescents in many regions have too rarely followed suit. For Americans aged 15 to 35 years, homicide is the second leading cause of death, and for young African Americans, 15 to 24 years, it is *the* leading cause of death. In the decade following the mid-1980s, the rate of murder committed by teenagers 14 to 17 more than doubled. The rates of injury suffered by small children are skyrocketing, with the number of seriously injured children nearly quadrupling from 1986 to 1993; and a proportion of these injuries are inflicted by children upon one another. Even homicides by children, once next to unknown, have escalated in recent decades.

America may be the only society on earth to have experienced what has been called an "epidemic of children killing children," which is ravaging some of its communities today. As in any epidemic, it is urgent to ask what it is that makes so many capable of such violence, victimizes so many others, and causes countless more to live in fear. Whatever role the media are found to play in this respect, to be sure, is but part of the problem. Obviously, not even the total elimination of media violence would wipe out the problem of violence in the United States or any other society. The same can be said for the proliferation and easy access to guns, or for poverty, drug addiction, and other risk factors. As Dr. Deborah Prothrow-Stith puts it, "It's not an either or. It's not guns or media or parents or poverty."

We have all witnessed the four effects that I have discussed . . .—fearfulness, numbing, appetite, and aggressive impulses—in the context of many influences apart from the media. Maturing involves learning to resist the dominion that these effects can gain over us; and to strive, instead, for greater resilience, empathy, self control, and respect for self and others. The process of maturation and growth in these respects is never completed for any of us; but it is most easily thwarted in childhood, before it has had chance to take root. Such learning calls for nurturing and education at first; then for increasing autonomy in making personal decisions about how best to confront the realities of violence.

Today, the sights and sounds of violence on the screen affect this learning process from infancy on, in many homes. The television screen is the lens through which most children learn about violence. Through the magnifying power of this lens, their everyday life becomes suffused by images of shootings, family violence, gang warfare, kidnappings, and everything else that contributes to violence in our society. It shapes their experiences long before they have had the opportunity to consent to such shaping or developed the ability to cope adequately with this knowledge. The basic nurturing and protection to prevent the impairment of this ability ought to be the birthright of every child.

PERSONAL RESPONSE

Has this essay in any way changed your views on the question of how media violence affects young people? Select a statement or passage that especially interests you, either positively or negatively, and discuss your response to it.

QUESTIONS FOR CLASS OR SMALL-GROUP DISCUSSION

1. Summarize the viewpoints of both John Grisham and Oliver Stone on the matter of "copycat" killings. What does Bok think that both men sidestep in their arguments? What do you think of Grisham's and Stone's arguments? Do you agree with either one? Do you think that Bok is correct in her comments on their arguments?
2. What do you understand Bok to mean by the term "'aggressor effect'" (paragraph 6). What do investigators have to say about violent pornography and the aggressor effect?
3. What is your response to this statement: "No reputable scholar accepts the view expressed by 21 percent of the American public in 1995, blaming television more than any other factor for teenage violence" (paragraph 9)? What does Bok have to say about the studies conducted by Brandon S. Centerwall?
4. Bok notes the difficulty of showing the precise causal relationships between tobacco smoking and cancer and between drunken driving and automobile

accidents, even though most people seem to accept that smoking causes cancer and that drunk driving is a chief cause of automobile accidents. What do you think of her application of the "'probabilistic causation'" factor to the matter of media violence? That is, how valid do you find her logic? Are you convinced that even though we cannot precisely pinpoint the direct causes of societal violence, we can still discuss and propose "efforts to curtail" the "risk factors in media violence" (paragraph 15)?

5. What, according to Bok, might be the effects on children of early and ongoing exposure to media violence? Are you persuaded by her argument that research on the causal links between exposure to media violence and violent behavior must continue?

VIOLENT MEDIA IS GOOD FOR KIDS

GERARD JONES

Gerard Jones is a veteran writer of comics, cartoons, and screenplays. He wrote a number of comic books, including Batman, Spider-Man, Ultraforce, Justice League, *and* Pokémon. *He is also author of several books, including* Honey I'm Home: Sitcoms Selling the American Dream *(1993);* Killing Monsters: Why Children Need Fantasy, Superheroes and Make-Believe Violence *(2002); and* Men of Tomorrow: Geeks, Gangsters and the Birth of the Comic Book *(2004). This piece was originally published on June 28, 2000, by* MotherJones.com.

At 13 I was alone and afraid. Taught by my well-meaning, progressive, English-teacher parents that violence was wrong, that rage was something to be overcome and cooperation was always better than conflict, I suffocated my deepest fears and desires under a nice-boy persona. Placed in a small, experimental school that was wrong for me, afraid to join my peers in their bumptious rush into adolescent boyhood, I withdrew into passivity and loneliness. My parents, not trusting the violent world of the late 1960s, built a wall between me and the crudest elements of American pop culture.

Then the Incredible Hulk smashed through it.

One of my mother's students convinced her that Marvel Comics, despite their apparent juvenility and violence, were in fact devoted to lofty messages of pacifism and tolerance. My mother borrowed some, thinking they'd be good for me. And so they were. But not because they preached lofty messages of benevolence. They were good for me because they were juvenile. And violent.

4 The character who caught me, and freed me, was the Hulk: overgendered and undersocialized, half-naked and half-witted, raging against a frightened world that misunderstood and persecuted him. Suddenly I had a fantasy self to carry my stifled rage and buried desire for power. I had a fantasy self who was a self: unafraid of his

desires and the world's disapproval, unhesitating and effective in action. "Puny boy follow Hulk!" roared my fantasy self, and I followed.

I followed him to new friends—other sensitive geeks chasing their own inner brutes—and I followed him to the arrogant, self-exposing, self-assertive, superheroic decision to become a writer. Eventually, I left him behind, followed more sophisticated heroes, and finally my own lead along a twisting path to a career and an identity. In my 30s, I found myself writing action movies and comic books. I wrote some Hulk stories, and met the geek-geniuses who created him. I saw my own creations turned into action figures, cartoons, and computer games. I talked to the kids who read my stories. Across generations, genders, and ethnicities I kept seeing the same story: people pulling themselves out of emotional traps by immersing themselves in violent stories. People integrating the scariest, most fervently denied fragments of their psyches into fuller senses of selfhood through fantasies of superhuman combat and destruction.

I have watched my son living the same story—transforming himself into a bloodthirsty dinosaur to embolden himself for the plunge into preschool, a Power Ranger to muscle through a social competition in kindergarten. In the first grade, his friends started climbing a tree at school. But he was afraid: of falling, of the centipedes crawling on the trunk, of sharp branches, of his friends' derision. I took my cue from his own fantasies and read him old Tarzan comics, rich in combat and bright with flashing knives. For two weeks he lived in them. Then he put them aside. And he climbed the tree.

But all the while, especially in the wake of the recent burst of school shootings, I heard pop psychologists insisting that violent stories are harmful to kids, heard teachers begging parents to keep their kids away from "junk culture," heard a guilt-stricken friend with a son who loved Pokémon lament, "I've turned into the bad mom who lets her kid eat sugary cereal and watch cartoons!"

8 That's when I started the research.

"Fear, greed, power-hunger, rage: these are aspects of our selves that we try not to experience in our lives but often want, even need, to experience vicariously through stories of others," writes Melanie Moore, Ph.D., a psychologist who works with urban teens. "Children need violent entertainment in order to explore the inescapable feelings that they've been taught to deny, and to reintegrate those feelings into a more whole, more complex, more resilient selfhood."

Moore consults to public schools and local governments, and is also raising a daughter. For the past three years she and I have been studying the ways in which children use violent stories to meet their emotional and developmental needs—and the ways in which adults can help them use those stories healthily. With her help I developed Power Play, a program for helping young people improve their self-knowledge and sense of potency through heroic, combative storytelling.

We've found that every aspect of even the trashiest pop-culture story can have its own developmental function. Pretending to have superhuman powers helps children conquer the feelings of powerlessness that inevitably come with being so young and small. The dual-identity concept at the heart of many superhero stories helps kids negotiate the conflicts between the inner self and the public self as they work through the early stages of socialization. Identification with a rebellious, even destructive, hero helps children learn to push back against a modern culture that cultivates fear and teaches dependency.

12 At its most fundamental level, what we call "creative violence"—head-bonking cartoons, bloody videogames, playground karate, toy guns—gives children a tool to master their rage. Children will feel rage. Even the sweetest and most civilized of them, even those whose parents read the better class of literary magazines, will feel rage. The world is uncontrollable and incomprehensible; mastering it is a terrifying, enraging task. Rage can be an energizing emotion, a shot of courage to push us to resist greater threats, take more control, than we ever thought we could. But rage is also the emotion our culture distrusts the most. Most of us are taught early on to fear our own. Through immersion in imaginary combat and identification with a violent protagonist, children engage the rage they've stifled, come to fear it less, and become more capable of utilizing it against life's challenges.

I knew one little girl who went around exploding with fantasies so violent that other moms would draw her mother aside to whisper, "I think you should know something about Emily . . . ." Her parents were separating, and she was small, an only child, a tomboy at an age when her classmates were dividing sharply along gender lines. On the playground she acted out "Sailor Moon" fights, and in the classroom she wrote stories about people being stabbed with knives. The more adults tried to control her stories, the more she acted out the roles of her angry heroes: breaking rules, testing limits, roaring threats.

Then her mother and I started helping her tell her stories. She wrote them, performed them, drew them like comics: sometimes bloody, sometimes tender, always blending the images of pop culture with her own most private fantasies. She came out of it just as fiery and strong, but more self-controlled and socially competent: a leader among her peers, the one student in her class who could truly pull boys and girls together.

I worked with an older girl, a middle-class "nice girl," who held herself together through a chaotic family situation and a tumultuous adolescence with gangsta rap. In the mythologized street violence of Ice T, the rage and strutting of his music and lyrics, she found a theater of the mind in which she could be powerful, ruthless, invulnerable. She avoided the heavy drug use that sank many of her peers, and flowered in college as a writer and political activist.

16 I'm not going to argue that violent entertainment is harmless. I think it has helped inspire some people to real-life violence. I am going to argue that it's helped hundreds of people for every one it's hurt, and that it can help far more if we learn to use it well. I am going to argue that our fear of "youth violence" isn't well-founded on reality, and that the fear can do more harm than the reality. We act as though our highest priority is to prevent our children from growing up into murderous thugs—but modern kids are far more likely to grow up too passive, too distrustful of themselves, too easily manipulated.

We send the message to our children in a hundred ways that their craving for imaginary gun battles and symbolic killings is wrong, or at least dangerous. Even when we don't call for censorship or forbid "Mortal Kombat," we moan to other parents within our kids' earshot about the "awful violence" in the entertainment they love. We tell our kids that it isn't nice to play-fight, or we steer them from some monstrous action figure to a pro-social doll. Even in the most progressive households, where we make such a point of letting children feel what they feel, we rush to substitute an enlightened discussion for the raw material of rageful fantasy. In the process, we risk confusing them about their natural aggression in the same way the Victorians confused their children about their sexuality. When we try to protect our children from their own feelings and fantasies, we shelter them not against violence but against power and selfhood.

PERSONAL RESPONSE

Write for a few minutes in response to Jones's remark that "modern kids are . . . likely to grow up too passive, too distrustful of themselves, too easily manipulated" (paragraph 16).

QUESTIONS FOR CLASS OR SMALL-GROUP DISCUSSION

1. Explain Jones's basic premise, that is, the assumption on which his argument is based.
2. Do your own experiences or observations confirm or contradict Jones's belief, as stated in his title, that "violent media is good for kids"? Do you know people who have gotten out of "emotional traps by immersing themselves in violent stories" (paragraph 5)?
3. What do you understand Jones to mean when he says that he and his colleagues have "found that every aspect of even the trashiest pop-culture story can have its own developmental function" (paragraph 11). Besides the examples he names, can you think of other ways in which that statement can be validated?
4. To what extent do you find Jones's conclusions about the role of violent images in children's lives convincing? Are you swayed by his argument? Explain your answer.

THE END OF ADMIRATION: THE MEDIA AND THE LOSS OF HEROES

PETER H. GIBBON

Peter H. Gibbon is a senior Research Fellow at Boston University's School of Education. He has done extensive research on the educational systems of Japan, China, and Germany and is coauthor, with Peter J. Gomes, of A Call to Heroism: Renewing America's Vision of

Greatness *(2002), about the disappearance of public heroes in American society. His articles have appeared in magazines such as* Newsweek *and* Time *and in a number of newspapers, including* the New York Times, Los Angeles Times, Philadelphia Inquirer, *and* Washington Post. *He has also made guest appearances on many television and radio programs and travels the country talking to both general audiences and students about heroism. This piece, based on a talk he delivered at a seminar on the history of journalism hosted by Hillsdale College, appeared in the May 1999 issue of* Imprimis.

I travel around the country talking to Americans about the loss of public heroes. I point out that New York City's Hall of Fame for Great Americans attracts only a few thousand visitors each year, while Cleveland's Rock and Roll Hall of Fame draws over one million.

I describe a 25-foot stained glass window in the Cathedral of St. John the Divine—dedicated in the 1920s to four athletes who exemplified good character and sportsmanship—and I offer a quick list of titles of contemporary books on sports: *Shark Attack,* on the short and bitter career of college coaches; *Meat on the Hoof,* about the mercenary world of professional football; *Personal Fouls,* on the mistreatment of college athletes; *The Courts of Babylon,* on the venality of the women's professional tennis circuit; and *Public Heroes, Private Felons,* on college athletes who break the law.

I contrast two westerns: *High Noon,* which won four Academy Awards in 1959, and *Unforgiven,* which was voted "Best Picture" in 1992. The hero of *High Noon,* Will Kane, is a U.S. marshal. The hero of *Unforgiven,* Will Munny, is a reformed killer and alcoholic reduced to pig farming.

4 I mention that our best-selling postage stamps feature Elvis Presley and Marilyn Monroe and that our most popular TV show was, until it left the air recently, *Seinfeld.*

I remind my audiences that Thomas Jefferson is now thought of as the president with the slave mistress and Mozart as the careless genius who liked to talk dirty.

I add that a recent biography of Mother Teresa is titled *The Missionary Position.*

I offer some reasons for the disappearance of public heroes. Athletes have given up on being team players and role models. Popular culture is often irreverent, sometimes deviant. Revisionist historians present an unforgiving, skewed picture of the past. Biographers are increasingly hostile toward their subjects. Social scientists stridently assert that human beings are not autonomous but are conditioned by genes and environment.

8 Hovering in the background are secularism, which suggests that human beings are self-sufficient and do not need God, and modernism—a complex artistic and literary movement that repudiates structure, form, and conventional values.

Finally, in an age of instant communication, in which there is little time for reflection, accuracy, balance or integrity—the media creates the impression that sleaze is everywhere, that nothing is sacred, that no one is noble, and that there are no heroes.

Nothing to Admire

Radio, television, and computers offer news with such speed that newspaper and magazine circulation has plummeted, and readers have smaller vocabularies. I recently wrote an op-ed piece syndicated in several newspapers. My title, "*Nil Admirari,*" which means "nothing to admire," came from the Roman lyric poet Horace.

None of the newspapers used the title, and one editor reminded me that newspaper stories are now aimed at a sixth-grade reading level.

12 In the Age of Information, the image reigns. There are 81 television sets for every 100 Americans. In the typical household, the television is on six hours a day. Television has become our chief source of local and national news, and broadcast journalists have become more prominent and more powerful than columnists. There used to be three channels. Now, there are over one hundred. When we weary of television channels, we can turn to countless radio stations, videotapes, and web pages.

This explosion of information means we now have a vast menu of choices that allows us to be transported to many different worlds and provides us with educational opportunities undreamed of thirty years ago. It also means that we spend more time in front of television and computer screens and less time reading to our children. It is no wonder that our children have shorter attention spans and smaller vocabularies.

A Wired World

Along with this vast menu of choices is the absence of gatekeepers. As parents, we need to realize that there are dangers that come with too many choices and too few guides. We need to remind ourselves that their well-being depends not only on nutrition, sunlight, and exercise; on friendship, work, and love; but also on *how they see the world.* Subtly and powerfully, the media helps shape their world view.

The media has a liberal bias, but its *central* bias is toward bad news. Accidents, crimes, conflict, and scandal are interesting. Normality is boring. The prevalence of bad news and the power of the image encourage children—and us—to overestimate the chance of an accident, the risk of disease, the rate of violence, the frequency of marital infidelity. The average policeman, for example, never fires a gun in action, and most Americans are monogamous.

16 In a wired world with no restraint, the media can misinform us. It can also make us suspicious, fearful, and cynical. It can lead us to lose faith in our nation, repudiate our past, question our leaders, and cease to believe in progress.

We know the worst about everyone instantly. Over and over again, we see clips of George Bush vomiting, Dan Quayle misspelling "potato," Gerald Ford tripping.

No longer do we want our child to grow up and become president. We harbor dark suspicions about the personal conduct of scoutmasters, priests, and coaches. We think army sergeants harass their subordinates. We have trouble calling any public figure a hero. A wired world becomes a world without heroes, a world of *nil admirari,* with no one to admire.

Americans tell pollsters the country is in moral and spiritual decline. In the midst of peace and prosperity, with equality increasing and health improving, we are sour. With our military powerful and our culture ascendant, pessimism prevails.

Crusaders or Rogues?

20 Should we blame journalists? It is certainly tempting. Just as we blame teachers for the poor performance of students, so we can blame reporters for the nation's malaise.

But just as teachers are not responsible for poverty and disintegrating families, journalists are not responsible for satellites, fiber optic cables, transistors, and microprocessors—the inventions that make possible instant information. Journalists did not cause the sexual revolution. They did not invent celebrity worship or gossip. Nor did they create leaders who misbehave and let us down.

At the same time, in the world of *nil admirari,* journalists are not innocent, and they know it. Roger Rosenblatt, a veteran of the *Washington Post, Time, Life,* and the *New York Times Magazine,* says, "My trade of journalism is sodden these days with practitioners who seem incapable of admiring others or anything." In his memoir, former presidential press secretary and ABC News senior editor Pierre Salinger writes, "No reporter can be famous unless they have brought someone down." And *New Yorker* writer Adam Gopnik comments, "The reporter used to gain status by dining with his subjects; now he gains status by dining on them."

Journalists can also be greedy. Eager for money, some reporters accept handsome speaking fees from organizations they are supposed to be covering. Some are dishonest, making up quotations, even inventing stories. No longer content with anonymity, many reporters seek celebrity, roaming the talk shows and becoming masters of the sound bite. They write autobiographies and give interviews to other journalists.

24 Just as our president is enamored of Hollywood, so are our journalists. Larry King recently spent a full hour interviewing singer Madonna. *Sixty Minutes* devoted much of a show to "bad boy" actor Sean Penn. Actors, supermodels, and musicians are no longer just entertainers. They are treated like philosopher–kings, telling us how to live. In a recent interview, actress Sharon Stone, star of *Basic Instinct,* advises parents to make condoms available to their teenagers.

Aggressive and anxious for ratings, television news shows feature hosts and guests who come armed with hardened opinions. Many are quick to judge and prone to offer easy solutions for complex problems. "Talking heads" argue, yell, interrupt, and rarely make concessions.

But in the world of *nil admirari,* journalists are now reviled more often than revered. In the 1980s, muckraker Steven Brill skewered lawyers. In his new magazine, *Brill's Content,* he lambastes journalists. In *Right in the Old Gazoo,* former Wyoming Senator Alan Simpson accuses journalists of becoming "lazy, complacent, sloppy, self-serving, self-aggrandizing, cynical and arrogant beyond belief." In *Breaking the News,* writer James Fallows comments that while movies once portrayed journalists as crusaders, they are now portrayed as rogues "more loathsome than . . . lawyers, politicians, and business moguls."

How much of this is new?

28 Since the founding of America, reporters have been harsh critics of public figures. George Washington did not like reading in pamphlets that the essence of his education had been "gambling, reveling, horse racing and horse whipping." Thomas Jefferson did not relish the label "effeminate." Abraham Lincoln did not appreciate being portrayed by cartoonists as a baboon.

Throughout our history, reporters have also received harsh criticism. Just after the Civil War, abolitionist Harriet Beecher Stowe claimed the press had become so vicious that no respectable American man would ever again run for president. In 1870, the British critic and poet Matthew Arnold toured America and concluded, "If one were searching for the best means . . . to kill in a whole nation . . . the feeling for what is elevated, one could not do better than take the American newspaper." At the turn of the century, novelist Henry James condemned what he called the "impudence [and] the shamelessness of the newspaper and the interviewer." In the early decades of the 20th century, "yellow journalism," "muckraking," and "debunking" became household words to describe newspaper stories that exaggerated and distorted events to make them more sensational.

Nor is the media's fascination with celebrities new. When silent screen idol Rudolph Valentino and educational reformer Charles William Eliot died within a day of each other in 1926, high-minded Americans complained that the press devoted too many columns to a celebrity and too few to a hero of education. Between 1925 and 1947, millions of Americans listened to Walter Winchell's radio program, *The Lucky Strike Hour* and read his column in the *New York Mirror.* Winchell hung out at the Stork Club, collecting gossip about celebrities and politicians from tipsters. He urged all newspaper offices to post these words on their walls: "Talk of virtue and your readers will become bored. Hint of gossip and you will secure perfect attention."

In short, media critics have always called reporters cynical. Reporters have always collected gossip and featured celebrities. And high-minded Americans have always warned that journalists could lower the nation's moral tone.

An Empire of Information

32 From the outset, thoughtful critics conceded that journalists had an obligation to inform and expose. But those same critics were afraid that reporters would eliminate privacy and slander leaders; that by repeating gossip and emphasizing crime and corruption, newspapers would coarsen citizens; and that journalists would become more influential than ministers, novelists, professors, and politicians. They were right.

Journalists *have* become more powerful than ministers, novelists, professors, and politicians. They preside over an empire of information unimaginable to our ancestors—an empire that reaches small villages in India and can change governments in China; an empire characterized by staggering choice, variety, and technological sophistication.

An empire of information ruled by the modern media *has* eliminated privacy. With recorders and cameras, reporters freely enter dugouts, locker rooms, board rooms, hotel rooms. There are neither secrets nor taboos. Some listen in on private telephone conversations and sift through garbage for incriminating documents.

Early critics were also right to worry that journalists could contribute to a decline in taste and judgment, could destroy the feeling for the elevated, could eliminate appetite for the admirable. The empire they have created is slick, quick, hard-hitting, entertaining, and inescapable. It makes us more knowledgeable, but it also leaves us overwhelmed, convinced that the world is a sleazy place, and mistrustful of authority and institutions. It all but extinguishes our belief in heroism.

Hope for the Future

36 Are there reasons to be hopeful about the future of America and the future of the media? I believe there are. Intent on exposing our faults, we forget what we do well. America is much better and healthier than the country portrayed in the media and in pessimistic opinion polls. The American people are basically hardworking, idealistic, compassionate, and religious.

American journalism is still biased, but it is slowly becoming more balanced. We have the *Washington Times* as well as the *Washington Post, U.S. News & World Report* as well as *Newsweek, National Review* as well as the *Nation,* the *Wall Street Journal* as well as the *New York Times.* We have prominent conservative and liberal commentators.

In the late 1990s, newspaper and television journalists have become more self-critical. Some recognize the need to become less cynical, less greedy, less celebrity oriented, less combative; and a few recognize the need to report the normal and the good rather than only the sensational and the deviant.

Reporters, editors, and publishers are influential, but they are not all-powerful. In America, the consumer is king. We choose our sources of information just as we purchase cars and potato chips. When CNN interrupted its coverage of the Lorena Bobbitt trial to report on the Chernobyl nuclear disaster, the number of angry callers caused the network's switchboard to crash. Reporters could be more courageous and less concerned with profits, but American citizens could be more high-minded.

40 In the Age of Information, journalists and citizens face the same challenges. We need to study the past so as not to become arrogant, to remember the good so as not to become cynical, and to recognize America's strengths so as not to dwell on her weaknesses. We need to be honest and realistic without losing our capacity for admiration—and to be able to embrace complexity without losing our faith in the heroic.

PERSONAL RESPONSE

Gibbon states that "we have trouble calling any public figure a hero" (paragraph 16). Are there public figures whom you admire as heroes, and if so, what makes them heroic? If you cannot think of any public hero whom you would regard as a hero, explore reasons why this is so.

QUESTIONS FOR CLASS OR SMALL-GROUP DISCUSSION

1. Assess the effectiveness of the series of contrasts that Gibbon makes in the first six paragraphs. Then discuss the explanations he gives to account for them in the next several paragraphs. Do you accept his explanations? Are there any that you would challenge?
2. Gibbon alleges that journalists can be greedy and dishonest, seeking celebrity status for themselves (paragraphs 24 and 25). To what extent do you agree with Gibbon? Can you give examples of journalists who either support or refute his claims?

3. In paragraph 34, Gibbon briefly summarizes both positive and negative views of journalists over time, with emphasis on the negative. He concludes that those who feared the worst "were right." To what extent do you agree with Gibbon that the worst fears of critics of journalists have been realized?
4. Explain whether you agree with Gibbon in this passage from paragraph 37: "The empire they created is slick, quick, hard-hitting, entertaining, and inescapable. It makes us more knowledgeable, but it also leaves us overwhelmed, convinced that the world is a sleazy place, and mistrustful of authority and institutions. It all but extinguishes our belief in heroism"? Do you think that he is wrong or unfair in any part of this passage?

ADVERTISING'S INFLUENCE ON MEDIA CONTENT

JEAN KILBOURNE

Jean Kilbourne is a social theorist who has lectured for many years on advertising images of women and on alcohol and liquor advertisements. A widely published writer and speaker who has twice been named Lecturer of the Year by the National Association of Campus Activities, she is perhaps best known for her award-winning documentaries on advertising images, Killing Us Softly, Slim Hopes, *and* Pack of Lies. *Her latest book, coauthored with Diane E. Levin, is* So Sexy So Soon: The New Sexualized Childhood and What Parents Can Do to Protect Their Kids *(2009). This piece is an excerpt from Chapter One of Kilbourne's* Can't Buy My Love: How Advertising Changes the Way We Think and Feel *(2000) (hard cover title:* Deadly Persuasion: Why Women and Girls Must Fight the Addictive Power of Advertising*). You can find additional resources and other information at Kilbourne's website: www.jeankilbourne.com.*

Advertising's influence on media content is exerted in two major ways: via the suppression of information that would harm or "offend the sponsor" and via the inclusion of editorial content that is advertiser-friendly, that creates an environment in which the ads look good. The line between advertising and editorial content is blurred by "advertorials" (advertising disguised as editorial copy) "product placement" in television programs and feature films, and the widespread use of "video news releases," corporate public-relations puff pieces aired by local television stations as genuine news. Up to 85 percent of the news we get is bought and paid for by corporations eager to gain positive publicity.

Although people have become used to news reporters popping up in commercials and movies (as Joan Lunden and Linda Ellerbee did in television commercials for Vaseline and Maxwell House coffee, respectively, and as almost everyone at CNN did in the movie *Contact*), many were shocked in late 1997 when retired newsman David Brinkley became the pitchman for agribusiness giant Archer Daniels Midland, a company that has been convicted of price fixing on an international scale.

In 1998 Nike's sponsorship of CBS's Olympic coverage was rewarded when the correspondents delivered the news wearing jackets emblazoned with Nike's symbolic swoosh. The president of CBS News vehemently denied that this sponsorship had anything to do with the thwarting of a follow-up to a hard-hitting investigative piece on Nike for *48 Hours*. The editor of *The San Francisco Examiner* likewise denied that Nike's co-sponsorship of their big annual promotion was in any way related to the decision to kill a column by a reporter that was highly critical of Nike.

4 In 1996 Chrysler Corporation set off a furor by demanding in writing that magazines notify it in advance about "any and all editorial content that encompasses sexual, political, social issues or any editorial that might be construed as provocative or offensive." According to Chrysler spokesman Mike Aberlich, placing an ad is like buying a house: "You decide the neighborhood you want to be in." Fear of losing the lucrative Chrysler account led *Esquire* to kill a long story with a gay theme, already in page proofs, by accomplished author David Leavitt. Will Blythe, the magazine's literary editor, promptly quit, saying in his letter of resignation that "in effect, we're taking marching orders (albeit, indirectly) from advertisers." Of course, had Blythe not gone public, the public would never have known what happened. When we don't get the story, we don't know what we're missing.

In reaction to the Chrysler letter, the American Society of Magazine Editors and Magazine Publishers of America issued a joint statement in the fall of 1997 calling for editorial integrity and barring magazines from giving advertisers a preview of stories, photos, or tables of contents for upcoming issues. This is to their credit, of course, but it won't protect us from similar phenomena occurring: According to an article in the *Columbia Journalism Review*, in 1997 a major advertiser (unnamed in the article) warned all three newsweeklies—*Time*, *Newsweek*, and *U.S. News & World Report*—that it would award all of its advertising to the magazine that portrayed its company's industry in the most favorable light during the upcoming quarter.

More often than not, self-censorship by magazine editors and television producers makes such overt pressure by corporations unnecessary. According to Kurt Andersen, the former editor of *New York* magazine, "Because I worked closely and happily with the publisher at *New York*, I was aware who the big advertisers were. My antennae were turned on, and I read copy thinking, 'Is this going to cause Calvin Klein or Bergdorf big problems?'" No doubt this is what ran through the minds of the CBS executives who canceled Ed Asner's series after two large corporate advertisers—Vidal Sassoon and Kimberly-Clark—withdrew their sponsorship because of Asner's association with Medical Aid for El Salvador.

Sometimes the self-censorship involves an entire industry rather than a specific company or corporation. For example, several radio stations in the Midwest not only refused to play a commercial advocating vegetarianism in which country singer k.d. lang appeared as a spokesperson, but also banned lang's songs from the air. Clearly this kind of thinking has more serious consequences than an occasional editorial omission or favorable mention—it warps a worldview and distorts the editorial content we read and the programs we listen to and watch.

8 Nowhere is this more obvious than in most women's and girls' magazines, where there is a very fine line, if any, between advertising and editorial content. Most of these magazines gladly provide a climate in which ads for diet and beauty products will be looked at with interest, even with desperation. And they suffer consequences from advertisers if they fail to provide such a climate.

Gloria Steinem provides a striking example of this in her article "Sex, Lies & Advertising," in which she discusses an award-winning story on Soviet women that was featured on the cover of the November 1980 issue of *Ms.* In those days, *Ms.,* like every other woman's magazine, depended on advertising. Following that story, *Ms.* lost all hope of ever getting Revlon ads. Why? Because the Soviet women on the cover weren't wearing makeup.

More recently, the editor of *New Woman* magazine in Australia resigned after advertisers complained about the publication's use of a heavyset cover girl, even though letters had poured in from grateful readers. According to *Advertising Age International,* her departure "made clear the influence wielded by advertisers who remain convinced that only thin models spur sales of beauty products." One prevalent form of censorship in the mass media is the almost complete invisibility, the eradication, of real women's faces and bodies.

No wonder women's magazines so often have covers that feature luscious cakes and pies juxtaposed with articles about diets. "85 Ways to Lose Weight," *Woman's Day* tells us—but probably one of them isn't the "10-minute ice cream pie" on the cover. This is an invitation to pathology, fueling the paradoxical obsession with food and weight control that is one of the hallmarks of eating disorders.

12 It can be shocking to look at the front and back covers of magazines. Often there are ironic juxtapositions. A typical woman's magazine has a photo of some rich food on the front cover, a cheesecake covered with luscious cherries or a huge slice of apple pie with ice cream melting on top. On the back cover, there is usually a cigarette ad, often one implying that smoking will keep women thin. Inside the magazine are recipes, more photos of fattening foods, articles about dieting—and lots of advertising featuring very thin models. There usually also is at least one article about an uncommon disease or trivial health hazard, which can seem very ironic in light of the truly dangerous product being glamorized on the back cover.

In February 1999, *Family Circle* featured on its front cover a luscious photo of "gingham mini-cakes," while promoting articles entitled "New! Lose-Weight, Stay-Young Diet," "Super Foods That Act Like Medicine," and "The Healing Power of Love." On the back cover was an ad for Virginia Slims cigarettes. The same week, *For Women First* featured a chocolate cake on its cover along with one article entitled "Accelerate Fat Loss" and another promising "Breakthrough Cures" for varicose veins, cellulite, PMS, stress, tiredness, and dry skin. On the back cover, an ad for Doral cigarettes said, "Imagine getting more." *The Ladies' Home Journal* that same month offered on its cover "The Best Chocolate Cake You Ever Ate," along with its antidote, "Want to Lose 10 lbs? Re-program Your Body." Concern for their readers' health was reflected in two articles highlighted on the cover, "12 Symptoms You Must Not Ignore" and "De-Stressors for Really Crazy Workdays"—and then undermined by the ad for Basic cigarettes on the back cover (which added to the general confusion by picturing the pack surrounded by chocolate candies).

The diseases and health hazards warned about in the women's magazines are often ridiculous. *Woman's Day* once offered a "Special Report on Deadly Appliances," which warned us about how our appliances, such as toasters, coffeemakers, baby monitors, and nightlights, can suddenly burst into flame. Lest we think this is not a serious problem, the article tells us that in 1993, the last year for which figures were available, 80 people died and 370 were injured by these killer appliances. I don't wish to minimize any death or injury. However, on the back cover of this issue of *Woman's Day* is an advertisement for cigarettes, a product that kills over four hundred thousand people, year in and year out.

The January 1995 issue of *Redbook* warns us on the cover about all sorts of pressing problems from frizzy hair to "erotic accidents" and promotes an article entitled "If Only They'd Caught It Sooner: The Tests Even Healthy Women Need." On the back cover, as always, an ad for Virginia Slims. Needless to say, being set afire from smoking in bed (one of the leading causes of fire deaths) does not make it into the "erotic accidents" article.

16 An informal survey of popular women's magazines in 1996 found cover stories on some of the following health issues: skin cancer, Pap smears, leukemia, how breast cancer can be fought with a positive attitude, how breast cancer can be held off with aspirin, and the possibility that dry-cleaned clothes can cause cancer. There were cigarette ads on the back covers of all these magazines—and not a single mention inside of lung cancer and heart disease caused by smoking. In spite of increasing coverage of tobacco issues in the late 1990s, the silence in women's magazines has continued, in America and throughout the world. In my own research, I continue to find scanty coverage of smoking dangers, no feature stories on lung cancer or on smoking's role in causing many other cancers and heart disease . . . and hundreds of cigarette ads.

Dr. Holly Atkinson, a health writer for *New Woman* between 1985 and 1990, recalled that she was barred from covering smoking-related issues, and that her editor struck any reference to cigarettes in articles on topics ranging from wrinkles to cancer. When Atkinson confronted the editor, a shouting match ensued. "Holly, who do you think supports this magazine?" demanded the editor. As Helen Gurley Brown, former editor of *Cosmopolitan,* said: "Having come from the advertising world myself, I think, 'Who needs somebody you're paying millions of dollars a year to come back and bite you on the ankle?'"

It is not just women's magazines that tailor their articles to match their ads. The July 1995 issue of *Life* magazine warns us of the dangers our children face, including drugs, and asks, "How can we keep our children safe?" On the back cover is a Marlboro ad. Our children are far more likely to die from tobacco-related diseases than from any other cause, but cigarettes are not mentioned in the article.

Americans rely on the media for our health information. But this information is altered, distorted, even censored on behalf of the advertisers—advertisers for alcohol, cigarettes, junk food, diet products. We get most of our information from people who are likely to be thinking, "Is this going to cause Philip Morris or Anheuser-Busch big problems?" Of course, in recent years there has been front-page coverage of the liability suits against the tobacco industry and much discussion about antismoking legislation. However, there is still very little information about the health consequences of smoking, especially in women's magazines. The Partnership for a Drug-Free America, made up primarily of media companies dependent on advertising, basically refuses to warn children against the dangers of alcohol and tobacco. The government is spending $195 million in 1999 on a national media campaign to dissuade adolescents from using illicit drugs, but not a penny of the appropriated tax dollars is going to warn about the dangers of smoking or drinking.

20 No wonder most people still don't understand that these heavily advertised drugs pose a much greater threat to our young people and kill far more Americans than all illicit drugs combined. Thirty percent of Americans still don't know that smoking shortens life expectancy, and almost 60 percent don't know it causes emphysema. There is still so much ignorance that, when I was invited recently to give a talk on tobacco advertising to students at a progressive private school outside Boston, the person extending the invitation said she was also going to invite someone from the tobacco industry to represent "the other side." I was tempted to ask her if she felt equally compelled to have a batterer on hand during a discussion of domestic violence.

The influence of these huge and powerful corporations on the media leads to a pernicious kind of censorship. The problem is exacerbated by the fact that many of these corporations own and control the media. In 1996 the Seagram Company ran a whiskey ad on an NBC affiliate in Texas, thus breaking the decades-old tradition of liquor ads not being carried on television. Although network television is leery of running liquor ads for fear of offending their beer advertisers, *Advertising Age* reported that Seagram might have a "winning card to play," since the company owns 50 percent of both the USA Network and the Sci-Fi Channel. Although both have a ban on hard-liquor advertising, a top executive for USA Network said, "If Seagram came to us with a hard-liquor ad, we'd have to look at it."

Today, Time Warner, Sony, Viacom, Disney, Bertelsmann, and News Corporation together control most publishing, music, television, film, and theme-park entertainment throughout the developed world. It is estimated that by the end of the millennium these companies will own 90 percent of the world's information, from newspapers to computer software to film to television to popular music. We may be able to change the channel, but we won't be able to change the message.

Almost everywhere we look these days, anywhere in the world, there is a message from one of these conglomerates. An ad in *Advertising Age* shows a huge picture of the earth and the headline, "Do you see the trillion dollar market?" The triumph of democracy is becoming the triumph of consumerism, as the global village is reduced to a "trillion dollar market."

24 "Why 6,000,000 women who used to carry a little red book now carry a little red lipstick," says an ad for *Allure,* an American beauty magazine, featuring a Chinese woman in a military uniform wearing bright red lipstick. The copy continues, "When

nail polish becomes political, and fashion becomes philosophy, *Allure* magazine will be there." In the world of advertising the political is only personal. Six million women carrying a book of political ideas might be a movement, even a revolution. The same women, carrying lipstick, are simply red-lipped consumers. Advertisers are adept at appropriating dissent and rebellion, slickly packaging it, and then selling it right back to us.

Although the conglomerates are transnational, the culture they sell is American. Not the American culture of the past, which exported writers like Ernest Hemingway and Edgar Allan Poe, musical greats like Louis Armstrong and Marian Anderson, plays by Eugene O'Neill and Tennessee Williams, and Broadway musicals like *West Side Story*. These exports celebrated democracy, freedom, and vitality as the American way of life.

Today we export a popular culture that promotes escapism, consumerism, violence, and greed. Half the planet lusts for Cindy Crawford, lines up for blockbuster films like *Die Hard 2* with a minimum of dialogue and a maximum of violence (which travels well, needing no translation), and dances to the monotonous beat of the Backstreet Boys. *Baywatch,* a moronic television series starring Ken and Barbie, has been seen by more people in the world than any other television show in history. And at the heart of all this "entertainment" is advertising. As Simon Anholt, an English consultant specializing in global brand development, said, "The world's most powerful brand is the U.S. This is because it has Hollywood, the world's best advertising agency. For nearly a century, Hollywood has been pumping out two-hour cinema ads for Brand U.S.A., which audiences around the world flock to see." When a group of German advertising agencies placed an ad in *Advertising Age* that said, "Let's make America great again," they left no doubt about what they had in mind. The ad featured cola, jeans, burgers, cigarettes, and alcohol—an advertiser's idea of what makes America great.

Some people might wonder what's wrong with this. On the most obvious level, as multinational chains replace local stores, local products, and local character, we end up in a world in which everything looks the same and everyone is Gapped and Starbucked. Shopping malls kill vibrant downtown centers locally and create a universe of uniformity internationally. Worse, we end up in a world ruled by, in John Maynard Keynes's phrase, the values of the casino. On this deeper level, rampant commercialism undermines our physical and psychological health, our environment, and our civic life and creates a toxic society. Advertising corrupts us and, I will argue, promotes a dissociative state that exploits trauma and can lead to addiction. To add insult to injury, it then co-opts our attempts at resistance and rebellion.

28 Although it is virtually impossible to measure the influence of advertising on a culture, we can learn something by looking at cultures only recently exposed to it. In 1980 the Gwich'in tribe of Alaska got television, and therefore massive advertising, for the first time. Satellite dishes, video games, and VCRs were not far behind. Before this, the Gwich'in lived much the way their ancestors had for a thousand generations. Within ten years, the young members of the tribe were so drawn by television they no longer had time to learn ancient hunting

methods, their parents' language, or their oral history. Legends told around campfires could not compete with *Beverly Hills 90210*. Beaded moccasins gave way to Nike sneakers, sled dogs to gas-powered skimobiles, and "tundra tea" to Folger's instant coffee.

Human beings used to be influenced primarily by the stories of our particular tribe or community, not by stories that are mass-produced and market-driven. As George Gerbner, one of the world's most respected researchers on the influence of the media, said, "For the first time in human history, most of the stories about people, life, and values are told not by parents, schools, churches, or others in the community who have something to tell, but by a group of distant conglomerates that have something to sell." The stories that most influence our children these days are the stories told by advertisers.

PERSONAL RESPONSE

What is your initial response to what Kilbourne tells readers that she will argue hin the rest of her book: "Advertising corrupts us and, I will argue, promotes a dissociative state that exploits trauma and can lead to addiction. To add insult to injury, it then co-opts our attempts at resistance and rebellion" (paragraph 27)? Are you skeptical or intrigued?

QUESTIONS FOR CLASS OR SMALL-GROUP DISCUSSION

1. What is your opinion on the matter of whether corporations should have the right to review editorial content of publications they advertise in and whether magazines should practice self-censorship? Is it just good business, or is it more than that, as Kilbourne claims? Do you think Kilbourne overreacts when she writes that this practice "warps a worldview and distorts the editorial content we read and the programs we listen to and watch" (paragraph 7)?
2. State in your own words the issues that Kilbourne is most concerned about in her allegations against women's and girls' magazines. Do you agree with her? Although she cites many examples, can you provide others that either support or refute her arguments? Summarize Kilbourne's point about alcohol and tobacco advertising. Is her argument valid? To what extent do you agree with her?
3. What do you think of Kilbourne's allegation that America exports "a popular culture that promotes escapism, consumerism, violence, and greed" (paragraph 26). Can you provide examples that either support or refute this view?
4. Without having read the rest of the book that this excerpt comes from *(Can't Buy My Love: How Advertising Changes the Way We Think and Feel)*, are you inclined to think that Kilbourne is right in her criticism of advertising, or do you find her argument in this excerpt unconvincing?

✧ PERSPECTIVES ON MEDIA STUDIES ✧

Suggested Writing Topics

1. Advertisers contend that they do not create problems, but simply reflect the values of society. Explain your position on the subject of how much responsibility advertisers should bear for the images they produce in their advertisements.
2. Describe a figure, character, recurring daydream, or escapist fantasy that gave you comfort or strength when you were growing up. Explain how it aided you then and how you view it now that you are grown up.
3. With Peter H. Gibbon's "The End of Admiration: The Media and the Loss of Heroes" in mind, argue either in support of or against the statement that America no longer has heroes.
4. Define the word "hero" and use a person you admire to illustrate the meaning of the word.
5. Survey a selection of magazines aimed at a specific audience—girls, women, boys, men—and apply the kind of analysis that Jean Kilbourne does in "Advertising's Influence on Media Content." Explain what you find and whether your conclusions agree with or differ from hers.
6. Use examples of well-known advertisements to explore the question of whether advertisers underestimate the intelligence of consumers.
7. With Sissela Bok's "Aggression: The Impact of Media Violence" in mind, select a particular film or television series and analyze its sexual or violent content How is sex or violence handled? Is there too much? Is it too graphic? How is it portrayed, and what is its relevance to the plot? Are sex and violence linked?
8. Listen to two radio talk shows or television programs, one liberal and one conservative, and compare the two. What subjects do they discuss? How do their approaches differ? Do you find yourself persuaded by one over the other? Why?
9. Select a news item in the headlines this week and follow the media's coverage of it, mixing media if possible. For instance, you could track the story as reported on an Internet site, on a national news program, and in a newspaper, or as it is handled by several different Internet sites, television programs, or newspapers. What conclusions can you draw about the media's handling of the story? Do you detect any bias in reporting it?
10. Write a paper in response to the central argument of any of the essays in this chapter.
11. Imagine that you are preparing to give a talk to a group of children about the possible dangers of exposure to media violence. Write an essay to that group as audience and include details, facts, or references to studies that you think would make an impression on them.

Research Topics

1. Research the subject of advertising ethics by locating articles and books representing the opinions of both those who are critical of advertisements and those who defend them. Argue your own position on the subject, supporting it with relevant source materials.
2. Research images of a specific group in advertising. For instance, you could focus on images of women, as Jean Kilbourne has done in "Advertising's Influence on Media Content," and locate additional research and opposing viewpoints. Consider also the topics of advertising images of men, advertisements that encourage destructive behavior, or advertisements aimed at children.
3. Take as your starting point any of the accusations that Jean Kilbourne makes in "Advertising's Influence on Media Content" about corporate sponsors, self-censorship, alcohol or tobacco advertisements, or conflicting messages in women's magazines. Locate sources, do some preliminary reading, and narrow your focus on one aspect of the broader topic.
4. Research the question of whether allegations that the media have a liberal bias are true. Is it simply a perception, or can such bias, if it exists, be documented?
5. Select a news story that got a great deal of media coverage and research how it was reported in a variety of media sources. Compare the handling of the news item by the different sources. What conclusions can you draw on whether there is bias in reporting the story?
6. Research any of the issues raised by Sissela Bok's article, perhaps including her book, *Mayhem: Violence as Public Entertainment,* as one of your sources. For instance, you may want to read more about the effects of violent entertainment on children's moral and psychological development, the debate between protecting children and preserving First Amendment rights, or the measures taken by other nations to control media violence without censorship. Because Bok's article was published over a decade ago, her research has probably been updated by other studies. Look for more recent studies for your research paper. Are the results similar to or markedly different from those of more dated research? Formulate your own position on the issue, and support it with references from your source materials.
7. Explain your perspective on some aspect of popular culture, taking into account the views expressed by any of the writers in this chapter. Focus on a specific issue about which you have formed an opinion after reading their views, refer to the other writers as a way of providing the context for your own essay, supplement those readings with additional research, and then explain in detail your own position. For instance, examine one form of popular entertainment, such as rock videos, popular music, television shows, advertising, or movies, for the ways in which it promotes or fosters an attitude of acceptance of violence.

Responding to Visuals

"I like it. It's dumb without trying to be clever."

1. What are the implications of this cartoon about consumers?
2. What aspects of advertising and consumers does the cartoon make fun of?
3. What does the cartoon imply about the role of advertisements?

Responding to Visuals

Effiect of TV advertising on children

1. Why does the figure coming out of the screen have a smile on his face and his hand over the child's eyes?
2. What sorts of things is the figure casting behind him? What do they represent?
3. What commentary does the image make on the effects of television advertising on children?

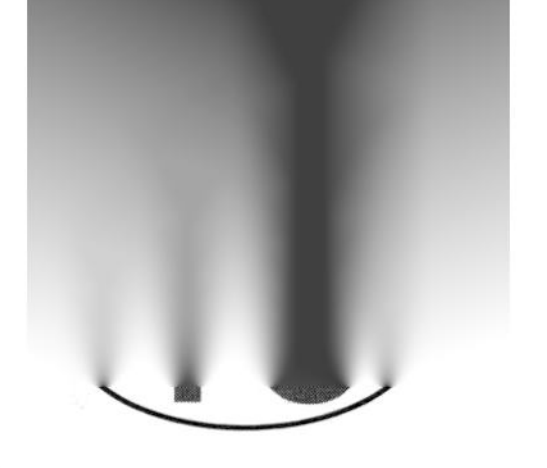

Film and Television

Makers of Hollywood films, television shows, and other products of the entertainment industry hope to tap into or even create trends that will have widespread appeal and thus result in huge profits. Because of its high visibility, ready availability, and ease of access to all age groups, the entertainment industry has always been closely scrutinized and subject to attack by its critics. Popular Hollywood films and television programs are particularly prime targets for both criticism and praise. Hollywood watchdogs and film critics pay attention not only to the craft of film production but also to the content of films. Indeed, the current film ratings system evolved in response to alarm at young viewers' exposure not only to scenes of graphic sex and violence but also to intensely frightening scenes. In recent years, many people have been sharply critical of films and television programs for what they see as irresponsible depiction of shocking images, excessive violence, and unnecessarily graphic sex. Defenders have been just as heated in their responses.

Television has been the target of suspicion, attack, and ridicule from the time it was invented. Though it is probably hard to believe now, when it was first invented, people thought "the tube" would never replace the radio, especially when its early live-only broadcasts included inevitable comical errors. Once the problems were resolved and television broadcasting became increasingly sophisticated in both technology and programming, television became a commonplace medium. Television programs now number in the thousands, with cable access and computer-controlled satellite dishes bringing a dizzying array of viewing choices into people's homes. Many families own two or three (or more) televisions and at least both a DVD and a CD player. It is commonplace to download television programs on computers and handheld electronic devices as well. With the seemingly endless demand for television shows from viewers, network producers and local station managers are always looking for programs that will attract viewers and draw sponsors.

One of the oldest debates about television programming has to do with its depiction of violence. Mike Males, in "Stop Blaming Kids and TV," expresses his opinion on whether television violence causes violent and criminal behavior. Although many people argue that television violence has enormous influence on children and bears large responsibility for the high U.S. homicide rate, Males argues that television does not cause violent behavior. He cites numerous studies, as well as his own personal observations from working with youths, to support his firm belief that critics are wrongheaded to blame teens and mass media for problems such as youth violence, excessive teenage drinking, and increased rates of smoking among teenagers. He argues that there are other, more plausible causes of these problems. Where do you stand on this issue?

Another area of television programming that researchers have begun to investigate is reality shows. These programs follow real people over time behaving in unscripted situations, such as surviving on a faraway and exotic island, selecting a potential mate from a group of twenty-five hopefuls, having a new home built for them, or competing to be the top singer or dancer in the nation. A couple of dozen such shows air during the regular television season and even more in the summer. The concept is not new: in the 1950s, for instance, *Queen for a Day* was an early variation, where contestants were selected to tell their sad stories and the winner was the one who garnered the loudest audience applause. But the proliferation of such programs is a twenty-first century phenomenon. In "Getting Real with Reality TV," Cynthia M. Frisby discusses research that helps explain why audiences view such television programs. After defining the social comparison theory developed in the 1950s, Frisby explains the results of a survey that she and others conducted to determine how that theory applies to reality-show viewers. As you read her article, think about your own viewing habits, particularly if you watch reality television shows.

The other two articles in this chapter discuss the subject of films. In "Creating Reel Change," Donovan Jacobs is interested in the positive effects of certain television and Hollywood films, especially documentaries, that deal with important social issues and that hope to influence audiences to take action in the interest of whatever cause the film is about. In contrast to so many critics of Hollywood films who believe that they promote antisocial behavior, Jacobs focuses on films that provide examples of pro-social behavior. As you read his article, see whether you have viewed any of the films he mentions, and if so, consider whether you responded in the way that companies who produce such films and documentaries hope viewers will respond.

Finally, Sady Doyle looks at the wild popularity among teen and preteen girls of the Twilight series of films and novels. The subtitle of her article reveals her position: "The unwarranted backlash against fans of the world's most popular vampire-romance series." If you have been accustomed to dismissing teenage girls as silly and overly romantic, consider whether this article makes you rethink your attitude.

STOP BLAMING KIDS AND TV

MIKE MALES

Mike Males, senior researcher for the Justice Policy Institute and sociology instructor at the University of California, Santa Cruz, describes himself as a writer of "unconventional articles on youth issues." His books include the following: The Scapegoat Generation: America's War on Adolescents *(1996);* Framing Youth: Ten Myths About the Next Generation *(1998);* Smoked: Why Joe Camel Is Still Smiling *(1999);* Juvenile Injustice: America's "Youth Violence" Hoax *(2000); and* Kids & Guns: How Politicians, Experts, and the Press Fabricate Fear of Youth *(2001). This essay first appeared in the October 1997 issue of the* Progressive. *Males can be reached through his homepage at* http://home.earthlink.net/~mmales/.

"Children have never been very good at listening to their elders," James Baldwin wrote in *Nobody Knows My Name*. "But they have never failed to imitate them." This basic truth has all but disappeared as the public increasingly treats teenagers as a robot-like population under sway of an exploitative media. White House officials lecture film, music, Internet, fashion, and pop-culture moguls and accuse them of programming kids to smoke, drink, shoot up, have sex, and kill.

So do conservatives, led by William Bennett and Dan Quayle. Professional organizations are also into media-bashing. In its famous report on youth risks, the Carnegie Corporation devoted a full chapter to media influences.

Progressives are no exception. *Mother Jones* claims it has "proof that TV makes kids violent." And the Institute of Alternative Media emphasizes, "the average American child will witness. . . . 200,000 acts of (TV) violence" by the time that child graduates from high school.

4 None of these varied interests note that during the eighteen years between a child's birth and graduation from high school, there will be fifteen million cases of *real* violence in American homes grave enough to require hospital emergency treatment. These assaults will cause ten million serious injuries and 40,000 deaths to children.

In October 1996, the Department of Health and Human Services reported 565,000 serious injuries that abusive parents inflicted on children and youths in 1993. The number is up four-fold since 1986.

The Department of Health report disappeared from the news in one day. It elicited virtually no comment from the White House, Republicans, or law enforcement officials. Nor from Carnegie scholars, whose 150-page study, "Great Transitions: Preparing Adolescents for a New Century," devotes two sentences to household violence. The left press took no particular interest in the story, either.

All sides seem to agree that fictional violence, sex on the screen, Joe Camel, beer-drinking frogs, or naked bodies on the Internet pose a bigger threat to children than do actual beatings, rape, or parental addictions. This, in turn, upholds the Clinton doctrine that youth behavior is the problem, and curbing young people's rights the answer.

8 Claims that TV causes violence bear little relation to real behavior. Japanese and European kids behold media as graphically brutal as that which appears on American screens, but seventeen-year-olds in those countries commit murder at rates lower than those of American seventy-year-olds.

Likewise, youths in different parts of the United States are exposed to the same media but display drastically different violence levels. TV violence does not account for the fact that the murder rate among black teens in Washington, D.C., is twenty-five times higher than that of white teens living a few Metro stops away. It doesn't explain why, nationally, murder doubled among nonwhite and Latino youth over the last decade, but declined among white Anglo teens. Furthermore, contrary to the TV brainwashing theory, Anglo sixteen-year-olds have lower violent-crime rates than black sixty-year-olds, Latino forty-year-olds, and Anglo thirty-year-olds. Men, women, whites, Latino, blacks, Asians, teens, young adults, middle-agers, and senior citizens in Fresno County—California's poorest urban area—display murder and violent-crime rates double those of their counterparts in Ventura County, the state's richest.

Confounding every theory, America's biggest explosion in felony violent crime is not street crime among minorities or teens of any color, but domestic violence among aging, mostly white baby boomers. Should we arm Junior with a V-chip to protect him from Mom and Dad?

12 In practical terms, media-violence theories are not about kids, but about race and class: If TV accounts for any meaningful fraction of murder levels among poorer, nonwhite youth, why doesn't it have the same effect on white kids? Are minorities inherently programmable?

The newest target is Channel One, legitimately criticized by the Unplug Campaign—a watchdog sponsored by the Center for Commercial-Free Public Education—as a corporate marketing ploy packaged as educational TV. But then the Unplug Campaign gives credence to claims that "commercials control kids" by "harvesting minds," as Roy Fox of the University of Missouri says. These claims imply that teens are uniquely open to media brainwashing.

Other misleading claims come from Johns Hopkins University media analyst Mark Crispin Miller. In his critique of Channel One in the May edition of *Extra!*, Miller invoked such hackneyed phrases as the "inevitable rebelliousness of adolescent boys," the "hormones raging," and the "defiant boorish behavior" of "young men." Despite the popularity of these stereotypes, there is no basis in fact for such anti-youth bias.

A 1988 study in the *Journal of Youth and Adolescence* by psychology professors Grayson Holmbeck and John Hill concluded: "Adolescents are *not* in turmoil, *not* deeply disturbed, *not* at the mercy of their impulses, *not* resistant to parental values, and *not* rebellious."

16 In the November 1992 *Journal of the American Academy of Child and Adolescent Psychiatry*, Northwestern University psychiatry professor Daniel Offer reviewed 150 studies and concluded, in his article "Debunking the Myths of Adolescence," that "the effects of pubertal hormones are neither potent nor pervasive."

If anything, Channel One and other mainstream media reinforce young people's conformity to—not defiance of—adult values. Miller's unsubstantiated claims that student consumerism, bad behaviors, and mental or biological imbalances are compelled by media ads and images could be made with equal force about the behaviors of his own age group. Binge drinking, drug abuse, and violence against children by adults over the age of thirty are rising rapidly.

The barrage of sexually seductive liquor ads, fashion images, and anti-youth rhetoric, by conventional logic, must be influencing those hormonally unstable middle-agers.

I worked for a dozen years in youth programs in Montana and California. When problems arose, they usually crossed generations. I saw violent kids with dads or uncles in jail for assault. I saw middle-schoolers molested in childhood by mom's boyfriend. I saw budding teen alcoholics hoisting forty-ouncers alongside forty-year old sots. I also saw again and again how kids start to smoke. In countless trailers and small apartments dense with blue haze, children roamed the rugs as grownups puffed. Mom and seventh-grade daughter swapped Dorals while bemoaning the evils of men.

A junior-high basketball center slept outside before a big game because a dozen elders—from her non-inhaling sixteen-year-old brother to her grandma—were all chain smokers. Two years later, she'd given up and joined the party.

20 As a rule, teen smoking mimicked adult smoking by gender, race, locale, era, and household. I could discern no pop-culture puppetry. My survey of 400 Los Angeles middle-schoolers for a 1994 *Journal of School Health* article found children of smoking parents three times more likely to smoke by age fifteen than children of nonsmokers. Parents were the most influential but not the only adults kids emulated. Nor did youngsters copy elders slavishly. Youths often picked slightly different habits (like chewing tobacco, or their own brands).

In 1989, the Centers for Disease Control lamented, "75 percent of all teenage smokers come from homes where parents smoke." You don't hear such candor from today's put-politics-first health agencies. Centers for Disease Control tobacco chieftain Michael Eriksen informed me that his agency doesn't make an issue of parental smoking. Nor do anti-smoking groups. Asked Kathy Mulvey, research director of INFACT: "Why make enemies of fifty million adult smokers" when advertising creates the real "appeal of tobacco to youth?"

Do ads hook kids on cigarettes? Studies of the effects of the Joe Camel logo show only that a larger fraction of teen smokers than veteran adult smokers choose the Camel brand. When asked, some researchers admit they cannot demonstrate that advertising causes kids to smoke who would not otherwise. And that's the real issue. In fact, surveys found smoking declining among teens (especially the youngest) during Joe's advent from 1985 to 1990.

The University of California's Stanton Glantz, whose exposure of 10,000 tobacco documents enraged the industry, found corporate perfidy far shrewder than camels and cowboys.

24 "As the tobacco industry knows well," Glantz reported, "kids want to be like adults." An industry marketing document advises: "To reach young smokers, present the cigarette as one of the initiations into adult life . . . the basic symbols of growing up."

The biggest predictor of whether a teen will become a smoker, a drunk, or a druggie is whether or not the child grows up amid adult addicts. Three-fourths of murdered kids are killed by adults. Suicide and murder rates among white teenagers resemble those of white adults, and suicide and murder rates among black teens track those of black adults. And as far as teen pregnancy goes, for minor mothers, four-fifths of the fathers are adults over eighteen, and half are adults over twenty.

The inescapable conclusion is this: If you want to change juvenile behavior, change adult behavior. But instead of focusing on adults, almost everyone points a finger at kids—and at the TV culture that supposedly addicts them.

Groups like Mothers Against Drunk Driving charge, for instance, that Budweiser's frogs entice teens to drink. Yet the 1995 National Household Survey found teen alcohol use declining. "Youths aren't buying the cute and flashy beer images," an in-depth *USA Today* survey found. Most teens found the ads amusing, but they did not consume Bud as a result.

28 By squabbling over frogs, political interests can sidestep the impolitic tragedy that adults over the age of twenty-one cause 90 percent of America's 16,000 alcohol-related traffic deaths every year. Clinton and drug-policy chief Barry McCaffrey ignore federal reports that show a skyrocketing toll of booze and drug-related casualties among adults in their thirties and forties—the age group that is parenting most American teens. But both officials get favorable press attention by blaming alcohol ads and heroin chic for corrupting our kids.

Progressive reformers who insist kids are so malleable that beer frogs and Joe Camel and Ace Ventura push them to evil are not so different from those on the Christian right who claim that *Our Bodies, Ourselves* promotes teen sex and that the group Rage Against the Machine persuades pubescents to roll down Rodeo Drive with a shotgun.

America's increasingly marginalized young deserve better than grownup escapism.

Millions of children and teenagers face real destitution, drug abuse, and violence in their homes. Yet these profound menaces continue to lurk in the background, even as the frogs, V-chips, and Mighty Morphins take center stage.

PERSONAL RESPONSE

Are you surprised by Males' defense of young people? Have you heard similar arguments before, or is his approach different from what you are used to hearing about television and its influence on young people?

QUESTIONS FOR CLASS OR SMALL-GROUP DISCUSSION

1. Males opens his essay with a quotation from James Baldwin and the following statement: "This basic truth has all but disappeared as the public increasingly treats teenagers as a robot-like population under sway of an exploitative media" (paragraph 1). State the "basic truth" that Males believes the quotation suggests. Then consider what Males seems to mean when he says that teenagers are treated "as a robot-like population." Do you agree with him on that point?
2. Males writes: "In practical terms, media-violence theories are not about kids, but about race and class" (paragraph 10). Are you persuaded by the evidence that Males presents to support this assertion? Can you add further proof or offer a counterargument?
3. Respond to this statement in paragraph 24: "If you want to change juvenile behavior, change adult behavior." Do you agree with Males?
4. How persuaded are you by Males's argument? Do you think that his personal observations strengthen or weaken his argument? What do you think about his use of loaded language and sarcasm? How would you assess the strengths and weaknesses of his argument overall?

GETTING REAL WITH REALITY TV

CYNTHIA M. FRISBY

Cynthia M. Frisby is associate professor of advertising at the University of Missouri School of Journalism, Columbia, and coeditor of Journalism Across Cultures (2003). *Her research interests include identifying the sources of American viewers' fascination with reality TV and the effects of idealized images on perceptions of body esteem among African American women. This essay appeared in the September 2004 issue of* USA Today *magazine.*

Every year, television networks vie to create cutting edge programming. New shows promise more drama, suspense, and laughter while pushing the envelope of what is morally and socially acceptable, funny, thrilling, and, of course, entertaining. Fitting all these criteria—at least according to the soaring ratings—is reality based television.

Reality TV is a genre of programming in which the everyday routines of "real life" people (as opposed to fictional characters played by actors) are followed closely by the cameras. Viewers cannot seem to help but become involved in the captivating plotlines and day-to-day drama depicted daily on their screens. Apparently, people simply take pleasure in watching other people's lives while those under scrutiny enjoy being on television enough to go on for free.

There are three major categories within the reality genre: game shows (e.g., "Survivor"), dating shows (e.g., "The Bachelor"), and talent shows (e.g., "American Idol"). While reality programming breeds fiercely during the regular season, in summer there is an even greater glut since such programs are cheap to produce and, if they fail to draw ratings, they quickly can be flushed away and replaced with something else.

4 It is becoming increasingly difficult to avoid contact with reality TV these days. In offices, hair salons, health clubs, restaurants, and bars, the general public is discussing what happened on television the night before—and it is not the world news they are dissecting. Rather, the hot topic may be what happened on "The Apprentice." Then again, it might be a "did-you-see" conversation concerning "The Bachelor" or "For Love or Money."

Shows such as "The Apprentice," "Survivor," "Fear Factor," "The Amazing Race," "American Idol," "American Girl," "Big Brother," "Extreme Makeover" "Temptation Island," "Cheaters," "The Simple Life," "Queer Eye for the Straight Guy," "The Bachelor," and "The Bachelorette" have reached out and grabbed today's American television viewer. During the 2003–04 season, 10 reality shows ranked among the top 25 prime-time programs in the audience-composition index for adults 18–49 with incomes of $75,000 or more. Nielsen ratings indicate that more than 18,000,000 viewers have been captivated by television programs that take ordinary people and place them in situations that have them competing in ongoing contests while being filmed 24 hours a day. What is it about these shows that attracts millions of loyal viewers week after week? Is it blatant voyeurism, or can their success be explained as a harmless desire for entertainment?

From "Survivor" to "Elimidate" to "Average Joe," to "Joe Millionaire," it seems that reality TV succeeds because it plays off of real-life concerns—looking for love, competing to win a job or big prize, or becoming a millionaire—situations (or dreams) that most people can relate to. However, as these shows become more pervasive, their grip on "reality" seems to be growing more tenuous.

"It's refreshing to see everyday people getting some of the spotlight, rather than just seeing movie stars all the time," maintains CBS News associate Presley Weir. According to CBS, the same element of being human that encourages people to gossip about the lives of their friends, family, and even total strangers is what fosters an audience for reality television. Much like a car crash on the side of the freeway, glimpses into the interior workings of other human beings is often shocking, yet impossible to turn away from. It was this theory that produced MTV's "The Real World," often referred to as "the forerunner of reality television shows." Seven strangers are selected to live together, and viewers watch to find out what happens when individuals with different backgrounds and points of view are left in close quarters.

Media Gratification

8 Researchers frequently refer to at least six gratifications of media use: information (also known as surveillance or "knowledge"), escape, passing time, entertainment, social viewing/status enhancement, and relaxation. Although the names or labels for these gratifications may change, various studies confirm that they hold up in and across all situations. So what type of gratifications do viewers receive from reality TV?

Actually, individuals compare themselves with others for a variety of reasons, including to: determine relative standing on an issue or related ability; emulate behaviors; determine norms; lift spirits or feel better about life and personal situations; and evaluate emotions, personality, and self-worth.

Those made with others who are superior to or better off than oneself are referred to as upward comparisons. Individuals engaging in upward comparison may learn from others, be inspired by their examples, and become highly motivated to achieve similar goals. Upward comparisons, research suggests, are invoked when a person is motivated to change or overcome difficulties. Self-improvement is the main effect of an upward comparison because the targets serve as role models, teaching and motivating individuals to achieve or overcome similar problems.

On the other hand, when a social comparison involves a target who is inferior, incompetent, or less fortunate, it is referred to as a downward comparison. Its basic principle is that people feel better about their own situation and enhance their subjective well-being when they make comparisons with others who are worse off. Supposedly, downward comparisons help individuals cope with personal problems by allowing them to see themselves and their difficulties in a more positive light by realizing there are others who face more difficult circumstances.

12 A social comparison does not mean that the individual has to give careful, elaborate, conscious thought about the comparison, but implies that there has to be, to some degree, an attempt to identify or look for similarities or differences between

the other and self on some particular dimension. There are theorists who might argue that, for a comparison to be considered a comparison, the individual must be aware of the comparison and come into direct contact with the other person. However, psychologists have discovered that social comparisons do not require conscious or direct personal contact because fictional characters illustrated in the media can represent meaningful standards of comparison.

Data on social comparisons and media use suggest that everyday encounters with media images may provide viewers with information that encourages them to engage in an automatic, spontaneous social comparison. This ultimately affects mood and other aspects of subjective well-being. People just might not be able to articulate consciously the comparison process or consciously register its effects (i.e., self-enhancement, self-improvement, etc.).

Reality TV allows audiences to laugh, cry, and live vicariously through so-called everyday, ordinary people who have opportunities to experience things that, until the moment they are broadcast, most individuals only dream about. Viewers may tune into these shows: because they contain elements the audience would like to experience themselves; to laugh at the mistakes of others and/or celebrate successes; or to feel better about themselves because they are at least not as "bad as the people on television."

Exposure to tragic events or bad news invites social comparison among viewers. It is believed that reality audiences may be encouraged to compare and contrast their own situation with those of the reality show stars, and that this comparison process eventually could produce a form of self-satisfaction.

16 In real-life, everyday situations, it would be extremely difficult to avoid making some type of comparison. Frequently, people may compare themselves with others in their immediate environment or in the mass media in order to judge their own personal worth.

We contacted 110 people and asked them to complete a uses and gratifications survey on reality television with two goals in mind: to demonstrate that social comparisons may be elicited by certain television content and to explore if viewers use reality television's content and images as a source for social comparison.

Of the respondents, 78.2% reported being regular viewers of reality television programs. A list of 37 reality shows was presented to the participants. They were asked to check those that they watch on a regular basis, and indicate on a scale of 1–5—number 1 signifying "liked a lot" and number five meaning "extreme dislike"—whether they liked or disliked each of the 37 programs. This paper-and-pencil test also asked respondents to identify the extent to which they considered themselves a "regular viewer of reality television." For purposes of conceptualization, a regular viewer was defined as "one who watches the show every week, and/or records episodes to avoid missing weekly broadcasts."

Data was obtained on other television viewing preferences by asking respondents to indicate how regularly they watch programs like news magazines, talk shows, reality programs, daytime serials, and other offerings and to identify the gratifications obtained from watching reality television.

20 To better understand the cognitive responses made when exposed to media content, a content analysis of the thoughts generated while watching reality TV was conducted. The researcher coded any and all thoughts that contained expressions of, or alluded to, social comparisons that participants "appeared to have" made spontaneously.

Participants were told that they later would see a segment of reality TV and encouraged to view that segment as if they were watching the program at home. While viewing the segment, participants were asked to record all their thoughts, and were given ample space to do so.

Data show that, of all the responses made concerning reality programming, most expressed some type of comparison between themselves and the reality show's stars. We conducted a content analysis of the thoughts and responses provided by the participants and found that, for the most part, men and women, as well as regular viewers and nonviewers, did not differ in terms of how they responded to people on reality shows.

We then compared mood ratings obtained prior to viewing the reality show with those from immediately following exposure to the program. Analysis clearly indicated that regular viewers and nonviewers alike experienced a significant mood enhancement after exposure to reality television.

Captivating Audiences

24 We know that reality television can captivate millions of viewers at any given time on any given day. Research has begun to document how people engage in automatic, spontaneous social comparisons when confronted by certain media images, particularly those of reality TV. We also know that one major effect of exposure to reality television is to feel better about one's own life circumstances, abilities, and talents. Reality TV also serves as a much-needed distraction from the ongoing parade of tragic world events. It allows viewers an outlet by watching others overcome hardships, escape danger, live in a rainforest, land a dream job, learn to survive in Corporate America, and yes, even find love.

Whether the aim is money, love, becoming a rock star, creative expression, or just a chance to be seen on TV, the effect on audiences is the same. People like knowing that there are others who are going through the same life experiences that they are and often make the same mistakes. Despite the shifting desires of society and the fickleness of television audiences, the human need to compare and relate has provided a market for this genre.

So, while viewers realize they are not America's Next Top Model, may not have a chance at becoming the next American Idol, or even an All American Girl, they do enjoy the fact that, through a vicarious social comparison process, they can fall in love, win $1,000,000, or get the office snitch fired.

PERSONAL RESPONSE

Do you watch any reality television shows? If so, explain their appeal. If not, explain why they do not appeal to you.

QUESTIONS FOR CLASS OR SMALL-GROUP DISCUSSION

1. What functions do the opening paragraphs serve? What is Frisby's thesis? How well organized and developed do you find her essay?
2. Explain in your own words what the social comparison theory is (paragraph 9) and how it applies in general to viewers of reality television programs, according to Frisby.
3. How do the terms "upward comparison" (paragraph 11) and "downward comparison" specifically apply to viewers who watch reality television shows, according to Frisby?
4. Summarize the results of the uses and gratifications survey (paragraph 18) that Frisby and colleagues conducted. Do you think that Frisby's observations accurately describe the people you know who view reality television programs?

CREATING REEL CHANGE

DONOVAN JACOBS

Donovan Jacobs, a story development consultant based in Los Angeles, has been script consultant for many motion picture production companies and television networks, including Warner Brothers, ABC, and Touchstone Pictures. A graduate of the prestigious Warner Bros. Writers Workshop for television, he specializes in the development of family movies for television. Jacobs contributed a chapter to a book by Act One: Training for Hollywood called Behind the Screen: Hollywood Insiders on Faith, Film and Culture *(2005). This piece was written for the November 2006 issue of* Sojourners.

Movie and television directors, producers, and writers interested in saying something of substance to their audiences have often been confronted with a quote generally attributed to former studio head Jack Warner: "If you want to send a message, call Western Union." Despite this adage's implication that films and TV programs should avoid the political and stick to entertaining (and make their studios and networks gobs of money), a number of movies and TV shows over the years have dealt with vital issues and encouraged pro-social behavior.

Now—whether because of, or in response to, opportunities offered by newer media such as the Internet and cable television—a variety of untraditional film and documentary makers seek to do more than portray positive action on the screen. These companies and artists want to motivate their audiences to get better informed on their issues, volunteer to help the subjects of the movie or program, and even advocate for legislation that offers protection to victims and tries to right the wrongs portrayed.

Probably the most publicized of these filmmakers is former eBay president Jeff Skoll, who through his company Participant Productions has committed an estimated $100 million to co-financing and producing a slate of theatrical releases. These movies include *An Inconvenient Truth,* Al Gore's documentary on global warming released earlier this year, and the current *Fast Food Nation,* about a marketing expert's odyssey to discover how his hamburger chain really makes its meat.

4 Participant's distinctiveness thus far hasn't been marked in Hollywood's traditional measures of achievement (four of the company's movies were nominated for Oscars in 2005 but have had mixed success at the box office). Rather, its chief innovation is creation of Internet-based campaigns for each film that allow viewers to join with established organizations to both make personal changes and call for social action in response to the movie's themes.

It's difficult to measure the success of these campaigns. Participant's October 2005 release of *North Country* (about a pioneering female coal miner harassed by male co-workers) was timed to allow audiences to support the National Organization for Women and other feminist groups in efforts to renew the federal Violence Against Women Act (VAWA). North Country only grossed $18 million, meaning about 2 million people saw it in theaters. But if even a small percentage of that number demanded approval of the act, the film may have contributed to the bill's passage in January 2006.

The TV industry has long been criticized for shying away from socially significant topics. But in recent years, the rise of cable television has allowed newer networks to present programs on controversial and vital issues of interest to their targeted audiences.

MTV, which has a reputation for offensive and sexually explicit programs, has also aired documentaries (many starring music and entertainment celebrities) intended to inform and inspire its teen and young adult audiences regarding issues—including discrimination and sexual health—that often escape mainstream media attention. Last summer, MTV announced plans for a special to feature hip-hop star Jay-Z and his efforts to raise awareness of the lack of safe drinking water in several countries during his September international concert tour. MTV's Web site will offer ways for viewers to contribute to building "Play-Pumps," playground carousels that pump fresh water as kids spin them.

8 Lifetime Television has gained solid ratings with its heavily female viewership for a series of issue-based movies and miniseries, including *A Girl Like Me: The Gwen Araujo Story,* about a Latina mother who first opposes then supports her son's determination to live as a woman. Premiering last June, the movie was followed by public service announcements offering suggestions for encouraging tolerance and ending discrimination against transgender persons.

Lifetime's public affairs office has emerged as a lobbying force in Washington, D.C., credited by Rep. Carolyn Maloney with assisting in the passage of legislation involving women's issues such as quick DNA testing of rape kits and video voyeurism (the latter the subject of a 2004 Lifetime movie).

Many of the most vibrant movies and documentaries committed to advocacy come from less prominent filmmakers who use technologies such as DVDs and

Web sites not only to inform supporters, but to distribute their work to much wider audiences than otherwise possible. Brave New Films, a Los Angeles-based company run by veteran television producer Robert Greenwald, has focused on creating documentaries (such as last year's *Wal-Mart: The High Cost of Low Price*) that premiere in theaters and then are shown in public DVD screenings with discussion sessions after the film.

The company's current release, *Iraq for Sale: The War Profiteers,* deals with corporations, including Halliburton and Blackwater, that collect billions in taxpayer funds while allegedly delivering shoddy services that endanger U.S. troops and Iraqi citizens. Brave New Films arranged screenings of the movie for thousands of groups in July, devoting each day of a particular week to different audiences and the causes supported by co-sponsoring groups. The timing of these screenings shortly before the 2006 elections was no accident: One of the moviemakers' goals was to aid "get out the vote" drives across the country.

12 The filmmakers also hope to generate support for two proposed bills. One would form a congressional investigative entity to root out corruption and expose wrongdoers, modeled after the World War II-era "Truman Committee." The other legislation is the Honest Leadership and Accountability in Contracting Act of 2006, which defines and demands stiff penalties for war profiteering.

The Social Action goals of the three 20-something filmmakers behind the DVD documentary *Invisible Children* are equally ambitious. After graduating from film school, Jason Russell convinced childhood friends Bobby Bailey and Laren Poole to travel with him to Africa in 2003 to make a movie. The trio stumbled upon the story of thousands of children in northern Uganda, many of them orphans in refugee camps, who must hide in the countryside and in basements each night to avoid abduction by the Lord's Resistance Army, a rebel force that turns its victims into child soldiers and maims or kills those who resist.

Invisible Children seems amateurish and silly in spots, but the film's irreverence may make its heavy subject matter more appealing to the thousands of groups (mainly high school and college students) who have attended screenings around the United States. The movie's Web site features stories of young people inspired by the documentary to raise thousands of dollars to fund educational programs set up by the filmmakers in Uganda. This school year, more than 600 Ugandan teenagers will have their schooling paid for by American student fundraisers and the sale of native bracelets through the Web site. Natalia Angelo, a spokesperson for the filmmakers, told *Sojourners* that one of the most gratifying aspects of the movie's success has been the opportunity to spotlight stories of altruism and sacrifice by teens and young adults, which counters the prevailing myth of the supposed selfishness and materialism of American youth.

The short movies available through the New York-based Media That Matters Film Festival may seem small in scope, but they still convey a strong sense of urgency regarding the subjects they explore. The 16 documentaries and fictional films in the festival are first screened on the Internet and then made available on DVD each fall to educators across the country, along with teachers' guides that can be downloaded from the festival Web site.

16 Internet links and information in the guides provide sources of detailed information and opportunities for volunteerism and advocacy relating to the movies' broad range of themes. The festival is also affiliated with MediaRights, an organization that helps non-profits and advocacy groups learn to use documentaries to reach out to potential supporters and create change.

One of the shorts in the festival is *In the Morning*, a prizewinning fictional movie based on the true story of an honor killing in Turkey, where a rape victim was murdered by her brother to prevent her from bringing further "shame" on the family. Filmmaker Danielle Lurie stresses that honor killings, which occur primarily in the Middle East, are not linked to Islam—the basis for the killings is tribal. Lurie hopes the movie—which, thanks to the Internet, can be seen in Turkey and throughout the world—might help persuade the young boys often chosen by their fathers to commit the murders (because they tend to get shorter sentences) to not kill their sisters.

Lurie might be echoing everyone from a Hollywood producer like Jeff Skoll to her fellow young filmmakers when she says, "I would be naive to say that any single film on its own could make a difference, but my hope is that a movie, along with other films and educational tools, could create enough awareness that those in positions of power could effect change." Increasingly, it looks like these and other movies are placing the audience in those positions of power.

PERSONAL RESPONSE

Write about a film that has made a difference to you, perhaps one that made you aware of a problem you did not know about before or that moved you to act or think differently.

QUESTIONS FOR CLASS OR SMALL-GROUP DISCUSSION

1. What, according to Jacobs, have nontraditional films and documentaries done to "promote pro-social behavior" (paragraph 2)?
2. How convincing do you find Jacobs' examples and his explanations of how they support his thesis?
3. Discuss the range of topics covered by the films that Jacobs mentions. If you have seen any of them, what did you think of them? If you haven't seen any of them, which might you be interested in viewing, based on Jacobs' comments about them?
4. Discuss additional topics that you think would make good subjects for the kinds of films that Jacobs is writing about.

GIRLS JUST WANNA HAVE FANGS: THE UNWARRANTED BACKLASH AGAINST FANS OF THE WORLD'S MOST POPULAR VAMPIRE-ROMANCE

SADY DOYLE

Sady Doyle is a writer living in New York. Her articles have appeared in online editions of The American Prospect *and London's* Guardian, *as well as other publications. This article was posted on November 19, 2009, at the online site* www.Prospect.org *and published in the November 2009 print issue of* The American Prospect.

When *New Moon*, the second film adaptation of Stephenie Meyer's four-part *Twilight* series, opens in theaters this month, those who see it will not be getting great art. The faults of Meyer's immensely popular teen vampire-romance novels have been endlessly, and publicly, rehashed: the retrograde gender roles, the plodding plotlines, the super-heated goofiness of Meyer's prose. I can confirm for you that these faults are real!

Yet I could not stop reading the series. The books—all about sexy teen vampire Edward Cullen, his sexy teen werewolf rival Jacob Black, and their joint quest to stalk, control, and condescend their way into the ever-turgid affections of sexy teen (human) narrator Bella Swan—are slow, repetitive, and often unintentionally hilarious. ("If I hadn't seen him undressed, I would have sworn there was nothing more beautiful than Edward in his khakis." Wait. Hold up. The vampire is wearing khakis?)

Twilight isn't a literary masterpiece and doesn't need to be. There is, I would argue, a place for fantasies like these—specifically, a place in the lives of adolescent girls, who often find actual teenage boys more intimidating than the fictional vampire variety, and for whom imaginary worlds (where no one has to grow up, where danger is the prelude to a rescue, where boys have no hidden agendas aside from loving you forever) can be a shelter from the terrors of puberty. The books are silly—and have been roundly critiqued by feminists—but they speak to a legitimate need.

4 Meyer's commitment to satisfying that need hasn't gone unrewarded. In the first quarter of 2009, *Twilight* novels composed 16 percent of all book sales—four out of every 25 books sold were part of the series. The final installment, *Breaking Dawn*, sold 1.3 million copies on the day of its release in August 2008.

And then there are the movies. The first, *Twilight*, made $70.6 million on its opening weekend last November and set the record for biggest opening weekend for a film by a female director. The soundtrack sold 2.2 million copies. The follow-up film, *New Moon*, began selling out screenings more than two months ago, and its soundtrack is expected to be one of the top-selling albums of 2009, even though it's composed mostly of songs by indie artists.

Twilight is more than a teen dream. It's a massive cultural force. Yet the very girliness that has made it such a success has resulted in its being marginalized and mocked. Of course, you won't find many critics lining up to defend Dan Brown or Tom Clancy, either; mass-market success rarely coincides with literary acclaim. But male escapist fantasies—which, as anyone who has seen *Die Hard* or read those Tom Clancy novels can confirm, are not unilaterally sophisticated, complex, or forward-thinking—tend to be greeted with shrugs, not sneers. The *Twilight* backlash is vehement, and it is just as much about the fans as it is about the books. Specifically, it's about the fact that those fans are young women.

Twilight fans (sometimes known as "Twi-Hards") are derided and dismissed, sometimes even by outlets that capitalize on their support. MTV News crowned "Twilighters" its Woman of the Year in 2008, but referred to them as "shrieking and borderline-stalker female fans." You can count on that word—shrieking—to appear in most articles about *Twilight* readers, from *New York* magazine's Vulture blog ("Teenage girls shrieking . . . before the opening credits even begin") to *Time* magazine ("Shrieking fangirls [outdoing] hooting fanboys . . . in number, ardor, and decibel level") to *The Onion*'s A.V. Club ("Squealing hordes of (mostly) teenage, female fans") to *The New York Times* ("Squeals! The 'Twilight Saga: New Moon' Teaser Trailer Is Here!"). Yes, Twi-Hards can be loud. But is it really necessary to describe them all by the pitch of their voices? It propagates the stereotype of teen girls as hysterical, empty-headed, and ridiculous.

8 Self-described geeks and horror fans are especially upset at how the series introduces the conventions of the romance novel—that most stereotypically feminine, most scorned of literary forms—into their far more highbrow and culturally relevant monster stories. At the 2009 Comic-Con, *Twilight* fans were protested and said to be "ruining" the event. Fans of *Star Wars*, *Star Trek*, *X-Men*, and *Harry Potter* are seen as dorks at worst, participants in era-defining cultural phenomena at best. Not so for *Twilight* fans. What sets *Twilight* apart from Marvel comics? The answer is fairly obvious, and it's not—as geeks and feminists might hope—the quality of the books or movies. It's the number of boys in the fan base.

Compare Meyer to J. K. Rowling. The *Harry Potter* author had her detractors, too. In a 2000 *Wall Street Journal* article, Harold Bloom turned up his nose at the *Harry Potter* series, calling the books "not well written" and an example of cultural "dumbing-down." The headline: "Can 35 Million Book Buyers Be Wrong? Yes." In 1999, *The New York Times* seemed bewildered by the popularity of *Harry Potter* and noted, in a hilariously late-'90s turn of phrase, that "the books have become the literary equivalent of Furby stuffed animals." Yet *Potter* fans were never mocked as much as *Twilight* fans are, and respect for the series grew along with its readership. The final three books in the series were given full-length considerations in the *Times* by that most respected of book reviewers, Michiko Kakutani. "J. K. Rowling's monumental, spellbinding epic, 10 years in the making, is deeply rooted in traditional literature," reads her review of the final *Potter* novel, published in 2007.

There's little doubt that Rowling's success stemmed from her talent. But she also benefited from escaping the girly ghetto to which *Twilight* has been confined. Her publishers, famously, asked her to bill herself as J. K. rather than Joanne so as not to alienate male readers, and her books focused on a male hero and included lots of boy-friendly elements such as sports and warfare. She won a male readership, and with it, praise for the "universality" of her work.

Meyer, meanwhile, decided to forgo a pen name in favor of Stephenie, and *Twilight* is largely narrated by a girl. The books don't strive to draw in straight, male readers: There's little action, lots of emotion, and much lavish description of Edward Cullen's beauty. The vampire heartthrob isn't exactly macho. He's smooth-skinned, delicate-featured, and his body even sparkles. Edward abstains from sex and human blood, turning down several opportunities to enjoy both, and talks about his feelings frequently. To be blunt, he's not much of a man by sexist standards. In less-civilized regions of the Internet, the words "gay," "faggot," and "pussy" are thrown around liberally in discussions of the series, and of Edward.

12 Is it any wonder that there are so few visible male *Twilight* fans? Although boys' lack of interest in the series is used to argue against its "universality," the fact is that boys who do like it may be legitimately scared to say so. The vitriol aimed at the series is often about policing gender and punishing girliness—and boys who dare to enjoy something so blatantly non-masculine would almost certainly find themselves harshly judged.

Yet, if the numbers are any indication, you don't need male fans to dominate the marketplace. In this decade, teen girls have backed the success of Taylor Swift (who ranks above every artist on the pop charts except for Michael Jackson), Miley Cyrus (responsible for multiple best-selling albums, a television series, a concert film, a movie, and various merchandise including a best-selling book), and the blockbuster movie franchise *High School Musical*. In the 1990s, teenage girls were responsible for the runaway success of Justin Timberlake, Britney Spears, and *Titanic*, the top-grossing movie of all time. A fan base of teen girls launched Madonna's multi-decade career. And there was that 1960s boy band—the one with all the catchy, cheery pop songs and the cute, nonthreatening members who made girls squeal. I believe they called themselves The Beatles.

Teen girls have the power to shape the market because they don't have financial responsibilities, tend to be passionate about their interests, and share those interests socially. If a girl likes something, she's liable to recommend it to her friends; a shared enthusiasm for Edward, or the Jonas Brothers, or anything else, becomes part of their bond. Marketers prize teenage girls, even as the media scoff at them.

If you want to matter, though, apparently you need boys. The third film adaptation of the *Twilight* series, *Eclipse*, will be helmed by horror director David Slade, who has made such movies as *Hard Candy* and *Thirty Days of Night*. Even though it will not hit theaters until June 2010, it is already being touted as "darker," more action-packed, and more "guy friendly." Because the popularity of the *Twilight* formula guarantees *Eclipse* will be a box-office smash, the decision to consciously appeal to boys seems more like a grab at credibility than at profit. Romance-loving Twi-Hards be damned! Who cares about disappointing a huge, passionate, lucrative fan base if they're all a bunch of *girls*?

16 As *Twilight* demonstrates, not everything girls like is good art—or, for that matter, good feminism. Still, the *Twilight* backlash should matter to feminists, even if the series makes them shudder. If we admit that girls are powerful consumers, then

we admit that they have the ability to shape the culture. Once we do that, we might actually start listening to them. And I suspect a lot of contemporary girls have more to talk about than Edward Cullen.

PERSONAL RESPONSE

If you have read the books and/or seen the films that Doyle discusses, explain your response to them. If you haven't read the books or seen the films, explain whether you are intrigued by them after reading this article.

QUESTIONS FOR CLASS OR SMALL-GROUP DISCUSSION

1. Why do you think Doyle begins her essays by pointing out the faults and weaknesses of the *Twilight* series? Do you consider it an effective strategy in her argument?
2. Summarize Doyle's argument. What evidence does she provide to support her position? Are you convinced that the backlash against fans of the *Twilight* series is "unwarranted" (subtitle)?
3. According to Doyle, what is the difference between teenage girl escapist fantasies and the escapist fantasies of males? Do you agree with her on this point?
4. In your own words, state the differences that Doyle sees between two successful female writers of popular series, Stephenie Meyer and J. K. Rowling. Can you add anything to her comparison? Are there any points on which you disagree with Doyle?

✧ PERSPECTIVES ON FILM AND TELEVISION ✧

Suggested Writing Topics

1. Argue for or against Sady Doyle's position that the backlash against "Twi-Hards" is "unwarranted" in "Girls Just Wanna Have Fangs: The Unwarranted Backlash Against Fans of the World's Most Popular Vampire-Romance."
2. Like advertisers, producers of television shows argue that they do not create problems but simply reflect the values of society. Explain your position on the subject of how much responsibility television producers should bear for the images portrayed in their programs.
3. Write an analysis of a popular television show or film. Your analysis can be either positive or negative, depending on your feelings about it. You may criticize it as ridiculous, boring, or poorly acted, for instance, or you may praise a brilliant, hilarious, or wonderfully acted one.
4. Do an analysis of any fairy tale or children's film for its depiction of female and male sex roles. Do you find stereotyped assumptions about masculinity and femininity? In what ways do you think the fairy tale or film reinforces or shapes cultural definitions of masculinity and femininity?

5. Explore the positive and negative aspects of a particular type of television programming, such as situation comedies, medical dramas, or soap operas. Use several programs of the type as examples.
6. Assess the quality of today's films by using examples of a film or films you have seen recently. Consider, for instance, evaluating the values endorsed by the film(s).
7. Write a position paper on the topic of sexually explicit and graphically violent Hollywood films by selecting one film for close analysis. You may want to mention two or three other examples to support your position.
8. Explore the effects on you, either positive or negative, of a movie or television program that you saw when you were growing up.
9. If you are a fan of reality shows on television, choose one that you particularly like and explain why it appeals to you. If you do not like reality shows, pick one that you particularly dislike and explain why you do not like it.
10. Examine portrayals of any of the following in several television programs: the American family, women, men, a particular ethnic group, or a particular age group.
11. Write a letter to the president of one of the major television networks in which you express your views on the nature and quality of its programming for children.
12. Write a letter to either or both the sponsors and the producer of a television program you find particularly violent, mindless, or vulgar, explaining your complaint and what you would like to see changed. Or, write a letter to the sponsors or producer of a television program you find intellectually stimulating, educational, or informative, praising the program and pointing out its best features.

Research Topics

1. Research the critical responses to the *Twilight* series of books or films and compare them with the critical responses to the Harry Potter series of books or films. As part of your research, read books or view films in both series and formulate a position on how the two compare.
2. Select a particular genre of film, such as comedy, western, romance, fantasy, or action, and research observations of various film historians, film critics, and/or other film commentators about the films in that genre. This is a broad topic, so be sure to narrow your focus early on. One approach is to assess the historical development of the genre and its current state. As you do your preliminary reading, look for a controversial issue on which to focus your research. Then draw your own conclusions after you thoroughly research your subject.
3. Select a particular type of television program, such as reality TV, news program, talk show, children's entertainment, drama, or situation comedy, and research what critics say about such programming currently and

historically. Is there a program that represents the best of the type? The worst of the type?

4. Film or television critics and commentators sometimes use the term "golden age" to refer to a period in the past when a particular type of film or program reached its peak of excellence. Select a medium—film or television—and a genre—comedy, drama, or another of your choice—and research what characterizes "golden age" for the type and which program(s) or film(s) represent the type. If possible, view representative programs or films and include your responses to them in your research paper.
5. Much has been written about certain images in films or on television, such as the portrayal of women, of minorities, and of class issues. Select a particular image or theme to research for its representation in films or on television. Choose a specific period (films/programs from this year or last year, or films/programs from a previous decade, for instance) and narrow your focus as much as possible. This task will become more manageable once you begin searching for sources and discover the nature of articles, books, and other materials on the general subject.
6. Research a recent film that generated controversy, or view any of the films mentioned in Donovan Jacobs's "Creating Reel Change." View the film yourself and read what critics and other authorities on the subject of film have to say about this particular one.
7. Research the Television Violence Act. Find out what it is and what critics, behaviorists, and media experts say about its potential effectiveness. Then explain your own opinion of the effectiveness of such an act.
8. In 1961, Newton N. Minow coined the term *vast wasteland* for what he saw as television's empty content and anti-intellectualism. Argue either that television remains a vast wasteland or that the phrase is unfair to television today. Base your position on research into the views of experts or others who have published opinions on the subject. Include the results of studies or any other relevant data you find.
9. Research any of the subjects relevant to this chapter that are suggested by the titles of books that Mike Males has written: *The Scapegoat Generation: America's War on Adolescents* (1996); *Framing Youth: Ten Myths About the Next Generation* (1998); *Smoked: Why Joe Camel is Still Smiling* (1999); *Juvenile Injustice: America's "Youth Violence" Hoax* (2000); or *Kids & Guns: How Politicians, Experts, and the Press Fabricate Fear of Youth* (2001). Refer to one or more of these books in your paper.

Responding to Visuals

A still image from director Mel Gibson's film The Passion of the Christ

1. What is your emotional response to this image? What details of the image contribute to your response to it?
2. Characterize the graphic violence represented by the picture. Do you see any paradox in people's accepting this kind of violence while ordinarily condemning violence in films?
3. Comment on the perspective from which the image is viewed. What is the effect of the close-up of Jesus' upper body?

Responding to Visuals

"In search of America's laziest man"

1. What do the man's clothing and the fact that he's asleep say about him as a television viewer?
2. How does the image of the man relate to the words coming from the television program?
3. What comment on reality television shows does this cartoon make?

CHAPTER 11

The Arts

Humans have always used a variety of creative ways in which to express themselves imaginatively through such forms as storytelling, drawing, painting, sculpture, and music. Researchers have discovered paintings in prehistoric caves that provide evidence of the earliest humans' compulsion to tell stories or depict significant aspects of their lives through pictures, while people today argue that videogames, Internet websites, and other digital forms are the latest developments in mankind's quest to express itself aesthetically.

Literature has long been regarded as a significant art form. Indeed, some would claim that imaginative writing, whether it be a short story, a novel, a poem, or some other form of creative expression, is just as crucial to the nurturing of the human soul as are visual arts and music. Certainly Michael Chabon in "Solitude and the Fortresses of Youth" believes this is so. He uses personal experience to explain why he believes young people should not be unduly punished for writing violent material. The force of his own imagination, he writes, was "nourished, stoked and liberated" by everything he read, including stories depicting "human beings in the most extreme situations and states of emotion—horror stories; accounts of madness and despair." Even people whose chief interests are science and scientific writing explore the nature of human intelligence as measured by an ability to create metaphor and to think in imaginative ways. Whatever its form, imagination and creativity are clearly important components of human identity. As you read Chabon's essay, think about the degree to which you would describe yourself as creative and consider whether you agree with his point about censorship and the arts.

Andrew D. Arnold, in "Comix Poetics," looks at the subject of graphic comics as a form of literature that he wishes to see legitimized as he explains his belief that comics achieve "the same artistic ambitions as poetry." Serious comic artists, he maintains, have much in common with traditional poets and should be given the credit they are due. As you read his essay, consider whether you accept his argument. Are you convinced that graphic literature operates with the same imaginative principles as poetry, or do you think that Arnold is stretching the comparison too far?

As you will see, the essays in this chapter raise some intriguing questions, such as, How do artists benefit society? Would society lose its soul without artists? How would society—or you personally—change without art? Discussing an artistic expression that does not use words or paper, Barbara Ehrenreich explains in "Dance, Dance, Revolution" some of the historical development of dance and argues for its importance in our lives. As you read her essay, consider your life without dance or music to dance to. How important are music and dance to you? Can you envision your life without them?

Many strong supporters of the arts believe that society would be lost without them. Such is the underlying assumption of Morris Dickstein's "How Song, Dance and Movies Bailed Us Out of the Depression." Demonstrating the role of artistic enterprises in shoring up the spirits of a desperate nation throughout the Great Depression, Dickstein argues that the creative arts may be called upon to do exactly the same thing in the current economic slump.

The subject of art and artists is so vast that these few readings serve only to indicate the breadth and depth of possible related topics and issues. Despite the persistence of art throughout time, the role of the artist in society and the relative value of art often are frequently debated topics. Tastes change and differ from generation to generation and individual to individual, as do values and beliefs about what is important to sustain and nurture a society and the standards by which people judge the merits of works of art. Determining what makes an artwork "good" or "bad" is often a subjective response to the art rather than a conscious application of objective standards. Do you have trouble determining whether a new movie, painting, or song is a good or bad one? How do you judge such works? As you consider the points made by the writers in this section, also think about the kinds of creative art that appeal to you, including what imaginative writing you like to read and perhaps write yourself. Think about the role that all of these forms of expression play in humans' lives: How might their absence affect humanity? Do you think your life would be impoverished without art, music, and literature? Why or why not?

SOLITUDE AND THE FORTRESSES OF YOUTH

Michael Chabon

Michael Chabon has written numerous articles, stories, novels, screenplays, and teleplays, including the screenplay for the second Spiderman *movie. His collections of short stories include* A Model World and Other Stories *(1991) and* Werewolves in Their Youth: Stories *(1999). His novels include* The Mysteries of Pittsburg *(1988);* Wonder Boys *(1995);* The Amazing Adventures of Kavalier & Clay *(2000), which won the Pulitzer Prize for fiction in 2001;* The Yiddish Policemen's Union *(2007), and* Gentlemen of the Road: A Tale of Adventure *(2007). A selection of his opinion essays is collected in* Manhood for Amateurs: The Pleasures and Regrets of a Husband, Father, and Son *(2009). This essay was published in the April 13, 2004, issue of the* New York Times.

Earlier this month my local paper, the *San Francisco Chronicle,* reported that a college student had been expelled from art school here for submitting a story "rife with gruesome details about sexual torture, dismemberment and bloodlust" to his creative writing class. The instructor, a poet named Jan Richman, subsequently found herself out of a job. The university chose not to explain its failure to renew Ms. Richman's contract, but she intimated that she was being punished for having set the tone for the class by assigning a well-regarded if disturbing short story by the MacArthur-winning novelist David Foster Wallace, "Girl with Curious Hair." Ms. Richman had been troubled enough by the student's work to report it to her superiors in the first place, in spite of the fact that it was not, according to the *Chronicle,* "the first serial-killer story she had read in her six semesters on the faculty at the Academy of Art University."

Homicide inspectors were called in; a criminal profiler went to work on the student.

The officers found no evidence of wrongdoing. The unnamed student had made no threat; his behavior was not considered suspicious. In the end, no criminal charges were brought.

4 In this regard, the San Francisco case differs from other incidents in California, and around the country, in which students, unlucky enough to have as literary precursor the Columbine mass-murderer Dylan Klebold, have found themselves expelled, even prosecuted and convicted on criminal charges, because of the violence depicted in their stories and poems. The threat posed by these prosecutions to civil liberties, to the First Amendment rights of our young people, is grave enough. But as a writer, a parent and a former teenager, I see the workings of something more iniquitous: not merely the denial of teenagers' rights in the name of their own protection, but the denial of their humanity in the name of preserving their innocence.

It is in the nature of a teenager to want to destroy. The destructive impulse is universal among children of all ages, rises to a peak of vividness, ingenuity and fascination in adolescence, and thereafter never entirely goes away. Violence and hatred, and the fear of our own inability to control them in ourselves, are a fundamental part of our birthright, along with altruism, creativity, tenderness, pity and love. It therefore requires an immense act of hypocrisy to stigmatize our young adults and teenagers as agents of deviance and disorder. It requires a policy of dishonesty about and blindness to our own histories, as a species, as a nation, and as individuals who were troubled as teenagers, and who will always be troubled, by the same dark impulses. It also requires that favorite tool of the hypocritical, dishonest and fearful: the suppression of constitutional rights.

We justly celebrate the ideals enshrined in the Bill of Rights, but it is also a profoundly disillusioned document, in the best sense of that adjective. It stipulates all the worst impulses of humanity: toward repression, brutality, intolerance and fear. It couples an unbridled faith in the individual human being, redeemed time and again by his or her singular capacity for tenderness, pity and all the rest, with a profound disenchantment about groups of human beings acting as governments, court systems, armies, state religions and bureaucracies, unchecked by the sting of individual conscience and only belatedly if ever capable of anything resembling redemption.

In this light the Bill of Rights can be read as a classic expression of the teenage spirit: a powerful imagination reacting to a history of overwhelming institutional repression, hypocrisy, chicanery and weakness. It is a document written by men who, like teenagers, knew their enemy intimately, and saw in themselves all the potential they possessed to one day become him. We tend to view idealism and cynicism as opposites, when in fact neither possesses any merit or power unless tempered by, fused with, the other. The Bill of Rights is the fruit of that kind of fusion; so is the teenage imagination.

8 The imagination of teenagers is often—I'm tempted to say always—the only sure capital they possess apart from the love of their parents, which is a force far beyond

their capacity to comprehend or control. During my own adolescence, my imagination, the kingdom inside my own skull, was my sole source of refuge, my fortress of solitude, at times my prison. But a fortress requires a constant line of supply; those who take refuge in attics and cellars require the unceasing aid of confederates; prisoners need advocates, escape plans, or simply a window that gives onto the sky.

Like all teenagers, I provisioned my garrison with art: books, movies, music, comic books, television, role-playing games. My secret confederates were the works of Monty Python, H. P. Lovecraft, the cartoonist Vaughan Bodé, and the Ramones, among many others; they kept me watered and fed. They baked files into cakes and, on occasion, for a wondrous moment, made the walls of my prison disappear. Given their nature as human creations, as artifacts and devices of human nature, some of the provisions I consumed were bound to be of a dark, violent, even bloody and horrifying nature; otherwise I would not have cared for them. Tales and displays of violence, blood and horror rang true, answered a need, on some deep, angry level that maybe only those with scant power or capital, regardless of their age, can understand.

It was not long before I began to write: stories, poems, snatches of autobiographical jazz. Often I imitated the work of my confederates: stories of human beings in the most extreme situations and states of emotion—horror stories; accounts of madness and despair. In part—let's say in large part, if that's what it takes to entitle the writings of teenagers to unqualified protection under the First Amendment—this was about expression. I was writing what I felt, what I believed, wished for, raged against, hoped and dreaded. But the main reason I wrote stories—and the reason that I keep on writing them today—was not to express myself. I started to write because once it had been nourished, stoked and liberated by those secret confederates, I could not hold back the force of my imagination. I had been freed, and I felt that it was now up to me to do the same for somebody else, somewhere, trapped in his or her own lonely tower.

We don't want teenagers to write violent poems, horrifying stories, explicit lyrics and rhymes; they're ugly, in precisely the way that we are ugly, and out of protectiveness and hypocrisy, even out of pity and love and tenderness, we try to force young people to be innocent of everything but the effects of that ugliness. And so we censor the art they consume and produce, and prosecute and suspend and expel them, and when, once in a great while, a teenager reaches for an easy gun and shoots somebody or himself, we tell ourselves that if we had only censored his journals and curtailed his music and video games, that awful burst of final ugliness could surely have been prevented. As if art caused the ugliness, when of course all it can ever do is reflect and, perhaps, attempt to explain it.

12 Let teenagers languish, therefore, in their sense of isolation, without outlet or nourishment, bereft of the only thing that makes it all bearable: knowing that somebody else has felt the way that you feel, has faced it, run from it, rued it, lamented it and transformed it into art; has been there, and returned, and lived, for the only good reason we have: to tell the tale. How confident we shall be, once we have done this, of never encountering the ugliness again! How happy our children will be, and how brave, and how safe!

PERSONAL RESPONSE

What do you think of the case that Chabon mentions in his opening paragraphs? In your opinion, should the student have been expelled for writing his gruesome story? If the teacher's termination was, indeed, a punishment for assigning a violent but disturbing story, as she thinks it was, do you think the punishment just?

QUESTIONS FOR CLASS OR SMALL-GROUP DISCUSSION

1. Explain in your own words what it is that bothers Chabon about the expulsion and/or prosecution of students for writing violent stories and poems. Do you agree with his position on this subject?
2. How do you respond to Chabon's assertion in paragraph 4 that "[i]t is in the nature of a teenager to want to destroy"? Is he correct about that, in your opinion?
3. Explain Chabon's analogy of the Bill of Rights "as a classic expression of the teenage spirit" (paragraph 6). How effective do you find that analogy as a strategy for developing his argument?
4. Comment on Chabon's strategy of using his own experience to further his argument. Does it work to strengthen or weaken the argument?

COMIX POETICS

ANDREW D. ARNOLD

Andrew D. Arnold was a Time.com *columnist from 2002 to 2007. He wrote in his final* Time.comix *column that he began doing the column when comics (or, as he prefers, "comix") and graphic novels were just being noticed by the mainstream press. Since then, the genre has gained a large audience of readers and is being taken somewhat seriously by critics and academics. His columns have also appeared in the weekly print magazine,* Time. *This article was published in the March/April 2007 edition of* World Literature Today, *a publication of the University of Oklahoma.*

The debate over comics' qualifications as art has been crushed, like an icky spider, under a pile of masterful books. Art Spiegelman's *Maus,* Chris Ware's *Jimmy Corrigan: The Smartest Kid on Earth,* and Marjane Satrapi's *Persepolis* are just a few of the ever-growing list of important works of graphical literature that prove comic art can carry as much truth, beauty, mystery, emotion, and smart entertainment as any of the other, more traditional, media of expression. Even the Ivory Tower has admitted "graphic novels" (an imperfect term that describes any book-length comic work, including nonfiction) onto course lists. So now we can turn our attention to more interesting comparative questions. For example, can comics create poetry like the works of Shakespeare, T. S. Eliot, or Aleksandr Pushkin?

In short, no, but not from lack of merit or ability. While comics have a similar delivery as poetry—books, paper, words, etc.—the language, syntax, and meaning of comics spring primarily through the relationship between images rather than words. This is not just a different ballgame but a different sport. However, this does not exclude comics from achieving the same artistic ambitions as poetry. Practically since their inception, comics have shown their ability to achieve powerful artistry through the inspired use of condensed, musical, and highly structured language. So, herewith a brief survey of some comic art that rivals the work of many a fine traditional poet.

Early on, during the explosion of newspaper strips in the early twentieth century, creators had the rare kind of artistic freedom that comes from a total lack of rules or precedent. As a result, some of the wildest feats of artistic imagination in the history of the medium occurred at its inception. Perhaps no pioneering comics artist came as close to poetic perfection as George Herriman (1880–1944), author of *Krazy Kat,* which appeared in newspapers from 1913 until the author's death. Like few others, Herriman developed his own "voice" both in his written and visual language to create a work beloved by some of the most highly regarded artists and intellectuals of the time. Gilbert Seldes, cultural essayist par excellence, praised it in his now-classic 1924 book *The Seven Lively Arts* as "the most amusing and fantastic and satisfactory work of art produced in America to-day."

4 Herriman used the core dynamic of his three principal characters—lovesick Krazy Kat, brick-throwing Ignatz Mouse, and dutiful Offica Pup—like a sonnet form, endlessly rifling on the characters' relationships to get at something profoundly tragic and funny about life. One full-page Sunday strip from 1937 exemplifies the many beauties of Krazy Kat. Over the course of several panels, Krazy seeks seclusion under a tree and begins writing in a diary. Little hearts bubble out of its pages as she does so. She speaks to herself in the oddball patois that is one of the strip's hallmarks. "I are alone," she says, "Jetz me . . . an' jetz my dee-dee diary." She puts the diary under a rock and incants over it, "Now beck into sigglution, witch only these kobbil rocks, this blue bin butch-the moon an' the dokk, dokk night know. An' they won't tell-you is illone." The final panel, stretching the width of the page, shows all the other characters reading the book after she has left. In a single page, Herriman creates not a traditional poem but its comic-art equivalent. It has playfulness about both the language ("dee dee diary," "dokk, dokk night") and the images (the background changes from panel to panel though the foreground remains consistent). It also examines great themes like love (those little hearts) and existentialism ("you is illone"). But the essence of the work, called the "gag" panel in this context but akin to a sonnet's final couplet, appears at the end. Herriman bursts the illusion of aloneness and privacy, emphasizing our existence in a community. And it's funny, too. Most important, he communicates this through a wordless image. Impossible in any other medium, here we see an example of cartoon poetry in its purest form.

The comic-book craze that began with the introduction of Superman in 1938 did about as much harm as good for the medium. While massively popularizing the comics' language, cheap comic books also commodified it, leading to a stultification of the form as a mode of personal expression. It wouldn't begin to develop its full potential until the 1960s, when a group of West Coast cartoonists began independently publishing comic books and selling them "underground" in head shops and record stores. Robert Crumb became the most famous member of this movement. Though he would go on to become comics' most brilliant polytechnic, constantly changing styles and subjects, his early work remains his most popular and the closest to what can be called comic poetry. "Freakout Funnies Presents I'm a Ding Dong Daddy," a two-pager that appeared in the premier issue of Zap in 1967, exemplifies the psychedelicized free-form style of the underground era. Wordless except for the onomatopoeia of "Snap!" "Bonk!" and "Pow!" it depicts a big-footed young man having an epiphany on the street. Ecstatic, his mind blown, he runs around hitting his head against the wall, eventually working himself up into such a cosmic frenzy that he explodes into stars. Captured in a thought bubble, the stars dissolve to emptiness as our man from the beginning returns to a state of ignorance. Like the best linguistic poetry, "Ding Dong Daddy" uses the comics language of the past (superhero and gag comics) in radically new ways to express something profound about the culture of its time.

The comics didn't begin to emerge from the "underground" until the 1980s. *Raw,* a magazine edited by Art Spiegelman and Francoise Mouly, became one of the main factors in the shift. Emphasizing works closer to self-aware "art" than salacious entertainment, *Raw* asserted itself as comics for grown-ups rather than merely "adults." Among the many brilliant pieces to have appeared in its pages, Richard McGuire's "Here" (1989) stands out as one of the most influential works of comics poetry ever published. Its method of using comics to split time into multiple layers that can be read simultaneously still has the shock of the new. It begins as a pregnant woman stands in her living room and announces to her husband, "Honey, I think it's time." Fixing the "camera" to the same location, McGuire begins jumping back and forth in time by generations, then centuries, then millennia, exploring the past and future of a single location in space. He does this in six pages by setting smaller panels inside larger ones, which are all labeled with a year, so one begins to read multiple timelines simultaneously, each with its own narrative. Using similarities of composition, movement, and language, McGuire ties it all together into a fluid comment on the nature of time using a form unique to comics.

The youngest comic-book poet of this survey, Anders Nilsen (b. 1973), has been gaining a major reputation among the comixcenti for his simple, enigmatic, and memorable work. One of his most interesting recent pieces appeared in the excellent biannual anthology series *Mome,* published by Fantagraphics books. . . . The fall 2005 issue included Nilsen's short work "Event." The design couldn't be simpler. Page 1 contains a single gray square with a black border, the size of a postage stamp, accompanying the text, "What you said you would do." On page. . . [2] a slightly smaller square broken into quadrants of different hues sits over the text "Your reasons for not doing it: stated." Page 3 contains a larger, dun-colored square over the word "Unstated." It continues like this, using squares of varying sizes and quantities to represent time, people, events, and consequences affected by and resulting from this original, unnamed inaction. A comics poem with a twist ending, the last panel switches its core geometry to feature red concentric circles over the label "Anxiety experienced every time you think back to this experience for the rest of your life." While lines like that will not win over any old-school poets, as a whole the work reads as a fascinatingly clever minimalist visual poem. The words and pictures are totally dependent on each other to convey the meaning of the work, which reads as a compressed, playful examination of regret. In sum, it is a graphic poem.

8 Culturally, at least, serious-minded comic artists have much in common with traditional poets. You could describe each the same way: an underappreciated author who spends years working on a thin volume to be published by a barely surviving independent press for a small, cultlike audience. Until recently, the difference could be measured in the level of respect accorded one over the other, at least in the United States. Comic artists, regardless of their subject matter, have traditionally hovered in the artistic hierarchy somewhere above pornographers but below children's book authors. But that seems to be changing. There are more comic poets today than at any time before, thanks to the comic medium's explosive growth in the last five years. Like traditional poets who work at the cutting edge of the English language, these artists create the pathways that others will follow.

PERSONAL RESPONSE

Do you read the kinds of comics that Arnold writes about here? If so, explain their appeal; if not, explain why you do not read them.

QUESTIONS FOR CLASS OR SMALL-GROUP DISCUSSION

1. Analyze the structure and development of this essay. What is Arnold's thesis? How well organized is it? What strategy does he use to prove his thesis?
2. Arnold writes in paragraph 5 that the comic book craze "did about as much harm as good for the medium." What do you understand him to mean by that statement?
3. Summarize the contributions, according to Arnold, to the comic art genre of each of the examples he names.
4. Are you convinced by Arnold's examples that comics "achieve the same artistic ambitions as poetry" (paragraph 2)? To what extent do you agree with him that comics qualify as art?

DANCE, DANCE, REVOLUTION

BARBARA EHRENREICH

Barbara Ehrenreich's articles appear in a variety of popular magazines and newspapers. Her books include Hearts of Men: American Dreams and the Flight from Commitment *(1984);* For Her Own Good: 150 Years of the Experts' Advice to Women *(with Deirdre*

English) (1989); Blood Rites: Origins and History of the Passions of War *(1997);* Fear of Falling: The Inner Life of the Middle Class *(2000);* Nickel and Dimed: On (Not) Getting by in America *(2001);* Global Woman, *a collection of essays co-edited with Arlie Russell Hochschild (2002);* Bait and Switch: The (Futile) Pursuit of the American Dream *(2005);* Dancing in the Streets: A History of Collective Joy *(2007);* This Land is Their Land: Reports from a Divided Nation *(2008); and* Bright-Sided: How the Relentless Promotion of Positive Thinking has Undermined America *(2009). This article appeared in the* New York Times *on June 3, 2007.*

Compared with most of the issues that the venerable civil liberties lawyer Norman Siegel takes up, this one may seem like the ultimate in urban frivolity: Late last month, he joined hundreds of hip-hoppers, salsa dancers, Lindy Hoppers and techno-heads boogying along Fifth Avenue to protest New York City's 80-year-old restrictions on dancing in bars.

But disputes over who can dance, how and where, are at least as old as civilization, and arise from the longstanding conflict between the forces of order and hierarchy on the one hand, and the deep human craving for free-spirited joy on the other.

New York's cabaret laws limit dancing to licensed venues. They date back to the Harlem Renaissance, which had created the unsettling prospect of interracial dancing.

4 For decades, no one paid much attention to the laws until Mayor Rudolph Giuliani, bent on turning Manhattan into a giant mall/food court, decided to get tough. Today, the city far more famous for its night life than its Sunday services has only about 170 venues where it is legal to get up and dance—hence last month's danced protest, as well as an earlier one in February.

Dust-ups over dancing have become a regular feature of urban life. Dance clubs all over the country have faced the threat of shutdowns because the dancing sometimes spills over into the streets. While neighbors annoyed by sleepless nights or the suspicion of illegal drug use may be justified in their concerns, conflict over public dancing has a long history—one that goes all the way back to the ancient Mediterranean world.

The Greeks danced to worship their gods—especially Dionysus, the god of ecstasy. But then the far more strait-laced Romans cracked down viciously on Dionysian worship in 186 B.C., even going on to ban dancing schools for Roman children a few decades later. The early Christians incorporated dance into their liturgy, despite church leaders' worries about immodesty. But at the end of the fourth century, the archbishop of Constantinople issued the stern pronouncement: "For where there is a dance, there is also the Devil."

The Catholic Church did not succeed in prohibiting dancing within churches until the late Middle Ages, and in doing so perhaps inadvertently set off the dance "manias" that swept Belgium, Germany and Italy starting in the 14th century. Long attributed to some form of toxin—ergot or spider venom—the manias drove thousands of people to the streets day and night, mocking and menacing the priests who tried to stop them.

8 In northern Europe, Calvinism brought a hasty death to the old public forms of dancing, along with the costuming, masking and feasting that had usually accompanied them. All that survived, outside of vestiges of "folk dancing," were the elites' tame, indoor ballroom dances, fraught, as in today's "Dancing With the Stars," with anxiety over a possible misstep. When Europeans fanned out across the globe in the 18th and 19th centuries, the colonizers made it a priority to crush the danced rituals of indigenous people, which were seen as savagery, devil worship and prelude to rebellion.

To the secular opponents of public dancing, it is always a noxious source of disorder and, in New York's case, noise. But hardly anyone talks about what is lost when the music stops and the traditional venues close. Facing what he saw as an epidemic of melancholy, or what we would now call depression, the 17th-century English writer Robert Burton placed much of the blame on the Calvinist hostility to "dancing, singing, masking, mumming and stage plays." In fact, in some cultures, ecstatic dance has been routinely employed as a cure for emotional disorders. Banning dancing may not cause depression, but it removes an ancient cure for it.

The need for public, celebratory dance seems to be hardwired into us. Rock art from around the world depicts stick figures dancing in lines and circles at least as far back as 10,000 years ago. According to some anthropologists, dance helped bond prehistoric people together in the large groups that were necessary for collective defense against marauding predators, both animals and human. While language also serves to forge community, it doesn't come close to possessing the emotional urgency of dance. Without dance, we risk loneliness and anomie.

Dancing to music is not only mood-lifting and community-building; it's also a uniquely human capability. No other animals, not even chimpanzees, can keep together in time to music. Yes, we can live without it, as most of us do most of the time, but why not reclaim our distinctively human heritage as creatures who can generate our own communal pleasures out of music and dance?

12 This is why New Yorkers—as well as all Americans faced with anti-dance restrictions—should stand up and take action; and the best way to do so is by high stepping into the streets.

PERSONAL RESPONSE

Ehrenreich comments that "the need for public, celebratory dance seems to be hardwired into us" (paragraph 10). Does your own attitude about dance support that comment? Do your observations of others support it? Can you "live without [music]" (paragraph 11)?

QUESTIONS FOR CLASS OR SMALL-GROUP DISCUSSION

1. Explain in your own words what the issue is that Ehrenreich writes about here. What action does she call for?
2. Summarize the long history of the conflict over public dancing. Can you think of other examples of that conflict?

3. Ehrenreich notes that "hardly anyone talks about what is lost when the music stops and the traditional venues close" (paragraph 9). What, according to her, is lost? Do you agree with her?
4. What value does Ehrenreich believe dance has? To what extent do you agree with her?

HOW SONG, DANCE AND MOVIES BAILED US OUT OF THE DEPRESSION

MORRIS DICKSTEIN

Morris Dickstein is Distinguished Professor of English at Queens College and teaches literature and film at the CUNY Graduate Center in New York. He is author of the following books: Gates of Eden: American Culture in the Sixties *(1977, 1997);* Double Agent: The Critic and Society *(1992);* Leopards in the Temple: The Transformation of American Fiction, *1945–1970 (2002); and* Dancing in the Dark: A Cultural History of the Great Depression *(2009). This article appeared in the April 1, 2009, issue of the* Los Angeles Times.

Many were surprised that the final stimulus legislation signed by President Obama preserved a $50-million increase in arts funding that had been the subject of a heated battle in Congress. Though it amounted to only a tiny fraction of the measure's total cost, it had become the target of conservatives, many of whom consider the arts frivolous, elitist and, frankly, left-wing. They showed their disdain in February when they pushed for—and passed—a Senate amendment ruling out stimulus funds for museums, arts centers and theaters.

That shortsighted decision was reversed at the last moment, after supporters made a good case that the arts are often the linchpin of downtown neighborhoods, creating jobs and providing many other economic benefits: stimulating business, promoting urban renewal and attracting tourists.

But was that really the point? Is that really why we need the arts? These days, it seems that every discussion of the economic situation includes the obligatory comparison to the prolonged crisis of the 1930s, yet what the Depression and the New Deal actually showed is that the value of the arts goes well beyond job creation and economic stimulus.

4 Studies of the 1930s have shown how the economic meltdown was accompanied by psychological depression: loss of morale, a sense of despair, grave fears for the future. Going to the movies or listening to the radio could not solve these problems, but they could ease them in the same way that President Franklin D. Roosevelt's intimate fireside chats boosted morale and restored confidence.

The most durable cliché about the arts in the 1930s is that despite the surge of social consciousness among writers, photographers and painters (some of it supported by federal dollars), the arts offered Depression audiences little more than fluffy escapism, which was just what they needed.

But that's not the whole story. It's certainly a paradox that dire economic times produced such a fizzy, buoyant popular culture. From the warring couples of screwball comedy and the magical dancing of Fred Astaire and Ginger Rogers to the sophisticated music and lyrics of Cole Porter, Rodgers and Hart, and the Gershwins, the '30s generated mass entertainment legendary for its wit, elegance and style. This culture had its roots in the devil-may-care world of the 1920s, but it took on new meaning as the Depression deepened.

The engine of the arts in the '30s was not escapism, as we sometimes imagine, but speed, energy and movement at a time of economic stagnation and social malaise. When Warner Bros.—which avoided bankruptcy with its lively and topical gangster films, backstage musicals and Depression melodramas—promised a "New Deal in Entertainment," it was offering the cultural equivalent of the New Deal, a psychological stimulus package that might energize a shaken public.

8 With his roots in the ethnic slums, the gangster was a dynamic figure who somehow mastered his own fate even as he trampled on other people's lives. Busby Berkeley's showgirls were at the center of glittering fables of success and failure, wondrous changes in fortunes that resonated for '30s audiences. Against all odds, the performers came together into a working community; so did the stricken victims in topical melodramas right up through "The Grapes of Wrath," who discovered that they were helpless on their own but had a chance if they banded together and helped one another.

If we look at the arts as a life-giving form of social therapy, many other fads and fashions of the 1930s fall into place. The thrust of the culture, like the aims of the New Deal, was to get the country moving again. At cross-purposes in conversation, Astaire and Rogers seem perfectly ill-matched. Endlessly bickering with each other, they can agree on nothing. But once they dance, a swirling poetry of movement takes over.

The public also loved comedies about the very rich. Everyone could feel superior to their silliness, the weightlessness of their lives, yet live vicariously through their energy, irresponsibility and freedom, the snap of their delicious dialogue. Meanwhile, musical standards created a seductive dreamland, somewhere "over the rainbow," a better world where cloudy skies and rainy days somehow promised "pennies from heaven."

The propulsive swing music of the big bands, produced by performers and band leaders such as Duke Ellington, Artie Shaw and Benny Goodman, brought jazz to a mass audience for the first time—jazz to dance to, not simply to listen to. It filled the airwaves, ballrooms, nightclubs, even concert halls.

12 The visual equivalent of swing music was Art Deco. Gifted designers such as Raymond Loewy, Donald Deskey, Walter Dorwin Teague and Norman Bel Geddes stimulated consumption by putting a fluid sense of movement into everything from locomotives to table radios, projecting the consumer into a streamlined future otherwise hard to imagine. This culminated in the design of the 1939 New York World's Fair, with its flowing crowds and futuristic visions of "The World of Tomorrow."

Today's economic and cultural climate is still a long way from the Depression, which was already in its fourth year when FDR kicked off the New Deal. A quarter of the workforce was unemployed. The stock market had crashed, and the banking system had failed. Yet there are eerie resemblances, especially in the crisis of confidence that froze credit markets and blasted consumer spending almost overnight in mid-September of last year.

There is little sign so far of how the arts will respond to the damage done to our confidence and morale this time around. But moviegoing has already increased by almost 16% this year. We know from the 1930s that the stimulating effect of art and entertainment comes not only in the jobs produced but in the emotional links with the public that absorbs this work and takes it to heart.

The arts can be a lifeline as well as a pleasant diversion, a source of optimism and energy as well as peerless insight, especially when so many people are stymied or perplexed by the unexpected changes in their world. As our troubles worsen, as stress morphs into anxiety and depression, we may desperately need the mixture of the real and the fantastic, the sober and the silly, that only the arts can bring us.

PERSONAL RESPONSE

How important are the arts to you? Which arts interest you most?

QUESTIONS FOR CLASS OR SMALL-GROUP DISCUSSION

1. State in your own words "How Song, Dance and Movies Bailed Us Out of The Depression" (title), according to Dickstein.
2. Dickstein reminds readers of a commonly held view of the arts during the Depression as "fluffy escapism" (paragraph 5). What argument does he make against that viewpoint? Are you convinced by his examples?
3. What is the New Deal (paragraph 3) that Dickstein refers to throughout his essay? What does he compare to the New Deal? Do you find the analogy effective?
4. Identify the following from paragraph 6: Fred Astaire and Ginger Rogers, Cole Porter, Rodgers and Hart, the Gershwins. Explain the reference to "Busby Berkeley's showgirls" (paragraph 8). Who are Duke Ellington, Artie Shaw, and Benny Goodman (paragraph 11)? What is Art Deco (paragraph 12)?

✧ PERSPECTIVES ON THE ARTS ✧

Suggested Writing Topics

1. Argue your viewpoint on the depiction of violence in any of the creative arts—poetry, drama, short story, novel, dance, the visual arts. Is the expulsion

of students or firing of teachers, as described in Michael Chabon's "Solitude and the Fortresses of Youth" justified in uncertain and dangerous times?

2. If you have found that a particular form of creative art is a way to express yourself or use your imagination, as Michael Chabon in "Solitude and the Fortresses of Youth" did with writing, explain what that art is and how it enables you to find self-expression.

3. One of the oldest forms of art is personal decoration. The body is still being used as a surface for symbolic expression by some young people, who use such techniques as branding, piercing, and tattooing. Defend or attack these practices by considering their relative artistic or creative merits.

4. Defend the central place of art in education.

5. Drawing on at least two of the selections in this chapter, explain your viewpoint on the importance of art. Be sure to defend your position by supplying evidence not only from the essays but also from your own observations.

6. Interview a group of your friends and acquaintances for their opinions on the place of an artist's private beliefs and behavior in judging the artist's work. Then report the results of your survey in an essay that synthesizes the comments of the people whom you survey.

7. Who do you think are today's most creative people? You might highlight a particular group of people (artists, musicians) or a particular person. Give supporting evidence to substantiate your viewpoint.

8. Define *excellence* in relation to a specific art form (for instance, a painting, a novel, a poem, a dance, a song, or a film) by stating the criteria you use for judging that abstract quality and by giving examples you believe best illustrate it.

9. Select a work of art in any medium—painting, music, graphic literature, the theatre, dance, literature—and analyze its importance as a work of art, including what it means to you personally.

10. Answer the question: In what ways do the arts—music, art, drama, literature—contribute to the culture of a people? What is the value of art?

11. Explore the question of what makes some art live for all time and other art disappear. What makes a "timeless" work of art? Select a particular painting as an example and explain, in as much detail as possible, why you believe as you do.

12. Explain what you think is gained by a culture's interest in and support of the arts and what you think would be lost without it. As an alternative, argue that nothing is gained by a culture's art and that little or nothing would be lost without it. Make sure you explain why you feel as you do on this subject.

Research Topics

1. Select an issue or question related to the broad subject of the role of the artist in society to research and then argue your position on that issue. For instance, what is the role of the arts in today's culture? Do we need the arts?
2. In recent years, some people have been highly critical of what they see as obscenity or immorality in contemporary art. Some time ago, the works of Robert Mapplethorpe, for instance, were the object of such widespread, heated public debate that the National Endowment for the Arts was threatened with funding cuts because of similar projects it had supported with grants. Research the issue of censorship in the arts, and write an opinion paper on the subject. Consider: Does society have a moral obligation to limit what people can say, do, or use in their art, or do First Amendment rights extend to any subject or medium an artist wants to use?
3. The discoveries of prehistoric cave drawings that are fairly sophisticated in technique and meaning have led some art historians to suggest that art did not necessarily develop progressively, as has been commonly believed. Research this topic by reading about some of the prehistoric cave drawings that have been discovered and the theories of art historians about their importance. Then weigh the evidence and arrive at your own opinion about the nature and purpose of prehistoric art or its place in the historical development of art.
4. Research the role of the arts in strengthening students' abilities in other subject areas.
5. Research the contributions to art of a well-known artist or performer. Although you will want to provide a brief biographical sketch, your paper should focus on assessing the particular way(s) the artist had an effect on not only his or her own specialty but also "the arts" in general.
6. Research the history of a particular dance form. You may want to use as one of your sources Barbara Ehrenreich's book *Dancing in the Streets: A History of Collective Joy*.
7. In "Dance, Dance, Revolution," Barbara Ehrenreich refers to "the dance 'manias' that swept Belgium, Germany, and Italy starting in the 14th century" (paragraph 7). Research the subject of dance manias during that period.
8. Andrew D. Arnold writes in "Comix Poetics" that "some of the wildest feats of artistic imagination in the history of the medium occurred at [the] inception" of newspaper strips (paragraph 3). Research that historical period and write a paper defending that statement. You will probably

want to include the artists that Arnold mentions, George Herriman and Gilbert Seldes.

9. Morris Dickstein in "How Song, Dance and Movies Bailed Us Out of the Depression" makes reference to many artists popular during the period of the Great Depression and the years following. Research either an art form or a particular person or group mentioned in his article on the role it/they played in helping people cope with the Depression. You may want to use his book *Dancing in the Dark: A Cultural History of the Great Depression* as one of your sources, or use it as a way to discover what interests you most about the role of the arts in that period.

RESPONDING TO VISUALS

Henderson Advertising for the South Carolina Ballet

"The new ballet will have quite an effect on you."

1. What is the purpose of this advertisement?
2. Does the stance of the mechanic strike you as amusing or odd?
3. How do the mechanic and his environment function in relation to what the advertisement is promoting?
4. What is the target audience of the advertisement? How effectively do you think it reaches that audience?

Responding to Visuals

Cover illustration of Superman comic book from DC Comics.

1. Analyze the cover by discussing how the artist conveys action, how Superman is represented, what he is doing, and where the action takes place. What story does the picture tell?
2. Why do you think that comic books and graphic novels are so popular? If you read graphic novels or comic books, explain why they appeal to you.
3. Do you think that graphic literature and/or comic books should be taught as legitimate forms of literature in schools?

PART • THREE

Social and Behavioral Sciences

CHAPTER 12

Education

Education is a complex and crucially important subject. Without education, people face obstacles to participating fully in society. Because of its importance, education is also the subject of controversy. People are divided on issues such as what materials and activities are appropriate for the classroom, what methods of delivering material work best, how much homework ought to be required of students, and what skills and knowledge students must demonstrate to go on to subsequent educational levels. Periodically, philosophies of education change, curricula are restructured, classrooms are transformed, and instructors learn new approaches to teaching their subject matter. As a student who has gone through many years of education, beginning in the primary grades, you are uniquely positioned to comment on this subject. You have been immersed in education and are presumably currently enrolled in at least one class, the course for which you are using this textbook. In the essays in this chapter, writers express their strong opinions on the subject of education and criticize certain aspects of the educational system in America, so you are likely to find yourself either nodding your head in agreement or shaking your head in disagreement with what they say.

In the first essay in this chapter, Judy Blume recounts her experiences with banned books as a child and her sometimes painful experience of having her own books banned, attacked, censored, and vilified. In "Censorship: A Personal View," which is her introduction to a collection of stories by writers who have been censored, Blume explains how she "found [her]self at the eye of a storm." She also asks the question, "What is censorship?" You might think that there is an obvious definition, but she maintains that if you ask a dozen people, you will get a dozen different definitions. So as you read her essay, ask yourself what you consider censorship to be. You also may be interested to note, if you have read any of the titles that she mentions, which have been banned from the classroom or school libraries. What sorts of things were banned or censored when you were in school?

Following Blume's thoughts on censorship and what to do about it is a *Boston Globe* opinion column by Diane Ravitch on the subject of what she describes as a skill-centered fad in K–12 education. In "Critical Thinking? You Need Knowledge," Ravitch explains why she is critical of the "21st-Century Skills" initiative in public schools. As you read her piece, consider how you would define an intelligent person. What skills and knowledge must a truly educated student have?

Next is an excerpt from Mike Rose's book *Why School?* in which he narrates an encounter with a slightly brain-damaged student in a community college basic skills program. As you read about Anthony's achievements, can you think of students you have known who might be similarly challenged and motivated? What does the example of Anthony add to your understanding of the importance of education?

Finally, in a short but pointed essay, David McCullough, well-known historian, public television host, and biographer, reminds us of the importance of reading books. In "No Time to Read?" McCullough urgently and fervently advises his audience to "read for pleasure. Read what you like and all that you like. Read literally to your heart's content." For him, books are our most important source of education.

As you read these selections, think about your own education, the courses you have taken, your classroom activities, the teachers who have taught you, and your own reading habits. Where do you find yourself agreeing with the authors, and where do you disagree? Are your experiences similar to or different from what they describe? What is your own philosophy of education? How important do you believe education is to your well-being and sense of self? How important is reading to you?

CENSORSHIP: A PERSONAL VIEW

JUDY BLUME

Judy Blume's novels have sold over 80 million copies and have been translated into over thirty languages worldwide. Hers are also among the most frequently banned or challenged books in America because of her frank treatment of issues relating to children and young adults. Among her more than two dozen novels are Are You There, God? It's Me, Margaret *(1970);* It's Not the End of the World *(1972);* Tales of a Fourth Grade Nothing *(1974);* Forever *(1975);* Wifey *(1978);* Summer Sisters *(1998); and* Double Fudge *(2002). Blume is founder of the charitable and educational foundation The Kids Fund. Because of her experiences with censorship, she edited* Places I Never Meant to Be: Original Stories by Censored Writers *(1999), a collection of short stories by authors who have been censored or banned. The introduction to that collection is reprinted here.*

When I was growing up I'd heard that if a movie or book was "Banned in Boston" everybody wanted to see it or read it right away. My older brother, for example, went to see such a movie—*The Outlaw,* starring Jane Russell—and I wasn't supposed to tell my mother. I begged him to share what he saw, but he wouldn't. I was intensely curious about the adult world and hated the secrets my parents, and now my brother, kept from me.

A few years later, when I was in fifth grade, my mother was reading a novel called *A Rage to Live,* by John O'Hara, and for the first time (and, as it turned out, the only time) in my life, she told me I was never to look at that book, at least not until I was *much* older. Once I knew my mother didn't want me to read it, I figured it must be really interesting!

So, you can imagine how surprised and delighted I was when, as a junior in high school, I found John O'Hara's name on my reading list. Not a specific title by John O'Hara, but *any* title. I didn't waste a minute. I went down to the public library in Elizabeth, New Jersey, that afternoon—a place where I'd spent so many happy hours as a young child, I'd pasted a card pocket on the inside back cover of each book I owned—and looked for *A Rage to Live.* But I couldn't find it. When I asked, the librarian told me *that* book was *restricted.* It was kept in a locked closet, and I couldn't take it out without written permission from my parents.

4 Aside from my mother's one moment of fear, neither of my parents had ever told me what I could or could not read. They encouraged me to read widely. There were no "Young Adult" novels then. Serious books about teenagers were published as adult novels. It was my mother who handed me *To Kill a Mockingbird* and Anne Frank's *Diary of a Young Girl* when they were first published.

By the time I was twelve I was browsing in the bookshelves flanking the fireplace in our living room where, in my quest to make sense of the world, I discovered J.D. Salinger's *The Catcher in the Rye,* fell in love with the romantic tragedies of Thomas Hardy and the Brontë sisters, and over-identified with "Marjorie Morningstar."

But at the Elizabeth Public Library the librarian didn't care. "Get permission in writing," she told me. When I realized she was not going to let me check out *A Rage to Live,* I was angry. I felt betrayed and held her responsible. It never occurred to me that it might not have been her choice.

At home I complained to my family, and that evening my aunt, the principal of an elementary school, brought me her copy of *A Rage to Live.* I stayed up half the night reading the forbidden book. Yes, it was sexy, but the characters and their story were what kept me turning the pages. Finally, my curiosity (about that book, anyway) was satisfied. Instead of leading me astray, as my mother must have feared, it led me to read everything else I could find by the author.

8 All of which brings me to the question *What is censorship?* If you ask a dozen people you'll get twelve different answers. When I actually looked up the word in *The Concise Columbia Encyclopedia* I found this definition: "[The] official restriction of any expression believed to threaten the political, social, or moral order." My thesaurus lists the following words that can be used in place of *ban* (as in book banning): *Forbid. Prohibit. Restrict.* But what do these words mean to writers and the stories they choose to tell? And what do they mean to readers and the books they choose to read?

I began to write when I was in my mid-twenties. By then I was married with two small children and desperately in need of creative work. I wrote *Are You There God? It's Me, Margaret* right out of my own experiences and feelings when I was in sixth grade. Controversy wasn't on my mind. I wanted only to write what I knew to be true. I wanted to write the best, the most honest books I could, the kinds of books I would have liked to read when I was younger. If someone had told me then I would become one of the most banned writers in America, I'd have laughed.

When *Margaret* was published in 1970 I gave three copies to my children's elementary school but the books never reached the shelves. The male principal decided on his own that they were inappropriate for elementary school readers because of the discussion of menstruation (never mind how many fifth- and sixth-grade girls already had their periods). Then one night the phone rang and a woman asked if I was the one who had written that book. When I replied that I was, she called me a communist and hung up. I never did figure out if she equated communism with menstruation or religion.

In that decade I wrote thirteen other books: eleven for young readers, one for teenagers, and one for adults. My publishers were protective of me during those years and didn't necessarily share negative comments about my work. They believed if I didn't know some individuals were upset by my books, I wouldn't be intimidated.

12 Of course, they couldn't keep the occasional anecdote from reaching me: the mother who admitted she'd cut two pages out of *Then Again, Maybe I Won't* rather than allow her almost thirteen-year-old son to read about wet dreams. Or the young librarian who'd been instructed by her male principal to keep *Deenie* off the shelf because in the book, Deenie masturbates. "It would be different if it were about a boy," he'd told her. "That would be normal."

The stories go on and on but really, I wasn't that concerned. There was no organized effort to ban my books or any other books, none that I knew of, anyway. The seventies were a good decade for writers and readers. Many of us came of age during those years, writing from our hearts and guts, finding editors and publishers who believed in us, who willingly took risks to help us find our audience. We were free to write about real kids in the real world. Kids with feelings and emotions, kids with real families, kids like we once were. And young readers gobbled up our books, hungry for characters with whom they could identify, including my own daughter and son, who had become avid readers. No mother could have been more proud to see the tradition of family reading passed on to the next generation.

Then, almost overnight, following the presidential election of 1980, the censors crawled out of the woodwork, organized and determined. Not only would they decide what *their* children could read but what *all* children could read. It was the beginning of the decade that wouldn't go away, that still won't go away almost twenty years later. Suddenly books were seen as dangerous to young minds. Thinking was seen as dangerous, unless those thoughts were approved by groups like the Moral Majority, who believed with certainty they knew what was best for everyone.

So now we had individual parents running into schools, waving books, demanding their removal—books they hadn't read except for certain passages. Most often their objections had to do with language, sexuality, and something called "lack of moral tone."

16 Those who were most active in trying to ban books came from the "religious right" but the impulse to censor spread like a contagious disease. Other parents, confused and uncertain, were happy to jump on the bandwagon. Book banning satisfied their need to feel in control of their children's lives. Those who censored were easily frightened. They were afraid of exposing their children to ideas different from their own. Afraid to answer children's questions or talk with them about sensitive subjects. And they were suspicious. They believed if kids liked a book, it must be dangerous.

Too few schools had policies in place enabling them to deal with challenged materials. So what happened? The domino effect. School administrators sent down the word: Anything that could be seen as controversial had to go. Often books were quietly removed from school libraries and classrooms or, if seen as potential troublemakers, were never purchased in the first place. These decisions were based not on what was best for the students, but what would not offend the censors.

I found myself at the center of the storm. My books were being challenged daily, often placed on *restricted* shelves (shades of Elizabeth, New Jersey, in 1955) and sometimes removed. A friend was handed a pamphlet outside a supermarket urging parents to rid their schools and libraries of Judy Blume books. Never once did the pamphlet suggest the books actually be read. Of course I wasn't the only target.

Across the country, the Sex Police and the Language Police were thumbing through books at record speed, looking for illustrations, words or phrases that, taken out of context, could be used as evidence against them.

Puberty became a dirty word, as if children who didn't read about it wouldn't know about it, and if they didn't know about it, it would never happen.

20 The Moral Tone Brigade attacked *Blubber* (a story of victimization in the classroom) with a vengeance because, as they saw it, in this book evil goes unpunished. As if kids need to be hit over the head, as if they don't get it without having the message spelled out for them.

I had letters from angry parents accusing me of ruining Christmas because of a chapter in *Superfudge* called "Santa Who?" Some sent lists showing me how easily I could have substituted one word for another: meanie for bitch; darn for damn; nasty for ass. More words taken out of context. A teacher wrote to say she blacked out offending words and passages with a felt-tip marker. Perhaps most shocking of all was a letter from a nine-year-old addressed to *Jew*dy Blume telling me I had no right to write about Jewish angels in *Starring Sally J. Freedman as Herself.*

My worst moment came when I was working with my editor on the manuscript of *Tiger Eyes* (the story of a fifteen-year-old girl, Davey, whose beloved father dies suddenly and violently). When we came to the scene in which Davey allows herself to *feel* again after months of numbness following her father's death, I saw that a few lines alluding to masturbation had been circled. My editor put down his pencil and faced me. "We want this book to reach as many readers as possible, don't we?" he asked.

I felt my face grow hot, my stomach clench. This was the same editor who had worked with me on *Are You There God? It's Me, Margaret; Then Again, Maybe I Won't; Deenie; Blubber; Forever*—always encouraging, always supportive. The scene was psychologically sound, he assured me, and delicately handled. But it also spelled trouble. I got the message. If you leave in those lines, the censors will come after this book. Librarians and teachers won't buy it. Book clubs won't take it. Everyone is too scared. The political climate has changed.

24 I tried to make a case for why that brief moment in Davey's life was important. He asked me *how* important? Important enough to keep the book from reaching its audience? I willed myself not to give in to the tears of frustration and disappointment I felt coming. I thought about the ways a writer brings a character to life on the page, the same way an artist brings a face to life on canvas—through a series of brush strokes, each detail adding to the others, until we see the essence of the person. I floundered, uncertain. Ultimately, not strong enough or brave enough to defy the editor I trusted and respected, I caved in and took out those lines. I still remember how alone I felt at that moment.

What effect does this climate have on a writer? *Chilling.* It's easy to become discouraged, to second-guess everything you write. There seemed to be no one to stand up to the censors. No group as organized as they were; none I knew of, anyway. I've never forgiven myself for caving in to editorial pressure based on fear, for playing into the hands of the censors. I knew then it was all over for me unless I took a stand. So I began to speak out about my experiences. And once I did, I found that I wasn't as alone as I'd thought.

My life changed when I learned about the National Coalition Against Censorship (NCAC) and met Leanne Katz, the tiny dynamo who was its first and longtime director. Leanne's intelligence, her wit, her strong commitment to the First Amendment and helping those who were out on a limb trying to defend it, made her my hero. Every day she worked with the teachers, librarians, parents and students caught in the cross fire. Many put themselves and their jobs on the line fighting for what they believed in.

In Panama City, Florida, junior high school teacher Gloria Pipkin's award-winning English program was targeted by the censors for using Young Adult literature that was *depressing, vulgar and immoral,* specifically *I Am the Cheese,* by Robert Cormier, and *About David,* by Susan Beth Pfeffer.

28 A year later, when a new book selection policy was introduced forbidding vulgar, obscene and sexually related materials, the school superintendent zealously applied it to remove more than sixty-five books, many of them classics, from the curriculum and classroom libraries. They included *To Kill a Mockingbird, The Red Badge of Courage, The Great Gatsby, Wuthering Heights,* and *Of Mice and Men.* Also banned were Shakespeare's *Hamlet, King Lear, The Merchant of Venice,* and *Twelfth Night.*

Gloria Pipkin fought a five-year battle, jeopardizing her job and personal safety (she and the reporter covering the story received death threats) to help reinstate the books. Eventually, the professional isolation as well as the watered-down curriculum led her to resign. She remains without a teaching position.

Claudia Johnson, Florida State University professor and parent, also defended classic books by Aristophanes and Chaucer against a censor who condemned them for promoting "women's lib and pornography." She went on to fight other battles—in defense of John Steinbeck's *Of Mice and Men,* and a student performance of Lorraine Hansberry's *A Raisin in the Sun.*

English teacher Cecilia Lacks was fired by a high school in St. Louis for permitting her creative writing students to express themselves in the language they heard and used outside of school everyday. In the court case that followed, many of her students testified on their teacher's behalf. Though she won her case, the decision was eventually reversed and at this time Lacks is still without a job.

32 Colorado English teacher Alfred Wilder was fired for teaching a classic film about fascism, Bernardo Bertolucci's *1900.*

And in Rib Lake, Wisconsin, guidance counselor Mike Dishnow was fired for writing critically of the Board of Education's decision to ban my book *Forever* from the junior high school library. Ultimately he won a court settlement, but by then his life had been turned upside down.

And these are just a few examples.

This obsession with banning books continues as we approach the year 2000. Today it is not only Sex, Swear Words and Lack of Moral Tone—it is Evil, which, according to the censors, can be found lurking everywhere. Stories about Halloween, witches, and devils are . . . [all] suspect for promoting Satanism. *Romeo and Juliet* is under fire for promoting suicide; Madeleine L'Engle's *A Wrinkle in Time,* for promoting New Age-ism. If the censors had their way it would be good-bye to Shakespeare as well as science fiction. There's not an *ism* you can think of that's not bringing some book to the battlefield.

36 What I worry about most is the loss to young people. If no one speaks out for them, if they don't speak out for themselves, all they'll get for required reading will be the most bland books available. And instead of finding the information they need at the library, instead of finding the novels that illuminate life, they will find only those materials to which nobody could possibly object.

Some people would like to rate books in schools and libraries the way they rate movies: G, PG, R, X, or even more explicitly. But according to whose standards would the books be rated? I don't know about you but I don't want anyone rating my books or the books my children or grandchildren choose to read. We can make our own decisions, thank you. Be wary of the censors' code words—*family friendly; family values; excellence in education.* As if the rest of us don't want excellence in education, as if we don't have our own family values, as if libraries haven't always been family-friendly places!

And the demands are not all coming from the religious right. No . . . the urge to decide not only what's right for their kids but for all kids has caught on with others across the political spectrum. Each year *Huckleberry Finn* is challenged and sometimes removed from the classroom because, to some, its language, which includes racial epithets, is offensive. Better to acknowledge the language, bring it out in the open, and discuss why the book remains important than to ban it. Teachers and parents can talk with their students and children about any book considered controversial.

I gave a friend's child one of my favorite picture books, James Marshall's *The Stupids Step Out,* and was amazed when she said, "I'm sorry, but we can't accept that book. My children are not permitted to use that word. Ever. It should be changed to 'The Sillies Step Out.'" I may not agree, but I have to respect this woman's right to keep that book from her child as long as she isn't trying to keep it from other people's children. Still, I can't help lamenting the lack of humor in her decision. *The Stupids Step Out* is a very funny book. Instead of banning it from her home, I wish she could have used it as an opportunity to talk with her child about why she felt the way she did, about why she never wanted to hear her child call anyone stupid. Even very young children can understand. So many adults are exhausting themselves worrying about other people corrupting their children with books, they're turning kids off to reading instead of turning them on.

40 In this age of censorship I mourn the loss of books that will never be written, I mourn the voices that will be silenced—writers' voices, teachers' voices, students' voices—and all because of fear. How many have resorted to self-censorship? How many are saying to themselves, "Nope . . . can't write about that. Can't teach that book. Can't have that book in our collection. Can't let my student write that editorial in the school paper."

PERSONAL RESPONSE

Describe an experience that you have had with being forbidden to read, watch, or listen to something because it was considered inappropriate. How did it make you feel? What was it like to finally read, watch, or listen to it?

QUESTIONS FOR CLASS OR SMALL-GROUP DISCUSSION

1. Blume asks "What is censorship?" (paragraph 8) and observes that it has different meanings to different people. How do you define "censorship"? Give examples to illustrate your definition.
2. Explain in your own words why Blume's books have been challenged or censored.
3. Discuss your own experience in junior and senior high school with banned or challenged books. Were your librarians and teachers free to choose any books they wanted for the library or classroom? If not, what books were not allowed?
4. Under what circumstances do you think it justifiable to forbid children or young adults to read something?
5. If you have read any of the novels that Blume mentions as having been challenged, banned, or censored, what did you think of them? What parts of the books do you think drew the attention of censors? Do you agree that the books should be withheld from children or young adults?

CRITICAL THINKING? YOU NEED KNOWLEDGE

DIANE RAVITCH

Diane Ravitch is a research professor of education at New York University and cochair of Common Core. She has published numerous articles and books, including The Language Police: How Pressure Groups Restrict What Students Learn *(2003);* The English Reader: What Every Literate Person Needs to Know *(edited with Michael Ravitch) (2006);* Edspeak: A Glossary of Education Terms, Phrases, Buzz Words, and Jargon *(2007); and* The Death and Life of the Great American School System: How Testing and Choice Are Undermining Education *(2010). This article was published in the* Boston Globe *on September 15, 2009.*

The latest fad to sweep K–12 education is called "21st-Century Skills." States—including Massachusetts—are adding them to their learning standards, with the expectation that students will master skills such as cooperative learning and critical thinking and therefore be better able to compete for jobs in the global economy. Inevitably, putting a priority on skills pushes other subjects, including history, literature, and the arts, to the margins. But skill-centered, knowledge-free education has never worked.

The same ideas proposed today by the 21st-Century Skills movement were iterated and reiterated by pedagogues across the 20th century. In 1911, the dean of the education school at Stanford called on his fellow educators to abandon their antiquated academic ideals and adapt education to the real life and real needs of students.

In 1916, a federal government report scoffed at academic education as lacking relevance. The report's author said black children should "learn to do by doing," which he considered to be the modern, scientific approach to education.

4 Just a couple of years later, "the project method" took the education world by storm. Instead of a sequential curriculum laid out in advance, the program urged that boys and girls engage in hands-on projects of their own choosing, ideally working cooperatively in a group. It required activity, not docility, and awakened student motivation. It's remarkably similar to the model advocated by 21st-century skills enthusiasts.

The list goes on: students built, measured, and figured things out while solving real-life problems, like how to build a playhouse, pet park, or a puppet theater, as part of the 1920s and 1930s "Activity Movement." From the "Life Adjustment Movement" of the 1950s to "Outcome-Based Education" in the 1980s, one "innovation" after another devalued academic subject matter while making schooling relevant, hands-on, and attuned to the real interests and needs of young people.

To be sure, there has been resistance. In Roslyn, Long Island, in the 1930s, parents were incensed because their children couldn't read but spent an entire day baking nut bread. The Roslyn superintendent assured them that baking was an excellent way to learn mathematics.

None of these initiatives survived. They did have impact, however: They inserted into American education a deeply ingrained suspicion of academic studies and subject matter. For the past century, our schools of education have obsessed over critical-thinking skills, projects, cooperative learning, experiential learning, and so on. But they have paid precious little attention to the disciplinary knowledge that young people need to make sense of the world.

8 For over a century we have numbed the brains of teachers with endless blather about process and abstract thinking skills. We have taught them about graphic organizers and Venn diagrams and accountable talk, data-based decision-making, rubrics, and leveled libraries.

But we have ignored what matters most. We have neglected to teach them that one cannot think critically without quite a lot of knowledge to think about. Thinking critically involves comparing and contrasting and synthesizing what one has learned. And a great deal of knowledge is necessary before one can begin to reflect on its meaning and look for alternative explanations.

Proponents of 21st-Century Skills might wish it was otherwise, but we do not restart the world anew with each generation. We stand on the shoulders of those who have gone before us. What matters most in the use of our brains is our capacity to make generalizations, to see beyond our own immediate experience. The intelligent person, the one who truly is a practitioner of critical thinking, has the capacity to understand the lessons of history, to grasp the inner logic of science and mathematics, and to realize the meaning of philosophical debates by studying them.

Through literature, for example, we have the opportunity to see the world through the eyes of another person, to walk in his shoes, to experience life as it was lived in another century and another culture, to live vicariously beyond the bounds of our own time and family and place.

12 Until we teach both teachers and students to value knowledge and to love learning, we cannot expect them to use their minds well.

PERSONAL RESPONSE QUESTION

Comment on your own high school education. Do you recall any particular approach to learning that teachers had in common? If so, what was it? If not, how would you characterize your teachers' educational philosophy? How well do you believe that your high school education prepared you for college?

QUESTIONS FOR CLASS OR SMALL-GROUP DISCUSSION

1. Summarize in your own words the approaches to teaching that Ravitch complains about.
2. What rhetorical purpose is served by Ravitch's review of twentieth-century educational movements?
3. What is that Ravitch feels is missing in the current educational movement? Do you agree with her?
4. Explain in your own words Ravitch's definition of an intelligent person. What, if anything, would you add to her definition?

EXCERPT FROM *WHY SCHOOL? A STUDENT IN A COMMUNITY COLLEGE BASIC SKILLS PROGRAM*

MIKE ROSE

Mike Rose, a professor of Social Research Methodology at UCLA, has a special interest in educational programs for economically impoverished or underprepared students. He has written extensively on language, literacy, and the teaching of writing. His books include Lives on the Boundary *(2005);* An Open Language: Selecting Writing on Literacy, Learning, and Opportunity *(2005); and* Writer's Block: The Cognitive Dimension *(2009). Rose posted this excerpt from his book* Why School? *(2009) at his blog on October 12, 2009.*

Food wrappers and sheets of newspaper were blowing in the wet wind across the empty campus. It was late in the day, getting dark fast, and every once in a while I'd look outside the library—which was pretty empty too—and imagine the drizzly walk to the car, parked far away.

Anthony was sitting by me, and I was helping him read a flyer on the dangers of cocaine. He wanted to give it to his daughter. Anthony was enrolled in a basic skills program, one of several special programs at this urban community college. Anthony was in his late-thirties, had some degree of brain damage from a childhood injury, worked custodial jobs most of his life. He could barely read or write, but was an informed, articulate guy, listening to FM radio current affairs shows while he worked, watching public television at home. He had educated himself through the sources available to him, compensating for the damage done.

The librarian was about to go off shift, so we gathered up our things—Anthony carried a big backpack—and headed past her desk to the exit. The wind pushed back on the door as I pushed forward, and I remember thinking how dreary the place was, dark and cold. At that moment I wanted so much to be home.

4 Just then a man in a coat and tie came up quickly behind us. "Hey man," he said to Anthony, "you look good. You lose some weight?" Anthony beamed, said that he had dropped a few pounds and that things were going o.k. The guy gave Anthony a cupping slap on the shoulder, then pulled his coat up and walked head down across the campus.

"Who was that?" I asked, ducking with Anthony back inside the entryway to the library. He was one of the deans, Anthony said, but, well, he was once his parole officer, too. He's seen Anthony come a long way. Anthony pulled on the straps of his backpack, settling the weight more evenly across his shoulders. "I like being here," he said in his soft, clear voice. "I know it can't happen by osmosis. But this is where it's at."

I've thought about this moment off and on for twenty years. I couldn't wait to get home, and Anthony was right at home. Fresh from reading something for his daughter, feeling the clasp on his shoulder of both his past and his future, for Anthony a new life was emerging on the threshold of a chilly night on a deserted campus.

These few minutes remind me of how humbling work with human beings can be. How we'll always miss things. How easily we get distracted—my own memories of cold urban landscapes overwhelmed the moment.

8 But I also hold onto this experience with Anthony for it contains so many lessons about development, about resilience and learning, about the power of hope and a second chance. It reminds us too of the importance of staying close to the ground, of finding out what people are thinking, of trying our best—flawed though it will be—to understand the world as they see it ... and to be ready to revise our understanding. This often means taking another line of sight on what seems familiar, seeing things in a new light.

And if we linger with Anthony a while longer, either in the doorway or back inside at a library table, we might get the chance to reflect on the basic question of what school is for, the purpose of education. What brought Anthony back to the classroom after all those years? To help his economic prospects, certainly. Anthony wanted to trade in his mop and pail for decent pay and a few benefits. But we also get a glimpse as to why else he's here. To be able to better guide his daughter. To be more proficient in reading about the events swirling around him—to add reading along with radio and television to his means of examining the world. To create a new life for himself, nurture this emerging sense of who he can become.

PERSONAL RESPONSE QUESTION

Write for a few minutes on your reasons for going to college.

QUESTIONS FOR CLASS OR SMALL-GROUP DISCUSSION

1. State in your own words the point or central purpose of this piece.
2. Comment on the rhetorical effectiveness of Rose's use of one extended example to achieve his purpose.
3. Rose says that his experience with Anthony contains "so many lessons" (paragraph 8). What do you understand those lessons to be, and how does Anthony illustrate them?
4. In the concluding paragraph, Rose suggests that the experience with Anthony raises "the basic question of what school is for, the purpose of education." Discuss how Rose answers the question of what school is for and whether you agree with him. Would you add other reasons to those that Rose names?

NO TIME TO READ?

DAVID McCULLOUGH

David McCullough is a biographer, historian, lecturer, and teacher. He holds twenty-one honorary degrees and has received many awards for his writing, including Pulitzer Prizes for his widely acclaimed biographies Truman *(1992) and* John Adams *(2001). His other books include* The Path Between the Seas *(1977), chronicling the building of the Panama Canal;* Mornings on Horseback *(1981), on the life of the young Theodore Roosevelt;* Brave Companions *(1992), essays on heroic figures of the past and present;* The Great Bridge: The Epic Story of Building the Brooklyn Bridge *(2001); and* 1776 *(2005). McCullough is also well known to viewers of PBS as the host of* The American Experience *and numerous PBS documentaries. "No Time to Read?" appeared in the April 18, 2000, issue of* Family Circle.

Once upon a time in the dead of winter in the Dakota territory, Theodore Roosevelt took off in a makeshift boat down the Little Missouri River in pursuit of a couple of thieves who had stolen his prized rowboat. After several days on the river, he caught up and got the draw on them with his trusty Winchester, at which point they surrendered. Then Roosevelt set off in a borrowed wagon to haul the thieves cross-country to justice. They headed across the snow-covered wastes of the Badlands to the railhead at Dickinson, and Roosevelt walked the whole way, the entire 40 miles.

It was an astonishing feat, what might be called a defining moment in Roosevelt's eventful life. But what makes it especially memorable is that during that time, he managed to read all of *Anna Karenina.*

4 I often think of that when I hear people say that they haven't time to read.

Reportedly, the average American does have time to watch 28 hours of television every week, or approximately four hours a day. The average person, I'm told, reads at a rate of 250 words per minute. So, based on these statistics, were the average American to spend those four hours a day with a book instead of watching television, he or she could, in a week, read: the complete poems of T. S. Eliot; two plays by Thornton Wilder, including *Our Town;* the complete poems of Maya Angelou; Faulkner's *The Sound and the Fury; The Great Gatsby;* and The Book of Psalms.

That's all in one week.

But a week is a long time by today's standards, when information is available at the touch of a finger. Information has become an industry, a commodity to be packaged, promoted and marketed incessantly. The tools for "accessing" data grow ever more wondrous and ubiquitous and essential if we're to keep in step, we've come to believe. All hail the web, the Internet, the Information Highway.

We're being sold the idea that information is learning, and we're being sold a bill of goods.

8 Information isn't learning. It isn't wisdom. It isn't common sense necessarily. It isn't kindness. Or good judgment. Or imagination. Or a sense of humor. Or courage. Information doesn't tell us right from wrong.

Knowing the area of the state of Connecticut in square miles, or the date on which the United Nations Charter was signed, or the jumping capacity of a flea may be useful, but it isn't learning of itself.

The greatest of all avenues to learning—to wisdom, adventure, pleasure, insight, to understanding human nature, understanding ourselves and our world and our place in it—is in reading books.

Read for life, all your life. Nothing ever invented provides such sustenance, such infinite reward for time spent, as a good book.

12 Read for pleasure. Read what you like, and all you like. Read literally to your heart's content. Let one book lead to another. They nearly always do.

Take up a great author, new or old, and read everything he or she has written. Read about places you've never been. Read biography, history. Read books that changed history: Tom Paine's *Common Sense;* the autobiography of Frederick Douglass; Rachel Carson's *Silent Spring.*

Read those books you know you're supposed to have read and imagine as dreary. A classic may be defined as a book that stays long in print, and a book stays long in print only because it is exceptional. Why exclude the exceptional from your experience?

Go back and read again the books written supposedly for children, especially if you think they are only for children. My first choice would be *The Wind in the Willows.* There's much, very much, you can learn in the company of Toad, Rat and Mole.

16 And when you read a book you love—a book you feel has enlarged the experience of being alive, a book that "lights the fire"—then spread the word.

To carry a book with you wherever you go is old advice and good advice. John Adams urged his son, John Quincy, to carry a volume of poetry. "You'll never be alone," he said, "with a poet in your pocket."

PERSONAL RESPONSE

Do you read books for pleasure during your leisure time? If so, what do you like to read? If not, why not?

QUESTIONS FOR CLASS OR SMALL-GROUP DISCUSSION

1. How effective do you find McCullough's opening anecdote about Theodore Roosevelt?
2. Do you agree with McCullough that, on the "idea that information is learning, [. . .] we're being sold a bill of goods" (paragraph 6)? Do you agree with him that "[i]nformation isn't learning" (paragraph 7)?
3. Discuss the extent to which you agree with McCullough's implication that people would have time to read books if they just took the time.
4. Have you read any of the books or any works by the authors that McCullough names? What authors have you heard about whose books you would like to read (paragraph 12)? What books do you "know you're supposed to have read and imagine as dreary" (paragraph 13)? Which of the books for children, besides *The Wind in the Willows*, do you think McCullough may have in mind when he says to read the "books written supposedly for children" (paragraph 14)?

✧ PERSPECTIVES ON EDUCATION ✧

Suggested Writing Topics

1. With Judy Blume's "Censorship: A Personal View" in mind, define "censorship," using your own experience with a banned, censored, forbidden, or challenged book.
2. Read one or more of the books that Judy Blume mentions in "Censorship: A Personal View" and write an essay explaining why you think it was challenged, censored or banned and whether you agree that it should have been.
3. Explain what you see as the role of parents in children's education.
4. Define *education*, using specific examples to illustrate general or abstract statements. You may want to focus specifically on high school education, as you experienced it, or higher education, which you are currently experiencing.
5. Distinguish among the words *education*, *knowledge*, and *wisdom*. How are they similar? How are they different? Would a standardized test measure any of them?

6. With Diane Ravitch's "Critical Thinking? You Need Knowledge" in mind, define an "intelligent person." You may want to include specific instances of someone you know who exemplifies that term for you.
7. Explain whether you think Diane Ravitch ("Critical Thinking? You Need Knowledge") would consider Anthony of Mike Rose's excerpt from *Why School?* "an intelligent person."
8. Argue in support of or against this statement from David McCullough's "No Time to Read?": "The greatest of all avenues to learning . . . is in reading books" (paragraph 9).
9. Write a paper about a book that had a profound effect on you. Explain briefly what the book is and what it is about, but focus on aspects of it that affected you. Perhaps it moved you emotionally as no other book has or it directed you on a specific path in life.
10. Write about a teacher who made an impression and had a significant effect on you. What made that teacher so important to you? Try to explain not only physical characteristics but, more importantly, personality features and admirable qualities. If a particular incident was especially significant in your relationship, narrate what happened.
11. Some people argue that not everyone deserves to go to college and that admitting average or mediocre students into colleges has debased American higher education. Argue in support of or against that position.
12. Imagine that the number of students admitted to college directly after high school has been limited to the upper 33 percent of all graduating seniors and that you do not meet the requirements for admission to college. Under special circumstances, students who fall below the 33 percent mark may be admitted. In a letter to the admissions officer at the college of your choice, argue that you should be admitted despite your class ranking and give reasons why you would make a good student.

Research Topics

1. Research the subject of governmental plans to measure learning in institutions of higher education by using a standardized test, and argue your position on the subject.
2. Research opinions for and against requiring students to write an essay as part of their qualifications for a degree, as some universities now do. Arrive at your own viewpoint based on your research, and argue your position.
3. Read one of the books that Judy Blume mentions in "Censorship: A Personal View," and research the controversy surrounding it. Explain the arguments both for and against banning or censoring the book, and then argue your own position.

4. Research the tracking systems used in many schools. Find opinions supporting and opposing such systems, consider their advantages and disadvantages, and arrive at your own conclusion based on your reading.
5. Spend some time searching the Internet or going through your library's catalog of books and periodicals on the subject of education. You will find a very large number of subtopics under that broad heading. Select a seemingly controversial subtopic that interests you. Keep searching until you have narrowed your focus to one specific aspect of the subject that is suitable for your research project.
6. Research the conflict of traditional versus revisionist curriculum. Interview educators and read periodical articles from the last several years on *political correctness*, defenses for or against *the canon*, or related topics.
7. David McCullough in "No Time to Read?" finds fault with the electronic media. Research the subject of the role of television or of the Internet in American popular culture in relationship to the reading habits of Americans.
8. Research the 21st-Century Skills movement. Define it, explain its purpose, and assess its usefulness in producing truly educated students.

Responding to Visuals

Boring class, circa 1950s.

1. What do you think the photographer wanted to convey with this picture?
2. Although the caption describes the photograph as that of a boring class, what other emotions do the facial expressions of the students suggest? What does their body language reveal about how they view this particular classroom experience?
3. If you had not been told the date that the photograph was taken, what aspects of the classroom and students would give you clues that it is not recent?
4. Why do you think the teacher is not shown in the photograph?

Responding to Visuals

Think for yourself.

1. How do the robots on the left and right differ from the middle robot? Why is the middle one smiling?
2. Discuss the effectiveness of this image as a comment on censorship. Do you think that is its only message, or are there other ways of interpreting the image?
3. Do you think books should be banned for school-aged children? If so, who should make the decision about which books to ban: parents, the administration, or teachers? What if one group believes a book should be banned while another defends it as literature and finds it acceptable?

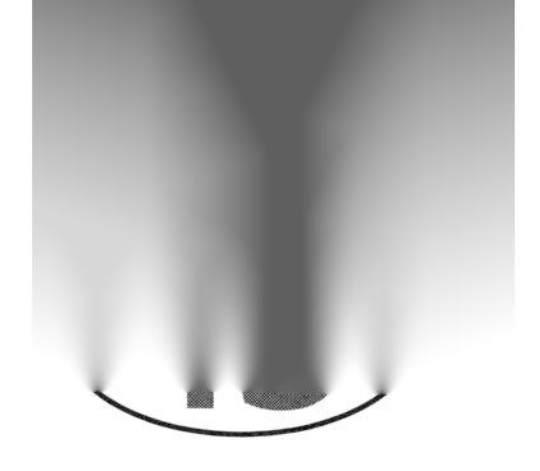

Poverty and Homelessness

Once largely ignored, the issues of poverty, homelessness, and welfare have prompted heated discussion in recent years. At the community level, social workers and staff members at shelters for the homeless and impoverished struggle to meet the needs of desperate people, while at the state and federal levels, legislators argue over whether to cut welfare funding. The numbers of people in poverty, especially women and children, continue to rise. Many families whose incomes provide just enough for basic necessities, such as shelter and food, are only a paycheck or two away from living on the streets. Worse, a growing number of the nation's poor actually work full-time. Compounding the difficulty of these issues are certain attitudes toward or stereotyped beliefs about people on welfare or living on the streets. Charges of laziness and fraud are often leveled at welfare recipients, despite studies that demonstrate that the vast majority of people on welfare want to work and live independent lives.

The essays in this chapter examine some of the issues associated with poverty and homelessness. First, Anna Quindlen in "Our Tired, Our Poor, Our Kids" looks at the plight of homeless mothers and children in America. She points out some of the effects of homelessness on children, emphasizes the importance of affordable housing, and touches on the effects of welfare reform on homelessness. In contrast to Quindlen's focus on homeless and impoverished children is Kevin Fagan's piece on an older population of people living on the street. "Homeless, Mike Dick Was 51, Looked 66" takes a close look at a man who is representative of "old folks who have no business living in the gutter," as Fagan describes them.

Next, Barbara Ehrenreich addresses the subject of the newly poor versus the working poor. She compares the situations of middle-class, white collar workers who have suffered in a slumped economy with those of people whose blue-collar jobs pay only enough for them to just manage to scrape by. Following up on some of the people she interviewed for her book *Nickel and Dimed*, Ehrenreich highlights the special problems faced by low-wage earners in a weak economy.

Finally, in "The Singer Solution to World Poverty," Peter Singer broadens the focus of the chapter to world poverty while addressing his essay to the American middle class. Using the logic of his training as a utilitarian philosopher, Singer offers a hypothetical ethical scenario to raise readers' awareness of what he sees as their moral responsibility to donate to world aid funds for poor and starving children.

As you read these essays, think about your own attitudes toward welfare, homelessness, and poverty. These are tough social problems that just about every society must face, but especially so in countries with large urban areas and great gaps between the rich and the poor. Do the Quindlen and Fagan essays in any way reinforce or change your attitudes about these issues? Are you moved by Ehrenreich's description of the desperately uncertain lives of the working poor? Does Singer persuade you to donate to charities?

OUR TIRED, OUR POOR, OUR KIDS

ANNA QUINDLEN

Anna Quindlen is a novelist, social critic, and journalist who began her career at the New York Post *and then became deputy metropolitan editor of the* New York Times. *In 1986, she began her syndicated column "Life in the Thirties" and a few years later "Public and Private," for which she won a Pulitzer Prize in 1992. She contributed to* Newsweek's *prestigious back-page column, "The Last Word," every other week until she retired in 2009. Her columns are collected in* Living Out Loud *(1988);* Thinking Out Loud *(1992); and* Loud and Clear *(2004). She has written the following novels:* Object Lessons *(1991);* One True Thing *(1994);* Black and Blue *(1998);* Blessings *(2003); and* Being Perfect *(2004). Among her nonfiction books are* How Reading Changed My Life *(1998);* A Short Guide to a Happy Life *(2000); and* Imagining London: A Tour of the World's Greatest Fictional City *(2004). This essay appeared in the March 12, 2001, issue of* Newsweek.

Six people live here, in a room the size of the master bedroom in a modest suburban house. Trundles, bunk beds, dressers side by side stacked with toys, clothes, boxes, in tidy claustrophobic clutter. One woman, five children. The baby was born in a shelter. The older kids can't wait to get out of this one. Everyone gets up at 6 a.m., the little ones to go to day care, the others to school. Their mother goes out to look for an apartment when she's not going to drug-treatment meetings. "For what they pay for me to stay in a shelter I could have lived in the Hamptons," Sharanda says.

Here is the parallel universe that has flourished while the more fortunate were rewarding themselves for the stock split with SUVs and home additions. There is a boom market in homelessness. But these are not the men on the streets of San Francisco holding out cardboard signs to the tourists. They are children, hundreds of thousands of them, twice as likely to repeat a grade or be hospitalized and four times as likely to go hungry as the kids with a roof over their heads. Twenty years ago New York City provided emergency shelter for just under a thousand families a day; last month it had to find spaces for 10,000 children on a given night. Not since the Great Depression have this many babies, toddlers and kids had no place like home.

Three mothers sit in the living room of a temporary residence called Casa Rita in the Bronx and speak of this in the argot of poverty. "The landlord don't call back when they hear you got EARP," says Rosie, EARP being the Emergency Assistance Rehousing Program. "You get priority for Section 8 if you're in a shelter," says Edna, which means federal housing programs will put you higher on the list. Edna has four kids, three in foster care; she arrived at Casa Rita, she says, "with two bags and a baby." Rosie has three; they share a bathroom down the hall with two other families.

Sharanda's five range in age from 13 to just over a year. Her eldest was put in the wrong grade when he changed schools. "He's humiliated, living here," his mother says.

4 All three women are anxious to move on, although they appreciate this place, where they can get shelter, get sober and keep their kids at the same time. They remember the Emergency Assistance Unit, the city office that is the gateway to the system, where hundreds of families sit every day surrounded by their bags, where children sleep on benches until they are shuffled off dull-eyed for one night in a shelter or a motel, only to return as supplicants again the next day.

In another world middle-class Americans have embraced new-home starts, the stock market and the Gap. But in the world of these displaced families, problems ignored or fumbled or unforeseen during this great period of prosperity have dovetailed into an enormous subculture of children who think that only rich people have their own bedrooms. Twenty years ago, when the story of the homeless in America became a staple of news reporting, the solution was presented as a simple one: affordable housing. That's still true, now more than ever. Two years ago the National Low Income Housing Coalition calculated that the hourly income necessary to afford the average two-bedroom apartment was around $12. That's more than twice the minimum wage.

The result is that in many cities police officers and teachers cannot afford to live where they work, that in Las Vegas old motels provide housing for casino employees, that in shelters now there is a contingent of working poor who get up off their cots and go off to their jobs. The result is that if you are evicted for falling behind on your rent, if there is a bureaucratic foul-up in your welfare check or the factory in which you work shuts down, the chances of finding another place to live are very small indeed. You're one understanding relative, one paycheck, one second chance from the street. And so are your kids.

So-called welfare reform, which emphasizes cutbacks and make-work, has played a part in all this. A study done in San Diego in 1998 found that a third of homeless families had recently had benefits terminated or reduced, and that most said that was how they had wound up on the street. Drugs, alcohol and domestic abuse also land mothers with kids in the shelter system or lead them to hand their children over to relatives or foster homes. Today the average homeless woman is younger than ever before, may have been in foster care or in shelters herself and so considers a chaotic childhood the norm. Many never finished high school, and have never held a job.

8 Ralph Nunez, who runs the organization Homes for the Homeless, says that all this calls for new attitudes. "People don't like to hear it, but shelters are going to be the low-income housing of the future," he says. "So how do we enrich the experience and use the system to provide job training and education?" Bonnie Stone of Women in Need, which has eight other residences along with Casa Rita, says, "We're pouring everything we've got into the nine months most of them are here—nutrition, treatment, budgeting. By the time they leave, they have a subsidized apartment, day care and, hopefully, some life skills they didn't have before."

But these organizations are rafts in a rising river of need that has roared through this country without most of us ever even knowing. So now you know. There are hundreds of thousands of little nomads in America, sleeping in the back of cars, on floors in welfare offices or in shelters five to a room. What would it mean, to spend your childhood drifting from one strange bed to another, waking in the morning to try to figure out where you'd landed today, without those things that confer security and happiness: a familiar picture on the wall, a certain slant of light through a curtained window? "Give me your tired, your poor," it says on the base of the Statue of Liberty, to welcome foreigners. Oh, but they are already here, the small refugees from the ruin of the American dream, even if you cannot see them.

PERSONAL RESPONSE

What image of the homeless did you have before reading this essay? Has your understanding of them changed in any way now that you have read it? If so, in what way has it changed? If not, explain why.

QUESTIONS FOR CLASS OR SMALL-GROUP DISCUSSION

1. Were you surprised by this statement: "Not since the Great Depression have this many babies, toddlers and kids had no place like home" (paragraph 2)? What do you think Quindlen hopes to achieve by the reference to the Great Depression?
2. Explain why, according to Quindlen, there are so many homeless women and children in America. What is the effect of homelessness on children? Are you persuaded of the seriousness of the problem?
3. What does Quindlen mean by the term *working poor* (paragraph 6)?
4. Quindlen uses the term *so-called* to describe welfare reform (paragraph 7). Why do you think she does that? What fault does she find with welfare reform? Do you agree with her?

HOMELESS, MIKE DICK WAS 51, LOOKED 66

KEVIN FAGAN

Kevin Fagan, a San Francisco Chronicle *staff writer, and photographer Brant Ward covered homelessness for* The Chronicle *locally and nationally from 2003 to 2006. They spent many nights outside with street people in San Francisco. This follow-up article on one of the men they followed during that period was published in the* San Francisco Chronicle *on March 2, 2008.*

Mike Dick looked like a thousand other old homeless guys—a lump of blankets, jacket and jeans so grimy-gray from the street you couldn't tell what color they used to be. And when Chronicle photographer Brant Ward and I strolled up to his doorway in downtown San Francisco two years ago for a chat, his response was the typical old-homeless-guy response.

A blank stare.

So Brant pulled out a cigarette. Mike allowed the hint of a smile, baring his only two teeth. He lit up and took a drag.

"Cold f-ing day, ain't it?" he eventually let out. Then he coughed violently. Which was no surprise, considering he had emphysema, bronchitis, a congestive heart condition and high blood pressure. Not to mention a cold.

4 But on the street, a cigarette is a luxury nobody refuses, especially if it isn't a scrounged butt. Besides, the crack habit he had was worse. As were the 22 years of horrific wear and tear Mike bore on his beanpole of a body from shivering under wet blankets on sidewalks and getting the tar kicked out of him fairly frequently. His right eye wandered from one of those kicks, and his forehead bore a ragged hole where doctors sliced out a cue-ball-size tumor. Battered, sad and hopeless-looking—that was Mike.

There are more like him on the street every day—old folks who have no business living in the gutter. And even if they're rescued, it's often way too late.

Brant and I knew Mike back during our years as the only newspaper team in the United States covering homelessness full time—him the photographer, me the word man. Mike was 51 when we met him, but that was really what counselors would call a "street 66"—meaning his years of homelessness made him look and function 15 years older than he was. He shuffled more than walked, had a bushy gray beard to his chest, and the worry lines in his face looked carved. Brant and I marveled that he was still alive, as we did when we met so many other "streets 66s," "street 70s," or even "street 80s."

Our worries, it turned out, were well-placed. Mike died Dec. 29.

8 The irony is that by then, he had been scooped off the street by city homelessness counselors and given a roof—the Coast Hotel, a supportive housing complex. There, residents live rent-free while on-site counselors help them wrestle the demons that put them on the street. Mike had been at the Coast for 15 months, probably the happiest period of his life, and if fate had been more benevolent, he would have passed many years there getting his act together.

But homeless decay doesn't leave your bones just because you leave the sidewalk.

He died sitting in the hotel's television lounge. His battered heart just finally gave out, and he looked so peaceful in the chair that his pals thought he was sleeping until one noticed his face was unusually pale two hours after his death.

I think what happened to Mike is that he finally relaxed the tensely clenched defense mechanisms he held in all those years, physically and mentally, to keep himself alive through thrashings, hunger and freezing cold. Once he got a safe, permanent roof and natural vulnerability was allowed to settle in, his body just allowed itself to surrender to death.

12 We're going to see more Mikes dying—in and out of housing—before we see fewer.

That's because Mike, and most of the old homeless folks you see panhandling or snoring outside, hit the streets back in the 1980s during what experts call the "big boom" of homelessness. Now, all these years later, they are simply aging toward a premature death—right where they sit, stand and sleep.

UCSF Assistant Professor Judy Hahn in 2006 led what is believed to be the most significant study of older homeless people in the United States, and she found that the median age of street people in San Francisco was 50—compared with 37 in 1990. They all had far more problems with emphysema and other ailments than non-homeless people their age, "the rates of disease you would expect in a much older population," Hahn said. She says the median age will go up every year.

Mike never knew what was coming.

16 "I feel better than ever," Mike told me last summer when I bought him a cup of coffee in the Tenderloin. "I never thought I'd get to really move inside, but I guess it was finally my time."

Clapton's Saddest Songs

Mike's gentleness that charmed me and Brant on the street, his fervor for reading Tom Clancy novels and listening to Eric Clapton's saddest songs—all characteristics invisible to those who would walk by him with revulsion—were even more vivid than before. But his lingering cough and the very way he stood, like a reed ready to fall over, told me he was either fooling himself or too happy to acknowledge how broken he was.

Mike wasn't even the worst off of the older street folks whom Brant and I have known. Our homeless beat included dozens of them known, like hoboes, by one-name handles: Georgia. Rhonda. Grimes. Peg. Red. And lots of Mikes and Mamas.

Several died before they could get inside. Others who did manage to find a roof are, like Mike, no longer with us—most notably Jill May, who last spring was beaten and set on fire by thugs.

20 They all had addiction and other hobbles in common—but one commonality stood out: Almost every one grew up poor and abused, and though they made stabs at normal life, they never had a chance.

In Mike's case, his mother died a month after giving birth to him, and his father was a drunk. Mike left his home in Idaho at 14 and wandered through janitor jobs and youth homes before hitting the gutter in 1984.

Odd jobs, of short duration

His demons were drugs and booze, and although he held odd jobs now and then as an adult—florist's aide was the pinnacle—they never lasted long. By the time we met Mike, he was scraping up $4 a day by recycling from trash cans.

In a rich country where *actors* can make millions of dollars pretending, on a movie screen, to be poor like Mike and then go home to one of their mansions at night, we can do better. San Francisco, like many cities, has made sincere efforts to get old homeless folks into housing—but the city can't fund enough of it alone. Huge cuts to federal housing and poverty programs over the past two decades have not been replaced with anything effective.

24 This is a problem that's not going away. The nation needs to commit, emotionally and economically, to saving these older folks. It's too late for Mike—but not for the hundreds of thousands like him.

PERSONAL RESPONSE

What is your emotional response to the life of Mike Dick? Do you feel sympathetic toward him? Is your attitude toward him different from or similar to the attitude you had toward the homeless living on the street before reading this article? Explain your answer.

QUESTIONS FOR CLASS OR SMALL-GROUP DISCUSSION

1. What is the rhetorical effect of focusing on one specific person, as Fagan has done here, rather than on older homeless people in general?
2. What do you think that Fagan hoped to achieve by writing about Mike Dick? Does he have a stated or an implied purpose?
3. What conclusions can you draw about the backgrounds of older homeless people and/or the reasons why they end up on the streets? What do they have in common?
4. What actions does Fagan call for to address the problem of homelessness? Can you suggest other solutions besides those he names?

TOO POOR TO MAKE THE NEWS

BARBARA EHRENREICH

Barbara Ehrenreich's articles appear in a variety of popular magazines and newspapers, including Time, *the* Progressive, *and the* New York Times. *Her books include the following:* Hearts of Men: American Dreams and the Flight from Commitment *(1984);* Blood Rites: Origins and History of the Passions of War *(1997);* Fear of Falling: The Inner Life of the Middle Class *(2000);* Nickel and Dimed: On (Not) Getting By in America *(2001);* Bait and Switch: The (Futile) Pursuit of the American Dream *(2006);* Dancing in the Streets: A History of Collective Joy *(2007);* This

Land Is Their Land: Reports from a Divided Nation *(2008); and* Bright-Sided: How the Relentless Promotion of Positive Thinking Has Undermined America *(2009). This article was first published in the June 15, 2009, issue of the* New York Times.

The human side of the recession, in the new media genre that's been called "recession porn," is the story of an incremental descent from excess to frugality, from ease to austerity. The super-rich give up their personal jets; the upper middle class cut back on private Pilates classes; the merely middle class forgo vacations and evenings at Applebee's. In some accounts, the recession is even described as the "great leveler," smudging the dizzying levels of inequality that characterized the last couple of decades and squeezing everyone into a single great class, the Nouveau Poor, in which we will all drive tiny fuel-efficient cars and grow tomatoes on our porches.

But the outlook is not so cozy when we look at the effects of the recession on a group generally omitted from all the vivid narratives of downward mobility—the already poor, the estimated 20 percent to 30 percent of the population who struggle to get by in the best of times. This demographic, the working poor, have already been living in an economic depression of their own. From their point of view "the economy," as a shared condition, is a fiction.

This spring, I tracked down a couple of the people I had met while working on my 2001 book, "Nickel and Dimed," in which I worked in low-wage jobs like waitressing and housecleaning, and I found them no more gripped by the recession than by "American Idol"; things were pretty much "same old." The woman I called Melissa in the book was still working at Wal-Mart, though in nine years, her wages had risen to $10 an hour from $7. "Caroline," who is increasingly disabled by diabetes and heart disease, now lives with a grown son and subsists on occasional cleaning and catering jobs. We chatted about grandchildren and church, without any mention of exceptional hardship.

4 As with Denise Smith, whom I recently met through the Virginia Organizing Project and whose bachelor's degree in history qualifies her for seasonal $10-an-hour work at a tourist site, the recession is largely an abstraction. "We were poor," Ms. Smith told me cheerfully, "and we're still poor."

But then, at least if you inhabit a large, multiclass extended family like my own, there comes that e-mail message with the subject line "Need your help," and you realize that bad is often just the stage before worse. The note was from one of my nephews, and it reported that his mother-in-law, Peg, was, like several million other Americans, about to lose her home to foreclosure.

It was the back story that got to me: Peg, who is 55 and lives in rural Missouri, had been working three part-time jobs to support her disabled daughter and two grandchildren, who had moved in with her. Then, last winter, she had a heart attack, missed work and fell behind in her mortgage payments. If I couldn't help, all four would have to move into the cramped apartment in Minneapolis already occupied by my nephew and his wife.

Only after I'd sent the money did I learn that the mortgage was not a subprime one and the home was not a house but a dilapidated single-wide trailer that, as a "used vehicle," commands a 12-percent mortgage interest rate. You could argue, without any shortage of compassion, that "Low-Wage Worker Loses Job, Home" is nobody's idea of news.

8 In late May I traveled to Los Angeles—where the real unemployment rate, including underemployed people and those who have given up on looking for a job, is estimated at 20 percent—to meet with a half-dozen community organizers. They are members of a profession, derided last summer by Sarah Palin, that helps low-income people renegotiate mortgages, deal with eviction when their landlords are foreclosed and, when necessary, organize to confront landlords and bosses. The question I put to this rainbow group was: "Has the recession made a significant difference in the low-income communities where you work, or are things pretty much the same?" My informants—from Koreatown, South Central, Maywood, Artesia and the area around Skid Row—took pains to explain that things were already bad before the recession, and in ways that are disconnected from the larger economy. One of them told me, for example, that the boom of the '90s and early 2000s had been "basically devastating" for the urban poor. Rents skyrocketed; public housing disappeared to make way for gentrification.

But yes, the recession has made things palpably worse, largely because of job losses. With no paychecks coming in, people fall behind on their rent and, since there can be as long as a six-year wait for federal housing subsidies, they often have no alternative but to move in with relatives. "People are calling me all the time," said Preeti Sharma of the South Asian Network. "They think I have some sort of magic."

The organizers even expressed a certain impatience with the Nouveau Poor, once I introduced the phrase. If there's a symbol for the recession in Los Angeles, Davin Corona of Strategic Actions for a Just Economy said, it's "the policeman facing foreclosure in the suburbs." The already poor, he said—the undocumented immigrants, the sweatshop workers, the janitors, maids and security guards—had all but "disappeared" from both the news media and public policy discussions.

Disappearing with them is what may be the most distinctive and compelling story of this recession. When I got back home, I started calling up experts, like Sharon Parrott, a policy analyst at the Center on Budget and Policy Priorities, who told me, "There's rising unemployment among all demographic groups, but vastly more among the so-called unskilled."

12 How much more? Larry Mishel, the president of the Economic Policy Institute, offers data showing that blue-collar unemployment is increasing three times as fast as white-collar unemployment. The last two recessions—in the early '90s and in 2001—produced mass white-collar layoffs, and while the current one has seen plenty of downsized real-estate agents and financial analysts, the brunt is being borne by the blue-collar working class, which has been sliding downward since deindustrialization began in the '80s.

When I called food banks and homeless shelters around the country, most staff members and directors seemed poised to offer press-pleasing tales of formerly middle-class families brought low. But some, like Toni Muhammad at Gateway Homeless Services in St. Louis, admitted that mostly they see "the long-term poor," who become even poorer when they lose the kind of low-wage jobs that had been so easy for me to find from 1998 to 2000. As Candy Hill, a vice president of Catholic Charities U.S.A., put it, "All the focus is on the middle class—on Wall Street and Main Street—but it's the people on the back streets who are really suffering."

What are the stations between poverty and destitution? Like the Nouveau Poor, the already poor descend through a series of deprivations, though these are less likely to involve forgone vacations than missed meals and medications. The *Times* reported earlier this month that one-third of Americans can no longer afford to comply with their prescriptions.

There are other, less life-threatening, ways to try to make ends meet. The Associated Press has reported that more women from all social classes are resorting to stripping, although "gentlemen's clubs," too, have been hard-hit by the recession. The rural poor are turning increasingly to "food auctions," which offer items that may be past their sell-by dates.

16 And for those who like their meat fresh, there's the option of urban hunting. In Racine, Wis., a 51-year-old laid-off mechanic told me he's supplementing his diet by "shooting squirrels and rabbits and eating them stewed, baked and grilled." In Detroit, where the wildlife population has mounted as the human population ebbs, a retired truck driver is doing a brisk business in raccoon carcasses, which he recommends marinating with vinegar and spices.

The most common coping strategy, though, is simply to increase the number of paying people per square foot of dwelling space—by doubling up or renting to couch-surfers. It's hard to get firm numbers on overcrowding, because no one likes to acknowledge it to census-takers, journalists or anyone else who might be remotely connected to the authorities. At the legal level, this includes Peg taking in her daughter and two grandchildren in a trailer with barely room for two, or my nephew and his wife preparing to squeeze all four of them into what is essentially a one-bedroom apartment. But stories of Dickensian living arrangements abound.

In Los Angeles, Prof. Peter Dreier, a housing policy expert at Occidental College, says that "people who've lost their jobs, or at least their second jobs, cope by doubling or tripling up in overcrowded apartments, or by paying 50 or 60 or even 70 percent of their incomes in rent." Thelmy Perez, an organizer with Strategic Actions for a Just Economy, is trying to help an elderly couple who could no longer afford the $600 a month rent on their two-bedroom apartment, so they took in six unrelated subtenants and are now facing eviction. According to a community organizer in my own city, Alexandria, Va., the standard apartment in a complex occupied largely by day laborers contains two bedrooms, each housing a family of up to five people, plus an additional person laying claim to the couch.

Overcrowding—rural, suburban and urban—renders the mounting numbers of the poor invisible, especially when the perpetrators have no telltale cars to park on the street. But if this is sometimes a crime against zoning laws, it's not exactly a victimless one. At best, it leads to interrupted sleep and long waits for the bathroom; at worst, to explosions of violence. Catholic Charities is reporting a spike in domestic violence in many parts of the country, which Candy Hill attributes to the combination of unemployment and overcrowding.

20 And doubling up is seldom a stable solution. According to Toni Muhammad, about 70 percent of the people seeking emergency shelter in St. Louis report they had been living with relatives "but the place was too small." When I asked Peg what it was like to share her trailer with her daughter's family, she said bleakly, "I just stay in my bedroom."

The deprivations of the formerly affluent Nouveau Poor are real enough, but the situation of the already poor suggests that they do not necessarily presage a greener, more harmonious future with a flatter distribution of wealth. There are no data yet on the effects of the recession on measures of inequality, but historically the effect of downturns is to increase, not decrease, class polarization.

The recession of the '80s transformed the working class into the working poor, as manufacturing jobs fled to the third world, forcing American workers into the low-paying service and retail sector. The current recession is knocking the working poor down another notch—from low-wage employment and inadequate housing toward erratic employment and no housing at all. Comfortable people have long imagined that American poverty is far more luxurious than the third world variety, but the difference is rapidly narrowing.

Maybe "the economy," as depicted on CNBC, will revive again, restoring the kinds of jobs that sustained the working poor, however inadequately, before the recession. Chances are, though, that they still won't pay enough to live on, at least not at any level of safety and dignity. In fact, hourly wage growth, which had been running at about 4 percent a year, has undergone what the Economic Policy Institute calls a "dramatic collapse" in the last six months alone. In good times and grim ones, the misery at the bottom just keeps piling up, like a bad debt that will eventually come due.

PERSONAL RESPONSE

Write about the degree to which you can identify with the working poor or with those who have had to scale back because of the economy. If you do not identify with either group, write for a few minutes about a job you have had and whether you think you were paid enough for it.

QUESTIONS FOR CLASS OR SMALL-GROUP DISCUSSION

1. Summarize the differences between the "Nouveau Poor" and the working poor, according to Ehrenreich. Do you think her descriptions of these groups of people are accurate? Would you add to or modify what she has said about them?

2. What is Ehrenreich's attitude toward the "Nouveau Poor" and the working poor? Is she more sympathetic toward one group than the other? How can you tell? What is her tone when writing about each of the groups?
3. Explain the title of this essay. Who is "too poor to make the news"? Why?
4. State in your own words what Ehrenreich describes as "the stations between poverty and destitution" (paragraph 14). What coping mechanisms do the working poor use, according to Ehrenreich?

THE SINGER SOLUTION TO WORLD POVERTY

PETER SINGER

Peter Singer, an Australian-born philosopher and bioethicist, is author of the highly influential book Animal Liberation *(1975), which has been translated into two dozen languages. He has served as president of the International Association of Bioethics and as editor of its official journal,* Bioethics. *Among his dozen or so other books are* How Are We to Live? Ethics in an Age of Self Interest *(1993);* Rethinking Life and Death: The Collapse of Our Traditional Ethics *(1995);* Writings on an Ethical Life *(2000);* The President of Good and Evil *(2004);* The Way We Eat: Why Our Food Choices Matter *(2006); and* Stem Cell Research, *coedited with Laura Grabel and Lori Gruen (2007). Singer is on the faculty at the Center for Human Values at Princeton University. You can visit his website at www.princeton.edu/~psinger. This essay appeared in the September 5, 1999, issue of the* New York Times Magazine.

In the Brazilian film *Central Station*, Dora is a retired schoolteacher who makes ends meet by sitting at the station writing letters for illiterate people. Suddenly she has an opportunity to pocket $1,000. All she has to do is persuade a homeless nine-year-old boy to follow her to an address she has been given. (She is told he will be adopted by wealthy foreigners.) She delivers the boy, gets the money, spends some of it on a television set, and settles down to enjoy her new acquisition. Her neighbor spoils the fun, however, by telling her that the boy was too old to be adopted—he will be killed and his organs sold for transplantation. Perhaps Dora knew this all along, but after her neighbor's plain speaking, she spends a troubled night. In the morning Dora resolves to take the boy back.

Suppose Dora had told her neighbor that it is a tough world, other people have nice new TVs too, and if selling the kid is the only way she can get one, well, he was only a street kid. She would then have become, in the eyes of the audience, a monster. She redeems herself only by being prepared to bear considerable risks to save the boy.

At the end of the movie, in cinemas in the affluent nations of the world, people who would have been quick to condemn Dora if she had not rescued the boy go home to places far more comfortable than her apartment. In fact, the average family in the United States spends almost one-third of its income on things that are no more necessary to them than Dora's new TV was to her. Going out to nice restaurants, buying new clothes because the old ones are no longer stylish, vacationing at beach resorts—so much of our income is spent on things not essential to the preservation of our lives and health. Donated to one of a number of charitable agencies, that money could mean the difference between life and death for children in need.

4 All of which raises a question: In the end, what is the ethical distinction between a Brazilian who sells a homeless child to organ peddlers and an American who already has a TV and upgrades to a better one—knowing that the money could be donated to an organization that would use it to save the lives of kids in need?

Of course, there are several differences between the two situations that could support different moral judgments about them. For one thing, to be able to consign a child to death when he is standing right in front of you takes a chilling kind of heartlessness; it is much easier to ignore an appeal for money to help children you will never meet. Yet for a utilitarian philosopher like myself—that is, one who judges whether acts are right or wrong by their consequences—if the upshot of the American's failure to donate the money is that one more kid dies on the streets of a Brazilian city, then it is, in some sense, just as bad as selling the kid to the organ peddlers. But one doesn't need to embrace my utilitarian ethic to see that, at the very least, there is a troubling incongruity in being so quick to condemn Dora for taking the child to the organ peddlers while, at the same time, not regarding the American consumer's behavior as raising a serious moral issue.

In his 1996 book, *Living High and Letting Die*, the New York University philosopher Peter Unger presented an ingenious series of imaginary examples designed to probe our intuitions about whether it is wrong to live well without giving substantial amounts of money to help people who are hungry, malnourished, or dying from easily treatable illnesses like diarrhea. Here's my paraphrase of one of these examples: Bob is close to retirement. He has invested most of his savings in a very rare and valuable old car, a Bugatti, which he has not been able to insure. The Bugatti is his pride and joy. In addition to the pleasure he gets from driving and caring for his car, Bob knows that its rising market value means that he will always be able to sell it and live comfortably after retirement. One day when Bob is out for a drive, he parks the Bugatti near the end of a railway siding and goes for a walk up the track. As he does so, he sees that a runaway train, with no one aboard, is running down the railway track. Looking farther down the track, he sees the small figure of a child very likely to be killed by the runaway train. He can't stop the train and the child is too far away to warn of the danger, but he can throw a switch that will divert the train down the siding where his Bugatti is parked. Then nobody will be killed—but the train will destroy his Bugatti. Thinking of his joy in owning the car and the financial security it represents, Bob decides not to throw the switch.

The child is killed. For many years to come, Bob enjoys owning his Bugatti and the financial security it represents.

Bob's conduct, most of us will immediately respond, was gravely wrong. Unger agrees. But then he reminds us that we, too, have opportunities to save the lives of children. We can give to organizations like Unicef or Oxfam America. How much would we have to give one of these organizations to have a high probability of saving the life of a child threatened by easily preventable diseases? (I do not believe that children are more worth saving than adults, but since no one can argue that children have brought their poverty on themselves, focusing on them simplifies the issues.) Unger called up some experts and used the information they provided to offer some plausible estimates that include the cost of raising money, administrative expenses, and the cost of delivering aid where it is most needed. By his calculation, $200 in donations would help a sickly two-year-old transform into a healthy six-year-old—offering safe passage through childhood's most dangerous years. To show how practical philosophical argument can be, Unger even tells his readers that they can easily donate funds by using their credit card and calling one of these toll-free numbers: (800) 367–5437 for Unicef; (800) 693–2687 for Oxfam America.

8 Now you, too, have the information you need to save a child's life. How should you judge yourself if you don't do it? Think again about Bob and his Bugatti. Unlike Dora, Bob did not have to look into the eyes of the child he was sacrificing for his own material comfort. The child was a complete stranger to him and too far away to relate to in an intimate, personal way. Unlike Dora, too, he did not mislead the child or initiate the chain of events imperiling him. In all these respects, Bob's situation resembles that of people able but unwilling to donate to overseas aid and differs from Dora's situation.

If you still think that it was very wrong of Bob not to throw the switch that would have diverted the train and saved the child's life, then it is hard to see how you could deny that it is also very wrong not to send money to one of the organizations listed above. Unless, that is, there is some morally important difference between the two situations that I have overlooked.

Is it the practical uncertainties about whether aid will really reach the people who need it? Nobody who knows the world of overseas aid can doubt that such uncertainties exist. But Unger's figure of $200 to save a child's life was reached after he had made conservative assumptions about the proportion of the money donated that will actually reach its target.

One genuine difference between Bob and those who can afford to donate to overseas aid organizations but don't is that only Bob can save the child on the tracks, whereas there are hundreds of millions of people who can give $200 to overseas aid organizations. The problem is that most of them aren't doing it. Does this mean that it is all right for you not to do it?

12 Suppose that there were more owners of priceless vintage cars—Carol, Dave, Emma, Fred and so on, down to Ziggy—all in exactly the same situation as Bob, with their own siding and their own switch, all sacrificing the child in order to preserve their own cherished car. Would that make it all right for Bob to do the same?

To answer this question affirmatively is to endorse follow-the-crowd ethics—the kind of ethics that led many Germans to look away when the Nazi atrocities were being committed. We do not excuse them because others were behaving no better.

We seem to lack a sound basis for drawing a clear moral line between Bob's situation and that of any reader of this article with $200 to spare who does not donate it to an overseas aid agency. These readers seem to be acting at least as badly as Bob was acting when he chose to let the runaway train hurtle toward the unsuspecting child. In the light of this conclusion, I trust that many readers will reach for the phone and donate that $200. Perhaps you should do it before reading further.

Now that you have distinguished yourself morally from people who put their vintage cars ahead of a child's life, how about treating yourself and your partner to dinner at your favorite restaurant? But wait. The money you will spend at the restaurant could also help save the lives of children overseas! True, you weren't planning to blow $200 tonight, but if you were to give up dining out just for one month, you would easily save that amount. And what is one month's dining out, compared to a child's life? There's the rub. Since there are a lot of desperately needy children in the world, there will always be another child whose life you could save for another $200. Are you therefore obliged to keep giving until you have nothing left? At what point can you stop?

Hypothetical examples can easily become farcical. Consider Bob. How far past losing the Bugatti should he go? Imagine that Bob had got his foot stuck in the track of the siding, and if he diverted the train, then before it rammed the car it would also amputate his big toe. Should he still throw the switch? What if it would amputate his foot? His entire leg?

16 As absurd as the Bugatti scenario gets when pushed to extremes, the point it raises is a serious one: Only when the sacrifices become very significant indeed would most people be prepared to say that Bob does nothing wrong when he decides not to throw the switch. Of course, most people could be wrong; we can't decide moral issues by taking opinion polls. But consider for yourself the level of sacrifice that you would demand of Bob, and then think about how much money you would have to give away in order to make a sacrifice that is roughly equal to that. It's almost certainly much, much more than $200. For most middle-class Americans, it could easily be more like $200,000.

Isn't it counterproductive to ask people to do so much? Don't we run the risk that many will shrug their shoulders and say that mortality, so conceived, is fine for saints but not for them? I accept that we are unlikely to see, in the near or even medium-term future, a world in which it is normal for wealthy Americans to give the bulk of their wealth to strangers. When it comes to praising or blaming people for what they do, we tend to use a standard that is relative to some conception of normal behavior. Comfortably off Americans who give, say, 10 percent of their income to overseas aid organizations are so far ahead of most of their equally comfortable fellow citizens that I wouldn't go out of my way to chastise them for not doing more. Nevertheless, they should be doing much more, and they are in no position to criticize Bob for failing to make the much greater sacrifice of his Bugatti.

At this point various objections may crop up. Someone may say: "If every citizen living in the affluent nations contributed his or her share I wouldn't have to make such a drastic sacrifice, because long before such levels were reached, the resources would have been there to save the lives of all those children dying from lack of food or medical care. So why should I give more than my fair share?" Another, related objection is that the government ought to increase its overseas aid allocations, since that would spread the burden more equitably across all taxpayers.

Yet the question of how much we ought to give is a matter to be decided in the real world—and that, sadly, is a world in which we know that most people do not, and in the immediate future will not, give substantial amounts to overseas aid agencies. We know, too, that at least in the next year, the United States government is not going to meet even the very modest United Nations–recommended target of 0.7 percent of gross national product; at a moment it lags far below that, at 0.09 percent, not even half of Japan's 0.22 percent or a tenth of Denmark's 0.97 percent. Thus, we know that the money we can give beyond that theoretical "fair share" is still going to save lives that would otherwise be lost. While the idea that no one need do more than his or her fair share is a powerful one, should it prevail if we know that others are not doing their fair share and that children will die preventable deaths unless we do more than our fair share? That would be taking fairness too far.

20 Thus, this ground for limiting how much we ought to give also fails. In the world as it is now, I can see no escape from the conclusion that each one of us with wealth surplus to his or her essential needs should be giving most of it to help people suffering from poverty so dire as to be life-threatening. That's right: I'm saying that you shouldn't buy that new car, take that cruise, redecorate the house, or get that pricey new suit. After all, a $1,000 suit could save five children's lives.

So how does my philosophy break down in dollars and cents? An American household with an income of $50,000 spends around $30,000 annually on necessities, according to the Conference Board, a nonprofit economic research organization. Therefore, for a household bringing in $50,000 a year, donations to help the world's poor should be as close as possible to $20,000. The $30,000 required for necessities holds for higher incomes as well. So a household making $100,000 could cut a yearly check for $70,000. Again, the formula is simple: Whatever money you're spending on luxuries, not necessities, should be given away.

Now, evolutionary psychologists tell us that human nature just isn't sufficiently altruistic to make it plausible that many people will sacrifice so much for strangers. On the facts of human nature, they might be right, but they would be wrong to draw a moral conclusion from those facts. If it is the case that we ought to do things that, predictably, most of us won't do, then let's face that fact head-on. Then, if we value the life of a child more than going to fancy restaurants, the next time we dine out we will know that we could have done something better with our money. If that makes living a morally decent life extremely arduous, well, then that is the way things are. If we don't do it, then we should at least know that we are failing to live a morally decent life—not because it is good to wallow in guilt but because knowing where we should be going is the first step toward heading in that direction.

When Bob first grasped the dilemma that faced him as he stood by that railway switch, he must have thought how extraordinarily unlucky he was to be placed in a situation in which he must choose between the life of an innocent child and the sacrifice of most of his savings. But he was not unlucky at all. We are all in that situation.

PERSONAL RESPONSE

Do you contribute to charities? If not, are you moved to start doing so after reading this essay? Why do you think more people do not contribute to charities, especially if they could, as Singer argues, help improve life for the world's impoverished children?

QUESTIONS FOR CLASS OR SMALL-GROUP DISCUSSION

1. What is the effect of the opening example from the film *Central Station?* Does it help clarify for you the thesis of Singer's essay? Do you agree with Singer that the failure to donate money to a charity that would save a Brazilian child from starvation is "just as bad as selling the kid to organ peddlers" (paragraph 5)?
2. Comment on the hypothetical scenario from Peter Unger's book that Singer paraphrases in paragraph 7. Do you agree that "Bob's conduct . . . was gravely wrong" and that failure to donate money to charities that would save children's lives is equally wrong (paragraph 8)? How persuasive do you find Singer's discussion of the ethical implications of failing to donate to charities?
3. Discuss your answer to this question: "While the idea that no one need to do more than his or her fair share is a powerful one, should it prevail if we know that others are not doing their fair share and that children will die preventable deaths unless we do more than our fair share?" (paragraph 20).
4. To what extent do you agree with Singer that "we ought to do things that, predictably, most of us won't do" (paragraph 23)? How persuasive do you find Singer's argument?

✧ PERSPECTIVES ON POVERTY AND HOMELESSNESS ✧

Suggested Writing Topics

1. Taking into consideration Anna Quindlen's "Our Tired, Our Poor, Our Children," explore the subject of the effects of poverty on self-esteem or other aspects of the well-being of children.
2. Drawing on at least two of the readings in this chapter, consider the problems associated with meeting the needs of welfare recipients, impoverished

families, or homeless people. What possible solutions are there to the problems? Can you propose additional suggestions for reducing the large numbers of people in poverty or without homes?

3. With the readings in this chapter in mind, write your own opinion piece on the subject of poverty and homelessness in America.
4. Write a letter to the editor in response to Kevin Fagan's profile of Mike Dick in "Homeless, Mike Dick Was 51, Looked 66."
5. If you have ever experienced the effects of poverty, too little income, not enough work, or a need to juggle child care with the demands of a job, write an essay describing that experience, how you felt about it, and how you handled it.
6. If you know someone who is homeless, describe that person and the situation he or she is in. Explain the conditions that led to the homelessness, if possible.
7. If you know someone who has lost his or her job because of the economy, write about that person's experiences and the effects of joblessness.
8. Create a different hypothetical situation similar to Peter Unger's scenario of Bob and his Bugatti in "The Singer Solution to World Poverty." Detail the moral dilemma of your own scenario and discuss the ethical implications of various responses to the dilemma.
9. Working in small groups and drawing on the essays in this chapter, create a scenario involving one or more of the following people: a welfare recipient or a homeless person, a welfare caseworker or a staff member at a homeless shelter, a police officer, and either or both a wealthy person and a working-class person with a regular income and a home. Provide a situation, create dialogue, and role-play in an effort to understand the varying perspectives of different people on the issue of welfare or homelessness. Then present your scenario to the rest of your classmates. For an individual writing project, do an analysis of the scenario or fully develop the viewpoint of the person whose role you played.

Research Topics

1. Research your state's policy on welfare, including residency requirements, eligibility for payments, monitoring of recipients, and related issues. Then write a paper outlining your opinion of your state's welfare policy, including any recommendations you would make for changing it.
2. From time to time, politicians propose establishing orphanages that would house not only orphaned children but also the children of single parents on welfare or parents deemed unfit to raise their children. Research this subject, and then write a paper in which you argue for or against the establishment of such orphanages. Make sure you consider as many perspectives as possible

on this complex issue, including the welfare of the child, the rights of the parent or parents, and society's responsibility to protect children.

3. Research the subject of poverty in America. Focus your research on a particular group, such as children, women, two-parent families, or single-parent families, or target a particular aspect of the subject such as the effects of race, parental education, or employment on poverty. Consider starting with one of these classic studies of homelessness and poverty in America and then reading more recent studies: Michael B. Katz's *The Undeserving Poor: From the War on Poverty to the War on Welfare* (1990); Jonathan Kozol's *Rachel and Her Children: Homeless Families in America* (1987); Elliot Liebow's *All Them Who I Am: The Lives of Homeless Women* (1995); or Peter H. Rossi's *Down and Out in America: The Origins of Homelessness* (1991).
4. Research an area of public policy on welfare reform, child welfare, homelessness, public housing, family welfare, food stamps, job training, or any other issue related to any reading in this chapter.

Responding to Visuals

"Some families go out for dinner every night."

1. What is the point of this public service advertisement?
2. In what ways does the ad engage readers?
3. The text of this advertisement reads: *This is not Calcutta. Or Rwanda. Or Haiti. This is your backyard. This is Greenville. And every night, hundreds, if not thousands of your neighbors go to sleep hungry. But many who might otherwise be hungry aren't, because of a place called Project Host. Project Host is a soup kitchen in downtown Greenville that served over 63,000 meals to the needy last year. Every weekday, Project Host offers homemade soup, a sandwich, fruit, and a beverage to those in our community who, for one reason or another, can't quite make it on their own right now. We don't ask why. We don't criticize. We don't judge. We simply feed. And if you'd like to help, we, and the host of hungry people we provide for would be eternally grateful.* Do you find the text of the advertisement effective?
4. What do you think is the story of the two people in the picture? Why does the photographer place them at the side of the picture instead of the center?

RESPONDING TO VISUALS

A homeless person begging for money.

1. What does the homeless person's body language say about him?
2. What can you tell about the man from the way he is dressed and his facial features? What does the man's sign add to your understanding of him?
3. How does the photographer's perspective affect the way viewers see and respond to the man's situation?
4. Is there any irony in the contrast between the man and the sign behind him?

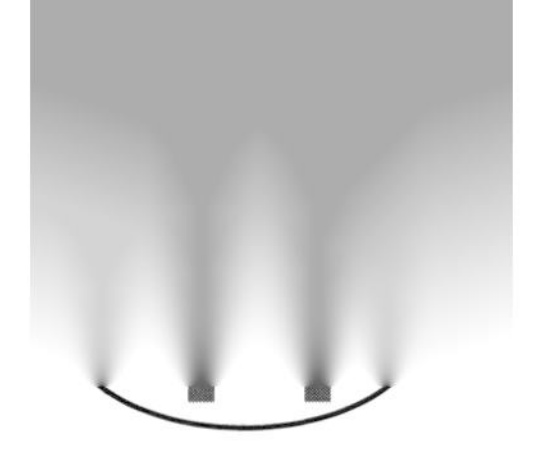

Gender and Sex Roles

Many people use the word *gender* interchangeably with the word *sex*, but the two have different meanings. Sex is a biological category; a person's sex—whether male or female—is genetically determined. On the other hand, gender refers to the socially constructed set of expectations for behavior based on one's sex. Masculinity and femininity are gender constructs whose definitions vary and change over time and with different cultures or groups within cultures. What is considered appropriate and even desirable behavior for men and women in one culture may be strongly inappropriate in another. Like other cultures, American culture's definitions of masculinity and femininity change with time, shaped by a number of influences, such as parental expectations, peer pressure, and media images. We are born either male or female, and most of us learn to behave in ways consistent with our society's expectations for that sex.

The chapter begins with a review of literature on the debate over what it means to grow up male in America. Thomas Bartlett's "The Puzzle of Boys" looks at a number of recent studies of boys and explains researchers' questions and conclusions about the nature of boyhood. His article gives a general overview of what has become a trend in gender studies toward looking at the difficulties boys face in American culture. This trend marks a shift from decades of studies on girls and women toward more inclusive or balanced efforts to understand both males and females. As you read the essay, consider your feelings about being male or female, recalling especially situations when you were identified on the basis of that characteristic alone.

Next is an article by Deborah Tannen, a professor whose research on the ways that people communicate and interact with one another has had broad appeal to general audiences as well as to academics and students. "Who Does the Talking Here?" touches on a topic that she has studied throughout her career, the differences in communication styles of males and females. In this piece, Tannen responds to an article she had recently read that "claims to lay to rest, once and for all, the stereotype that women talk more than men, by proving—scientifically—that women and men talk equally." As you read her article, think about the ways that the men and women you know talk to one another when they are in a group of their own sex or in mixed-sex gatherings. Do your own observations support or refute those that Tannen makes?

The focus of the chapter shifts from comparing males and females to looking at the ways in which important federal legislation during the women's movement of the 1970s led to vastly increased opportunities for girls and women in sports. Elinor Nauen's "A Sporting Chance: Title IX and the Seismic Shift in Women's Sports" gives an overview of the history and background of Title IX, legislation that changed the way women participate in sports. You may be surprised to learn of the restrictions that faced girls and young women before 1972. As you read of all the benefits that resulted from Title IX, think about schools you have attended and the programs that they offered to girls. Have girls' sports achieved full equality with boys' sports?

One of the many topics in the broad subject area of gender and sex roles is marriage, both hetero- and homosexual. No doubt the more heated debate has occurred over gay marriage, but the nature of marriage itself often comes up for discussion. The chapter ends with an opinion piece on the subject of marriage, Howard Moody's "Sacred Rite or Civil Right?" Moody asserts that gay marriages show why we need to separate church and state. He gives a historical overview of the roles

that both church and state have played in establishing the nature of heterosexual marriage, stressing the differences between the religious definition of marriage and the state's definition. At the heart of his essay is the question of what marriage is, so you may want to think about your own definition of marriage as you read the essay.

THE PUZZLE OF BOYS

THOMAS BARTLETT

Thomas Bartlett, a senior writer for the Chronicle of Higher Education *since 2001, has covered such subjects as teaching, religion, tenure, plagiarism, diploma mills, and other forms of cheating. He regularly contributes to the* Chronicle's *Off Beat column, which takes a look at funny or unusual trends in higher education. This piece appeared in the* Chronicle of Higher Education *on November 22, 2009.*

My son just turned 3. He loves trains, fire trucks, tools of all kinds, throwing balls, catching balls, spinning until he falls down, chasing cats, tackling dogs, emptying the kitchen drawers of their contents, riding a tricycle, riding a carousel, pretending to be a farmer, pretending to be a cow, dancing, drumming, digging, hiding, seeking, jumping, shouting, and collapsing exhausted into a Thomas the Tank Engine bed wearing Thomas the Tank Engine pajamas after reading a Thomas the Tank Engine book.

That doesn't make him unusual; in fact, in many ways, he couldn't be more typical. Which may be why a relative recently said, "Well, he's definitely all boy." It's a statement that sounds reasonable enough until you think about it. What does "all boy" mean? Masculine? Straight? Something else? Are there partial boys? And is this relative aware of my son's fondness for Hello Kitty and tea sets?

These are the kinds of questions asked by anxious parents and, increasingly, academic researchers. Boyhood studies—virtually unheard of a few years ago—has taken off, with a shelf full of books already published, more on the way, and a new journal devoted to the subject. Much of the focus so far has been on boys falling behind academically, paired with the notion that school is not conducive to the way boys learn. What motivates boys, the argument goes, is different from what motivates girls, and society should adjust accordingly.

4 Not everyone buys the boy talk. Some critics, in particular the American Association of University Women, contend that much of what passes for research about boyhood only reinforces stereotypes and arrives at simplistic conclusions: Boys are competitive! Boys like action! Boys hate books! They argue that this line of thinking miscasts boys as victims and ignores the very real problems faced by girls.

But while this debate is far from settled, the field has expanded to include how marketers target boys, the nature of boys' friendships, and a host of deeper, more philosophical issues, all of which can be boiled down, more or less, to a single question: Just what are boys, anyway?

One of the first so-called boys' books, Michael Gurian's *The Wonder of Boys*, was not immediately embraced by publishers. In fact, it was turned down by 25 houses before finally being purchased by Tarcher/Putnam for a modest sum. This was in the mid-1990s, and everyone was concerned about girls. Girls were drowning in the "sea of Western culture," according to Carol Gilligan. In *Reviving Ophelia*, Mary Pipher bemoaned a "girl-poisoning" culture that emphasized sexiness above all else.

Boys weren't the story. No one wanted to read about them.

8 Or so publishers thought. *The Wonder of Boys* has since sold more than a half-million copies, and Gurian, who has a master's degree in writing and has worked as a family counselor, has become a prominent speaker and consultant on boys' issues. He has written two more books about boys, including *The Purpose of Boys*, published this year, which argues that boys are hard-wired to desire a sense of mission, and that parents and teachers need to understand "boy biology" if they want to help young men succeed.

Drawing on neuroscience research done by others, Gurian argues that boy brains and girl brains are fundamentally dissimilar. In the nature versus nurture debate, Gurian comes down squarely on the side of the former. He catches flak for supposedly overinterpreting neuroscience data to comport with his theories about boys. In *The Trouble with Boys*, a former *Newsweek* reporter, Peg Tyre, takes him to task for arguing that female brains are active even when they're bored, while male brains tend to "shut down" (a conclusion that Ruben Gur, director of the Brain Behavior Laboratory at the University of Pennsylvania, tells Tyre isn't supported by the evidence). Gurian counters that his work has been misrepresented and that the success of his programs backs up his scientific claims.

Close on Gurian's heels was *Real Boys*, by William Pollack. Pollack, an associate clinical professor of psychology at Harvard Medical School and director of the Centers for Men and Young Men, writes that behind their facade of toughness, boys are vulnerable and desperate for emotional connection. Boys, he says, tend to communicate through action. They are more likely to express empathy and affection through an activity, like playing basketball together, than having a heart-to-heart talk. Pollack's view of what makes boys the way they are is less rooted in biology than Gurian's. "What neuroscientists will tell you is that nature and nurture are bonded," says Pollack. "How we nurture from the beginning has an effect." *Real Boys* earned a stamp of approval from Mary Pipher, who writes in the foreword that "our culture is doing a bad job raising boys."

Pollack's book, like Gurian's, was an enormous success. It sold more than 750,000 copies and has been published in 13 countries. Even though it came out a decade ago, Pollack says he still receives e-mail every week from readers. "People were hungry for it," he says.

12 The following year, *Raising Cain*, by Dan Kindlon, an adjunct lecturer in Harvard's School of Public Health, and Michael Thompson, a psychologist in private practice, was published and was later made into a two-hour PBS documentary. Their book ends with seven recommendations for dealing with boys, including "recognize and accept the high activity level of boys and give them safe boy places to express it." The book is partially about interacting with boys on their own terms, but it also

encourages adults to help them develop "emotional literacy" and to counter the "culture of cruelty" among older boys. It goes beyond academic performance, dealing with issues like suicide, bullying, and romance.

Perhaps the most provocative book of the bunch is *The War Against Boys: How Misguided Feminism Is Harming Our Young Men,* by Christina Hoff Sommers. As the subtitle suggests, Sommers believes that she's found the villain in this story, making the case that it's boys, not girls, who are being shortchanged and that they need significant help if they're going to close the distance academically. But that does not mean, according to Sommers, that they "need to be rescued from their masculinity."

Those books were best sellers and continue to attract readers and spirited debate. While the authors disagree on the details, they share at least two broad conclusions: (1) Boys are not girls, and (2) Boys are in trouble. Why and how they're different from girls, what's behind their trouble, and what if anything to do about it—all that depends on whom you read.

A backlash was inevitable. In 2008 the American Association of University Women issued a report, "Where the Girls Are: The Facts about Gender Equity in Education," arguing not only that the alleged academic disparity between boys and girls had been exaggerated, but also that the entire crisis was a myth. If anything, the report says, boys are doing better than ever: "The past few decades have seen remarkable gains for girls and boys in education, and no evidence indicates a crisis for boys in particular."

16 So how could the boys-in-trouble crowd have gotten it so wrong? The report has an answer for that: "Many people remain uncomfortable with the educational and professional advances of girls and women, especially when they threaten to outdistance their peers." In other words, it's not genuine concern for boys that's energizing the movement but rather fear of girls surpassing them.

The dispute is, in part, a dispute over data. And like plenty of such squabbles, the outcome hinges on the numbers you decide to use. Boys outperform girls by more than 30 points on the mathematics section of the SAT and a scant four points on the verbal sections (girls best boys by 13 points on the recently added writing section). But many more girls actually take the test. And while it's a fact that boys and girls are both more likely to attend college than they were a generation ago, girls now make up well over half of the student body, and a projection by the Department of Education indicates that the gap will widen considerably over the next decade.

College isn't the only relevant benchmark. Boys are more likely than girls to be diagnosed with attention-deficit disorder, but girls are more likely to be diagnosed with depression. Girls are more likely to report suicide attempts, but boys are more likely to actually kill themselves (according to the Centers for Disease Control and Prevention, 83 percent of suicides between the ages of 10 and 24 are male). Ask a representative of the AAUW about a pitfall that appears to disproportionately affect boys, like attention-deficit disorder, and the representative will counter that the disparity is overplayed or that girls deal with equally troubling issues.

But it's not statistics that have persuaded parents and educators that boys are in desperate straits, according to Sara Mead, a senior research fellow with the New America Foundation, a public-policy institute. Mead wrote a paper in 2006 that argued, much like the later AAUW report, that the boys' crisis was bunk. "What seems to most resonate with teachers and parents is not as much the empirical evidence but this sense of boys being unmoored or purposeless in a vaguely defined way," Mead says in an interview. "That's a really difficult thing to validate more beyond anecdote." She also worries that all this worrying—much of it, she says, from middle-class parents—could have a negative effect on boys, marking them as victims when they're nothing of the sort.

20 Pollack concedes, as Mead and others point out, that poor performance in school is also tied to factors like race and class, but he insists that boys as a group—including white, middle-class boys—are sinking, pointing to studies that suggest they are less likely to do their homework and more likely to drop out of high school. And he has a hunch about why some refuse to acknowledge it: "People look at the adult world and say, 'Men are still in charge.' So they look down at boys and say, 'They are small men, so they must be on the way to success,'" says Pollack. "It's still a man's world. People make the mistake of thinking it's a boy's world."

If the first round of books was focused on the classroom, the second round observes the boy in his natural habitat. The new book *Packaging Boyhood: Saving Our Sons from Superheroes, Slackers, and Other Media Stereotypes* offers an analysis of what boys soak in from TV shows, video games, toys, and other facets of boy-directed pop culture. The news isn't good here, either. According to the book, boys are being taught they have to be tough and cool, athletic and stoic. This starts early with toddler T-shirts emblazoned with "Future All-Star" or "Little Champion." Even once-benign toys like Legos and Nerf have assumed a more hostile profile with Lego Exo-Force Assault Tigers and the Nerf N-Strike Raider Rapid Fire CS-35 Dart Blaster. "That kind of surprised us," says one of the book's three authors, Lyn Mikel Brown, a professor of education and human development at Colby College. "What happened to Nerf? What happened to Lego?"

Brown also co-wrote *Packaging Girlhood.* In that book, the disease was easier to diagnose, what with the Disney princess phenomenon and sexy clothes being marketed to pre-adolescent girls. Everyone was worried about how girls were being portrayed in the mass media and what that was doing to their self-esteem. The messages about boys, however, were easier to miss, in part because they're so ubiquitous. "We expect a certain amount of teasing, bullying, spoofing about being tough enough, even in animated films for the littlest boys," Brown says.

For *Packaging Boyhood,* the authors interviewed more than 600 boys and found that models of manhood were turning up in some unexpected places, like the Discovery Channel's *Man vs. Wild,* in which the star is dropped into the harsh wilderness and forced to forage. They're concerned that such programs, in order to compete against all the stimuli vying for boys' attentions, have become more aggressively in-your-face, more fearlessly risk-taking, manlier than thou. Says Brown: "What really got us was the pumping up of the volume."

24 Brown thinks boys are more complicated, and less single-minded, than adults give them credit for. So does Ken Corbett, whose new book, *Boyhoods: Rethinking Masculinities,* steers clear of generalizations and doesn't try to elucidate the ideal boyhood (thus the plural "masculinities"). Corbett, an assistant professor of psychology

at New York University, wants to remind us not how boys are different from girls but how they're different from one another. His background is in clinical psychoanalysis, feminism, and queer studies—in other words, as he points out in the introduction, "not your father's psychoanalysis."

In a chapter titled "Feminine Boys," he writes of counseling the parents of a boy who liked to wear bracelets and perform a princess dance. The father, especially, wasn't sure how to take this, telling Corbett that he wanted a son, not a daughter.

To show how boys can be difficult to define, Corbett tells the story of Hans, a 5-year-old patient of Sigmund Freud, who had a fear of being castrated by, of all things, a horse. Young Hans also fantasizes about having a "widdler," as the boy puts it, as large as his father's. Freud (typically) reads the kid's issues as primarily sexual, and his desire to be more like his father as Oedipal. Corbett, however, doesn't think Hans's interest in his penis is about sex, but rather about becoming bigger, in developing beyond the half-finished sketch of boyhood. "Wishing to be big is wishing to fill in the drawing," Corbett writes.

Corbett disputes the idea that boys as a group are in peril. They have troubles, sure, but so do other people. Treating boys as problems to be solved, rather than subjects to be studied, is a mistake, he says, and much of the writing on boys "doesn't illuminate the experience of being a boy, but it does illuminate the space between a boy and a parent."

28 The experience of being a boy is exactly what Miles Groth wants to capture. Groth, a psychology professor at Wagner College, is editor of *Thymos: Journal of Boyhood Studies,* founded in 2007. An article he wrote in the inaugural issue of the journal, "Has Anyone Seen the Boy? The Fate of the Boy in Becoming a Man," is a sort of call to arms for boyhood-studies scholars. For years, Groth says, academics didn't really discuss boys. They might study a certain subset of boys, but boys per se were off the table. "I think there was some hesitancy for scholars to take up the topic, to show that they're paying attention to guys when we should be paying attention to girls," says Groth. "Now I think there's less of that worry. People don't see it as a reactionary movement."

That has opened the door for scholars like Niobe Way. A professor of applied psychology at New York University, Way recently finished a book, scheduled to be published next year by Harvard University Press, on how boys communicate. She's been interviewing teenage boys about their friendships, and what she's found is remarkable. While it's common wisdom that teenage boys either can't express or don't possess strong feelings about their friends, Way has discovered that boys in their early teens can be downright sentimental when discussing their friendships. When asked what they liked about their best friends, boys frequently said: "They won't laugh at me when I talk about serious things." What has emerged from her research is a portrait of emotionally intelligent boys who care about more than sports and cars. Such an observation might not sound revolutionary, but what boys told her and her fellow researchers during lengthy, probing interviews runs counter to the often one-dimensional portrayal of boys in popular culture. "They were resisting norms of masculinity," she says.

Note the past tense. At some point in high school, that expressiveness vanishes, replaced with a more defensive, closed-off posture, perhaps as boys give in to messages about what it means to be a man. Still, her research undermines the stereotype that boys are somehow incapable of discussing their feelings. "And yet," she says, "this notion of this emotionally illiterate, sex-obsessed, sports-playing boy just keeps getting spit out again and again."

Touchy-feely talk about friendships may seem disconnected from boys' academic woes, but Way insists they're pieces of the same puzzle. "If you don't understand the experience of boyhood," she says, "you'll never understand the achievement gaps."

Books cited in this article:

The Wonder of Boys, by Michael Gurian
(Tarcher/Putnam, 1996)

Real Boys, by William Pollack
(Random House, 1998)

Raising Cain, by Dan Kindlon and Michael Thompson
(Ballantine Books, 1999)

The War Against Boys, by Christina Hoff Sommers
(Simon & Schuster, 2000)

The Trouble with Boys, by Peg Tyre
(Crown Publishers, 2008)

Packaging Boyhood, by Lyn Mikel Brown, Sharon Lamb, and Mark Tappan
(St. Martin's Press, 2009)

Boyhoods: Rethinking Masculinities, by Ken Corbett
(Yale University Press, 2009)

PERSONAL RESPONSE

Select a passage about one of the books that Bartlett reviews and write for a few minutes on your response to the conclusions about boyhood that the author makes.

QUESTIONS FOR CLASS OR SMALL-GROUP DISCUSSION

1. What assumptions about the traditional definitions of sex and gender does Bartlett point out? What do you think it means when a child is described as "all boy" or "all girl"? How do you feel about such labels?
2. Summarize the chief interests of the recent books on boys that Bartlett covers in his article. What are researchers primarily interested in learning about boys? What conclusions have they drawn?

3. State your understanding of the different approaches among researchers in the area of "boyhood studies." On what points do they seem to agree and disagree? How does Bartlett account for the differences?
4. Do you think it possible for any society, but especially American society, to do away with assigning sex roles? How possible do you think it would be to raise a child not to be conscious of gender? Is such a goal desirable? Explain your answer.

WHO DOES THE TALKING HERE?

DEBORAH TANNEN

Deborah Tannen is a professor of linguistics at Georgetown University. Author of many scholarly articles and books on subjects in her field, she is probably best known for her general-audience books beginning with You Just Don't Understand: Women and Men in Conversation *(1990). Her other books include* Talking from 9 to 5: Women and Men at Work *(1994);* The Argument Culture: Stopping America's War on Words *(1999);* I Only Say This Because I Love You: Talking to Your Parents, Partner, Sibs and Kids When You're All Adults *(2002);* You're Wearing That? Understanding Mothers and Daughters in Conversation *(2006); and* You Were Always Mom's Favorite! Sisters in Conversation Throughout Their Lives" *(2009). This article appeared in the July 15, 2009, edition of the* Washington Post.

It's no surprise that a one-page article published this month in the journal *Science* inspired innumerable newspaper columns and articles. The study, by Matthias Mehl and four colleagues, claims to lay to rest, once and for all, the stereotype that women talk more than men, by proving—scientifically—that women and men talk equally.

The notion that women talk more was reinforced last year when Louann Brizendine's *The Female Brain* cited the finding that women utter, on average, 20,000 words a day, men 7,000. (Brizendine later disavowed the statistic, as there was no study to back it up.) Mehl and his colleagues outfitted 396 college students with devices that recorded their speech. The female subjects spoke an average of 16,215 words a day, the men 15,669. The difference is insignificant. Case closed.

Or is it? Can we learn who talks more by counting words. No, according to a forthcoming article surveying 70 studies of gender differences in talkativeness. (Imagine—70 studies published in scientific journals, and we're still asking the question.) In their survey, Campbell Leaper and Melanie Ayres found that counting words yielded no consistent differences, though number of words per speaking turn did (Men, on average, used more).

4 This doesn't surprise me. In my own research on gender and language, I quickly surmised that to understand who talks more, you have to ask: What's the situation? What are the speakers using words for?

The following experience conveys the importance of situation. I was addressing a small group in a suburban Virginia living room. One man stood out because he talked a lot, while his wife, who was sitting beside him, said nothing at all. I described to the group a complaint common among women about men they live with: At the end of a day she tells him what happened, what she thought and how she felt about it. Then she asks, "How was your day?"—and is disappointed when he replies, "Fine," "Nothing much" or "Same old rat race."

The loquacious man spoke up. "You're right," he said. Pointing to his wife, he added, "She's the talker in our family." Everyone laughed. But he explained, "It's true. When we come home, she does all the talking. If she didn't, we'd spend the evening in silence."

The "how was your day?" conversation typifies the kind of talk women tend to do more of: spoken to intimates and focusing on personal experience, your own or others'. I call this "rapport-talk." It contrasts with "report-talk"—giving or exchanging information about impersonal topics, which men tend to do more.

8 Studies that find men talking more are usually carried out in formal experiments or public contexts such as meetings. For example, Marjorie Swacker observed an academic conference where women presented 40 percent of the papers and were 42 percent of the audience but asked only 27 percent of the questions; their questions were, on average, also shorter by half than the men's questions. And David and Myra Sadker showed that boys talk more in mixed-sex classrooms—a context common among college students, a factor skewing the results of Mehl's new study.

Many men's comfort with "public talking" explains why a man who tells his wife he has nothing to report about his day might later find a funny story to tell at dinner with two other couples (leaving his wife wondering, "Why didn't he tell me first?").

In addition to situation, you have to consider what speakers are doing with words. Campbell and Ayres note that many studies find women doing more "affiliative speech" such as showing support, agreeing or acknowledging others' comments. Drawing on studies of children at play as well as my own research of adults talking, I often put it this way: For women and girls, talk is the glue that holds a relationship together. Their best friend is the one they tell everything to. Spending an evening at home with a spouse is when this kind of talk comes into its own. Since this situation is uncommon among college students, it's another factor skewing the new study's results.

Women's rapport-talk probably explains why many people think women talk more. A man wants to read the paper, his wife wants to talk; his girlfriend or sister spends hours on the phone with her friend or her mother. He concludes: Women talk more.

12 Yet Leaper and Ayres observed an overall pattern of men speaking more. That's a conclusion women often come to when men hold forth at meetings, in social groups or when delivering one-on-one lectures. All of us—women and men—tend to notice others talking more in situations where we talk less.

Counting may be a start—or a stop along the way—to understanding gender differences. But it's understanding when we tend to talk and what we're doing with words that yields insights we can count on.

PERSONAL RESPONSE

What do you own informal observations reveal about who talks more, males or females?

QUESTIONS FOR CLASS OR SMALL-GROUP DISCUSSION

1. Tannen opens with references to studies on who talks more, men or women. What is her opinion of these works? How might a study of college students skew the results of research into which sex talks more? Why do you think there have been so many studies about women's and men's talkativeness? What is the issue?
2. Explain why Tannen believes that *situation* is important when considering who talks more, men or women. How effective do you find her personal anecdote in illustrating her point?
3. What do you understand Tannen to mean when she says that studies on gender and language must ask *what the speakers are using words for*?
4. What is the difference between "rapport talk" and "report talk," according to Tannen? What is "affiliative speech" (paragraph 10)? Do your own observations support or refute her comments on these ways of speaking?

A SPORTING CHANCE: TITLE IX AND THE SEISMIC SHIFT IN WOMEN'S SPORTS

ELINOR NAUEN

Elinor Nauen is editor of Diamonds Are a Girl's Best Friend: Women Writers on Baseball *(1994) and* Ladies Start Your Engines: Women Writers on Cars and the Road *(1997). She is a teacher, poet, and journalist who has written about sports, mostly baseball, for many publications. This essay was first published in the October 20, 2008, edition of* America magazine.

Imagine: if only the boys at your school could play on the football, track, wrestling, basketball and baseball teams, and the girls had . . . synchronized swimming. Or imagine a coach saying, "There's a place for women's athletics: after 7 p.m. and before 6 a.m." Or a judge remarking, as he legally barred girls from competing on a boys' high school cross-country team even though there was no girls' team: "Athletic competition builds character in our boys. We do not need that kind of character in our girls." Imagine that people believed women runners would be unable to bear children, would grow a mustache or wanted to be men.

Actually, you do not have to imagine any of this. These are true examples from the world before 1972. Marj Snyder, chief program officer of the Women's Sports

Foundation, remembers those days. She also remembers two boys being admitted to a college that had rejected her, even though her test scores and grades were better. But they had team experience, an option that did not exist for her. As Dolly Brumfield White, who played in the 1940s All-American Girls Professional Baseball League, recalls: "We weren't allowed in the weight room—it was as bad as going to a pool hall."

Then as now, sports were a microcosm of society. The lack of teams, facilities and encouragement went hand in hand with narrower opportunities in other areas; women became teachers and nurses, not principals and doctors. Without coaches or practice times and subject to being teased or hassled when they tried or even wanted to play sports, is it any wonder that so many girls did not see themselves as strong, vigorous, talented, capable beings?

Then Things Changed

4 What jumpstarted a seismic shift in American life was a law Congress passed in 1972 known as Title IX. Its text read: "No person in the United States shall, on the basis of sex, be excluded from participation in, be denied the benefits of, or be subjected to discrimination under any educational program or activity receiving federal financial assistance." In essence, Title IX prohibits any and every institution that receives government money from practicing gender discrimination. That was and is nearly all of them.

The statistics illustrate an important part of the transformation since the law went into effect. In 1971, fewer than 300,000 high school girls participated in athletics. Today that number is close to three million, with almost half of all female high school students on a team. In 1972 about 16,000 young women participated in college athletics, a number that has grown to over 180,000. The number of women's teams per campus has increased from an average of 2.5 before 1972 to 8.5 in 2006.

"Title IX built a base for sports that led to the 1999 World Cup and women's professional basketball—so many things that go beyond the traditional women's sports of figure skating, tennis and golf," notes Snyder of the Women's Sports Foundation. "Once schools realized they had to open their doors to women and let them onto the playing fields, they added sports like softball, track, field hockey and soccer, sports with high participation numbers." The Summer Olympics have also witnessed a sharp increase in the number of women athletes that began two decades ago. In 1972, 1,058 (or 16 percent) of 7,123 athletes in total were women. In the 2008 games in China, that number rose to 4,746 (or 42 percent) of the total of 11,196 athletes.

The Benefits

Numbers are only part of the story, of course. Consider the benefits to the athletes. "We've always said sports are opportunities for boys and men to benefit from fun, to build character and confidence, to become physically fit and healthy. And to network—your teammates are your future colleagues," says Snyder. "Lots of evidence demonstrates that girls also benefit. Girls who participate in sports have less osteoporosis, less obesity and better heart health. Psychologically, they have a better body image, higher self-confidence and self-esteem, and they do better in business. They are less likely to get pregnant, more likely to delay sexual activity till later, more likely to have fewer sexual partners and less likely to use drugs and smoke." Snyder concludes: "If you don't play on a team, where do you learn risk-taking in a safe environment? Now girls have access to that training ground."

8 An analysis from the Department of Education backs this up. Its 1997 report *Title IX: 25 Years of Progress* noted that "the critical values learned from sports participation—including teamwork, standards, leadership, discipline, self-sacrifice and pride in accomplishment—are being brought to the workplace as women enter employment in greater numbers, and at higher levels than ever before. For example, 80 percent of female managers of Fortune 500 companies have a sports background."

Note too that Title IX was not meant to apply exclusively to sports but was also intended to combat quotas that kept women out of law, medical and engineering programs. It has worked there too. Before Title IX, more than a quarter of men but less than a fifth of women completed college; that gap has disappeared. Five times as many women receive medical degrees now as 35 years ago, six times as many earn law degrees and almost twice as many are awarded doctoral degrees.

By Title IX's 25th anniversary in 1997, Richard W. Riley, the U.S. Secretary of Education, could say that "America is a more equal, more educated and more prosperous nation because of the far-reaching effects of this legislation. . . . What strikes me the most about the progress that has been achieved since Title IX was passed in 1972 is that there has been a sea change in our expectations of what women can achieve. More important, women have shown skeptics again and again that females are fully capable of being involved as successful and active participants in every realm of American life."

Many coaches are well aware of this. Bruce Rasmussen graduated from college in 1971 and began teaching in a small town in southern Iowa. "I was low on the totem pole, so when the women's coach left, I took that on," he recalls. "What I found was that the girls were much more receptive to coaching. The boys thought they knew it before they knew it, but the girls were appreciative of any commitment and attention. It was 'we *get* to practice' versus 'we *have* to practice.' It was an eye-opener." Now director of athletics at Creighton University in Omaha, Rasmussen says: "I see our female athletes have embraced and grown and learned from values such as attention to detail, playing a role on a team and discipline just as much as males, if not more. For years people believed in the value of athletics for what men can achieve. If we believe athletics has a value beyond wins and losses, then that value is there for female athletes as much as male. There are benefits at home, on the job—everywhere."

12 Jean Hastings Ardell, author of *Breaking Into Baseball: Women and the National Pastime*, puts it this way: "Title IX blew apart the old limitations for half the population of this country."

Enforcement and Challenges

Not surprisingly, implementing such sweeping legislation caused plenty of confusion, foot-dragging and challenges. Courts have upheld Title IX at every turn, in cases of school athletics and also in regard to sexual harassment, standardized tests, pregnant students and much more. In 1997 a Supreme Court ruling sent a clear message that just offering women's sports was not enough. Educational institutions had to provide facilities, equipment, practice and game times, as well as encouragement.

"I don't think the men who wrote the law envisioned that this is how it would turn out," Snyder says. One of the three ways the law is enforced is by proportionality—you must demonstrate that sports programs are offered to men and women in percentages equivalent to their enrollment. "The men probably thought they would always have a big advantage, because in 1972 only 35 percent of college undergrads were women. Today, it's 57 percent." (Compliance is also gauged by whether opportunities for women are increasing and whether the school satisfies the athletic interests and abilities of its female students. Schools need to meet only one of the three criteria.)

Despite what some critics claim, Title IX does not require any college to eliminate men's teams in order to be compliant. Adding women's opportunities is not supposed to be done by taking them away from men, but by expanding them for everybody. In fact, last year more college participation opportunities were added for men than for women. Schools drop or add sports for many reasons, not only because of Title IX. Money is a key factor. The cost of insurance, equipment, facilities or team travel may determine what can be offered.

16 Rasmussen came to Creighton as the women's basketball coach in 1980. "We had a team but there were no scholarships, no budget, no assistance," he recalls. "Now there's a full complement of coaches, we're fully funded the same as the men, we play a national schedule, and we get just as much priority in workout times." Creighton is currently building a $40 million facility for women's basketball and volleyball.

Before Title IX, only a handful of women got athletic scholarships. Donna de Varona may have won two gold medals in the 1964 Olympics, but that did not mean she could garner a college swimming scholarship. Today, college women receive about 42 percent of college athletic scholarship dollars. Much less is spent on women's operating expenses, recruiting costs and head coaching salaries, according to the 2000–01 Gender Equality Study. Full equality still lies ahead.

Tim Wiles, director of research for the Baseball Hall of Fame, served on the Title IX Compliance Committee at the University of Northern Iowa when he was librarian there in 1994. When the committee circulated a draft report, he says he was visited by one assistant athletic director who "tried to pressure us to write something different. This was 22 years after IX passed, and they still didn't know what to do with it. They still were trying to keep the status quo."

"I was born in 1964," Wiles added. "There were girls in Little League and Biddy Basketball but there was no prohibition against denigrating the skills or participation of females in sports. It was very socially acceptable to consider women participants second-class. It was expected that if you were a boy you'd get better times and fields. I'm sorry to say I was one of those kids who had the general idea that sports were for boys and 'you girls should go away and do your own thing.' No one would go to a girls' game in high school."

20 How that has changed! One anecdote from Marj Snyder illustrates the shift in attitude. "When my sister was coaching her older daughter in basketball, she took both girls to high school basketball games and taped women's basketball. One day her five-year-old daughter asked, 'Do boys play basketball too?'"

"If there's something you want to do, you should have the opportunity. Thank goodness, we mostly have the opportunities today. That's what Title IX did: It put pressure on schools to offer facilities and opportunities for girls," concludes Dolly White, who played, then taught and coached from the 1940s through the 1990s. "How do you know what you can do until you try?"

What About Women's Schools?

Although single-sex schools are not bound by the provisions of Title IX, they have been greatly affected. "Title IX was and is a great, great piece of legislation to protect women's rights," says Patricia McGuire, who is in her 20th year as president of Trinity College, a women's school in Washington, D.C. But, she adds, Title IX is "one of the forces that contributed to decline in enrollment in women's colleges." Before Title IX, only women's colleges had gyms readily available to women. Title IX equalized resources, "but because we were a single-sex college, we didn't have to equalize our facilities."

Eventually, McGuire says, "We saw it was hurting us—it was an excuse not to keep up. A college that says it stands for women's rights and advancements can't take a pass. We have to do the same as big universities to give equal opportunities." In Trinity's case, that meant building its Center for Women and Girls in Sports, which opened in 2002—the first new building on campus in 40 years.

24 "Whether we like it or not, sports in higher education drives perceptions of institutional liveliness and attractiveness," McGuire adds. "Being able to offer high-class sports has turned our enrollment around. Women expect to have that and Title IX created that expectation."

PERSONAL RESPONSE

Write about your experience with school sports, whether as a participant or as an observer.

QUESTIONS FOR CLASS OR SMALL-GROUP DISCUSSION

1. Comment on the effectiveness of Nauen's opening paragraph. Does it capture your attention? State in your own words the conditions for girls' and women's sports participation before Title IX. Were you aware that such conditions were commonplace before 1972? In what other areas were there restrictions on women's participation?
2. Nauen writes in paragraph 2: "Then as now, sports were a microcosm of society." What do you understand her to mean by that statement? How were sports before 1972 a "microcosm of society" and how are they now?
3. What are the benefits of sports, according to Nauen? Do you agree with her on this point? Are there other benefits that she does not mention? Are there any drawbacks to sports participation?
4. Why does Nauen say that "full equality still lies ahead" (paragraph 17)? Is she correct, in your opinion, or do your observations and experiences indicate otherwise?

SACRED RITE OR CIVIL RIGHT?

HOWARD MOODY

Howard Moody, minister emeritus of Judson Memorial Church in New York City, is often referred to as the Harriet Tubman of the abortion rights movement. Author of several books, including two with Arlene Carmen on abortion rights and prostitution, as well as a collection of essays, The God-Man of Galilee: Studies in Christian Living *(1983), he lectures, preaches, and writes often on issues of ethics and social policy. "Sacred Rite or Civil Right?" was first published in the July 5, 2004, issue of the* Nation.

If members of the church that I served for more than three decades were told I would be writing an article in defense of marriage, they wouldn't believe it. My reputation was that when people came to me for counsel about getting married, I tried to talk them out of it. More about that later.

We are now in the midst of a national debate on the nature of marriage, and it promises to be as emotional and polemical as the issues of abortion and homosexuality have been over the past century. What all these debates have in common is that they involved both the laws of the state and the theology of the church. The purpose of this writing is to suggest that the gay-marriage debate is less about the legitimacy of the loving relationship of a same-sex couple than about the relationship of church and state and how they define marriage.

In Western civilization, the faith and beliefs of Christendom played a major role in shaping the laws regarding social relations and moral behavior. Having been nurtured in the Christian faith from childhood and having served a lifetime as an ordained Baptist minister, I feel obligated first to address the religious controversy concerning the nature of marriage. If we look at the history of religious institutions regarding marriage we will find not much unanimity but amazing diversity—it is really a mixed bag. Those who base their position on "tradition" or "what the Bible says" will find anything but clarity. It depends on which "tradition" in what age reading from whose holy scriptures.

4 In the early tradition of the Jewish people, there were multiple wives and not all of them equal. Remember the story of Abraham's wives, Sara and Hagar. Sara couldn't get pregnant, so Hagar presented Abraham with a son. When Sara got angry with Hagar, she forced Abraham to send Hagar and her son Ishmael into the wilderness. In case Christians feel superior about their "tradition" of marriage, I would remind them that their scriptural basis is not as clear about marriage as we might hope. We have Saint Paul's conflicting and condescending words about the institution: "It's better not to marry." Karl Barth called this passage the Magna Carta of the single person. (Maybe we should have taken Saint Paul's advice more seriously. It might have prevented an earlier generation of parents from harassing, cajoling and prodding our young until they were married.) In certain religious branches, the church doesn't recognize the licensed legality of marriage but requires that persons meet certain religious qualifications before the marriage is recognized by the church. For members

of the Roman Catholic Church, a "legal divorce" and the right to remarry may not be recognized unless the first marriage has been declared null and void by a decree of the church. It is clear that there is no single religious view of marriage and that history has witnessed some monumental changes in the way "husband and wife" are seen in the relationship of marriage.

In my faith-based understanding, if freedom of choice means anything to individuals (male or female), it means they have several options. They can be single and celibate without being thought of as strange or psychologically unbalanced. They can be single and sexually active without being labeled loose or immoral. Women can be single with child without being thought of as unfit or inadequate. If these choices had been real options, the divorce rate may never have reached nearly 50 percent.

The other, equally significant choice for people to make is that of lifetime commitment to each other and to seal that desire in the vows of a wedding ceremony. That understanding of marriage came out of my community of faith. In my years of ministry I ran a tight ship in regard to the performance of weddings. It wasn't because I didn't believe in marriage (I've been married for sixty years and have two wonderful offspring) but rather my unease about the way marriage was used to force people to marry so they wouldn't be "living in sin."

The failure of the institution can be seen in divorce statistics. I wanted people to know how challenging the promise of those vows was and not to feel this was something they had to do. My first question in premarital counseling was, "Why do you want to get married and spoil a beautiful friendship?" That question often elicited a thoughtful and emotional answer. Though I was miserly in the number of weddings I performed, I always made exceptions when there were couples who had difficulty finding clergy who would officiate. Their difficulty was because they weren't of the same religion, or they had made marital mistakes, or what they couldn't believe. Most of them were "ecclesiastical outlaws," barred from certain sacraments in the church of their choice.

8 The church I served had a number of gay and lesbian couples who had been together for many years, but none of them had asked for public weddings or blessings on their relationship. (There was one commitment ceremony for a gay couple at the end of my tenure.) It was as though they didn't need a piece of paper or a ritual to symbolize their lifelong commitment. They knew if they wanted a religious ceremony, their ministers would officiate and our religious community would joyfully witness.

It was my hope that since the institution of marriage had been used to exclude and demean members of the homosexual community, our church, which was open and affirming, would create with gays and lesbians a new kind of ceremony. It would be an occasion that symbolized, between two people of the same gender, a covenant of intimacy of two people to journey together, breaking new ground in human relationships—an alternative to marriage as we have known it.

However, I can understand why homosexuals want "to be married" in the old fashioned "heterosexual way." After all, most gays and lesbians were born of married parents, raised in a family of siblings; many were nourished in churches and synagogues, taught about a living God before Whom all Her creatures were equally loved. Why wouldn't they conceive their loving relationships in terms of marriage and family and desire that they be confirmed and understood as such? It follows that if these gays and lesbians see their relationship as faith-based, they would want a religious ceremony that seals their intentions to become lifelong partners, lovers and friends, that they would want to be "married."

Even though most religious denominations deny this ceremony to homosexual couples, more and more clergy are, silently and publicly, officiating at religious rituals in which gays and lesbians declare their vows before God and a faith community. One Catholic priest who defied his church's ban said: "We can bless a dog, we can bless a boat, but we can't say a prayer over two people who love each other. You don't have to call it marriage, you can call it a deep and abiding friendship, but you can bless it."

12 We have the right to engage in "religious disobedience" to the regulations of the judicatory that granted us the privilege to officiate at wedding ceremonies, and suffer the consequences. However, when it comes to civil law, it is my contention that the church and its clergy are on much shakier ground in defying the law.

In order to fully understand the conflict that has arisen in this debate over the nature of marriage, it is important to understand the difference between the religious definition of marriage and the state's secular and civil definition. The government's interest is in a legal definition of marriage—a social and voluntary contract between a man and woman in order to protect money, property and children. Marriage is a civil union without benefit of clergy or religious definition. The state is not interested in why two people are "tying the knot," whether it's to gain money, secure a dynasty or raise children. It may be hard for those of us who have a religious or romantic view of marriage to realize that loveless marriages are not that rare. Before the Pill, pregnancy was a frequent motive for getting married. The state doesn't care what the commitment of two people is, whether it's for life or as long as both of you love, whether it's sexually monogamous or an open marriage. There is nothing spiritual, mystical or romantic about the state's license to marry—it's a legal contract.

Thus, George W. Bush is right when he says that "marriage is a sacred institution" when speaking as a Christian, as a member of his Methodist church. But as President of the United States and leader of all Americans, believers and unbelievers, he is wrong. What will surface in this debate as litigation and court decisions multiply is the history of the conflict between the church and the state in defining the nature of marriage. That history will become significant as we move toward a decision on who may be married.

After Christianity became the state religion of the Roman Empire in AD 325, the church maintained absolute control over the regulation of marriage for some 1,000 years. Beginning in the sixteenth century, English kings (especially Henry VIII, who found the inability to get rid of a wife extremely oppressive) and other monarchs in Europe began to wrest control from the church over marital regulations. Ever since, kings, presidents and rulers of all kinds have seen how important the control of marriage is to the regulation of social order. In this nation, the government has always been in charge of marriage.

16 That is why it was not a San Francisco mayor licensing same-sex couples that really threatened the President's religious understanding of marriage but rather the

Supreme Judicial Court of Massachusetts; declaring marriage between same-sex couples a constitutional right, that demanded a call for constitutional amendment. I didn't understand how important that was until I read an op-ed piece in the *Boston Globe* by Peter Gomes, professor of Christian morals and the minister of Memorial Church at Harvard University, that reminds us of a seminal piece of our history:

> The Dutch made civil marriage the law of the land in 1590, and the first marriage in New England, that of Edward Winslow to the widow Susannah White, was performed on May 12, 1621, in Plymouth by Governor William Bradford, in exercise of his office as magistrate.

There would be no clergyman in Plymouth until the arrival of the Rev. Ralph Smith in 1629, but even then marriage would continue to be a civil affair, as these first Puritans opposed the English custom of clerical marriage as unscriptural. Not until 1692, when Plymouth Colony was merged into that of Massachusetts Bay, were the Clergy authorized by the new province to solemnize marriages. To this day in the Commonwealth the clergy, including those of the archdiocese, solemnize marriage legally as agents of the Commonwealth and by its civil authority. Chapter 207 of the General Laws of Massachusetts tells us who may perform such ceremonies.

Now even though it is the civil authority of the state that defines the rights and responsibilities of marriage and therefore who can be married, the state is no more infallible than the church in its judgments. It wasn't until the mid-twentieth century that the Supreme Court declared anti-miscegenation laws unconstitutional. Even after that decision, many mainline churches, where I started my ministry, unofficially discouraged interracial marriages, and many of my colleagues were forbidden to perform such weddings.

The civil law view of marriage has as much historical diversity as the church's own experience because, in part, the church continued to influence the civil law. Although it was the Bible that made "the husband the head of his wife," it was common law that "turned the married pair legally into one person—the husband," as Nancy Cott documents in her book *Public Vows: A History of Marriage and the Nation* (an indispensable resource for anyone seeking to understand the changing nature of marriage in the nation's history). She suggests that "the legal doctrine of marital unity was called coverture . . . [which] meant that the wife could not use legal avenues such as suits or contracts, own assets, or execute legal documents without her husband's collaboration." This view of the wife would not hold water in any court in the land today.

20 As a matter of fact, even in the religious understanding of President Bush and his followers, allowing same-sex couples the right to marry seems a logical conclusion. If marriage is "the most fundamental institution of civilization" and a major contributor to the social order in our society, why would anyone want to shut out homosexuals from the "glorious attributes" of this "sacred institution"? Obviously, the only reason one can discern is that the opponents believe that gay and lesbian people are not worthy of the benefits and spiritual blessings of "marriage."

At the heart of the controversy raging over same-sex marriage is the religious and constitutional principle of the separation of church and state. All of us can probably agree that there was never a solid wall of separation, riddled as it is with breaches. The evidence of that is seen in the ambiguity of tax-free religious institutions, "in God we trust" printed on our money and "under God" in the Pledge of Allegiance to our country. All of us clergy, who are granted permission by the state to officiate at legal marriage ceremonies, have already compromised the "solid wall" by signing the license issued by the state. I would like to believe that my authority to perform religious ceremonies does not come from the state but derives from the vows of ordination and my commitment to God. I refuse to repeat the words, "by the authority invested in me by the State of New York, I pronounce you husband and wife," but by signing the license, I've become the state's "handmaiden."

It seems fitting therefore that we religious folk should now seek to sharpen the difference between ecclesiastical law and civil law as we beseech the state to clarify who can be married by civil law. Further evidence that the issue of church and state is part of the gay-marriage controversy is that two Unitarian ministers have been arrested for solemnizing unions between same-sex couples when no state licenses were involved. Ecclesiastical law may punish those clergy who disobey marital regulations, but the state has no right to invade church practices and criminalize clergy under civil law. There should have been a noisy outcry from all churches, synagogues and mosques at the government's outrageous contravention of the sacred principle of the "free exercise of religion."

I come from a long line of Protestants who believe in "a free church in a free state." In the issue before this nation, the civil law is the determinant of the regulation of marriage, regardless of our religious views, and the Supreme Court will finally decide what the principle of equality means in our Constitution in the third century of our life together as a people. It is likely that the Commonwealth of Massachusetts will probably lead the nation on this matter, as the State of New York led to the Supreme Court decision to allow women reproductive freedom.

24 So what is marriage? It depends on whom you ask, in what era, in what culture. Like all words or institutions, human definitions, whether religious or secular, change with time and history. When our beloved Constitution was written, blacks, Native Americans and, to some extent, women were quasi-human beings with no rights or privileges, but today they are recognized as persons with full citizenship rights. The definition of marriage has been changing over the centuries in this nation, and it will change yet again as homosexuals are seen as ordinary human beings.

In time, and I believe that time is now, we Americans will see that all the fears foisted on us by religious zealots were not real. Heterosexual marriage will still flourish with its statistical failures. The only difference will be that some homosexual couples will join them and probably account for about the same number of failed relationships. And we will discover that it did not matter whether the couples were joined in a religious ceremony or a secular and civil occasion for the statement of their intentions.

PERSONAL RESPONSE

Explain whether you believe that the issue of how marriage is defined by church and state is relevant to the issue of same-sex marriage.

QUESTIONS FOR CLASS OR SMALL-GROUP DISCUSSION

1. Locate Moody's central purpose and discuss whether you are persuaded that his position is valid.
2. What distinctions does Moody draw between the state's definition of marriage and that of the church?
3. To what extent are you convinced that "the state has no right to invade church practices and criminalize clergy under civil law" (paragraph 20)?
4. How would you answer the question, "So what is marriage?" (paragraph 22)?

✧ PERSPECTIVES ON GENDER AND SEX ROLES ✧

Suggested Writing Topics

1. Read any of the books or articles mentioned by writers in this chapter and write a critique of it.
2. Define "marriage," taking into account Howard Moody's article "Sacred Rite or Civil Right?"
3. Write an essay defining and distinguishing among the terms "sex," "gender," and "sexuality."
4. Drawing on two or more of the essays in this chapter, write a reflective essay in which you explore your own concepts of masculinity and femininity (and perhaps androgyny) and the way in which that concept has shaped the way you are today. Did your parents or care givers treat you differently on the basis of your sex? Were you assigned a "gender identity" that you were comfortable with?
5. Consider to what degree you think that sex determines destiny.
6. Conduct an investigative analysis of any of the following for their depiction of female and male sex roles: fairy tales, children's stories, advertising images, music videos, television programs, or film. Do you find stereotyped assumptions about masculinity and femininity? In what ways do you think the subject of your analysis reinforces or shapes cultural definitions of masculinity and femininity?
7. Examine media images for the ways in which gays and lesbians are portrayed. Focus on a particular medium, such as print advertisements, television situation comedies, or film.
8. Explore ways in which you would like to see definitions of masculinity and femininity changed. How do you think relationships between the sexes would be affected if those changes were made?

9. Write a personal narrative recounting an experience in which you felt you were being treated unfairly or differently from persons of the other sex. What was the situation, how did you feel, and what did you do about it?
10. Explain the degree to which you consider gender issues to be important. Do you think too much is made of gender? Does it matter whether definitions of masculinity and femininity are rigid?
11. Argue the case for or against same-sex marriage to an audience of judges sitting on a state's Supreme Court, trying to decide whether to legalize it.
12. Interview at least two people who grew up in the 1950s or 1960s about the sports that girls were allowed to participate in. Do they have memories of girls and women who were not allowed to play when they wanted to or who were denied access to professional schools because of the quota system?

Research Topics

1. Thomas Bartlett in "The Puzzle of Boys" refers to the "nature versus nurture debate" (paragraph 10). Research some aspect of this debate. As with any research topic, you will need to narrow your focus after doing some preliminary reading on the nature and scope of this issue.
2. Deborah Tannen in "Who's Doing the Talking Here" refers to some 70 studies published in scientific journals on "gender differences in talkativeness" (paragraph 3). Research the subject by reading some of the studies done on it and arrive at your own conclusions. Include at least one work by Deborah Tannen.
3. Research the history of the contemporary women's movement, the men's movement, or the gay rights movement in America and report on its origins, goals, and influence. You will have to narrow your scope, depending on the time you have for the project and the nature of your purpose.
4. Research the subject of bisexuality, making sure to include differing viewpoints, and then explain your own viewpoint on the topic, supporting your position with relevant source materials.
5. Through research and interviews, write a paper on some aspect of the gay and lesbian experience in America.
6. Research the subject of sex-role stereotyping in books, movies, or other media.
7. Research the shifting views of both the church and the state on marriage. You may want to begin with Nancy Cott's *Public Vows: A History of Marriage and the Nation* that Howard Moody recommends in "Sacred Rite or Civil Right?"
8. Conduct research on the subject of sex-role stereotyping and its influence on boys and/or girls. You may want to focus just on girls or just on boys or do a comparative analysis. Consider beginning your research by looking at some of the books mentioned by Thomas Bartlett in "The Puzzle of Boys."

9. Research some aspect of women's sports before and after Title IX, taking Elinor Nauen's "A Sporting Chance: Title IX and the Seismic Shift in Women's Sports" as a starting point. Or, you may want to track women's entrance into such professions as law or medicine before and after Title IX. Consider reading the experiences of women who were denied access to medical or law school before the female quota system was abandoned and compare those experiences with what is available to women today.
10. Elinor Nauen in "A Sporting Chance: Title IX and the Seismic Shift in Women's Sports" writes about women's and men's college sports that "full equality still lies ahead" (paragraph 17)? Conduct research that either supports or refutes that statement.

Responding to Visuals

Department of Defense photo by PH2 J. Alan Elliott

A Marine steadies a child playing with the M60 Maremount machine gun mounted atop an M998 High-mobility Multipurpose Wheeled Vehicle (HMMWV). The vehicle is one of the displays on the pier outside the battleship USS IOWA (BB 61) during Navy Appreciation Week.

1. How do the various components of the photograph contribute to its overall impression? For instance, what is the effect of the position of the American flag?
2. What do the looks on the faces of the man and child contribute to the overall effect?
3. Is there any irony in the contrast between the child and the Marine?

Responding to Visuals

Woman climber looking back at view of mountains, elevated view.

1. What emotions do you imagine the woman in the photograph might be having?
2. How does the composition of the photograph convey what this climber has achieved?
3. In what ways could the image be symbolic of the journey girls and women have made in sports in the last several decades?

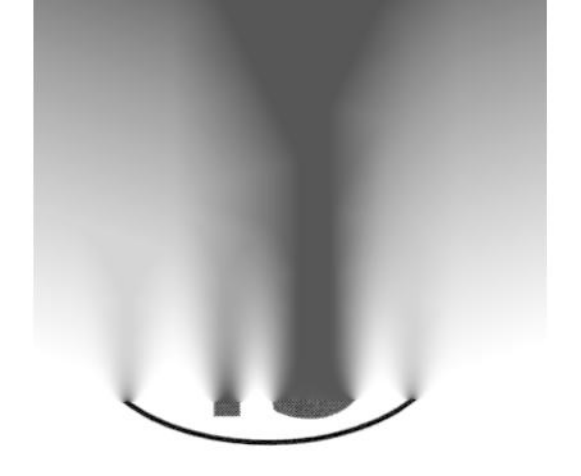

Race and Ethnicity in America

Racial or ethnic heritage is as important to shaping identity as are sex and social class. One's race or ethnicity can also influence quality of life, educational opportunity, and advancement in employment. American society has a long history of struggling to confront and overcome racism and discrimination on the basis of ethnic heritage. Beginning well before the Civil War, American antislavery groups protested the enslavement of African Americans and worked to abolish slavery in all parts of the country. Other groups besides African Americans have experienced harsh treatment and discrimination solely because of their color or ethnic heritage.

These groups include Chinese men brought to America to help construct a cross-country railroad in the nineteenth century, European immigrants who came to America in large numbers near the end of the nineteenth century in search of better lives than they could expect in their homelands, Japanese men who came in the twentieth century to work at hard labor for money to send home, and Latinos/Latinas and Hispanics migrating north to America. As a result of the heightened awareness of the interplay of race, class, and gender, schools at all levels, from elementary through postgraduate, have incorporated course materials on or created whole courses devoted to those important components of individual identity and history. The readings in this chapter focus on immigrants and minority groups in a country that still struggles with racial inequities and discrimination.

The chapter begins with the first article in a series by the *Washington Post* on the effects of increases in the numbers of immigrants on American life in the last decade of the twentieth century and in the future. William Booth's "One Nation, Indivisible: Is It History?" contrasts the effects of the first great wave of immigration to America in the period between 1890 and 1920 with the recent second great wave of immigration, as he explores the question of whether America is truly a "melting pot." As you read his article, keep in mind the question posed by its title and consider whether you think, as the writer implies, that the concept of America as a single, indivisible nation is soon to be a matter of history, not fact.

Following Booth's piece, John J. Savant's "Imagining the Immigrant: Why Legality Must Give Way to Humanity" addresses the issue of what to do about undocumented illegal immigrants in America. He argues that our common humanity is a prime reason for us to use our imagination, which "speaks to both heart and mind" and will "lead to right action." Consider as you read Savant's article whether you are convinced by his argument. Next, Raina Kelley in "Playing the Race Card" expresses her opinion on the subject of why race is not discussed in the aftermath of the election of President Barack Obama. She insists that avoiding the subject is not going to help solve the problem of racism in America. As you read her piece, think about whether you agree that talking about the race of America's first African American president and the racist remarks of his detractors might help achieve racial equality.

The chapter ends with an essay by Maryann Cusimano Love, who points out a number of social problems that indicate that America is far from solving its racial problem. In "Race in America: 'We Would Like to Believe We Are Over the Problem,'" she takes exception to a statement by a Virginia legislator who believes that "'blacks need to get over' slavery." Think about how you would you reply to the legislator and whether you agree with Love's response.

ONE NATION, INDIVISIBLE: IS IT HISTORY?

WILLIAM BOOTH

William Booth, a Washington Post *writer who previously reported for the science and styles desks, now lives in Mexico and reports for the* Post's *Foreign Service. This article was the first in a series examining the effects of changing demographics on American life. It appeared in the Sunday, February 22, 1998, issue of the* Washington Post.

At the beginning of this century, as steamers poured into American ports, their steerages filled with European immigrants, a Jew from England named Israel Zangwill penned a play whose story line has long been forgotten, but whose central theme has not. His production was entitled "The Melting Pot," and its message still holds a tremendous power on the national imagination—the promise that all immigrants can be transformed into Americans, a new alloy forged in a crucible of democracy, freedom, and civic responsibility. In 1908, when the play opened in Washington, the United States was in the middle of absorbing the largest influx of immigrants in its history—Irish and Germans, followed by Italians and East Europeans, Catholics and Jews—some 18 million new citizens between 1890 and 1920.

Today, the United States is experiencing its second great wave of immigration, a movement of people that has profound implications for a society that by tradition pays homage to its immigrant roots at the same time it confronts complex and deeply ingrained ethnic and racial divisions. The immigrants of today come not from Europe but overwhelmingly from the still developing world of Asia and Latin America. They are driving a demographic shift so rapid that within the lifetimes of today's teenagers, no one ethnic group—including whites of European descent—will comprise a majority of the nation's population.

This shift, according to social historians, demographers, and others studying the trends, will severely test the premise of the fabled melting pot, the idea, so central to national identity, that this country can transform people of every color and background into "one America." Just as possible, they say, is that the nation will continue to fracture into many separate, disconnected communities with no shared sense of commonality or purpose. Or perhaps it will evolve into something in between, a pluralistic society that will hold onto some core ideas about citizenship and capitalism, but with little meaningful interaction among groups.

4 The demographic changes raise other questions about political and economic power. Will that power, now held disproportionately by whites, be shared in the new America? What will happen when Hispanics overtake blacks as the nation's single largest minority? "I do not think that most Americans really understand the historic changes happening before their very eyes," said Peter Salins, an immigration scholar who is provost of the State Universities of New York. "What are we going to become? Who are we? How do the newcomers fit in—and how do the natives handle it—this is the great unknown."

Fear of strangers, of course, is nothing new in American history. The last great immigration wave produced a bitter backlash, epitomized by the Chinese Exclusion Act of 1882 and the return, in the 1920s, of the Ku Klux Klan, which not only targeted blacks, but Catholics, Jews, and immigrants, as well. But despite this strife, many historians argue that there was a greater consensus in the past on what it meant to be an American, a yearning for a common language and culture, and a desire—encouraged, if not coerced by members of the dominant white Protestant culture—to assimilate. Today, they say, there is more emphasis on preserving one's ethnic identity, of finding ways to highlight and defend one's cultural roots.

Difficult to Measure

More often than not, the neighborhoods where Americans live, the politicians and propositions they vote for, the cultures they immerse themselves in, the friends and spouses they have, the churches and schools they attend, and the way they view themselves are defined by ethnicity. The question is whether, in the midst of such change, there is also enough glue to hold Americans together. Black community activist Nathaniel J. Wilcox in Miami says, "Hispanics don't want some of the power, they want all the power." "As we become more and more diverse, there is all this potential to make that reality work for us," said Angela Oh, a Korean American activist who emerged as a powerful voice for Asian immigrants after the Los Angeles riots in 1992. "But yet, you witness this persistence of segregation, the fragmentation, all these fights over resources, this finger-pointing. You would have to be blind not to see it."

It is a phenomenon sometimes difficult to measure, but not observe. Houses of worship remain, as the Rev. Martin Luther King Jr. described it three decades ago, among the most segregated institutions in America, not just by race but also ethnicity. At high school cafeterias, the second and third generation children of immigrants clump together in cliques defined by where their parents or grandparents were born. There are television sit-coms, talk shows, and movies that are considered black or white, Latino or Asian. At a place like the law school of the University of California at Los Angeles, which has about 1,000 students, there are separate student associations for blacks, Latinos, and Asians with their own law review journals.

8 It almost goes without saying that today's new arrivals are a source of vitality and energy, especially in the big cities to which many are attracted. Diversity, almost everyone agrees, is good; choice is good; exposure to different cultures and ideas is good. But many scholars worry about the loss of community and shared sense of reality among Americans, what Todd Gitlin, a professor of culture and communications at New York University, calls "the twilight of common dreams." The concern is echoed by many on both the left and the right, and of all ethnicities, but no one seems to know exactly what to do about it.

Academics who examine the census data and probe for meaning in the numbers already speak of a new "demographic balkanization," not only of residential segregation, forced or chosen, but also of a powerful preference to see ourselves through a racial prism, wary of others, and, in many instances, hostile. At a recent school board meeting in East Palo Alto, California, police had to break up a fight between Latinos and blacks, who were arguing over the merits and expense of bilingual education in a school district that has shifted over the past few years from majority African American to majority Hispanic. One parent told reporters that if the Hispanics wanted to learn Spanish they should stay in Mexico.

The demographic shifts are smudging the old lines demarcating two historical, often distinct societies, one black and one white. Reshaped by three decades of rapidly rising immigration, the national story is now far more complicated. Whites currently account for 74 percent of the population, blacks 12 percent, Hispanics 10 percent, and Asians 3 percent. Yet according to data and predictions generated by the U.S. Census Bureau and social scientists poring over the numbers, Hispanics will likely surpass blacks early in the next century. And by the year 2050, demographers predict, Hispanics will account for 25 percent of the population, blacks 14 percent, Asians 8 percent, with whites hovering somewhere around 53 percent. As early as next year, whites will no longer be the majority in California; in Hawaii and New Mexico this is already the case. Soon after, Nevada, Texas, Maryland, and New Jersey are also predicted to become "majority minority" states, entities where no one ethnic group remains the majority.

Effects of 1965 Law

The overwhelming majority of immigrants come from Asia and Latin America—Mexico, the Central American countries, the Philippines, Korea, and Southeast Asia. What triggered this great transformation was a change to immigration law in 1965, when Congress made family reunification the primary criterion for admittance. That new policy, a response to charges that the law favored white Europeans, allowed immigrants already in the United States to bring over their relatives, who in turn could bring over more relatives. As a result, America has been absorbing as many as 1 million newcomers a year, to the point that now almost 1 in every 10 residents is foreign born. These numbers, relative to the overall population, were slightly higher at the beginning of this century, but the current immigration wave is in many ways very different, and its context inexorably altered, from the last great wave.

12 This time around tensions are sharpened by the changing profile of those who are entering America's borders. Not only are their racial and ethnic backgrounds more varied than in decades past, their place in a modern postindustrial economy has been recast. The newly arrived today can be roughly divided into two camps: those with college degrees and highly specialized skills, and those with almost no education or job training. Some 12 percent of immigrants have graduate degrees, compared to 8 percent of Native Americans. But more than one-third of the immigrants have no high school diploma, double the rate for those born in the United States. Before 1970, immigrants were actually doing better than natives overall, as measured by education, rate of home ownership, and average income. But those arriving after 1970 are younger, more likely to be underemployed, and live below the poverty level. As a group, they are doing worse than natives. About 6 percent of new arrivals receive some form of welfare, double the rate for U.S.-born citizens. Among some newcomers—Cambodians and Salvadorans, for example—the numbers are even higher.

With large numbers of immigrants arriving from Latin America, and segregating in barrios, there is also evidence of lingering language problems. Consider that in Miami, three-quarters of residents speak a language other than English at home, and 67 percent of those say that they are not fluent in English. In New York City, 4 of every 10 residents speak a language other than English at home, and of these, half said they do not speak English well.

It is clear that not all of America is experiencing the impact of immigration equally. Although even small midwestern cities have seen sharp changes in their racial and ethnic mix in the past two decades, most immigrants continue to cluster into a handful of large, mostly coastal metropolitan areas: Los Angeles, New York, San Francisco, Chicago, Miami, Washington, D.C., and Houston. They are home to more than a quarter of the total U.S. population and more than 60 percent of all foreign-born residents. But as the immigrants arrive, many American-born citizens pour out of these cities in search of new homes in more homogeneous locales. New York and Los Angeles each lost more than 1 million native-born residents between 1990 and 1995, even as their populations increased by roughly the same numbers with immigrants. To oversimplify, said University of Michigan demographer William Frey, "For every Mexican who comes to Los Angeles, a white native-born leaves."

Most of the people leaving the big cities are white, and they tend to be working class. This is an entirely new kind of "white flight," whereby whites are not just fleeing the city centers for the suburbs but also are leaving the region and often the state. "The Ozzies and Harriets of the 1990s are skipping the suburbs of the big cities and moving to more homogeneous, mostly white smaller towns and smaller cities and rural areas," Frey said. They're headed to Atlanta, Las Vegas, Phoenix, Portland, Denver, Austin, and Orlando, as well as smaller cities in Nevada, Idaho, Colorado, and Washington. Frey and other demographers believe the domestic migrants—black and white—are being "pushed" out, at least in part, by competition with immigrants for jobs and neighborhoods, political clout and lifestyle. Frey sees in this pattern "the emergence of separate Americas, one white and middle-aged, less urban and another intensely urban, young, multicultural, and multiethnic. One America will care deeply about English as the official language and about preserving social security. The other will care about things like retaining affirmative action and bilingual education."

Ethnic Segregation

16 Even within gateway cities that give the outward appearance of being multicultural, there are sharp lines of ethnic segregation. When describing the ethnic diversity of a bellwether megacity such as Los Angeles, many residents speak roaringly of the great mosaic of many peoples. But the social scientists who look at the hard census data see something more complex. James P. Allen, a cultural geographer at California State University–Northridge, suggests that while Los Angeles, as seen from an airplane, is a tremendously mixed society, on the ground, racial homogeneity and segregation are common. This is not a new phenomenon; there have always been immigrant neighborhoods. Ben Franklin, an early proponent of making English the official language, worried about close-knit German communities. Sen. Daniel

Patrick Moynihan (D–N.Y.) described the lingering clannishness of Irish and other immigrant populations in New York in *Beyond the Melting Pot,* a benchmark work from the 1960s that he wrote with Nathan Glazer.

But the persistence of ethnic enclaves and identification does not appear to be going away and may not in a country that is now home to not a few distinct ethnic groups, but to dozens. Hispanics in Los Angeles, to take the dominant group in the nation's second largest city, are more segregated residentially in 1990 than they were ten or twenty years ago, the census tracts show. Moreover, it is possible that what mixing of groups that does occur is only a temporary phenomenon as one ethnic group supplants another in the neighborhood.

If there is deep-seated ethnic segregation, it clearly extends to the American workplace. In many cities, researchers find sustained "ethnic niches" in the labor market. Because jobs are often a matter of whom one knows, the niches were enduring and remarkably resistant to outsiders. In California, for example, Mexican immigrants are employed overwhelmingly as gardeners and domestics, in apparel and furniture manufacturing, and as cooks and food preparers. Koreans open small businesses. Filipinos become nurses and medical technicians. African Americans work in government jobs, an important niche that is increasingly being challenged by Hispanics who want in.

UCLA's Roger Waldinger and others have pointed to the creation, in cities of high immigration, of "dual economies." For the affluent, which includes a disproportionate number of whites, the large labor pool provides them with a ready supply of gardeners, maids, and nannies. For businesses in need of cheap manpower, the same is true. Yet there are fewer "transitional" jobs—the blue-collar work that helped Italian and Irish immigrants move up the economic ladder—to help newcomers or their children on their way to the jobs requiring advanced technical or professional skills that now dominate the upper tier of the economy.

A Rung at a Time

20 Traditionally, immigration scholars have seen the phenomenon of assimilation as a relentless economic progression. The hard-working new arrivals struggle along with a new language and at low-paying jobs in order for their sons and daughters to climb the economic ladder, each generation advancing a rung. There are many cases where this is true. More recently, there is evidence to suggest that economic movement is erratic and that some groups—particularly in high immigration cities—can get "stuck." Among African Americans, for instance, there emerge two distinct patterns. The black middle class is doing demonstrably better—in income, home ownership rates, education—than it was when the demographic transformation (and the civil rights movement) began three decades ago. But for African Americans at the bottom, research indicates that immigration, particularly of Latinos with limited education, has increased joblessness and frustration.

In Miami, where Cuban immigrants dominate the political landscape, tensions are high between Hispanics and blacks, said Nathaniel J. Wilcox, a community activist there. "The perception in the black community, the reality, is that Hispanics don't want some of the power, they want all the power," Wilcox said. "At least when we were going through this with the whites during the Jim Crow era, at least they'd hire us. But Hispanics won't allow African Americans to even compete. They have this feeling that their community is the only community that counts."

Yet many Hispanics too find themselves in an economic "mobility trap." While the new immigrants are willing to work in low-end jobs, their sons and daughters, growing up in the barrios but exposed to the relentless consumerism of popular culture, have greater expectations, but are disadvantaged because of their impoverished settings, particularly the overwhelmed inner-city schools most immigrant children attend. "One doubts that a truck-driving future will satisfy today's servants and assemblers. And this scenario gets a good deal more pessimistic if the region's economy fails to deliver or simply throws up more bad jobs," writes Waldinger, a professor of sociology and director of center for regional policy studies at the University of California–Los Angeles.

Though there are calls to revive efforts to encourage "Americanization" of the newcomers, many researchers now express doubt that the old assimilation model works. For one thing, there is less of a dominant mainstream to enter. Instead, there are a dozen streams, despite the best efforts by the dominant white society to lump groups together by ethnicity. It is a particularly American phenomenon, many say, to label citizens by their ethnicity. When they lived in El Salvador, for example, they saw themselves as a nationality. When they arrive in the United States, they become Hispanic or Latino. So too with Asians. Koreans and Cambodians find little in common, but when they arrive here they become "Asian," and are counted and courted, encouraged or discriminated against as such. "My family has had trouble understanding that we are now Asians, and not Koreans, or people from Korea or Korean Americans, or just plain Americans," said Arthur Lee, who owns a dry cleaning store in Los Angeles. "Sometimes, we laugh about it. Oh, the Asian students are so smart! The Asians have no interest in politics! Whatever. But we don't know what people are talking about. Who are the Asians?"

24 Many immigrant parents say that while they want their children to advance economically in their new country, they do not want them to become "too American." A common concern among Haitians in South Florida is that their children will adopt the attitudes of the inner city's underclass. Vietnamese parents in New Orleans often try to keep their children immersed in their ethnic enclave and try not to let them assimilate too fast.

Hyphenated Americans

One study of the children of immigrants, conducted six years ago among young Haitians, Cubans, West Indians, Mexicans, and Vietnamese in South Florida and southern California, suggests the parents are not alone in their concerns. Asked by researchers Alejandro Portes and Ruben Rumbauthow how they identified themselves, most chose categories of hyphenated Americans. Few choose "American" as their identity. Then there was this—asked if they believe the United States is the best country in the world, most of the youngsters answered: no.

PERSONAL RESPONSE

Does the fact that many immigrant parents say "they do not want [their children] to become 'too American'" (paragraph 24) surprise you? How important do you consider your race or ethnicity to your identity? Is the neighborhood where you grew up largely composed of a particular racial or ethnic group, or does it have a mixed population?

QUESTIONS FOR CLASS OR SMALL-GROUP DISCUSSION

1. State in your own words what is meant by the terms *melting pot* (paragraphs 1 and 3) and *pluralistic society* (paragraph 3). What does *demographic balkanization* (paragraph 9) mean?
2. How, according to Booth, does the second great wave of immigration differ from the first great wave? What possible effect do social historians and demographers see in this second wave? How has the 1965 immigration law affected American demographics?
3. In what ways, according to Booth, is America still a highly segregated country? Explain whether your own observations and/or experiences support his assertions.
4. Summarize Booth's discussion of terminology for various racial or ethnic groups (paragraphs 23–25). What effect do you think labels or identity markers have on members of those groups?

IMAGINING THE IMMIGRANT: WHY LEGALITY MUST GIVE WAY TO HUMANITY

JOHN J. SAVANT

John J. Savant, an emeritus professor of English at Dominican University of California, writes on the issues of philosophy, ethics, and morality. This essay was first published in the October 26, 2009, issue of America *magazine.*

Great detectives, we are told, are able to think like criminals. Similarly, effective therapists learn to enter into the fantasies of their patients. These behaviors are a function of that supreme and godlike faculty we call imagination. Unlike daydream or fancy—a centrifugal spinning away from reality, the mind on holiday—imagination is centripetal, a disciplined contemplation of reality that takes us beneath appearances and into the essence of what we contemplate. Imagination, therefore, can lead to moral clarification. In issues where law and morality seem to clash, as in the current debate over undocumented immigrants, imagination (which speaks to both heart and mind) can lead to right action.

Law and morality are not always commensurate; a law that is just in one context may be inappropriate in another, because laws function more often to allow a workable social order than to represent absolute moral imperatives. We hear it argued, for example, that granting amnesty and a path to citizenship for illegal aliens encourages disrespect for the law—a legitimate concern within the context of normal civic life. What this argument does not address, however, are the social and economic circumstances that significantly alter the normal civic context—for example, the abnormal circumstances that lie at the heart of major migration movements.

Even in very modest circumstances, people prefer their home turf and the comforts of custom to the trauma of dislocation and the uncertainty of the unfamiliar. There will always be adventurers who are at home anywhere in the world, but when populations begin to cross borders in significant numbers, it is almost always out of dire economic necessity or because of severe political persecution. In light of our common humanity—a familial bond with its own intuitions and responsibilities—we cannot make the moral urgings of this bond subservient to the civil proscriptions of law.

Legality Versus Starvation

4 Against the compelling urgency of the plight of immigrants, therefore, the claims of legal compliance must give way to the more fundamental claims of our common humanity. If numerous immigrants are here because their families would otherwise live in abject poverty, the issue boils down to legal conformity versus possible starvation. Here is where abstractions must give way to concrete reality. But as any poet or artist will tell you, the concrete is the realm of the imagination. In attempting to understand what is just, we have to imagine real persons and their concrete situations.

Let's imagine a man named Eusebio. If deported as an illegal alien and thus deprived of an income, he could likely witness the decline of a sickly daughter whose medicines he can no longer purchase, or he might have to face the possibility that her despondent older sister will opt for whatever income prostitution might provide. Ironically, a few miles across the border, some of his countrymen are earning more in a day than he does in a month. He sees his tired wife scrubbing one of her three dresses, his pretty daughter staring glumly at nothing and the streets outside bleak and empty of promise. He does not think, at this moment, of breaking laws. He thinks of his paternal duty and acts not out of greed but out of desperation.

Or imagine a woman named Marta, whose husband has been "disappeared" by a rival faction. Possessing only domestic skills, she tries to support her mother and children by selling gum and postcards to tourists. It is not enough. She leaves her two youngest children and her meager savings with her mother and makes the harrowing journey with her son across the Rio Grande, more desperate than hopeful, driven more by a primal affirmation of life and the panic of love than by any plan. In our concern for "respect for law," can we demote these and many similar tragedies to a category of lesser urgency, considering them the "collateral effects" of market forces?

A Nation of Imagination

America was at one time described as a "City upon a Hill," the "New Zion," a beacon to the world. Many in the mid-19th century would have agreed with the Unitarian minister William Ellery Channing, who proclaimed that our nation represented God's plan for humankind, its freedoms guaranteeing a nobler, more resilient and more just society. He said this, of course, not long before we engaged in one of history's bloodiest civil wars, a war that jarred our self-perception of national innocence and historical exception. Now, with the closing of the frontier and the unparalleled opportunities it made possible for the rugged individual, we have been snatched out of our timeless dream and back into history. The world now watches to see how well our behavior will match our lofty rhetoric.

8 What America has been is largely the product of a historical windfall—the confluence of revolutionary European theory, geographical separation from centers of control, the necessity of (and gradual education in) self-governance and an unimaginable expanse of continent in which to carry out our democratic experiment. What America can become will be the result of the new culture we form in the far more restricted (and realistic) circumstances of a closed frontier. Will we continue to manifest the daring, idealism, generosity and openness to the new and the difficult that marked our frontier forebears at their best? Or will we respond to challenges like the current influx of immigrants with a narrow sense of proprietorship and a very un-American fear of the unknown and the unfamiliar? If we reduce justice to legality and culture to security, we take the first steps toward a state driven not by enthusiasm but by caution, not by daring but by fear. We will prove that our vaunted magnanimity has been not the natural and characteristic expression of a free and democratic people, but the specious (and transient) product of a magnificent frontier blessed with material plenty.

The American dream has run headlong into a historical crunch time. If we are not to betray the dream, we simply must imagine better. Just as we imagined our dogged pilgrim pioneers and our daring frontier ancestors in creating a heroic mythology and a resourceful and generous self-image, so too does the bond of our common humanity require that we imagine today the blood ties with our immigrant population that render their desperation our own. Historically, humankind finds this a supremely difficult challenge, for our loyalties to family, clan and nation are the schools of our first imaginings in culture, ritual and governance. We tend to resist other ways of living, other cultures, despite the fact that, as cultural historians will affirm, travel, trade and periodic immigrations have ever tended to enrich their host cultures. In the matter of our growing immigrant population, then, can we not imagine better than to build fences and expand border patrols?

The world is rapidly growing smaller, more intimate and more dangerous. Gerald Vann, O.P., in *The Heart of Man*, writes that in true love, "the lover becomes the beloved." Such becoming is truly an act of the imagination. Can we imagine the immigrant in our midst? Can we become the third world citizen whose longings, not unlike our own, still appear so remote? Such becoming can lead to a moral imagination that gives primacy to radical human need over legal compliance. The survival and growth of our own civilization may well depend upon our imagining better.

PERSONAL RESPONSE

Respond to this sentence: "In the matter of our growing immigrant population, then, can we not imagine better than to build fences and expand border patrols?" (paragraph 9).

QUESTIONS FOR CLASS OR SMALL-GROUP DISCUSSION

1. Analyze the structure of Savant's argument. What does he want his audience to do? Where does he acknowledge those opposed to his position and how does he counter them?
2. What appeals does Savant make? (Recall from Chapter 5 that common appeals are to logic, ethics, emotion, and/or shared values). State specifically where those appeals are made. Do you find them effective?
3. What use does Savant make of the hypothetical examples of Eusebio and Marta? How effective do you find those examples? Do they convince you to agree with Savant?
4. Are you convinced that "legality must give way to humanity"? Why or why not?

PLAY THE RACE CARD

RAINA KELLEY

Raina Kelley, a staff writer for Newsweek *magazine, writes often about racial issues. This opinion piece was published in the September 28, 2009, issue of* Newsweek.

Let me say this clearly so there are no misunderstandings: some of the protests against President Obama are howls of rage at the fact that we have an African-American head of state. I'm sick of all the code words used when this subject comes up, so be assured that I am saying exactly what I mean. Oh, and in response to the inevitable complaints that I am playing the race card—race isn't a political parlor game. It is a powerful fault line in a nation that bears the scars of slavery, a civil war, Jim Crow, a mind-numbing number of assassinations, and too many riots to count. It is naive and disingenuous to say otherwise.

So when Idaho gubernatorial candidate Rex Rammell jokes about hunting the president or South Carolina GOP activist Rusty DePass calls an escaped gorilla one of Michelle Obama's ancestors, it's racist. Which, in case of confusion, is the "ideology that all members of each racial group possess characteristics or abilities specific to that race, especially to distinguish it as being either superior or inferior to another racial group." (That's from the Oxford English Dictionary, but leave the Brits out of this.) When "Tea Party" leader Mark Williams appears on CNN and speaks of "working-class people" taking "their" country back from a lawfully elected president, he is not just protesting Obama's politics; he is griping over the fact that this country's most powerful positions are no longer just for white men. No, I do not believe that everyone who disagrees with Obama is racist. But racists do exist in this country, and they don't like having a black president.

Did anyone think it would be otherwise? There were always going to be aftershocks in an Obama presidency. Landmark events that change the paradigm between black and white people don't happen without repercussions—some are still complaining about *Brown v. Board of Education*. Black skin has meant something very specific in this country for hundreds of years. It has meant "less than," "not as good as," "separate than," and even "equal to." It has never meant "better than" unless you were talking about dancing, singing, or basketball. Obama represents "better than," and that's scary for people who think of black people as shaved gorillas.

4 So color me a little offended when the "mainstream media" suddenly discovered that there might be a racial element to the attacks on Obama. Maureen Dowd's Sept. 13 column in *The New York Times* is a perfect example: "I've been loath to admit that the shrieking lunacy of the summer—the frantic efforts to paint our first black president as the Other, a foreigner, socialist, fascist, Marxist, racist, Commie, Nazi; a cad who would snuff old people; a snake who would indoctrinate kids—had much to do with race." But at least she did acknowledge it. A *Times* piece just a day earlier explained why Obama is so unpopular in Louisiana and somehow managed to omit race as a factor. It took 20 paragraphs for a Politico column titled "What's the Matter With South Carolina?" to mention race. This hesitancy to even speak of racism widens the divide between readers and the journalists who are supposed to be covering the world as it is, not as they want it to be. It also explains, at least in part, the popularity of alternative news sources like *The Daily Show* or the *Huffington Post* that love to identify racist double-talk.

I had actually been looking forward to the aftershocks of an Obama victory. Maybe I'm the one who's naive, but I thought of the election of the first African-American president as the ultimate teachable moment. I wasn't expecting a holiday. But almost anything, really, would be better than all this "post-racial" and "Kumbaya" crap we're being peddled. Even though Oprah and Will Smith are beloved by Americans of all hues, they are still exceptions in a country where judging people based on the color of their skin is a habit we've yet to break.

I get it. Race issues are scary. There are few souls brave enough to say what they think about race relations outside the privacy of their homes or the anonymity of the Internet. But rather than deal with the discomfort of talking about race, we've continued to follow outdated rules about what words can be said by whom or, even worse, to stay silent. As if not speaking of racism will somehow make it go away. Silence, even the well-meaning kind, rarely wins an argument. It just allows the lunatic fringe to fill the vacuum in the public debate. And this reluctance doesn't help the effort to achieve racial equality, it hurts it.

PERSONAL RESPONSE

Write about your views on racism. Do you see it in your daily life? Have you experienced it? How do you respond to it when you see or experience it?

QUESTIONS FOR CLASS OR SMALL-GROUP DISCUSSION

1. What is Kelley's purpose for writing this essay? Does she achieve that purpose, in your opinion? Are you convinced by her argument?
2. Comment on Kelley's language: is it appropriate for her purpose? Does she use language effectively? How would you characterize her tone?
3. Discuss this statement: "Black skin has meant something very specific in this country for hundreds of years" (paragraph 3). Can you give examples other than the ones Kelley names that support or refute her point?
4. How do you respond to Kelley's assertion that "judging people based on the color of their skin is a habit we've yet to break" (paragraph 5)?

RACE IN AMERICA: "WE WOULD LIKE TO BELIEVE WE ARE OVER THE PROBLEM"

MARYANN CUSIMANO LOVE

Maryann Cusimano Love is an award-winning educator and a New York Times *best-selling author of children's books. A professor of international politics at Catholic University, she has also taught courses in globalization, terrorism, and security at the Pentagon. As a member of the Council on Foreign Relations, Love has been advising Canadian, Caribbean, and U.S. government and private sector leaders on security issues since 1998. This essay appeared in the February 12, 2007, edition of the Catholic weekly* America.

As Senator Barack Obama explores a presidential bid, media headlines across the country ask, "Is America ready for an African-American president?" Between 50 percent and 62 percent of Americans polled answer yes, that race is no longer a barrier in the United States. But that this is considered a newsworthy headline by all the major media outlets and that around 40 percent of those polled answer no suggests otherwise.

A recent controversy in Virginia echoes the issue. A Virginia state legislator, Delegate Frank D. Hargrove Sr., a Republican from a suburb of Richmond, gave a newspaper interview on Martin Luther King Jr. Day in which he said that "blacks need to get over" slavery. He was stating his opposition to a resolution in the Virginia legislature to apologize for slavery and promote racial reconciliation as part of Virginia's activities marking the 400th anniversary of the English settlement at Jamestown in 1607. Officials tout Jamestown's founding as the birthplace of our nation (predating the pilgrims' landing in Plymouth Rock by 13 years), of representative government, of the rule of law and of American entrepreneurism. (Jamestown was settled by the Virginia Company of London in order to bring profits back to shareholders.) But Jamestown was also the birthplace of slavery in our country. Government time and tax money are being spent on the commemoration. One sponsor of the resolution, state Senator Henry Marsh, notes that while "the whole world's attention is on Virginia" because of the Jamestown anniversary, "Virginia can take a leadership role in promoting racial harmony." Delegate Hargrove disagrees. He argues it is "counterproductive to dwell on it," noting that "not a soul today had anything to do with slavery."

Some of Delegate Hargrove's argument is attractive. It lets us all off the hook for the inequities of the past. My Sicilian and Irish great-grandparents emigrated to the United States in the 1900's. By Hargrove's logic, my family is not responsible for slavery or its aftermath, because we were not here when it happened. On the other hand, my husband's family moved from Scotland and Ireland to the Chesapeake Bay region in the 1600's. We know little of the family history, but the name is common in these parts, on both black and white faces. I laugh in the grocery checkout lane with an African-American over our shared name, Love. Did someone in my family tree own someone in your family tree?

4 The flaw in Hargrove's argument is that the inequities of the past persist today. Noting achievements of African-Americans like Senator Obama, we would like to believe we "are over" the race problem. But the statistics paint a more sobering picture. Dr. David Satcher, the 16th surgeon general of the United States, notes that 85,000 African-Americans died in the year 2000 due to inequality in health care. The infant mortality rate of black babies is double the infant mortality rate of white babies in the United States. African-Americans have lower life expectancies than white Americans by six or seven years. Twenty-five percent of black Americans live in poverty. One-third of African-American children live in poverty. Black poverty rates are triple those of whites. Tavis Smiley's book, *Covenant with Black America*, explores many other disturbing inequities that persist in the United States today in housing, education and the criminal justice system. The Hatewatch Web site lists cross burnings and activities of white supremacist groups today, and it is possible to track the hate groups currently active in each state. The Harvard online racial bias tests have shown that millions of Americans harbor racial preconceptions. And 16-year-old Kiri Davis repeated the "doll test" used in the 1954 Brown v. Board of Education case with the same infamous results: 4- and 5-year-old black children in Harlem overwhelmingly said that the black dolls were bad and the white dolls were good and pretty. As past inequities continue into the present, we have a moral responsibility to address them.

To "get over" racial problems in America today, we need to understand them and their roots. But we don't. A recent survey conducted by the University of Connecticut found that more than 19 percent of the 14,000 college students in 50 U.S. universities surveyed believed that Martin Luther King Jr.'s "I Have a Dream" speech was advocating the abolition of slavery. I teach a course at Catholic University on the civil rights movement. Our students, most of them graduates of Catholic elementary and high schools, know little of U.S. or Catholic racial history.

The United States is not alone. Such debates are hallmarks of peace-building efforts in post-conflict societies from South Africa to Colombia. We all face these choices, balancing apologies, reconciliation, redress for past wrongs, with attention to present and future problems.

Delegate Hargrove's suggestion that we "get over" the past by not bringing it up can be tempting because it is easy. Senator Obama's vision of a post-racial politics is inviting because it is hopeful. But we are not there yet, and the only way to get there is to work through the present-day ramifications of our persistent past, not only as individuals ("I don't condone racism") but as communities ("What are we doing to end unacceptable racial inequities?").

PERSONAL RESPONSE

What is your response to Delegate Hargrove's statement that "'blacks need to get over slavery'"?

QUESTIONS FOR CLASS OR SMALL-GROUP DISCUSSION

1. State in your own words why Delegate Hargrove is opposed to a resolution in the Virginia legislature to apologize to blacks for slavery. To what extent do you agree that he has a valid point?
2. Summarize the concessions that Love makes to Hargrove's argument.
3. What does Love offer as proof to support her opposition to Hargrove? Do you find her argument valid?
4. What action does Love propose to help America "'get over' racial problems" (paragraph 5)? Can you think of ways to "work through the present-day ramifications of [America's] persistent past" (paragraph 7)?

✧ PERSPECTIVES ON RACE AND ETHNICITY IN AMERICA ✧

Suggested Writing Topics

1. Refer to the comments of at least two writers in this chapter in an essay on some aspect of the subject of stereotyping and prejudice. As you plan your essay, consider the following questions: Where do people get prejudices? What aspects of American culture reinforce and/or perpetuate stereotypes? How can you personally work against stereotyping and prejudice?
2. Explore your position on the issue of a "melting pot" (a society in which minorities are assimilated into the dominant culture) versus pluralism (a society in which ethnic and racial groups maintain separate identities, with no dominant culture). Take into consideration the views of two or more authors in this chapter.
3. Explore the subject of the role that labels play in one's identity, self-esteem, and/or self-concept.
4. Interview at least one other person whose racial or ethnic heritage is different from yours about some of the points raised in at least two of the essays in this chapter. Then write an essay explaining what you learned and how the interview has in any way changed your own views on the issue of racism.

5. Write a reflective essay on your own cultural heritage, explaining your family's background and how you feel about that heritage.
6. Explain the importance of race or ethnicity to your own self-identity. Is it as important as your sex, your job, your socioeconomic level, or your educational level?
7. Write a letter to the editor of *Newsweek* magazine in which you explain your response to Raina Kelley's viewpoint in "Play the Race Card," or, referring to her article where relevant, explain your own theory on the conditions that prevent blacks and whites in America from understanding one another's perspectives.
8. Write an essay explaining your viewpoint on illegal immigration, with John J. Savant's "Imagining the Immigrant: Why Legality Must Give Way to Humanity" in mind. Explain how immigration is a social problem, what its complexities are, and why the problem is dire.
9. Explore the role of racial and ethnic diversity in your educational experiences in high school and college. Consider these questions: How diverse are the student populations of schools you have attended? How large a component did multiculturalism play in the curricula of courses you have taken? Have you been satisfied with that aspect of your education?
10. Narrate your first experience with prejudice, discrimination, or bigotry, as either a witness or a victim. Describe in detail the incident and how it made you feel.
11. Explain the effects of racial prejudice on a person or a group of people familiar to you.
12. Interview people who have immigrated to America to learn their reasons for coming to this country. Find out what images they had of America before they came and whether their impressions have changed now that they are living here.
13. If you are familiar with the difficulties a foreigner has had adjusting to life in your own country, tell about that person's experiences. Or, if you have personally experienced life as a foreigner in a country not your own, describe that experience.

Research Topics

1. Research the subject of a public policy like affirmative action, welfare, or bilingual public education as an effective (or ineffective) way to address racial or ethnic inequities in American society.
2. As a starting point for a research project, read Alex Kotlowitz's *There Are No Children Here: The Story of Two Boys Growing Up in the Other America* or *The Other Side of the River: A Story of Two Towns, a Death, and America's Dilemma.* You may decide to find out more about a major point the author makes, or something the author mentions may lead you to a suitable

topic. If the book has a bibliography, you have an excellent list of potential resources for your project.

3. Research one aspect of the subject of immigration mentioned by William Booth in “One Nation, Indivisible: Is It History?” or John J. Savant in “Imagining the Immigrant: Why Legality Must Give Way to Humanity.”
4. Research one of the following topics related to some of the essays in this chapter: Jim Crow; the influx of Chinese immigrants to America in the nineteenth century; the Chinese Exclusion Act of 1882 and its implications for Japanese immigrants; the Japanese religion Shinto; the internment of people of Japanese ancestry in America during World War II; or the economic, political, or historical relationship of the United States with Puerto Rico, Cuba, Central America, or Mexico.
5. Research the subject of multiculturalism in American education by reading differing opinions on the subject.
6. Research the subject of whether America is a classless society. Do certain factors such as culture, ethnicity, demographics, nativity, citizenship, mother tongue, religion, skin color, or race play a role in an individual’s prospects for social mobility?
7. Select a topic from any of the suggested writing topics above and expand it to include library research, Internet research, and/or interviews.
8. Select one of the following groups to whom the U.S. federal government has made reparations and research reasons why those reparations were made: Japanese Americans interned in American prisons camp during World War II or the Sioux Indians whose lands were confiscated in 1877.

Responding to Visuals

A friend comforts the Iraqi-born owner, right, of a restaurant burned by apparently racially motivated arson, Plymouth, Massachusetts, September 19, 2001.

1. What emotions does the photograph evoke in you?
2. The restaurant owner had received threatening telephone calls for days before the fire. How does that knowledge affect your understanding of this photograph?
3. Why did the photographer choose this particular moment to take his picture? What does it convey that a picture of the restaurant ruins alone would not?

Responding to Visuals

Vince Gonzalez, from left, of Scranton, PA; Kevin Gonzalez, 9, of Scranton, PA; Jeanne Brolan from United Neighborhood Centers; Estrella Gonzalez, 6, of Scranton, PA; Charlotte Lewis of Scranton, PA; and Chris Walters of Brooklyn, NY; participate in a rally organized by the Pennsylvania Immigration and Citizenship Coalition in Scranton, PA, Monday, March 12, 2007. The rally was held directly across from the William J. Nealon Federal Building and United States Courthouse during opening day of the first federal trial in the nation to address whether local government can enact ordinances that punish employers and landlords that do business with illegal immigrants.

1. Does the fact that children are being used as part of the protest strengthen or weaken the protest?
2. Do you agree that the two children are "America," as the signs they are holding state?
3. Do you agree that "no one is illegal," as the sign on the right states?
4. Do you believe that children of illegal immigrants should have rights? What about the illegal immigrants themselves? Where do you position yourself on the issue of illegal immigration?

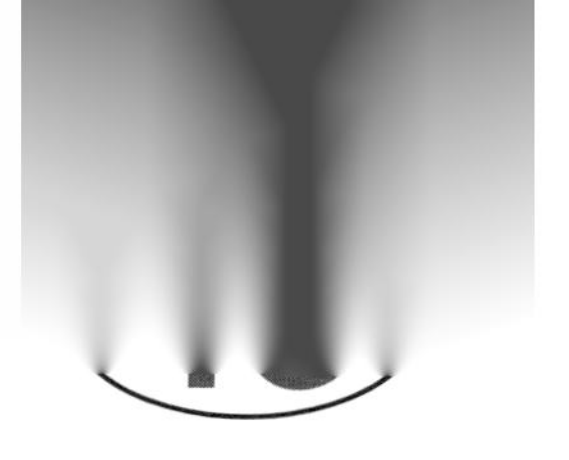

American Foreign Policy

In recent years, international relations have become an extremely important branch of political science, the study of politics, and the workings of the government. America's role as a superpower puts it in the position of being closely scrutinized by leaders, journalists, and ordinary citizens around the world. What America does politically is extremely important to other countries because America's actions are likely to affect them either directly or indirectly in many ways, especially economically and politically. The term *global village*, coined a few decades ago to describe the myriad links among the world's nations, is particularly apt when considering international relations and the perception that other countries have of America. Its political events are reported almost instantaneously around the globe by satellite, and magazines and newspapers also play crucial roles in conveying certain images of America and Americans to other nations.

How to deal with terrorism and prevent terrorist activities figures prominently in the making of American foreign policy. America is one of many nations that have experienced terrorism both abroad and at home. For instance, in 1979, militant students in Tehran stormed the U.S. Embassy there and held fifty-two hostages for 444 days. In 1983, a suicide-bomb attack destroyed the U.S. Embassy in Beirut, killing sixty-three. That same year, also in Beirut, Hezbollah suicide bombers claimed responsibility for blowing up U.S. and French military headquarters, killing 241 U.S. and fifty-eight French servicemen. In 1988, Pan Am flight 103, on its way to the United States, exploded over Lockerbie, Scotland, killing 270 people. On American soil, in 1993 a bomb in the underground garage of the World Trade Center killed six and injured more than 1,000 people; in 1995, a truck bomb destroyed a federal building in Oklahoma City, killing 168 and injuring more than 600.

By far the largest acts of terrorism, in terms of lives lost and effects on the economy, the way people live, and American society in countless ways, have been the September 11, 2001, attacks on the World Trade Center in New York City and the Pentagon in Washington, D.C. Those attacks have had profound effects on America and both its allies and foes. Many countries around the world expressed not only their shock and outrage at the terrorism on American soil but also their deep sympathy for the families, friends, and loved ones of those who lost their lives or were injured in the attacks.

The essays in this chapter address some of the issues involved in American foreign policy and its war on terrorism. First, Paul Johnson in "American Idealism and Realpolitik" comments on America's role as "the reluctant sheriff of a wild world" and the dilemma it finds itself in as it plays that role. As a nation founded on idealism, America is frequently faced with being both a benign champion of weak and oppressed countries while at the same time having to make practical and sometimes Machiavellian decisions about how to deal with the aggressors against the countries it defends. (Note that "realpolitik" refers to politics or diplomacy based primarily on practical considerations, rather than ideological notions.) Johnson raises some intriguing points about this moral dilemma.

Next, Thomas Friedman urges Americans not to let down their guard against terrorists in his essay "Still Not Tired." Citing examples of individual terrorist acts to remind us that the enemy is still active, he calls for vigilance against such acts. Beyond the immediate, though, Friedman believes we must make a long-term commitment to the war on terrorism. Following Friedman's piece, Cathy Young explains in "Lessons from World War II" what we can learn from that war, which she says continues to be a living past with important implications for us today. The war, she contends, reminds us "of the limits of idealism," among other things, and raises the question of how far a nation can allow itself to go in the cause of liberty. Both Friedman and Young make thoughtful observations on the difficult subjects of how we approach the war on terrorism and what we can learn from a devastating world war that occurred more than 70 years ago.

An influential aspect of America that has enormous influence on how foreigners perceive it is popular culture. The image of America conveyed abroad as represented by such products as movies, songs, magazines, T-shirts, and celebrities helps perpetuate certain notions about America as a land of glamour, wealth, excess, excitement, and even a kind of innocence. Hollywood has had particular influence in conveying this image. Martha Bayles takes as her subject the way that American popular culture projects a negative image of the country and wonders if that is responsible for the decline in America's reputation around the world. In "Now Showing: The Good, the Bad and the Ugly Americans," she notes that funding for cultural diplomacy was shrinking in America at the same time that Hollywood become very aggressive in its exports abroad. She notes: "American popular culture is no longer a beacon of freedom to huddled masses in closed societies. Instead, it's a glut on the market and . . . our de facto ambassador to the world." As you read her essay, think about what Hollywood suggests to you. Do you think of glamour, of classic films and famous stars, or do you think of cheap sensationalism, escapism, and money-hungry exploiters out to become rich in any way they can? What picture of America do you think today's Hollywood stars, pop recording artists, and other popular culture representatives project?

AMERICAN IDEALISM AND REALPOLITIK

PAUL JOHNSON

Paul Johnson, eminent British historian and author, has written columns for decades for such British publications as the Spectator, *the* Daily Mail, *and the* Daily Telegraph. *He also contributes to such American publications as* National: The Founding Father Review, *the* Wall Street Journal, *and the* New York Times. *He has written over forty books, primarily on history but also on religion and travel.*

His most recent are Napoleon *(2002);* George Washington *(2005);* Creators *(2006);* Heroes *(2007); and* Churchill *(2009). In 2006, Johnson was awarded the Presidential Medal of Freedom. This article was published in the March 12, 2007, issue of* Forbes.

America is the reluctant sheriff of a wild world that sometimes seems mired in wrongdoing. The UN has nothing to offer in the way of enforcing laws and dispensing justice, other than spouting pious oratory and initiating feeble missions that usually do more harm than good. NATO plays a limited role, as in Afghanistan, but tends to reflect the timidity (and cowardice) of Continental Europe. Britain and a few other nations such as Australia are willing to follow America's lead but are too weak to act on their own.

That leaves the U.S. to shoulder the responsibility. Otherwise—what? Is brute force to replace the rule of law in the world because there's no one to enforce it? I wish some of those who constantly criticize America's efforts and the judgment of President Bush would ask themselves this simple question: Would you really like to live in a world where the U.S. sits idly by and lets things happen?

Life in such a world would be like the bestial existence described in Thomas Hobbes' great work, *Leviathan.* If people "live without a common power to keep them all in awe, they are in that condition which is called war, and such a war as is of every man against every man." In that lawless state there will be "continual fear and danger of violent death, and the life of man solitary, poor, nasty, brutish and short."

4 In the 350 years since Hobbes wrote his book nothing essential has changed. For proof, look at the poor people of Sudan, in whose struggle the U.S. has not been willing to intervene and whose lives are exactly as Hobbes described. The same is true in Somalia, where the U.S. has been indecisive and vacillating. And this was the case in the former Yugoslavia until the U.S., with great misgiving, finally responded to pressure and sent in its forces.

It's fortunate for the world that in areas in which international law doesn't operate and rogue states do as they please, America will sometimes agree to play Leviathan in order to establish law, at the risk of huge financial expense and its soldiers' lives. It does so because it is a country founded on idealism. A majority of Americans have always believed that a society, under God, must come to the rescue of the poor, weak and oppressed if it has the means to do so. The U.S. has applied this idealism systematically to the world as a whole and in many different ways, from the Marshall Plan, which helped raise Europe from ruin in 1948, to declaring war on international terrorism five years ago.

On the Horns of a Dilemma

America is fundamentally and instinctively idealistic. But following these ideals and acting as the world's policeman raises moral issues. We all agree that the sheriff must be righteous, brave and resolute. But should he also, if the situation demands, be cunning, devious and Machiavellian? In short, should America, along with its idealism, also practice realpolitik? And won't these two forces be in constant practical and moral conflict?

It's difficult to exercise authority in large parts of the world and, to use Hobbes' phrase, "keep them all in awe," without a touch of realpolitik. Britain discovered this in the 19th century, just as the Romans had two millennia before. Moreover, as British statesmen such as Benjamin Disraeli and Robert Cecil, Lord Salisbury, found, imperial realpolitik expressed itself principally in two cynical maxims: "Divide and rule" and "My enemy's enemy is my friend." These two maxims are rearing their heads again in the Middle East, and almost unwittingly—and certainly not from any set purpose—the U.S. finds itself following them.

U.S. intervention in Iraq has had the inevitable consequence of fueling the Sunni-Shia feud, which has raged in Islam for 1,000 years at varying degrees of intensity. It's now running hotter than ever, and likely to get worse, as more and more of the Middle East is drawn into it. Of course, with the Sunnis fighting the Shia, they have less time and energy to fight the West, and America finds it easier to rule. But this raises moral dilemmas that the U.S. has so far failed to resolve or publicly recognize.

8 Another situation where realpolitik could come into play is Iran's nuclear power quest. The moment Iran possesses and can deliver nuclear bombs it will use them against Israel, destroying the entire country and its inhabitants. If this danger becomes imminent, Israel has the means—if suitably assisted—to launch a preemptive strike. Should the U.S. provide such assistance and moral encouragement?

China's progress in advanced military technology, especially Star Wars–like rocket defenses, is also giving American strategists problems: How should the U.S. react? The realpolitik answer would be to assist India, China's natural rival and potential antagonist in east and central Asia, to achieve technological parity. But would it be right to do so?

These kinds of questions can arise almost anywhere but do so especially around ruthless totalitarian regimes that are attempting to acquire more military power than is safe to allow them. North Korea is a case in point. It's one thing for the U.S. to make clear that it will defend its allies, such as South Korea and Japan, from nuclear threats. That is straightforward and honorable. But the realpolitik solution would be to assist and encourage China to deal with the problem of a nuclear-armed and aggressive North Korea, the strategy being based on another old maxim: "Set a thief to catch a thief."

I don't envy those in Washington whose duty it is to resolve the dilemma between idealism and realpolitik. But they will not go far wrong if they respect the great tripod on which all geopolitical wisdom rests: the rule of law, the consultation of the people and the certitude that, however strong we may be, we are answerable to a higher power.

PERSONAL RESPONSE

How do you answer Johnson's question in paragraph 2: "Would you really like to live in a world where the U.S. sits idly by and lets things happen?"

QUESTIONS FOR CLASS OR SMALL-GROUP DISCUSSION

1. Explain the title. In what ways is America idealistic? In what ways must it practice realpolitik, according to Johnson? Do you agree with Johnson on these points?

2. Johnson writes that America's idealism conflicts with its role as "the world's policeman," which "raises moral issues" (paragraph 6)? What do you understand him to mean by that?
3. Johnson mentions several examples of the U.S.'s efforts to help other countries and the "practical and moral conflict" that results. Can you provide other, similar examples to illustrate that point?
4. Comment on the effectiveness of Johnson's conclusion.

STILL NOT TIRED

THOMAS L. FRIEDMAN

Thomas L. Friedman has written for the New York Times *since 1981. In 1995, he became the paper's foreign affairs columnist. Friedman was awarded the 1983 Pulitzer Prize for international reporting (from Lebanon) and the 1988 Pulitzer Prize for international reporting (from Israel). In 2002, he won the Pulitzer Prize for commentary. His book* From Beirut to Jerusalem *(1989) won the National Book Award for nonfiction in 1989.* The Lexus and the Olive Tree: Understanding Globalization *won the 2000 Overseas Press Club award for best nonfiction book on foreign policy and has been published in twenty languages. He is also author of* Longitudes and Attitudes: Exploring the World after September 11 *(2002);* The World is Flat: A Brief History of the Twenty-First Century *(2005);* Hot, Flat, and Crowded: Why We Need a Green Revolution—and How it Can Renew America *(2008). This op-ed column was published in the October 4, 2009, issue of the* New York Times.

He didn't want to wear earplugs. Apparently, he wanted to enjoy the blast.

That is what *The Dallas Morning News* reported about Hosam Maher Husein Smadi, the 19-year-old Jordanian accused of trying to blow up a downtown Dallas skyscraper. He was caught by an F.B.I. sting operation that culminated in his arrest nearly two weeks ago—after Smadi parked a 2001 Ford Explorer Sport Trac, supplied by the F.B.I., in the garage of a Dallas office tower.

"Inside the S.U.V. was a fake bomb, designed to appear similar to one used by Timothy McVeigh in the 1995 Oklahoma City bombing," *The News* wrote. "Authorities say Smadi thought he could detonate it with a cellphone. After parking the vehicle, he got into another vehicle with one of the agents, and they drove several blocks away. An agent offered Smadi earplugs, but he declined, 'indicating that he wanted to hear the blast,' authorities said. He then dialed the phone, thinking it would trigger the bomb. . . . Instead, the agents took him into custody."

4 If that doesn't send a little shiver down your spine, how about this one? BBC.com reported that "it has emerged that an Al Qaeda bomber who died last month

while trying to blow up a Saudi prince in Jeddah had hidden the explosives inside his body." He reportedly inserted the bomb and detonator in his rectum to elude metal detectors. My God.

Or how about this? Two weeks ago in Denver, the F.B.I. arrested Najibullah Zazi, a 24-year-old Afghan immigrant, and indicted him on charges of planning to set off a bomb made of the same home-brewed explosives used in the 2005 London transit bombings. He allegedly learned how to do so on a training visit to Pakistan. The *Times* reported that Zazi "had bought some bomb ingredients in beauty supply stores, the authorities said, after viewing instructions on his laptop on how to build such a bomb. When an employee of the Beauty Supply Warehouse asked about the volume of materials he was buying, he remembered Mr. Zazi answering, 'I have a lot of girlfriends.'"

These incidents are worth reflecting on. They tell us some important things. First, we may be tired of this "war on terrorism," but the bad guys are not. They are getting even more "creative."

Second, in this war on terrorism, there is no "good war" or "bad war." There is one war with many fronts, including Europe and our own backyard, requiring many different tactics. It is a war within Islam, between an often too-silent Muslim mainstream and a violent, motivated, often nihilistic jihadist minority. Theirs is a war over how and whether Islam should embrace modernity. It is a war fueled by humiliation—humiliation particularly among young Muslim males who sense that their faith community has fallen behind others, in terms of both economic opportunity and military clout. This humiliation has spawned various jihadist cults, including Al Qaeda, which believe they have the God-given right to kill infidels, their own secular leaders and less pious Muslims to purify Islam and Islamic lands and thereby restore Muslim grandeur.

8 Third, the newest and maybe most active front in this war is not Afghanistan, but the "virtual Afghanistan"—the loose network of thousands of jihadist Web sites, mosques and prayer groups that recruit, inspire and train young Muslims to kill without any formal orders from Al Qaeda. The young man in Dallas came to F.B.I. attention after espousing war on the U.S. on jihadist Web sites.

Fourth, in the short run, winning this war requires effective police/intelligence action, to kill or capture the jihadists. I call that "the war on terrorists." In the long run, though, winning requires partnering with Arab and Muslim societies to help them build thriving countries, integrated with the world economy, where young people don't grow up in a soil poisoned by religious extremists and choked by petro-dictators so they can never realize their aspirations. I call this "the war on terrorism." It takes a long time.

Our operation in Afghanistan after 9/11 was, for me, only about "the war on terrorists." It was about getting bin Laden. Iraq was "the war on terrorism"—trying to build a decent, pluralistic, consensual government in the heart of the Arab-Muslim world. Despite all we've paid, the outcome in Iraq remains uncertain. But it was at least encouraging to see last week's decision by Prime Minister Nuri Kamal al-Maliki to run in the next election with a nonsectarian, multireligious coalition—a rare thing in the Arab world.

So, what President Obama is actually considering in Afghanistan is shifting from a "war on terrorists" there to a "war on terrorism," including nation-building. I still have serious doubts that we have a real Afghan government partner for that. But if Mr. Obama decides to send more troops, the most important thing is not the number. It is his commitment to see it through. If he seems ambivalent, no one there will stand with us and we'll have no chance. If he seems committed, maybe—maybe—we'll find enough allies. Remember, the bad guys are totally committed—and they are not tired.

PERSONAL RESPONSE

Write about your emotional responses to the news of terrorist attacks. Do you have a vivid memory of the events of September 11, 2001, or of more recent terrorist activities?

Questions for Class or Small-Group Discussion

1. Explain the title. Who is "still not tired"?
2. Comment on the effectiveness of Friedman's opening paragraph. Why do you think he used those two sentences rather than other details he might have chosen? How does his opening relate to his central point?
3. Discuss the organization of this essay. Why do you think Friedman begins with a series of brief sketches or examples? How do they lead to his central purpose? What is gained or lost by not beginning with his thesis or central point?
4. State in your own words the distinction that Friedman makes between "the war on terrorists" and "the war on terrorism." Do you agree with him that there is a difference? Do you view the two types of war as he does, or do you view them differently?

LESSONS FROM WORLD WAR II

CATHY YOUNG

Cathy Young (Ekaterina Jung) is a journalist and writer. Born in Russia, she immigrated to the United States with her family in 1980 at the age of seventeen and is a graduate of Rutgers University. She writes a monthly column for Reason *magazine and a weekly one for both the* Boston Globe *and* RealClearPolitics.com. *Young is author of* Growing Up in Moscow: Memories of a Soviet Girlhood *(1989) and* Cease Fire: Why Women and Men Must Join Forces to Achieve Equality *(1999). This article was published on May 14, 2009, at* RealClearPolitics.com.

This past weekend marked 64 years since the surrender of Nazi Germany and the Allied victory in Europe in World War II (May 8, except in Russia and a few other former Soviet republics where it is commemorated on May 9). In the United States, this date generally receives little notice except on the major anniversaries; in Russia, Victory Day is the most important public holiday, celebrated with much pomp and circumstance. Yet in any country directly affected by World War II, that war holds a unique place in our collective cultural and historical consciousness—a living past that continues to influence the way we see the present.

In modern-day Russia, victory in "the Great Patriotic War" is probably the only major event of the last hundred years that everyone can celebrate, regardless of political beliefs. The war, which took up to 14 million lives in Russia (and as many as 27 million in the entire Soviet Union), and caused untold hardship and suffering to most survivors, is a sacred memory, a source of both grief and rightful pride. For people who saw the collapse of Communism and were suddenly told that the Soviet experiment had not been a glorious struggle for a better future but a 70-year road to nowhere, it means a great deal to know that their country's role in the defeat of Nazism is still a victory they can believe in.

There is, however, a darker side to this legacy. Russian apologists for Communism use the victory in World War II as a validation of the Soviet regime—and sometimes as an excuse for the odious rule of Joseph Stalin, Hitler's rival in butchery. In recent years, the Russian government has exploited the war to promote the image of Russia as a benign power and denigrate the claims of Eastern European countries and former Soviet republics which see themselves as victims not only of Nazi Germany but of Soviet Communism as well.

4 The glorified official Russian view of the war also ignores the extent to which the wartime suffering of the Russian people was inflicted by their own leadership. There is little mention of the fact that untrained, ill-equipped draftees were used as cannon fodder, that regular troops were routinely followed by special units which shot at soldiers who tried to retreat, or Soviet soldiers taken prisoner by the Germans were branded traitors for surrendering and often sent to the gulag prison camps for their homecoming.

But we too have our World War II blind spots—sometimes, ironic mirror images of the Russian ones. Russians commonly downplay the role of American and British allies in defeating the German war machine; Americans, much to the annoyance of Russians, often talk as if we almost single-handedly liberated Europe from Nazism. We, too, remain in thrall to the myth of "The Good War" that often glosses over some of the less noble actions taken on our own side. Even those on the left who denounce the bombing of Hiroshima and the internment of Japanese-Americans rarely mention the firebombing of German cities or the well-documented mistreatment of German civilians and POWs. Little is said about the morality of handing over Eastern Europe to Stalin, or of forcibly repatriating to the USSR Soviet POWs and other Soviet nationals who faced harsh punitive measures and sometimes execution without trial.

The "Good War," like the Good Book, can be put in the service of any agenda. Conservatives invoke it to justify military action: "What about Hitler?" is a devastating, if cliché, rebuttal to the pacifist insistence that there is never a good reason to start a war. It is, to some extent, an unfair argument that much too easily confers the status of Hitler on our enemy of the day. But it also makes a valid and important point: evil does exist (if usually on a smaller scale than Nazism), and to refuse to fight it is to ensure its triumph.

For liberals, particularly in response to the War on Terror and its excesses, World War II is the foremost example of how we were able to defeat a formidable enemy without abandoning our core principles, such as humane treatment of prisoners. But that is not so simple, either. After President Obama's statement attributing the line, "We do not torture," to Sir Winston Churchill, there were revelations that at least one British facility for captive Germans did, in fact, use brutal methods that qualify as torture—though probably without Churchill's knowledge. Besides, are brutal interrogation methods a worse departure from our moral principles than killing civilians in indiscriminate air raids?

8 Despite its darkest moments, World War II remains "the Good War"—not because we were impeccably good, but because we fought an enemy that was as close as one can be to pure evil. It also belies the popular notion that if we cross certain moral lines to achieve our war aims, we will become just as bad as the enemy: the staggering casualties in the firebombing of Dresden notwithstanding, Churchill did not "sink to the level" of the leaders of the Third Reich.

World War II reminds us about the limits of idealism. Looking back, many people wonder if we would have won the war with the level of media openness and respect for human rights that we have today. That's a legitimate question—but its seamy side is a dangerous nostalgia for a "simpler" time when soldiers could do their job without having to think of sissy stuff like rights and legalities.

Perhaps the real lesson of World War II is that a free, civilized society at war will always seek to strike some balance between self-defense and principle. Sometimes, it will err badly. To defend these errors as fully justified is to betray our own values and start on a road that leads to the kind of authoritarian mindset so rampant in Putin's Russia. To condemn them with no understanding of their context is a self-righteous utopian posture that, in the end, does liberal values a disservice.

PERSONAL RESPONSE

Thinking about what you have studied in school or been told about it, write about what World War II means to you.

QUESTIONS FOR CLASS OR SMALL-GROUP DISCUSSION

1. According to Young, how do Russia and the United States differ in the way they commemorate the Allied victory in Europe in World War II? How does that contrast relate to her thesis?
2. What do you understand the phrase "The Good War" to mean? Why does Young call it a "myth" (paragraph 5)?

3. In what ways, according to Young, does World War II remind us of "the limits of idealism" (paragraph 8). Do you agree with her?
4. What are the "lessons from World War II" (title)?

NOW SHOWING: THE GOOD, THE BAD AND THE UGLY AMERICANS

MARTHA BAYLES

Martha Bayles teaches humanities at Boston College. She is author of Hole in Our Soul: The Loss of Beauty and Meaning in American Popular Music *(1994) and* The Ugly Americans: How Not to Lose the Global Cultural War *(2009). This essay first appeared in the* Washington Post *on August 28, 2005.*

When Benjamin Franklin went to France in 1776, his assignment was to manipulate the French into supporting the American war for independence. This he accomplished with two stratagems: First, he played the balance-of-power game as deftly as any European diplomat; and second, he waged a subtle but effective campaign of what we now call public diplomacy, or the use of information and culture to foster goodwill toward the nation. For Franklin, this meant turning his dumpy self into a symbol. "He knew that America had a unique and powerful meaning for the enlightened reformers of France," writes historian Bernard Bailyn, "and that he himself . . . was the embodiment, the palpable expression, of that meaning." Hence the fur cap and rustic manner that made Franklin a celebrity among the powdered wigs and gilded ornaments of the court of Louis XVI.

Today, as we witness the decline of America's reputation around the world, we're paying far more attention to Franklin's first stratagem than to his second. Indeed, despite a mounting stack of reports recommending drastic changes in the organization and funding of public diplomacy, very little of substance has been done. And most Americans, including many who make it their business to analyze public diplomacy, seem unmindful of the negative impression that America has recently been making on the rest of humanity—via our popular culture.

A striking pattern has emerged since the end of the Cold War. On the one hand, funding for public diplomacy has been cut by more than 30 percent since 1989, the National Science Board reported last year. On the other hand, while Washington was shrinking its funding for cultural diplomacy, Hollywood was aggressively expanding its exports. The Yale Center for the Study of Globalization reports that between 1986 and 2000 the fees generated by the export of filmed and taped entertainment went from $1.68 billion to $8.85 billion—an increase of 427 percent. Foreign box-office revenue has grown faster than domestic, and now approaches a 2-to-1 ratio. The pattern is similar for music, TV and video games.

4 This massive export of popular culture has been accompanied by domestic worries about its increasingly coarse and violent tone—worries that now go beyond the polarized debates of the pre-9/11 culture war. For example, a number of prominent African Americans, such as Bill Stephney, co-founder of the rap group Public Enemy, have raised concerns about the normalization of crime and prostitution in gangsta and "crunk" rap. And in April 2005, the Pew Research Center reported that "roughly six-in-ten [Americans] say they are very concerned over what children see or hear on TV (61%), in music lyrics (61%), video games (60%) and movies (56%)."

These worries now have a global dimension. The 2003 report of the U.S. House of Representatives Advisory Group on Public Diplomacy for the Arab and Muslim World stated that "Arabs and Muslims are . . . bombarded with American sitcoms, violent films, and other entertainment, much of which distorts the perceptions of viewers." The report made clear that what seems innocuous to Americans can cause problems abroad: "A Syrian teacher of English asked us plaintively for help in explaining American family life to her students. She asked, 'Does "Friends" show a typical family?'"

One of the few efforts to measure the impact of popular culture abroad was made by Louisiana State University researchers Melvin and Margaret DeFleur, who in 2003 polled teenagers in 12 countries: Saudi Arabia, Bahrain, South Korea, Mexico, China, Spain, Taiwan, Lebanon, Pakistan, Nigeria, Italy and Argentina. Their conclusion, while tentative, is nonetheless suggestive: "The depiction of Americans in media content as violent, of American women as sexually immoral and of many Americans engaging in criminal acts has brought many of these 1,313 youthful subjects to hold generally negative attitudes toward people who live in the United States."

Popular culture is not a monolith, of course. Along with a lot of junk, the entertainment industry still produces films, musical recordings, even television shows that rise to the level of genuine art. The good (and bad) news is that censorship is a thing of the past, on both the producing and the consuming end of popular culture. Despite attempts by radical clerics in Iraq to clamp down on Western influences, pirated copies of American movies still make it onto the market there. If we go by box office figures, the most popular films in the world are blockbusters like "Harry Potter." But America is also exporting more than enough depictions of profanity, nudity, violence and criminal activity to violate norms of propriety still honored in much of the world.

8 But instead of questioning whether Americans should be super-sizing to others the same cultural diet that is giving us indigestion at home, we still seem to congratulate ourselves that our popular culture now pervades just about every society on Earth, including many that would rather keep it out. Why this disconnect? Partly it is due to an ingrained belief that what's good for show business is good for America's image. During both world wars, the movie studios produced propaganda for the government, in exchange for government aid in opening resistant foreign markets. Beginning in 1939, the recording industry cooperated with the Armed Forces Network to beam jazz to American soldiers overseas, and during the Cold War it helped the Voice of America (VOA) do the same for 30 million listeners behind the Iron Curtain.

In his book, *Cultural Exchange & the Cold War,* veteran foreign service officer Yale Richmond quotes the Russian novelist Vasily Aksyonov, for whom those VOA jazz broadcasts were "America's secret weapon number one." Aksyonov said that "the snatches of music and bits of information made for a kind of golden glow over the horizon . . . the West, the inaccessible but oh so desirable West."

To my knowledge, this passage has not been quoted in defense of Radio Sawa, the flagship of the U.S. government's new fleet of broadcast channels aimed at reaching young, largely Arab audiences. But even if it were, who could imagine such a reverent, yearning listener in the Middle East, South Asia or anywhere else today? The difference is not just between short-wave radio and unlimited broadband; it is also between Duke Ellington and 50 Cent.

During the Cold War, Washington also boosted the commercial export of popular culture, adhering to the view set forth in a 1948 State Department memo: "American motion pictures, as ambassadors of good will—at no cost to the American taxpayers—interpret the American way of life to all the nations of the world, which may be invaluable from a political, cultural, and commercial point of view."

12 And this boosterism continued through the 1960s and '70s, even as movies and rock music became not just unruly but downright adversarial. During the 1970s, the government worked so hard to pry open world markets to American entertainment that UNESCO and the Soviet Union led a backlash against "U.S. cultural imperialism." In 1967, the VOA began to broadcast rock and soul. And while a provocative figure like Frank Zappa was hardly a favorite at diplomatic receptions, many in the foreign service understood his symbolic importance to dissidents, including Czech playwright (and later president) Vaclev Havel. In general, the U.S. political establishment was content to let America's homegrown counterculture do its subversive thing in Eastern Europe and Russia.

In the 1980s, the mood changed. Under Ronald Reagan appointee Charles Z. Wick, the United States Information Agency (USIA), the autonomous agency set up in 1953 to disseminate information and handle cultural exchange, was more generously funded and invited to play a larger role in policymaking—but at the price of having its autonomy curbed and the firewall between cultural outreach and policy advocacy thinned. It is noteworthy that these changes occurred amid the acrimony of the culture wars. Like the National Endowment for the Arts and public broadcasting, the USIA eventually found itself on Sen. Jesse Helms's list of artsy agencies deserving of the budgetary ax. And while the others managed to survive, the USIA did not. In 1999 it was absorbed into the very different bureaucratic culture of the State Department.

Today we witness the outcome: an unwarranted dismissal of elite-oriented cultural diplomacy, combined with an unquestioned faith in the export of popular culture. These converge in the decision to devote the bulk of post-9/11 funding to Radio Sawa and the other commercial-style broadcast entities, such as al-Hurra (a U.S.-based satellite TV network aimed at Arab listeners) and Radio Farda (which is broadcast in Farsi to Iran). Because the establishment of these new channels has been accompanied by the termination of the VOA's Arabic service, critics have focused largely on their news components. But what benefit is there in Radio Sawa's heavy rotation of songs by sex kitten Britney Spears and foul-mouthed rapper Eminem?

To the charge that the Bush administration is peddling smut and profanity to Arab teens, Radio Sawa's music director, Usama Farag, has stated that all the offensive lyrics are carefully edited out. Yet there is something quaint about the U.S. government's censoring song lyrics in a world where most people have ready access to every product of the American entertainment industry, including the dregs.

14 American popular culture is no longer a beacon of freedom to huddled masses in closed societies. Instead, it's a glut on the market and, absent any countervailing cultural diplomacy, our de facto ambassador to the world. The solution to this problem is far from clear. Censorship is not the answer, because even if it were technologically possible to censor our cultural exports, it would not be politic. The United States must affirm the crucial importance of free speech in a world that has serious doubts about it, and the best way to do this is to show that freedom is self-correcting—that Americans have not only liberty but also a civilization worthy of liberty.

From Franklin's days, U.S. cultural diplomacy has had both an elite and a popular dimension. Needless to say, it has rarely been easy to achieve a perfect balance between the two. What we could do is try harder to convey what the USIA mandate used to call "a full and fair picture of the United States." But to succeed even a little, our new efforts must counter the negative self-portrait we are now exporting. Along with worrying about what popular culture is teaching our children about life, we need also to worry about what it is teaching the world about America.

PERSONAL RESPONSE

What is your opinion of America's pop culture exports, particularly Hollywood films? Do you think they convey a negative image of America?

QUESTIONS FOR CLASS OR SMALL-GROUP DISCUSSION

1. How does the opening paragraph about Franklin relate to the rest of the essay?
2. Bayles writes in paragraph 2 of "the negative impression that America has recently been making on the rest of humanity—via our popular culture." What examples of popular culture can you give that support or refute this statement?
3. State in your own words what you understand Bayles to mean when she writes that we have "an unwarranted dismissal of elite-oriented cultural diplomacy, combined with an unquestioned faith in the export of popular culture" (paragraph 14).
4. Bayles believes that the solution to the problem of the negative image that popular culture gives to people in other countries "is far from clear" (paragraph 16) and concludes that we could "try harder to convey . . . 'a full and fair picture of the United States'" (paragraph 17). Discuss possible solutions to the problem and ways to convey a better, fuller picture of America.

✧ PERSPECTIVES ON AMERICA FOREIGN POLICY ✧

Suggestions for Writing

1. Explain your position on the question of whether America should be responsible for defending weaker countries from oppression.
2. Respond to Paul Johnson's "American Idealism and Realpolitik," either agreeing or disagreeing with him and using examples to support your position.
3. Support or argue against this statement by Thomas Friedman in "Still Not Tired": "[I]n this war on terrorism, there is no 'good war' or 'bad war.' There is one war with many fronts" (paragraph 7).
4. Expand on, explain, or respond to this statement by Cathy Young in "Lessons from World War II": "[A] free, civilized society at war will always seek to strike some balance between self-defense and principle" (paragraph 9).
5. Drawing on Martha Bayles's "Now Showing: The Good, the Bad and the Ugly Americans," explain what you think ordinary American citizens can do to help improve the image of America abroad.
6. Explain the effect that America's wealth, power, commercialism, or any other aspect of its culture has on the way America is perceived by people in other nations.
7. Select a recent popular film and analyze the image of America that it projects, or, do a close analysis of a person or object from popular culture that you think represents an aspect of American culture.
8. Analyze an American book or story for the image it projects of America. Try to view the book or story objectively, as if you were a foreigner looking for information about America. What impression do you think a foreigner reading the same book or story would get of America?
9. Explore the effects of the September 11, 2001, terrorist attacks on America. In what ways did they change America?
10. Analyze the responses of people in other nations to the September 11, 2001, terrorist attacks.
11. Explain your viewpoint on the issue of how far the state should be allowed to restrict civil liberties for the sake of national security.
12. Write a personal essay explaining your feelings about the September 11, 2001, terrorist attacks and/or how you see them affecting you or your generation in the years to come.
13. Explore the effects on people of a serious event like a terrorist attack, an automobile accident, an encounter with random violence, or a close brush with death. How does such an event affect their sense of security and the way in which they think about their own lives? Use personal experience or observation to write your essay.

Research Topics

1. Research the subject of America's "soft power" in the period following the September 11, 2001, terrorist attacks on American soil.

2. Research the subject of anti-Americanism in countries other than America, whether it exists and, if so, why it exists and how strong it is.
3. Conduct library research to expand on the views expressed by writers in this chapter on America's foreign policy, America's war on terrorism, or the lessons that a previous war has for us today. You should be able to narrow your focus and determine a central idea for your paper after your preliminary search for sources and early review of the materials.
4. Research the subject of U.S. relations with Japan, China, the Soviet Union, the Middle East, or another foreign country that may figure importantly in the future of the United States. On the basis of your research, assess the importance to the United States of strengthening such relations and the potential effects of allowing relations with that country to deteriorate.
5. Research the conditions surrounding America's involvement in Bosnia, Kuwait, or Kosovo. Limit your focus to one aspect of the subject, such as what led to America's involvement, what America's involvement meant to American citizens, or effects on the country of America's intervention. Then argue the extent to which you support that involvement.
6. Martha Bayles in "Now Showing: The Good, the Bad and the Ugly Americans" opens her essay with a reference to Benjamin Franklin's public diplomacy in France. Research the subject of Franklin's success at diplomacy. What were his goals, what strategies did he use, and do you think they have application to the United States' efforts to improve public diplomacy today?
7. Research the effects of the September 11, 2001, terrorist attacks in New York and Washington on the American economy, the American image abroad, or America's role in international politics. All of these topics are broad, so after selecting one, narrow it down further. For instance, you might begin by asking what the economic effects of the attacks were on the airline industry, investment firms, or the stock exchange, and then further narrow your focus as you begin reading on the subject.
8. Research the subject of what led to the events of September 11, 2001, or to another large-scale act of terrorism. What motivated the terrorist attacks? How can one explain why they happened?
9. Research the impact of the events of September 11, 2001, and the war on terrorism on Muslim Americans.
10. Research the role of other nations in coalition-building following the terrorist attacks in New York and Washington on September 11, 2001.
11. Research the subject of how extremist Muslims contrast with moderate and secularist Muslims. Look at the beliefs and actions of both and identify major areas of difference.
12. Following the terrorist attacks against New York and Washington on September 11, 2001, the North Atlantic Treaty Organization (NATO) invoked article 5 of its mutual defense treaty. Research the purpose of NATO and assess its role in the aftermath of the September 11 attacks.

Responding to Visuals

12th March 1946: Commuters boarding a tram in bomb-damaged Dresden, Germany

1. What is the overall effect of the people boarding a tram amidst the rubble of their damaged city?
2. What image of war does the photograph convey?
3. Comment on the contrast between the buildings that are still standing in the background and the rubble.

Responding to Visuals

Protesters burn American flag during demonstrations in the western Pakistani city of Peshawar, October 12, 2001

1. What is going on in this picture? Select details that convey the overall meaning of the picture.
2. What are the implications of the many cameras and video recorders at this event? Does the rhetorical effectiveness of flag burning depend on its being photographed? Does a gesture such as burning a flag need to be recorded visually in order to be effective? How does capturing the event on film or tape aid its effectiveness as a public expression of protest?
3. How would the meaning of the image change if the photographer had done a close-up of the burning flag, excluding the crowd?

PART • FOUR

Science and Technology

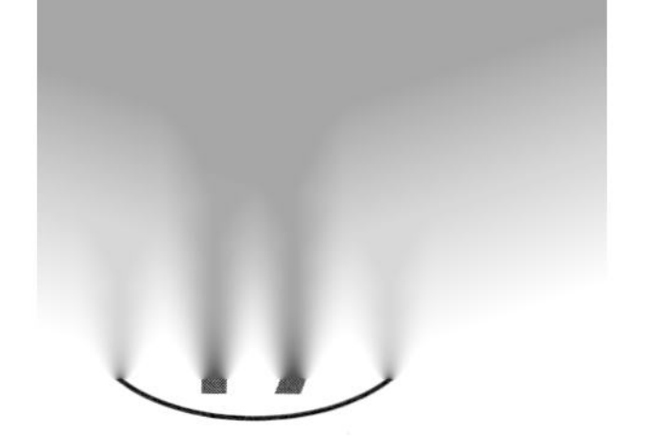

Digital Technology and the Internet

Digital technology is constantly changing, with exciting new, ever-faster programs emerging frequently. Although early researchers recognized the potential of computers, no doubt few of them envisioned the staggering capabilities of what they can do or the extent to which they would be so closely and inextricably linked with people's everyday lives. Increasingly sophisticated computers make child's play of activities that just a few years ago were challenging or impossible tasks. Young children today learn skills—sometimes before they enter school—that many of their grandparents and certainly their great-grandparents will never even try to learn. Indeed, computer technology has advanced at such a rapid rate that its powers seem unlimited, a prospect that fills some with eager anticipation and leaves others feeling intimidated and frightened.

Cyberspace, a word coined by author William Gibson in his sci-fi novel *Neuromancer*, commonly refers to the nonphysical space and sense of community created by Internet users around the world, the virtual "world" that users inhabit when they are online. People can communicate and share files on the Internet through e-mail and at websites; they can conduct research, shop, play games, and do any number of activities that people have been accustomed to do in physical space. The difference, of course, is that all those activities take place by pressing keys on a keyboard, moving a mouse around, or using a touchpad. Such convenience has changed the way many people conduct their lives, most would say in a positive way. However, the high-tech capabilities of the Internet have also led to problems. The readings in this chapter look at some of those problems as well as the benefits of such technology.

The first two readings focus on the Internet and other technological advances with an article on MySpace and one that muses on the importance in education of twenty-first-century technology. Cindy Long writes to an audience of educators about the benefits and potential dangers of MySpace, a social networking site founded in 2003, that originally appealed primarily to high school, middle school, and even grade school students, but now is a site used by just about anyone, including politicians, movie stars, and other celebrities. Many schools have blocked students from using MySpace because of its potential as a site where sexual predators could lurk and because some students post questionable content, such as too much personal information or obscene, damaging, or hurtful language. Long's essay cites the opinions of students and teachers on both positive and negative aspects of MySpace. Although the popularity of MySpace has been eclipsed by Facebook and Twitter, the benefits and drawbacks remain virtually the same for all social networking sites.

Then, a high school educator responds to a widespread belief that, given all the technology available in the classroom today, this is perhaps "The Most Important Moment of All Time" in education. Technology has certainly brought changes to the classroom, but Grant Calder wonders whether this is really the dawn of a new age: "Will more computers in schools, more Internet access, more curricular materials in varied media, more 'tweeting,' more use of social networking tools, and more globally oriented curricula transform this generation of students in some world-changing way?" As you read his answer to that question, consider how you would answer it.

Following Calder is an essay by Steven Johnson, a writer very much interested in the intersection of technology and the personal, that is, the ways in which the incredible advances in technology affect individual lives. In "Social Connections," Johnson responds to an op-ed piece by Thomas Friedman, in which Friedman suggests that our abilities to communicate instantly because of all the technological devices available to us might actually prevent one-on-one personal communication. Technology, Friedman wrote, actually drives us apart rather than brings us together. Johnson takes exception to this view and explains why he feels just the opposite of Friedman. As you read Johnson's argument, consider whose position you find yourself agreeing with.

The chapter concludes with a look at a relatively new concern in digital technology, aspects of which raise grave concerns for many people, the implantation of a radio frequency identification (RFID) microchip into humans that emits a radio signal with an identification number. The device was originally designed to be linked to medical records for use by heart patients, people with implanted medical devices such as defibrillators, patients who need frequent medical care, and the mentally impaired. Since the FDA approved chip implantation for these uses in 2004, there has been much discussion about the ethics of such chips, particularly concerning privacy. The concern is that the wrong people might gain access to the patient's information or that the information can be used against the patient, such as by an employer or insurance company. Todd Lewan's article "Chips: High Tech Aids or Tracking Tools?" is particularly interested in the privacy issues raised by the relatively new use of RFIDs as human tracking devices and as identification for people in certain high-security positions. He looks at the opinions of both supporters and detractors of their use and identifies a number of the questions that people have about them. As you read his article, consider whether you might agree to have such a device implanted in your body.

I NEED MY SPACE!

CINDY LONG

Cindy Long is a Washington, D.C.–based writer who covers education and technology. This essay appeared in the April 2007 issue of NEA Today, *a publication for educators who are members of the National Education Association.*

When Caitlyn McNeill started high school last year, she wished she could take all of her middle school friends with her. Unfortunately, only half of the 16-year-old's friends joined her at Northern High in Owings, Maryland, while the other half went to school in the neighboring town. They still manage to keep in close touch, chatting almost as often as they did when they walked the halls and ate lunch together. The only difference is that now they hang out on MySpace.com, the Web site that has become the 21st century's answer to the 1950s soda shop.

Caitlyn and her friends log on to MySpace to catch up with each other, post bulletins about what's new, and chat about friends, school, weekend plans, and, of course, boys. They decorate their MySpace pages the way they might decorate their bedrooms, complete with colorful, patterned backgrounds and photos; Caitlyn's page is greenish-blue with a star pattern. "It's bright and really cute," she says. Along with posting pictures of themselves and their friends, they link to videos and MP3 files. "My friend has a video from the Fresh Prince of Bel-Air, where Will and Carlton are doing a dance," says Caitlyn. "It's hilarious."

It's all part of the social networking revolution, in which users build personal pages and use those pages to share information, chat online, and keep in touch with others. Hundreds of such sites exist, but MySpace leads the way. It's the third most visited Web site in the United States (behind Yahoo! and Google), averaging 36 million page views a day. Of the millions, many are students. Right now, more than half of American kids online use social networking sites, according to a Pew Internet & American Life Project survey of teenagers.

4 Making connections is what powers the popularity of sites like MySpace, but it can also be cause for concern. News stories abound of online predators stalking young girls and boys by way of their profiles and luring teens, even preteens, into dangerous situations. Some kids post photographs of themselves in less-than-virtuous poses, in barely-there outfits—or worse, in incriminating situations—for all the world to see, including college admissions officers and potential employers. Students have also posted nasty comments about their classmates and teachers. In fact, more than one in three educators surveyed by the National School Boards Association (NSBA)—some 36 percent—said social networking sites have been disruptive at school.

But tell students about the concerns surrounding sites like MySpace, and the common refrain is one adults have been hearing from teenagers since the Stone Age: "You worry too much!" As media-savvy technophiles, they realize some of their peers misuse the Web, but they're asking us to trust that most of them use it safely and responsibly. What's more, research backs up their claims. Most students take steps to protect their privacy, and in some schools, safety and social networking have become part of the curriculum. "Simply blocking access to MySpace at school is not the end of the story," said NSBA Executive Director Anne Bryant. "Students need to be educated about these sites and what the impact of misuse is on themselves as well as others."

Kathy Schrock, who helps educate students on technology issues in Nauset Public Schools on Cape Cod, comes at the problems of social networking with firsthand experience. For an entire year, she had an "imposter page," or fake profile, posted about her on MySpace by five students at a Catholic high school.

"The page they created for me was basically harmless, but it wasn't authentic and I wanted it taken down," says Schrock, the district's administrator for technology, whose "Guide for Educators" is found at www.discoveryschool.com. "I had to call the teacher, who didn't even know about MySpace. I wrote to the school, but the principal wouldn't take care of it. MySpace wouldn't even take it down."

8 That was a year ago. The bogus page has since come down, and MySpace is now quick to remove imposter pages. In fact, its frequently asked questions include, "How do we remove an imposter profile for a teacher/faculty member" and "Someone is pretending to be me—what do I do?"

While high-profile cases involving teenagers creating imposter pages for teachers and classmates have surfaced, Schrock is more concerned about students' safety. Her message to students is simple: if you have a profile, keep it private.

MySpace requires users to be at least 14, and profiles of MySpace users under 16 are automatically set to "private," so only the users they've allowed access can view their profile, send instant messages and e-mails, or add them to their blog list. But kids routinely lie about their ages—either that, or there are a surprising number of high school freshmen and sophomores age 20 or above on MySpace.

Last June, MySpace announced that privacy options would be available to users of all ages and that all users could block others from contacting them, conceal their "online now" status, and prevent others from e-mailing direct links to their images. MySpace users 18 or older can no longer add users under 16 to their friends list unless they already know the person's full name or e-mail address.

12 The new privacy options were announced after a 16-year-old girl tricked her parents into getting her a passport and then flew to the Mideast to be with a man she met on the site. It's one of the most extreme stories—of which there are only a smattering, considering the tens of millions of young people who visit the site regularly.

How often is regularly? "I go on MySpace every chance I get," Caitlyn McNeill says. She's not alone. According to the Pew study, 48 percent of teens visit social networking sites at least once every day.

Most of Caitlyn's MySpace habits align closely with the Pew findings, which show that young people are wise to the dangers posed by social networking sites. Caitlyn and her friends set their profiles to private; Pew found that 66 percent of teens have done the same. Caitlyn uses MySpace to keep in touch with her friends from school and to make plans; Pew found that 91 percent of teens use social networking sites to keep in touch with friends they see a lot, while 72 percent use the site to make plans with those friends. In fact, the tagline of the MySpace site is, "A place for friends."

Caitlyn is also a fairly savvy Internet user. "There are a lot of creeps out there, and I know it," she says. "I don't let anybody add me to their friends list, and I don't accept messages from anybody I haven't met in person. Also, if your profile is set to private, the people at school you don't like can't find out information about you."

16 Sarah Mortimer, who lives in New Hampshire, uses MySpace to keep in touch with friends both near and far. "Since I have switched schools a lot, I am able to keep in touch with kids from my old schools," the 16-year-old says. "It's just really nice to see someone I haven't talked to in, like, 10 years and remember them from my childhood." She has her profile set to private so "rapist killers don't get me," she says half-jokingly. But her profile also says she lives in Zimbabwe so that anyone searching in her town or ZIP code won't find her.

That's exactly the kind of Internet shrewdness Kim Conner, the computer teacher at Nauset Middle School, is trying to instill among her sixth-, seventh-, and eighth-graders. "One student put up Albert Einstein as his profile photo to help hide his identity," Conner says. "I thought that was rather clever."

Conner has worked social networking safety into the curriculum as a way to "make the kids aware of the different things that can happen when they use the sites without thinking," she says.

As is the case in most districts, Conner and her students can't access MySpace or other social networking sites at school, but she's saved screen shots that she uses to demonstrate how profiles that aren't set to private can reveal identifying details. For example, when kids allow their profiles and instant messages to be open, anyone can read plans they might make online. She uses the following as an example:

NAUSETGIRL (5:09:55): wotz ^? wnt 2 go out?
WARRIOR08 (5:09:56): yS, whr do wnt 2 go?
NAUSETGRIL (5:09:57): How bout the chocl@ Sparrow n Orleans?

20 Suddenly, anyone logged onto the page can see where the girls are meeting.

Conner also uses an example of a profile of a girl who thought she hadn't posted anything identifiable, except for a photo gallery image of her wearing her school's field hockey uniform.

But once students are aware of the dangers and are taught to think carefully about how they use sites like MySpace, Conner believes that the advantages outweigh the disadvantages. "It's really a great way for kids to stay connected outside of school," she says, adding that sometimes students get online and help each other with homework or work on assignments together. But the main benefit of sites like MySpace is that they "allow young people to express themselves, be creative, and show their friends who they really are," says Conner. "It gives them a common venue."

Chris Luty, a senior at Kennedy High School in Silver Spring, Maryland, expresses himself on his MySpace profile with photos, videos, music files, and different fonts and backgrounds. Parents and teachers beware—what kids like Chris might find appealing about their profiles would probably cross the eyes of most adults. On many teen profiles, backgrounds are a blur of vibrant colors, patterns, and clashing, often unreadable fonts, splattered with links and images. But their friends can tell a lot about their sense of humor by the videos they post, or about their musical tastes by the bands they promote.

24 Chris's profile includes an Adam Sandler video and videos of live performances by three of his favorite bands—Godsmack, 44, and Patent Pending. He says that all of his friends on MySpace are people he knows in "real life." Otherwise, he says, "I'd have no idea who was sitting behind that keyboard."

Kim Conner acknowledges that there have been problems with abuses of MySpace, but she says she approaches it with "the one bad apple doesn't spoil the whole bushel theory."

"Some really good things can come out of this," Conner says. "It gives all students a way to connect and be together in a safe environment. MySpace can be a very safe and positive thing."

PERSONAL RESPONSE

If you have (or have had) a MySpace or other social network account, write about your experiences with it. If you have never personally had an account, what have you observed of those you know who do have one?

QUESTIONS FOR CLASS OR SMALL-GROUP DISCUSSION

1. Comment on Long's use of examples. For instance, how effective do you find her opening paragraphs? How do they advance the development of her essay? Note other uses of example throughout the essay.
2. Long reports that over a third of the educators surveyed by the National School Boards Association (NSBA) said that "social networking sites have been disruptive at school" (paragraph 4). In what ways might such sites be disruptive? Do you believe they are disruptive?
3. Long quotes NSBA director Anne Bryant as saying that "'students need to be educated'" about sites like MySpace and their potential misuse. What sorts of things do you imagine that such an education would include? What warning or advice would you give a young person interested in such a site?
4. What, according to Long, are the benefits and drawbacks of a social networking account like MySpace? Long notes that Computer Teacher Kim Connor "believes [of sites like MySpace] that the advantages outweigh the disadvantages" (paragraph 21). Do you agree with her?

THE MOST IMPORTANT MOMENT OF ALL TIME?

GRANT CALDER

Grant Calder teaches history and is codirector of college counseling at Friends' Central School in Wynnewood, PA. This opinion piece was published in the Philadelphia Inquirer *on November 29, 2009.*

Many educators and education theorists seem to have bought into the notion that the early 21st century marks some kind of watershed in the history of the field. We do have some powerful new technologies to bring to bear on the learning process. And the daunting societal and environmental challenges that seem to lie ahead may demand some rethinking of our approach to educating our youth. On the other hand, our tendency to overestimate our importance as molders of young minds and our limited capacity to see into the future should suggest a cautious approach to these heralds of a new age.

One pedagogical pundit, Marc Prensky, believes that the brains of today's teenagers have already been physically altered by their use of computer-chip-driven devices of all sorts. "Digital natives" he calls them, and he says there is strong "indirect evidence" of this transformation. He goes on to claim that as their teachers, we cannot hope to effectively bridge the divide that separates us from this new breed unless we are willing to meet them on their turf (presumably somewhere in cyberspace). The old methods will no longer work.

I started teaching exactly 30 years ago, two years before IBM brought out its first PC. I told my current students that they had been dubbed "digital natives" and asked them whether they felt it was difficult to relate to someone of my pre-digital vintage. They thought I was joking.

4 Another contingent of innovators has latched on to training-our-children-for-global-citizenship as the new critical need. Advocates emphasize the central role technologies must play in creating a new generation of humans who perceive of themselves first as citizens of the world.

The presenters at a Global Education seminar I attended last spring repeatedly referred to this moment in history as pivotal, citing new data on population growth, environmental degradation, poverty, and the like. One of them quoted a British scientist who apparently believes that we live at the most important juncture not just in the four-billion-year history of the planet, but in the history of the cosmos! As far as I could tell, he was serious. I looked around at the audience and a few of them were nodding. None seemed to find the statement hard to swallow.

The catchiest phrase of the daylong event was a line taken from H.G. Wells, who once described humanity as in "a race between education and catastrophe." It perfectly fit the agenda of the session's designers and I can certainly see why they borrowed it. Context matters, however, particularly in subjects such as social studies.

I believe the phrase appeared in the introduction to the first edition of his 1,000-page volume, *The Outline of History*. The book traced the growth and development of the human family from its prehistoric origins to the 20th century. Wells wrote it in the immediate aftermath of the Great War (1914–1918). Wells believed, as did many contemporaries, that civilization might not survive another conflict on that scale and that a way must be found to prevent a repeat of this disaster. Wells saw education as the answer and hoped that a better understanding of our cultural and historical origins would help the world's people deal with each other more constructively and peacefully.

8 One can only applaud his efforts. Sadly, the name by which we now refer to that conflict—World War One—reflects the reality that many of the same people were at it again, killing millions more of each other and their children, two decades later.

Wells's reputation today rests primarily on his authorship of works of science fiction mostly written over a century ago. They include *War of the Worlds* and *The Island of Doctor Moreau*. These stories contained brilliantly prescient references to technologies that were often generations away from realization, yet Wells himself had no great hopes for a high-tech future. He famously said, "Every time I see an adult on a bicycle, I no longer despair for the human race."

The comment reminds me that many solutions to current problems can be found in already established technologies. The much greater challenge remains persuading people to commit to them. In the nation's classrooms, good teachers have been encouraging their students to think globally for decades. I still remember the special events held on the first Earth Day in 1970. We left the classroom and spent the day participating in rallies and cleanup projects. The experience helped shape my belief in the importance of finding ways to minimize our impact on the natural environment.

Is the early 21st century the most important moment in the history of the cosmos? Unlikely. Will more computers in schools, more Internet access, more curricular materials in varied media, more "tweeting," more use of social networking tools, and more globally oriented curricula transform this generation of students in some world-changing way? Probably not. Is there work to do? Absolutely. One worthwhile effort might be to get more kids (and adults) away from their digital devices and onto bikes.

PERSONAL RESPONSE

Grant notes that there are "powerful new technologies" in the classroom (paragraph 1). Write about the technologies available to you in the classroom, either now or when you were in high school.

QUESTIONS FOR CLASS OR SMALL-GROUP DISCUSSION

1. In paragraph 2, Calder explains the view of Marc Prensky that today's young people are "'digital natives'" and that the old methods of teaching "will no longer work." Do you agree with Prensky? Do you find it difficult to relate to teachers of "pre-digital vintage" (paragraph 3)?
2. Discuss your viewpoint on the argument of some that a critical need in education today is to train students for global citizenship and that "the new technologies must play" a central role in that process (paragraph 4).
3. State in your own words Calder's position on the role of the new technologies in the classroom. Do you agree with him?
4. What do you understand the H.G. Wells quotation in paragraph 9 to mean? How do the Wells quotation and Calder's concluding statement that it would be worthwhile to get kids and adults "away from their digital devices and onto bikes" relate to his central idea?

SOCIAL CONNECTIONS

STEVEN JOHNSON

Steven Johnson writes for a number of periodicals, including Wired, Discover, *and the* New York Times Magazine. *His books include* Mind Wide Open: Your Brain and the Neuroscience of Everyday Life *(2004);* Everything Bad is Good for You *(2005);* The Ghost Map: The Story of London's Most Terrifying Epidemic and How It Changed Science, Cities, and the Modern World *(2006), and* The Invention of Air: A Story of Science, Faith, and the Birth of America *(2008). This article was published in the* New York Times *on November 28, 2006.*

Earlier this month, Thomas Friedman began his column in *The New York Times* with a story about being chauffeured from Paris Charles De Gaulle Airport by a young, French-speaking African driver who chatted on his mobile phone the entire trip, while simultaneously watching a movie on the dashboard. Friedman, for his part, was writing a column on his laptop and listening to Stevie Nicks on the iPod.

Friedman wrote, "There was only one thing we never did: Talk to each other. . . . I relate all this because it illustrates something I've been feeling more and more lately—that technology is dividing us as much as uniting us. Yes, technology can make the far feel near. But it can also make the near feel very far."

This is the lament of iPod Nation: we've built elaborate tools to connect us to our friends—and introduce us to strangers—who are spread across the planet, and at the same time, we've embraced technologies that help us block out the people we share physical space with, technologies that give us the warm cocoon of the personalized soundtrack. We wear white earbuds that announce to the world: whatever you've got to say, I can't hear it.

4 Cities are naturally inclined to suffer disproportionately from these trends, since cities historically have produced public spaces where diverse perspectives can engage with each other—on sidewalks and subways, in bars and, yes, in taxicabs. Thirty years ago, the typical suburban commuter driving solo to work was already listening to his own private soundtrack on the car radio. (If anything, cell phones have made car-centric communities more social.) But for the classic vision of sidewalk urbanism articulated by Jane Jacobs, the activist and author, the bubble of permanent connectivity poses a real threat. There can be no Speaker's Corner if everyone's listening to his own private podcast.

I take these threats seriously, but let me suggest two reasons I am a bit less worried than Friedman is about the social disconnection of the connected age. One has to do with the past, the other the future.

First, there's a tendency to sentimentalize the public spaces of traditional cities. More than a few commentators have remarked on the ubiquity of the white earbuds on the New York City subways as a sign of urban disconnection. (Steven Levy summarizes and rebuts these objections elegantly in his recent book *The Perfect Thing*.) I rode the subways for almost 15 years before Apple introduced the iPod, and I can say with confidence that the subway system, for all its merits, was not exactly a hotbed of civic discourse even then. On the good days, most everyone was engrossed in their newspaper or their book. (On bad days, we were just trying to steer clear of all the subway vigilantes.) Now at least we have an excuse for not talking to each other.

It's telling that Friedman draws upon that very distinct form of social contact—the cabbie and the fare—since there are few other conventional urban situations that regularly produce substantive political conversation between strangers. The barstool conversation and the public hearing also come to mind, but I'm fairly sure the iPod hasn't infiltrated those zones yet.

8 Then there's the question of where all this technology is taking us. Friedman rightly celebrates "having lots of contacts and easy connectivity." Still, there's an underlying assumption in his piece—appropriate for someone who writes so powerfully about globalization—that connectivity is largely a matter of bringing disparate parts of the planet into closer contact. Yet that is not the whole story. Connectivity—in most instances the specific form of connectivity offered by the Web—has also greatly enhanced and amplified the kinds of conversations that

happen in real-world neighborhoods. "Placebloggers" are writing about the micronews of shared communities: the new playground that's just opened up, or the latest the city council election. The discussion forums at Chowhound are dissecting every change of menu in every hot restaurant in most American cities. Real estate blogs dish about last week's open houses, and trade statistics debating the inevitability of the post-bubble dark ages. (Full disclosure: I have, as James Baker likes to say, a dog in this hunt, in form of a new Web site I helped create called *outside.in*, which tries to organize all those conversations.)

So the idea that the new technology is pushing us away from the people sharing our local spaces is only half true. To be sure, iPods and mobile phones give us fewer opportunities to start conversations with people of different perspectives. But the Web gives us more of those opportunities, and for the most part, I think it gives us *better* opportunities. What it doesn't directly provide is face-to-face connection. So the question becomes: how important is face-to-face? I don't have a full answer to that—clearly it's important, and clearly we lose something in the transition to increasingly virtual interactions.

But just as clearly, we gain. I think of the online debate over the Atlantic Yards project here in Brooklyn—hundreds of voices working through their differences in sometimes excruciating detail. I've made a few volleys in that debate, and while it's true I haven't had face-to-face encounters with the other participants, the intensity and depth of the discussion has been far greater than any conversation on any topic that I've ever had with a stranger on a subway. The conversations unfolding across these sites are, for the most part, marvelous examples of strangers exchanging ideas and values, even without the subtleties of facial expressions and vocal intonation, and the ideas and values they're exchanging all eventually come back to a real-world place. Yes, they can sometimes get contentious. But so can Speaker's Corner. Contentiousness is what it's all about.

PERSONAL RESPONSE

How important to you are such things as a cell phone, laptop, and/or iPod? Would you be lost without them, or would you feel liberated if they were all taken away from you?

QUESTIONS FOR CLASS OR SMALL-GROUP DISCUSSION

1. Explain the controversy about technology that is at the heart of Johnson's opinion piece.
2. Summarize the first point that Johnson makes in his response to critics of the communication technology. Do you agree with him?
3. Summarize the second point in Johnson's response to critics of communication technology. Do you agree with him?
4. What is the "Speaker's Corner" that Johnson mentions in paragraphs 4 and 10? How does his concluding reference to it relate to his central point? How is "[c]ontentiousness . . . what it's all about"?

CHIPS: HIGH TECH AIDS OR TRACKING TOOLS?

TODD LEWAN

Todd Lewan joined the Associated Press as a correspondent, became an international editor for a time, and now serves as a national features writer. He is author of The Last Run: A True Story of Rescue and Redemption on the Alaskan Seas *(2005). This article was posted on the AP wire on July 22, 2007, and appeared in newspapers nationwide.*

CityWatcher.com, a provider of surveillance equipment, attracted little notice itself—until a year ago, when two of its employees had glass-encapsulated microchips with miniature antennas embedded in their forearms.

The "chipping" of two workers with RFIDs—radio frequency identification tags as long as two grains of rice, as thick as a toothpick—was merely a way of restricting access to vaults that held sensitive data and images for police departments, a layer of security beyond key cards and clearance codes, the company said.

"To protect high-end secure data, you use more sophisticated techniques," Sean Darks, chief executive of the Cincinnati-based company, said. He compared chip implants to retina scans or fingerprinting. "There's a reader outside the door; you walk up to the reader, put your arm under it, and it opens the door."

4 Innocuous? Maybe.

But the news that Americans had, for the first time, been injected with electronic identifiers to perform their jobs fired up a debate over the proliferation of ever-more-precise tracking technologies and their ability to erode privacy in the digital age.

To some, the microchip was a wondrous invention—a high-tech helper that could increase security at nuclear plants and military bases, help authorities identify wandering Alzheimer's patients, allow consumers to buy their groceries, literally, with the wave of a chipped hand.

To others, the notion of tagging people was Orwellian, a departure from centuries of history and tradition in which people had the right to go and do as they pleased, without being tracked, unless they were harming someone else.

8 Chipping, these critics said, might start with Alzheimer's patients or Army Rangers, but would eventually be suggested for convicts, then parolees, then sex offenders, then illegal aliens—until one day, a majority of Americans, falling into one category or another, would find themselves electronically tagged.

The concept of making all things traceable isn't alien to Americans. Thirty years ago, the first electronic tags were fixed to the ears of cattle, to permit ranchers to track a herd's reproductive and eating habits. In the 1990s, millions of chips were implanted in livestock, fish, dogs, cats, even racehorses.

Microchips are now fixed to car windshields as toll-paying devices, on "contactless" payment cards (Chase's "Blink," or MasterCard's "PayPass"). They're embedded in Michelin tires, library books, passports, work uniforms, luggage, and, unbeknownst to many consumers, on a host of individual items, from Hewlett Packard printers to Sanyo TVs, at Wal-Mart and Best Buy.

But CityWatcher.com employees weren't appliances or pets: They were people made scannable.

12 "It was scary that a government contractor that specialized in putting surveillance cameras on city streets was the first to incorporate this technology in the workplace," says Liz McIntyre, co-author of "Spychips: How Major Corporations and Government Plan to Track Your Every Move with RFID."

Darks, the CityWatcher.com executive, dismissed his critics, noting that he and his employees had volunteered to be chip-injected. Any suggestion that a sinister, Big-Brother-like campaign was afoot, he said, was hogwash.

"You would think that we were going around putting chips in people by force," he told a reporter, "and that's not the case at all."

Yet, within days of the company's announcement, civil libertarians and Christian conservatives joined to excoriate the microchip's implantation in people.

16 RFID, they warned, would soon enable the government to "frisk" citizens electronically—an invisible, undetectable search performed by readers posted at "hotspots" along roadsides and in pedestrian areas. It might even be used to squeal on employees while they worked; time spent at the water cooler, in the bathroom, in a designated smoking area could one day be broadcast, recorded and compiled in off-limits, company databases.

"Ultimately," says Katherine Albrecht, a privacy advocate who specializes in consumer education and RFID technology, "the fear is that the government or your employer might someday say, 'Take a chip or starve.'"

Some Christian critics saw the implants as the fulfillment of a biblical prophecy that describes an age of evil in which humans are forced to take the "Mark of the Beast" on their bodies, to buy or sell anything.

Gary Wohlscheid, president of These Last Days Ministries, a Roman Catholic group in Lowell, Mich., put together a Web site that linked the implantable microchips to the apocalyptic prophecy in the book of Revelation.

20 "The Bible tells us that God's wrath will come to those who take the Mark of the Beast," he says. Those who refuse to accept the Satanic chip "will be saved," Wohlscheid offers in a comforting tone.

In post-9/11 America, electronic surveillance comes in myriad forms: in a gas station's video camera; in a cell phone tucked inside a teen's back pocket; in a radio tag attached to a supermarket shopping cart; in a Porsche automobile equipped with a LoJack anti-theft device.

"We're really on the verge of creating a surveillance society in America, where every movement, every action—some would even claim, our very thoughts—will be tracked, monitored, recorded and correlated," says Barry Steinhardt, director of the Technology and Liberty Program at the American Civil Liberties Union in Washington, D.C.

RFID, in Steinhardt's opinion, "could play a pivotal role in creating that surveillance society."

24 In design, the tag is simple: A medical-grade glass capsule holds a silicon computer chip, a copper antenna and a "capacitor" that transmits data stored on the chip when prompted by an electromagnetic reader.

Implantations are quick, relatively simple procedures. After a local anesthetic is administered, a large-gauge hypodermic needle injects the chip under the skin on the back of the arm, midway between the elbow and the shoulder.

"It feels just like getting a vaccine—a bit of pressure, no specific pain," says John Halamka, an emergency physician at Beth Israel Deaconess Medical Center in Boston.

He got chipped two years ago, "so that if I was ever in an accident, and arrived unconscious or incoherent at an emergency ward, doctors could identify me and access my medical history quickly." (A chipped person's medical profile can be continuously updated, since the information is stored on a database accessed via the Internet.)

28 Halamka thinks of his microchip as another technology with practical value, like his BlackBerry. But it's also clear, he says, that there are consequences to having an implanted identifier.

"My friends have commented to me that I'm 'marked' for life, that I've lost my anonymity. And to be honest, I think they're right."

Indeed, as microchip proponents and detractors readily agree, Americans' mistrust of microchips and technologies like RFID runs deep. Many wonder:

Do the current chips have global positioning transceivers that would allow the government to pinpoint a person's exact location, 24–7? (No; the technology doesn't yet exist.)

32 But could a tech-savvy stalker rig scanners to video cameras and film somebody each time they entered or left the house? (Quite easily, though not cheaply. Currently, readers cost $300 and up.)

How about thieves? Could they make their own readers, aim them at unsuspecting individuals, and surreptitiously pluck people's IDs out of their arms? (Yes. There's even a name for it—"spoofing.")

What's the average lifespan of a microchip? (About 10–15 years.) What if you get tired of it before then—can it be easily, painlessly removed? (Short answer: No.)

Presently, Steinhardt and other privacy advocates view the tagging of identity documents—passports, drivers' licenses and the like—as a more pressing threat to Americans' privacy than the chipping of people. Equipping hospitals, doctors' offices, police stations and government agencies with readers will be costly, training staff will take time, and, he says, "people are going to be too squeamish about having an RFID chip inserted into their arms, or wherever."

36 But that wasn't the case in March 2004, when the Baja Beach Club in Barcelona, Spain—a nightclub catering to the body-aware, under-25 crowd—began holding "Implant Nights."

In a white lab coat, with hypodermic in latex-gloved hand, a company chipper wandered through the throng of the clubbers and clubbettes, anesthetizing the arms of consenting party goers, then injecting them with microchips.

The payoff?

Injectees would thereafter be able to breeze past bouncers and entrance lines, magically open doors to VIP lounges, and pay for drinks without cash or credit cards. The ID number on the VIP chip was linked to the user's financial accounts and stored in the club's computers.

40 After being chipped himself, club owner Conrad K. Chase declared that chip implants were hardly a big deal to his patrons, since "almost everybody has piercings, tattoos or silicone."

VIP chipping soon spread to the Baja Beach Club in Rotterdam, Holland, the Bar Soba in Edinburgh, Scotland, and the Amika nightclub in Miami Beach, Fla.

That same year, Mexico's attorney general, Rafael Macedo, made an announcement that thrilled chip proponents and chilled privacy advocates: He and 18 members of his staff had been microchipped as a way to limit access to a sensitive records room, whose door unlocked when a "portal reader" scanned the chips.

But did this make Mexican security airtight?

44 Hardly, says Jonathan Westhues, an independent security researcher in Cambridge, Mass. He concocted an "emulator," a hand-held device that cloned the implantable microchip electronically. With a team of computer-security experts, he demonstrated—on television—how easy it was to snag data off a chip.

Explains Adam Stubblefield, a Johns Hopkins researcher who joined the team: "You pass within a foot of a chipped person, copy the chip's code, then with a push of the button, replay the same ID number to any reader. You essentially assume the person's identity."

The company that makes implantable microchips for humans, VeriChip Corp., of Delray Beach, Fla., concedes the point—even as it markets its radio tag and its portal scanner as imperatives for high-security buildings, such as nuclear power plants.

"To grab information from radio frequency products with a scanning device is not hard to do," Scott Silverman, the company's chief executive, says. However, "the chip itself only contains a unique, 16-digit identification number. The relevant information is stored on a database."

48 Even so, he insists, it's harder to clone a VeriChip than it would be to steal someone's key card and use it to enter secure areas.

VeriChip Corp., whose parent company has been selling radio tags for animals for more than a decade, has sold 7,000 microchips worldwide, of which about 2,000 have been implanted in humans. More than one-tenth of those have been in the U.S., generating "nominal revenues," the company acknowledged in a Securities and Exchange Commission filing in February.

Although in five years VeriChip Corp. has yet to turn a profit, it has been investing heavily—up to $2 million a quarter—to create new markets.

The company's present push: tagging of "high-risk" patients—diabetics and people with heart conditions or Alzheimer's disease.

52 In an emergency, hospital staff could wave a reader over a patient's arm, get an ID number, and then, via the Internet, enter a company database and pull up the person's identity and medical history.

To doctors, a "starter kit"—complete with 10 hypodermic syringes, 10 VeriChips and a reader—costs $1,400. To patients, a microchip implant means a $200, out-of-pocket expense to their physician. Presently, chip implants aren't covered by insurance companies, Medicare or Medicaid.

For almost two years, the company has been offering hospitals free scanners, but acceptance has been limited. According to the company's most recent SEC quarterly filing, 515 hospitals have pledged to take part in the VeriMed network, yet only 100 have actually been equipped and trained to use the system.

Some wonder why they should abandon noninvasive tags such as MedicAlert, a low-tech bracelet that warns paramedics if patients have serious allergies or a chronic medical condition.

56 "Having these things under your skin instead of in your back pocket—it's just not clear to me why it's worth the inconvenience," says Westhues.

Silverman responds that an implanted chip is "guaranteed to be with you. It's not a medical arm bracelet that you can take off if you don't like the way it looks . . ."

In fact, microchips can be removed from the body—but it's not like removing a splinter.

The capsules can migrate around the body or bury themselves deep in the arm. When that happens, a sensor X-ray and monitors are needed to locate the chip, and a plastic surgeon must cut away scar tissue that forms around the chip.

60 The relative permanence is a big reason why Marc Rotenberg, of the Electronic Privacy Information Center, is suspicious about the motives of the company, which charges an annual fee to keep clients' records.

The company charges $20 a year for customers to keep a "one-pager" on its database—a record of blood type, allergies, medications, driver's license data and living-will directives. For $80 a year, it will keep an individual's full medical history.

In recent times, there have been rumors on Wall Street, and elsewhere, of the potential uses for RFID in humans: the chipping of U.S. soldiers, of inmates, or of migrant workers, to name a few.

To date, none of this has happened.

64 But a large-scale chipping plan that was proposed illustrates the stakes, pro and con.

In mid-May, a protest outside the Alzheimer's Community Care Center in West Palm Beach, Fla., drew attention to a two-year study in which 200 Alzheimer's patients, along with their caregivers, were to receive chip implants. Parents, children and elderly people decried the plan, with signs and placards.

"Chipping People Is Wrong" and "People Are Not Pets," the signs read. And: "Stop VeriChip."

Ironically, the media attention sent VeriChip's stock soaring 27 percent in one day.

68 "VeriChip offers technology that is absolutely bursting with potential," wrote blogger Gary E. Sattler, of the AOL site Bloggingstocks, even as he recognized privacy concerns.

Albrecht, the RFID critic who organized the demonstration, raises similar concerns on her AntiChips.com Web site.

"Is it appropriate to use the most vulnerable members of society for invasive medical research? Should the company be allowed to implant microchips into people whose mental impairments mean they cannot give fully informed consent?"

Mary Barnes, the care center's chief executive, counters that both the patients and their legal guardians must consent to the implants before receiving them. And the chips, she says, could be invaluable in identifying lost patients—for instance, if a hurricane strikes Florida.

72 That, of course, assumes that the Internet would be accessible in a killer storm. VeriChip Corp. acknowledged in an SEC filing that its "database may not function properly" in such circumstances.

As the polemic heats up, legislators are increasingly being drawn into the fray. Two states, Wisconsin and North Dakota, recently passed laws prohibiting the forced implantation of microchips in humans. Others—Ohio, Oklahoma, Colorado and Florida—are studying similar legislation.

In May, Oklahoma legislators were debating a bill that would have authorized microchip implants in people imprisoned for violent crimes. Many felt it would be a good way to monitor felons once released from prison.

But other lawmakers raised concerns. Rep. John Wright worried, "Apparently, we're going to permanently put the mark on these people."

76 Rep. Ed Cannaday found the forced microchipping of inmates "invasive . . . We are going down that slippery slope."

In the end, lawmakers sent the bill back to committee for more work.

PERSONAL RESPONSE

Discuss whether you would consider getting an ID chip.

QUESTIONS FOR CLASS OR SMALL-GROUP DISCUSSION

1. This article was written as an Associated Press wire story and published in newspapers across the nation. Assess its effectiveness by considering whether Lewan is impartial and fair in his coverage. Are there aspects of the subject that you think he should have covered but did not?
2. Summarize the arguments for and against chip implants.
3. Several people quoted in the article speak of the potential uses and/or misuses of RFID chips. Discuss ways in which you see such chips being used and explain their relative advantages and disadvantages.
4. How would you answer the question posed by the title? Why?

✧ PERSPECTIVES ON DIGITAL TECHNOLOGY AND THE INTERNET ✧

Suggested Writing Topics

1. Explore the positive and negative aspects of social networking like MySpace and Facebook and state your conclusions about their suitability for young people.
2. Explain whether you agree with H.G. Wells's description of humanity as in "'a race between education and catastrophe'" (paragraph 6, Grant Calder's "The Most Important Moment of All Time?")
3. Answer the question, "Is the early 21st century the most important moment in the history of the cosmos?" (paragraph 11, Grant Calder's "The Most Important Moment of All Time?") Explain why you feel as you do.

4. In a discussion of whether technology drives us further apart or brings us closer together, Steven Johnson in "Social Connections" admits that "face-to-face" interaction is lost but wonders: "[H]ow important is face-to-face?" (paragraph 9). Write an essay that answers that question. You may want to read Thomas L. Friedman's "The Taxi Driver," which appeared in the *New York Times* on November 1, 2006, and include the views of both Johnson and Friedman in your essay.
5. Read and respond to Steven Levy's *The Perfect Thing*, as mentioned in paragraph 6 of Steven Johnson's "Social Connections."
6. Argue your position on the issue of radio frequency identification implants.
7. Explain the characteristics of a blog that you particularly like to visit, or follow the postings at one blog for a week and do an analysis of the site. Or analyze a website that you think is especially well done.
8. Read and write a critical response to *Spychips: How Major Corporations and Government Plan to Track Your Every Move with RFID* by Liz McIntyre and Katherine Albrecht, as mentioned in Todd Lewan's "Chips: High Tech Aids or Tracking Tools?"
9. Drawing on at least one of the readings in this chapter, explore the impact of digital technology on an aspect of contemporary culture.
10. Drawing on at least one of the readings in this chapter, explain how digital technology raises issues for copyright holders.
11. Write an essay explaining what you see as the benefits and/or dangers of the Internet.
12. Explain the direction that you see digital technology going in over the next decade or two.

Research Topics

1. Research the social impact of networking sites like MySpace and Facebook or video sharing sites like YouTube.
2. Research the controversy over implanted radio frequency devices, investigate the pros and cons on the issue, and arrive at your own conclusion.
3. Research the efforts of rock groups such as Metallica and Pearl Jam to use the Internet to distribute their music while protecting themselves from piracy. Or do a similar thing with Hollywood films.
4. Research an area of computer technology that is still in the experimental stages or still being refined.
5. Research the impact of technology in one of the following areas: social networking, medicine, marketing, shopping, entertainment, scholarship/research, American culture, education, or government and politics. You will have to narrow your focus considerably for this subject.
6. Research a problem associated with the Internet such as the availability of pornography for children, the potential dangers of e-mail, the possibility of its use by terrorists, or privacy issues.

Responding to Visuals

"It turns out I just wasted the whole morning networking with a dog."

1. What do you suppose the artist intended by making the characters babies?
2. What is the implication of the speaker's having networked with a dog?
3. What comment on the accessibility of the Internet does the cartoon make?

RESPONDING TO VISUALS

Tribal boys with a laptop in Australia

1. What is your reaction to this picture?
2. What is the purpose of the picture?
3. What contrasts in the picture does the photographer emphasize?
4. What do you think the boys are doing with the laptop? Does it matter that we do not know?

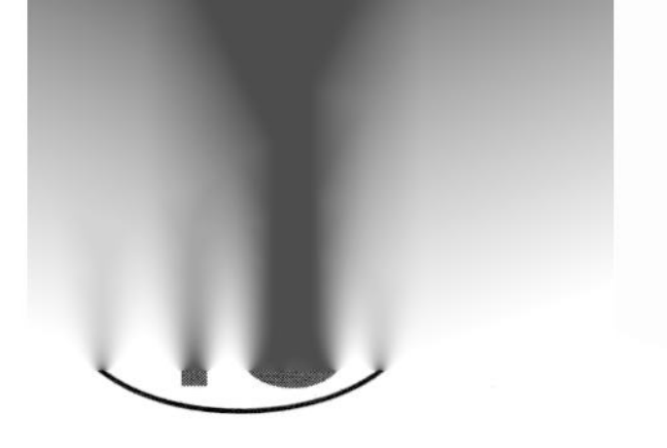

Bioethics

Bioethics has been a growing area of academic interest for the past thirty years or more. Broadly speaking, it refers to the ethics of biological and health sciences, and its scope encompasses dozens of moral and ethical issues in those areas. Bioethical concerns surround such controversial practices as cloning, cryonics, human genetic engineering, euthanasia, artificial life, transexuality, chip implants inserted into the brains of humans, and genetically modified foods as well as issues concerning organ donation, life support, population control, medical research, and the like. Of great interest to bioethicists has been the mapping of the human genome and what to do with the knowledge that resulted.

Research into the complex structure of the human body since James D. Watson and Francis Crick discovered in 1953 that deoxyribonucleic acid (DNA) molecules arrange themselves in a double helix has made enormous advances. The discovery of this pattern in DNA, a substance that transmits the genetic characteristics from one generation to the next, earned Watson and Crick a Nobel Prize in 1962. Their discovery led other scientists to work on such things as recombinant DNA and gene splicing in the 1970s and eventually to the Human Genome Project, whose goal was to map the entire sequence of human DNA. A genome is the complete set of instructions for making a human being. Each nucleus of the 100 trillion cells that make up the human body contains this set of instructions, which is written in the language of DNA. This major undertaking by scientists around the world promises to provide medical doctors with the tools to predict the development of human diseases. When the project began in 1988, scientists thought that it would take fifteen years to complete, but the project progressed faster than first predicted and was finished well ahead of schedule.

Now that the human code has been mapped, scientists can begin to better understand how humans grow, what causes human diseases, and what new drugs would combat those diseases by either preventing or curing them. Scientists already are able to identify variations or defects in the genetic makeup of certain cells in human bodies that may result in diseases with genetic origins. Eventually, they will be able to develop tests of an individual's likelihood of developing one of thousands of inherited diseases such as sickle-cell anemia, cystic fibrosis, or muscular dystrophy, and even heart disease or cancer. Because more than 30,000 genes make up the "instruction manual" for the human body, it will take some time before all of them are codified and their functions known. The Human Genome Project raised a number of difficult ethical questions, however, as the essays in this chapter indicate. One of the most controversial steps forward in the potential of scientists to manipulate genes is the capacity to clone living creatures, though gene therapy has other potential uses.

The first two essays are about the same subject, the selling of human organs for transplant, in this case, kidneys. In "About That New Jersey Organ Scandal," Sally Satel, herself a recipient of a kidney from a friend, argues for increased legal incentives for organ donation and stricter punishments for brokering them. Reporter Deborah Kotz picks up on Satel's opinion piece and asks, "Women Sell Their Eggs, So Why Not a Kidney?" Do these writers convince you that more incentives should be offered to encourage legal kidney donations?

Then, in "Patenting Life," Michael Crichton takes up one of the ethical issues that grew out of the success of the Human Genome Project, when he explains why genes are allowed to be patented and how that affects everyone's lives, not just those suffering from particular medical problems. As he raises objections to the patenting of genes and urges support of a House Bill introduced to stop it, consider whether you are persuaded by his arguments that patenting genes is a bad practice.

One highly controversial issue in bioethics is human embryonic stem cell research, in large part because of the techniques used to harvest stem cell lines, which involve either destroying a human embryo or using somatic cell nuclear transfer, often referred to as therapeutic cloning. One of the arguments used by opponents of stem cell research is that it destroys embryonic life and will inevitably lead to human cloning, while supporters argue that the benefits of such research far outweigh the costs. In "Bioethics and the Stem Cell Research Debate," Robyn S. Shapiro gives an overview of the issues involved in the controversy over stem cell research. You will no doubt find as you read the essay that the issue is more complex than you might have thought.

As you read the essays in this chapter, ask yourself the questions that their authors raise: Just how far should science be allowed to go?

ABOUT THAT NEW JERSEY ORGAN SCANDAL

SALLY SATEL

Sally Satel is a resident scholar at the American Enterprise Institute and the staff psychaitrist at the Oasis Clinic in Wshington. She has taught psychaitry at Yale and served as a Robert Wood Johnson policy fellow with the Senate Labor and Human Resources Committee. She is author of Drug Treatment: The Case for Coercion *(1999) and* PC, M.D.: How Political Correctness Is Corrupting Medicine *(2001); coauthor of* One Nation under Therapy *(2005) and* The Health Disparity Myth *(2006); and editor of* When Altruism Isn't Enough: The Case for Compensating Kidney Donors *(2009). Dr. Satel received a kidney from a friend in 2006. This article was published in the* Wall Street Journal *on July 26, 2009.*

Even by New Jersey standards, Thursday's roundup of three mayors, five rabbis and 36 others on charges of money laundering and public corruption was big. But what put this FBI dragnet head and shoulders above the rest are the charges of trafficking in human body parts.

According to a federal criminal complaint filed in district court in New Jersey, Levy Izhak Rosenbaum of Brooklyn conspired to broker the sale of a human kidney for a transplant. The cost was $160,000 to the recipient of the transplant, of which the donor got $10,000. According to the complaint, Mr. Rosenbaum said he had brokered such sales many times over the past 10 years.

"That it could happen in this country is so shocking," said Dr. Bernadine Healy, former head of the Red Cross.

4 No, it isn't. When I needed a kidney several years ago and had no donor in sight, I would have considered doing business with someone like Mr. Rosenbaum. The current law—the National Organ Transplant Act of 1984—gave me little choice. I would be a felon if I compensated a donor who was willing to spare me years of life-draining dialysis and premature death.

The early responses to the New Jersey scandal leave me dismayed, though not surprised. "We really have to crack down," the co-director of the Joint Council of Europe/United Nations Study on Trafficking in Organs and Body Parts told MSNBC. That strategy is doomed, of course. It ignores the time-tested fact that efforts to stamp out underground markets either drive corruption further underground or cause it to flourish elsewhere.

The illicit organ trade is booming across the globe. It will only recede when the critical shortage of organs for transplants disappears. The best way to make that happen is to give legitimate incentives to people who might be willing to donate. Instead, I fear that Congress will merely raise the penalties for underground organ sales without simultaneously establishing a legal mechanism to incentivize donors.

Al Gore, then a Tennessee congressman who spearheaded the National Organ Transplant Act, spoke of using "a voucher system or a tax credit to a donor's estate" if "efforts to improve voluntary donation are unsuccessful." After 25 years, it is clear they have been unsuccessful.

8 More than 80,000 Americans now wait for a kidney, according to the United Network for Organ Sharing. Thirteen of them die daily; the rest languish for years on dialysis. The number of donors last year was lower than in 2005, despite decades of work to encourage people to sign donor cards and donate to loved ones.

Sen. Arlen Specter (D., Pa.) is circulating a draft bill (the Organ Trafficking Prohibition Act), cosponsored by Sens. Bob Casey Jr. (D., Pa.) and Tom Harkin (D., Iowa), to enable governmental entities to offer donor benefits while raising penalties for brokering. States could offer health and life insurance to living donors, or funeral benefits to families of posthumous donors. Donors could also be offered a tax credit or perhaps a very generous contribution to a charity of their choice.

The rewards could come from state governments or approved charities, not from individuals, and the organs would be distributed according to formulas already in place. That means organs will not be available only to the wealthy.

What Mr. Rosenbaum is accused of doing is indeed against the law, and if he is found guilty he will be held accountable. But his alleged actions were a symptom of a deeper problem: the dire organ shortage.

12 Congress must permit donors to accept third-party benefits for saving the life of a stranger. Otherwise desperate patients and donors will continue to be reluctant co-conspirators in crime.

PERSONAL RESPONSE

Do you know of anyone who needs or has had an organ transplant? Write for a bit about what you know about the organ transplant issue.

QUESTIONS FOR CLASS OR SMALL-GROUP DISCUSSION

1. State in your own words what Satel is arguing for.
2. Assess Satel's argument. Does she adequately support or prove her position?
3. What do you think of the options that Satel mentions in paragraph 9? Could you add more options, or do you not agree that such options are a good idea?
4. Satel quotes the head of the Red Cross as being shocked that such a thing as the New Jersey organ scandal could happen in America and then says that it is not shocking to her (paragraph 3-4). Is it to you? What do you know about trafficking of human organs?

WOMEN SELL THEIR EGGS, SO WHY NOT A KIDNEY?

DEBORAH KOTZ

Deborah Kotz is a senior writer in the Health section of U.S. News & World Report *whose work focuses on women's health issues. This piece was published in the July 28, 2009, issue of* U.S. News & World Report.

I was as upset as anyone by the allegations of organ selling that are associated with a New Jersey corruption scandal resulting in more than 40 arrests last week. But a *Wall Street Journal* column this week calling for more incentives for folks to donate organs makes the issue seem more complex than at first blush. "More than 80,000 Americans now wait for a kidney . . . thirteen of them die daily; the rest languish for years on dialysis," writes Sally Satel. She says she would have gladly considered paying an organ broker to get a kidney several years back when she needed one and there was no donor. That is, if it hadn't been illegal. (She eventually received a kidney from a friend.)

While most of us find it revolting to pay for an organ, we readily accept allowing women to sell their eggs to an infertile couple. In fact, just a few weeks ago, New York State became the first in the nation to allow federally funded researchers to pay women for their eggs for embryonic stem cell research. While men typically donate their sperm free of charge, women expect to get paid for their eggs because of the hassle and risk of injecting themselves with hormones to ripen multiple eggs at once and of having those eggs surgically extracted. The reality is, few donors would go through that if there were no financial incentive. While it's not illegal for women in the United States to get payments for egg donations (it is in Europe), the American Society for Reproductive Medicine has established ethical guidelines for egg donor compensation—a cap of $10,000 per cycle—which most fertility clinics follow.

16 So taking this one step further, why shouldn't willing donors be allowed to charge reasonable rates for their organs?

"I'm on the fence, I have to say. I'm really torn about this," says Jonathan Moreno, a professor of bioethics at the University of Pennsylvania. "People are understandably uncomfortable and uncertain about selling kidneys, but there really is a shortage." He says if there were a non-exploitative way of doing this, he'd like to see it tried within the framework of a research study. (Most shocking were allegations that poor donors were forced to give up their kidneys for $10,000, while the middlemen received $150,000.)

Trouble is, Moreno admits, it's hard to say whether setting up an ethical and legal system reduces exploitation or increases it. He still sees advertisements at Penn offering students $40,000 for their Ivy League eggs and notes that the legalization of prostitution in Amsterdam's red-light district has led to a spike in criminal activity like money laundering just outside the district. Donating a kidney is also a riskier procedure than egg donation because it involves more-invasive surgery and long-term risks of having a malfunction in the one remaining kidney.

But some, like Satel, argue that living kidney donors need to be given more incentives. She favors a bill being put forth by Democratic Sen. Arlen Specter of Pennsylvania that would enable state governments to provide donor benefits while also raising penalties for brokering. Donors could get health and life insurance, tax credits, or a generous contribution to the charity of their choice. I've written before about those who altruistically donate their kidneys to strangers, but those folks are, unfortunately, few and far between.

PERSONAL RESPONSE

Would you be willing to donate an organ to a close friend or relative? Write for a few minutes explaining your answer.

QUESTIONS FOR CLASS OR SMALL-GROUP DISCUSSION

1. Reporters try to remain objective, no matter how controversial their subject. How objective do you find Kotz? Does she reveal her own viewpoint?
2. How well does Kotz answer the question posed in her title? Summarize what she says are the arguments for and against allowing women "to charge reasonable rates for their organs" (paragraph 3). State your own view on the arguments for and against allowing people to sell their kidneys.
3. Kotz concludes by mentioning that she has written elsewhere about donors who "altruistically" give kidneys to strangers. What does she mean by "altruistically"? What have you heard of such donations? Do you know anyone who has donated or received a kidney—or any organ? If so, share your story with the rest of your class or group.

4. Discuss this statement: "It's hard to say whether setting up an ethical and legal system reduces exploitation or increases it" (paragraph 5). How might such a system increase exploitation? Can you give examples of situations where that might be the case?

PATENTING LIFE

MICHAEL CRICHTON

Michael Crichton (1942–2008), was an author, critic, and film producer. While earning his degree from Harvard Medical School, he began writing novels. Among his twenty-five novels are such bestsellers as The Andromeda Strain *(1969),* The Terminal Man *(1972),* The Great Train Robbery *(1975),* Sphere *(1987),* Jurassic Park *(1990),* Airframe *(1996), and his last,* Pirate Latitudes *(2009). He was also creator and coproducer of the long-running television drama* ER. *This essay appeared as an op-ed piece in the February 13, 2007, edition of the* New York Times.

You, or someone you love, may die because of a gene patent that should never have been granted in the first place. Sound far-fetched? Unfortunately, it's only too real.

Gene patents are now used to halt research, prevent medical testing and keep vital information from you and your doctor. Gene patents slow the pace of medical advance on deadly diseases. And they raise costs exorbitantly: a test for breast cancer that could be done for $1,000 now costs $3,000.

Why? Because the holder of the gene patent can charge whatever he wants, and does. Couldn't somebody make a cheaper test? Sure, but the patent holder blocks any competitor's test. He owns the gene. Nobody else can test for it. In fact, you can't even donate your own breast cancer gene to another scientist without permission. The gene may exist in your body, but it's now private property.

4 This bizarre situation has come to pass because of a mistake by an underfinanced and understaffed government agency. The United States Patent Office misinterpreted previous Supreme Court rulings and some years ago began—to the surprise of everyone, including scientists decoding the genome—to issue patents on genes.

Humans share mostly the same genes. The same genes are found in other animals as well. Our genetic makeup represents the common heritage of all life on earth. You can't patent snow, eagles or gravity, and you shouldn't be able to patent genes, either. Yet by now one-fifth of the genes in your body are privately owned.

The results have been disastrous. Ordinarily, we imagine patents promote innovation, but that's because most patents are granted for human inventions. Genes aren't human inventions, they are features of the natural world. As a result these patents can be used to block innovation, and hurt patient care.

For example, Canavan disease is an inherited disorder that affects children starting at 3 months; they cannot crawl or walk, they suffer seizures and eventually become paralyzed and die by adolescence. Formerly there was no test to tell parents if they were at risk. Families enduring the heartbreak of caring for these children engaged a researcher to identify the gene and produce a test. Canavan families around the world donated tissue and money to help this cause.

8 When the gene was identified in 1993, the families got the commitment of a New York hospital to offer a free test to anyone who wanted it. But the researcher's employer, Miami Children's Hospital Research Institute, patented the gene and refused to allow any health care provider to offer the test without paying a royalty. The parents did not believe genes should be patented and so did not put their names on the patent. Consequently, they had no control over the outcome.

In addition, a gene's owner can in some instances also own the mutations of that gene, and these mutations can be markers for disease. Countries that don't have gene patents actually offer better gene testing than we do, because when multiple labs are allowed to do testing, more mutations are discovered, leading to higher-quality tests.

Apologists for gene patents argue that the issue is a tempest in a teapot, that patent licenses are readily available at minimal cost. That's simply untrue. The owner of the genome for Hepatitis C is paid millions by researchers to study this disease. Not surprisingly, many other researchers choose to study something less expensive.

But forget the costs: why should people or companies own a disease in the first place? They didn't invent it. Yet today, more than 20 human pathogens are privately owned, including haemophilus influenza and Hepatitis C. And we've already mentioned that tests for the BRCA genes for breast cancer cost $3,000. Oh, one more thing: if you undergo the test, the company that owns the patent on the gene can keep your tissue and do research on it without asking your permission. Don't like it? Too bad.

12 The plain truth is that gene patents aren't benign and never will be. When SARS was spreading across the globe, medical researchers hesitated to study it—because of patent concerns. There is no clearer indication that gene patents block innovation, inhibit research and put us all at risk.

Even your doctor can't get relevant information. An asthma medication only works in certain patients. Yet its manufacturer has squelched efforts by others to develop genetic tests that would determine on whom it will and will not work. Such commercial considerations interfere with a great dream. For years we've been promised the coming era of personalized medicine—medicine suited to our particular body makeup. Gene patents destroy that dream.

Fortunately, two congressmen want to make the full benefit of the decoded genome available to us all. Last Friday, Xavier Becerra, a Democrat of California, and Dave Weldon, a Republican of Florida, sponsored the Genomic Research and Accessibility Act, to ban the practice of patenting genes found in nature. Mr. Becerra has been careful to say the bill does not hamper invention, but rather promotes it. He's right. This bill will fuel innovation, and return our common genetic heritage to us. It deserves our support.

PERSONAL RESPONSE

Crichton believes that "you shouldn't be able to patent genes" (paragraph 5). Do you agree with him? Explain your answer.

QUESTIONS FOR CLASS OR SMALL-GROUP DISCUSSION

1. What are the negative effects of gene patents, according to Crichton?
2. What do supporters of gene patents argue, according to Crichton? Do you think that Crichton effectively addresses those arguments?
3. How well do you think that Crichton argues his position? What argumentative strategies does he use?
4. Do you believe that Crichton has considered all sides of the issue? If not, what do you think he has overlooked?

BIOETHICS AND THE STEM CELL RESEARCH DEBATE

ROBYN S. SHAPIRO

Robyn S. Shapiro is Ursula von der Ruhr Professor of Bioethics and Director of the Center for the Study of Bioethics at the Medical College of Wisconsin in Milwaukee. She is also a health law partner at Gardner Carton & Douglas LLP in Milwaukee. She publishes and speaks frequently on ethical issues in science and medicine, especially in relation to the law. This essay was first published in the May–June 2006 issue of Social Education, *the journal of the National Council for Social Studies.*

Since its birth in the 1970s, bioethics—the study of ethical issues in science and medicine—has grown to become a significant academic and service-oriented discipline with its own research centers, conferences, journals, and degree programs. As these issues have moved to the center of public debate, the law has assumed an increasingly important place in the discipline of bioethics.

The growing importance of the law as a forum for the debate and mediation of bioethical issues is apparent on several fronts. In the United States Supreme Court, bioethical issues have been central to key reproductive privacy cases, from the Court's 1973 decision in Roe v. Wade, 410 U.S. 113, to its 2000 decision in Stenberg v. Carkart, 530 U.S. 914, which struck down a controversial Nebraska partial-birth abortion law. In state courts, bioethical considerations inform judges' balancing of patient health care confidentiality with a "duty to warn" of potentially dangerous patient behavior (see, for example, the California Supreme Court's landmark 1976 decision, Tarasoff v. Regents of the University of California, 17 Cal. 3d 425). At both the state and federal levels, bioethical debates help shape end-of-life statutes and court cases, including Cruzan v. Missouri Dept. of Health, 497 U.S. 261 (1990), in which the U.S. Supreme Court upheld the State of Missouri's requirement for clear and convincing evidence that a person in a persistent vegetative state had expressed a wish not to be kept alive by life-sustaining equipment.

Today, embryonic stem cell research stands out as a critically important issue about which we have neither ethical consensus nor clear, comprehensive regulation. The ethical debate centers on the fact that stem cell research involves the destruction of very early human embryos. On the federal level, funding for stem cell research has been limited to research using stem cells derived from a limited number of stem cell "lines." On the state level, approaches range from legislative restrictions on stem cell research to the State of California's plan to provide $3 billion in stem cell research funding through the voter-approved California Institute for Regenerative Medicine.

4 In order for potentially revolutionary stem cell research to progress, scientists' long-term needs must be effectively coordinated with appropriate and effective ethical and legal guidance. This article provides brief scientific background and then discussion of key ethical and legal/regulatory issues that surround embryonic stem cell research.

Background

Embryonic stem cells are precursor cells that have the capacity to divide for indefinite periods of time in culture and to give rise to virtually any type of specialized cells in the body. They are derived from the inner cell mass of a 100-cell blastocyst—a very early embryo, usually only 3–4 days old—long before the cells have started to specialize to create a nervous system, spine and other features that, with further development, would transform the embryo into a fetus. Typically, these cells are derived from embryos that originally were created for infertility treatment purposes through in vitro fertilization, but that are no longer desired or needed by the infertile couple for treatment. The extraction of the stem cells from the blastocyst necessarily requires the destruction of that blastocyst.

Because embryonic stem cells are capable of self-renewal and can differentiate into a wide variety of cell types, potential applications of embryonic stem cell research are far-reaching. For example, embryonic stem cell research holds out great promise to those suffering from Type I diabetes. Type I diabetes is an autoimmune disease characterized by destruction of insulin-producing cells in the pancreas. Some of the current efforts to treat these patients use donated human pancreases for transplantation of islets—clusters of cells on the pancreas that produce insulin—in an effort to restore the insulin-secreting function. Islet transplantation efforts are limited by the small numbers of available donated pancreases, as well as the toxicity of immunosuppressive drug treatments that are required to prevent graft rejection. Use of embryonic stem cells that are instructed to differentiate into pancreatic islet cells has the potential to overcome the shortage of effective material to transplant.

Similarly, embryonic stem cell research offers tremendous potential to those suffering from nervous system diseases that result from loss of nerve cells. Since mature cells cannot divide to replace cells that are lost, therapeutic possibilities do not exist in the absence of a new source of functioning nerve tissue. Conceivably, however, with embryonic stem cell research, nerve cells that make the chemical dopamine could be created for individuals with Parkinson's disease, cells responsible for the production of certain neuro-transmitters could be reconstituted for individuals with Alzheimer's, the motor cells that activate muscles could be replaced for ALS patients, and glia (cells that perform numerous functions within the human nervous system) could be formed for individuals with multiple sclerosis.

8 In addition to these promising therapeutic applications of embryonic stem cell research, such research also could provide new insights into how human beings, organs and tissues develop. It also has the potential to substantially change the development and testing of pharmaceutical products. New medications could be tested initially on cells or tissues developed from embryonic stem cells, and only those drugs initially found to be safe and effective would be tested further on animals and humans.

Ethical Issues

Notwithstanding the promise of embryonic stem cells, several ethical issues have made stem cell research controversial. The most vexing ethical issues surrounding embryonic stem cell research, which focus on the moral status of the very early embryo, arise from the fact that isolating embryonic stem cells requires destruction of the embryo.

Some who condemn embryonic stem cell research believe that the embryo is a full person or human subject, with full rights and interests from the moment of conception. Others take a developmental view of personhood, believing that the embryo only gradually becomes a full human being and that the very early embryo is not entitled to the same moral protections to which it would be entitled at a later developmental stage. Still others hold that while the embryo represents human life, such life is not a "person" at any time prior to birth.

The role of science in deciding the difficult ethical question of the moral status of the very early embryo is unresolved. Key issues in deciding this question include the following:

- How significant is it that at less than 14 days a blastocyst has no neural tissue? Some contend that this fact makes derivation of stem cells from a blastocyst prior to this developmental stage no different than allowing organ donation at the point of brain death.
- Is it ethically significant that until formation of the primitive streak at 14 days, a blastocyst can undergo complete fission to form an identical twin? One commentator contends that since "individuality is a sine qua non for personhood, it seems safe to consider 14 days of normal embryonic development to be the minimum requirement for a human being to emerge."
- Is the argument for the protection of the "potential" for human life affected by scientific assertions that an embryo does not have such potential unless it is implanted in a uterus?
- Is it ethically significant that a blastocyst created by somatic cell nuclear transfer, if implanted, would be extremely unlikely to develop into a human being? As one commentator notes, "cytoplasmic factors would have to act on an adult nucleus to produce the same patterns of gene activation that are critical for early embryonic development."

Legal Issues

12 Federal and state legislatures have begun to grapple with the ethical questions involved in stem cell research, but to date, there is no comprehensive or consistent regulation of stem cell research in the United States. Since 1996, riders to federal appropriations language (known as the "Dickey Amendment") have prohibited use of federal funds for "the creation of a human embryo or embryos for research purposes," as well as "research in which a human embryo or embryos are destroyed, disabled or knowingly subjected to a risk of injury or death greater than allowed for research on fetuses in utero . . ." In January 1999, however, the General Counsel of the Department of Health and Human Services (HHS) determined that federal law does not prohibit public funding of embryonic stem cell research as long as the research to be funded does not include derivation of the stem cells from the embryo (and, therefore, destruction of the embryo). In other words, cells could be derived from embryos destroyed in private labs with private money, and then shipped to federally funded scientists for study.

Following this legal clearance from HHS, the director of the National Institutes of Health (NIH) convened a 13-member working group to draw up guidelines for research using embryonic stem cells. This group's guidelines, which became effective August 2000, state that research involving embryonic stem cells is acceptable as long as

- the stem cells come from spare embryos that were originally created through in vitro fertilization for infertility treatment purposes,
- the embryos have not reached the developmental state at which the mesoderm is formed,
- the researcher is not involved in the infertility treatment for which the embryos were created and has not played any role in the donors' decision to donate the embryos for research,
- there is no directed donation of embryos for the derivation of stem cells for eventual use in transplantation, and
- the stem cells are not added to human or animal eggs or embryos via somatic cell nuclear transfer.

On August 9, 2001, however, President Bush effectively suspended the NIH 2000 guidelines. He announced that federal funding for embryonic stem cell research would be available only under the following conditions:

- the stem cells are derived from stem cell lines existing as of August 9, 2001,
- the lines were derived with proper informed consent of the embryo donors,
- the embryos used were originally created through in vitro fertilization for infertility treatment purposes, and
- there were no financial inducements made to the embryo donors.
- No federal funds may be used for derivation or use of stem cells derived from newly destroyed embryos, creation of human embryos for research purposes, or cloning of human embryos for any purpose.

Many contend that the president's restrictions on federal funding of embryonic stem cell research are inhibiting the ability to unlock the potential of embryonic stem cells. One concern relates to recently discovered chromosomal rearrangements in embryonic stem cells over time, which suggest that the federally approved lines may have limited therapeutic potential. Additional concerns relate to the limited number and the narrow racial diversity of the federally approved stem cell lines.

16 Moreover, in addition to the federal funding restrictions, embryonic stem cell research is also subject to some restrictive state laws. While California is providing government funding for stem cell research through the California Institute for Regenerative Medicine, and New Jersey, Massachusetts, Illinois, Wisconsin, and Texas are considering funding measures, other states—including Iowa, Louisiana, Michigan, Arkansas, Nebraska, North Dakota, South Dakota, and Virginia—have laws that limit embryonic stem cell research.

On the other hand, stem cells, as well as their derivation and their uses, are eligible for federal patent protections. In fact, a number of patents relating to human embryonic stem cells have been filed—the most fundamental of which are the "Thomson" patents, named after the University of Wisconsin researcher who led a group that developed the technique for isolating and growing human embryonic stem cells. Thomson patents relate to the methods of deriving and maintaining human embryonic stem cells in vitro, and the products of those methods. These patents were assigned by the inventors to the Wisconsin Alumni Research Foundation, which exclusively licensed their commercial applications within certain fields of use to Geron Corporation, and made licenses to practice under the patent rights for research purposes available through a non-profit corporation.

Some have questioned the ethical acceptability of patenting embryonic stem cells. For example, one commentator has questioned whether the federal government's opposition to direct federal funding of post-August 2001 stem cell lines is consistent with its sanction of exclusive property rights in such lines, since these patent-protected rights can create "indirect research funding" through rewarding market investments. However, such qualms collide with the United States Supreme Court's declaration that "everything under the sun" isolated or manipulated by humanity may be patented and that patent law is not intended to displace the police powers of the states with respect to safety, health and morality. Ironically, then, the current federal position is to allow sensitive ethical questions on stem cell research to be decided by the marketplace, with private money developing products that receive patent protection without the regulatory oversight that would apply to federally funded research.

Conclusion

Stem cell research has emerged as a potential political issue that could play a role in the 2006 mid-term elections and beyond. In his 2006 State of the Union speech, President Bush called upon Congress "to pass legislation to prohibit the most egregious abuses of medical research," including "human cloning in all its forms." Some commentators have criticized this statement for failing to distinguish between human reproductive cloning, which most experts oppose, and therapeutic cloning, in which cloning techniques are used to produce blastocysts for stem cell extraction, not embryos for implantation. In Congress, there are signs of division in the Republican majority on the question of stem cell research. A bill easing current federal restrictions on stem cell research passed the Republican-controlled House of Representatives in 2005 but stalled in the Senate, which is scheduled to take up the bill sometime in 2006. Several key senators, including Senate Majority Leader Bill Frist (R-Tenn.), have spoken in support of the bill.

20 In the meantime, there is no consensus concerning ethical questions surrounding embryonic stem cell research. Continued careful attention to ethical review of the issues that surround this promising research, and consistent incorporation of such analysis into evolving laws and regulations, will assure the appropriate and effective use of this emerging knowledge.

PERSONAL RESPONSE

What is your position on the subject of human embryonic stem cell research?

QUESTIONS FOR CLASS OR SMALL-GROUP DISCUSSION

1. Summarize in your own words the arguments in favor of and those opposed to human embryonic stem cell research.
2. State in your own words the ethical issues surrounding the subject of human embryonic stem cell research.
3. Summarize the various legal questions raised in state and federal legislatures surrounding the subject of human embryonic stem cell research.
4. Select and discuss a particular comment, fact, or statement that you find intriguing, argumentative, or in need of explanation or clarification.

✧ PERSPECTIVES ON BIOETHICS ✧

Suggested Writing Topics

1. Drawing on Michael Crichton's "Patenting Life" and Robyn S. Shapiro's "Bioethics and the Stem Cell Research Debate," explain where you stand on one of the questions raised in the readings about the implications and dangers of genetics research.
2. Write a response to either Sally Satel ("About That New Jersey Organ Scandal") or Deborah Kotz ("Women Sell Their Eggs, So Why Not a Kidney?"). Explain where you agree, where you disagree, and where you have real concerns about what the writer says.
3. Argue your position on any of the issues raised by the essays in this chapter.

4. Write an essay on another issue, besides the ones identified by the authors of the articles in this chapter, that needs to be looked at closely. For instance, do you think care must be taken to make the results of genetic research available to everyone while protecting the rights of both researchers who make the discoveries and companies that want to profit from them?
5. Conduct a class forum on the ethical, social, and/or legal problems that are associated with the Human Genome Project, human cloning, stem cell research, or other genetics research. For a writing project, summarize the views of your classmates, and state your own position on the subject.
6. Interview professionals such as a molecular biologist, an ethics professor, or someone else familiar with genetics research or the Human Genome Project on the ethical, social, and/or legal problems associated with the Human Genome Project or stem cell research. Draw on the views of the professionals whom you interview as you explain your own position on the subject.

Research Topics

1. Research the National Organ Transplant Act of 1984—what it restricts and allows, what its impact has been on organ transplants, and whether you think it should remain in effect as it is, be amended or revised, or be repealed. Consider the opinion of Sally Satel in "About That New Jersey Organ Scandal" in your research.
2. Starting with Robyn S. Shapiro's "The Bioethics and the Stem Cell Research Debate," update the state of the controversy over stem cell research by finding out what state and federal laws have been passed since 2006; then state your own position on the subject, given its current ethical and legal status.
3. Research one of the issues suggested by the readings in this chapter: legalizing the selling of certain organs, increasing incentives for organ donation, stem cell research, physician-assisted suicide, universal health care, access to expensive treatments for self-induced health problems, embryo research, mandatory testing for HIV diseases, compulsory genetic screening for certain risk groups or during premarital examinations, or the status of genetic disease and genetic therapy.
4. Research the Human Genome Project, and write a paper in which you elaborate on its main objectives, provide representative views on the controversy surrounding it, and explain your own position and why you believe as you do.
5. Research the Genomic Research and Accessibility Act mentioned by Michael Crichton in "Patenting Life." Find out what conditions led to its proposal, what arguments have been made in support of or against it, whether it has passed the House and gone to the Senate, and/or other aspects of the proposed bill.

6. Research the question: Should scientists create human life? Consider pros and cons and arrive at your own conclusion.
7. Select an issue in the area of neurotechnology, such as transcranial magnetic stimulation, implantable brain chips, brain imaging, cochlear implants, lie detection technologies, deep brain stimulators, brain computer interfaces, forensic neuroscience, or neuromarketing. Research the controversy over the issue and arrive at your own conclusion.
8. Research some aspect of the history and/or practice of eugenics, such as the program of Nazi Germany under Hitler or U.S. programs for forced sterilization for mentally ill patients.

Responding to Visuals

Baby boy's face on eggs in box.

1. What message, if any, does this image convey?
2. What is the significance of identical babies in an egg box?
3. What fears about human cloning does the image seem to play on?

Responding to Visuals

Stan Schmunk protests as a truck passes by carrying anti-stem cell research messages outside the Stem Cells and Regenerative Medicine: Commercial Implications for the Pharmaceutical and Biotech Industries meeting, October 8, 2002, in San Diego, California. The protesters are demonstrating on behalf of the anti-abortion California Life Coalition that opposes all embryonic stem cell research.

1. What comment does the photograph make on opposition to stem cell research?
2. To what extent does this photograph summarize the reasons some people are opposed to stem cell research?
3. To what extent do you agree with the messages photographed here?

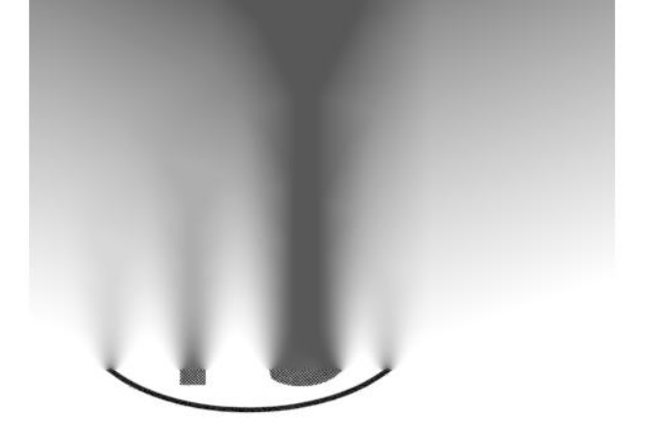

Public Health

Epidemics, pandemics, and plagues have been much dreaded realities from the very beginning of human existence. Consider such major outbreaks of disease as the bubonic plague in thirteenth- and fourteenth-century Europe; cholera epidemics in various parts of the world from time to time, up to the present; the smallpox epidemic that swept Sweden in 1764; the typhus epidemic that killed more than 3 million Russians during World War I; or the influenza plague of 1918 to 1919 that killed more than 20 million people around the world. More recently, untreatable, deadly viruses have infected populations in certain areas of the world, worrying health officials that they may spread elsewhere. The Ebola virus in Africa, for instance, produces acute suffering in its victims, most of whom die within days of being infected. Viruses are particularly difficult to contain, because they live inside body cells, where antibiotics cannot reach them. Worse, once a person is infected with a virus, it can continue to live in the body's cells, waiting to strike again many years later.

Even such previously treatable diseases as herpes, hepatitis, and chicken pox are becoming resistant to treatment and causing deaths in increasingly higher numbers. Cases of deaths caused by herpes simplex 1 (HSV1) and related members of the herpes family, such as cytomegalovirus (CVM), chicken pox, and genital herpes (HSV2), have been reported. Although certain groups such as pregnant women are particularly vulnerable to these diseases, these and other viruses pose a considerable threat to the general population. More than 3 million Americans are believed to harbor the mysterious and deadly hepatitis C virus, for instance, with even more people harboring the less-mysterious but potentially life-threatening hepatitis A and hepatitis B viruses.

This chapter features articles on issues related to several aspects of public health, both national and global, beginning with two opinions on the issue of whether the HPV vaccine should be mandatory. In response to Texas governor Rick Perry's issuing an executive order in 2007 mandating the vaccination of young girls with the HPV vaccine, Mike Adams created the cartoon and wrote the commentary for "HPV Vaccine Texas Tyranny." His stand on the issue is clear from the nature of the cartoon and from the beginning of the commentary. Arthur Allen, on the other hand, though not inclined to endorse mandatory vaccinations for the virus, looks at the issue by comparing it to mandates for other viruses, like Hepatitis B. In "The HPV Debate Needs an Injection of Reality" he urges a cautious approach to the issue.

The focus then shifts to global health concerns with Richard D. Smith's "Global Public Goods and Health." Smith explains what "global public goods" are and suggests applying that model to global health issues. Finally, Jessica Reaves in "What the Rest of Africa Could Learn About AIDS" reports on the success that the African nation Senegal has had in reducing the spread of AIDS. She explains how the Senegalese model works in three separate areas: government involvement, religious attitudes, and the country's legalization and regulation of prostitution. From Senegal, she suggests, the rest of the continent can learn much about aggressively fighting this devastating disease.

HPV VACCINE TEXAS TYRANNY

MIKE ADAMS

Counterthink Cartoons *are NaturalNews.com parodies or satirical commentary on various matters that the owners of the website believe to be of public concern. This cartoon and commentary were posted on Wednesday, February 7, 2007, by Mike Adams and Dan Berger. The link to the NaturalNews website is www.naturalnews.com.*

Commentary by Mike Adams, the creator of this cartoon:

FACT: THE PUSH FOR MANDATORY HPV VACCINES WAS BANKROLLED BY DRUG COMPANIES. TEXAS GOV. RICK PERRY ACCEPTED THOUSANDS FROM MERCK.

On Friday, Feb. 2, Texas governor Rick Perry issued an executive order that bypassed the will of the people and the entire Texas legislature, mandating the vaccination of young girls with the HPV vaccine sold by Merck—the same drug company that reportedly gave thousands to Perry's campaign efforts. The vaccine is absolutely worthless as a medical treatment according to top docs in the alternative health field, and in my opinion, the so-called "science" supporting the vaccine as the only prevention for cervical cancer is an outright fraud.

But the story gets even more interesting when you start connecting the dots. A key Merck lobbyist, a man named Mike Toomey, actually served as the governor's chief of staff. In other words, a former top power person for the governor now works for Merck, the drug company that gave money to the campaign of the governor who essentially used dictatorial power to mandate, without any public debate whatsoever, the mass vaccination of young girls with a drug that will earn tens of millions of dollars in profits for Merck. Sound suspicious? It should.

4 The "dirty money connection" seems obvious to many readers who have been following this story, including one who posted, *"Only a man, Rick Perry especially,*

would sign an executive order, bypassing legislation, to inject girls with chemicals made by one of his contributors even though most parents have never seen sufficient information about this vaccine. Perry should be impeached as a threat to the safety of our children." (See http://blogs.chron.com/texaspolitics/archives/2007/02/lawmakers_resci.html)

The humanitarian cover story. Drug companies are experts at framing their profit pursuits as public health initiatives. "We have to protect the little girls!" they insist, but what's really going on behind closed doors is a far less altruistic push—the push for profits. Requiring millions of young girls to get these new vaccines just happens to generate enormous profits for Merck. But Merck officials, and even the governor of Texas, would have you believe that has nothing to do with this. Apparently, the fact that Merck will earn obscene profits from this initiative never entered their minds.

Nonsense. If Merck really wants to help these teenage girls, **why don't they pledge to give away all their vaccines free of charge?** In fact, if they're such a humanitarian organization, why don't they give away all their drugs, and release third world countries from patent protection at the same time? The answer, of course, is because **this is all about money, not public health.** If Merck was really about "patients first," they should convert to a 501(c)3 non-profit, stop paying their CEOs $10 million salaries, and give all their drugs away for free as a gift to humankind, shouldn't they?

That will never happen, of course, because it really is about the money. The sick care industry is a for-profit industry, and the more people drug companies can target as being sick today—or even possibly someday being sick at some future date that "justifies" treatment right now—the more money they can sock away in the bank. When it comes to money, it seems drug companies will stop at nothing to get more of it, including influencing state officials to mandate vaccine consumption policies that have nothing whatsoever to do with evidence-based medicine or genuine compassion for the health and lives of human beings.

8 What's happening in Texas right now is a form of **medical tyranny**, and it's only the beginning of what may prove to be a monumental battle between personal freedoms vs. the corporate-controlled State.

We must stop the medical tyranny. If we let Texas get away with this medical tyranny, forcing all young girls to undergo these HPV vaccinations even against their parents' wishes, more states will follow suit. Merck is right now lobbying hard to pass similar measures in over twenty other states, and if we don't put a stop to the Texas situation, Merck will feel emboldened and likely urge other governors to make the same declarations in their states, calling it a "public health" measure but actually pocketing the profits from massive sales of these vaccines.

What can you do? I say we fight the tyranny by exposing it. You can **take action to spread the word on this issue.** POST this cartoon to your website and LINK to our articles on this topic. We give you full permission to reprint this cartoon and forward it to your friends. Expose this medical madness before we all end up prisoners under a system of medical tyranny that turns the bodies of teenage girls into profit centers for Big Pharma! And unlike Merck, we don't care about the intellectual property royalties on this comic. Make as many copies as you want. Print up T-shirts. Add it to your book. Use it as you wish, and you don't owe me a dime. Why? Because I actually do care about my fellow human beings and I'm here to help stop the medical madness sweeping America today.

Speak up now or surrender your health freedoms forever. You see, if we don't stand up to this kind of medical tyranny, it will only get worse. This debate is not merely about one vaccine, it's about surrendering your health freedom to a medical system that is owned and controlled by Big Pharma. Drug companies practically run the FDA, the EPA and even control the FTC (when was the last time the FTC investigated and prosecuted drug company monopolies?). Drug companies influence the DEA to keep their own drugs legal while the exact same "street" drugs are illegal. They own our elected officials, almost all of which accepted at least some money from drug companies in their last election campaign. Drug companies also own the mainstream media by propping up television networks, cable networks, newspapers, magazines and websites with literally billions of dollars in advertising. On top of that, drug companies heavily influence the medical journals and medical schools, and have effectively limited the entire conventional medical industry to a "drugs and surgery" approach to health, practically censoring nutritional knowledge out of existence.

12 Given this environment, is anyone supposed to believe we will see anything resembling honest debate or genuine science about this HPV vaccine? The entire industry, including drug companies, doctors, medical journals and the mainstream media, is twisting the facts to create the illusion that these vaccines are both safe and effective when, in reality, they are probably neither. Nor are they necessary. Cervical cancer is prevented in a hundred other ways, including adequate sunlight exposure and vitamin D consumption, supplementation with probiotics, adequate intake of selenium and zinc, increased consumption of trace minerals and iodine, regular physical exercise and many other safe, natural, non-patented strategies.

America is being hoodwinked over the HPV vaccine. To call this anything resembling genuine public health policy is an absolute joke. **It's really just a grand moneymaking scheme that exploits the bodies of young girls, marketed to look like compassionate health care.** Supporters of this policy are shameless, ignorant and devious in framing their nonsensical arguments using carefully-chosen words and phrases that make them seem like they're delivering a cancer cure from God. But in reality, mandatory HPV vaccines are a deal with the devil.

Consider this: With all the drugs being prescribed, all the toxic chemicals being consumed, and all the diseases now ravaging America—a country with the highest rates of degenerative disease in the world—does anybody really think that injecting one more drug is the answer? You'd have to be crazy to think so.

PERSONAL RESPONSE

What do you think of the cartoon?

QUESTIONS FOR CLASS OR SMALL-GROUP DISCUSSION

1. Comment on the cartoon as a persuasive tool.
2. What strategies does Adams use to advance his argument? What evidence does he give to support his position? Does he make any unsupported claims?
3. Comment on Adams' tone and language. Discuss their appropriateness, given the context of the cartoon and commentary and their intended audience.
4. What actions does Adams call for? Are you persuaded to act?

THE HPV DEBATE NEEDS AN INJECTION OF REALITY

ARTHUR ALLEN

Arthur Allen, a Washington-based writer and journalist, is the author of Vaccine: The Controversial Story of Medicine's Greatest Lifesaver *(2007). He has written about the subject of vaccines for such publications as the* New York Times, *the* Washington Post, *and the* Atlantic Monthly. *This article appeared in the April 7, 2007, issue of the* Washington Post.

The recommendation was that all children be given a vaccine for a carcinogenic virus whose spread is associated, in many minds, with sinful activities. Here's what some leading pediatricians had to say about it: "We are notably poor soothsayers in predicting which child will be put at high risk by future behavior. Pediatricians must initiate, then, an insurance policy for young patients that matures in adulthood."

That statement was made in 1992. Its authors were Neal Halsey and Caroline Breese Hall of the American Academy of Pediatrics' infectious-disease committee. They called for universal vaccination of newborns and adolescents against hepatitis B, a disease that, in the United States, spreads mainly through sex and shared hypodermic needles. Halsey and Hall were pushing universal vaccination because earlier programs to immunize at-risk groups—drug users, prostitutes, prisoners, gay males—had been a miserable failure.

The choice to vaccinate infants was controversial, but the virus is a deadly one. In the early 1990s, about 250,000 Americans were infected with hepatitis B each year. About a fifth would become chronic carriers and suffer, in some cases, scarring of the liver. About 6,000 died each year of liver cancer associated with hepatitis B. And although children represented a small percentage of those infected, they were more likely to become chronic hepatitis B carriers.

4 There was controversy in the medical community over the hepatitis B vaccination program, but it was implemented, in that pre-Internet era, with minimal public fretting. Nearly every state now requires the vaccination for entry to primary school.

Now there are questions about mandatory vaccination of girls for the human papilloma virus, which can cause cervical cancer. This vaccine offers similar, if slightly less dramatic, hope to a large population of neglected Americans. But politically, it's a very different story this time. A powerful movement has sprung up to oppose mandatory HPV immunization. Much of this resistance is, I believe, misguided. Yet I have my own reservations about mandating the HPV vaccine at this time.

The results of the hepatitis B vaccination program that began in the 1990s have been dramatic. In the Morbidity and Mortality Weekly Report of March 16, the Centers for Disease Control and Prevention reported that the number of new cases had fallen to about 50,000 in 2005. New infections were most reduced in the vaccinated groups—98 percent among elementary-school children and young teenagers, and 90 percent among 15- to 24-year-olds.

Similarly, in trials completed last year, the HPV vaccine was shown to prevent 70 percent of the growths that lead to cervical cancer, which strikes 14,000 American women each year, killing one-fourth of them. The 20,000 women who received the vaccine in trials by Merck, the manufacturer, experienced no major side effects. By preventing precancerous growths, the vaccine also can reduce the need for extra gynecological visits and painful procedures.

8 This all sounds good. It helps explain why liberal groups such as Women in Government accepted funding from Merck this year to help the drug firm lobby state legislatures to make the HPV vaccine mandatory for sixth-grade girls.

So what's wrong with ordering parents to get their children immunized by a product that has the power, like the hepatitis B vaccine, to help prevent a deadly disease? Plenty, according to the many activists who have whipped up a firestorm on the issue in places from California to Maryland and the District, where the city council last week took the first step toward requiring HPV vaccination. (Virginia acted this year to require the immunizations but made it fairly easy for parents to opt out.)

In my view, the fact that HPV is sexually transmitted is no reason to keep children from being vaccinated against it. Immunizing infants against hepatitis B has clearly shown that public health campaigns can prevent disease without causing moral turpitude. In any case, HPV's spread is not linked to risky sexual behavior. The virus is as common as influenza: About 80 percent of women will be exposed to it at some point.

When the CDC led a drive to enforce mandatory vaccination against measles in the 1970s, it discovered that immunization rates increased by as much as 20 percent. The parents who had their kids vaccinated only when their schools required it often had been unaware of the vaccine, unable to afford it, or too overwhelmed to get their children to a clinic. Those who strongly opposed the vaccination could usually opt out under state laws. The same would be true of the HPV vaccine.

12 Most cervical cancers can be prevented with regular pap smear tests, which find precancerous growths that can be excised. Most of the women who get cervical cancer

haven't had the test done in at least three years. It stands to reason that, without a mandatory vaccination, many of the girls who don't get vaccinated will belong to the same groups that fall through the cracks of the patchy U.S. health-care system.

During a recent radio interview about this issue, I was dismayed to hear callers claim that proposed HPV mandates would make their children "guinea pigs" in a contemporary Tuskegee—a reference to the notorious experiments in which black men with syphilis were studied but not given penicillin. I responded by asking whether it was better to be neglected by the medical mainstream than to be enrolled in a measure that covers all girls—rich, poor, black, white, Hispanic and Asian.

Sadly, as long as the HPV vaccine is not required, the people who need it most probably won't get it. "Those who are well-informed with good families, parents involved with their children, will go ahead," said Hall, who is with the University of Rochester Medical Center in New York. "Those who are not as well informed or involved in the care of their children will not get the vaccine."

So why, given all these arguments, do I think that requiring HPV vaccination for school-age girls is a mistake at the present time? The most obvious reason is that when a vaccine is mandated, it must be available for free to those who can't afford it. But state health officials are already struggling to provide for existing mandated vaccines such as DTP (diphtheria, tetanus and pertussis), MMR (measles, mumps and rubella) and chickenpox. They simply don't have the money to buy the HPV immunization for girls whose families can't afford it.

16 Second, the vaccine, while promising, has no track record. Merck's hepatitis B vaccine was licensed in 1986, which allowed plenty of time to observe its efficacy and safety before it became mandatory—and forestalled the "guinea pig" argument. While the hepatitis B vaccine proved quite safe, there's no guarantee that the HPV immunization won't provoke a rare side effect.

But there is a third, less tangible reason for holding off—one that has to do with the kind of public perceptions that are essential to successful vaccination programs and are magnified in this era of instant blogging.

With only Merck and a few activists pushing the HPV vaccine, it lacks credibility. This has opened the door to critics of immunization in general, who are gaining support among people who fear an HPV-vaccine mandate.

Our rickety pediatric vaccination system is a three-legged stool whose stability relies on the participation of drug companies, which need a profit incentive; the government, which buys about half of all childhood vaccines; and parents, who are called on to submit their children to vaccination not only to protect them but to diminish the spread of disease.

20 In failing to include two legs of the system, those pushing for immediate mandatory vaccination are risking its collapse. The HPV vaccine may do great things, but we shouldn't rush it.

PERSONAL RESPONSE

Where do you position yourself on the issue of mandatory HPV vaccinations?

QUESTIONS FOR CLASS OR SMALL-GROUP DISCUSSION

1. How effective do you find Allen's opening paragraphs about the hepatitis B vaccine? Why does he start with that subject when his main focus is on the HPV vaccine?
2. Where does Allen make concessions in his argument?
3. What do you think of Allen's answers to the question he asks at the beginning of paragraph 15?
4. Comment on the effectiveness of Allen's metaphor in the closing paragraphs.

GLOBAL PUBLIC GOODS AND HEALTH

RICHARD D. SMITH

Richard D. Smith is Professor of Health System Economics and head of the School of Health Policy and Practice, University of East Anglia, England. He has written and spoken extensively on health issues, particularly those affecting the elderly and disadvantaged, and the effects of globalization on health care. "Global Public Goods and Health" is an editorial that appeared in the July, 2003, issue of Bulletin of the World Health Organization.

Health improvement requires collective as well as individual action, and the health of poor populations in particular requires collective action between countries as well as within them. Initiatives such as the Global Fund to Fight AIDS, Tuberculosis and Malaria reflect a growing awareness of this fact. However, initiating, organizing and financing collective actions for health at the global level presents a challenge to existing international organizations *(1)*.

The concept of "global public goods" (GPGs) suggests one possible framework for considering these issues *(2)*. In this expression, "goods" encompass a range of physical commodities (such as bread, books and shoes) but include services (such as security, information and travel), distinguishing between private and public goods. Most goods are "private" in the sense that their consumption can be withheld until a payment is made in exchange for them, and once consumed they cannot be consumed again. In contrast, once "public" goods are provided no one can be excluded from consuming them (they are non-excludable), and one person's consumption of them does not prevent anyone else's (they are non-rival in consumption) *(3)*. For example, no one in a population can be excluded from benefiting from a reduction in risk of infectious disease when its incidence is reduced, and one person benefiting from this reduction in risk does not prevent anyone else from benefiting from it as well.

Global public goods are goods of this kind whose benefits cross borders and are global in scope. For example, reductions in carbon dioxide emissions will slow global warming. It will be impossible to exclude any country from benefiting from this, and each country will benefit without preventing another from doing so. Similarly, the eradication of infectious diseases of global scope, such as smallpox or polio, provides a benefit from which no country is excluded, and from which all countries will benefit without detriment to others.

4 However, these attributes of public goods give rise to a paradox: although there is significant benefit to be gained from them by many people, there is no commercial incentive for producing them, since enjoyment cannot be made conditional on payment. With national public goods, the government therefore intervenes either financially, through such mechanisms as taxation or licensing, or with direct provision. But for global public goods this is harder to do, because no global government exists to ensure that they are produced and paid for. The central issue for health-related GPGs is how best to ensure that the collective action necessary, for health is taken at the international level.

Globalization of travel, changes in technology, and the liberalization of trade all affect health. Communicable diseases spread more rapidly, often in drug-resistant form *(4)*, environmental degradation reduces access to clean air and water, and knowledge of traditional and modern health technologies is increasingly patented and thus made artificially excludable *(5)*. However, discussion of GPGs to date has typically been broad-based and multisectoral (for instance on the environment, international security and trade agreements), and most of the discussion within the health sector has been focused on medical technologies *(3, 6, 7)*.

This has left many questions unanswered *(8)*. For example, is health itself a GPG? To what extent does my (national) health depend on your (national) health? How many of the actions necessary to global health—communicable disease control, generation and dissemination of medical knowledge, public health infrastructure—constitute GPGs? What contribution can the GPG concept make to fulfilling these needs? Is international financing for these GPGs best coordinated through voluntary contributions, global taxation systems, or market-based mechanisms? Does the concept of GPGs undermine or support concepts of equity and human rights?

The first large-scale study of the application of the GPG concept to the health sector examines questions such as these, and has just been published *(8)*. The study finds that, while the concept has important limitations, for some areas of health work it can offer guidance in the financing and provision of global health programmes. In these areas it provides a framework for collective action at the global level, demonstrates the advantages for the rich in helping the poor, and provides a rationale for industrialized countries to use national health budgets to complement traditional aid (as seen in the Polio Eradication Initiative *(9)*). Overall, the GPG concept will be increasingly important as a rationale and a guide for public health work in an era of globalization.

Endnotes[1]

1. Drager N, Beaglehole R. Globalization: Changing the public health landscape. *Bulletin of the World Health Organization* 2001; 79:803.
2. Kaul I, Faust M. Global public goods and health: Taking the agenda forward. *Bulletin of the World Health Organization* 2001; 79:869–74.
3. Kaul I, Grunberg I, Stern, MA, editors. *Global public goods: International cooperation in the 21st century*. New York: Oxford University Press; 1999.
4. Smith RD, Coast J. Antimicrobial resistance: a global response. *Bulletin of the World Health Organization* 2002; 80:126–33.
5. Thorsteinsdottir H, Daar A, Smith RD, Singer P. Genomics—a global public good? *Lancet* 2003; 361:891–2.
6. Kaul I, Conceicao P, Le Goulven K, Mendoza RU, editors. *Providing global public goods: managing globalization*. New York: Oxford University Press; 2003.
7. *Macroeconomics and health: investing in health for economic development. Report of the Commission on Macroeconomics and Health*. Geneva: World Health Organization; 2001.
8. Smith RD, Beaglehole R, Woodward D, Drager N, editors. *Global public goods for health: a health economic and public health perspective*. Oxford: Oxford University Press; 2003.
9. Aylward B, Acharya A, England S, et al. Achieving global health goals: the politics and economics of polio eradication, *Lancet* (forthcoming).

PERSONAL RESPONSE

Do you agree that the issue of health care requires collective rather than individual action (paragraph 1)? How would you answer Smith's question in paragraph 6: "Is health itself a GPG [global public goods]"?

QUESTIONS FOR CLASS OR SMALL-GROUP DISCUSSION

1. Does Smith clearly define the concept of "global public goods"? How well do his examples in paragraphs 2 and 3 serve to illustrate that concept?
2. How well does Smith explain the paradox that he mentions in paragraph 4?
3. Do you agree with Smith that the GPG model would work in the health sector?
4. What is the rhetorical effect of the series of questions in paragraph 6?

[1]Endnotes are reproduced as originally published and do not conform to either MLA or APA style. [Ed.]

WHAT THE REST OF AFRICA COULD LEARN ABOUT AIDS

JESSICA REAVES

Jessica Reaves is a staff writer and reporter for the Chicago Tribune, *where she has worked since 2004. Before joining the* Tribune, *she wrote for Time.com in New York and as a reporter for* Ms. Magazine. *She appears regularly on CNN, MSNBC, Fox News, and NPR. This article was published in the April 27, 2007, issue of the* Chicago Tribune.

KOLDA, Senegal—The open-air classroom, buffeted by a stiff, dusty wind, rang with the sound of children's laughter and excited chatter as their teacher paced in front of the blackboard, brandishing colored chalk. He raised his hand, and the room fell silent.

He pointed to a poster with an illustration of a man in a bar, leaning suggestively toward a woman holding a condom in her hand. "What do we think is happening here?" he asked.

The 12- and 13-year-olds raised their hands eagerly, some bouncing up and down in their seats. The teacher called on a girl sitting in the back of the room.

4 "He wants to have sex with her," she said.

"And what will she say to him?" asked the teacher.

There was some mumbling, and then a boy raised his hand.

"Not without a condom."

8 This is a scene I witnessed recently in the West African country of Senegal, one of the continent's success stories in the fight against HIV/AIDS. The infection rate in Senegal is 0.9 percent—similar to the rate in the U.S. (0.6 percent), and far lower than the soaring tolls in African countries such as Namibia (19.6 percent), South Africa (18.8 percent) and Botswana (24.1 percent).

What is Senegal doing right, I wondered, and could those practices be replicated in other countries?

I arrived in Senegal with plenty of questions and, like most Americans, a few misconceptions about Islamic West Africa. As far as AIDS in Senegal was concerned, I knew there were a few factors to consider: government involvement, religious attitudes and the country's long-standing legalization and regulation of prostitution.

The Senegalese government has taken a remarkably active role in the sex education of its citizens. In 1986, immediately after the first case of AIDS was confirmed in Senegal, the government launched a massive prevention program, pouring resources into AIDS education.

12 The Senegalese brand of Islam dictates a certain social conservatism, and there is little opportunity for teenagers to be alone together. The lack of alcohol certainly plays a role in disease prevention; drunken sex is statistically far less likely to involve condom use than sober sex. And Senegal's sex worker registration system, in place since 1969, provides prostitutes with weekly health care and free condoms. In a

recent academic report, 100 percent of Senegalese sex workers surveyed (all of whom had taken part in government-sponsored classes on AIDS and sexually transmitted disease prevention) said they use condoms with every customer.

But there are plenty of other reasons for the country's low AIDS rate, including the early and intensive efforts by the country's powerful imams, some of whom use Friday services to educate their congregations about AIDS. This growing trend is a powerful indicator of the partnership between the medical community and religious leaders: While imams limit their sermons to discussions of abstinence and fidelity, doctors are often on hand to handle practical instruction and clinical questions.

One particularly warm day during my trip, I went to speak with the imam who presides over the Grand Mosque in Kolda, a city in Senegal's Casamance region, where the AIDS rate is six times higher (3 percent) than it is in the capital of Dakar (0.5 percent). I took note of the imam's kind eyes, grizzled hair and easy smile and asked him, through a translator, whether he had any hesitation incorporating AIDS into his sermons, which reach about 3,000 people each week. "We treat this like any other disease," he replied. "If someone is sick, we want to help them."

And when it comes to talking about condoms? "Teaching people to use condoms is a contradiction of Islamic law," he said. "We teach fidelity in marriage and abstinence before marriage." Outside the mosque, he said, he can discuss HIV and AIDS more directly and, like many Senegalese imams, he refers congregants to a local clinic or doctor where practical advice about contraception is readily available.

16 Imams enjoy enormous political and cultural power in Senegal. In involving its religious leaders—a process that has taken patience, time and government funding—Senegal's anti-AIDS strategy provides a useful blueprint for other countries struggling to contain the spread of the disease.

Another of Senegal's successful HIV/AIDS prevention techniques should also be duplicated and exported: Frank, open and comprehensive sex education beginning at age 12, and AIDS awareness training starting as early as 1st grade.

The emphasis on education is deeply ingrained. In 1994, Senegal's Ministry of Education requested—and received—funding from UNFPA (the United Nations Population Fund) to begin the Group for the Study and Teaching of Population Issues, or GEEP. GEEP's mandate: to bring information about sex, contraception, health and family planning to children in Senegal's schools.

Over 13 years, GEEP has expanded; it now provides peer counselors to students and sponsors family life education clubs in schools. Since GEEP's inception, Senegalese girls have delayed sex three years longer than their mothers' generation, and a recent survey shows that condom use has risen threefold from 10 years ago, to nearly 70 percent.

20 The message is clear: Comprehensive sex education—including information about condoms and how to use them—is one of the most important weapons in the fight against AIDS.

Teaching kids about condoms doesn't promote sex. (Anyone who's been a high school student knows this makes some sense: If there's anything less romantic than unrolling condoms in front of your classmates, it's seeing graphic photographs of

STD-infected genitals—available at any Senegalese health kiosk.) But the Bush administration exports a restrictive, abstinence-only agenda used in many American schools.

PEPFAR, the United States President's Emergency Plan for AIDS Relief, has made funding of sex education projects contingent on the use of extremely limited language when talking about contraception and sex. To receive PEPFAR funding, countries must severely constrain teaching about condoms in favor of abstinence-based lessons.

In Senegal and in Uganda, where the HIV infection rate has fallen from 15 percent to about 6 percent, the governments were quick to implement the "ABC" approach, which advocates "Abstinence, Be Faithful and Use Condoms." This trifecta is consistent with the teaching I saw in Senegal, where middle school pupils were told that abstinence and monogamy were the best choices—though if they were unable to maintain either, they should always use a condom.

24 That doesn't jibe with PEPFAR's logic, which hinges on "targeted" messaging. By their calculations, only sex workers and other "high risk" populations should receive information about condoms. And even then, PEPFAR policy dictates that the message has to include an abstinence component.

Many African nations, including AIDS-ravaged Botswana and South Africa, continue to receive PEPFAR money, a dependency that stifles the free exchange of information and could cost more lives than it saves. Senegal's policy of legalized prostitution means the country is ineligible for PEPFAR funding, so it relies instead on donations from the UNFPA and the Global Fund, an independent grant-making consortium of governmental, non-governmental and private-sector groups. That means Senegal's teachers and community leaders are free to discuss condom use as part of a larger prevention message—a message, it must be noted, that has been far more successful than what is offered in any of the PEPFAR recipient countries.

The hot March day when I visited a classroom in Kolda, I was struck, as the kids answered their teacher's questions without embarrassment, by their sophisticated understanding of AIDS and of the ways, including abstinence until marriage and condom use, they could prevent the disease from spreading.

As the class period ended and the kids filed out of the room, the girls whispering and giggling and the boys whooping on their way to the dirt field for a game of soccer, their teacher suddenly let out an exclamation.

28 "I forgot the condom demonstration," he said, shaking his head ruefully. "I got so wrapped up in the lesson I forgot to bring out the condoms."

"Oh, well," he said, sitting down at his desk to rewrite the next day's lesson plans. "We'll tackle that tomorrow."

PERSONAL RESPONSE

Reaves mentions that she arrived in Senegal with "a few misconceptions about Islamic West Africa," although she does not say what those misconceptions were. What do you suppose they were? What impressions or even "misconceptions," if any, did you have about Senegal before reading this article?

QUESTIONS FOR CLASS OR SMALL-GROUP DISCUSSION

1. Assess the effectiveness of Reaves's opening description of the classroom scene and her returning to it at the end of her article. What function do those references serve in relation to the rest of her article?
2. What does Reaves think that the rest of Africa could learn about AIDS from Senegal?
3. Are you persuaded by Reaves's evidence that Senegal's policy toward HIV/AIDS education is a model for other countries? How likely do you think it is that other countries will adopt Senegal's policies in AIDS prevention? Explain your answer.
4. Discuss Reaves's suggestion that the U.S. policy for giving aid to African countries (PEPFAR) creates "a dependency that stifles the free exchange of information and could cost more lives than it saves" (paragraph 25). Do you agree with her?

✧ PERSPECTIVES ON PUBLIC HEALTH ✧

Suggested Writing Topics

1. Argue for or against making HPV vaccinations mandatory.
2. Argue for or against the right of pharmaceutical companies to hold patents and continue to make large profits on drugs that could help fight AIDS in sub-Saharan countries.
3. Explore the role of drug companies in fighting the global AIDS epidemic.
4. Discuss your views on providing universal access to health care in light of the high cost of health care.
5. Explain your views on how best to educate the public about preventing sexually transmitted diseases.
6. Explain the role you believe that schools and other public institutions should play in disseminating information about sexually transmitted diseases.
7. Argue either for or against programs to distribute free condoms to high school students.
8. If you know someone with AIDS or another grave illness, describe that person's condition, the problems it poses for the person's family, and your concerns about the person and the illness.
9. Many writers suggest that social inequalities, such as poverty, the class system, or women's lower social status, help spread AIDS in Third World countries. Select one of those subjects and explain how working to overcome the problems associated with it is an important component in the fight against AIDS. For instance, how would helping lift people out of poverty work against the spread AID? How might improving women's rights help control the spread of AIDS?

Research Topics

1. Research the controversy over mandatory HPV vaccination. You might want to begin with the two essays in this chapter on the subject, or have a look at Arthur Allen's *Vaccine: The Controversial Story of Medicine's Greatest Lifesaver* as a starting point.
2. Research the viewpoints of drug companies, economists, and health workers, among others, on this question: Should drug companies bear the financial burden of sending lifesaving drugs to developing countries?
3. In combination with library and Internet research, interview public health officials or representatives from the health center at your campus about a public health issue. Narrow your focus to one aspect of public health and explain your own view on the topic.
4. Research the controversy over government funding for AIDS research.
5. Research and assess the importance or success of the work of either a national health agency, such as the U.S. Centers for Disease Control (CDC), or an international health agency, such as the World Health Organization (WHO).
6. Research some aspect of the AIDS epidemic in the United States (or another country) and responses by public health officials to the disease. You will discover many controversies on this subject, so identify one major controversy, explore the issues involved, and arrive at your own position on the subject. You may want to take a historical approach, for instance, by exploring various theories on the origin of AIDS, or you may want to focus on controversial treatments for the disease.
7. Research one of the many contributing factors in the spread of AIDS in Africa, such as poverty, gender, class inequality, ignorance, urbanization, colonialism, or the collapse of rural economies.
8. Research some aspect of a recent epidemic, such as SARS or the H1N1 virus. Consider such things as how widespread it was, who suffered most from it, and how it was brought under control.
9. Research a major plague of the past, such as the bubonic plague in thirteenth- and fourteenth-century Europe, cholera epidemics, the smallpox epidemic that swept Sweden in 1764, the typhus epidemic that killed more than 3 million Russians during World War I, or the influenza plague of 1918 to 1919 that killed more than 20 million people around the world. Determine the consequences for the country (or countries) affected by the plague as well as its possible origins and how it was finally conquered.

Responding to Visuals

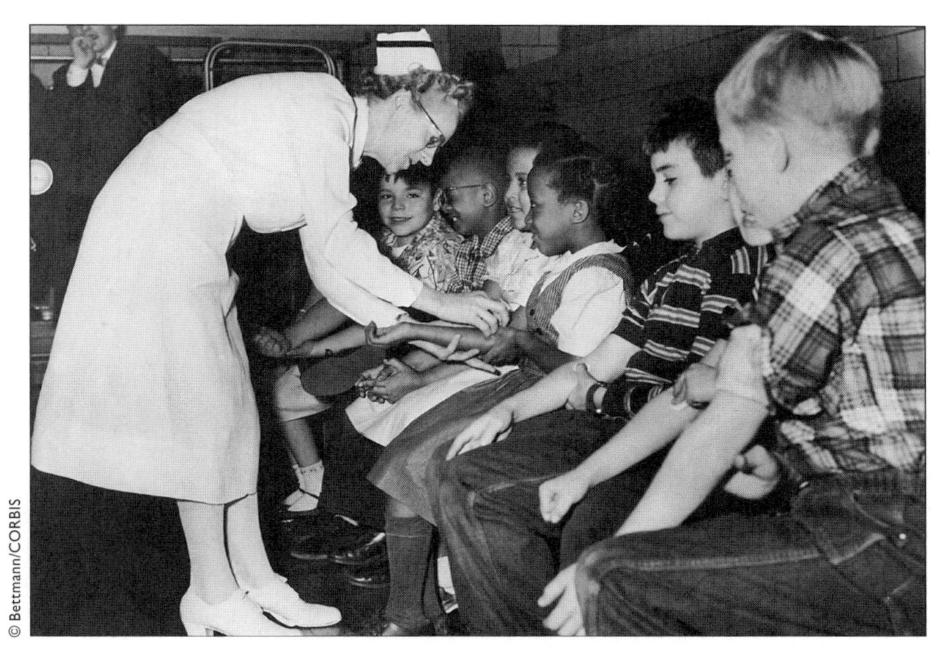

A nurse prepares children for a polio vaccine as part of a city-wide testing of vaccine on elementary school students, February 23, 1954, Pittsburgh, Pennsylvania.

1. What is going on in this photograph? State the details that explain what is happening.
2. What aspects of the scene does the photographer emphasize?
3. What do the facial expressions and body language indicate about how both the nurse and the children view this experience?
4. What details give clues that this picture is not current? Could you tell that the photograph was taken in the 1950s if you were not told that in the caption?

Responding to Visuals

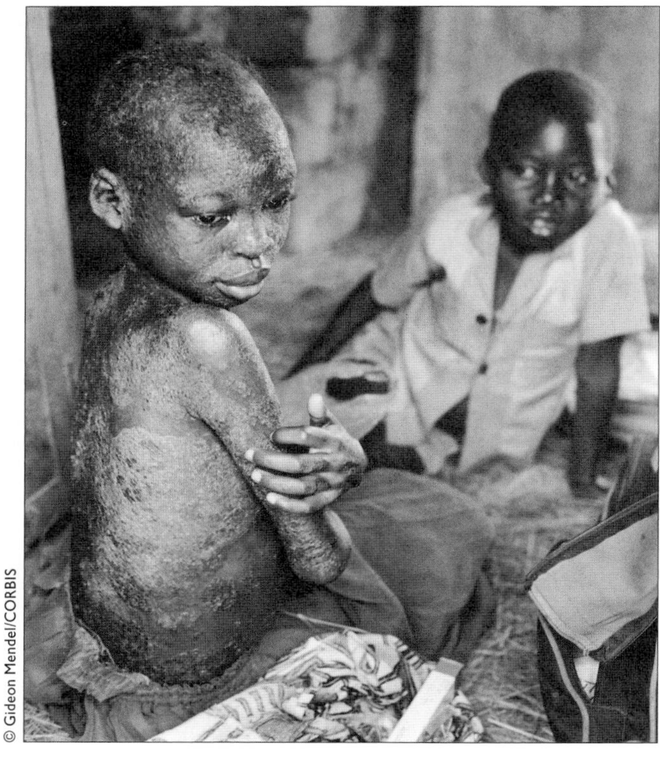

A 13-year old Tanzanian girl suffering from an AIDS-related skin infection, at her home near Bukoba, Tanzania. She was transmitted AIDS from a blood transfusion from her father to treat malarial anemia. Her father died from AIDS-related syndrome, and her mother is severely ill from the disease

1. What is your emotional response to the picture?
2. What is the effect of the perspective from which the photograph was taken? What details about the children are revealed from that perspective?
3. Why does the photographer include the child who apparently is not ill? What is the effect of the juxtaposition of the two children?

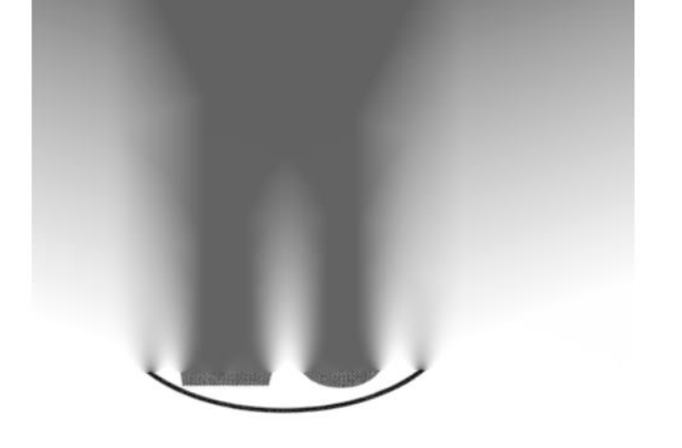

Environmental Studies

Environmental issues such as depletion of the ozone layer, global warming, deforestation, and air and water pollution are just a few of the many causes for concern over the health of animal and vegetable life on Earth. Closely connected to these environmental problems is the rapid rate of increase in the world population. As the number of people grows, pressure increases on natural resources. Will Earth provide enough food for everyone? How can water supplies be kept safe for drinking? How does pollution produced by so many humans affect the quality of the air they breathe? How can people stop the ever-widening hole in the ozone layer that protects us from the harmful rays of the sun? How will future generations sustain the rapidly increasing worldwide population? These are just some of the questions confronting scientists, civic leaders, and ordinary people everywhere.

Although most people recognize that humans must keep their environments safe, not everyone agrees on either the nature of the problems or the severity of their consequences. For instance, resource depletion and global warming are the subjects of many debates. Researchers and scientists differ in their beliefs on questions such as Earth's ability to sustain life indefinitely and whether Earth is experiencing global warming and, if so, whether the phenomenon is cause for alarm.

In the first piece in this chapter, Aaron Sachs profiles the nineteenth-century scientist Baron Alexander von Humboldt, who, he says, is "the man most responsible for bringing the practice of science into mainstream Western culture." In "Humboldt's Legacy and the Restoration of Science," Sachs maintains that modern science would do well to adopt Humboldt's integrated vision of nature. He laments the relatively low federal allocation for furthering the understanding of the environment, and he believes that ecologists and environmentalists should adopt a broader, interdisciplinary approach to environmental problems. Although the essay was first published a decade and a half ago, you will no doubt see that what Sachs says about Humboldt resonates yet today for anyone concerned about environmentalism.

Then, Bill McKibben makes an impassioned plea for activism in "Global Warming: Get Up! Stand Up!" Pointing out that previously identified environmental problems were fixable with both changes in behavior as well as legislatively mandated changes, he maintains that Congress has "failed to take on the single greatest challenge human civilization has ever faced." His subtitle, "How to Build a Mass Movement to Halt Climate Change," is a clear indication of the subject of his essay. As you read McKibben's piece, notice his argumentative strategies and ask yourself whether you are persuaded to take action as he so urgently presses his readers to do.

Two more argumentative essays complete the chapter, with each writer seeking to persuade audiences to action. Jeff Corwin in "The Sixth Extinction" gives startling facts about the rapid extinction of species. He points out that somewhere on Earth, "every 20 minutes we lose an animal species." With examples of dying species from several areas of the globe, Corwin hopes to persuade readers to "rise to the cause." Finally, in "Accounting 101 for the 21st Century: A Liberal Arts Education in Carbon," John Petersen urges administrators, instructors, and students on college and university campuses across the nation to respond to the environmental challenge. Using the example of his own institution, Oberlin College, he explains how across the curriculum and across the campus, colleges and universities can act positively to meet the challenges to ensure global environmental health.

HUMBOLDT'S LEGACY AND THE RESTORATION OF SCIENCE

AARON SACHS

Aaron Sachs is an assistant professor in the Department of History at Cornell University. He is author of Eco-Justice: Linking Human Rights and the Environment *(1994) and* The Humboldt Current: Nineteenth-Century Exploration and the Roots of American Environmentalism *(2006), and coauthor of* The Next Efficiency Revolution: Creating a Sustainable Materials Economy *(1990) and* State of the World 1995 *(1995). This essay is from the March/April 1995 issue of* World Watch *magazine.*

On September 15, 1869, *The New York Times* ran a one-word headline: "HUMBOLDT." Every literate American knew the name. "The One Hundredth Birthday of the Philosopher," explained the subtitle. "Celebration Generally Throughout the Country." The story took up the entire front page.

It is unthinkable today that Americans would celebrate the birthday of any dead philosopher, let alone a foreign one. Yet from San Francisco to Peoria to New York, on that Tuesday afternoon, people read speeches, unrolled banners, and unveiled statues in honor of the late Baron Alexander von Humboldt. Of course, Humboldt was much more than a philosopher: He was also an explorer, a geographer, a writer, a naturalist—and the man most responsible for bringing the practice of science into mainstream Western culture.

The word *scientist* first entered the English language in the 1830s, specifically in reference to Humboldt and his disciples—Charles Darwin among them. Originally, then, the term meant "natural scientist." The new profession Humboldt had carved out and popularized took as its goal the transformation of natural history studies, to cover not just the detailed cataloging of the phenomena of the physical world, but also the formulation of a grand, unifying theory that would link all those phenomena together. Humboldt wanted to know what tied the rivers to the trees, how climate influenced vegetation, why particular animals thrived only in particular habitats; he also wanted to reveal humanity's place within these interdependent relationships. And in an early nineteenth-century culture of amateur naturalists obsessed with the romance of the wilderness, his quest struck many chords.

4 Initially, Humboldt earned his fame by exploring the New World between 1799 and 1804, when he surveyed the headwaters of the Orinoco in the jungles of Venezuela and scaled the Andes to heights never before attained in any of the world's mountain ranges. On that trip, between the ages of thirty and thirty-five, the "Rediscoverer of America" witnessed the immense diversity of humanity and nature. He saw just how different life was among the natives of the Venezuelan rainforest and the politicians of the newly formed U.S. Congress—among the insects swarming in marshlands along the Colombian coast and the birds floating above Ecuadorean volcanoes and the wildflowers lining fertile Cuban valleys. Yet he never wavered in his belief that there existed a "chain of connection," that all elements of earthly life,

including humans, were "mutually dependent"—and that a knowledge of that interdependence was the "noblest and most important result" of all scientific inquiry. For the last fifty-five years of his life—he lived to age ninety—he struggled to "recognize unity in the vast diversity of physical phenomena." While acknowledging the world's chaos, he saw within it what the ancient Greeks called a *kosmos*, a beautifully ordered and harmonious system, and he coined the modern word *cosmos* to use as the title of his final, multivolume work—a book Walt Whitman kept on his desk as he was writing *Leaves of Grass*.

Today, most environmentalists would be shocked to learn that nature's interrelationships were once in the mainstream of scientific thought. The dominant theme in science over the past century has been *fission*, the breaking down of life and matter and ideas into their smaller components: Life science and its organic theories have given way to specialization, to microbiology and nuclear physics. In our rush to gain in-depth knowledge about particular elements of a complicated, seemingly chaotic world, we have tacitly decided that it would be futile to try to tie those elements together. Science has lost its delicate balance between chaos and cosmos, between diversity and unity.

It now seems clear that this century-old imbalance is inextricably linked to our global ecological crisis. If we assume that the world on which we depend is utterly chaotic, there is no reason to do anything but try to control and conquer it—which has become science's new goal. And though specialization has proved itself invaluable in the pursuit of knowledge, its narrow, short-range focus, in the absence of a complementary organic approach, is extremely dangerous. We have directed society's accumulated scientific knowledge toward constantly improving our exploitation of each individual natural resource, without recognizing the threat we are posing to the basic ecosystems that create those resources. As Rachel Carson observed in her classic *Silent Spring*, we failed to predict the environmental impacts of extensive pesticide use because chemical companies paid researchers simply to kill pests—and not to worry about the pesticides' effects on other plants and animals, or groundwater supplies, or farm workers' lungs. Perhaps the highest goal of the environmental movement, then, is to reclaim science, to ensure that we use it not for the domination of nature but for the appreciation of our connectedness to it—to restore, in other words, the legacy that Humboldt tried to leave us.

In the nineteenth century, Humboldt's appeal was wide-ranging. Many people saw him as the world's historian, the man who would explain where we came from and how we fit into the universe. He provided an enthralled public with glimpses of exotic natural worlds they would never see for themselves. Scholars flocked to his study in Germany to soak up his wisdom, to examine his field notes and sprawling maps and native artifacts. And laypeople gathered at the newly opened natural history museums to which Humboldt had donated his famous collections of intricate jungle plants and multicolored birds. By organizing lectures and workshops all over the world, he made huge numbers of people feel involved in the progress of science. Moreover, his theories themselves were attractive for their inclusiveness, their ambitious attempts at painting a unified picture of all the world's complexities.

8 Just as every lowly plant and minute insect had a crucial role in Humboldt's vision of the world, so too did every type of human being, no matter how powerless or marginalized.

Humboldt was a hero to Simon Bolivar, who used the scientist's writings in his campaigns for Latin American independence, to help prove that colonialism was wreaking havoc on both the people and the environment of the New World. And Humboldt was especially popular among Americans, by the time of the 1869 centennial, because he had been one of the world's most outspoken opponents of slavery. "In maintaining the unity of the human race," he had written, "we also reject the disagreeable assumption of superior and inferior peoples." Four years after the end of the Civil War, Americans found in Humboldt's scientific work a parallel to the political heroism of President Lincoln. Both men had staked everything on the concept of Union.

In 1869, Humboldt was as well-known and respected, globally, as Lincoln and Bolivar; he had been as influential in nineteenth-century science as Beethoven had been in music, as Napoleon had been in politics. Darwin once wrote that "my whole career is due to having read and reread" Humboldt's *Personal Narrative to the Equinoctial Regions of America*, and he often sent his manuscripts to the older scientist for comment. When the great theoretician of evolution set off on his voyage aboard *The Beagle*, he brought with him only three books: the Bible, a copy of Milton, and Humboldt's *Narrative*. Humboldt's magnum opus, *Cosmos*, bore the daunting subtitle, "A Sketch of a Physical Description of the Universe," and it had an index that ran to more than one thousand pages. But it was translated into all the major languages and sold hundreds of thousands of copies. "The demand is epoch-making," Humboldt's publisher claimed. "Book parcels destined for London and St. Petersburg were torn out of our hands by agents who wanted their orders filled for the bookstores in Vienna and Hamburg." Science, it seems, could easily have gone in the direction Humboldt was taking it.

Today, Humboldt's name is woven tightly into our geographical fabric: The index of a good atlas might list it some twenty-five times, referring not only to towns like Humboldt, Iowa, and Humboldt, South Dakota, but also to the Humboldt Mountains in China, Venezuela, and Nevada; the Humboldt Current off the coast of Peru; and even a Humboldt Glacier in Greenland. But almost no one today has any idea who Humboldt was.

Science, and Western society in general, underwent a huge transformation toward the end of the nineteenth century. In 1859, Humboldt died, Darwin published *On the Origin of Species*, and the modern age was born—though the full implications of evolution did not become clear until 1871, when Darwin delivered the ultimate comeuppance of his own species in *The Descent of Man*. The theory of evolution was revolutionary both because it directly undermined the centuries-old assumption that there was a divine plan separating human beings from the lowly animals, and because it posed a significant threat to the dearly held Humboldtian notion that nature was fundamentally a harmonious, unified entity. To most educated Westerners, the Darwinian concept of "the struggle for existence" meant that humanity's origins were steeped in animal violence and conflict—that the different facets of nature were not working together to form an organic whole but were competing with each other, fighting over ecological niches, fighting just to survive.

12 The one redeeming element of Darwinism, for many shocked Victorians, was that their civilization had at least seemed to come out of the competition victorious. In the hands of so-called Social Darwinists, "the struggle for existence" became "the

survival of the fittest," and theorizers were quick to assert that Darwin's explanation of biological fitness proved the superiority of white, Christian Europeans. After all, they argued, a careful reading of *On the Origin of Species* revealed that the successful animals were those that had bodies perfectly designed to perform a particular function or adapt to a particular environment. The key to a species' success, in other words, was *specialization*—a word Darwin probably coined in the 1840s. And Europeans were without question becoming the world's experts in specialization.

By the second half of the nineteenth century, specialization was beginning to seep into almost every aspect of Western culture and thought. Graduate schools were offering highly specialized training in narrow professions. Huge new businesses were dividing their production processes into the smallest possible components, with the aim of improving efficiency and becoming more fit competitors in the capitalist economy. Laborers no longer saw products through from start to finish, but rather performed their one limited function, over and over again. By the turn of the century, someone had to coin the term *Renaissance man* to refer to that rare person who hearkened back to the era before intense specialization was the norm, back when most people cultivated a variety of linked interests and skills.

Gradually, Humboldt's bigger picture came to seem neither appealing nor important, since specialization was paying off so well by making labor and the exploitation of nature so much more efficient. Now, Darwinists reasoned, man might be on his way to breaking his connections with animal savagery and freeing himself from all the other harsh forces of nature. Evolutionary progress came to mean the conquest of the natural world by science and technology, and distancing oneself from nature became a cultural imperative. Survival depended on winning an all-out competition with other living things—including other members of our own species. And knowledge depended on the ability to observe nature purely as object, as something unrelated to us and best understood when broken down mechanistically into its smallest components.

The embrace of Darwinism and the transformation of science, then, went hand in hand with rapid industrialization, the rise of free-market capitalism, and the expansion of colonialism. Social Darwinists defended empire-building on the grounds that vigorous self-aggrandizement was only natural. And they used similar arguments to validate their racism: The affluence and technological prowess of the Western world, they argued, proved that the races and nations of the "Third World" really were "less developed." As C. S. Lewis, the British writer and critic, once pointed out, the ironies of this new world order ran deep: "At the moment, then, of man's victory over nature, we find the whole human race subjected to some individual men, and individuals subjected to that in themselves which is purely 'natural'—to their irrational impulses." The leaders of a culture that worshipped civilization and science were calmly calling for the massacre or repression of several indigenous nations in the Americas, the methodical deforestation of the United States, and the military invasion of most of Africa.

16 Of course, given Humboldt's direct influence on Darwin, there had to be elements of the theory of evolution that hearkened back to the elder scientist's approach.

Indeed, the most significant implication of the *Origin* may have been its assertion that man, on the most fundamental level, was but a part of nature—as Humboldt had argued for decades. Some nineteenth-century thinkers, accordingly, managed to find in evolutionary theory a spirit of cooperation and union. To the author and naturalist W. H. Hudson, for instance, Darwin's work meant that "we are no longer isolated, standing like starry visitors on a mountain-top, surveying life from the outside; but are on a level with and part and parcel of it."

Darwin was fascinated with the idea of nature as a "web"—"we may all be netted together," he mused in the late 1830s—and strong ecological currents run through many of his early writings. The word *oecologie* was in fact coined in 1866 by Germany's foremost Darwinian scientist, Ernst Haeckel. And when Haeckel defined his new scientific discipline, he invoked his mentor by name: ecology, he explained, was "the body of knowledge concerning the economy of nature . . . , the study of all those complex interrelations referred to by Darwin."

In the end, however, Darwin chose to focus on the violent, competitive aspects of his theory. He was explicitly lending his support to the colonialist ethic when he asserted the evolutionary doctrine that an "endless number of lower races" had to be "beaten and supplanted" by "the higher civilized races." Such competitive replacement was inevitable, Darwin argued, because niches in the economy of nature were only so big—as he had learned from the work of the Reverend Thomas Malthus. To Darwin, Malthus's 1798 *Essay on Population* proved that no species could rely on the myth of nature's abundance. Since our population seems to grow at a much faster rate than our food supply, Malthus argued, human society is destined to face starvation on a massive scale. Darwin made this doomsday theme the engine of his theory of evolution: Crises caused by environmental constraints brutally forced out the species that could not compete. He considered it part of his mission to convince naive Romantics that, in the words of the evolutionary biologist Stephen Jay Gould, "we should never have sought solace or moral instruction in Nature."

20 Humboldt, conversely, held up the natural world as a model, as something worthy of our ultimate respect. In his writings, he sought "to depict the contemplation of natural objects as a means of exciting a pure love of nature." Yet he was no naive Romantic. Just as Darwin recognized the organicist ecological perspective, so too did Humboldt recognize the elements of violence, competition, and disunity in nature. After all, he had cut his way through the swarming, dripping jungles of South America, had witnessed such bizarre events as the mass electrocution of several horses by a colony of eels—and he had seen men enslaving other men. While Darwin focused on the disunity, though, and the specialized adaptations of species to local environments, Humboldt focused on the unity, and the global forces that link different environments and their inhabitants together. Both perspectives reveal important truths.

Humboldt's ideas were marginalized simply because Darwin's were more fit in the late nineteenth century—because Darwinism in effect captured the essence of the modernizing Western world.

In general, Humboldt's work is still marginalized, but where it is known, experts accept it as good, hard science. One representative contribution he made to the development of ecology was his theory relating the geographical distribution of plants to the effects of climate—a radical idea that remains a cornerstone of our understanding of plant ecosystems. At the base of peaks like Mount Chimborazo in the Ecuadorean Andes, he found the vines and bright orchids and tall hardwoods of the rainforest, while on the snow-clad summit he found only the hardiest mosses and lichens. On mountain after mountain, vegetation got sparser at higher altitudes, as if during his ascent he were walking from the equator to one of the poles: vertical geography mirrored horizontal geography. Humboldt was the first to classify forests as tropical, temperate, or boreal. Climate, he realized, seemed to govern the development of life everywhere; all plants and animals were "subject to the same laws" of temperature.

Humboldt had traveled to a continent less touched by human influence in order to look into the past and discover the forces that had shaped nature into its present form. "In the New World," he wrote, "man and his productions almost disappear amidst the stupendous display of wild and gigantic nature. . . . On no other part of the globe is [the naturalist] called upon more powerfully to raise himself to general ideas on the cause of phenomena and their mutual connection." This historical technique and his "habit of viewing the Globe as a great whole" allowed Humboldt to identify climate as a unifying global force, proving, in a sense, that we all live under the same roof. Changes in one locale, he pointed out, might cause, or at least signal, changes somewhere else. And by drawing lines on the map connecting points with the same mean temperature—he coined the word *isotherm*—he established permanent scientific structures that would enable future generations to think globally. Humboldt's innovations in the field of comparative climatology underlie current attempts to understand the threat of global warming.

24 Long before any suspicion of change in the atmosphere, Humboldt was worrying about the effect of humanity's actions on terra firma; his knowledge of ecology translated into a nascent environmentalism. Again, the New World taught him an important lesson. European systems of commerce insulated the wealthy from the ecological consequences of their consumption, but the less developed economies of the Americas could not hide their dependence on surrounding natural systems. A year in Mexico, for instance, showed Humboldt that "the produce of the earth is in fact the sole basis of permanent opulence"—and that we could not afford to use that produce wastefully.

Studying a lake in Venezuela, Humboldt used his ecological perspective to relate the lake's decline to the deforestation of the surrounding watershed. Once deprived of the trees' root systems, he explained, the surrounding soils had a greatly diminished capacity for water retention, so they could no longer recharge the springs that fed the lake. And, meanwhile, because the area was deforested, "the waters falling in rain are no longer impeded in their course; and instead of slowly augmenting the level of the rivers by progressive filtrations, they furrow [the hillsides with] sudden inundations," causing widespread soil erosion. "Hence it results that the destruction of the forests, the want of permanent springs, and the existence of torrents are three phenomena closely connected together." Humboldt saw the social consequences as well: "by felling trees . . . , men in every climate prepare at once two calamities for future generations: the want of fuel and a scarcity of water."

Humboldt's fear of resource scarcity reflects his own reading of Malthus's essay, which he called "one of the most profound works of political economy ever written." Yet Humboldt's analysis of environmental limits was far more sophisticated than

Malthus's: To Humboldt, increases in resource consumption reflected not inevitable demographic pressures but simple, conscious decisions. If our population increased to several billion, then perhaps our basic needs might become too much for the earth to handle, but Humboldt realized that the resource scarcities of his own day were caused by overconsumption and mismanagement. Those trees in Venezuela didn't have to be chopped down.

Even more radical was Humboldt's interest in linking such problems to the injustices of colonialism. In his analysis of the resource base of Mexico, which he published as *A Political Essay on the Kingdom of New Spain*—and which ventured into the fields of demography, medicine, anthropology, sociology, political science, economics, agriculture, biology, geology, and geography—Humboldt took great pains to show that it was not necessary for so many Mexicans to go without land and food. His multifaceted approach helped him to see that such outrages were being driven not by population pressures but by basic socioeconomic structures. Many peasants were landless, he explained, because "the property in New Spain . . . is in a great measure in the hands of a few powerful families who have gradually absorbed the smaller estates." And impoverished Mexicans were starving because wealthy landlords grew cash crops for export instead of food crops for domestic consumption. "Whenever the soil can produce both indigo and maize," Humboldt noted indignantly, "the former prevails over the latter, although the general interest requires that a preference be given to those vegetables which supply nourishment to man over those which are merely objects of exchange with strangers."

28 Humboldt was still a man of his time: In general, he approved of the development of the New World, and he never openly demanded that the Spanish American colonies receive full independence. But his interdisciplinary research did lead him to a scathing critique of colonialism. With the conviction of one who knows his subject thoroughly, Humboldt asserted that "the restless and suspicious colonial policies of the nations of Europe . . . have thrown insurmountable obstacles in the way of the . . . prosperity of their distant possessions. . . . A colony has for ages been considered useful to the parent state only in so far as it supplied a great number of raw materials." Because Humboldt was so aware of the interdependent relationships that governed the world, his science could never have been used to validate dominance over other people or the environment; he knew the Europeans' abuse of other lands would come back to haunt them. Later in the nineteenth century, politicians would repeatedly refer to Darwinism in claiming that certain human and natural resources were expendable for the sake of the evolutionary progress of "the higher civilized races." But according to Humboldt, nothing was expendable.

Today, the destruction of the developing world's environment—the burning of the rainforest, the strip-mining of mountain ranges, the appropriation of valuable croplands for the raising of tradable commodities—is still largely driven by the demands of the world's wealthiest countries. The structure of the global economy dictates that developing nations put all their efforts into raising cash—usually by exporting whatever virgin resources the industrial world might desire. They need the cash to pay off their "debt."

Even Humboldt accepted Darwinian conflict and chaos as basic facts of life. The whole time he was working on *Cosmos*—during the last thirty years of his life—he knew that the grand, unifying theory he sought was unattainable, because the world was too complicated and chaotic and contingent. "Experimental sciences," he wrote, "based on the observation of the external world, cannot aspire to completeness; the nature of things, and the imperfection of our organs, are alike opposed to it. . . . The attempt perfectly to represent unity in diversity must therefore necessarily prove unsuccessful."

The existence of chaos, however, does not invalidate the search for a cosmos. "Even a partial solution," Humboldt wrote, "—the tendency toward a comprehension of the phenomena of the universe—will not the less remain the eternal and sublime aim of every investigation of nature." And modern chaos theory has in fact demonstrated that beneath almost every manifestation of disorder lurks some sort of pattern or equilibrium. As Daniel Botkin, author of *Discordant Harmonies: A New Ecology for the Twenty-First Century,* has noted, it is important for us to realize, with Darwin, that nature is not calm and balanced but rather constantly changing; but we must also understand that "certain rates of change are natural, desirable, and acceptable, while others are not." It is possible to differentiate between natural and unnatural rates of change and to seek to uphold nature's dynamic equilibrium.

32 Up to now, unfortunately, scientists and policy makers have put far too much emphasis on bracing for disorder—on exploiting and stockpiling natural resources in ever greater quantities, and on stockpiling weapons to defend those resources. The United States, for instance, spends $50 billion annually on the development of defense and space technologies, but less than $2 billion in furthering our understanding of the environment. There is a perfectly straightforward reason why we have more sophisticated techniques for planting land mines in the desert than for planting corn on an erodible hillside.

Restoring the balance of modern science, then, would entail devoting more time and money to the search for order in nature, to the mapping of the world's interconnections. more prominent, better-funded environmental science could help stop over-exploitation by forcing people to realize that each part of the living world is equally valuable. And a major redistribution of research dollars could produce creative, long-term solutions to the problems inherent in resource extraction. New studies could help us, for instance, to pinpoint sustainable yields from fisheries and water supplies; to harvest crops, including trees, without losing so much soil to erosion; and to harness renewable, efficient forms of energy instead of going to war to ensure a steady supply of oil.

In lobbying for the research dollars they deserve, ecologists and environmentalists should begin by spreading an ethic of interdisciplinary cooperation. Their unique perspective, which emphasizes holistic, synthetic thinking, is crucial to scientists and developers alike, who need to understand the full impacts of their work over the long term. Even more important, though, ecologists and environmentalists should extend their interdisciplinary approach to include the public at large. People everywhere need to realize that they have a stake in the direction science is taking. All over the world, people concerned about their environments are already clamoring for more information, so that they can hold developers, corporations, and governments accountable for their actions. But they need more help from the scientists themselves, who too often come across as aloof experts with little interest in the public sphere. Only by bridging the gap between "laypeople" and "specialists," only by building connections among ourselves, will we be able to alter the scientific research agenda and rebuild our connections with the natural world.

So far, what limited success environmentalists have had in broadening their coalitions and garnering more research grants has been due to their eloquent public warnings about the dangers of ignoring the ecological perspective. Over the last few years, for instance, by pointing out that most rainforests are probably nurturing valuable medicines, food crops, fibers, soil-restoring vegetation, or petroleum substitutes, environmentalists have convinced major drug companies and agribusiness firms to join with indigenous peoples in conserving tropical ecosystems. As the wilderness philosopher Aldo Leopold once noted, "To keep every cog and wheel is the first precaution of intelligent tinkering."

36 Unfortunately, though, ecological warnings sometimes deteriorate into scare tactics, and a public that already has too much to worry about is quickly becoming disdainful of doomsday scenarios. Well-meaning environmentalists too often claim that if we don't do the right thing immediately, we'll end up fighting each other for whatever resources remain—in other words, we'll be stuck in a world of Malthusian scarcity and Darwinian conflict. Yet the goal of ecological thinking should be to offer an alternative to conflict. If environmentalists truly want to restore science's balance, they will have to go beyond warnings and give us a positive reason to take an interest in scientific research priorities. They will have to popularize science the way Humboldt did—by conveying to people the exhilaration of understanding one's place in the world, the "intellectual delight and sense of freedom" that comes of "insight into universal nature."

Humboldt considered himself above all an educator, and his ultimate goal was to teach people a basic love of nature, something today's environmental movement rarely seems to do. All his life, he encouraged people simply to leave their houses and escape their specialized lifestyles, to experience the wide-open land. Once we were surrounded by nature, Humboldt felt sure, an awareness of our dependence on it would arise in us "intuitively . . . , from the contrast we draw between the narrow limits of our own existence and the image of infinity revealed on every side—whether we look upward to the starry vault of heaven, scan the far-stretching plain before us, or seek to trace the dim horizon across the vast expanse of ocean." That intuition of our indebtedness to the natural world, that recognition of our own smallness, should be the force driving scientific research.

PERSONAL RESPONSE

What did you know about Humboldt before you read this essay? What is your impression of him now that you have read about his work and his importance?

QUESTIONS FOR CLASS OR SMALL-GROUP DISCUSSION

1. What is the impact of Sachs's opening paragraph? What details does Sachs provide throughout the essay to explain why Humboldt was so highly regarded? Locate a passage that you consider especially significant in describing Humboldt and his influence.
2. Sachs writes in paragraph 19 that the perspectives of both Darwin and Humboldt "reveal important truths." Summarize the different perspectives of those two, and then discuss what truths their differing perspectives reveal.
3. Sachs reports that the United States "spends $50 billion annually on the development of defense and space technologies, but less than $2 billion on furthering our understanding of the environment" (paragraph 30). Are you comfortable with that ordering of priorities? Explain whether you would make any changes in allocations if you had the authority to do so.
4. Sachs maintains that ecologists and environmentalists should spread "an ethic of interdisciplinary cooperation" (paragraph 32). How do you think that might be done?

GLOBAL WARNING: GET UP! STAND UP!

BILL MCKIBBEN

Bill McKibben, author, educator, and environmentalist, is contributing editor of OnEarth. *His books include* The End of Nature, *the first book for a general audience on global warming (1989);* The Age of Missing Information *(1992);* Hope, Human and Wild: True Stories of Living Lightly on Earth *(1995);* Maybe One: The Case for Smaller Families *(1998);* Long Distance: Testing the Limits of Body and Spirit in a Year of Living Strenuously *(2000);* Enough: Staying Human in an Engineering Age *(2003);* Deep Economy: The Wealth of Communities and the Durable Future *(2007); and* EAARTH *[sic]*: Making a Life on a Tough New Planet *(2008).* OnEarth, *the quarterly journal of the Natural Resources Defense Council, explores politics, nature, wildlife, culture, science, health, the challenges that confront our planet, and the solutions that promise to heal and protect it. This article appeared in the Spring 2007 issue of* OnEarth.

Here's a short list of the important legislation our federal government has enacted to combat global warming in the years since 1988, when a NASA climatologist, James Hansen, first told Congress that climate change was real:

1.
2.
3.

And what do you know? That bipartisan effort at doing nothing has been highly successful: Our emissions of carbon dioxide have steadily increased over that two-decade span.

Meanwhile, how have the lone superpower's efforts at leading international action to deal with climate change gone? Not too well. We refused to ratify the Kyoto treaty, while the rest of the developed world finally did so. And while we've pressured China over world-shaking issues like DVD piracy, we've happily sold them the parts to help grow their coal-fired electric utility network to a size that matches ours.

In other words, Washington has utterly and completely failed to take on the single greatest challenge human civilization has ever faced.

4 What's more, Washington, at least so far, couldn't care less about the failure. A flurry of legislation has been introduced in the last couple of months, but scarcely a member of Congress felt compelled to answer in the last election for failing to deal with climate change. A simple "I'm concerned" was more than enough.

Not only that, but scientists revealed last December that a piece of ice the size of 11,000 football fields had broken off an Arctic ice shelf.

So, and here I use a technical term that comes from long study of the intricate science, we're screwed. Unless.

If we're going to change any of those nasty facts, we need a movement. A real, broad-based public movement demanding transformation of the way we power our world. A movement as strong, passionate, and willing to sacrifice as the civil rights movement that ended segregation more than a generation ago. This essay is about the possible rise of such a movement—about the role that you might play in making it happen.

8 It's not the fault of our environmental organizations that such a movement doesn't yet exist. It's the fault of the molecular structure of carbon dioxide.

Modern environmentalism arose in the early 1960s in the wake of *Silent Spring*. That's the moment advocates of "conservation"—the idea that we should protect some areas as refuges amid a benign modernity—began to realize that modernity itself might be a problem, that the bright miracles of our economic life came with shadows. First DDT, but before long phosphates in detergent and sulfur in the smoke stream of coal plants and chlorofluoro-carbons (CFCs) in our air conditioners. And carbon monoxide, carbon with one oxygen atom, the stuff that was helping turn the air above our cities brown.

All were alike in one crucial way: You could take care of the problems they caused with fairly easy technical fixes. Different pesticides that didn't thin eggshells; scrubbers on smokestacks. DuPont ended up making more money on the stuff that replaced CFCs, which had been tearing a hole in the ozone layer. None of these battles was easy: The Natural Resources Defense Council (NRDC) and Greenpeace and Environmental Defense and the Sierra Club and the Union of Concerned Scientists and a thousand Friends of the You-Name-It had to fight like hell to make sure that the fixes got made. But that was the war we armed for: We had the lawyers and the scientists and the regulatory experts and the lobbyists and the fund-raisers. We didn't always win, but the batting average was pretty high: You can swim in more rivers, breathe in more cities. It was a carbon monoxide movement, and the catalytic converter, which washed that chemical from your exhaust, was its emblem. You could drive your car; you just needed the right gear on your tailpipe.

But carbon dioxide—carbon with two oxygen atoms—screwed everything up. Carbon dioxide in itself isn't exactly a pollutant. It doesn't hurt you when you breathe it; in fact, for a very long time engineers described a motor as "clean-burning" if it gave off only CO_2 and water vapor. The problem that emerged into public view in the late 1980s was that its molecular structure trapped heat near the planet that would otherwise radiate back out to space. And, worse, there wasn't a technofix this time—CO_2 was an inevitable by-product of burning fossil fuels. That is to say, the only way to deal with global warming is to move quickly away from fossil fuels.

12 When you understand that, you understand why Congress has yet to act, and why even big and talented environmental organizations have been largely stymied. Fossil fuel is not like DDT or phosphates or CFCs. It's the absolute center of modern life. An alien scientist arriving on our planet might well conclude that Western human beings are devices for burning coal and gas and oil, since that is what we do from dawn to dusk, and then on into the brightly lit night. When societies get richer, they start reducing other pollutants—even in China some cities have begun to see reductions in sulfur and nitrogen as people demand better pollution controls. But as the Harvard economist Benjamin Friedman conceded in a landmark book in 2005, *The Moral Consequences of Economic Growth*, carbon dioxide is the only pollutant that economic growth doesn't reduce. It is economic growth. It's no accident that the last three centuries, a time of great prosperity, have also been the centuries of coal and oil and gas.

Which means that this is a war that environmentalism as currently constituted simply can't win. Our lobbyists can sit down with congressional staffers and convince them of the need for, say, lower arsenic levels in water supplies; they have enough support to win those kinds of votes. We've managed, brilliantly, to save the Arctic National Wildlife Refuge from drilling. But we lack (by a long shot) the firepower to force, say, a carbon tax that might actually cut fossil fuel use. We've been outgunned by the car companies and the auto unions when it comes to gasoline mileage. We can save the Arctic refuge from oil drilling, but we can't save it from thawing into a northern swamp no caribou would ever wander through. In essence, we have a problem opposite to that of the American military: Well armed for small battles with insurgent polluters, we suddenly find ourselves needing to fight World War II.

What we have now is the superstructure of a movement. We have brilliant scientists, we have superb economists, we have some of the most battle-hardened lawyers and lobbyists you could hope for. The only thing the climate movement lacks is the movement part.

Consider this: Last Labor Day weekend, a few of us led a five-day, 50-mile march across our home state of Vermont to demand that our candidates for federal office take stronger stands on climate legislation. We started at Robert Frost's summer writing cabin high in the Green Mountains, happy with the symbolism of choosing a road less taken. As we wandered byways and main roads, we were happy too with the reception we got—crowds waiting to greet us at churches and senior centers and farms, motorists waving and honking even from the largest SUVs. By the time we reached Burlington, the state capital, we had a thousand marchers. (It was more than enough to convince all our candidates, even the conservative Republicans, to endorse strong carbon reductions; they all signed a pledge backing 80 percent cuts in carbon emissions by 2050.) But here's the not-so-happy thing: The newspapers said that a rally of 1,000 people was the largest that had yet taken place in this nation against global warming. That's pathetic.

16 But not hopeless. Because that movement is starting to gather, less inside the main environmental organizations than on their fringes.

The student movement, for instance, has come out of nowhere in the last three years. All of a sudden there are hundreds of high schools and college campuses where kids are working for real change in how their dorms and classrooms are heated and lit. And emboldened by their success on campus, they're increasingly involved in state and national and international efforts. Whenever I'm feeling disheartened about how slowly change is coming, I stop by a meeting of the Sunday Night Group at Middlebury College, the campus where I work. A hundred or more students show up for the weekly meetings, and they get right down to business—some on making sure that every light bulb in town is a compact fluorescent, some on making sure that every legislator in the state is a climate convert. On the national level, the group Energy Action has joined 16 student organizations into an effective force. The group's Campus Climate Challenge will soon involve a thousand schools, and its leaders are planning a summer of marches and a platoon of youth to bird-dog presidential candidates.

Or look at the churches and synagogues. Ten years ago there was no religious environmental movement to speak of. Now, "creation care" is an emerging watchword across the spectrum, from Unitarians to evangelicals among the Christian traditions and in Jewish, Buddhist, and Muslim communities as well. And the rhetoric is increasingly matched by action: Groups such as Interfaith Power and Light are organizing congregations to cut energy use, and groups such as Religious Witness for the Earth are organizing people of faith for marches of their own.

There's even one very sweet by-product of the roadblock in Washington: In cities and states across the union, big environmental groups and local citizen activists have focused their energy on mayors and governors and learned a good deal in the process. Including this: It's possible to win. If California's Republican governor can decide it's in his interest to embrace strong climate legislation, you know people have done good groundwork. They've worked in public as well as behind the scenes. Activists from the Maryland-based Chesapeake Climate Action Network were arrested last fall for blocking the doors to federal offices to demand more accurate federal science.

20 The moment is ripe. Hurricane Katrina blew open the door of public opinion, and Al Gore walked valiantly through it with his movie. There are, finally, lots and lots of people who want to know how they can make a difference. Not 51 percent of the people, but we don't need 51 percent. We can do just fine with 15 percent. As long as they're active. As long as they're a movement.

Which brings me, finally, to the point. It's time to unleash as much passion and energy as we can. It's movement time.

What we need is nothing less than a societal transformation. Not a new gizmo, not a few new laws, but a commitment to wean America from fossil fuels in our lifetime and to lead the rest of the world, especially India and China, in the same direction. The shorthand we're using in our April stepitup07.org campaign is the same as it was in our Vermont march: 80 percent cuts by 2050. What we need is big change, starting right now.

And that's a message Congress needs to hear. Though the November elections opened new possibilities, they also raised new perils. Instead of James Inhofe, who thought global warming was a hoax, the relevant Senate committee now answers to Barbara Boxer, who understands that it's very real. But the very chance of a deal raises the specter of a bad deal—some small-potatoes around-the-edges kind of action that substitutes the faux realism of Washington politics for the actual physics-and-chemistry realism of our predicament. For instance, when John McCain introduced legislation five years ago that asked for small and more or less voluntary cuts, it was a step forward, and I saluted him on the cover of this magazine. But the current draft of his bill is fairly weak. Even the strongest bills, introduced by Henry Waxman and Bernie Sanders, barely meet the test for what the science demands. And chances are, unless we really do our job on the ground, the measures they're proposing will barely be discussed.

24 NASA's James Hansen—our premier climatologist—has made it clear we have 10 years to reverse the flow of carbon into the atmosphere. Actually, he made it clear in the fall of 2005, so we have eight and a half years before we cross certain thresholds (Arctic melt, for instance) that commit us to an endless cycle of self-reinforcing feedback loops and, in Hansen's words, a "totally different planet."

That requires transformation, not tinkering. It's not like carbon monoxide or DDT—it's like the women's movement or the civil rights movement, which changed the basic taken-for-granted architecture of our nation. Except it's harder, because this time we don't need the system to accommodate more people; we need the system to change in profound ways.

The only chance is for those of us who see the risk and the opportunity to act—as quickly and as powerfully as ever we can.

PERSONAL RESPONSE

How committed are you to the kind of activism that McKibben calls for?

QUESTIONS FOR CLASS OR SMALL-GROUP DISCUSSION

1. Describe the tone in the opening paragraphs. What is the effect of that tone? Where does the tone change?
2. In paragraph 7, McKibben writes that Washington has failed "to take on the single greatest challenge human civilization has ever faced." What is that challenge? Do you agree that it is the greatest challenge humans have faced? If not, what other challenge(s) are greater?
3. The subtitle of this essay is "How to Build a Mass Movement to Halt Climate Change." Summarize in your own words the actions that McKibben recommends for building a mass movement to halt climate change. Do you agree with him that such a movement will work?
4. How persuasive do you find this article? Are you moved to act?

THE SIXTH EXTINCTION

JEFF CORWIN

Jeff Corwin, biologist, Emmy-Award winning producer, and television host is the author of 100 Heartbeats: The Race to Save the World's Most Endangered Animal Species *(2009), a book about his experiences tracking the sixth extinction. A companion documentary to the book aired on MSNBC in 2009. This article was published in the* Los Angeles Times *on November 30, 2009.*

There is a holocaust happening. Right now. And it's not confined to one nation or even one region. It is a global crisis.

Species are going extinct en masse.

Every 20 minutes we lose an animal species. If this rate continues, by century's end, 50% of all living species will be gone. It is a phenomenon known as the sixth extinction. The fifth extinction took place 65 million years ago when a meteor smashed into the Earth, killing off the dinosaurs and many other species and opening the door for the rise of mammals. Currently, the sixth extinction is on track to dwarf the fifth.

4 What—or more correctly—who is to blame this time? As Pogo said, "We have met the enemy, and he is us."

The causes of this mass die-off are many: overpopulation, loss of habitat, global warming, species exploitation (the black market for rare animal parts is the third-largest illegal trade in the world, outranked only by weapons and drugs). The list goes on, but it all points to us.

Over the last 15 years, in the course of producing television documentaries and writing about wildlife, I have traveled the globe, and I have witnessed the grim carnage firsthand. I've observed the same story playing out in different locales.

In South Africa, off the coast of Cape Horn, lives one of the most feared predators of all—the great white shark. Yet this awesome creature is powerless before the mindless killing spree that is decimating its species at the jaw-dropping rate of 100 million sharks a year. Many are captured so that their dorsal fins can be chopped off (for shark fin soup). Then, still alive, they are dropped back into the sea, where they die a slow and painful death.

8 Further east, in Indonesia, I witnessed the mass destruction of rain forests to make way for palm oil plantations. Indonesia is now the world's leading producer of palm oil—a product used in many packaged foods and cosmetic goods—and the victims are the Sumatran elephant and orangutan. These beautiful creatures are on the brink of extinction as their habitats go up in smoke, further warming our planet in the process.

One day while swimming off the coast of Indonesia, I came across a river of refuse and raw sewage stretching for miles. These streams and islands of refuse now populate all our oceans; in the middle of the Pacific, there is an island of garbage the size of Texas. This floating pollution serves to choke off and kill sea turtles—driving them closer to extinction. At the same time, the coral reefs where sea turtles get their food supply are dying due to rising sea temperatures from global warming. To top it off, sea turtles are hunted and killed for their meat—considered a delicacy in many Asian countries. It is an ugly but altogether effective one-two-three punch for this unique species.

It's important to understand that this is not just a race to save a handful of charismatic species—animals to which we attach human-inspired values or characteristics. Who wouldn't want to save the sea otter, polar bear, giant panda or gorilla? These striking mammals tug at our heartstrings and often our charitable purse strings. But our actions need to be just as swift and determined when it comes to the valley elderberry longhorn beetle or the distinctly uncuddly, pebbly-skinned Puerto Rican crested toad or the black-footed ferret, whose fate is inextricably intertwined with that of the prairie dog. The reality is that each species, no matter how big, small, friendly or vicious, plays an important and essential role in its ecosystem. And we're in a race to preserve as much of the animal kingdom as possible.

Meanwhile, around the planet there are massive die-offs of amphibians, the canaries in our global coal mine. When frogs and other amphibians, which have existed for hundreds of millions of years, start to vanish, it is a sign that our natural world is in a state of peril. Bat and bee populations are also being decimated. Without bees, there will be no pollination, and without pollination, the predator that is decimating these other species—humankind—will also be headed toward its own extinction. Yes, there is a certain irony there.

12 This was all brought home to me in an intimate way after a recent trip to Panama. My young daughter, Maya, asked if she could accompany me on my next trip there so that she could see one of her favorite animals—the Panamanian golden frog—up close and personal in the jungle. Sadly, I had to tell her no. This small, beautiful frog—the national symbol of Panama—no longer exists in the wild. Only a few live in captivity.

Is there hope? Yes. Because in every place I visited to witness the sixth extinction unfold, I met brave and selfless conservationists, biologists and wildlife scientists working hard to save species.

In Panama, biologist Edgardo Griffith has set up an amphibian rescue center to protect and quarantine rare frogs (including the Panamanian golden frog) before they are all wiped out by the deadly fungus *Chytrid*, which is rapidly killing off frogs on a global scale. In Africa, zoologist Iain Douglas Hamilton is one of many seeking to stop the illegal trade in elephant ivory and rhino horn. In Namibia, zoologist Laurie Marker is making strides to save the cheetah before it goes the way of the saber tooth tiger (or India's Bengal tiger, which is also on the precipice of extinction). In Indonesia, Ian Singleton is raising orphaned orangutans, training them to return to the remaining rain forest—giving them a second chance at living in the wild. In South Africa, Alison Kock is leading a crusade to educate the world about the wholesale destruction of sharks.

Here in the United States, Chris Lucash of the U.S. Fish and Wildlife Service, is working to reintroduce the red wolf, now found only in captivity, to the woods of North Carolina. They are just a few of the many who are trying to reverse the species holocaust that threatens the future of our natural world.

16 These committed scientists bring great generosity and devotion to their respective efforts o stop the sixth extinction. But if we don't all rise to the cause and join them in action, they cannot succeed. The hour is near, but it's not too late.

PERSONAL RESPONSE

Write for a few minutes about a detail in this essay that impressed you in some way.

QUESTIONS FOR CLASS OR SMALL-GROUP DISCUSSION

1. Explain what Corwin means by his title, "The Sixth Extinction."
2. Where does Corwin's use examples effectively? What do you understand Corwin to mean by the metaphor of canaries in a coal mine (paragraph 11)?
3. What argumentative strategies does Corwin use to persuade his reader to action? Are you persuaded?
4. In his concluding paragraph, Corwin urges readers to "rise to the cause and join [scientists] in action." How do you think readers can practically join scientists around the globe? What else might individuals do to help stop species extinction?

ACCOUNTING 101 FOR THE 21ST CENTURY: A LIBERAL ARTS EDUCATION IN CARBON

JOHN PETERSEN

John Petersen is Associate Professor of Environmental Studies and Biology and Director of Oberlin College's Environmental Studies Program. A systems ecologist by training, his research has appeared in the journals Ecology, American Naturalist and BioScience *and in books that he has authored and contributed to. His current research focuses on flows of energy, cycles of matter, and feedback control mechanisms operating in the built environment. This article was published in the* Chronicle of Higher Education *on June 20, 2008.*

Recent graduates have a lot to learn about budgeting when they leave college. Many are financially on their own for the first time, and so rent, grocery bills, taxes, and, of course, student loans are expenditures they will need to balance against their incomes. In addition to those personal budgetary challenges, the lives of our graduates will be profoundly affected by impending national budget crises associated with the costs of war, a trade imbalance, Social Security, and health care. And as if those burdens were not enough, the graduates must concern themselves with a new category of budgeting, one that relates not to money but to carbon.

Today's college graduates confront the first truly worldwide environmental challenge, that of balancing the carbon budget—the stocks and flow of carbon through the biosphere—to ameliorate the negative consequences of global climate change. Colleges and universities have an obligation to ensure that we provide our students with the knowledge and experience necessary to accomplish that challenging task. Many of those essential lessons can take place in classrooms, while an equally educational, parallel curriculum is embodied in the management and development of campus infrastructure, the maintenance of grounds, and the provisioning of food and transportation for our students.

On college campuses and in our modern industrial economy as a whole, each bite we eat, each item we discard, each e-mail message we send, and each purchase we make entails a conversion of fossil-fuel carbon to carbon dioxide. Our growing use of fossil fuels has resulted in a sharp increase in atmospheric carbon dioxide, and the carbon budget tips farther out of balance each day.

4 Institutions of higher education are poised to play a leading role in developing and executing climate-neutral policies. The good news is that the emergence of carbon as a universal environmental currency provides a unique and exciting opportunity to integrate economy, ecology, and culture to solve many vexing environmental and cultural problems. That opportunity, in turn, provides many avenues for our colleges, students, and graduates to play a role in developing such solutions.

Like an increasing number of our peer institutions, Oberlin College has adopted a comprehensive environmental policy on energy use, purchasing, building construction and management, food, transportation, waste, grounds management, and education. Although not a perfect measure, the transition to environmental sustainability in every one of these areas can be quantified in terms of reductions in the college's carbon emissions. Examples of carbon-balancing policies and projects at Oberlin include:

- A green-energy purchasing agreement with our local utility that simultaneously reduces the college's carbon-dioxide emissions by 25 percent and generates a "sustainable energy reserve fund" to encourage community-based projects that lead to further carbon-dioxide savings. Community projects carried out thus far include research on the feasibility of local wind power and a grant that helped open a local gas station that now sells only biofuels.
- A green building policy ensures that all new campus construction achieves a Leadership in Energy and Environmental Design Silver or better rating. The LEED rating system is the nationally accepted benchmark for the design, construction, and operation of buildings that minimize energy use (and encourage other practices that minimize greenhouse-gas emissions) and maximize a range of environmental benefits.
- City Wheels, a car-sharing program, provides access to fuel-efficient automobiles on campuses.
- Our Campus Resource Monitoring System provides students with a minute-by-minute online display of electricity use and associated carbon-dioxide

emissions in their residence halls. During a two-week competition, students in residence halls provided with this real-time feedback were able to reduce their electricity use by 56 percent, and the campus as a whole reduced emissions by 148,000 pounds of carbon dioxide.

- Oberlin's Lewis Center for Environmental Studies contains the largest photovoltaic array in Ohio. On an annual basis, the solar cells in the array capture more energy than the total amount that the center uses. The excess emissions-free electricity is sold back to the power company.
- An experimental local "carbon offset" program balances some on-campus greenhouse-gas emissions through projects that reduce emissions in the larger community. For example, in this spring's "Lightbulb Brigade," students provided 10,000 compact fluorescent bulbs to residents in predominantly low-income neighborhoods in exchange for their incandescent bulbs, resulting in savings of about 6,500 tons of carbon dioxide, which could then be credited to Oberlin College.

Many institutions are beginning to recognize such creative campus actions as an imperative. In 2006, Oberlin was the first of its peer institutions to sign the American College and University President's Climate Commitment. By April 2008, the presidents of more than 520 public and private institutions had signed the pledge. Each college commits to develop a budget that will account for all carbon-emissions-associated campus operations, and a long-term plan for balancing that budget to achieve carbon neutrality.

College campuses can serve as laboratories for exploring and developing policies, technologies, attitudes, and behaviors necessary to achieve carbon neutrality. Through class projects, independent research, and student activism, Oberlin students have been key players in all of the environmental initiatives described above. And they have learned a great deal in the process.

Institutions across the country are expanding course offerings on the science and policy of climate change. A number of colleges, including Oberlin, Harvard University, the University of Colorado at Boulder, and the University of California at Berkeley now offer courses in campus sustainability in which students and faculty members engage with administrators and staff members to analyze, explore, and develop strategies to reduce greenhouse-gas emissions at their institutions.

Further, the Disciplinary Associations Network for Sustainability (www.aashe.org/dans) now includes more than 20 national disciplinary associations that have committed to focusing on climate change and environmental sustainability in curricula, research, and professional development. The group includes such diverse organizations as the American Chemical Society, the American Psychological Association, the American Philosophical Association, and the American Academy of Religion. Still needed are mechanisms for easily sharing the creative approaches that instructors and institutions are now developing for teaching climate change across the curriculum.

No one would argue for a monomaniacal focus on carbon or climate in the curriculum, but the fact is that the climate change now under way will touch the personal and professional lives of all of today's students, whether they major in neuroscience, Romance languages, or studio art. Courses that focus directly on climate change are crucial to building expertise, but a systemic approach is necessary to ensure that the entire campus community and the full spectrum of disciplinary perspectives are brought to bear on the challenge before us.

The creativity and critical-thinking skills that emerge from training in the arts and humanities may play a particularly important role in helping students grapple with the meaning of a rapidly changing climate. Literature, religion, sculpture, photography, and language all provide windows for understanding the relationship between humans and their environment.

Faculty members need not have expertise in climate science or policy to begin exploring the implications of a changing world with their students. With a bit of creativity, the importance and relevance of climate change can be linked with content of most natural and social-science classes and introduced for discussion without fundamentally altering existing syllabi. What is vital is that students feel empowered to openly discuss their questions, concerns, and ideas so that they are prepared to address personal, professional, and political choices related to climate change as informed citizens.

A key goal of a liberal-arts education in the 21st century must be to equip graduates with a diversity of intellectual tools and learning experiences needed to ensure the health of our planet. The challenge that our students face is daunting, but with the help of supportive institutions and faculty members, they have the opportunity to construct a world and a culture that are vast improvements on the ones they inherit.

PERSONAL RESPONSE

Explain your position on the subject of individual responsibility for environmental health and/or reducing your carbon footprint.

QUESTIONS FOR CLASS OR SMALL-GROUP DISCUSSION

1. Explain Peterson's opening analogy of college graduates needing to budget. Do you find it an effective lead-in to his main focus?
2. Discuss the steps that Peterson's own college has taken to reduce carbon emissions and enhance environmental sustainability. How does your campus compare?
3. What actions does Peterson call on college administrators, faculty, and students to take? Do you think that such actions are possible?
4. Peterson's final paragraph begins with this statement: "A key goal of a liberal-arts education in the 21st century must be to equip graduates with . . . tools and learning experiences . . . to ensure the health of our planet." Do you agree with him? Explain your answer.

✧ PERSPECTIVES ON ENVIRONMENTAL STUDIES ✧

Suggested Writing Topics

1. Explain your own position on the issue of global warming or any of the environmental issues mentioned in the readings in this chapter.
2. Write an essay that offers possible solutions to one of the major environmental issues confronting people today.
3. Write an essay in response to the author of any of the essays in this chapter.
4. Argue the extent to which you think pressure from lobbyists should influence the thinking of legislators considering measures that would tighten regulations on environmental issues.
5. Write a letter to the editor of your campus or community newspaper in which you urge students on your campus and citizens in the community to take actions to reverse the current abuse of natural resources.
6. Propose practical conservation steps that students on your campus can take.
7. Write a letter to the president of a corporation that you know abuses the environment urging him or her to make changes in the way the company produces its product. If you refuse to buy the product because of its production methods, say so.
8. Although the writers in this chapter address a wide range of environmental issues, these selections do not provide exhaustive coverage. Select an environmental issue that is not addressed in these essays, explain the problem in detail, and if possible, offer solutions.

Research Topics

1. Research the work of Baron Alexander von Humboldt, Charles Darwin, or Thomas Malthus and write a paper arguing the relevance of their ideas to today's environmental issues.
2. Find out more about the sixth extinction and focus on one specific aspect of it to research.
3. Conduct library research on the impact of socioeconomic inequities on environmental issues and argue your position on the subject. Consider including interviews of environmentalists, sociologists, and/or economists from your campus in your research.
4. Research the Kyoto Treaty, explain the controversy that surrounds the treaty, and explain your own viewpoint on it.
5. Select any of the environmental issues mentioned in this chapter as a research subject. Make sure that you fairly present both sides of the issue as you explain your own position.

Responding to Visuals

Editorial cartoon

1. What issue is the subject of the cartoon?
2. This cartoon appeared as on the editorial page of the *Augusta Chronicle*. What position does the editor take on that issue?
3. What details of the cartoon support the editorial position?

Responding to Visuals

Man blocking the flow of toxic waste in the river with smoke emitting from handgun

1. What do the smokestacks in the shape of guns represent?
2. What does the man in the river represent?
3. How effective do you find this image as a statement on environmentalism?

PART • FIVE

Business and Economics

Marketing and the American Consumer

In their characteristic consumption and materialism, Americans are both the envy of people in other nations and the objects of their criticism. America has long been regarded as the "land of plenty," with a plethora of products to buy and a standard of living that allows most citizens to buy them. Yet such plenitude can lead to over-consumption, creating a need to buy for the sake of buying that can become a kind of obsession. Some people seek psychological counseling for this compulsion, whereas others seek financial counseling to manage the debts they have built up as a result of their need to buy things.

Indeed, shopping is so central to the lives of Americans that malls have become more than places to find virtually any product people want and need; they have become social centers, where people gather to meet friends, eat, hang out, exercise, and be entertained. Some regard this penchant for spending money and acquiring goods as a symptom of some inner emptiness, with malls, shopping strips, and discount stores replacing the spiritual centers that once held primary importance in people's lives. Others, especially manufacturers of products and the people who sell them, regard consumerism as a hearty indicator of the nation's economic health.

In the first selection in this chapter, Gary Ruskin and Juliet Schor discuss the negative effects of the pervasive spread of commercialism throughout far too many aspects of American life. "Every Nook and Cranny: The Dangerous Spread of Commercialized Culture" cites numerous examples of the commercialization of government and culture and argues that the effects are almost all negative. Noting that advertising has only recently "been recognized as having political and social merit," Ruskin and Schor complain that it now invades "nearly every nook and cranny of life." You may find yourself nodding in agreement as they mention many ways in which advertising has invaded everyday life. Whether you agree with them that such pervasiveness is dangerous is something you will have to decide for yourself.

The next reading, "Marketing to the Millennials," by Suzy Menkes, explains the new approaches to marketing that upscale luxury and fashion brands are taking. She asks, "If the exclusivity inherent in traditional luxury is an obsolete factor, how do you market to the Millennials?" Part of the explanation lies in the differences in consumer habits among Millennials, Generation X members, and Baby Boomers. No matter what category of consumer you fit into, you will likely be interested in what she has to say about how advertisers profile these groups and shape their strategies as a result.

Then, Anna Quindlen in "Stuff Is Not Salvation" comments on Americans' inclination to buy things that they don't need. Writing just before Christmas, she asks: "[W]hy in the world did we buy all this junk in the first place?" As you read what Quindlen has to say about "addiction to consumption," ask yourself about your own buying habits. Do you see yourself in Quindlen's description of the behavior of shoppers? Do you like to buy for the sake of buying, whether you need a product or not?

Finally, Phyllis Rose takes an amused look at consumerism in America in "Shopping and Other Spiritual Adventures in America Today." Although her essay was written in 1991, her astute observations on why people shop remain relevant today. Using her own experiences, Rose elaborates on what she means when she writes, "It is a misunderstanding of the American retail store to think we go there necessarily to buy. Some of us shop. There's a difference." As you read what Rose has to say about shoppers, think about your own shopping behavior. Do you see yourself in her description of the behavior of shoppers?

EVERY NOOK AND CRANNY: THE DANGEROUS SPREAD OF COMMERCIALIZED CULTURE

GARY RUSKIN AND JULIET SCHOR

Gary Ruskin is Executive Director of Commercial Alert. Juliet Schor is a professor of sociology at Boston College, and author of The Overworked American: The Unexpected Decline of Leisure *(1991)*; The Overspent American: Upscaling, Downshifting and the New Consumer *(1998)*; and Born to Buy: The Commercialized Child and the New Consumer Culture *(2004). She serves on the Board of Directors of Commercial Alert. This article was first published in the January/February 2005 issue of* Multinational Monitor, *a publication that tracks activity in the corporate world, especially in third world countries.*

In December, many people in Washington, D.C., paused to absorb the meaning in the lighting of the National Christmas Tree, at the White House Ellipse. At that event, President George W. Bush reflected that the "love and gifts" of Christmas were "signs and symbols of even a greater love and gift that came on a holy night."

But these signs weren't the only ones on display. Perhaps it was not surprising that the illumination was sponsored by MCI, which, as MCI WorldCom, committed one of the largest corporate frauds in history. Such public displays of commercialism have become commonplace in the United States.

The rise of commercialism is an artifact of the growth of corporate power. It began as part of a political and ideological response by corporations to wage pressures, rising social expenditures, and the successes of the environmental and consumer movements in the late 1960s and early 1970s. Corporations fostered the anti-tax movement and support for corporate welfare, which helped create funding crises in state and local governments and schools, and made them more willing to carry commercial advertising. They promoted "free market" ideology, privatization and consumerism, while denigrating the public sphere. In the late 1970s, Mobil Oil began its decades-long advertising on the *New York Times* op-ed page, one example of a larger corporate effort to reverse a precipitous decline in public approval of corporations. They also became adept at manipulating the campaign finance system, and weaknesses in the federal bribery statute, to procure influence in governments at all levels.

4 Perhaps most importantly, the commercialization of government and culture and the growing importance of material acquisition and consumer lifestyles was hastened by the co-optation of potentially countervailing institutions, such as churches (papal visits have been sponsored by Pepsi, Federal Express and Mercedes-Benz), governments, schools, universities and nongovernmental organizations.

While advertising has long been an element in the circus of U.S. life, not until recently has it been recognized as having political or social merit. For nearly two centuries, advertising (lawyers call it commercial speech) was not protected by the U.S. Constitution. The U.S. Supreme Court ruled in 1942 that states could regulate commercial speech at will. But in 1976, the Court granted constitutional protection to commercial speech. Corporations have used this new right of speech to proliferate advertising into nearly every nook and cranny of life.

Entering the Schoolhouse

During most of the twentieth century, there was little advertising in schools. That changed in 1989, when Chris Whittle's Channel One enticed schools to accept advertising, by offering to loan TV sets to classrooms. Each school day, Channel One features at least two minutes of ads, and 10 minutes of news, fluff, banter and quizzes. The program is shown to about 8 million children in 12,000 schools.

Soda, candy and fast food companies soon learned Channel One's lesson of using financial incentives to gain access to schoolchildren. By 2000, 94 percent of high schools allowed the sale of soda, and 72 percent allowed sale of chocolate candy. Energy, candy, personal care products, even automobile manufacturers have entered the classroom with "sponsored educational materials"—that is, ads in the guise of free "curricula."

8 Until recently, corporate incursion in schools has mainly gone under the radar. However, the rise of childhood obesity has engendered stiff political opposition to junk food marketing, and in the last three years, coalitions of progressives, conservatives and public health groups have made headway. The State of California has banned the sale of soda in elementary, middle and junior high schools. In Maine, soda and candy suppliers have removed their products from vending machines in all schools. Arkansas banned candy and soda vending machines in elementary schools. Los Angeles, Chicago and New York have city-wide bans on the sale of soda in schools. Channel One was expelled from the Nashville public schools in the 2002–3 school year, and will be removed from Seattle in early 2005. Thanks to activist pressure, a company called ZapMe!, which placed computers in thousands of schools to advertise and extract data from students, was removed from all schools across the country.

Ad Creep and Spam Culture

Advertisers have long relied on 30-second TV spots to deliver messages to mass audiences. During the 1990s, the impact of these ads began to drop off, in part because viewers simply clicked to different programs during ads. In response, many advertisers began to place ads elsewhere, leading to "ad creep"—the spread of ads throughout social space and cultural institutions. Whole new marketing sub-specialties developed, such as "place-based" advertising, which coerces captive viewers to watch video ads. Examples include ads before movies, ads on buses and trains in cities (Chicago, Milwaukee and Orlando), and CNN's Airport channel. Video ads are also now common on ATMs, gas pumps, in convenience stores and doctors' offices.

Another form of ad creep is "product placement," in which advertisers pay to have their product included in movies, TV shows, museum exhibits, or other forms of media and culture. Product placement is thought to be more effective than the traditional 30-second ad because it sneaks by the viewer's critical faculties. Product placement has recently occurred in novels, and children's books. Some U.S. TV programs (*American Idol, The Restaurant, The Apprentice*) and movies (*Minority Report, Cellular*) are so full of product placement that they resemble infomercials. By contrast, many European nations, such as Austria, Germany, Norway and the United Kingdom, ban or sharply restrict product placement on television.

Commercial use of the Internet was forbidden as recently as the early 1990s, and the first spam wasn't sent until 1994. But the marketing industry quickly penetrated this sphere as well, and now 70 percent of all e-mail is spam, according to the spam filter firm Postini Inc. Pop-ups, pop-unders and ad-ware have become major annoyances for Internet users. Telemarketing became so unpopular that the corporate-friendly Federal Trade Commission established a National Do Not Call Registry, which has brought relief from telemarketing calls to 64 million households.

12 Even major cultural institutions have been harnessed by the advertising industry. During 2001–2002, the Smithsonian Institution, perhaps the most important U.S. cultural institution, established the General Motors Hall of Transportation and the Lockheed Martin Imax Theater. Following public opposition and Congressional action, the commercialization of the Smithsonian has largely been halted. In 2000, the Library of Congress hosted a giant celebration for Coca-Cola, essentially converting the nation's most important library into a prop to sell soda pop.

Targeting Kids

For a time, institutions of childhood were relatively uncommercialized, as adults subscribed to the notion of childhood innocence, and the need to keep children from the "profane" commercial world. But what was once a trickle of advertising to children has become a flood. Corporations spend about $15 billion marketing to children in the United States each year, and by the mid-1990s, the average child was exposed to 40,000 TV ads annually.

Children have few legal protections from corporate marketers in the United States. This contrasts strongly to the European Union, which has enacted restrictions. Norway and Sweden have banned television advertising to children under 12 years of age; in Italy, advertising during TV cartoons is illegal, and toy advertising is illegal in Greece between 7 AM and 11 PM. Advertising before and after children's programs is banned in Austria.

Government Brought to You by . . .

As fiscal crises have descended upon local governments, they have turned to advertisers as a revenue source. This trend began inauspiciously in Buffalo, New York, in 1995 when Pratt & Lambert, a local paint company, purchased the right to call itself the city's official paint. The next year the company was bought by Sherwin-Williams, which closed the local factory and eliminated its 200 jobs.

16 In 1997, Ocean City, Maryland, signed an exclusive marketing deal to make Coca-Cola the city's official drink, and other cities have followed with similar deals with Coke or Pepsi. Even mighty New York City has succumbed, signing a $166 million exclusive marketing deal with Snapple, after which some critics dubbed it the "Big Snapple."

At the United Nations, UNICEF made a stir in 2002 when it announced that it would "team up" with McDonald's, the world's largest fast food company, to promote "McDonald's World Children's Day" in celebration of the anniversary of the United Nations adoption of the Convention on the Rights of the Child. Public health and children's advocates across the globe protested, prompting UNICEF to decline participation in later years.

Another victory for the anti-commercialism forces, perhaps the most significant, came in 2004, when the World Health Organization's Framework Convention on Tobacco Control became legally binding. The treaty commits nations to prohibit tobacco advertising to the extent their constitutions allow it.

Impacts

Because the phenomenon of commercialism has become so ubiquitous, it is not surprising that its effects are as well. Perhaps most alarming has been the epidemic of marketing-related diseases afflicting people in the United States, and especially children, such as obesity, type 2 diabetes and smoking-related illnesses. Each day, about 2,000 U.S. children begin to smoke, and about one-third of them will die from tobacco-related illnesses. Children are inundated with advertising for high calorie junk food and fast food, and, predictably, 15 percent of U.S. children aged 6 to 19 are now overweight.

20 Excessive commercialism is also creating a more materialistic populace. In 2003, the annual UCLA survey of incoming college freshmen found that the number of students who said it was a very important or essential life goal to "develop a meaningful philosophy of life" fell to an all-time low of 39 percent, while succeeding financially has increased to a 13-year high, at 74 percent. High involvement in consumer culture has been show (by Schor) to be a significant cause of depression, anxiety, low self-esteem and psychosomatic complaints in children, findings which parallel similar studies of materialism among teens and adults. Other impacts are more intangible. A 2004 poll by Yankelovich Partners, found that 61 percent of the U.S. public "feel that the amount of marketing and advertising is out of control," and 65 percent "feel constantly bombarded with too much advertising and marketing." Is advertising diminishing our sense of general well-being? Perhaps.

The purpose of most commercial advertising is to increase demand for a product. As John Kenneth Galbraith noted 40 years ago, the macro effect of advertising is to artificially boost the demand for private goods, thereby reducing the "demand" or support for unadvertised, public goods. The predictable result has been the backlash to taxes, and reduced provision of public goods and services.

This imbalance also affects the natural environment. The additional consumption created by the estimated $265 billion that the advertising industry will spend in 2004 will also yield more pollution, natural resource destruction, carbon dioxide emissions and global warming.

Finally, advertising has also contributed to a narrowing of the public discourse, as advertising-driven media grow ever more timid. Sometimes it seems as if we live in an echo chamber, a place where corporations speak and everyone else listens.

24 Governments at all levels have failed to address these impacts. That may be because the most insidious effect of commercialism is to undermine government integrity. As governments adopt commercial values, and are integrated into corporate marketing, they develop conflicts of interest that make them less likely to take stands against commercialism.

Disgust Among Yourselves

As corporations consolidate their control over governments and culture, we don't expect an outright reversal of commercialization in the near future.

That's true despite considerable public sentiment for more limits and regulations on advertising and marketing. However, as commercialism grows more intrusive, public distaste for it will likely increase, as will political support for restricting it. In the long run, we believe this hopeful trend will gather strength.

In the not-too-distant future, the significance of the lighting of the National Christmas Tree may no longer be overshadowed by public relations efforts to create goodwill for corporate wrongdoers.

PERSONAL RESPONSE

Ruskin and Schor ask in paragraph 20: "Is advertising diminishing our sense of general well-being?" Look at the examples they give in that and the previous paragraph and then answer the question by examining whether your own general well-being has been affected by advertising.

QUESTIONS FOR CLASS OR SMALL-GROUP DISCUSSION

1. Ruskin and Schor mention ways in which commercialism has entered the schoolroom (paragraphs 6–8). Were any of the examples they cite part of your own school experience? Can you give other examples of the invasion of commercialism into schools?

2. What other examples of "ad creep" (paragraph 9) can you give besides the ones that Ruskin and Schor mention? Discuss whether you believe that such advertising should be banned or restricted in the United States, as it is in other countries.
3. Summarize the effects cited by Ruskin and Schor of the "ubiquitous" nature of commercialization (paragraph 19). Do you think that they provide enough evidence to support their contention?
4. Are you convinced by Ruskin's and Schor's argument that the spread of commercialism is "dangerous"? Explain your answer.

MARKETING TO THE MILLENNIALS

SUZY MENKES

Suzy Menkes is Fashion Editor of the International Herald Tribune *and travels the world covering international designer collections. She is also an expert on jewelry and the British royal family and has written the following books:* The Royal Jewels *(1985),* The Windsor Style *(1987), and* Queen and Country *(1992). Menkes was named an officer of the Order of the British Empire for her services to journalism and also named a chevalier of the Legion of Honor by President Jacques Chirac of France. This article was published March 2, 2010, in the* New York Times.

The model Lily Donaldson's hair coils, floats and springs across the screen, creating arresting images in slow motion. As the last strand fades, you brace yourself for the hair spray advertisement that will batter away the emotion and kill the dream.

But it doesn't happen. Nor at the close of a video of a Rodarte woman—all distressed glamour in a techno-thriller of hallucinatory tension. Not even when you give your personal verdict by clicking on the love/don't love buttons. There are no distractions, just an intriguing feeling of an experience without blandishments and no e-commerce in sight.

Nowness.com, the Web site unveiled by LVMH Moët Hennessy Louis Vuitton last week, is as different as could be imagined from the group's defunct eluxury.com, which it replaces. Instead of urgent offers to buy, each video clip, artistic image and cultural commentary creates a mood and suggests that you have entered an exclusive world where you can absorb and be informed. The pleasure is measured by the time you choose to spend in this enfolding world of art laced with the fashionable.

4 If you search for the LVMH name or any indication that the site is underwritten by the world's biggest luxury group, the nearest you get is a fleeting reference to Fendi or another brand that the cognoscenti would recognize as part of the group.

Behind the concept of this interactive platform to create a luxury experience online is Kamel Ouadi, the digital vice president of Nowness. He describes the site as a subtle, discreet and elegant way to offer original, interesting and ever-changing content to intelligent and aspirational people—and those who are already embedded in the digital culture.

"It is not a commercial platform, although we hope that when we have raised the traffic, we can have partnerships with others as well as give animated and customized information," says Mr. Ouadi, explaining how a visitor's viewing choices will be streamlined into a personal portfolio.

Finding a way to reach a generation that is eager to be entertained and informed, yet resistant to the familiar, in-your-face 20th-century approach, is the focus of every smart luxury and fashion brand. As the fourth and final round of the international collections opens in Paris on Wednesday, the buzz is more around live-streaming shows and 3-D technology than about seasonal trends.

8 The target is the Millennials, defined as those born in the 1980s who came of age with the new century and are now between 18 and 28. The fact that they have grown up wired—linked as soon as they start to socialize via cellphones, computers and video games—is not the only defining characteristic. They have a different mind-set, making former methods of approach obsolete. This is the generation of free downloads, easy access to everything—what the American psychologist Nathan Brody calls "the entitled generation."

If the exclusivity inherent in traditional luxury is an obsolete factor, how do you market to the Millennials?

"We think a lot about the mind-set of the consumers—what are the youngsters doing, does it differ country by country, region by region—we need a deep understanding because that is crucial for the future," says Robert Polet, president and chief executive of Gucci Group.

Like other executives, Mr. Polet refers to the definitive report by the Pew Research Center, a U.S.-based nonprofit public opinion research group, that explored the behaviors, values and opinions of the teens and 20-somethings that make up the Millennial Generation.

12 One of the most evident changes is social networking, which is embraced by 75 percent of the Millennials, compared with 50 percent of the Generation X members (ages 30 to 45) and just 30 percent of Baby Boomers (aged 46 to 64).

"These unique factors make them very savvy consumers, who pay great attention to the value of what they buy and require a different way to interact with brands," says Mr. Polet. "At Gucci Group, we recognize their transformative power in the way they engage with luxury brands. We are embracing different ways of creating dialogue through social media. Some of our brands have launched Facebook and Twitter pages and iPhone applications."

The executive was referring particularly to products, playlists and videos introduced by Gucci, with the active involvement of Frida Giannini, its 38-year-old creative director.

Angela Ahrendts, chief executive of Burberry, sees Christopher Bailey, the brand's 38-year-old chief creative officer, as "a bridge into the Millennial consumer." Their joint embrace of new technology is already legendary within the fashion world.

16 It encompasses the wired interiors of the London and New York headquarters, the embrace of videos, Skype-ing between design team and factory, as well as the more outwardly visible live-streaming and 3-D filming of recent shows and the "Art of the Trench," the Web site set up specifically to promote the iconic Burberry trench coat with the photo blogger Scott Schuman, known as the Sartorialist.

"Attracting the Millennial customer to luxury started two years ago—I said that we can either get crushed or ride the greatest wave of our life," says Ms. Ahrendts. "We brought people on the team who were Millennials. I knew it was not my mother tongue—and I don't have time to learn it."

One savvy move was to make Emma Watson, born in 1990 and who famously plays Hermione in the Harry Potter movie series, the new face of Burberry.

"She was 19. She is a Millennial. And it is all about attitude," says Ms. Ahrendts. She also explained that the idea of global Internet reach was particularly important for countries like India and South America, where the young population is burgeoning and where Burberry has not yet opened brick-and-mortar stores.

20 Although youth is always cited as the key to the Millennium generation, the digital state of mind encompasses a broader reach than might be expected. If Generation X is, as Pew's research claims, 50 percent techno-savvy enough to be involved in social media, those members could be well-paid consumers who are much more important to fashion retailers than the younger Millennials.

Mr. Ouadi says that LVMH's Nowness Web site is aimed at 35 to 40 year olds. It seems to reach out to a cross-culture generation more aware of art as an interesting and pleasurable experience than the clubbing/music/movies pursuits detailed on Twitter and Facebook.

So age is not necessarily the only guarantee of belonging to the wired world.

Giorgio Armani, 75, is not actively involved with the Internet, and yet he has been adamant that his company must reach out to the new generation, via Facebook, YouTube and more.

24 "Our goal is always to create a seamless brand experience, especially with our younger lines, communicating the brand wherever the customer wants to touch it—on their mobile devices, via a social network, on blogs, in store, in print and outdoor media," says John Hooks, deputy chairman of the Armani company.

The executive referred to the mobile phone applications that were follow-ups to the introduction of the Emporio Armani e-commerce site in 2007. Emporio customers can buy by phone, browse information and view backstage videos of runway shows. Similarly, there is an Emporio YouTube channel.

And the A/X Armani brand, aimed at young customers, has focused on "m-commerce," or mobile phone shopping, which includes the A/X music label. Lady Gaga's recent appearance in a space age Armani creation seems to have revved up the brand's Facebook site, with 50,000 of its 268,000 "friends" joining in the last month.

What about designers themselves? Are they all deeply involved on the technology as well as the creative side? Paradoxically, they often say that they try to stay clear of techno-babble, seeing it as a distraction or an overload of information.

28 Raf Simons, 42, had street smarts when he started his career, even basing a men's collection on the backpacking generation. But, even though his clothes are modernist, even futuristic, he admits he is now out of the loop.

"I feel like an oldie—when I started there was no computer and no mobile phones—I can't follow the kids these days," says Mr. Simons. "Do I miss something?"

"I am very old school," he adds. "Not that I regret it."

The designer, who also works for the Jil Sander label, says he does not believe that the fashion world has changed so radically in recent years, except in certain respects.

32 "The only thing that has changed a lot is that we were always defined as elite—and everybody is going to have access to everything at any time," he says. "It can kill the actual experience in its own time."

Traditionally, magazines have been the conduit that filtered fashion and delivered it to the consumer. Now those same publications are acutely aware that there are other ways to deliver fashion directly, not least by the brands themselves.

Significantly, the LVMH site debuted publicly on the same day as Vogue.it, the new Web site of Italian Vogue. That Condé Nast site was introduced at an event that projected images from the magazine on the façade of a Milan palazzo and drew an overwhelming number of fashion influentials to see its pages spring to life on screen.

Forward-looking magazines are hyper-aware of the need for a digital experience. Terry Jones started the hip British magazine i-D with his wife, Tricia, 30 years ago and has kept its youthful, edgy quality. He sees dramatic change in the medium—but not necessarily in the soul of the Millennial generation.

36 "Fundamentally, I think human nature is the same—but the condition of the generation of today is different," says Mr. Jones, "The idea is to have easy access to everything, compared to when everything in fashion was kept under corporate control."

As Nowness.com shows, it is the smart minds in the corporate luxury world who are trying to get back control from the chaotic cacophony that is the Internet. Only this time, the idea is to listen to consumers, instead of talking at them—especially if they are 20-something Millennials who are set to take over a digitalized world.

PERSONAL RESPONSE

Do advertisements influence you to buy products? Whether you can afford luxury items or not, how appealing do you find advertisements for such products?

QUESTIONS FOR CLASS OR SMALL-GROUP DISCUSSION

1. State in your own words the approach that venders of luxury and fashion items are taking to market their products to Millennials.
2. Menkes characterizes traditional approaches to advertising as "batter[ing] away the emotion and kill[ing] the drama" (paragraph 1) and as "in-your-face" (paragraph 7). Do you agree with her on this point? Can you give examples that either support or refute her statements?

3. Menkes quotes designer Giorgio Armani as saying "'our goal is always to create a seamless brand experience'" (paragraph 24). What do you understand him to mean by that? What is a "seamless brand experience"?
4. Menkes reports that designer Raf Simons feels that he is "out of the loop" because when he started, "there was no computer and no mobile phones. . . . Do I miss something?'" How would you answer his question? What is he missing, if anything, by being "out of the loop"?

STUFF IS NOT SALVATION

ANNA QUINDLEN

Anna Quindlen is a novelist, social critic, and journalist. In 1986, she began her syndicated column "Life in the Thirties" in the New York Times, *and a few years later "Public and Private," for which she won a Pulitzer Prize in 1992. She contributed to* Newsweek's *prestigious back-page column, "The Last Word," every other week until she retired in 2009. Her columns are collected in* Living Out Loud *(1988);* Thinking Out Loud *(1992); and* Loud and Clear *(2004). She has written the following novels:* Object Lessons *(1991);* One True Thing *(1994);* Black and Blue *(1998);* Blessings *(2003); and* Being Perfect *(2004). Among her nonfiction books are* How Reading Changed My Life *(1998);* A Short Guide to a Happy Life *(2000); and* Imagining London: A Tour of the World's Greatest Fictional City *(2004). This essay appeared in the December 22, 2008, issue of* Newsweek.

As the boom times fade, an important holiday question surfaces: why in the world did we buy all this junk in the first place?

What passes for the holiday season began before dawn the day after Thanksgiving, when a worker at a Wal-Mart in Valley Stream, N.Y., was trampled to death by a mob of bargain hunters. Afterward, there were reports that some people, mesmerized by cheap consumer electronics and discounted toys, kept shopping even after announcements to clear the store.

These are dark days in the United States: the cataclysmic stock-market declines, the industries edging up on bankruptcy, the home foreclosures and the waves of layoffs. But the prospect of an end to plenty has uncovered what may ultimately be a more pernicious problem, an addiction to consumption so out of control that it qualifies as a sickness. The suffocation of a store employee by a stampede of shoppers was horrifying, but it wasn't entirely surprising.

4 Americans have been on an acquisition binge for decades. I suspect television advertising, which made me want a Chatty Cathy doll so much as a kid that when I saw her under the tree my head almost exploded. By contrast, my father will be

happy to tell you about the excitement of getting an orange in his stocking during the Depression. The depression before this one.

A critical difference between then and now is credit. The orange had to be paid for. The rite of passage for a child when I was young was a solemn visit to the local bank, there to exchange birthday money for a savings passbook. Every once in a while, like magic, a bit of extra money would appear. Interest. Yippee.

The passbook was replaced by plastic, so that today Americans are overwhelmed by debt and the national savings rate is calculated, like an algebra equation, in negatives. By 2010 Americans will be a trillion dollars in the hole on credit-card debt alone.

But let's look, not at the numbers, but the atmospherics. Appliances, toys, clothes, gadgets. Junk. There's the sad truth. Wall Street executives may have made investments that lost their value, but, in a much smaller way, so did the rest of us. "I looked into my closet the other day and thought, why did I buy all this stuff?" one friend said recently. A person in the United States replaces a cell phone every 16 months, not because the cell phone is old, but because it is oldish. My mother used to complain that the Christmas toys were grubby and forgotten by Easter. (I didn't even really like dolls, especially dolls who introduced themselves to you over and over again when you pulled the ring in their necks.) Now much of the country is made up of people with the acquisition habits of a 7-year-old, desire untethered from need, or the ability to pay. The result is a booming business in those free-standing storage facilities, where junk goes to linger in a persistent vegetative state, somewhere between eBay and the dump.

8 Oh, there is still plenty of need. But it is for real things, things that matter: college tuition, prescription drugs, rent. Food pantries and soup kitchens all over the country have seen demand for their services soar. Homelessness, which had fallen in recent years, may rebound as people lose their jobs and their houses. For the first time this month, the number of people on food stamps will exceed the 30 million mark.

Hard times offer the opportunity to ask hard questions, and one of them is the one my friend asked, staring at sweaters and shoes: why did we buy all this stuff? Did anyone really need a flat-screen in the bedroom, or a designer handbag, or three cars? If the mall is our temple, then Marc Jacobs is God. There's a scary thought.

The drumbeat that accompanied Black Friday this year was that the numbers had to redeem us, that if enough money was spent by shoppers it would indicate that things were not so bad after all. But what the economy required was at odds with a necessary epiphany. Because things are dire, many people have become hesitant to spend money on trifles. And in the process they began to realize that it's all trifles.

Here I go, stating the obvious: stuff does not bring salvation. But if it's so obvious, how come for so long people have not realized it? The happiest families I know aren't the ones with the most square footage, living in one of those cavernous houses with enough garage space to start a homeless shelter. (There's a holiday suggestion right there.) And of course they are not people who are in real want. Just because consumption is bankrupt doesn't mean that poverty is ennobling.

12 But somewhere in between there is a family like one I know in rural Pennsylvania, raising bees for honey (and for the science, and the fun, of it), digging a pond out of the downhill flow of the stream, with three kids who somehow, incredibly, don't spend six months of the year whining for the toy du jour. (The youngest once

demurred when someone offered him another box on his birthday; "I already have a present," he said.) The mother of the household says having less means her family appreciates possessions more. "I can give you a story about every item, really," she says of what they own. In other words, what they have has meaning. And meaning, real meaning, is what we are always trying to possess. Ask people what they'd grab if their house were on fire, the way our national house is on fire right now. No one ever says it's the tricked-up microwave they got at Wal-Mart.

PERSONAL RESPONSE

What would you grab if your house or apartment were on fire (paragraph 12)? Why?

QUESTIONS FOR CLASS OR SMALL-GROUP DISCUSSION

1. What is Quindlen's thesis or central idea? Do you agree with her that "stuff is not salvation"?
2. Quindlen writes: "Now much of the country is made up of people with the acquisition habits of a 7-year-old . . ." (paragraph 7). What does she mean? Do your observations support or contradict her statement?
3. What contrast does Quindlen draw between real need and a need for "junk" (paragraph 7). To what extent do you agree with her?
4. How effective do you find Quindlen's conclusion?

SHOPPING AND OTHER SPIRITUAL ADVENTURES IN AMERICA TODAY

PHYLLIS ROSE

Phyllis Rose is author of the following books: Woman of Letters: A Life of Virginia Woolf *(1978);* Parallel Lives: Five Victorian Marriages *(1983);* Jazz Cleopatra: Josephine Baker in Her Time *(1989);* The Norton Book of Women's Lives *(1993);* The Year of Reading Proust: A Memoir in Real Time *(1999); and* Never Say Goodbye: Essays *(1991), from which this essay is taken.*

Last year a new Album's Food Mart opened in the shopping mall on Route 66. It belongs to the new generation of super-duper markets open twenty-four hours that have computerized checkout. I went to see the place as soon as it opened and I was impressed. There was trail mix in Lucite bins. There was freshly made pasta. There were coffee beans, four kinds of tahini, ten kinds of herb teas, raw shrimp in shells and cooked shelled shrimp, fresh-squeezed orange juice. Every sophistication known to the big city, even goat's cheese covered with ash, was now available in Middletown,

Conn. People raced from the warehouse aisle to the bagel bin to the coffee beans to the fresh fish market, exclaiming at all the new things. Many of us felt elevated, graced, complimented by the presence of this food palace in our town.

This is the wonderful egalitarianism of American business. Was it Andy Warhol who said that the nice thing about Coke is, no can is any better or worse than any other? Some people may find it dull to cross the country and find the same chain stores with the same merchandise from coast to coast, but it means that my town is as good as yours, my shopping mall as important as yours, equally filled with wonders.

Imagine what people ate during the winter as little as seventy-five years ago. They ate food that was local, long-lasting, and dull, like acorn squash, turnips, and cabbage. Walk into an American supermarket in February and the world lies before you: grapes, melons, artichokes, fennel, lettuce, peppers, pistachios, dates, even strawberries, to say nothing of ice cream. Have you ever considered what a triumph of civilization it is to be able to buy a pound of chicken livers? If you lived on a farm and had to kill a chicken when you wanted to eat one, you wouldn't ever accumulate a pound of chicken livers.

4 Another wonder of Middletown is Caldor, the discount department store. Here is man's plenty: tennis racquets, panty hose, luggage, glassware, records, toothpaste. Timex watches, Cadbury's chocolate, corn poppers, hair dryers, warm-up suits, car wax, light bulbs, television sets. All good quality at low prices with exchanges cheerfully made on defective goods. There are worse rules to live by. I feel good about America whenever I walk into this store, which is almost every midwinter Sunday afternoon, when life elsewhere has closed down. I go to Caldor the way English people go to pubs: out of sociability. To get away from my house. To widen my horizons. For culture's sake. Caldor provides me too with a welcome sense of seasonal change. When the first outdoor grills and lawn furniture appear there, it's as exciting a sign of spring as the first crocus or robin.

Someone told me about a Soviet émigré who practices English by declaiming, at random, sentences that catch his fancy. One of his favorites is, "Fifty percent off all items today only." Refugees from Communist countries appreciate our supermarkets and discount department stores for the wonders they are. An Eastern European scientist visiting Middletown wept when she first saw the meat counter at Waldbaum's. On the other hand, before her year in America was up, her pleasure turned sour. She wanted everything she saw. Her approach to consumer goods was insufficiently abstract, too materialistic. We Americans are beyond a simple, possessive materialism. We're used to abundance and the possibility of possessing things. The things, and the possibility of possessing them, will still be there next week, next year. So today we can walk the aisles calmly.

It is a misunderstanding of the American retail store to think we go there necessarily to buy. Some of us shop. There's a difference. Shopping has many purposes, the least interesting of which is to acquire new articles. We shop to cheer ourselves up. We shop to practice decision making. We shop to be useful and productive members of our class and society. We shop to remind ourselves how much is available to us. We shop to remind ourselves how much is to be striven for. We shop to assert our superiority to the material objects that spread themselves before us.

Shopping's function as a form of therapy is widely appreciated. You don't really need, let's say, another sweater. You need the feeling of power that comes with buying or not buying it. You need the feeling that someone wants something you have—even if it's just your money. To get the benefit of shopping, you needn't actually purchase the sweater, any more than you have to marry every man you flirt with. In fact, window-shopping, like flirting, can be more rewarding, the same high without the distressing commitment, the material encumbrance. The purest form of shopping is provided by garage sales. A connoisseur goes out with no goal in mind, open to whatever may come his or her way, secure that it will cost very little. Minimum expense, maximum experience. Perfect shopping.

8 I try to think of the opposite, a kind of shopping in which the object is all important, the pleasure of shopping at a minimum. For example, the purchase of blue jeans. I buy new blue jeans as seldom as possible because the experience is so humiliating. For every pair that looks good on me, fifteen look grotesque. But even shopping for blue jeans at Bob's Surplus on Main Street—no frills, bare-bones shopping—is an event in the life of the spirit. Once again I have to come to terms with the fact that I will never look good in Levi's. Much as I want to be mainstream, I never will be.

In fact, I'm doubly an oddball, neither Misses nor Junior, but Misses Petite. I look in the mirror, I acknowledge the disparity between myself and the ideal, I resign myself to making the best of it: I will buy the Lee's Misses Petite. Shopping is a time of reflection, assessment, spiritual self-discipline.

It is appropriate, I think, that Bob's Surplus has a communal dressing room. I used to shop only in places where I could count on a private dressing room with a mirror inside. My impulse then was to hide my weaknesses. Now I believe in sharing them. There are other women in the dressing room at Bob's Surplus trying on blue jeans who look as bad as I do. We take comfort from one another. Sometimes a woman will ask me which of two items looks better. I always give a definite answer. It's the least I can do. I figure we are all in this together, and I emerge from the dressing room not only with a new pair of jeans but with a renewed sense of belonging to a human community.

When a Solzhenitsyn rants about American materialism, I have to look at my digital Timex and check what year this is. Materialism? Like conformism, a hot moral issue of the fifties, but not now. How to spread the goods, maybe. Whether the goods are the Good, no. Solzhenitsyn, like the visiting scientist who wept at the beauty of Waldbaum's meat counter but came to covet everything she saw, takes American materialism too materialistically. He doesn't see its spiritual side. Caldor, Waldbaum's, Bob's Surplus—these, perhaps, are our cathedrals.

PERSONAL RESPONSE

Explain your attitude toward shopping. Do you go to discount stores or malls to shop or to buy? Does shopping give you the pleasure that Rose says it gives most Americans?

QUESTIONS FOR CLASS OR SMALL-GROUP DISCUSSION

1. How does the list of foods that Rose mentions in paragraph 1 relate to her central point? What function do the references to the Soviet émigré and the Eastern European scientist in paragraph 5 serve?
2. Discuss whether you get the pleasure from shopping in American discount stores and supermarkets that Rose describes in her essay. Consider, for instance, Rose's comment in paragraph 9 that "shopping is a time of reflection, assessment, spiritual self-discipline."
3. What criticisms of American consumerism does Rose imply in her ironic descriptions of shopping as a spiritual adventure and department stores as America's cathedrals?
4. In paragraph 10, Rose describes trying on jeans in a communal dressing room and of taking comfort from other women there. Do men experience the same kind of camaraderie when shopping that women often do? To what extent do you think there are differences between the way men and women view shopping in general?

✧ PERSPECTIVES ON MARKETING AND THE AMERICAN CONSUMER ✧

Suggested Writing Topics

1. Argue against or in support of the contention of Gary Ruskin and Juliet Schor in "Every Nook and Cranny" that commercialism is "dangerous" to the public.
2. Drawing on any of the readings in the chapter, write an essay on the importance of young consumers to the American economy.
3. Drawing on readings in this chapter, explain the pressures you think America's high-consumption society puts on young people and the effects of those pressures.
4. Write an essay on the image you think that American consumerism presents to the rest of the world and whether you think that image is good or a bad.
5. Argue for or against the proposition that the United States should "ban or sharply restrict product placement on television" (Gary Ruskin and Juliet Schor, "Every Nook and Cranny," paragraph 10).
6. Classify consumers' shopping and buying habits on the basis of what generation they belong to, using Millennials, Generation X members, and Baby Boomers as your three groups.
7. Write an essay in response to the statement in Anna Quindlen's "Stuff Is Not Salvation" that Americans have "an addiction to consumption so out of control that it qualifies as a sickness" (paragraph 3).

8. Phyllis Rose suggests in "Shopping and Other Spiritual Adventures in America Today" that malls, discount stores, and supermarkets are America's cathedrals. Write an essay explaining the extent to which you agree with her. Can you name other structures that would be more appropriate symbols of America's spiritual center? Is consumerism America's main religion?
9. In "Shopping and Other Spiritual Adventures in America Today," Phyllis Rose refers to the "wonderful egalitarianism of American business" (paragraph 2). Using that comment as a starting point, write an essay on American consumerism as a social equalizer.
10. Imagine that you are marketing a product that has traditionally been sold to one particular segment of the market, such as white, middle-class males. Now you want to increase your sales by targeting other groups. Select a particular group and create a sales campaign aimed at that group.
11. Explain the effects on you or someone you know of a change in income, suddenly coming into money, or acquiring some coveted material possession.
12. Analyze the positive and negative effects of America's emphasis on consumerism on one particular group of people, such as young people, the elderly, working-class people, the wealthy, or those living in poverty.
13. Explain what you think shopping malls, discount stores, and overstocked supermarkets suggest about Americans' values. For instance, what impression do you think that foreign visitors get of America when they see the sizes of and selections in those marketplaces?

Research Topics

1. Research one of the many subjects raised by Gary Ruskin and Juliet Schor in "Every Nook and Cranny," such as their assertion in paragraph four that "the commercialization of government and culture and the growing importance of material acquisition and consumer lifestyles was hastened by the co-optation of potentially countervailing institutions, such as churches, . . . governments, schools, universities, and nongovernmental organizations."
2. Research the marketing strategies of a major business, perhaps one mentioned in this chapter. Assess what you see as its successes and/or failures in promoting its products.
3. Select a particular product (such as automobiles, cosmetics, clothing, or beer) or a particular target population (such as children, overweight women, or the elderly) and research the market strategies used by major companies for that particular product or group.

4. Research the recent advertising campaign of a major corporation whose product poses a threat to the environment or to human health and well-being.
5. Research the subject of American consumerism and arrive at your own conclusion about its effects on Americans and American values. This is a broad subject, so look for ways to narrow your focus as quickly as you can.
6. Research the impact of suburban malls on city-center or small "Mom and Pop," neighborhood businesses.

Responding to Visuals

©AP Photo/Mary Altaffer

A pedestrian looks at an advertisement featuring Eva Longoria at the New York & Co. store on Lexington Ave in New York, Thursday, December 1, 2005. New York & Co.'s November same-store sales rose 13 percent as the company's merchandise assortments and advertising campaign helped boost traffic.

1. How does the ad make use of the fame of actress Eva Longoria? How effective do you find celebrity endorsement as a selling tool?
2. In what ways does the advertisement use sex to sell its product?
3. What details of the advertisement do you find persuasive?

Responding to Visuals

Blow-up bald eagle wrapped with American flag

1. What do the most obvious components of this picture represent—the bald eagle wrapped in an American flag and the "sale" sign on its chest?
2. What comment on American commercialism does this image make or imply?
3. Can you tell what is being sold? Does it matter?

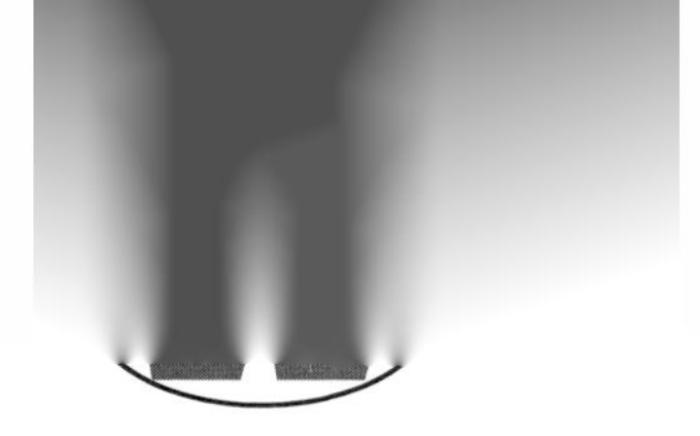

The Workplace

The workplace can have enormous influence on people's lives. Most Americans work outside the home, either full-time or part-time, spending significant portions of their lives on the job. The physical atmosphere of the workplace, the friendliness of coworkers, wages and benefits, and the attitudes of supervisors or bosses play pivotal roles not only in the way workers perform but also in the way they feel about themselves. Tension, anxiety, and stress in the workplace can lower production for the company and produce actual illnesses in workers, whereas a pleasant atmosphere, good benefits, and relatively low stress can boost production and make employees look forward to going to work. Research has demonstrated that the quality of life in the workplace has a direct effect on the quality of work employees do and on their general well-being.

If, like most college students, you have had a job or are currently working, think about your own experiences as a worker. Do you feel a sense of community in your workplace? Is your work fun? Tedious? Challenging? How would you characterize the relationship between management and employees where you work (or have worked)? Is what you earn adequate enough to meet your financial needs? Do you have benefits with your job? These questions all relate to the quality of your work experience, and how you answer them reveals a great deal about your workplace.

The first essay in this chapter focuses on an issue of particular importance for mothers who work outside the home. In "You've Been Mommified," Ellen Goodman looks at "family responsibility discrimination," specifically discrimination against women workers who are also mothers. Suggesting that such women are looked at almost as a "third gender," she reports on the findings of a research center on worklife law and on the results of a study to determine if there is a "motherhood penalty in the job market." Given that a large portion of women in the workforce also have children, this subject is a compelling one. As you read Goodman's piece, think about the women you know who are mothers and work outside the home. Does what Goodman says ring true to your own observations or even your own experience?

Then Judith Warner takes up the subject of working mothers who wish that they could afford to work part-time, but in the course of her piece expands her focus to include all workers. In "The Full-Time Blues," she notes that most part-time work does not have the pay and benefits to make it a viable choice for those women who prefer not to work full time because of the demands of family. In proposing solutions to the problem, Warner calls for the adoption of the kind of family-friendly practices and even legislation currently operative in many European countries. Consider whether you agree with her that flexible scheduling, better benefits and pay for part-time workers, or even paid family leave would benefit all workers, male or female, with or without children.

Next, Jody Greenstone Miller writes about temporary workers, but her subject is high-level executives, not minimum wage workers. It is an interesting perspective on the workplace in that she argues for an end to discrimination against temporary workers and advocates greater rights and more respect for them. Finally, Jeff Jacoby's "Oh, Brother" takes a different look at the subject of employees' rights in the workplace by siding with the employer in a case before a Superior Court in Massachusetts. As you no doubt know, Big Brother is a reference to the fictional director of Oceania in the George Orwell novel *1984*. Oceania is a totalitarian state where citizens are always under surveillance and are constantly being reminded that "Big Brother is watching you." As you read his piece, consider whether you agree with Jacoby's position on the case or whether you take the opposite position on it.

YOU'VE BEEN MOMMIFIED

ELLEN GOODMAN

Ellen Goodman began her career as a reporter for Newsweek, *worked for a time at the* Detroit Free Press, *and became a columnist for the* Boston Globe *in 1967. Her column, "At Large," has been syndicated by the* Washington Post *Writers Group since 1976. In 1980, she won a Pulitzer Prize for distinguished commentary. She has published a study of human change,* Turning Points *(1979), and many of her columns have been collected in* Close to Home *(1979),* At Large *(1981),* Keeping in Touch *(1985),* Making Sense *(1989),* Value Judgments *(1993), and* Paper Trail *(2004). She is author, with Patricia O'Brien, of* I Know Just What You Mean: The Power of Friendship in Women's Lives *(2000). This article was published in the May 10, 2007, issue of the* Boston Globe.

It's become a Mother's Day tradition on a par with candy, flowers and guilt. While advertisers wax poetically about the priceless work of motherhood, economists tally up the paycheck for the services she performs.

This year, salary.com estimates the value of a full-time mom at $138,095, up 3 percent from last year. The monetary value of a second-shift mom is $85,939, on top of her day job.

But, alas, the check is not in the mail. Nor will mom find it next to the maple syrup on her bed tray. Motherhood is what the economists call a monopsony, a job for which there is only one employer. And it's a rare child who's saved up to fill mom's piggybank, let alone a 401(k).

4 The real story of the Mother's Day economy is less rosy. This is what to expect when you are expecting—expecting to be a mom and a paid worker at the same time. You can expect to be mommified.

Mothers are still treated as if they were a third gender in the workplace. Among people ages 27 to 33 who have never had children, women's earnings approach 98 percent of men's. Many women will hit the glass ceiling, but many more will crash into the maternal wall.

Here's a Mother's Day card from a study just published by Shelley Correll in the American Journal of Sociology. Correll performed an experiment to see if there was a motherhood penalty in the job market. She and her colleagues at Cornell University created an ideal job applicant with a successful track record, an uninterrupted work history, a boffo resume, the whole deal.

Then they tucked a little telltale factoid into some of the resumes with a tip-off about mom-ness. It described her as an officer in a parent–teacher association. And—zap—she was mommified.

8 Moms were seen as less competent and committed. Moms were half as likely to be hired as childless women or men with or without kids. Moms were offered $11,000 less in starting pay than non-moms. And, just for good measure, they were also judged more harshly for tardiness.

"Just the mention of the PTA had that effect," says Correll. "Imagine the effect of a two-year absence from the work force or part-time work."

If this is true in the lab, it's true in real life. Joan C. Williams, who runs the Center for WorkLife Law at Hastings Law School, says discrimination against women may have gone underground but "the discrimination against mothers is breathtakingly open. Mothers are told, 'You belong at home with the kids, you're fired.'"

In the stories from the center's hot line and in the growing case law they've accumulated on family responsibility discrimination, you hear about women overtly denied promotions for having a child, told to have an abortion to keep a job, or rejected for a new job because "it was incompatible with being a mother." Family emergencies are treated differently than other timeouts. And things are at least as bad for dads when they take on mommy's work of caregiving.

12 I'm not suggesting that mothers quit the PTA, hide the kids or even sue, although the 400 percent increase in FRD suits has, um, raised some corporate consciousness. But at the very least, we have to turn the story line around.

No, mothers are not actually a third gender. More than 80 percent of American women have children and 80 percent of those are employed by the time their kids are 12. The reality of the workplace affects us all.

The much-touted mommy wars are as useful in solving our problems as a circular firing squad. And tales of women "opting out" of professional careers squeeze out the tales of women being pushed out.

As for the idea that women's lives are an endless array of choices? Williams says ruefully, "An awful lot of what gets interpreted as a mother's choice to drop out is really a 'take this job and shove it' reaction by mothers who encounter discrimination."

16 How many mothers would choose to spend more time at home if the fear of re-entry weren't so daunting? How many would choose to stay in the work force except for one sick child, one snow day, one emergency room visit? And how many dads would choose to live up to their own family ideals?

On Mother's Day 2007 there is still a deep-seated bias that puts the image of a "good mother" at odds with that of an "ideal worker." Until we wrestle down the beliefs and the rules of the workplace, our annual homage to the family values keeper will be as sentimental as this year's $138,095 paycheck.

PERSONAL RESPONSE

How would you define a "'good mother'" and an "'ideal worker'" (paragraph 17). Do you believe that the two are incompatible?

QUESTIONS FOR CLASS OR SMALL-GROUP DISCUSSION

1. What do you understand Goodman to mean by the term "mommified" (title and paragraph 7)?
2. How effective do you find Goodman's opening paragraphs about the monetary value of a full-time mother? How do they relate to her central idea?
3. Define in your own words what you believe the terms "glass ceiling" and "maternal wall" mean (paragraph 5).
4. Discuss whether you agree with Goodman when she says that "the reality of the workplace affects us all" (paragraph 13).

THE FULL-TIME BLUES

JUDITH WARNER

Judith Warner writes the "Domestic Disturbances" column for the New York Times *and is the host of "The Judith Warner Show" on XM Satellite Radio. She is also the author of the best-selling biography* Hillary Clinton: The Inside Story *(1993);* You Have the Power: How to Take Back Our Country and Restore Democracy to America *(with Howard Dean) (2004); and* Perfect Madness: Motherhood in the Age of Anxiety *(2005). A former special correspondent for* Newsweek *in Paris, she reviews books for the* New York Times *and has written about politics and women's issues for magazines including the* New Republic *and* Elle. *This piece was published in the July 24, 2007, issue of the* New York Times.

The news from the Pew Research Center this month—that 60 percent of working mothers say they'd prefer to work part time—was barely out before it was sucked up into the fetid air of the mommy wars, with all the usual talk on "opting out" and guilting out, and the usual suspects lining up to slug it out on morning talk TV.

But the conversation we should be having these days really isn't one about What Mothers Want. (This has been known for years; surveys dating back to the early 1990s have shown that up to 80 percent of mothers—working and at-home alike—consistently say they wish they could work part time.) The interesting question is, rather, why they're not getting it.

Only 24 percent of working mothers now work part time. The reason so few do isn't complicated: most women can't afford to. Part-time work doesn't pay.

4 Women on a reduced schedule earn almost 18 percent less than their full-time female peers with equivalent jobs and education levels, according to research by Janet Gornick, a professor of sociology and political science at City University of New York, and the labor economist Elena Bardasi. Part-time jobs rarely come with benefits. They tend to be clustered in low-paying fields like the retail and service industries. And in

better-paid professions, a reduced work schedule very often can mean cutting down from 50-plus hours a week to 40-odd—hardly a "privilege" worth paying for with a big pay cut.

It doesn't have to be this way. In Europe, significant steps have been made to make part-time work a livable reality for those who seek it. Denying fair pay and benefits to part-time workers is now illegal. Parents in Sweden have the right to work a six-hour day at prorated pay until their children turn 8 years old. Similar legislation helps working parents in France, Austria, and Belgium and any employee in Germany and the Netherlands who wants to cut back.

Even Britain has a (comparatively tame) pro-family law that guarantees parents and other caregivers the right to request a flexible schedule from their employers. European employers have the right to refuse workers' requests, but research shows that very few actually do. And workers have the right to appeal the denials.

None of this creates a perfect world. Feminists have long been leery of part-time work policies, which tend to be disproportionately used by women, mommy-tracking them and placing them at an economic disadvantage within their marriages and in society. The American model of work-it-out-for-yourself employment is Darwinian, but women's long working hours have gone a long way toward helping them advance up the career ladder.

8 "We know that family-friendly policies encourage work force participation," says Professor Gornick, who has extensively studied family policy on both sides of the Atlantic. "But do they lower the glass ceiling or make it thicker? That's the million-euro question."

I think that when it comes to setting priorities for (currently nonexistent) American work-family policy, we ought to go for the greatest good for the greatest number.

The place to start, ideally, would be universal health care, which is really the necessary condition for making freedom of choice a reality for working parents. European-style regulations outlawing wage and benefit discrimination against part-time workers would be nice, too, though it's not a terribly realistic goal for the U.S., where even unpaid family leave is still a hot-button issue for employers.

A British-style "soft touch" law could, however, be within the realm of the possible. Senator Edward Kennedy and Representative Carolyn Maloney are circulating draft legislation modeled on the British workplace flexibility law that would give employees—all workers, not just moms or parents—the right to request a flexible schedule. The legislation—which would require employers to discuss flexibility with workers who request it, but wouldn't require them to honor the requests—has a little bit of something for everyone: protection from retaliation for workers who fear letting on that they're eager to cut back, protection from "unfunded mandates" for businesses.

12 Critics might say the proposed legislation's touch is so soft as to be almost imperceptible, but it's a start. At the very least, it's a chance to stop emoting about maternal love and war and guilt and have a productive conversation.

PERSONAL RESPONSE

Discuss whether you think the United States should make it illegal to deny fair pay and benefits to part-time workers, as some European countries have done.

QUESTIONS FOR CLASS OR SMALL-GROUP DISCUSSION

1. Comment on the effectiveness as an argumentative strategy of Warner's use of statistics in the first four paragraphs.
2. What do you think the term "mommy-tracking" means in the context of paragraph 7? What does Warner mean by the term "Darwinian" (paragraph 7)?
3. How likely do you think it is that the United States will enact universal health care, as some European countries have done (paragraph 10)?
4. To what extent are you convinced by Warner's proposal that the United States enact a law "modeled on the British workplace flexibility law" (paragraph 11)? Do you agree that flexibility in scheduling would be a good option for all employees to have available to them?

TEMPORARY WORKERS AND THE 21ST CENTURY ECONOMY

JODY GREENSTONE MILLER

Jody Greenstone Miller is the founder and CEO of the Business Talent Group. She served as a special assistant to President Bill Clinton from 1993 to 1995. This piece was first published in the Wall Street Journal *on November 30, 2009.*

The White House is turning its nose up at last month's spurt in temporary work—the one bright spot in an otherwise grim jobs report. It claims that such work is proof that the economy is still malfunctioning. The truth is that this surge in temporary workers is not only good news for the economy, it's the future of the 21st century labor market. If Washington wants to jump start job growth for the 3.5 million white-collar workers who have lost jobs in this recession, it should start by scrapping the outdated legal and regulatory hurdles to temporary work.

I know something about this because I run a business that places talented individuals into temporary consulting and interim executive assignments. Amid the worst recession in decades, our business is up 70%. Yet there would be much more growth in this sector if Americans—from the White House down to the personnel department—stopped discriminating against temporary work as inferior or anomalous.

Today, demand for high-end temporary business talent is not focused on cost-cutting projects, as some might suspect. Instead, firms use temporary executives to drive innovation. In uncertain times, firms are simply more comfortable with deploying talent on a flexible basis.

4 Temporary work also boosts economic efficiency because not all executive roles require permanent staff. For example, one pharmaceutical company client took on a temporary marketing executive to help launch a new drug. The old way of doing this

was to make a new permanent hire (or a small team) who would have been underutilized after the launch. The availability of temporary staff who can get the job done quickly means that firms can rethink how work is organized.

Which brings us to another case for temporary work: Top business talent increasingly wants to work this way. In one situation, a VP-level executive we placed was developing his own new business. He valued the way a part-time senior role allowed him to support his family while he worked on his own project. For others, working in a series of temporary assignments may be their preferred full-time occupation.

Given the contribution that temporary work makes to the economy, it's time Washington embraced it. Here are three things the feds could do immediately to make it easier for firms and executives to work this way:

First, the Obama administration should create a two-year "safe harbor" for independent professionals doing temporary work. Currently, the rules governing independent contractors are determined on a case-by-case basis and are subject to state law variations. This leaves risk-averse personnel departments wary of hiring temporary executives for fear that they could be reclassified as employees, saddling employers with liabilities. The solution is to create a two-year safe harbor provision that lays out a clear test for being classified as an independent contractor. The White House could streamline these rules, beginning with the IRS, if it made it a priority.

8 Second, Washington should apply any new employment tax subsidy to temporary jobs. There is much talk of a new jobs tax subsidy, but as it currently stands it would exclude temporary work. This is 20th century thinking. Any new subsidy should seek to boost temporary roles as well.

Third, the feds should let independent workers buy into the congressional health plan. A huge barrier to temporary employment for professionals who prefer to work this way is their inability to access group health coverage outside the permanent employment setting. Though Congress may pass health reform this year, the new insurance exchanges that would remedy this problem won't come into play until at least 2013. Congress should allow temporary workers to buy into the congressional health plan until then. As we reboot the great American jobs machine, it's time to shelve outdated assumptions and accept that a portfolio of multiple assignments is what growing legions of companies and executives want. This new relationship between talent and firms isn't a failure to be stigmatized, but the latest sign of our economy's endless capacity for renewal and innovation.

PERSONAL RESPONSE

What is your response to Miller's statement that temporary work is "the future of the 21st century labor market" (paragraph 1)?

QUESTIONS FOR CLASS OR SMALL-GROUP DISCUSSION

1. What advantages does Greenstone mention in her argument for protecting high-level temporary workers? What disadvantages does she mention?

2. Greenstone urges the federal government to do three things. Summarize what each of those things is and comment on whether you think it a good idea.
3. What reactions to Greenstone's essay do you imagine she received after its publications? Do you think that readers of the *Wall Street Journal* would support her position?
4. What do you think of Greenstone's argument? Do you see any flaws in her reasoning?

OH, BROTHER

JEFF JACOBY

Jeff Jacoby was chief editorial writer for the Boston Herald *from 1987 until becoming an op-ed columnist for the* Boston Globe *in 1994. Trained as a lawyer, he has been a political commentator for Boston's National Public Radio affiliate and was host of "Talk of New England," a weekly television program, for several years. In 1999, Jacoby became the first recipient of the Breindel Award for Excellence in Opinion Journalism. This opinion piece was first published in the* Boston Globe *on December 10, 2006.*

BIG BROTHER has been busy.

New York City's board of health voted last week to ban the use of trans fats in restaurants, a step that will force many of the Big Apple's 26,000 eating establishments to radically alter the way they prepare food. The prohibition is being called a model for other cities, such as Chicago, where similar bans have been proposed.

Is it a good idea to avoid food made with trans fats? That depends on what you consider good. Trans fats raise the risk of heart disease by increasing levels of LDL ("bad") cholesterol. They also contribute to the appealing taste of many baked and fried foods, and provide an economical alternative to saturated fats. As with most things in life, trans fats carry both risks and benefits. Do the long-term health concerns outweigh the short-term pleasures? That's a question of values—one that scientists and regulators aren't competent to answer.

4 Different people have different priorities. They make different choices about the fats in their diet, just as they make different choices about whether to drive a Toyota, drink their coffee black, or get a tattoo. In a free society, men and women decide such things for themselves. In New York, men and women are now a little less free. And since a loss of liberty anywhere is a threat to liberty everywhere, the rest of us are now a little less free as well.

But that doesn't trouble the lifestyle bullies. They are quite sure that they have the right to dictate people's eating habits. "It's basically a slow form of poison," sniffs David Katz of the Yale Prevention Research Center. "I applaud New York City, and frankly, I think there should be a nationwide ban."

Yes, why go through the trouble of making your own decision about trans fats or anything else when officious bureaucrats are willing to make it for you? It's so much easier to prohibit something—smoking in bars, say, or cycling without a helmet, or using marijuana, or gambling, or working a job for less than some "minimum" wage—than to allow adults the freedom to choose.

But Big Brother doesn't always appear as a hectoring nanny. Indeed, sometimes he comes disguised as a victim of the bullies.

8 Consider the plight of Scott Rodrigues, who lost his job with the Scotts lawn-care corporation when a drug test showed that he had violated a company rule against smoking at any time—on or off the job. Scotts no longer hires tobacco users, since they drive up the cost of medical insurance, and Rodrigues, a former pack-a-day smoker, knew about the policy and was trying to kick his habit. He was down to about six cigarettes daily when he was fired.

Now he claims that Scotts violated his privacy and civil rights, and is suing his ex-employer in Superior Court.

"How employees want to lead their private lives is their own business," his lawyer told the *Boston Globe*. "Next they're going to say, 'you don't get enough exercise'. . . . I don't think anybody ought to be smoking cigarettes, but as long as it's legal, it's none of the employer's business as long as it doesn't impact the workplace."

It's hard not to feel a measure of sympathy for Rodrigues. Many activities endanger health and can drive up the cost of health insurance, from drag-racing to overeating to promiscuous sex, yet none of them appears to be grounds for termination at Scotts. It seems capricious to treat smokers so harshly.

12 But capricious or not, Scotts is entitled to condition its employment on any criteria it wishes. (With the exception of the "protected categories"—race, religion, etc.—itemized in civil rights statutes) Rodrigues has not been cheated. Scotts is a private firm, and if it chooses not to employ smokers—or skiers, or Socialists, or "Seinfeld" fans—its decision should stand. Rodrigues is free to vent his disappointment, to criticize Scotts, even to organize a boycott. But forcing the company to defend itself against a groundless lawsuit goes too far. It is an abuse of governmental power—an assault on the liberty of employers to operate freely in the market. It is a different kind of bullying than the ban on trans fats, but it's an act of bullying nonetheless.

The price of liberty, Thomas Jefferson warned, is eternal vigilance. But too few of us have been vigilant, and the bullies keep gaining ground.

PERSONAL RESPONSE

Write about an experience in which you felt that being prevented from doing something—or being told not to do it—was unfair.

QUESTIONS FOR CLASS OR SMALL-GROUP DISCUSSION

1. How is the allusion to George Orwell's novel *1984* relevant to Jacoby's essay?
2. Why do you think Jacoby begins with a discussion of New York City's ban on trans fats in restaurants? How is that subject related to his discussion of the lawsuit that Scott Rodrigues filed against the Scotts lawn care company?

3. Jacoby believes that "Scotts is entitled to condition its employment on any criteria it wishes. . . . Rodrigues has not been cheated" (paragraph 12). To what extent do you agree with him?
4. Why does Jacoby call Rodrigues a bully (paragraph 12)? Do you agree with Jacoby on this point?

✧ PERSPECTIVES ON THE WORKPLACE ✧

Suggested Writing Topics

1. Ellen Goodman, in "You've Been Mommified," writes that "there is still a deep-seated bias that puts the image of a 'good mother' at odds with that of an 'ideal worker'" (paragraph 17). Define each of those terms—"good mother" and "ideal worker"— and explain whether you agree that there is a bias.
2. Write in favor of or opposed to the proposals in either Judith Warner's "The Full-Time Blues" or Jody Greenstone Miller's "Temporary Workers and the 21st Century Economy."
3. Write an editorial in reply to Jeff Jacoby's opinion piece "Oh, Brother."
4. Explain what you value most in a job and why. Is it having fun, making lots of money, meeting challenges, or some other aspect of it? Or conduct your own informal interview on the subject of expectations for a job and report your results.
5. Drawing on at least one of the essays in this chapter, describe what you see as the ideal job or ideal working conditions.
6. Describe your work experiences and the extent to which self-satisfaction or self-motivation contributes to your performance.
7. Argue in support of or against the contention made by many workers and implied by a couple of the authors in this chapter that employers unfairly violate the basic rights of workers.
8. Argue in support of or against drug testing in the workplace.

Research Topics

1. Both Ellen Goodman and Judith Warner use the term "mommy wars" ("You've Been Mommified," paragraph 14; "The Full-Time Blues," paragraph 1). Research the subject of the "mommy wars," report your conclusions, and, if possible, take a position on the subject.
2. Research the topic of "family responsibility discrimination" (Ellen Goodman's "You've Been Mommified," paragraph 11).
3. Research the "European-style regulations outlawing wage and benefit discrimination against part-time workers" referred to by Judith Warner in "The Full-Time Blues" (paragraph 10) and argue whether you think the United States ought to have such a goal and, if so, whether it could realistically attain it.

4. Conduct research to prove or disprove Jody Greenstone Miller's contention that temporary work "is the future of the 21st century labor market."
5. Combine library research and personal interviews with area employers on the subject of employer attitudes toward female employees with children. Then report your conclusions.
6. Research the topic of the differences between women's and men's managerial styles.
7. Research the topic of the effect of workplace environment on employee productivity and morale.
8. Research the subject of the right to free speech or the right to privacy in the work place.
9. Research workers' perceptions of their workplaces. If possible, interview people who work full-time about their work place experiences and combine the results of your interview(s) with your other sources.

Responding to Visuals

Sign for "SANTA'S WORKSHOP" lists schedule for workshops on "Conflicts in the Workplace," "Deadlines and Stress," and "Post-Christmas Letdown."

1. What makes this cartoon funny?
2. What play on words is at work in the heading "Santa's Workshop"?
3. What serious subject related to the workplace does the cartoon comment on?

Responding to Visuals

Working mother with baby in arms, home office.

1. What image of working at home does the photograph convey?
2. What do the looks on the faces of both mother and child suggest about how each felt at the moment the photograph was taken?
3. What details of the photograph convey the tensions between being simultaneously a mother and a worker?
4. Do you think that companies should accommodate working parents?

CHAPTER 23

American Business in the Global Marketplace

If we live in a global village, we also buy and sell in a global marketplace. Manufacturers that once exported goods to other nations now build plants and sell goods directly in those countries. American businesses that once limited themselves to the domestic market are now expanding operations beyond the United States as they compete in foreign markets. Indeed, most trade analysts predict that the twenty-first century will see enormous growth in global prosperity as businesses compete for foreign trade and increase their expansion in the global marketplace. Certainly, the ease of international travel makes the process of conducting business with other countries not much more difficult than travel from state to state was in former days, and the fax machine and Internet capabilities have had enormous impact on business communication. Combine those factors with the rise in market economies in previously communist countries, and you have some compelling reasons to account for optimistic forecasts for the global economy in the twenty-first century.

It is not just sales to other countries that contribute to the globalization of the marketplace but production as well. Throughout the twentieth century, American wholesalers and retailers imported goods that were made abroad. American consumers were used to seeing the words "made in China" or "made in Taiwan," for instance, on the products that they purchased. Then, it became popular in the last decades of the century for American manufacturers to either outsource the labor to make their products in a foreign country or physically to move abroad. Workers in other countries could be hired to make parts and/or assemble products at wages considerably less than what manufacturers would have to pay workers in the United States, and many American manufacturers found it just as cost-effective to relocate their factories. Central and South America were particularly appealing for such moves because transportation of the products into the United States was fairly easy.

Now, with the development of high-tech telecommunications and the globalization of the economy, many businesses are outsourcing their work to countries all over the world, or they are offshoring completely. Now not only Central and South America, but also India, Eastern Europe, North and South Africa, Asia Pacific, and New Zealand have all become outsourcing centers for American businesses.

The practice of outsourcing—that is, hiring people outside one's own company to do work previously done on-site, or offshoring, physically relocating to another country—has always been subject to criticism from American workers and consumers. These critics charge that it is unethical, unfair, and damaging to the U.S. economy. Its defenders point out that such a practice is highly beneficial to the company's economic health. The articles in this chapter look at both sides of the issue and explore some of the economic benefits and drawbacks of offshore outsourcing.

The first reading, Benjamin Powell's "In Defense of 'Sweatshops,'" takes what some may consider an unusual approach to the subject of sweatshop labor. We hear much from activists protesting sweatshops in third world countries, but Powell, an economist who has researched wages, benefits, and alternatives available to workers in those countries, believes there should be more, not fewer, sweatshops. His defense of sweatshops may surprise you, but read his piece with an open mind and consider his evidence. His approach, he tells us, does not rely on anecdotal evidence but rather on a systematic quantification of data.

The next two pieces in this chapter look at specific aspects of the outsourcing controversy. "The Wal-Mart You Don't Know," by Charles Fishman, examines the world's largest retailer in terms of what being able to offer products at low cost actually costs Wal-Mart's suppliers and the people who work for them. Wal-Mart exerts enormous pressure on its suppliers to outsource in order to sell at low wholesale prices to Wal-Mart. Fishman wonders, Are we shopping our way straight to the unemployment line? Then, Thomas L. Friedman in "30 Little Turtles" reports on his visit to a training center in India where young Indians are being taught to speak with a Canadian accent for their telephone service jobs. Friedman describes it as "an uplifting experience" and explains why he believes there is more to outsourcing than economics: "There's also geopolitics." The last reading in this chapter, John Boudreau's "Dominant Elsewhere, Google Struggles in China," looks at how well an Internet giant, Google, is doing as a competitor in the global Internet market. His article reports on the successes and failures of Google in China and the implications that Google's story has for other international giants attempting to gain a large share of the market there.

IN DEFENSE OF "SWEATSHOPS"

BENJAMIN POWELL

Benjamin Powell is Assistant Professor of Economics at Suffolk University in Boston and Senior Economist with the Beacon Hill Institute. He is editor of Making Poor Nations Rich: Entrepreneurship and the Process of Development *(2007) and coeditor (with Randall Holcombe) of* Housing America: Building out of a Crisis *(2009). This article was published in the Library of Economics and Liberty on June 2, 2008.*

I do not want to work in a third world "sweatshop." If you are reading this on a computer, chances are you don't either. Sweatshops have deplorable working conditions and extremely low pay—compared to the alternative employment available to me and probably you. That is why we choose not to work in sweatshops. All too often the fact that we have better alternatives leads first world activists to conclude that there must be better alternatives for third world workers too.

Economists across the political spectrum have pointed out that for many sweatshop workers the alternatives are much, much worse.[1] In one famous 1993 case U.S. senator Tom Harkin proposed banning imports from countries that employed children in sweatshops. In response a factory in Bangladesh laid off 50,000 children. What was their next best alternative? According to the British charity Oxfam a large number of them became prostitutes.[2]

The national media spotlight focused on sweatshops in 1996 after Charles Kernaghan, of the National Labor Committee, accused Kathy Lee Gifford of exploiting children in Honduran sweatshops. He flew a 15 year old worker, Wendy Diaz, to the United States to meet Kathy Lee. Kathy Lee exploded into tears and apologized on the air, promising to pay higher wages.

4 Should Kathy Lee have cried? Her Honduran workers earned 31 cents per hour. At 10 hours per day, which is not uncommon in a sweatshop, a worker would earn $3.10. Yet nearly a quarter of Hondurans earn less than $1 per day and nearly half earn less than $2 per day.

Wendy Diaz's message should have been, "Don't cry for me, Kathy Lee. Cry for the Hondurans not fortunate enough to work for you." Instead the U.S. media compared $3.10 per day to U.S. alternatives, not Honduran alternatives. But U.S. alternatives are irrelevant. No one is offering these workers green cards.

What Are the Alternatives to Sweatshops?

Economists have often pointed to anecdotal evidence that alternatives to sweatshops are much worse. But until David Skarbek and I published a study in the 2006 *Journal of Labor Research*, nobody had systematically quantified the alternatives[3] We searched U.S. popular news sources for claims of sweatshop exploitation in the third world and found 43 specific accusations of exploitation in 11 countries in Latin America and Asia. We found that sweatshop workers typically earn much more than the average in these countries. Here are the facts:

We obtained apparel industry hourly wage data for 10 of the countries accused of using sweatshop labor. We compared the apparel industry wages to average living standards in the country where the factories were located. Figure 1 summarizes our findings.[4]

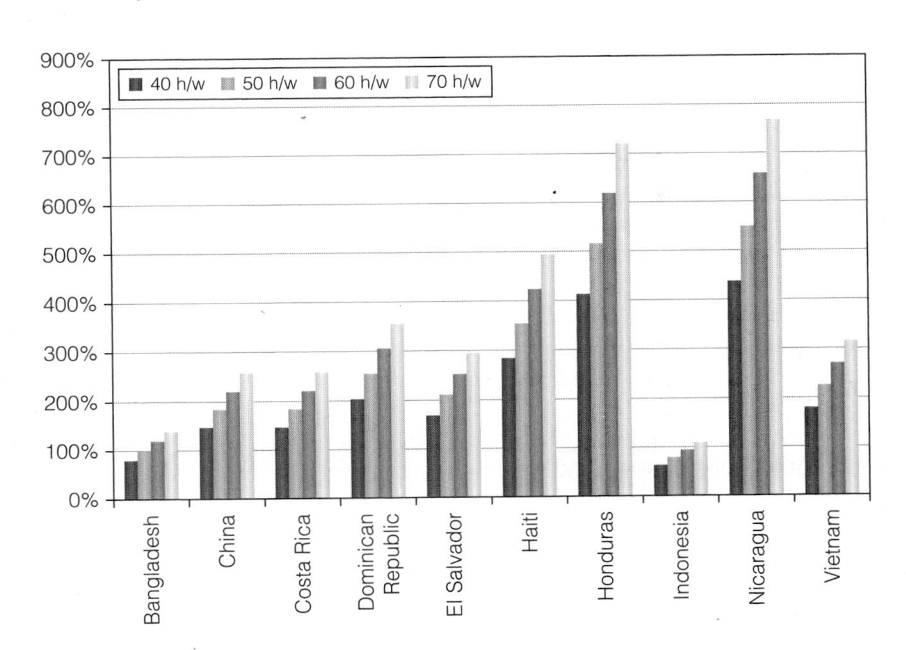

8 Working in the apparel industry in any one of these countries results in earning more than the average income in that country. In half of the countries it results in earning more than three times the national average.[5]

Next we investigated the specific sweatshop wages cited in U.S. news sources. We averaged the sweatshop wages reported in each of the 11 countries and again compared them to average living standards. Figure 2 summarizes our findings.

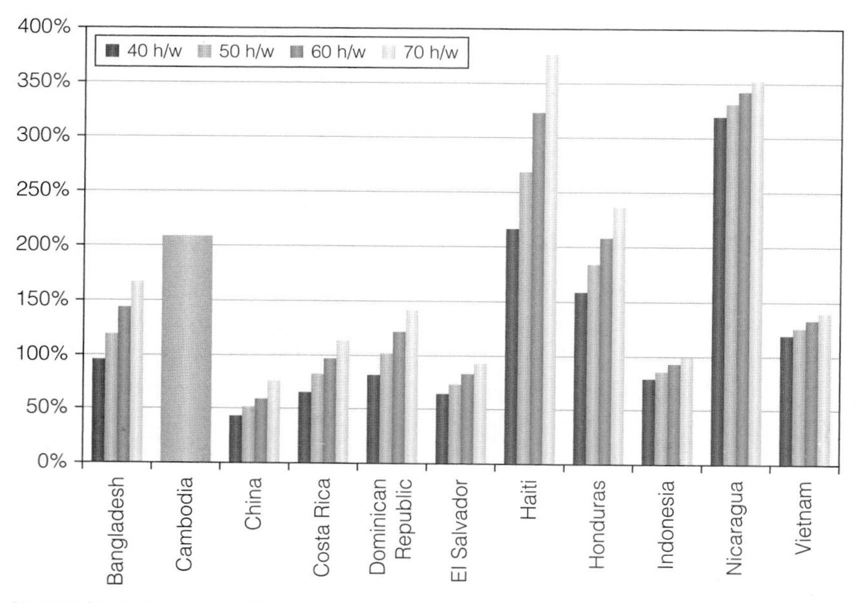

Note: In Combodia only weekly sweatshop wage data were available

Even in specific cases where a company was allegedly exploiting sweatshop labor we found the jobs were usually better than average. In 9 of the 11 countries we surveyed, the average reported sweatshop wage, based on a 70-hour work week, equaled or exceeded average incomes. In Cambodia, Haiti, Nicaragua, and Honduras, the average wage paid by a firm accused of being a sweatshop is more than double the average income in that country. The Kathy Lee Gifford factory in Honduras was not an outlier—it was the norm.

Because sweatshops are better than the available alternatives, any reforms aimed at improving the lives of workers in sweatshops must not jeopardize the jobs that they already have. To analyze a reform we must understand what determines worker compensation.

What Determines Wages and Compensation?

12 If a Nicaraguan sweatshop worker creates $2.50 per hour worth of revenue (net of non-labor costs) for a firm then $2.50 per hour is the absolute most a firm would be willing to pay the worker. If the firm paid him $2.51 per hour, the firm would lose

one cent per hour he worked. A profit maximizing firm, therefore, would lay the worker off.

Of course a firm would want to pay this worker less than $2.50 per hour in order to earn greater profits. Ideally the firm would like to pay the worker nothing and capture the entire $2.50 of value he creates per hour as profit. Why doesn't a firm do that? The reason is that a firm must persuade the worker to accept the job. To do that, the firm must offer him more than his next best available alternative.[6]

The amount a worker is paid is less than or equal to the amount he contributes to a firm's net revenue and more than or equal to the value of the worker's next best alternative. In any particular situation the actual compensation falls somewhere between those two bounds.

Wages are low in the third world because worker productivity is low (upper bound) and workers' alternatives are lousy (lower bound). To get sustained improvements in overall compensation, policies must raise worker productivity and/or increase alternatives available to workers. Policies that try to raise compensation but fail to move these two bounds risk raising compensation above a worker's upper bound resulting in his losing his job and moving to a less-desirable alternative.

16 What about non-monetary compensation? Sweatshops often have long hours, few bathroom breaks, and poor health and safety conditions. How are these determined?

Compensation can be paid in wages or in benefits, which may include health, safety, comfort, longer breaks, and fewer working hours. In some cases, improved health or safety can increase worker productivity and firm profits. In these cases firms will provide these benefits out of their own self interest. However, often these benefits do not directly increase profits and so the firm regards such benefits to workers as costs to itself, in which case these costs are like wages.

A profit-maximizing firm is indifferent between compensating workers with wages or compensating them with health, safety, and leisure benefits of the same value when doing so does not affect overall productivity. What the firm really cares about is the overall cost of the total compensation package.

Workers, on the other hand, do care about the mix of compensation they receive. Few of us would be willing to work for no money wage and instead take our entire pay in benefits. We want some of each. Furthermore, when our overall compensation goes up, we tend to desire more non-monetary benefits.

20 For most people, comfort and safety are what economists call "normal goods," that is, goods that we demand more of as our income rises. Factory workers in third world countries are no different. Unfortunately, many of them have low productivity, and so their overall compensation level is low. Therefore, they want most of their compensation in wages and little in health or safety improvements.

Evaluating Anti-Sweatshop Proposals

The anti-sweatshop movement consists of unions, student groups, politicians, celebrities, and religious groups.[7] Each group has its own favored "cures" for sweatshop conditions. These groups claim that their proposals would help third world workers.

Some of these proposals would prohibit people in the United States from importing any goods made in sweatshops. What determines whether the good is made in a sweatshop is whether it is made in any way that violates labor standards. Such standards typically include minimum ages for employment, minimum wages, standards of occupational safety and health, and hours of work.[8]

Such standards do nothing to make workers more productive. The upper bound of their compensation is unchanged. Such mandates risk raising compensation above laborers' productivity and throwing them into worse alternatives by eliminating or reducing the U.S. demand for their products. Employers will meet health and safety mandates by either laying off workers or by improving health and safety while lowering wages against workers' wishes. In either case, the standards would make workers worse off.

24 The aforementioned Charles Kernaghan testified before Congress on one of these pieces of legislation, claiming:

> Once passed, this legislation will reward decent U.S. companies which are striving to adhere to the law. Worker rights standards in China, Bangladesh and other countries across the world will be raised, improving conditions for tens of millions of working people. Your legislation will for the first time also create a level playing field for American workers to compete fairly in the global economy.[9]

Contrary to his assertion, anti-sweatshop laws would make third world workers worse off by lowering the demand for their labor. As his testimony alludes to though, such laws would make some American workers better off because they would no longer have to compete with third world labor: U.S. consumers would be, to some extent, a captive market. Although Kernaghan and some other opponents of sweatshops claim that they are attempting to help third world workers, their true motives are revealed by the language of one of these pieces of legislation: "Businesses have a right to be free from competition with companies that use sweatshop labor." A more-honest statement would be, "U.S. workers have a right not to face competition from poor third world workers and by outlawing competition from the third world we can enhance union wages at the expense of poorer people who work in sweatshops."

Kernaghan and other first world union members pretend to take up the cause of poor workers but the policies they advocate would actually make those very workers worse off. As economist David Henderson said, "[s]omeone who intentionally gets you fired is not your friend."[10] Charles Kernaghan is no friend to third world workers.

Conclusion

28 Not only are sweatshops better than current worker alternatives, but they are also part of the process of development that ultimately raises living standards. That process took about 150 years in Britain and the United States but closer to 30 years in the Japan, South Korea, Hong Kong, and Taiwan.

When companies open sweatshops they bring technology and physical capital with them. Better technology and more capital raise worker productivity. Over time this raises their wages. As more sweatshops open, more alternatives are available to workers raising the amount a firm must bid to hire them.

The good news for sweatshop workers today is that the world has better technology and more capital than ever before. Development in these countries can happen even faster than it did in the East Asian tigers. If activists in the United States do not undermine the process of development by eliminating these countries' ability to attract sweatshops, then third world countries that adopt market friendly institutions will grow rapidly and sweatshop pay and working conditions will improve even faster than they did in the United States or East Asia. Meanwhile, what the third world so badly needs is more "sweatshop jobs," not fewer.

Endnotes

1. Walter Williams, "Sweatshop Exploitation." January 27, 2004. Paul Krugman, "In Praise of Cheap Labor, Bad Jobs at Bad Wages Are Better Than No Jobs at All." *Slate*, March 20, 1997.
2. Paul Krugman, *The New York Times*. April 22, 2001.
3. Benjamin Powell and David Skarbek, "Sweatshop Wages and Third World Living Standards: Are the Jobs Worth the Sweat?" *Journal of Labor Research*. Vol. 27, No. 2. Spring 2006.
4. All figures are reproduced from our *Journal of Labor Research* article. See the original article for notes on data sources and quantification methods.
5. Data on actual hours worked were not available. Therefore, we provided earnings estimates based on various numbers of hours worked. Since one characteristic of sweatshops is long working hours, we believe the estimates based on 70 hours per week are the most accurate.
6. I am excluding from my analysis any situation where a firm or government uses the threat of violence to coerce the worker into accepting the job. In those situations, the job is not better than the next best alternative because otherwise a firm wouldn't need to use force to get the worker to take the job.
7. It is a classic mix of "bootleggers and Baptists." Bootleggers in the case of sweatshops are the U.S. unions who stand to gain when their lower priced substitute, 3rd world workers, is eliminated from the market. The "Baptists" are the true but misguided believers.
8. These minimums are determined by laws and regulations of the country of origin. For a discussion of why these laws should not be followed see Benjamin Powell, "In Reply to Sweatshop Sophistries." *Human Rights Quarterly*. Vol. 28. No.4. Nov. 2006.
9. Testimonies at the Senate Subcommittee on Interstate Commerce, Trade and Tourism Hearing. Statement of Charles Kernaghan. February 14, 2007.
10. David Henderson, "The Case for Sweatshops." *Weekly Standard*, 7 February 2000.

PERSONAL RESPONSE

With whom do you find yourself siding: those like Powell, who believes that third world sweatshop labor is good for workers in those countries, or those like Charles Kernaghan of the National Labor Committee, who believes that sweatshops are bad for workers?

QUESTIONS FOR CLASS OR SMALL-GROUP DISCUSSION

1. How does Powell define "sweatshop"?
2. Explain in your own words how the two graphs included in the article support Powell's position.
3. Analyze the structure of Powell's argument. Where does he state his thesis? Where does he acknowledge the opposition? What proof does he offer to support his position? What conclusions does he draw from his evidence?
4. Are you convinced by Powell's defense of sweatshops? Explain your answer.

THE WAL-MART YOU DON'T KNOW

CHARLES FISHMAN

Charles Fishman began his writing career at the Washington Post *and held positions on the* Orlando Sentinel *and* Raleigh News & Observer *before joining the staff of* Fast Company, *where he is a senior writer. He is author of The Wal-Mart Effect (2006). Andrew Moesel provided research assistance for this story, which appeared in the December 2003 issue of* Fast Company. The article *won Best Business Magazine Story of 2004 from the New York Press Club.*

A gallon-sized jar of whole pickles is something to behold. The jar is the size of a small aquarium. The fat green pickles, floating in swampy juice, look reptilian, their shapes exaggerated by the glass. It weighs 12 pounds, too big to carry with one hand. The gallon jar of pickles is a display of abundance and excess; it is entrancing, and also vaguely unsettling. This is the product that Wal-Mart fell in love with: Vlasic's gallon jar of pickles.

Wal-Mart priced it at $2.97—a year's supply of pickles for less than $3! "They were using it as a 'statement' item," says Pat Hunn, who calls himself the "mad scientist" of Vlasic's gallon jar. "Wal-Mart was putting it before consumers, saying, This represents what Wal-Mart's about. You can buy a stinkin' gallon of pickles for $2.97. And it's the nation's number-one brand."

Therein lies the basic conundrum of doing business with the world's largest retailer. By selling a gallon of kosher dills for less than most grocers sell a quart, Wal-Mart may have provided a service for its customers. But what did it do for

Vlasic? The pickle maker had spent decades convincing customers that they should pay a premium for its brand. Now Wal-Mart was practically giving them away. And the fevered buying spree that resulted distorted every aspect of Vlasic's operations, from farm field to factory to financial statement.

4 Indeed, as Vlasic discovered, the real story of Wal-Mart, the story that never gets told, is the story of the pressure the biggest retailer relentlessly applies to its suppliers in the name of bringing us "every day low prices." It's the story of what that pressure does to the companies Wal-Mart does business with, to U.S. manufacturing, and to the economy as a whole. That story can be found floating in a gallon jar of pickles at Wal-Mart.

Wal-Mart is not just the world's largest retailer. It's the world's largest company—bigger than ExxonMobil, General Motors, and General Electric. The scale can be hard to absorb. Wal-Mart sold $244.5 billion worth of goods last year. It sells in three months what number-two retailer Home Depot sells in a year. And in its own category of general merchandise and groceries, Wal-Mart no longer has any real rivals. It does more business than Target, Sears, Kmart, J.C. Penney, Safeway, and Kroger combined. "Clearly," says Edward Fox, head of Southern Methodist University's J.C. Penney Center for Retailing Excellence, "Wal-Mart is more powerful than any retailer has ever been." It is, in fact, so big and so furtively powerful as to have become an entirely different order of corporate being.

Wal-Mart wields its power for just one purpose: to bring the lowest possible prices to its customers. At Wal-Mart, that goal is never reached. The retailer has a clear policy for suppliers: On basic products that don't change, the price Wal-Mart will pay, and will charge shoppers, must drop year after year. But what almost no one outside the world of Wal-Mart and its 21,000 suppliers knows is the high cost of those low prices. Wal-Mart has the power to squeeze profit-killing concessions from vendors. To survive in the face of its pricing demands, makers of everything from bras to bicycles to blue jeans have had to lay off employees and close U.S. plants in favor of outsourcing products from overseas.

Of course, U.S. companies have been moving jobs offshore for decades, long before Wal-Mart was a retailing power. But there is no question that the chain is helping accelerate the loss of American jobs to low-wage countries such as China. Wal-Mart, which in the late 1980s and early 1990s trumpeted its claim to "Buy American," has doubled its imports from China in the past five years alone, buying some $12 billion in merchandise in 2002. That's nearly 10% of all Chinese exports to the United States.

8 One way to think of Wal-Mart is as a vast pipeline that gives non-U.S. companies direct access to the American market. "One of the things that limits or slows the growth of imports is the cost of establishing connections and networks," says Paul Krugman, the Princeton University economist. "Wal-Mart is so big and so centralized that it can all at once hook Chinese and other suppliers into its digital system. So—wham!—you have a large switch to overseas sourcing in a period quicker than under the old rules of retailing."

Steve Dobbins has been bearing the brunt of that switch. He's president and CEO of Carolina Mills, a 75-year-old North Carolina company that supplies thread, yarn, and textile finishing to apparel makers—half of which supply Wal-Mart.

Carolina Mills grew steadily until 2000. But in the past three years, as its customers have gone either overseas or out of business, it has shrunk from 17 factories to 7, and from 2,600 employees to 1,200. Dobbins's customers have begun to face imported clothing sold so cheaply to Wal-Mart that they could not compete even if they paid their workers nothing.

"People ask, 'How can it be bad for things to come into the U.S. cheaply? How can it be bad to have a bargain at Wal-Mart?' Sure, it's held inflation down, and it's great to have bargains," says Dobbins. "But you can't buy anything if you're not employed. We are shopping ourselves out of jobs."

The gallon jar of pickles at Wal-Mart became a devastating success, giving Vlasic strong sales and growth numbers—but slashing its profits by millions of dollars.

12 There is no question that Wal-Mart's relentless drive to squeeze out costs has benefited consumers. The giant retailer is at least partly responsible for the low rate of U.S. inflation, and a McKinsey & Co. study concluded that about 12% of the economy's productivity gains in the second half of the 1990s could be traced to Wal-Mart alone.

There is also no question that doing business with Wal-Mart can give a supplier a fast, heady jolt of sales and market share. But that fix can come with long-term consequences for the health of a brand and a business. Vlasic, for example, wasn't looking to build its brand on a gallon of whole pickles. Pickle companies make money on "the cut," slicing cucumbers into spears and hamburger chips. "Cucumbers in the jar, you don't make a whole lot of money there," says Steve Young, a former vice president of grocery marketing for pickles at Vlasic, who has since left the company.

At some point in the late 1990s, a Wal-Mart buyer saw Vlasic's gallon jar and started talking to Pat Hunn about it. Hunn, who has also since left Vlasic, was then head of Vlasic's Wal-Mart sales team, based in Dallas. The gallon intrigued the buyer. In sales tests, priced somewhere over $3, "the gallon sold like crazy," says Hunn, "surprising us all." The Wal-Mart buyer had a brainstorm: What would happen to the gallon if they offered it nationwide and got it below $3? Hunn was skeptical, but his job was to look for ways to sell pickles at Wal-Mart. Why not?

And so Vlasic's gallon jar of pickles went into every Wal-Mart, some 3,000 stores, at $2.97, a price so low that Vlasic and Wal-Mart were making only a penny or two on a jar, if that. It was showcased on big pallets near the front of stores. It was an abundance of abundance. "It was selling 80 jars a week, on average, in every store," says Young. Doesn't sound like much, until you do the math: That's 240,000 gallons of pickles, just in gallon jars, just at Wal-Mart, every week. Whole fields of cucumbers were heading out the door.

16 For Vlasic, the gallon jar of pickles became what might be called a devastating success. "Quickly, it started cannibalizing our non-Wal-Mart business," says Young. "We saw consumers who used to buy the spears and the chips in supermarkets buying the Wal-Mart gallons. They'd eat a quarter of a jar and throw the thing away when they got moldy. A family can't eat them fast enough."

The gallon jar reshaped Vlasic's pickle business: It chewed up the profit margin of the business with Wal-Mart, and of pickles generally. Procurement had to scramble to find enough pickles to fill the gallons, but the volume gave Vlasic strong sales numbers, strong growth numbers, and a powerful place in the world of pickles at Wal-Mart. Which accounted for 30% of Vlasic's business. But the company's profits from pickles had shriveled 25% or more, Young says—millions of dollars.

The gallon was hoisting Vlasic and hurting it at the same time.

Young remembers begging Wal-Mart for relief. "They said, 'No way,'" says Young. "We said we'll increase the price"—even $3.49 would have helped tremendously—"and they said, 'If you do that, all the other products of yours we buy, we'll stop buying.' It was a clear threat." Hunn recalls things a little differently, if just as ominously: "They said, 'We want the $2.97 gallon of pickles. If you don't do it, we'll see if someone else might.' I knew our competitors were saying to Wal-Mart, 'We'll do the $2.97 gallons if you give us your other business.'" Wal-Mart's business was so indispensable to Vlasic, and the gallon so central to the Wal-Mart relationship, that decisions about the future of the gallon were made at the CEO level.

20 Finally, Wal-Mart let Vlasic up for air. "The Wal-Mart guy's response was classic," Young recalls. "He said, 'Well, we've done to pickles what we did to orange juice. We've killed it. We can back off.'" Vlasic got to take it down to just over half a gallon of pickles, for $2.79. Not long after that, in January 2001, Vlasic filed for bankruptcy—although the gallon jar of pickles, everyone agrees, wasn't a critical factor.

By now, it is accepted wisdom that Wal-Mart makes the companies it does business with more efficient and focused, leaner and faster. Wal-Mart itself is known for continuous improvement in its ability to handle, move, and track merchandise. It expects the same of its suppliers. But the ability to operate at peak efficiency only gets you in the door at Wal-Mart. Then the real demands start. The public image Wal-Mart projects may be as cheery as its yellow smiley-face mascot, but there is nothing genial about the process by which Wal-Mart gets its suppliers to provide tires and contact lenses, guns and underarm deodorant at every day low prices. Wal-Mart is legendary for forcing its suppliers to redesign everything from their packaging to their computer systems. It is also legendary for quite straightforwardly telling them what it will pay for their goods.

John Fitzgerald, a former vice president of Nabisco, remembers Wal-Mart's reaction to his company's plan to offer a 25-cent newspaper coupon for a large bag of Lifesavers in advance of Halloween. Wal-Mart told Nabisco to add up what it would spend on the promotion—for the newspaper ads, the coupons, and handling—and then just take that amount off the price instead. "That isn't necessarily good for the manufacturer," Fitzgerald says. "They need things that draw attention."

It also is not unheard of for Wal-Mart to demand to examine the private financial records of a supplier, and to insist that its margins are too high and must be cut. And the smaller the supplier, one academic study shows, the greater the likelihood that it will be forced into damaging concessions. Melissa Berryhill, a Wal-Mart spokeswoman, disagrees: "The fact is Wal-Mart, perhaps like no other retailer, seeks to establish collaborative and mutually beneficial relationships with our suppliers."

24 For many suppliers, though, the only thing worse than doing business with Wal-Mart may be not doing business with Wal-Mart. Last year, 7.5 cents of every dollar spent in any store in the United States (other than auto-parts stores) went to the retailer. That means a contract with Wal-Mart can be critical even for the largest

consumer-goods companies. Dial Corp., for example, does 28% of its business with Wal-Mart. If Dial lost that one account, it would have to double its sales to its next nine customers just to stay even. "Wal-Mart is the essential retailer, in a way no other retailer is," says Gib Carey, a partner at Bain & Co., who is leading a yearlong study of how to do business with Wal-Mart. "Our clients cannot grow without finding a way to be successful with Wal-Mart."

Many companies and their executives frankly admit that supplying Wal-Mart is like getting into the company version of basic training with an implacable Army drill sergeant. The process may be unpleasant. But there can be some positive results.

"Everyone from the forklift driver on up to me, the CEO, knew we had to deliver [to Wal-Mart] on time. Not 10 minutes late. And not 45 minutes early, either," says Robin Prever, who was CEO of Saratoga Beverage Group from 1992 to 2000, and made private-label water sold at Wal-Mart. "The message came through clearly: You have this 30-second delivery window. Either you're there, or you're out. With a customer like that, it changes your organization. For the better. It wakes everybody up. And all our customers benefited. We changed our whole approach to doing business."

But you won't hear evenhanded stories like that from Wal-Mart, or from its current suppliers. Despite being a publicly traded company, Wal-Mart is intensely private. It declined to talk in detail about its relationships with its suppliers for this story. More strikingly, dozens of companies contacted declined to talk about even the basics of their business with Wal-Mart.

28 Here, for example, is an executive at Dial: "We are one of Wal-Mart's biggest suppliers, and they are our biggest customer by far. We have a great relationship. That's all I can say. Are we done now?" Goaded a bit, the executive responds with an almost hysterical edge: "Are you meshuga? Why in the world would we talk about Wal-Mart? Ask me about anything else, we'll talk. But not Wal-Mart."

No one wants to end up in what is known among Wal-Mart vendors as the "penalty box"—punished, or even excluded from the store shelves, for saying something that makes Wal-Mart unhappy. (The penalty box is normally reserved for vendors who don't meet performance benchmarks, not for those who talk to the press.)

"You won't hear anything negative from most people," says Paul Kelly, founder of Silvermine Consulting Group, a company that helps businesses work more effectively with retailers. "It would be committing suicide. If Wal-Mart takes something the wrong way, it's like Saddam Hussein. You just don't want to piss them off."

As a result, this story was reported in an unusual way: by speaking with dozens of people who have spent years selling to Wal-Mart, or consulting to companies that sell to Wal-Mart, but who no longer work for companies that do business with Wal-Mart. Unless otherwise noted, the companies involved in the events they described refused even to confirm or deny the basics of the events.

32 To a person, all those interviewed credit Wal-Mart with a fundamental integrity in its dealings that's unusual in the world of consumer goods, retailing, and groceries. Wal-Mart does not cheat suppliers, it keeps its word, it pays its bills briskly. "They are tough people but very honest; they treat you honestly," says Peter Campanella, who ran the business that sold Corning kitchenware products, both at Corning and then at World Kitchen. "It was a joke to do business with most of their competitors. A fiasco."

But Wal-Mart also clearly does not hesitate to use its power, magnifying the Darwinian forces already at work in modern global capitalism. What does the squeeze look like at Wal-Mart? It is usually thoroughly rational, sometimes devastatingly so.

John Mariotti is a veteran of the consumer-products world—he spent nine years as president of Huffy Bicycle Co., a division of Huffy Corp., and is now chairman of World Kitchen, the company that sells Oxo, Revere, Corning, and Ekco brand housewares.

He could not be clearer on his opinion about Wal-Mart: It's a great company, and a great company to do business with. "Wal-Mart has done more good for America by several thousand orders of magnitude than they've done bad," Mariotti says. "They have raised the bar, and raised the bar for everybody."

36 Mariotti describes one episode from Huffy's relationship with Wal-Mart. It's a tale he tells to illustrate an admiring point he makes about the retailer. "They demand you do what you say you are going to do." But it's also a classic example of the damned-if-you-do, damned-if-you-don't Wal-Mart squeeze. When Mariotti was at Huffy throughout the 1980s, the company sold a range of bikes to Wal-Mart, 20 or so models, in a spread of prices and profitability. It was a leading manufacturer of bikes in the United States, in places like Ponca City, Oklahoma; Celina, Ohio; and Farmington, Missouri.

One year, Huffy had committed to supply Wal-Mart with an entry-level, thin margin bike—as many as Wal-Mart needed. Sales of the low-end bike took off. "I woke up May 1"—the heart of the bike production cycle for the summer—"and I needed 900,000 bikes," he says. "My factories could only run 450,000." As it happened, that same year, Huffy's fancier, more-profitable bikes were doing well, too, at Wal-Mart and other places. Huffy found itself in a bind.

With other retailers, perhaps, Mariotti might have sat down, renegotiated, tried to talk his way out of the corner. Not with Wal-Mart. "I made the deal up front with them," he says. "I knew how high was up. I was duty-bound to supply my customer." So he did something extraordinary. To free up production in order to make Wal-Mart's cheap bikes, he gave the designs for four of his higher-end, higher-margin products to rival manufacturers. "I conceded business to my competitors, because I just ran out of capacity," he says. Huffy didn't just relinquish profits to keep Wal-Mart happy—it handed those profits to its competition. "Wal-Mart didn't tell me what to do," Mariotti says. "They didn't have to." The retailer, he adds, "is tough as nails. But they give you a chance to compete. If you can't compete, that's your problem."

In the years since Mariotti left Huffy, the bike maker's relationship with Wal-Mart has been vital (though Huffy Corp. has lost money in three out of the last five years). It is the number-three seller of bikes in the United States. And Wal-Mart is the number-one retailer of bikes. But here's one last statistic about bicycles: Roughly 98% are now imported from places such as China, Mexico, and Taiwan. Huffy made its last bike in the United States in 1999.

40 As Mariotti says, Wal-Mart is tough as nails. But not every supplier agrees that the toughness is always accompanied by fairness. The Lovable Company was founded in 1926 by the grandfather of Frank Garson II, who was Lovable's last president. It did business with Wal-Mart, Garson says, from the earliest days of founder Sam

Walton's first store in Bentonville, Arkansas. Lovable made bras and lingerie, supplying retailers that also included Sears and Victoria's Secret. At one point, it was the sixth largest maker of intimate apparel in the United States, with 700 employees in this country and another 2,000 at eight factories in Central America.

Eventually Wal-Mart became Lovable's biggest customer. "Wal-Mart has a big pencil," says Garson. "They have such awesome purchasing power that they write their own ticket. If they don't like your prices, they'll go vertical and do it themselves—or they'll find someone that will meet their terms."

In the summer of 1995, Garson asserts, Wal-Mart did just that. "They had awarded us a contract, and in their wisdom, they changed the terms so dramatically that they really reneged." Garson, still worried about litigation, won't provide details. "But when you lose a customer that size, they are irreplaceable."

Lovable was already feeling intense cost pressure. Less than three years after Wal-Mart pulled its business, in its 72nd year, Lovable closed. "They leave a lot to be desired in the way they treat people," says Garson. "Their actions to pulverize people are unnecessary. Wal-Mart chewed us up and spit us out."

44 Believe it or not, American business has been through this before. The Great Atlantic & Pacific Tea Co., the grocery-store chain, stood astride the U.S. market in the 1920s and 1930s with a dominance that has likely never been duplicated. At its peak, A&P had five times the number of stores Wal-Mart has now (although much smaller ones), and at one point, it owned 80% of the supermarket business. Some of the antipredatory-pricing laws in use today were inspired by A&P's attempts to muscle its suppliers.

There is very little academic and statistical study of Wal-Mart's impact on the health of its suppliers and virtually nothing in the last decade, when Wal-Mart's size has increased by a factor of five. This while the retail industry has become much more concentrated. In large part, that's because it's nearly impossible to get meaningful data that would allow researchers to track the influence of Wal-Mart's business on companies over time. You'd need cooperation from the vendor companies or Wal-Mart or both—and neither Wal-Mart nor its suppliers are interested in sharing such intimate detail.

Bain & Co., the global management consulting firm, is in the midst of a project that asks, How does a company have a healthy relationship with Wal-Mart? How do you avoid being sucked into the vortex? How do you maintain some standing, some leverage of your own?

Bain's first insights are obvious, if not easy. "Year after year," Carey, a partner at Bain & Co., says, "for any product that is the same as what you sold them last year, Wal-Mart will say, 'Here's the price you gave me last year. Here's what I can get a competitor's product for. Here's what I can get a private-label version for. I want to see a better value that I can bring to my shopper this year. Or else I'm going to use that shelf space differently.'"

48 Carey has a friend in the umbrella business who learned that. One year, because of costs, he went to Wal-Mart and asked for a 5% price increase. "Wal-Mart said, 'We were expecting a 5% decrease. We're off by 10%. Go back and sharpen your pencil.'" The umbrella man scrimped and came back with a 2% increase. "They said, 'We'll go with a Chinese manufacturer'—and he was out entirely."

The Wal-Mart squeeze means vendors have to be as relentless and as microscopic as Wal-Mart is at managing their own costs. They need, in fact, to turn themselves into shadow versions of Wal-Mart itself. "Wal-Mart won't necessarily say you have to reconfigure your distribution system," says Carey. "But companies recognize they are not going to maintain margins with growth in their Wal-Mart business without doing it."

The way to avoid being trapped in a spiral of growing business and shrinking profits, says Carey, is to innovate. "You need to bring Wal-Mart new products—products consumers need. Because with those, Wal-Mart doesn't have benchmarks to drive you down in price. They don't have historical data, you don't have competitors, they haven't bid the products out to private-label makers. That's how you can have higher prices and higher margins."

Reasonable advice, but not universally useful. There has been an explosion of "innovation" in toothbrushes and toothpastes in the past five years, for instance; but a pickle is a pickle is a pickle.

52 Bain's other critical discovery is that consumers are often more loyal to product companies than to Wal-Mart. With strongly branded items people develop a preference for—things like toothpaste or laundry detergent—Wal-Mart rarely forces shoppers to switch to a second choice. It would simply punish itself by seeing sales fall, and it won't put up with that for long.

But as Wal-Mart has grown in market reach and clout, even manufacturers known for nurturing premium brands may find themselves overpowered. This July, in a mating that had the relieved air of lovers who had too long resisted embracing, Levi Strauss rolled blue jeans into every Wal-Mart doorway in the United States: 2,864 stores. Wal-Mart, seeking to expand its clothing business with more fashionable brands, promoted the clothes on its in-store TV network and with banners slipped over the security-tag detectors at exit doors.

Levi's launch into Wal-Mart came the same summer the clothes maker celebrated its 150th birthday. For a century and a half, one of the most recognizable names in American commerce had survived without Wal-Mart. But in October 2002, when Levi Strauss and Wal-Mart announced their engagement, Levi was shrinking rapidly. The pressure on Levi goes back 25 years—well before Wal-Mart was an influence. Between 1981 and 1990, Levi closed 58 U.S. manufacturing plants, sending 25% of its sewing overseas.

Sales for Levi peaked in 1996 at $7.1 billion. By last year, they had spiraled down six years in a row, to $4.1 billion; through the first six months of 2003, sales dropped another 3%. This one account—selling jeans to Wal-Mart—could almost instantly revive Levi.

56 Last year, Wal-Mart sold more clothing than any other retailer in the country. It also sold more pairs of jeans than any other store. Wal-Mart's own inexpensive house brand of jeans, Faded Glory, is estimated to do $3 billion in sales a year, a house brand nearly the size of Levi Strauss. Perhaps most revealing in terms of Levi's strategic blunders: In 2002, half the jeans sold in the United States cost less than $20 a pair. That same year, Levi didn't offer jeans for less than $30.

For much of the last decade, Levi couldn't have qualified to sell to Wal-Mart. Its computer systems were antiquated, and it was notorious for delivering clothes late to retailers. Levi admitted its on-time delivery rate was 65%.When it announced the deal with Wal-Mart last year, one fashion-industry analyst bluntly predicted Levi would simply fail to deliver the jeans.

But Levi Strauss has taken to the Wal-Mart Way with the intensity of a near death religious conversion—and Levi's executives were happy to talk about their experience getting ready to sell at Wal-Mart. One hundred people at Levi's headquarters are devoted to the new business; another 12 have set up in an office in Bentonville, near Wal-Mart's headquarters, where the company has hired a respected veteran Wal-Mart sales account manager.

Getting ready for Wal-Mart has been like putting Levi on the Atkins diet. It has helped everything—customer focus, inventory management, speed to market. It has even helped other retailers that buy Levis, because Wal-Mart has forced the company to replenish stores within two days instead of Levi's previous five-day cycle.

60 And so, Wal-Mart might rescue Levi Strauss. Except for one thing.

Levi didn't actually have any clothes it could sell at Wal-Mart. Everything was too expensive. It had to develop a fresh line for mass retailers: the Levi Strauss Signature brand, featuring Levi Strauss's name on the back of the jeans.

Two months after the launch, Levi basked in the honeymoon glow. Overall sales, after falling for the first six months of 2003, rose 6% in the third quarter; profits in the summer quarter nearly doubled. All, Levi's CEO said, because of Signature.

But the low-end business isn't a business Levi is known for, or one it had been particularly interested in. It's also a business in which Levi will find itself competing with lean, experienced players such as VF and Faded Glory. Levi's makeover might so improve its performance with its non-Wal-Mart suppliers that its established business will thrive, too. It is just as likely that any gains will be offset by the competitive pressures already dissolving Levi's premium brands, and by the cannibalization of its own sales. "It's hard to see how this relationship will boost Levi's higher-end business," says Paul Farris, a professor at the University of Virginia's Darden Graduate School of Business Administration. "It's easy to see how this will hurt the higher-end business."

64 If Levi clothing is a runaway hit at Wal-Mart, that may indeed rescue Levi as a business. But what will have been rescued? The Signature line—it includes clothing for girls, boys, men, and women—is an odd departure for a company whose brand has long been an American icon. Some of the jeans have the look, the fingertip feel, of pricier Levis. But much of the clothing has the look and feel it must have, given its price (around $23 for adult pants): cheap. Cheap and disappointing to find labeled with Levi Strauss's name. And just five days before the cheery profit news, Levi had another announcement: It is closing its last two U.S. factories, both in San Antonio, and laying off more than 2,500 workers, or 21% of its workforce. A company that 22 years ago had 60 clothing plants in the United States—and that was known as one of the most socially responsible corporations on the planet—will, by 2004, not make any clothes at all. It will just import them.

In the end, of course, it is we as shoppers who have the power, and who have given that power to Wal-Mart. Part of Wal-Mart's dominance, part of its insight, and part of its arrogance, is that it presumes to speak for American shoppers.

If Wal-Mart doesn't like the pricing on something, says Andrew Whitman, who helped service Wal-Mart for years when he worked at General Foods and Kraft, they simply say, "At that price we no longer think it's a good value to our shopper. Therefore, we don't think we should carry it."

Wal-Mart has also lulled shoppers into ignoring the difference between the price of something and the cost. Its unending focus on price underscores something that Americans are only starting to realize about globalization: Ever-cheaper prices have consequences. Says Steve Dobbins, president of thread maker Carolina Mills: "We want clean air, clear water, good living conditions, the best health care in the world—yet we aren't willing to pay for anything manufactured under those restrictions."

68 Randall Larrimore, a former CEO of MasterBrand Industries, the parent company of Master Lock, understands that contradiction too well. For years, he says, as manufacturing costs in the United States rose, Master Lock was able to pass them along. But at some point in the 1990s, Asian manufacturers started producing locks for much less. "When the difference is $1, retailers like Wal-Mart would prefer to have the brand-name padlock or faucet or hammer," Larrimore says. "But as the spread becomes greater, when our padlock was $9, and the import was $6, then they can offer the consumer a real discount by carrying two lines. Ultimately, they may only carry one line."

In January 1997, Master Lock announced that, after 75 years making locks in Milwaukee, it would begin importing more products from Asia. Not too long after, Master Lock opened a factory of its own in Nogales, Mexico. Today, it makes just 10% to 15% of its locks in Milwaukee—its 300 employees there mostly make parts that are sent to Nogales, where there are now 800 factory workers.

Larrimore did the first manufacturing layoffs at Master Lock. He negotiated with Master Lock's unions himself. He went to Bentonville. "I loved dealing with Wal-Mart, with Home Depot," he says. "They are all very rational people. There wasn't a whole lot of room for negotiation. And they had a good point. Everyone was willing to pay more for a Master Lock. But how much more can they justify? If they can buy a lock that has arguably similar quality, at a cheaper price, well, they can get their consumers a deal."

It's Wal-Mart in the role of Adam Smith's invisible hand. And the Milwaukee employees of Master Lock who shopped at Wal-Mart to save money helped that hand shove their own jobs right to Nogales. Not consciously, not directly, but inevitably. "Do we as consumers appreciate what we're doing?" Larrimore asks. "I don't think so. But even if we do, I think we say, Here's a Master Lock for $9, here's another lock for $6—let the other guy pay $9."

PERSONAL RESPONSE

Do you shop at Wal-Mart? Has this article changed in any way your view of Wal-Mart?

QUESTIONS FOR CLASS OR SMALL-GROUP DISCUSSION

1. Comment on the effectiveness as a rhetorical strategy of Fishman's references to the gallon-sized jar of whole pickles throughout the essay.
2. What is "the real story of Wal-Mart, the story that never gets told" (paragraph 4)?
3. Comment on Fishman's use of examples. How do they work to illustrate his major points? Which do you think are the most effective or most dramatic examples?
4. Fishman reveals that he had trouble finding sources to corroborate his findings (paragraph 31). Does that weaken his article? Does he provide enough evidence to outweigh the drawbacks of uncooperative sources?

30 LITTLE TURTLES

THOMAS L. FRIEDMAN

Thomas L. Friedman has written for the New York Times *since 1981. In 1995, he became the paper's foreign affairs columnist. Friedman was awarded the 1983 Pulitzer Prize for international reporting (from Lebanon) and the 1988 Pulitzer Prize for international reporting (from Israel). In 2002, he won the Pulitzer Prize for commentary. His book* From Beirut to Jerusalem *(1989) won the National Book Award for nonfiction in 1989.* The Lexus and the Olive Tree: Understanding Globalization *(2000) won the 2000 Overseas Press Club award for best nonfiction book on foreign policy and has been published in twenty languages. He is also author of* Longitudes and Attitudes: Exploring the World after September 11 *(2002);* The World is Flat: A Brief History of the Twenty-first Century *(2005); and* Hot, Flat, and Crowded: Why We Need a Green Revolution—and How it Can Renew America *(2008). This op-ed column was published in the February 29, 2004, issue of the* New York Times.

Indians are so hospitable. I got an ovation the other day from a roomful of Indian 20-year-olds just for reading perfectly the following paragraph: "A bottle of bottled water held 30 little turtles. It didn't matter that each turtle had to rattle a metal ladle in order to get a little bit of noodles, a total turtle delicacy. The problem was that there were many turtle battles for less than oodles of noodles."

I was sitting in on an "accent neutralization" class at the Indian call center 24/7 Customer. The instructor was teaching the would-be Indian call center operators to suppress their native Indian accents and speak with a Canadian one—she teaches British and U.S. accents as well, but these youths will be serving the Canadian market. Since I'm originally from Minnesota, near Canada, and still speak like someone out of the movie "Fargo," I gave these young Indians an authentic rendition of "30 Little Turtles," which is designed to teach them the proper Canadian pronunciations. Hence the rousing applause.

Watching these incredibly enthusiastic young Indians preparing for their call center jobs—earnestly trying to soften their t's and roll their r's—is an uplifting experience, especially when you hear from their friends already working these jobs how they have transformed their lives. Most of them still live at home and turn over part of their salaries to their parents, so the whole family benefits. Many have credit cards and have become real consumers, including of U.S. goods, for the first time. All of them seem to have gained self-confidence and self-worth.

4 A lot of these Indian young men and women have college degrees, but would never get a local job that starts at $200 to $300 a month were it not for the call centers. Some do "outbound" calls, selling things from credit cards to phone services to Americans and Europeans. Others deal with "inbound" calls—everything from tracing lost luggage for U.S. airline passengers to solving computer problems for U.S. customers. The calls are transferred here by satellite or fiber optic cable.

I was most taken by a young Indian engineer doing tech support for a U.S. software giant, who spoke with pride about how cool it is to tell his friends that he just spent the day helping Americans navigate their software. A majority of these call center workers are young women, who not only have been liberated by earning a decent local wage (and therefore have more choice in whom they marry), but are using the job to get M.B.A.'s and other degrees on the side.

I gathered a group together, and here's what they sound like: M. Dinesh, who does tech support, says his day is made when some American calls in with a problem and is actually happy to hear an Indian voice: "They say you people are really good at what you do. I am glad I reached an Indian." Kiran Menon, when asked who his role model was, shot back: "Bill Gates—I dream of starting my own company and making it that big." I asked C. M. Meghna what she got most out of the work: "Self-confidence," she said, "a lot of self-confidence, when people come to you with a problem and you can solve it—and having a lot of independence." Because the call center teams work through India's night—which corresponds to America's day—"your biological clock goes haywire," she added. "Besides that, it's great."

There is nothing more positive than the self-confidence, dignity and optimism that comes from a society knowing it is producing wealth by tapping its own brains—men's and women's—as opposed to one just tapping its own oil, let alone one that is so lost it can find dignity only through suicide and "martyrdom."

8 Indeed, listening to these Indian young people, I had a déjà vu. Five months ago, I was in Ramallah, on the West Bank, talking to three young Palestinian men, also in their 20's, one of whom was studying engineering. Their hero was Yasir Arafat. They talked about having no hope, no jobs and no dignity, and they each nodded when one of them said they were all "suicide bombers in waiting."

What am I saying here? That it's more important for young Indians to have jobs than Americans? Never. But I am saying that there is more to outsourcing than just economics. There's also geopolitics. It is inevitable in a networked world that our economy is going to shed certain low-wage, low-prestige jobs. To the extent that they go to places like India or Pakistan—where they are viewed as high-wage, high-prestige jobs—we make not only a more prosperous world, but a safer world for our own 20-year-olds.

PERSONAL RESPONSE

Are you sympathetic with Friedman's view of the young Indians whom he describes in his essay?

QUESTIONS FOR CLASS OR SMALL-GROUP DISCUSSION

1. Do you think that Friedman anticipated an audience who would be supportive or critical of him? How can you tell?
2. Do you find the title effective? How does it relate to the essay?
3. How well do Friedman's examples of individual Indians help convey his view that being with them was an "uplifting experience" (paragraph 2)?
4. How adequately does Friedman make his case that "there is more to outsourcing than just economics" (paragraph 8)? Are you convinced?

DOMINANT ELSEWHERE, GOOGLE STRUGGLES IN CHINA

JOHN BOUDREAU

John Boudreau is a staff writer covering global business and technology for the San Jose Mercury News. *This article was published in the October 8, 2009, issue of the* Mercury News.

In China Google means underdog. While the Mountain View company dominates the search market in the United States, it is not part of the pop lexicon on the other side of the Pacific. In its nine years in China, which now has the world's largest Internet audience, Google has struggled.

It has seen its services temporarily shut down by the government, and has been accused of purveying porn. Google China has also been outmaneuvered by a nimble rival, Baidu.com, the look-alike site that claims more than 60 percent of the market in China.

"It's a constant struggle," said Yuke, a Google employee who goes by one name. He was Google's lead product manager in China before managing the social responsibility department. "Sometimes we move ahead; sometimes we lose ground. It's a tough fight."

4 In many ways, Google's experience in China is typical of what international companies face when trying to tap into the emerging wealth of this vast nation of 1.3 billion. They learn, often at great cost, that their China enterprises need "a lot of hand-holding," said Mark Natkin, managing director of Beijing-based Marbridge Consulting.

Google's China business represented just a sliver of its 2008 revenue of $21.8 billion, "a rounding error" of not more than $300 million, according to RBC Capital Markets analyst Ross Sandler.

Other Silicon Valley global giants have been humbled here, as well. In 2005, Yahoo handed over operations of Yahoo China to Alibaba after the Sunnyvale, Calif., company took a $1 billion, 40 percent stake in its erstwhile Chinese competitor. Five years ago, eBay appeared untouchable in China after acquiring EachNet, China's then-leading online auctioneer. Now, though, eBay ranks far behind Taobao, which controls about 80 percent of the online retail market.

"I call it the Pacific Ocean gap," said Victor Koo, chief executive of Youku.com, a Beijing-based online video site. "If you have to wait for a conference call across the Pacific (before making a decision), it can take days. You can't compete. We make decisions faster and we understand the market better."

8 Though Google launched a Chinese version of its search engine in 2000, before Baidu showed up, it wasn't until 2005 that the Mountain View, Calif., company dispatched an on-the-ground team led by the charismatic Kai-Fu Lee, who just left the company to start a venture fund. Under his leadership, Google nearly doubled its share of the market to 31 percent.

But Baidu dominates China's online culture and has trumpeted its Chinese roots in commercials appealing to nationalism.

"In China, everybody uses Baidu," said Meya Hsu, a 20-year-old college student sitting in a cafe with her MacBook laptop. She uses Google only as a last resort, such as to look up information about American pop stars.

Until recently, Google has done next to no marketing, said Kaiser Kuo, a Beijing writer and China Internet expert. Most people can't even spell Google and are unaware that there's a simpler URL, g.cn.

12 Google's ramp-up is an acknowledgment of a rapidly growing market: China's 700 million mobile phone subscribers and 338 million Internet users dwarf those of any other country.

Google's 500 employees in China share a 10-story complex in Tsinghua Science Park in Beijing's high-tech Haidian district. The company has transported its valley culture here—workers curl up on brightly colored couches with laptops, play pingpong, take belly dancing lessons and nibble throughout the day on free snacks and meals prepared by a chef. Teams of engineers devise China-specific products, including a free music service that features lyrics for karaoke-loving Chinese.

Google now is "putting up a fight. They have made good progress," said Youku.com's Koo.

But Google may always face special scrutiny from the government, which is wary of foreign Internet companies. It not only has shut down Google on occasions but also has redirected Internet traffic to Baidu.

16 Google has been careful not to provide products—such as blog services—that require it to gather personal data on users for fear of being forced to turn over information to the government, a decision that hurts it in the market, analysts say. Google runs its Gmail service on servers located outside China, making it more secure from government eyes.

"They are haunted by the ghost of Tom Lantos," said Kuo, referring to the late San Mateo, Calif., congressman who berated Yahoo executives during congressional hearings after the company handed over e-mail records of journalist Shi Tao, who was accused by the Chinese authorities of leaking state secrets abroad and sentenced in 2007 to 10 years in prison.

This summer, online activists relied on Google's Gmail to successfully campaign against the government's efforts to require PC makers to install Internet filtering software on all new machines. "We always tell Chinese people to use non-China-based services," said a Shanghai-based researcher who goes by the name Isaac Mao.

While sometimes running afoul of the Chinese government, Google has been hammered by human rights organizations for cooperating with the government's efforts to block politically sensitive search results. Google searches in China filter out findings objectionable to the government, but users are told they are not getting access to all information because of government restrictions.

20 "I think Google has tried to strike a balance between protecting access to as much information as possible and to expand that while at the same time not being purer than the pope so people don't get access to information in China," said Susan Shirk, a former deputy assistant secretary of state in the Clinton administration responsible for U.S. relations with China. Google, she added, is playing an important role in China's online civil society.

"Any foreign company that does content online is in for a rough period," said Rebecca MacKinnon, an expert on the Internet in China at the University of Hong Kong. "If you want to beat the Chinese competitors, you have to really lower your ethical standards in terms of how you are going to treat your users. I don't see any other way to do it."

China-based Googlers, however, believe time is on their side. As China's telecom giants invest an estimated $59 billion in 3G infrastructure in 200 cities during the next three years, Google hopes to capture leadership in mobile search. Its partnership with China Mobile, the country's largest mobile carrier, will deploy Google's Android operating system on handsets.

"From a pure technology point of view, it's very hard to compete with Google," said Feng Hong, the company's product manager of music search. "There is a long, long way for Google to go.

PERSONAL RESPONSE

Write for a few minutes in response to the information that international giants such as Google, eBay, and Yahoo are not doing well in the Chinese market. Are you surprised?

QUESTIONS FOR CLASS OR SMALL-GROUP DISCUSSION

1. Comment on the effectiveness of the opening paragraph. This is a newspaper article, which means that the reporter has been trained to make the first paragraph an attention grabber and also a succinct statement of what the entire article is about. How successfully do you think Boudreau has been at capturing reader attention?
2. State in your own words why Baidu is doing better in China than Google.
3. What has Google done to improve its business in China?
4. In what ways might Google's struggle to dominate in China be representative of the competition of all international businesses to dominate in the global marketplace?

✧ PERSPECTIVES ON AMERICAN BUSINESS IN THE GLOBAL MARKETPLACE ✧

Suggested Writing Topics

1. Write an essay in response to Benjamin Powell's defense of sweatshops.
2. In response to Charles Fishman's "The Wal-Mart You Don't Know," defend Wal-Mart's business practices.
3. Write a critique of Thomas L. Friedman's "30 Little Turtles."
4. Describe your own buying habits in terms of whether you are socially conscious or not. Do you consciously buy only "fair trade" products, for instance? Do you boycott products of companies that employ sweatshop labor?
5. Select a statement from any of the essays in this chapter that you would like to respond to, elaborate on, or argue for or against.
6. Compare and contrast the benefits of offshore outsourcing.
7. If you know someone who has lost a job because the company moved offshore, narrate that person's experience.
8. Discuss the implications for both American consumers and American businesses of the rapid expansion of the global marketplace.
9. Explain how you see changes in the global economy affecting you personally, both as a consumer and as a (perhaps future) member of the workforce.
10. Assess the impact of foreign products on a typical day in your life. Which imported items are important to your daily life?
11. Interview a specialist in international marketing or economics about the global market and its importance for the American economy in the twenty-first century. Then write an essay on America's future in the global economy in which you include both the specialist's remarks and those of any of the authors in this chapter.

12. Write an essay from the point of view of a market researcher for a new corporation looking for rapid growth through global marketing. Make up a product and a corporation name; then prepare a report for the board of directors of your company in which you recommend expanding efforts in one of the world's newest market areas.

Research Topics

1. Using Benjamin Powell's "In Defense of 'Sweatshops'" as a starting point, research some aspect of the issues surrounding sweatshop labor.
2. Research the subject of outsourcing and draw your own conclusions about the extent to which outsourcing should be cause for concern.
3. Research Wal-Mart's business practices that make it a model of success.
4. Research one of the companies that supplies products to Wal-Mart, as mentioned in Charles Fishman's "The Wal-Mart You Don't Know," and chart its progress or decline.
5. Using John Boudreau's "Dominant Elsewhere, Google Struggles in China" as a starting point, research Google's struggle to gain a stronghold in China, or select another international giant such as Yahoo or eBay and research its success or failure to dominate in the Chinese market.
6. Research the economic impact of outsourcing by focusing on one particular type of business.
7. Research the subject of the non-economic benefits or drawbacks to outsourcing. For instance, some researchers say that outsourcing has resulted in creating allies in the war on terrorism. Can you confirm or refute that claim?
8. Research the effects of the North American Free Trade Agreement (NAFTA) on the American economy and workers.
9. Research the subject of trade protectionism and state your conclusions on its positive or negative effects.
10. Research the economic changes in the past decade in any of these geographic areas: Asia, Asia Pacific, Latin America, Eastern Europe, or sub-Saharan Africa. Read about developments in the area and projections for the future, and then report your findings and conclusions.
11. Research the global investment strategies of any major American corporation. Draw some conclusions about the effectiveness of such strategies in your paper.
12. Analyze the connections between the information revolution and the global spread of market economies. How do they affect or influence one another?
13. Select an area such as politics, technology, or economics. Then conduct library research to determine both the positive and negative implications of the enormous global changes in that area, including a prediction of the effects of these changes on the American economy in the next decade.

RESPONDING TO VISUALS

Business relay race.

1. What comment on the business world does this image make?
2. What details extend the implication of the image to include the global marketplace?
3. Why is this a "relay race" rather than just a race?

Responding to Visuals

A Taiwanese manager, left, walks past seamstresses in the Chentex factory in Tipitata, Nicargua, near Managua, December 13, 2000. Four hundred of the plant's 2,000 workers were fired in August after a four-day strike to demand better pay and working conditions at a factory that sews blue jeans for the U.S. military.

1. What impression of the workplace does the photograph convey?
2. What does the fact that 20 percent of the plant's workers were fired after striking for better pay and working conditions add to the image of workers in this plant?
3. What does the information that the factory sews blue jeans for the U.S. military add to the impact of the photograph?

APPENDIX 1

Glossary of Terms

abstract. A summary of the essential points of a text. It is usually quite short, no more than a paragraph.

***ad hominem* arguments.** Attacking the character of the arguer rather than the argument itself.

analysis. Dividing a subject into its separate parts for individual study.

appeal. A rhetorical strategy used in argumentation to be persuasive; a persuasive technique that goes beyond fact or logic to engage audience's sympathy, sense of higher power or authority, or reasoning. Classic persuasion relies on a combination of ethical, logical, and emotional appeals to sway an audience.

argument/persuasion. An argument is an attempt to prove the validity of a position by offering supporting proof. Persuasion takes argument one step further by convincing an audience to adopt a viewpoint or take action.

attributive tag. A short identifying phrase or clause that identifies ("attributes") the source of a quotation or paraphrase: *Mugabane explains . . . ; According to Sissela Bok, . . . ; Singer, a Princeton University professor who publishes widely on bioethics issues, recommends . . . .*

backing. According to the Toulmin model of reasoning, the support or evidence for a warrant.

begging the question (circular reasoning). Making a claim that simply rephrases another claim in other words.

blog. A personal website which the owner uses for whatever purpose he or she likes, such as a daily record of thoughts or experiences or links to other sites. The term derives from the phrase "web log."

book review. A report that summarizes only the main ideas of a book and provides critical commentary on it. Usually in a book review, you will also be asked to give your personal response to the book, including both your opinion of the ideas it presents and an evaluation of its worth or credibility.

brainstorming. Writing for a short, set period of time everything related to a general subject in order to generate a workable topic for a paper.

case study. A situation or profile of a person or persons, for which you provide a context and background information.

citation. A reference that provides supporting illustrations or examples for your own ideas; the authority or source of that information is identified.

comparison. A likeness or strong similarity between two things.

concession. Agreement with an opponent on certain points or acknowledging that an opposing argument cannot be refuted.

contrast. A difference or strong dissimilarity between two things.

critique. An evaluation of a work's logic, rhetorical soundness, and overall effectiveness.

debate. A discussion involving opposing points in an argument. In formal debate, opposing teams defend and attack a specific proposition.

deductive reasoning. In argumentation, the movement from a general principle or shared premise to a conclusion about a specific instance.

description. A conveyance through words of the essential nature of a thing.

diction. A writer's word choice and level of usage, which varies in informal and formal language; slang, regional, nonstandard, and colloquial language; and jargon.

dropped quotation. A quotation that appears without an introduction, as if it had just been dropped into a paper.

either–or reasoning. Admitting only two sides to an issue and asserting that the writer's is the only possible correct one.

ellipsis points. Used in quoting source material, three spaced periods indicate that words have been omitted.

evaluation. A judgment about worth, quality, or credibility.

exemplification. Showing by example; using specific details or instances to illustrate, support, or make specific.

fallacy. A component of argument that is false or misleading, thus making the reasoning illogical and the argument essentially invalid.

false analogy. Falsely claiming that, because something resembles something else in one way, it resembles it in all ways.

figurative language. Nonliteral or imaginative language used to make abstract words or ideas more concrete. ***Simile*** and ***metaphor*** are two common figures of speech.

forum. An open discussion or exchange of ideas among many people.

freewriting. The act of writing down every idea that occurs to you about your topic without stopping to examine what you are writing.

hasty or faulty generalization. The drawing of a broad conclusion on the basis of very little evidence.

hypothesis. A tentative explanation to account for some phenomenon or set of facts. It is in essence a theory or an assumption that can be tested by further investigation and is assumed to be true for the purpose of argument or investigation.

illustration. An explanation or clarification, usually using example or comparison.

inductive reasoning. In argumentation, the movement from a number of specific instances to a general principle.

introduction. The opening words, sentences, or paragraphs that begin a piece of writing.

invention. Generating ideas for writing.

journal. A personal record of experiences, thoughts, or responses to something, usually kept separate from other writings, as in a diary or notebook.

listserv. An e-mail based discussion group of a specific topic.

literature search. A process of locating titles of articles, books, and other material on a specific subject.

loaded words (emotionally charged language). Language guaranteed to appeal to audiences on an emotional rather than an intellectual level. A loaded word has highly charged emotional overtones or connotations that evoke a strong response, either positive or negative, that goes beyond the denotation or specific definition given in a dictionary. Often the meaning or emotional association of the words varies from person to person or group to group.

metaphor. An implied comparison; comparing one thing to another without using the words "like" or "as." For instance, the metaphor "my love is a rose" makes the comparison between love and rose without explicitly saying so.

narration. Telling a story.

non sequitur. Drawing inferences or conclusions that do not follow logically from available evidence.

oversimplification. Offering a solution or an explanation that is too simple for the problem or issue being argued.

panel discussion. A small group of people (usually between three and six) gathered to discuss a topic. Often each member of a panel is prepared to represent a certain position or point of view on the subject of discussion, with time left after the presentations for questions from audience members.

paraphrase. A restatement of a passage in your own words. A paraphrase is somewhat shorter than the original but retains its essential meaning.

point of view. The perspective from which a piece is written: first person (I, we), second person (you), or third person (he/she/it/one, they).

position paper. A detailed report that explains, justifies, or recommends a particular course of action.

***post hoc, ergo propter hoc* reasoning.** Assuming that something happened simply because it followed something else without evidence of a causal relationship.

premise. An assumption or a proposition on which an argument is based or from which a conclusion is drawn.

prewriting. The first stage of the writing process, when writers determine their purpose, identify their audience, discover their subject, narrow their focus, and plan their writing strategy.

proposition. A statement of a position on a subject, a course of action, or a topic for discussion or debate.

rebuttal. Response addressed to opposing arguments, such as demonstrating a flaw in logic or reasoning or exposing faulty or weak supporting evidence.

red herring. Diverting the audience's attention from the main issue at hand to an irrelevant issue.

reflective writing. A process of drawing on personal experience to offer your own response to something. For this kind of writing, use the first person.

report. A detailed account of something.

rhetoric. The art or study of using language effectively.

rhetorical method. The strategy used to organize and develop ideas in a writing assignment.

simile. An express comparison; using the words "like" or "as" to make a comparison. For instance, "My love is like a red, red rose" is a simile.

slanted word. A word whose connotations (suggestive meaning as opposed to actual meaning) is used to advance an argument for its emotional association.

stereotyping. A form of generalization or oversimplification in which an entire group is narrowly labeled or perceived on the basis of a few in the group.

strategy. A plan of action to achieve a specific goal; the way that an assignment is organized and developed.

subject. A general or broad area of interest.

summary. A shortened version of a passage, stated in your own words. A summary resembles a paraphrase in that you are conveying the essence of the original, but it is shorter than a paraphrase.

syllogism. Traditional form of deductive reasoning that has two premises and a conclusion.

synthesis. Combining the ideas of two or more authors and integrating those ideas into your own discussion.

thesis statement. A statement of the specific purpose of a paper. A thesis is essentially a one-sentence summary of what you will argue, explain, illustrate, define, describe, or otherwise develop in the rest of the paper. It usually comes very early in a paper.

tone. A writer's attitude toward the subject and the audience, conveyed through word choice and diction.

topic. A specific, focused, and clearly defined area of interest. A topic is a narrow aspect of a subject.

topic sentence. Sentence stating the focus or central idea of a paragraph.

warrant. According to the Toulmin model of reasoning, the underlying assumptions or inferences that are taken for granted and that connect the claim to the data.

workshop. Similar in intent to a forum, a workshop is characterized by exchanges of information, ideas, and opinions, usually among a small group of people. Both workshops and forums involve interaction and exchange of ideas more than panel discussions, which typically allot more time to panel members than to audience participants.

Formatting Guidelines for Course Papers

Your instructor may give you formatting guidelines for your papers, but if not, the following guidelines should serve you well in most cases. They follow MLA recommended guidelines for student papers, as do the student papers that appear in this textbook.

MARGINS, SPACING, AND PAGE NUMBERS

Leave a one-inch margin on both sides and at the top and bottom of each page, except for the page number. Double-space everything throughout the paper. Number pages consecutively throughout the paper. MLA guidelines show the page number on the first page, but if your instructor asks you not to put it there, follow the instructor's directions. Place page numbers on the right-hand side, one-half inch from the top of the paper, flush with the right margin. MLA guidelines require your last name with each page number, including the first.

HEADING AND TITLE ON FIRST PAGE

If your instructor tells you to put the endorsement on the first page of your paper rather than on a separate title page, drop down one inch from the top of the first page and write all the information your instructor requires flush with the left margin. This information includes your name, your instructor's name, the course number and section, and the date (using day/month/year format). Then write your title, centered on the page. Double space between all lines, including between the date and the title and between the title and the first line of the paper. Do not underline your own title or put it in quotation marks.

Elizabeth Konrad Konrad 1

Professor Lee

English 102-12

28 November 2010

The Place of Spirituality in the College Curriculum

Education today is more complicated than ever before. The rapid rate at which knowledge increases and the almost constantly changing nature of our society and the jobs required to sustain it put great pressure on institutions of higher education and students alike.

TITLE PAGE

If your instructor requires a title page, center your title about a third of the way down the page. Do not underline your title or use quotation marks around it. Underneath the title, about halfway down, write your name. Then drop down the page and put your instructor's name, the course number and section, and the date.

The Place of Spirituality in the College Curriculum

Elizabeth Konrad

Professor Lee

English 102-12

28 November 2010

Adams, Mike (concept), and Dan Berger (art). "HPV Vaccine Texas Tyranny" (cartoon and commentary). 2007 Truth Publishing. www.naturalnews.com.

Allen, Arthur. "The HPV Debate Needs an Injection of Reality." From *The Washington Post,* April 8, 2007. Reprinted by permission of The Wylie Agency LLC.

Arnold, Andrew D. "Comix Poetics," from *World Literature Today,* March–April 2007, vol. 4, p. 12. Copyright 2007 by The University of Oklahoma Board of Regents. Reprinted by permission.

Bartlett, Thomas. "The Puzzle of Boys." The Chronicle of Higher Education. Copyright 2009. Reprinted with permission.

Bayles, Martha. "Now Showing: The Good, the Bad, and the Ugly Americans." First appeared in *The Washington Post,* August 28, 2005. Reprinted by permission of the author.

Begley, Josanne. "The Gettysburg Address and the War Against Terrorism." Reprinted with permission from Josanne Begley.

Blume, Judy. "Censorship: A Personal View." Reprinted with the permission of Simon & Schuster Books for Young Readers, an imprint of Simon & Schuster Children's Book Division, from *Places I Never Meant to Be* by Judy Blume. Copyright 1999 by Judy Blume. All rights reserved.

Bok, Sissela. "Aggression: The Impact of Media Violence." From *Mayhem: Violence as Public Entertainment by Sissela Bok.* Copyright 1998 by Sissela Bok. Reprinted by permission of Da Capo Press, a member of Perseus Books Group.

Booth, William. "One Nation Indivisible: Is It History?" *The Washington Post*, February 22, 1998. All rights reserved. Used by permission and protected by the Copyright Laws of the United States. The printing, copying, redistribution, or retransmission of the Material without express written permission is prohibited.

Boudreau, John. "Google Struggles in China." Used with permission of San Jose Mercury News. Copyright © 2010. All rights reserved.

Calder, Grant. "The Most Important Moment of All Time?" Originally appeared in *The Philadelphia Inquirer,* November 29, 2009. Reprinted with permission from Grant Calder. See his blog at fromtheclassroom.com.

Chabon, Michael. "Solitude and the Fortresses of Youth." Copyright 2004 by Michael Chabon. Originally appeared in *The New York Times.* All Rights Reserved. Reprinted by arrangement with Mary Evans Inc.

Corwin, Jeff . "The Sixth Extinction," *Los Angeles Times*, November 2009. Reprinted with permission from the author.

Crichton, Michael. "Patenting Life." *The New York Times,* February 13, 2007. Copyright 2007 The New York Times. All rights reserved. Used by permission and protected by the Copyright Laws of the United States. The printing, copying, redistribution, or retransmission of the Material without express written permission is prohibited.

Dickstein, Morris. "How Song, Dance and Movies Bailed Us Out of the Depression." Reprinted with permission from the author.

Doyle, Sady. "Girls Just Wanna Have Fun." Reprinted with permission from Sandy Doyle, "Girls Just Want to Have Fangs," *The American Prospect,* November 19, 2009. Issue 10, Volume 20. www.prospect.org. The American Prospect, 1710 Rhode Island Avenue, NW, 12th Floor, Washington, DC 20036. All rights reserved.

Ehrenreich, Barbara. "Dance, Dance Revolution," *The New York Times,* June 3, 2007. Copyright 2007 The New York Times. All rights reserved. Used by permission and protected by the Copyright Laws of the United States. The printing, copying, redistribution, or retransmission of the Material without express written permission is prohibited.

Ehrenreich, Barbara. "Too Poor to Make the News," *The New York Times,* June 13, 2008. Op-Ed Contribution. Reprinted by permission of The New York Times Syndicate.

Fagan, Kevin. "Homeless, Mike Dick was 51, Looked 66," *San Francisco Chronicle.* Reproduced with permission of San Francisco Chronicle via Copyright Clearance Center.

Fishman, Charles. "The Wal-Mart You Don't Know." Copyright 2004 Gruner + Jahr USA Publishing. First published in *Fast Company* Magazine. Reprinted with permission.

Friedman Thomas. "Still Not Tired," *The New York Times,* February 29, 2004. All rights reserved. Used by permission and protected by the Copyright Laws of the United States. The reprinting, copying, redistribution, or retransmission of the Material without express written permission is prohibited.

Frisby, Cynthia. "Getting Real with Reality TV," *USA Today,* September 2004. Reprinted with permission from Cynthia M. Frisby.

Gibbon, Peter H. "The End of Admiration: The Media and the Loss of Heroes," *Imprimis,* May 1999. Reprinted by permission from *Imprimis,* the monthly journal of Hillsdale College.

Goodman, Ellen. "You've been Mommified," *The Washington Post,* May 10, 2007. All rights reserved. Used by permission and protected by the Copyright Laws of the United States. The printing, copying, redistribution, or retransmission of the Material without express written permission is prohibited.

Greenstone Miller, Jody. "Temporary Workers and the 21st Century Economy," *The Wall Street Journal.* Copyright 2009 by Dow Jones & Company, Inc. Reproduced with permission of Dow Jones & Company via Copyright Clearance Center.

Jacobs, Donovan. "Creating Reel Change." *Sojourners* Magazine, November 2006. Reprinted by permission from Sojourners, (800) 714-7474, www. sojo.net.

Jacoby, Jeff. "Oh, Brother," *The Boston Globe,* December 10, 2006. All rights reserved. Used by permission and protected by the Copyright Laws of the United States. The printing, copying, redistribution, or retransmission of the Material without express written permission is prohibited.

Jenkins, Henry. "Art Form for the Digital Age," *Technology Review: MIT's National Magazine of Technology and Innovation*, September 2000. Copyright 2000 by MIT Technology Review. Reproduced with permission of MIT Technology Review via Copyright Clearance Center.

Johnson, Paul. "American Idealism and Realpolitik," *Forbes,* March 12, 2007. Reprinted by permission of Forbes Media LLC © 2010.

Johnson, Steven. "Social Connections," from the "Urban Planet" series, *The New York Times,* November 28, 2006. Reprinted by permission of Paradigm on behalf of the author.

Jones, Gerard. "Violent Media Is Good for Kids," *Mother Jones,* June 27, 2000. Copyright 2000, Foundation for National Progress. Reprinted with permission.

Kelley, Raina. "Play the Race Card: Why Avoiding the Issue Doesn't Help," *Newsweek,* September 19, 2008. Newsweek. All rights reserved. Used by permission and protected by the Copyright Laws of the United States. The printing, copying, redistribution, or retransmission of the Material without express written permission is prohibited.

Kilbourne, Jean. "Advertising's Influence on Media Content." Reprinted with the permission of The Free Press, a Division of Simon & Schuster, Inc., from *Can't Buy My Love: How Advertising Changes the Way We Think and Feel* (originally published as *Deadly Persuasion*) by Jean Kilbourne. Copyright 1999 by Jean Kilbourne. All rights reserved.

Kotz, Deborah. "On Women: Women Sell Their Eggs, So Why Not a Kidney?" *U.S. News & World Report.* U.S. News & World Report, L.P. Reprinted with permission.

Krauthammer, Charles. "The Moon We Left Behind, *The Washington Post,* July 17, 2009. The Washington Post. All rights reserved. Used by permission and protected by the Copyright Laws of the United States. The printing, copying, redistribution, or retransmission of the Material without express written permission is prohibited.

Lewan, Todd. "CHIPS: High-Tech Aids or Tracking Tools?" AP Wire Service, July 22, 2007. Used with permission of The Associated Press. Copyright 2010. All rights reserved.

Long, Cindy. "I Need My Space!" *NEA Today,* April 2007. Reprinted by permission.

Love, MaryAnn Cusimano. "Race in America: We Would Like to Believe We Are Over the Problem," *America,* February 12, 2007. Copyright 2007 by America Press, Inc. Reproduced with permission of America Press, Inc.

Males, Mike. "Stop Blaming Kids and TV." Reprinted by permission from the October, 1997 issue of *The Progressive,* 409 East Main Street, Madison, WI 53703.

McCullough, David. "No Time to Read?" Reprinted with the permission of *Family Circle* magazine.

McLune, Jennifer. "Hip-Hop's Betrayal of Black Women," Z Magazine online. July/August 2006. Reprinted by permission.

Menkes, Suzy. "Marketing to the Millenials," *The New York Times,* March 2, 2010. The New York Times. All rights reserved. Used by permission and protected by the Copyright Laws of the United States. The printing, copying, distribution, or retransmission of the Material without express written permission is prohibited.

Moody Howard. "Sacred Rite or Civil Right?" Reprinted with permission from the June 5, 2004 issue of *The Nation.* For subscription information, call 1-800-333-8536. Portions of each week's Nation magazine can be accessed at http://www.thenation.com.

Nauen, Elinor. "A Sporting Chance: Title IX and the Seismic Shift in Women's Sports," *American Magazine,* October 20, 2008. Reprinted with permission from America Press.

Petersen, John. "A Green Curriculum Involves Everyone on the Campus." Reprinted with permission from the author.

Powell, Benjamin. "In Defense of Sweatshops." Reprinted from Liberty Fund, Inc. http://www.libertyfund.org on June 2, 2008 and with permission from the author. Liberty Fund is a private educational dedicated to increased knowledge of a society of free and responsible individuals.

Powell, Benjamin, and David Skarbek. Figure 1, "Apparel Industry Wages as a Percent of Average National Income," from "Sweatshop Wages and Third World Living Standards" by Benjamin Powell and David Skarbek. From *The Journal of Labor Research,* Spring 2006, Vol. 27, No. 2. Reprinted by permission from Springer Publishing Company.

Quindlen, Anna. "Our Tired, Our Poor, Our Kids," *Newsweek.* Copyright 2001 by Anna Quindlen. Reprinted by permission of International Creative Management, Inc.

Ravitch, Diane. "Critical Thinking? You Need Knowledge." Reprinted with permission from the author,

Reaves, Jessica. "What the Rest of Africa Could Learn About AIDS." *Chicago Tribune.* All rights reserved. Used by permission and protected by the Copyright Laws of the United States. The printing, copying, redistribution, or retransmission of the Material without express written permission is prohibited.

Rose, Mike. "A Student in a Community College Basic Skills Program." Copyright © 2009 "Why School? Reclaiming Education for All of Us" by Mike Rose. Reprinted by permission of The New Press. www.thenewpress.com.

Rose, Phyllis. "Shopping and Other Spiritual Adventures in America Today," from *Never Say Goodbye* by Phyllis Rose. Copyright 1984, 1987, 1989, 1990 by Phyllis Rose.

Rountree, Cathleen, Ph.D. "In Defense of Hip-Hop," *Santa Cruz Sentinel,* May 19, 2007. Reprinted by permission of the author.

Ruskin, Gary, and Juliet Schor. "Every Nook and Cranny: The Dangerous Spread of Commercialized Culture," *Multinational Monitor,* January/February 2005. Copyright 2005 by Multinational Monitor. Reprinted with permission.

Sachs, Aaron. "Humboldt's Legacy," *Worldwatch Magazine,* vol. 8, no. 2, copyright 1995. www.worldwatch.org. Reprinted by permission.

Saltzman, Joe. "What's in a Name? More Than You Think." From *USA Today Magazine,* July 2003. Reprinted by permission of the author.

Satel, Sally. "About That New Jersey Organ Scandal," *America Magazine,* October 26, 2009. Reprinted by permission of America Magazine.

Shapiro, Robyn S. "Bioethics and the Stem Cell Research Debate." *Social Education,* May-June 2006. © National Council for the Social Studies. Reprinted by permission.

Singer, Peter. "The Singer Solution to World Poverty." Originally published in *The New York Times Magazine,* September 4, 1999. Reprinted by permission of Peter Singer.

Smith, Richard D. "Global Public Goods and Health." From *Bulletin of the World Health Organization,* July 2003, p. 475. Reprinted by permission of the WHO.

Sternheimer, Karen. "Do Video Games Kill?" *Contexts,* winter 2007, vol. 6, no. 1, pp. 13–17. Copyright 2007 American Sociological Society. Reproduced by permission of the publisher via Copyright Clearance Center, Inc.

"Still Hungry, Still Homeless." *America* editorial. Originally published in *America,* February 5, 2001. Reprinted with permission of America Press, Inc. Copyright 2001. All rights reserved

Sollod, Robert. "The Hollow Curriculum," from *The Chronicle of Higher Education,* 1992. Reprinted by permission of the author.

Tannen, Deborah. "Who Does the Talking Here," *The Washington Post,* July 15, 2007. The Washington Post. All rights reserved. Used by permission and protected by the Copyright Laws of the United States. The printing, copying, redistribution, or retransmission of the Material without express written permission is prohibited.

Warner, Judith. "The Full-Time Blues." *The New York Times,* July 24, 2007. Copyright 2007 New York Times. Reprinted by permission.

Young, Cathy. "Lessons from World War II," Real Clear Politics, May 24, 2009. Reprinted with permission from the author.

PHOTO/REALIA CREDITS

Cover and chapter opener patterns: Mark Ruchlewicz/Superstock; p. 17: Herb Watson/CORBIS; p. 167: Courtesy of USGS National Center for EROS and NASA Landsat Project Science; p. 220: Jon Feingersh/Blend Images/CORBIS; p. 221: Steve Skjold/Alamy; p. 248: The New Yorker Collection 1993 Warren Miller from cartoonbank.com All rights; p. 249: Alberto Ruggieri/Illustration Works/CORBIS; p. 271: Icon Prod./Marquis Films/The Kobal Collection/Antonello; p. 272: Jack Corbett/Cartoonstock.com; p. 290: Henderson Advertising for the South Carolina Ballet; p. 291: DC Comics. Image courtesy of the Advertising Archives; p. 312: H. Armstrong Roberts/CORBIS; p. 313: Used with permission from the American Library Association; p. 334: Henderson Advertising for Project Host Soup Kitchen; p. 336: Cengage Learning/Heinle Image Research Bank; p. 361: Department of Defense PH2 J. Alan Elliott; p. 362: Philip and Karen Smith/Digital Vision/Jupiter Images; p. 382: William B. Plowman/Getty Images; p. 383: AP Photo/The Citizen's Voice, Kristen Mullen; p. 400: Fred Ramage/Keystone/Getty Images; p. 401: Reuters/CORBIS; p. 423: Zachary Kanin/The New Yorker Collection/www.cartoonbank.com; p. 424: Robert Essel NYC/CORBIS; p. 441: Lars Borges/Stone/Getty Images; p. 442: David McNew/Getty Images; p. 445: Copyright © 2007 Truth Publishing. www.NaturalNews.com; p. 459: Bettmann/CORBIS; p. 460: Gideon Mendel/CORBIS; p. 484: Rick McKee/Staff/The Augusta Chronicle; p. 508: AP Photo/Mary Altaffer; p. 509: Simon Willms/Stone/Getty Images; p. 522: Mike Twohy/The New Yorker Collection/www.cartoonbank.com; p. 523: Ariel Skelley/Jupiter Images; p. 549: Images.com/CORBIS; p. 550: AP Photo/Mario Lopez.

INDEX

Ten Habits of Successful Students

excerpted from

Kirszner & Mandell, The Brief Handbook, 4/e

Ten Habits of Successful Students

As you have probably already observed, the students who are most successful in school are not always the ones who enter with the best grades. In fact, successful students have *learned* to be successful: they have developed specific strategies for success, and they apply those strategies to their education. If you take the time, you too can learn the habits of successful students and apply them to your own college education—and, later on, to your career.

1. Successful students manage their time.
2. Successful students put studying first.
3. Successful students understand what is required of them.
4. Successful students are active learners in the classroom.
5. Successful students are active learners outside the classroom.
6. Successful students use college services.
7. Successful students use the library.
8. Successful students use technology.
9. Successful students make contacts.
10. Successful students are lifelong learners.

Learn to Manage Your Time Effectively

One of the most difficult things about college is the demands it makes on your time. It is hard, especially at first, to balance studying, course work, family life, friendships, and a job. But if you do not take control of your schedule, it will take control of you; if you do not learn to manage your time, you will always be struggling to catch up.

Fortunately, there are two tools you can use to help you manage your time: a personal organizer and a calendar. Of course, simply buying an organizer and a calendar will not solve your time-management problems—you have to *use* them. Moreover, you have to use them effectively and regularly.

First of all, carry your organizer with you at all times, and post your calendar in a prominent place (perhaps above your desk or next to your phone). Then, remember to record *in both places* not only school-related deadlines, appointments, and reminders (every assignment due date, study group meeting, conference appointment, and exam) but also outside responsibilities like work hours and dental appointments. Record items as soon as you learn of them; if you do not write something down immediately, you are likely to forget it. (If you make an entry in your organizer while you are in class, be sure to copy it onto your calendar when you get back from school.)

You can also use your organizer to help you plan a study schedule. You do this by blocking out times to study or to complete assignment-related tasks—such as an Internet search for a research paper—in addition to appointments and deadlines. (It is a good idea to make these entries in pencil so you can adjust your schedule as new responsibilities arise.) If you have a schedule, you will be less likely to procrastinate—and therefore less likely to become overwhelmed.

The bottom line is this: your college years can be a very stressful time, but although some degree of stress is inevitable, it can be kept in check. If you are an organized person, you will be better able to handle the pressures of a college workload.

Put Studying First

? To be a successful student, you need to understand that studying is something you do *regularly,* not just right before an exam. You also need to know that studying does not mean memorizing facts; it means reading, rereading, and discussing ideas until you understand them.

To make studying a regular part of your day, set up a study space that includes everything you need (supplies, good light, a comfortable chair) and does not include anything you do not need (clutter, distractions). Then, set up a tentative study schedule. Try to designate at least two hours each day to complete assignments due right away, to work on those due later on, and to reread class notes. Then, when you have exams and papers to do, you can adjust your schedule accordingly.

Successful students often form study groups, and this is a strategy you should use whenever you can—particularly in a course you find challenging. A study group of four or five students who meet regularly (not just the night before an exam) can make studying more focused and effective as well as more enjoyable and less stressful. By discussing concepts with your classmates, you can try out your ideas and get feedback, clarify complex concepts, and formulate questions for your instructor.

Be Sure You Understand School and Course Requirements

To succeed in school, you need to know what is expected of you—and, if you are not sure, to ask.

When you first arrived at school, you probably received a variety of orientation materials—a student handbook, library handouts, and so on—that set forth the rules and policies of your school. Read these documents carefully (if you have not already done so), and be sure you understand what they ask of you. If you do not, ask your peer counselor or your adviser for clarification.

You also need to understand the specific requirements of each course you take. Education is a series of contracts between you and your instructors, and each course syllabus explains the terms of a particular contract. In a syllabus, you learn each instructor's policies about attendance and lateness, assignments and deadlines, plagiarism, and classroom etiquette. In addition, a syllabus may explain penalties for late assignments or missed quizzes, tell how much each assignment is worth, or note additional requirements, such as fieldwork or group projects. Requirements vary significantly from course to course, so read each syllabus very carefully—and also pay close attention to any supplementary handouts your instructors distribute.

As the semester progresses, your instructors will give you additional information about their expectations. For example, before an exam you will be told what material will be covered, how much time you will have to complete the test, and whether you will be expected to write an essay or fill in an answer sheet that will be graded electronically. When a paper is assigned, you may be given specific information not only about its content, length, and due date but also about its format (font size, line spacing, and margin width, for example). If your instructor does not give you this information, it is your responsibility to find out what is expected of you.

Be an Active Learner in the Classroom

Education is not about sitting passively in class and waiting for information and ideas to be given to you. It is up to you to be an active participant in your own education.

First, take as many small classes as you can. These classes give you the opportunity to interact with other students and with your instructor. If a large course has recitation sections, be sure to attend these regularly, even if they are not required. Also be sure to take as many classes as possible that require writing. Good writing skills are essential to your success as a student, and you need all the practice you can get.

Take responsibility for your education by attending class regularly and arriving on time. Listen attentively, and take careful, complete notes. (Try to review these notes later with other students to make sure you have not missed anything important.) Do your homework on time, and keep up with the reading. When you read an assignment, apply the techniques of active reading, interacting with the text instead of just seeing what is on the page. If you have time, read beyond the assignment, looking on the Internet and in books, magazines, and newspapers for related information that interests you.

As important as it is to listen and take notes in class, it is just as important (particularly in small classes and recitations) to participate in class discussions: to ask and answer questions, volunteer opinions, and give helpful feedback to other students. By participating in such discussions, you learn more about the subject matter being discussed, and you also learn to listen to other points of view, to test your ideas, and to respect the ideas of others.

Be an Active Learner Outside the Classroom

Taking an active role in your education is also important outside the classroom. Do not be afraid to approach your instructors; take advantage of their office hours, and keep in touch with them by e-mail. Get to know your major adviser well, and be sure he or she knows who you are and where your academic interests lie. Make appointments, ask questions, explore possible solutions to problems: this is how you learn.

Participate in the life of your school. Read your school newspaper, check the Web site regularly, join clubs, and apply for internships. This participation in life outside the classroom can help you develop new interests and friendships as well as enhance your education.

Finally, participate in the life of your community. Take service learning courses, if they are offered at your school, or volunteer at a local school or social agency. As successful students know, education is more than just attending classes.

Take Advantage of College Services

?

Colleges and universities offer students a wide variety of support services. Most students will need help of one kind or another at some point during their college careers; if help is available, it makes sense to use it.

For example, if you are struggling with a particular course, you can go to the tutoring service offered by your school's academic support center or by an individual department. Often, the tutors are students who have done well in the course, and their perspective will be very helpful. If you need help with writing or revising a paper, you can make an appointment with the writing lab, where tutors will give you advice (but will *not* rewrite or edit your paper for you). If you are having trouble deciding on what courses to take or what to major in, see your academic adviser. If you are having trouble adjusting to college life, your peer counselor or (if you live in a dorm) your resident adviser may be able to help you. If not, or if you have a personal or family problem you would rather not discuss with another student, make an appointment at your school's counseling center, where you can get advice from professionals who understand student problems.

Many other services are available at your school's computer center, job placement service, financial aid office, and elsewhere. Your academic adviser or instructors can tell you where to find the help you need, but it is up to you to make the appointment.

Use the Library

As more and more material becomes available on the Internet, you may begin to think of your college library as outdated or even obsolete. But learning to use the library is an important part of your education.

The library has a lot to offer. First, the library can provide a quiet place to study—something you may need if you have a large family or noisy roommates. The library also contains materials that cannot be found online—rare books, special collections, audiovisual materials—as well as electronic databases that contain material you will not find on the Internet. (At some schools, you will be able to access the library's electronic databases on your home computer; at others, you will not.)

Finally, the library is the place where you have access to the experience and expert knowledge of your school's reference librarians. These professionals can answer questions, guide your research, and point you to sources that you might never have found on your own.

Use Technology

As technology has become more and more important in the world, technological competence has become essential to success in college.

Naturally, it makes sense to develop good word-processing skills and to be comfortable with the Internet. You should also know how to send and receive e-mail from your university account as well as how to attach files to your e-mail. Beyond the basics, learn how to manage the files you download, how to evaluate Internet sources, and how to use the electronic resources of your library. You might also find it helpful to know how to scan documents, (images as well as text) and how to paste these files into your documents. If you do not have these skills, you need to find someone (in the library or in the computer lab) who can help you get them.

Finally, you need to know not only how to use technology to enhance a project—for example, how to use PowerPoint for an oral presentation—but also *when* to use technology (and when not to).

Make Contacts—and Use Them

One of the most important things you can do for yourself, both for the short term and for the long term, is to make contacts while you are in school and to use them both during college and after you graduate.

Your first contacts are your fellow students. Be sure you have the names, phone numbers, and e-mail addresses of at least two students in each of your classes. These contacts will be useful to you if you miss class, if you need help understanding your notes, or if you want to find someone to study with.

You should also build relationships with students with whom you participate in college activities, such as the college newspaper or the tutoring center. These people are likely to share your goals and interests, and so you may want to get feedback from them as you move on to choose a major, consider further education, and make career choices.

Finally, develop relationships with your instructors, particularly those in your major area of study. One of the things cited most often in studies of successful students is the importance of **mentors,** experienced individuals whose advice you trust. Long after you leave college, you will find these contacts useful. Keep in touch; it will pay off.

Be a Lifelong Learner

Your education should not stop when you graduate from college, and this is something you should be aware of from the first day you set foot on campus. To be a successful student, you need to see yourself as a lifelong learner.

Get in the habit of reading newspapers; know what is happening in the world outside school. Talk to people outside the college community, so you remember there are issues that have nothing to do with courses and grades. Never miss an opportunity to learn: try to get in the habit of attending plays and concerts sponsored by your school or community and lectures offered at your local library or bookstore.

And think about your future, the life you will lead after college. Think about who you want to be and what you have to do to get there. This is what successful students do.

✓ checklist Becoming a successful student

✓ Do you have a personal organizer? a calendar? Do you use them regularly?
✓ Have you set up a comfortable study space?
✓ Have you made a study schedule?

continued on the following page

Ten Habits of Successful Students

continued from the previous page

- ✓ Have you joined a study group?
- ✓ Have you read your course syllabi and orientation materials carefully?
- ✓ Are you attending classes regularly and keeping up with your assignments?
- ✓ Do you take advantage of your instructors' office hours?
- ✓ Do you participate in class?
- ✓ Do you participate in college life?
- ✓ Do you know where to get help if you need it?
- ✓ Do you know how to use your college library? Do you use it?
- ✓ Are you satisfied with your level of technological expertise? Do you know where to get additional instruction?
- ✓ Are you trying to make contacts and find mentors?
- ✓ Do you see yourself as a lifelong learner?